CRIMINAL PROCEDURE

AUSTRALIA
The Law Book Company Ltd.
Sydney : Melbourne : Brisbane

CANADA AND U.S.A.
The Carswell Company Ltd.
Agincourt, Ontario

INDIA
N. M. Tripathi Private Ltd.
Bombay

ISRAEL
Steimatzky's Agency Ltd.
Jerusalem : Tel Aviv : Haifa

MALAYSIA : SINGAPORE : BRUNEI
Malayan Law Journal (Pte.) Ltd.
Singapore

NEW ZEALAND
Sweet & Maxwell (N.Z.) Ltd.
Wellington

PAKISTAN
Pakistan Law House
Karachi

CRIMINAL PROCEDURE

BY

CELIA HAMPTON

of Gray's Inn, Barrister

SECOND EDITION

LONDON

SWEET & MAXWELL

1977

First Edition 1973
Second Edition 1977

Published by Sweet & Maxwell Ltd. of 11, New Fetter Lane and printed in Great Britain by The Eastern Press Ltd. of London and Reading

SBN Hardback 0421 21770 7
Paperback 0421 21780 4

PREFACE

THE aim of this book is to provide a straightforward account of the procedure in criminal cases. As far as possible I have followed the chronological sequence of events from detection to appeal, first for indictable offences and secondly for summary offences. This was originally designed to make lucid reading for students, but I hope that the book may also be of use to practitioners and others involved in the criminal process. In such a subject the major points of interest in theory and in practice tend to coincide—the legality of arrest and the preparation of indictments are obvious examples. I also hope that readers will find an ample citation of authorities for all propositions of importance, though in a book of this size I have had to concentrate by and large on modern decisions in which the older authorities are discussed.

The section on the general law of evidence included in the first edition has been omitted. It is a subject in which excellent works for all types of readership abound and could not be treated with justice or in a depth equivalent to that given to procedure in this book. Readers will nevertheless find that a great many aspects of the law of evidence are touched on; in any event it is often impossible to separate the two subjects—it would be curious to describe the legality of a procedure for search without considering the admissibility in evidence of the product of the search.

This book is published as a counterpart on the criminal side to Langan and Lawrence's *Civil Procedure* (second edition 1976). Readers will find that certain topics of peripheral importance to criminal procedure, which are omitted here, are dealt with at length in Langan and Lawrence, *e.g.* references to the European Court under article 177 of the EEC Treaty (which might be made following a recommendation for the deportation of a citizen of an EEC Member State).

The major charges in the law since the first edition have been in bail and sentence, though scarcely a single topic has remained unaffected by change in the four years or so between editions. The section on bail is based on the 1976 Act, although at the time of writing it was not in force. Rules of court implementing the Act were anticipated but failed to materialise in time for inclusion. The chapters on sentence had to be significantly expanded to take account of the new powers under the Criminal Justice Act 1972 as consolidated in the Powers of Criminal Courts Act 1973. Other matters which arose too late for inclusion were the Sexual Offences (Amendment) Act 1976 (which has a bearing on the publicity of proceedings and cross-examination in rape cases) and the Criminal Law Bill. A short summary of the second, however, is included as an appendix since it will have a radical effect on the classification and differential treatment of offences when enacted. The law is stated, generally speaking, as it stood on October 1, 1976. It was possible to make some small additions up to April 1, 1977, however.

I would like to express my gratitude to my husband for his guidance on the practical details discussed in this book, and to the editorial staff of Sweet and Maxwell for the advice, assistance and patience extended to me in the preparation of this edition.

London, CELIA HAMPTON
April 1977

CONTENTS

	page
Preface	v
Table of Cases	xi
Table of Statutes	xxix
Table of Statutory Instruments	xlii
Table of Rules of the Supreme Court	xliii

1. INTRODUCTION 1

PART ONE

MATTERS PRELIMINARY TO TRIAL

2. CRIMINAL JURISDICTION 9
   - A. General Territorial Jurisdiction 9
   - B. Time Limits 13
   - C. Immunity from Prosecution 14
   - D. Preliminary Administrative Action 15
   - E. Local Jurisdiction 16
3. PREPARATION FOR PROSECUTION 17
   - A. Prosecuting Authorities 17
   - B. Investigation by the Police 20
   - C. Powers of Search 25
   - D. Witnesses 29
   - E. Evidence of Identity and Miscellaneous Matters 34
   - F. Coroners' Inquests 37
   - G. Remedies for Wrongful Process 40
   - H. Supervisory Jurisdiction of the High Court 43
4. INITIATION OF PROCEEDINGS 48
   - A. The Magistrate and His Jurisdiction 48
   - B. Laying an Information 54
   - C. Summons 55
   - D. Warrant of Arrest 57
   - E. Extradition 60
   - F. Arrest without a Warrant 62
   - G. Powers and Duties Ancilliary to Arrest 64
   - H. Remand 67
   - I. Bail 68

PART TWO

TRIAL ON INDICTMENT

5. COURTS 85
   - A. Examining Justices 85
   - B. The Crown Court 86
   - C. The High Court 91
   - D. Courts-Martial 91
6. COMMITTAL PROCEEDINGS 93
   - A. Committal Proceedings—Preliminary 93
   - B. Written Statements of Evidence 96
   - C. Oral Committal Proceedings 97

page

Committal Proceedings—*cont.*
D. Section 1 Committal 100
E. Time and Place of Trial 101
F. Committal for Trial 103
G. Witnesses 105
H. Other Forms of Evidence 106
I. Extradition 115

7. The Indictment 117
A. Drafting an Indictment 117
B. Duplicity 128
C. Joinder of Offences 131
D. Joinder of Defendants 137
E. The Substance of the Indictment 142
F. Preferring the Indictment 144
G. Amendment 146
H. Quashing the Indictment 148

8. Trial on Indictment 150
A. Presence and Representation of the Accused: Presence of the Public 150
B. Arraignment and Plea 154
C. The Jury 171
D. The Order of Proceedings 176
E. Verdict 208
F. Procedure on a Plea of Guilty 215

9. Sentence 216
A. Judgment 216
B. Punishments 223
C. Non-Punitive Orders 233
D. Miscellaneous Orders 245
E. Combinations of Punishments and Orders 255
F. Pardon, Release, etc. 256

10. Appeals 260
A. Courts 260
B. Appeal against Conviction 262
C. Appeal against Sentence and Other Matters 274
D. Attorney-General's Reference on a Point of Law 279
E. Appeal to the House of Lords 280
F. Drafting Grounds of Appeal 283

PART THREE

SUMMARY TRIAL

11. Magistrates' Courts 289
A. Constitution 289
B. General Jurisdiction 290
C. Criminal Jurisdiction and the Classification of Offences 292
D. Non-Criminal Jurisdiction 300

12. Summary Trial 301
A. Presence and Representation of Parties: Presence of Public 301
B. The Information 303
C. Preliminary Procedure, Adjournment and Evidence 306
D. Order of Proceedings 308
E. Plea of Guilty 316

page

13. Sentence 317
  A. Procedure before Sentence 317
  B. Punishments and Orders 319
  C. Committal for Sentence 330

14. Appeals 340
  A. Courts 340
  B. Appeal to the Crown Court 344
  C. Appeal to the High Court 349
  D. Appeal to the House of Lords 352
  E. Appeal to the Court of Appeal 353
  F. Drafting a Case Stated 355

PART FOUR

SPECIAL CASES

15. Juveniles 361
  A. The Responsibility of Juveniles 362
  B. Trial on Indictment 364
  C. Summary Trial by Magistrates 368
  D. The Juvenile Court 370
  E. Procedure before Juvenile Courts 371
  F. Care Proceedings 382
  G. Appeals 387
  H. Juvenile Adults 388

16. Corporations, Contempt and Perjury 390
  A. Corporations 390
  B. Contempt of Court 392
  C. Perjury 394

PART FIVE

LEGAL AID

17. Legal Aid Orders 399
  A. Availability 400
  B. Extent 402
  C. Contributions 404
  D. The Application 405

Appendix 407

Index 411

TABLE OF CASES

ABBATTO AND HEALEY [1955] Crim.L.R. 645 108
Abbott [1955] 2 Q.B. 497; 3 W.L.R. 369; 2 All E.R. 899; 39 Cr.App.R. 141 .... 202, 267
—— [1964] 1 Q.B. 489; [1963] 2 W.L.R. 1011; 1 All E.R. 738; 47 Cr.App. R. 110 367
Aberdare Justices, *ex p.* Jones [1973] Crim.L.R. 45 314
Adams [1969] 1 W.L.R. 106; [1968] 3 All E.R. 437; 52 Cr.App.R. 588 212
Adamson (1875) 1 Q.B.D. 201 53
Aitken [1966] 1 W.L.R. 1076; 2 All E.R. 453; 50 Cr.App.R. 204 226
Akan [1973] 1 Q.B. 491; [1972] 3 W.L.R. 866; 3 All E.R. 285; 56 Cr.App.R. 716 .... 240, 256
Alderson *v.* Booth [1969] 2 Q.B. 216; 2 W.L.R. 1252; 2 All E.R. 271; 53 Cr.App.R. 301 64
Aldus *v.* Watson [1973] Q.B. 902; 3 W.L.R. 1007; 2 All E.R. 1018; Crim. L.R. 443 304
Alexander [1974] 1 W.L.R. 422; 1 All E.R. 539 .... 205, 209
Algar [1954] 1 Q.B. 279; [1953] 3 W.L.R. 1007; 2 All E.R. 1381; 37 Cr. App.R. 200 30
Ali [1972[Crim.L.R. 255; 56 Cr.App.R. 301 252
All Saints, Worcester (Inhabitants) (1817) 6 M. & S. 194 32
Allan *v.* Wiseman [1975] R.T.R. 217; Crim.L.R. 37 305
Alt [1972] Crim.L.R. 552; 56 Cr.App.R. 457 129
Amos [1961] 1 W.L.R. 308; 1 All E.R. 191; 45 Cr.App.R. 42 335
Ampleford [1975] Crim.L.R. 593; 61 Cr.App.R. 325 .... 220, 225
Anderson (1868) L.R.I.C.C.R. 161; 11 Cox 198 10
—— (1930) 20 Cox 102; 21 Cr.App.R. 178 178
—— (1958) 42 Cr.App.R. 91 221
Andrews [1967] 1 W.L.R. 439; 1 All E.R. 170; 51 Cr.App.R. 42 136
Ankers [1975] Crim.L.R. 402; 61 Cr.App.R. 170 233
Annesley [1976] 1 W.L.R. 106 222
Antypas [1973] Crim.L.R. 130; 56 Cr.App.R. 207 245
Arkle [1972] Crim.L.R. 582 227
Arron [1973] 1 W.L.R. 1238; 2 All E.R. 1221; Crim.L.R. 572 274
Arrowsmith [1975] 2 W.L.R. 484; 1 All E.R. 463 19
Artfield (1961) 45 Cr.App.R. 309 197
Ashdown [1974] 1 W.L.R. 270; 1 All E.R. 800; Crim.L.R. 130; 58 Cr. App.R. 339 271
Assim [1966] 2 Q.B. 249; 3 W.L.R. 55; 2 All E.R. 881; 50 Cr.App.R. 224 139, 140
Atkinson [1976] Crim.L.R. 307 26
—— *v.* U.S. Government [1971] A.C. 197; [1969] 3 W.L.R. 1074; 3 All E.R. 1317 349
Attorney-General for Northern Ireland *v.* Gallagher [1963] A.C. 349; [1961] 3 W.L.R. 619; 3 All E.R. 299; 45 Cr.App.R. 316 282
Aubrey-Fletcher, *ex p.* Thompson [1969] 1 W.L.R. 872; 2 All E.R. 846; 53 Cr.App.R. 380 328
Aughet (1918) 26 Cox 232; 13 Cr.App.R. 101 .... 163, 164
Auker-Howlett [1974] R.T.R. 109; [1973] Crim.L.R. 52 155
Austin [1973] Crim.L.R. 778; 58 Cr.App.R. 163 213

BADGER (1843) 4 Q.B. 468; 12 L.J.M.C. 66 78
Badjan (1966) 50 Cr.App.R. 141 266
Bagg *v.* Colquhoun [1904] 1 K.B. 554 314
Bailey [1924] 2 K.B. 300; 93 L.J.K.B. 989; 27 Cox 692; 18 Cr.App.R. 42 134
Baisie (1970) unreported 153
Baker (1912) 7 Cr.App.R. 217 158

Baldwin (1925) 28 Cox 17; 18 Cr.App.R. 175 184
Ball, Loughlin (1966) 50 Cr.App.R. 266 357
Balls (1871) L.R.I.C.C.R. 328 132
Ballysingh (1953) 37 Cr.App.R. 28 133
Balogh *v.* St. Albans Crown Court [1975] Q.B. 73; [1974] 3 W.L.R. 314; 3 All E.R. 283 392
Barber (1844) 1 C.W.K. 434; 1 Cox 62 199
Barker [1976] Crim.L.R. 324 202
Barnes (1971) 55 Cr.App.R. 100 .... 155, 268
Barnes and Richards [1940] 2 All E.R. 229; 27 Cr.App.R. 154 201
Barraclough [1906] 1 K.B. 201; 75 L.J.K.B. 77; 21 Cox 91 .... 118, 125
Barron [1914] 2 K.B. 570; 83 L.J.K.B. 786; 10 Cr.App.R. 81 ... 162, 163, 166
Barry [1975] 1 W.L.R. 1190; 2 All E.R. 760; 61 Cr.App.R. 172.......... 209, 213
Barton [1972] 2 All E.R. 1192 33
—— [1974] Crim.L.R. 43 33
Bashir [1969] 1 W.L.R. 1303; 3 All E.R. 692; 54 Cr.App.R. 1.......... 186
Bass [1953] 1 Q.B. 680; 1 All E.R. 1064; 37 Cr.App.R. 51 187
Bateson [1969] 3 All E.R. 1372; 54 Cr.App.R. 11 209
Baxter [1972] 1 Q.B. 1; [1971] 2 W.L.R. 1138; 2 All E.R. 359; 55 Cr.App.R. 214 9
Baylis *v.* Lucas (1779) 1 Cowp. 112 175
Baynes *v.* Brewster (1841) 2 Q.B. 375 62
Beamon [1948] 1 All E.R. 947; 31 Cr.App.R. 181 230
Beard [1974] 1 W.L.R. 1549; Crim.L.R. 92 .... 252, 255
Beever (1971) 115 S.J. 465 226
Beezley (1830) 4 C.& P. 220 188
Bennett [1968] 1 W.L.R. 988; 2 All E.R. 753; 52 Cr.App.R. 514 .... 235, 277
Beresford (1952) 36 Cr.App.R. 1 .... 39, 40
—— (1971) 56 Cr.App.R. 143 269
Berry (1897) 104 L.T.J. 110 150
Bidwell, *Ex p.* [1937] 1 K.B. 304 93
Biggin [1920] 1 K.B. 213; 89 L.J.K.B. 99; 26 Cox 545; 14 Cr.App.R. 87 194
Bircham [1972] Crim.L.R. 430 195
Bird *v.* Jones (1845) 7 Q.B. 742; 15 L.J.Q.B. 82 41
Birtles [1974] 1 W.L.R. 1047 24
—— [1975] 1 W.L.R. 1623; 3 All E.R. 395; Crim.L.R. 589...... 331, 341, 354
Bishop [1975] Q.B. 274; [1974] 3 W.L.R. 308; 2 All E.R. 1206; Crim.L.R. 546 .... 192, 194
Black [1963] 1 W.L.R. 1311; 3 All E.R. 682; 48 Cr.App.R. 52 196
Blackpool Justices, *ex p.* Charlson [1972] 1 W.L.R. 1456; 3 All E.R. 854; Crim.L.R. 641; 56 Cr.App.R. 823 333
—— *ex p.* Beaverbrook Newspapers Ltd. [1972] 1 W.L.R. 95; 1 All E.R. 388 95
Blackwood [1974] Crim.L.R. 437; 59 Cr.App.R. 170 234
Blake [1962] 2 Q.B. 377; [1961] 3 W.L.R. 744; 3 All E.R. 125; 45 Cr.App.R. 292 229
Blanchard [1952] 1 All E.R. 114; 35 Cr.App.R. 183 30
Blandford and Freestone [1955] 1 W.L.R. 331; 1 All E.R. 681; 39 Cr.App.R. 51 52
Blank [1972] Crim.L.R. 176.......... 197
Boardman *v.* D.P.P. [1975] A.C. 421; [1974] 3 W.L.R. 673; 3 All E.R. 887; [1975] Crim.L.R. 36 .... 134, 135
Bodmin Justices, *ex p.* McEwen [1947] K.B. 321; 1 All E.R. 109 297
Bonner [1974] Crim.L.R. 479 147
Borro [1973] Crim.L.R. 513.......... 10
Bosomworth [1973] Crim.L.R. 456; 57 Cr.App.R. 708 367
Bourne (1952) 36 Cr.App.R. 125 211
Box and Box [1964] 1 Q.B. 430; [1963] 3 W.L.R. 696; 3 All E.R. 240; 47 Cr.App.R. 284 .... 205, 267
Boyle [1954] 2 Q.B. 292; 3 W.L.R. 364; 2 All E.R. 721; 38 Cr.App.R. 111 ... 154
Bradburn [1973] Crim.L.R. 705; 57 Cr.App.R. 948 251

Bradburn *v.* Richards [1976] R.T.R. 275; Crim.L.R. 62 315
Bradfield and Sonning Justices, *ex p.* Jones [1976] R.T.R. 144; [1975] Crim.L.R. 518 .... 298, 351
Brangwynne *v.* Evans [1962] 1 W.L.R. 267; 1 All E.R. 446 .... 304, 320
Brentford Justices, *ex p.* Catlin [1975] Q.B. 455; 2 W.L.R. 506; 2 All E.R. 201 Crim.L.R. 233 .... 55, 305
Bridgend Justices, *ex p.* Randall [1975] Crim.L.R. 287 314
Brigden [1973] Crim.L.R. 579 198
Bristol Coroner, *ex p.* Kerr [1974] Q.B. 652; 2 W.L.R. 816; 2 All E.R. 719; Crim.L.R. 363 39
Bristol Riots Case (1832) 3 St.Tr.(N.S.) 1 62
Brogan [1975] 1 W.L.R. 393; 1 All E.R. 879 .... 333, 355
Brook [1949] 2 K.B. 138; 1 All E.R. 787; 33 Cr.App.R. 92 233
Brooker (1976) 120 S.J. 250 .... 101, 140
Brown (1971) 55 Cr.App.R. 478 196
—— [1972] 2 Q.B. 229; 3 W.L.R. 11; 2 All E.R. 1328; 56 Cr.App.R. 564 ... 197
—— [1975] R.T.R. 36; Crim.L.R. 293 247
Brunson, *Ex p.* [1953] 1 Q.B. 503 107
Bryant and Dickson (1946) 31 Cr.App.R. 146 114
Bryson [1974] Crim.L.R. 197; 58 Cr.App.R. 464 367
Buchan [1964] 1 W.L.R. 365; 1 All E.R. 502; 48 Cr.App.R. 126 22
Buggy (1961) 45 Cr.App.R. 298 139
Bullock [1964] 1 Q.B. 481; [1963] 3 W.L.R. 911; 3 All E.R. 506; 47 Cr.App.R. 288 348
Burles [1970] 2 Q.B. 191; 2 W.L.R. 597; 1 All E.R. 642; 54 Cr.App.R. 196 ... 171
Burnham Justices [1959] 1 W.L.R. 1041; 3 All E.R. 505 309
Butler *v.* Board of Trade [1971] Ch. 680; [1970] 3 W.L.R. 822; 3 All E.R. 593 33
Butters (1971) 55 Cr.App.R. 515 230

CAIN [1976] Q.B. 496; [1975] 3 W.L.R. 131; 2 All E.R. 900; [1976] Crim.L.R. 464; 61 Cr.App.R. 186 .... 15, 156
Callis *v.* Gunn [1964] 1 Q.B. 495; [1963] 3 W.L.R. 931; 3 All E.R. 677; 48 Cr.App.R. 36 36
Cameron [1973] Crim.L.R. 520 197
Canabe *v.* Walton-on-Thames U.D.C. [1914] A.C. 102 352
Carter (1960) 44 Cr.App.R. 225 199
Casement [1917] 1 K.B. 98; 86 L.J.K.B. 467; 12 Cr.App.R. 99; 25 Cox 480, 503 12
Cavanagh and Shaw [1972] 1 W.L.R. 676; 2 All E.R. 704; Crim.L.R. 389 115, 179
Central Funds Costs Order, *Re* [1975] 1 W.L.R. 1227; 3 All E.R. 238; Crim. L.R. 646 18
Chairman of London Quarter Sessions, *ex p.* Downes [1954] 1 Q.B. 1; [1953] 3 W.L.R. 586; 2 All E.R. 750; 37 Cr.App.R. 148 166
Chandler [1964] 2 Q.B. 322; 2 W.L.R. 689; 1 All E.R. 761; 48 Cr.App.R. 143 174
—— [1976] 1 W.L.R. 585; Crim.L.R. 308 .... 23, 198
—— *v.* Horne (1842) 2 Mood & R. 423 181
Chapman [1960] 1 W.L.R. 147; 1 All E.R. 452; 44 Cr.App.R. 115 239
Charles [1976] 1 W.L.R. 248; 1 All E.R. 659 197
Chic Fashions (West Wales) Ltd. *v.* Jones [1968] 2 Q.B. 299; 2 W.L.R. 201; 1 All E.R. 229 .... 26, 27
Christie *v.* Leachinsky [1947] A.C. 573; 1 All E.R. 567 64
Clayton-Wright [1948] 2 Cr.App.R. 763; 33 Cr.App.R. 22 .... 133, 135
Cleghorn [1967] 2 Q.B. 584; 2 W.L.R. 1421; 1 All E.R. 996; 51 Cr.App.R. 291 189
Clemo [1973] R.T.R. 176 198
Clewer (1953) 37 Cr.App.R. 37 189
Close [1977] Crim.L.R. 107 168
Clow [1965] 1 Q.B. 598; [1963] 3 W.L.R. 84; 2 All E.R. 216; 47 Cr.App.R. 136 .... 130, 132, 133
Cockermouth Justices, *ex p.* Patterson [1971] R.T.R. 216 247

Coe [1968] 1 W.L.R. 1950; [1969] 1 All E.R. 65; 53 Cr.App.R. 66 ... 73, 298, 333
Cokar [1960] 2 Q.B. 207; 2 W.L.R. 836; 2 All E.R. 175; 44 Cr.App.R. 165... 191
Cole [1965] 2 Q.B. 388; 3 W.L.R. 263; 2 All E.R. 29; 49 Cr.App.R. 199...... 158
Collins [1976] Crim.L.R. 249 161
Commissioner of Police for the Metropolis, *ex p.* Blackburn [1973] Q.B. 241; 2 W.L.R. 43; 1 All E.R. 324; Crim.L.R. 185 19
Conn *v.* Turnbull (1925) 89 J.P. 300 .... 294, 299, 305
Connelly *v.* D.P.P. [1964] A.C. 1254; 2 W.L.R. 1145; 2 All E.R. 401; 48 Cr.App.R. 183 .... 134, 159–161, 166, 167
Conti (1973) 58 Cr.App.R. 387; [1974] Crim.L.R. 247 .... 31, 200
Conway *v.* Hotten [1976] 2 All E.R. 213........ 22
—— *v.* Rimmer [1968] A.C. 910; 2 W.L.R. 998; 1 All E.R. 874 33
Coombes (1785) 1 Leach 388; 1 East P.C. 367 10
Cooper [1969] 1 Q.B. 267; 3 W.L.R. 1225; 1 All E.R. 32; 53 Cr.App.R. 82 ... 267
—— (1975) 61 Cr.App.R. 215 280
Corke, *Re* [1954] 1 W.L.R. 899; 2 All E.R. 440 44
Corless [1972] Crim.L.R. 314; 56 Cr.App.R. 341 .... 189, 204
Coughlan [1976] Crim.L.R. 631 .... 162, 190
Courvoisier (1840) 9 C. & P. 362 178
Cox *v.* Army Council [1963] A.C. 48; [1962] 2 W.L.R. 950; 1 All E.R. 880; 46 Cr.App.R. 258 13
Craig [1967] 1 W.L.R. 645; 1 All E.R. 1052; 51 Cr.App.R. 8 276
Crisp (1912) 7 Cr.App.R. 173 209
Cross [1973] Q.B. 937; 2 W.L.R. 1049; 2 All E.R. 920; Crim.L.R. 433; 57 Cr.App.R. 660 263
Croydon Juvenile Court Justices, *ex p.* Croydon L.B.C. [1973] 1 Q.B. 406; 2 W.L.R. 61; 1 All E.R. 476 367
Crozier *v.* Cundy (1827) 6 B. & C. 232 27
Culbertson [1970] Crim.L.R. 302; 54 Cr.App.R. 310 195
Curtis (1848) 2 C. & K. 763 114

DALLISON *v.* Caftery [1965] 1 Q.B. 348; [1964] 3 W.L.R. 385; 2 All E.R. 610 .... 64, 67, 114
Daly [1974] 1 W.L.R. 133; 1 All E.R. 290 251
Damer *v.* Davison [1975] Crim.L.R. 522; 61 Cr.App.R. 232 247
Darke (1937) 26 Cr.App.R. 85........ 171
Davies [1906] 1 K.B. 32 392
—— *v.* D.P.P. [1954] A.C. 378; 2 W.L.R. 343; 1 All E.R. 507; 38 Cr.App. R. 11 .... 30, 266
Davis (1837) 7 C. & P. 785 178
—— [1943] K.B. 274; 112 L.J.K.B. 355; 1 All E.R. 305; 29 Cr.App.R. 35 ... 221
—— (1959) 43 Cr.App.R. 215 198
—— [1975] 1 W.L.R. 345; 1 All E.R. 233 201
Dawson [1960] 1 W.L.R. 163; 1 All E.R. 558; 44 Cr.App.R. 87 143
Day [1940] 1 All E.R. 402; 27 Cr.App.R. 168 .... 203, 312
Deacon [1973] 1 W.L.R. 696; 2 All E.R. 1145; Crim.L.R. 432; 57 Cr.App.R. 688 .... 30, 272
Deakin [1972] 1 W.L.R. 1618; 3 All E.R. 803; Crim.L.R. 781; 56 Cr.App.R. 841 129
Deary, *The Times*, June 9, 1976 88
De Courcy [1964] 1 W.L.R. 1245; 3 All E.R. 251; 48 Cr.App.R. 323 270
De Marny [1907] 1 K.B. 388; 76 L.J.K.B. 210; 21 Cox 371 9
Denbigh Justices, *ex p.* Williams [1974] Q.B. 759; 3 W.L.R. 45; 2 All E.R. 1052; Crim.L.R. 392 303
Deputy Chairman of Inner London Quarter Sessions [1970] 2 Q.B. 80; 2 W.L.R. 95; [1969] 3 All E.R. 1537; 54 Cr.App.R. 49 159
Derby Justices, *ex p.* Kooner [1971] 1 Q.B. 147; [1970] 3 W.L.R. 598; 3 All E.R. 399; 54 Cr.App.R. 455 .... 402, 403
Devine [1956] 1 W.L.R. 236; 1 All E.R. 548; 40 Cr.App.R. 45 .... 207, 239
Dewing *v.* Cummings [1971] R.T.R. 295 349

Dick [1972] Crim.L.R. 58 230
Dickson [1969] 1 W.L.R. 405; 1 All E.R. 729; 53 Cr.App.R. 263 114
Dillon *v.* O'Brien and Davis (1887) 16 Cox 245 27
Disney [1933] 2 K.B. 138; 102 L.J.K.B. 381; 29 Cox 635; 24 Cr.App.R. 49... 130
Dolan [1971] Crim.L.R. 297 276
Doran [1972] Crim.L.R. 392; 56 Cr.App.R. 429 .... 179, 189, 203
Downes, *ex p.* [19541] Q.B. 1 148
D.P.P. *v.* Bladey [1912] 2 K.B. 89; 81 L.J.K.B. 613; 22 Cox 715 30
—— *v.* Boardman, see Boardman *v.* D.P.P.
—— *v.* Burgess [1971] Q.B. 432; [1970] 3 W.L.R. 805; 3 All E.R. 266 342
—— *v.* Doot [1973] A.C. 807; 2 W.L.R. 532; 1 All E.R. 940; Crim.L.R. 292; 57 Cr.App.R. 600 .... 10, 155
—— *v.* Hester [1973] A.C. 296; [1972] 3 W.L.R. 910; 3 All E.R. 1056; [1973] Crim.L.R. 43; 57 Cr.App.R. 212 30
—— *v.* Humphrys [1976] 2 W.L.R. 857; 2 All E.R. 497 .... 166–168, 181
—— *v.* Merriman [1973] A.C. 584; [1972] 3 W.L.R. 545; 3 All E.R. 42; Crim.L.R. 784; 56 Cr.App.R. 766 .... 138, 210, 281
—— *v.* Lamb [1941] 2 K.B. 89 349
—— *v.* Nasralla [1967] 2 A.C. 238; 3 W.L.R. 13; 2 All E.R. 161 160
—— *v.* Shannon [1975] A.C. 717; [1974] 3 W.L.R. 155; 2 All E.R. 1009; 59 Cr. App.R. 250 .... 138, 155, 168, 197, 210, 265, 266, 268
Drummond (1975) 119 S.J. 575 174
Drury (1849) 3 C. & K. 193 164
Dudley Crown Court, *ex p.* Smith [1973] Crim.L.R. 178; 58 Cr.App.R. 184 .... 86, 221
Duncan *v.* Cammell Laird and Co. Ltd. [1942] A.C. 624 33
Durante [1972] 1 W.L.R. 1612 210
Dwyer [1925] 2 K.B. 799; 95 L.J.K.B. 109; 18 Cr.App.R. 145; 27 Cox 697... 35
—— (1975) 60 Cr.App.R. 39 243

East Kerrier Justices, *ex p.* Mandy [1952] 2 Q.B. 719; 2 All E.R. 666........ 290
Edgar (1958) 42 Cr.App.R. 192 107
Eggington *v.* Pearl (1875) 40 J.P. 56 305
Elia [1968] 2 All E.R. 587; 52 Cr. App.R. 342 .... 212, 214
Elias *v.* Pasmore [1934] 2 K.B. 164; 103 L.J.K.B. 223 27
Ellis [1899] 1 Q.B. 230; 68 L.J.Q.B. 103; 19 Cox 210 9
—— [1973] Crim.L.R. 389; 57 Cr.App.R. 571 155
—— *v.* Burton [1975] 1 W.L.R. 386; 1 All E.R. 395; Crim.L.R. 32 164
Emery (1943) 29 Cr.App.R. 47 158
—— *ex p.* [1909] 2 K.B. 81 170
Entick v' Carrington (1765) 19 St.Tr. 1029 57
Epping and Harlow Justices, *ex p.* Massaro [1973] 1 Q.B. 433; 2 W.L.R. 158; 1 All E.R. 1011; Crim.L.R. 109; 57 Cr.App.R. 499 98
Errington (1922) 16 Cr.App.R. 148 146
Essex Justices, *ex p.* Final [1963] 2 Q.B. 816; 2 W.L.R. 38; [1962] 3 All E.R. 924 312
Evans [1963] 1 Q.B. 412; [1962] 3 W.L.R. 1457; 3 All E.R. 1086; 47 Cr.App.R. 62 356
—— *v.* Hemingway (1887) 52 J.P. 134 351
—— *v.* Macklen [1976] Crim.L.R. 120 64
Everitt *v.* Griffiths [1921] 1 A.C. 631 53
Ewer *v.* Ambrose (1825) 3 B. & C. 746 182

Fairford Justices, *ex p.* Brewster [1975] 3 W.L.R. 59; 2 All E.R. 757 306
Fairhead [1975] 2 All E.R. 737; 61 Cr.App.R. 102 242
Falconer-Atlee (1973) 58 Cr.App.R. 348 .... 198, 202
Fareham Justices, *ex p.* Long [1976] Crim.L.R. 269 310
Farndale [1974] Crim.L.R. 135; 59 Cr.App.R. 336 231
Farrow *v.* Tunnicliffe [1976] Crim.L.R. 127 .... 21, 25
Featherstone [1942] 2 All E.R. 672; 28 Cr.App.R. 176........ 199

Fenwick (1953) 54 S.R.N.S.W. 147 138
Ferguson [1970] 1 W.L.R. 1246; 2 All E.R. 820; 54 Cr.App.R. 410 252
Ferrara (1971) 55 Cr.App.R. 199 190
Finch (1962) 47 Cr.App.R. 58 244
Fisher [1965] 1 W.L.R. 464; 1 All E.R. 677; 49 Cr.App.R. 116 196
—— [1969] 2 Q.B. 114; 2 W.L.R. 453; 1 All E.R. 265 213
Fitzpatrick [1963] 1 W.L.R. 7; [1962] 3 All E.R. 840; 47 Cr.App.R. 16 134
Flack [1969] 1 W.L.R. 937; 2 All E.R. 784; 53 Cr.App.R. 166 134
Flanders [1969] 1 Q.B. 148; [1968] 3 W.L.R. 873; 3 All E.R. 534; 52 Cr.App. R. 676 230
Flannagan *v.* Shaw [1920] 3 K.B. 96 342
Flannigan (1884) 15 Cox 403 114
Flatman *v.* Light [1946] K.B. 414; 115 L.J.K.B. 353; 2 All E.R. 368 163
Flemming [1973] 2 All E.R. 401; Crim.L.R. 383; 57 Cr.App.R. 524 226
Flower (1956) 40 Cr.App.R. 189 164
Flynn [1972] Crim.L.R. 428 .... 184, 192
Forde [1923] 2 K.B. 400; 92 L.J.K.B. 501; 27 Cox 406; 17 Cr.App.R. 99 265
Foster [1975] R.T.R. 553 198
Foy [1962] 1 W.L.R. 609; 2 All E.R. 246; 46 Cr.App.R. 290 230
Frank Truman Export Ltd. *v.* Metropolitan Police Commissioner, *The Times*, December 22, 1976 27
Fraser (1923) 17 Cr.App.R. 182 .... 146, 159
Fraser and Warren (1956) 40 Cr.App.R. 160 183
French's Dairies (Sevenoaks) Ltd. *v.* Davis [1973] Crim.L.R. 630 314
Furlong [1962] 2 Q.B. 161; 2 W.L.R. 796; 1 All E.R. 656; 46 Cr.App.R. 122 294
Furlong, French and Pickard [1950] 1 All E.R. 636; 34 Cr.App.R. 79 209

GAISFORD [1892] 1 Q.B. 381 50
Gallagher [1974] 1 W.L.R. 1204; 3 All E.R. 118; Crim.L.R. 543 198
Gardiner [1967] 1 W.L.R. 464; 1 All E.R. 895; 51 Cr.App.R. 187 326
Garfield *v.* Maddocks [1974] Q.B. 7; [1973] 2 W.L.R. 888; 2 All E.R. 303; Crim.L.R. 231; 57 Cr.App.R. 372 305
Garman *v.* Plaice [1969] 1 W.L.R. 19; 1 All E.R. 62 304
Gash (No. 2) [1967] 1 W.L.R. 454; 1 All E.R. 811; 51 Cr.App.R. 37 267
Gee [1936] 2 K.B. 442; 105 L.J.K.B. 739; 2 All E.R. 89; 30 Cox 432; 25 Cr.App.R. 198 107
Genese [1976] 2 All E.R. 600 233
Ghani *v.* Jones [1970] 1 Q.B. 693; [1969] 3 W.L.R. 1158; 3 All E.R. 1700 .... 27, 28
Gibbs [1965] 2 Q.B. 281; [1964] 3 W.L.R. 1272; 3 All E.R. 776; 49 Cr.App.R. 42 .... 294, 295
Giddings (1842) C. & M. 634 132
Gilbert [1975] 1 W.L.R. 1012; 1 All E.R. 742; 60 Cr.App.R. 220 230
Gilby [1975] 1 W.L.R. 924; 2 All E.R. 743; 61 Cr.App.R. 112 .... 327, 334
Gillespie [1973] 1 W.L.R. 1483; [1974] 1 All E.R. 113; Crim.L.R. 57 222
Glinski *v.* McIver [1962] A.C. 726; 2 W.L.R. 832; 1 All E.R. 696 42
Goddard [1962] 1 W.L.R. 1282; 3 All E.R. 582; 46 Cr.App.R. 456 197
—— *v.* Smith (1704) 6 Mod.Rep. 261; 11 Mod.Rep. 56; 1 Salk. 21; 3 Salk. 245 19
Godstone Justices, *ex p.* Dickson [1971] Crim.L.R. 602; 115 S.J. 246 313
Golder [1960] 1 W.L.R. 1169; 3 All E.R. 457; 45 Cr.App.R. 5 .... 183, 197
Goodlad [1973] 1 W.L.R. 1102; 2 All E.R. 1200; Crim.L.R. 586; 57 Cr.App. R. 717 231
Goodson [1975] 1 W.L.R. 549; 1 All E.R. 760; 60 Cr.App.R. 266 ... 205, 209, 268
Gould (1840) C. & P. 364 161
—— [1968] 2 Q.B. 65; 2 W.L.R. 643; 1 All E.R. 849; 52 Cr.App.R. 152 260
Governor of Brixton Prison, *ex p.* Gardner [1968] 2 Q.B. 399; 2 W.L.R. 512; 1 All E.R. 636 116
Governor of Winson Green Prison, *ex p.* Littlejohn [1975] 1 W.L.R. 893; 3 All E.R. 208; Crim.L.R. 344 59
Gowerton Justices, *ex p.* Davies [1974] Crim.L.R. 253 309
Graham [1975] Crim.L.R. 699 267

Grant [1936] 2 All E.R. 1156; 30 Cox 453; 26 Cr.App.R. 8 164
—— [1958] Crim.L.R. 42 ..... 189, 203
Graves, *The Times*, April 7, 1976 334
Gray (1891) 17 Cox 299 209
—— (1973) 58 Cr.App.R. 177 196
Great Marlborough Street Magistrate, *ex p.* Fraser [1974] Crim.L.R. 47 ... 312
Greater Manchester Justices, *ex p.* Martyn [1976] Crim.L.R. 574 296
Green (1856) Dears. & B. 113; 26 L.J.M.C. 17; 7 Cox 186 164
—— [1950] 1 All E.R. 38; 34 Cr.App·R. 33 208
—— [1968] 1 W.L.R. 673; 2 All E.R. 77; Crim.L.R. 264; 52 Cr.App.R. 208 402
Greenberg (1919) 121 L.T. 288; 26 Cox 466 34
Greene, *Re* (1941) 57 T.L.R. 533 44
Greenough *v.* Eccles (1859) 5 C.B.(N.S.) 786; 28 L.J.C.P. 160 183
Greenwich Justices, *ex p.* Carter [1973] Crim.L.R. 444 98
Gregory [1972] 1 W.L.R. 991; 2 All E.R. 861; Crim.L.R. 509; 56 Cr.App.R. 441 ..... 123, 147
—— *v.* Tavernor (1833) 6 C. & P. 280 188
Griffiths (1932) 23 Cr.App.R. 153 158
—— *v.* Freeman [1970] 1 W.L.R. 659; 1 All E.R. 1117 ..... 120, 129
Grondkowski and Malinowski [1946] K.B. 369; 31 Cr.App.R. 116 141
Groom [1976] 1 W.L.R. 618; 2 All E.R. 321 ..... 137, 140, 142, 145
Grundy [1974] 1 W.L.R. 139; 1 All E.R. 292; Crim.L.R. 128 251
Guest [1961] 3 All E.R. 1118 68
Guildhall Justices, *ex p.* Marshall [1976] 1 W.L.R. 335 ..... 402, 403
Gunewardene [1951] 2 K.B. 600; 2 All E.R. 290; 35 Cr.App.R. 80 201
Gurney [1976] Crim.L.R. 567 204

HADDOCK [1976] Crim.L.R. 374 210
Hall [1968] 2 Q.B. 787; 3 W.L.R. 359; 2 All E.R. 1009; Crim.L.R. 403; 52 Cr.App.R. 528 147
Halse [1971] 3 All E.R. 1149; [1972] Crim.L.R. 59; 56 Cr.App.R. 47 231
Hammerton Cars Ltd. *v.* Redbridge L.B.C. [1974] 1 W.L.R. 484; 2 All E.R. 216; Crim.L.R. 241 250
Hammond [1941] 3 All E.R. 318; 28 Cr.App.R. 84 178
Hannigan [1971] Crim.L.R. 302 336
Harden [1963] 1 Q.B. 8; [1962] 2 W.L.R. 553; 1 All E.R. 286; 46 Cr.App.R. 90 147
Harper, de Haan [1968] 2 Q.B. 108; 2 W.L.R. 626; 52 Cr.App.R. 21 223
Harris (1897) 61 J.P. 792 170
—— [1969] 1 W.L.R. 745; 2 All E.R. 599; 53 Cr.App.R. 376 ..... 136, 162
—— (1976) 62 Cr.App.R. 28 147
—— *v.* D.P.P. [1952] A.C. 694; 1 All E.R. 1044; 36 Cr.App.R. 39 ..... 23, 191
—— *v.* Tippett (1811) 2 Camp. 637 186
Harrison [1954] Crim.L.R. 39 144
Harrow Justices, *ex p.* Morris [1973] 1 Q.B. 672; [1972] 3 W.L.R. 699; 3 All E.R. 494; Crim.L.R. 636 76
Hart (1932) 23 Cr.App.R. 202 184
—— (1958) 42 Cr.App.R. 47 188
—— [1960] Crim.L.R. 277 231
Haslam (1916) 85 L.J.K.B. 1511; 25 Cox 344; 12 Cr.App.R. 10 192
Hassan [1970] 1 Q.B. 423; 2 W.L.R. 82; 1 All E.R. 745; 54 Cr.App.R. 56 ... 112
Haughton *v.* Harrison [1976] R.T.R. 208 14
Hawkes (1931) 22 Cr.App.R. 172 209
Hawkins (1896) Q.B.D., unreported 114
Haycraft (1973) 58 Cr.App.R. 121 263
Hayden [1975] 1 W.L.R. 852; 2 All E.R. 558; 60 Cr.App.R. 304 275
Haygarth, *Ex p.*, *The Times*, October 29, 1975 316
Hazeltine [1967] 2 Q.B. 857; 3 W.L.R. 209; 2 All E.R. 671; 51 Cr.App.R. 351 157
Henderson *v.* Preston (1888) 21 Q.B.D. 362; 57 L.J.Q.B. 607; 16 Cox 445 ... 41

Hendon Justices, *ex p.* Gorchein [1973] 1 W.L.R. 1502; 1 All E.R. 168; Crim.L.R. 754 328
Hepworth and Fearnley [1955] 2 Q.B. 600; 3 W.L.R. 331; 2 All E.R. 918; 39 Cr.App.R. 152 196
Hertfordshire Justices, *ex p.* Larsen [1926] 1 K.B. 191 86
Hetherington [1972] Crim.L.R. 703 169
Hewitt (1971) 55 Cr.App.R. 433 233
Heyes [1951] K.B. 29; [1950] 2 All E.R. 587; 34 Cr.App.R. 161 .... 155, 169
Hill *v.* Baxter [1958] 1 Q.B. 277; 2 W.L.R. 76; 1 All E.R. 193; 42 Cr.App.R. 51 .... 343, 356
Hilton [1972] 1 Q.B. 421; [1971] 3 W.L.R. 625; 3 All E.R. 541; 55 Cr.App.R. 466 200
Hinds, *Ex p.* [1961] 1 W.L.R. 325; 1 All E.R. 707 44
Hoare [1966] 1 W.L.R. 762; 2 All E.R. 846; 50 Cr.App.R. 166 198
Hodgson [1973] 1 Q.B. 565; 2 W.L.R. 570; 2 All E.R. 552; 57 Cr.App.R. 502 213
Hogan [1960] 2 Q.B. 513; 3 W.L.R. 426; 3 All E.R. 149; 44 Cr.App.R. 255 ... 165
Hoggins [1967] 1 W.L.R. 1223; 3 All E.R. 334; 51 Cr.App.R. 444 .... 140, 141
Hollis [1971] Crim.L.R. 525 .... 120, 213
Hood [1968] 1 W.L.R. 773; 2 All E.R. 56; 52 Cr.App.R. 265 33
Hornett [1975] R.T.R. 256 9
Horseferry Road Stipendiary Magistrate, *ex p.* Pearson [1976] 1 W.L.R. 511; 2 All E.R. 264; Crim.L.R. 304 82
Hove Justices, *ex p.* Donne [1967] 2 All E.R. 1253 98
Howes [1964] 2 Q.B. 459; 1 W.L.R. 576; 2 All E.R. 172; 48 Cr.App.R. 172 ... 402
Howitt [1975] Crim.L.R. 588 274
Hudson [1912] 2 K.B. 464; 81 L.J.K.B. 861; 23 Cox 61; 7 Cr.App.R. 256 194
Hulusi (1973) 58 Cr.App.R. 378 189
Hunt [1968] 2 Q.B. 433; 3 W.L.R. 231; 2 All E.R. 1056; 52 Cr.App.R. 580 ... 210
Hussey (1924) 18 Cr.App.R. 121 158
Hutchison [1972] 1 W.L.R. 398 215

Ikpong [1972] Crim.L.R. 432 129
Ingle [1974] 3 All E.R. 811; Crim.L.R. 609; 59 Cr.App.R. 306 242
Ingleson [1915] 1 K.B. 512; 84 L.J.K.B. 280; 24 Cox 527; 11 Cr.App.R. 21... 158
Inman [1967] 1 Q.B. 140; [1966] 3 W.L.R. 567; 3 All E.R. 414; 50 Cr.App.R. 247 129
Inner London Quarter Sessions, *see* Deputy Chairman of Inner London Quarter Sessions
Inns [1975] Crim.L.R. 182; 60 Cr.App.R. 231 .... 157, 266
Inwood [1973] 1 W.L.R. 647; 2 All E.R. 645; Crim.L.R. 290 65
Ioannou [1975] 1 W.L.R. 1297 275
Isherwood [1974] Crim.L.R. 485; 59 Cr.App.R. 162 237
Ithell [1969] 1 W.L.R. 272; 2 All E.R. 449; 53 Cr.App.R. 210 230

Jackson [1953] 1 W.L.R. 591; 1 All E.R. 872; 37 Cr.App.R. 43 .... 32, 197
—— [1974] Q.B. 517; 2 W.L.R. 641; 2 All E.R. 211; Crim.L.R. 323; 59 Cr.App.R. 23 335
—— [1974] Q.B. 802; 2 W.L.R. 352; 1 All E.R. 640; Crim.L.R. 195; 58 Cr.App.R. 405 227
—— [1974] Crim.L.R. 718 157
Jackson and Robertson [1973] Crim.L.R. 356 112
Jacobs (1975) 62 Cr.App.R. 116 242
James [1960] 1 W.L.R. 812; 2 All E.R. 863 335
—— [1970] 1 W.L.R. 1304; 3 All E.R. 263; 54 Cr.App.R. 423 239
Jameson [1896] 2 Q.B. 425; 65 L.J.M.C. 218; 18 Cox 392 211
Jamieson [1975] Crim.L.R. 248 223
Jeffries [1969] 1 Q.B. 120; [1968] 3 W.L.R. 830; 3 All E.R. 238; 52 Cr.App.R. 654 270
Jemmison *v.* Priddle [1972] 1 Q.B. 489; 2 W.L.R. 293; 1 All E.R. 539 132
Jennings (1949) 33 Cr.App.R. 143 146

Johal [1973] 1 Q.B. 475; [1972] 3 W.L.R. 210; 2 All E.R. 449; 56 Cr.App.R. 348 147
John Lewis & Co. Ltd. *v.* Tims [1952] A.C. 676; 1 All E.R. 1203 64
Johnson (1805) 6 East 583; 29 St.Tr. 359 159
—— [1972] Crim.L.R. 180 196
—— [1976] 1 W.L.R. 426; 1 All E.R. 869 226
Jones [1969] 2 Q.B. 53; 2 W.L.R. 105; 1 All E.R. 325; 53 Cr.App.R. 87 354
—— [1971] 2 Q.B. 456; 2 W.L.R. 1485; 2 All E.R. 731; 55 Cr.App.R. 321 310
—— (No. 2) [1972] 1 W.L.R. 887; 56 Cr.App.R. 413 150
—— *ex p.* Thomas [1921] 1 K.B. 632; 90 L.J.K.B. 543; 26 Cox 706 132
—— *v.* D.P.P. [1962] A.C. 635; 2 W.L.R. 575; 1 All E.R. 569; 46 Cr.App.R. 129 .... 191, 192, 193
Joseph (1971) 56 Cr.App.R. 60 189
Joyce *v.* D.P.P. [1946] A.C. 347; 115 L.J.K.B. 146; 1 All E.R. 186; 31 Cr.App.R. 57 13

KALIA [1975] Crim.L.R. 181; 60 Cr.App.R. 200 .... 208, 249, 263
Karamat *v.* R. [1956] A.C. 256; 2 W.L.R. 412; 1 All E.R. 415; 40 Cr.App.R. 13 204
Keane *v.* Governor of Brixton Prison [1972] A.C. 204; [1971] 2 W.L.R. 1243; 1 All E.R. 1163 115
Keelan [1976] Crim.L.R. 455; 61 Cr.App.R. 212 354
Kelly [1950] 2 K.B. 164; 1 All E.R. 806; 34 Cr.App.R. 95 205
—— [1965] 2 Q.B. 409; 3 W.L.R. 571; 3 All E.R. 162; 49 Cr.App.R. 352 ... 157
Kendall *v.* Wilkinson (1855) 19 J.P. 467 347
Kent Justices, *ex p.* Lye [1967] 2 Q.B. 153; 2 W.L.R. 765; 1 All E.R. 560 11
——, *ex p.* Machin [1952] 2 K.B. 355; 1 All E.R. 1123; 36 Cr.App.R. 23 ... 296, 298
Kettering Justices, *ex p.* Patmore [1968] 1 W.L.R. 1436; 3 All E.R. 167 293
King [1897] 1 Q.B. 214; 18 Cox 447 .... 134, 162
—— [1970] 1 W.L.R. 1016; 2 All E.R. 249; 54 Cr.App.R. 362 233
Kinglake (1870) 11 Cox 499 32
King's Lynn Justices [1969] 1 Q.B. 488; [1968] 3 W.L.R. 1210; 3 All E.R. 858; 53 Cr.App.R. 42 332
Kingston (1948) 32 Cr.App.R. 183 153
Kirby (1972) 56 Cr.App.R. 758 210
Kirkham [1968] Crim.L.R. 210 .... 218, 220
Kneeshaw [1975] Q.B. 57; [1974] 2 W.L.R. 432; 1 All E.R. 896 252
Knightsbridge Crown Court *ex p.* Martin [1976] Crim.L.R. 463 347
Krausz [1973] Crim.L.R. 581; 57 Cr.App.R. 466 186
Kruger [1973] Crim.L.R. 133 276
Kray [1970] Q.B. 125; [1969] 3 W.L.R. 831; 3 All E.R. 941; 52 Cr.App.R. 581 .... 133, 134, 135, 145
——, *Re* [1965] Ch.736; 2 W.L.R. 626; 1 All E.R. 710; 40 Cr.App.R. 164 ... 78, 80
Kupferberg (1918) 13 Cr.App.R. 166 162
Kuruma *v.* R. [1955] A.C. 197; 2 W.L.R. 223; 1 All E.R. 236 .... 24, 29, 36
Kwame [1975] R.T.R. 106; 60 Cr.App.R. 65 77

LAMB [1968] 1 W.L.R. 1946; [1969] 1 All E.R. 45; Crim.L.R. 30 143
—— (1974) 59 Cr.App.R. 196 209
Langham [1972] Crim.L.R. 457 189
Larbin [1943] K.B. 174; 112 L.J.K.B. 163; 1 All E.R. 217; 29 Cr.App.R. 18 .... 198, 211
Lashbrooke (1958) 43 Cr.App.R. 86 171
Latham *v.* R. (1864) 5 B. & S. 635; 33 L.J.M.C. 197; 9 Cox 516 .... 143, 154
Lattimore [1976] Crim.L.R. 45; 62 Cr.App.R. 53 269
Lawrence [1968] 1 W.L.R. 341; 1 All E.R. 578; 57 Cr.App.R. 163 204
—— *v.* Same [1968] 2 Q.B. 93; 2 W.L.R. 1062; 1 All E.R. 1191 .... 304, 305, 315
Leach *v.* Money (1765) 19 St.Tr. 1001 57
Lee [1976] 1 W.L.R. 71; 1 All E.R. 570; Crim.L.R. 191; 62 Cr.App.R. 33 .... 193, 194

Lee Kun [1916] 1 K.B. 337; 85 L.J.K.B. 515; 25 Cox 304; 11 Cr.App.R. 293 151
Leeds Prison Governor, *ex p.* Huntley [1972] 1 W.L.R. 1016; 2 All E.R. 783; Crim.L.R. 373 324
Leigh and Harrison [1966] 1 All E.R. 687 140
Lennox-Wright [1973] Crim.L.R. 529 224
Lesley (1860) Bell 220; 8 Cox 269 41
Levene *v.* Pearcey [1976] Crim.L.R. 63 125
Levy and Tait [1966] Crim.L.R. 454; 50 Cr.App.R. 198 203
Lewis [1969] 2 Q.B. 1; 2 W.L.R. 55; 1 All E.R. 79; 53 Cr.App.R. 76 113
—— [1973] Crim.L.R. 576; 57 Cr.App.R. 860 198
——, *Ex p.* (1888) 21 Q.B.D. 191; 57 L.J.M.C. 108,; 16 Cox 449 53
—— *v.* Morgan [1943] K.B. 376; 112 L.J.K.B. 313; 2 All E.R. 272 165
Lidster [1976] R.T.R. 240; Crim.L.R. 80 255
Lillis [1972] 2 Q.B. 236; 2 W.L.R. 1409; 2 All E.R. 1209; Crim.L.R. 458; 56 Cr.App.R. 573 213
Linford *v.* Fitzroy (1849) 13 Q.B. 240; 18 L.J.M.C. 108 78
Linley [1959] Crim.L.R. 123 108
Linnell [1969] 1 W.L.R. 1514; 3 All E.R. 849; 53 Cr.App.R. 585 129
Lishman [1971] Crim.L.R. 548 226
Liskerrett Justices, *ex p.* Child [1972] R.T.R. 141; 135 J.P. 693 310
Liverpool Justices, *ex p.* Molyneux [1972] 2 Q.B. 384; 2 All E.R. 471 ...... 10, 12
Lock [1975] Crim.L.R. 35 196
London Quarter Sessions, *ex p.* Downes, *see* Chairman of London Quarter Sessions
London Sessions, *ex p.* Rogers [1951] 2 K.B. 74; 1 All E.R. 343 ... 331, 341, 345
Lovett [1973] 1 W.L.R. 241; 1 All E.R. 744; Crim.L.R. 176; 57 Cr.App.R. 332 267
Ludlow *v.* Burgess [1971] Crim.L.R. 238 43
—— *v.* Metropolitan Police Commissioner [1971] A.C. 29; [1970] 2 W.L.R. 521; 54 Cr.App.R. 233 .... 133, 135
Lycett [1968] 1 W.L.R. 1245; 2 All E.R. 1021; 52 Cr.App.R. 507 223
Lymm Justices, *ex p.* Brown [1973] 1 W.L.R. 1039; 1 All E.R. 716; Crim.L.R. 52 .... 297, 332

Maguire and Enos (1956) 40 Cr.App.R. 92 224
Maizone [1974] Crim.L.R. 112 295
Mallon *v.* Allon [1964] 1 Q.B. 385; [1963] 3 W.L.R. 1053; 3 All E.R. 843...... 130
Malvisi (1909) 2 Cr.App.R. 251 190
Mann [1972] Crim.L.R. 704; 56 Cr.App.R. 750 183
March [1970] 2 W.L.R. 998; 2 All E.R. 536; 54 Cr.App.R. 313 230
Marks *v.* Beyfus (1890) 25 Q.B.D. 494; 59 L.J.Q.B. 479; 17 Cox 196 34
Marquis (1951) 35 Cr.App.R. 33 218
—— [1974] 1 W.L.R. 1087 2 All E.R. 1216; Crim.L.R. 556; 59 Cr.App.R. 228 .... 237, 275
Marsden [1968] 1 W.L.R. 785; 2 All E.R. 341; 52 Cr.App.R. 301 277
Marshall [1972] Crim.L.R. 231; 56 Cr.App.R. 263 129
Marsham [1912] 2 K.B. 362; 81 L.J.K.B. 957; 23 Cox 77 164
Martin [1956] 2 Q.B. 272; 2 W.L.R. 975; 2 All E.R. 86; 40 Cr.App.R. 68...... 11
—— [1962] 1 Q.B. 221; [1961] 3 W.L.R. 17; 2 All E.R. 747; 45 Cr.App.R. 199 147
Maskell (1970) 54 Cr.App.R. 429 168
Maxwell *v.* D.P.P. [1935] A.C. 309; 103 L.J.K.B. 301; 30 Cox 160; 24 Cr.App.R. 152 192
Mayer [1975] R.T.R. 411 64
McCauliffe [1970] Crim.L.R. 660; 54 Cr.App.R. 516 .... 225, 367
McCormack [1969] 2 Q.B. 442; 3 W.L.R. 175; 3 All E.R. 371; 53 Cr.App.R. 514 .... 213, 272
McDonnell [1966] 1 Q.B. 233; [1965] 3 W.L.R. 1138; 1 All E.R. 193; 50 Cr.App.R. 5 .... 142, 148

McEvilly [1974] Crim.L.R. 239; 60 Cr.App.R. 320 24
McFarlane *v.* Sharp [1972] N.Z.L.R. 64; [1974] Crim.L.R. 218 28
McGinlay (1975) 62 Cr.App.R. 156 225
McGregor [1975] Crim.L.R. 514 65
McKenna [1960] 1 Q.B. 411; 2 W.L.R. 306; 1 All E.R. 326; 44 Cr.App.R. 63 211
—— [1974] 1 W.L.R. 267; 1 All E.R. 637 226
McNally [1954] 1 W.L.R. 933; 2 All E.R. 372; 38 Cr.App.R. 90 .... 164, 169
McQuaide [1975] Crim.L.R. 246; 60 Cr.App.R. 239 242
Mealey and Sheridan [1975] Crim.L.R. 154; 60 Cr.App.R. 59 280
Medway [1976] 2 W.L.R. 528; 1 All E.R. 527; Crim.L.R. 118; 62 Cr.App.R. 85 270
Meese [1973] 1 W.L.R. 675; 2 All E.R. 1103; 57 Cr.App.R. 568 247
Melville [1976] 1 W.L.R. 181; 1 All E.R. 395; Crim.L.R. 247; 62 Cr.App.R. 100 269
Mendy, *The Times*, June 29, 1976 185–186
Merry [1971] Crim.L.R. 91; 54 Cr.App.R. 274 269
Messingham (1830) 1 Mood C.C. 357 139
Michael [1975] 3 W.L.R. 731; [1976] 1 All E.R. 629 248
Middlesex Crown Court, *ex p.* Riddle [1975] Crim.L.R. 731 .... 199, 312
Midhurst Justices, *ex p.* Thompson [1974] Q.B. 137; [1973] 3 W.L.R. 715; 3 All E.R. 1164; Crim.L.R. 755 316
Miele [1976] R.T.R. 238 254
Miles (1890) 24 Q.B.D. 423; 59 L.J.M.C. 56; 17 Cox 9 .... 161, 164
—— (1909) 3 Cr.App.R. 13 162
Miller [1952] 2 All E.R. 667; 36 Cr.App.R. 169 201
Mills [1962] 1 W.L.R. 1152; 3 All E.R. 298; 46 Cr.App.R. 336 36
Mitchell (1848) 3 Cox 93; 6 St.Tr.(N.S.) 545 19
Moore [1968] 1 W.L.R. 397; 1 All E.R. 790; 52 Cr.App.R. 180 354
—— *v.* Clerk of Assize, Bristol [1971] 1 W.L.R. 1669; [1972] 1 All E.R. 58; Crim.L.R. 231 392
Moorhead [1973] Crim.L.R. 36 157
Morgan [1972] 1 Q.B. 436; 2 W.L.R. 123; 1 All E.R. 348; 56 Cr.App.R. 181 122
Morris (1867) L.R.1 C.C.R. 90; 36 L.J.M.C. 84; 10 Cox 480 162
—— *v.* The Crown Office [1970] 2 Q.B. 114; 2 W.L.R. 792; 1 All E.R. 1079 .... 393, 394
Morry [1946] K.B. 153; 115 L.J.K.B. 1; [1945] 2 All E.R. 632; 31 Cr.App.R. 19 143
Morsom [1976] Crim.L.R. 323; 62 Cr.App.R. 236 285
Moss *v.* Moss [1963] 2 Q.B. 799; 3 W.L.R. 171; 2 All E.R. 829; 47 Cr.App.R. 222 30
Moylan [1970] 1 Q.B. 143; [1969] 3 W.L.R. 814; 3 All E.R. 783; 53 Cr.App.R. 590 229
Muir [1938] 2 All E.R. 516; 26 Cr.App.R. 164 134
Munday (1971) 56 Cr.App.R. 220 229
——, *Ex p.* [1970] Crim.L.R. 601 296
Munisamy [1975] 1 All E.R. 910; Crim.L.R. 645; 60 Cr.App.R. 289 270
Murdoch *v.* Taylor [1965] A.C. 574; 2 W.L.R. 425; 1 All E.R. 406; 49 Cr.App.R. 119 200
Murtagh and Kennedy (1955) 39 Cr.App.R. 72 .... 196, 266
Mutch [1973] 1 All E.R. 178; Crim.L.R. 111; 57 Cr.App.R. 196 198
Mutford and Lothingland Justices, *ex p.* Harber [1971] 2 Q.B. 291; 2 W.L.R. 460; 1 All E.R. 81; 55 Cr.App.R. 57 344

NELSON [1967] 1 W.L.R. 449; 1 All E.R. 358; 51 Cr.App.R. 98 221
Neville [1971] Crim.L.R. 589 223
Newcastle-upon-Tyne Justices, *ex p.* John Bryce [1976] 1 W.L.R. 517 305
——, *ex p.* Swales [1972] Crim.L.R. 111; R.T.R. 57 315
Newham Justices, *ex p.* Knight [1976] Crim.L.R. 323 363
Nicholson [1974] 2 All E.R. 535; 32 Cr.App.R. 98 .... 165, 221

Nisbet [1972] Q.B. 37; [1971] 3 W.L.R. 455; 3 All E.R. 307; Crim.L.R. 532; 55 Cr.App.R. 490 .... 104, 143, 294
Nixon [1968] 1 W.L.R. 577; 3 All E.R. 33; 52 Cr.App.R. 218 .... 204, 209
Noble [1974] 1 W.L.R. 894; 2 All E.R. 811; Crim.L.R. 545; 59 Cr.App.R. 209 30
Noor Mohammed *v*. R. [1949] A.C. 182; 1 All E.R. 365 23
Norman [1915] 1 K.B. 341 134
North [1971] Crim.L.R. 429 247
North London Metropolitan Magistrate, *ex p*. Haywood [1973] 1 W.L.R. 965; 3 All E.R. 50; Crim.L.R. 442 328
Northamptonshire Justices, *ex p*. Nicholson [1974] R.T.R. 97; [1973] Crim.L.R. 762 316
Norton (1910) 5 Cr.App.R. 197 161
Norwich Rating Authority *v*. Norwich Assessment Committee [1941] 2 K.B. 326 352
Noseda [1958] 1 W.L.R. 793; 2 All E.R. 567; 42 Cr.App.R. 221 .... 232, 259

O'Brien (1974) 59 Cr.App.R. 222 .... 24, 210
O'Coigley (1798) 26 St.Tr. 1191 175
O'Connor [1976] 1 W.L.R. 368; 2 All E.R. 327 335
—— *v*. Isaacs [1956] 2 Q.B. 288; 3 W.L.R. 172; 2 All E.R. 417 53
Oddy [1974] 1 W.L.R. 1212; 2 All E.R. 666; Crim.L.R. 435; 59 Cr.App.R. 66 251
O'Doherty (1848) 6 St.Tr.(N.S.) 831 175
Ogden [1963] 1 W.L.R. 274; 1 All E.R. 574 292
Oldroyd (1805) R. & R. 88 108
Oliphant [1905] 2 K.B. 67; 74 L.J.K.B. 591; 21 Cox 192 9
Oliva [1965] 1 W.L.R. 1028; 3 All E.R. 116; 49 Cr.App.R. 298 179
Olympia Press *v*. Hollis [1973] 1 W.L.R. 1520; [1974] 1 All E.R. 108; [1973] Crim.L.R. 757 314
O'Neill (1950) 34 Cr.App.R. 108 184
Orpin [1975] Q.B. 283; [1974] 3 W.L.R. 252; 2 All E.R. 1211; Crim.L.R. 598; 59 Cr.App.R. 231 88
Osbourne [1973] 1 Q.B. 678; 2 W.L.R. 209; 1 All E.R. 649; Crim.L.R. 178... 21
O'Sullivan [1969] 1 W.L.R. 497; 2 All E.R. 237; 53 Cr.App.R. 274 36
Oteri *v*. The Queen, [1976] 1 W.L.R. 1272; [1976] Crim.L.R. 737 10
Owen, *The Times*, April 21, 1970 124
—— [1976] 1 W.L.R. 840; 3 All E.R. 5 392

Paprika Ltd. *v*. Board of Trade [1944] 1 K.B. 327 347
Parc [1974] Crim.L.R. 720 231
Parker [1970] 1 W.L.R. 1003; 2 All E.R. 458; 54 Cr.App.R. 339 275
Parkes *v*. The Queen [1976] 3 All E.R. 380 198
Parry (1837) 7 C. & P. 836; 2 Mood. 9 174
Payne [1963] 1 W.L.R. 637; 1 All E.R. 848; 47 Cr.App.R. 122 .... 23, 36
Peace [1976] Crim.L.R. 119 266
Peach [1974] Crim.L.R. 245 197
Peckham (1935) 30 Cox 353; 25 Cr.App.R. 125 205
Peel (1943) 29 Cr.App.R. 73 243
Perks [1973] Crim.L.R. 388 189
Peters (1973) 58 Cr.App.R. 328 270
Phelan *v*. Back [1972] 1 W.L.R. 273; 1 All E.R. 901; 56 Cr.App.R. 257 189
Phillips [1953] 2 Q.B. 14; 1 All E.R. 968; 37 Cr.App.R. 65 294
—— *v*. Eyre (1870) L.R. 6 Q.B. 1; 38 L.J.Q.B. 113 62
—— and Quayle [1939] 1 K.B. 63; 26 Cr.App.R. 200 .... 95, 107
Picker [1970] 2 Q.B. 161; 2 W.L.R. 1038; 2 All E.R. 226; 54 Cr.App.R. 330... 226
Pico [1971] Crim.L.R. 531 198
Piggott *v*. Sims [1973] R.T.R. 15; [1972] Crim.L.R. 595 313
Pilcher (1974) 60 Cr.App.R. 1 203
Pink [1971] 1 Q.B. 508; [1970] 3 W.L.R. 903; 3 All E.R. 897; 55 Cr.App.R. 16 .... 199, 268

Piracy Jure Gentium, *Re* [1934] A.C. 586; 103 L.J.P.C. 153 12
Plain [1967] 1 W.L.R. 565; 1 All E.R. 614; 51 Cr.App.R. 91 202
Platt Bros. [1970] Crim.L.R. 656..................... 232
Plimmer (1975) 61 Cr.App.R. 264 .... 156, 157, 199
Podola [1960] 1 Q.B. 325; [1959] 3 W.L.R. 718; 3 All E.R. 418; 43 Cr.App.R. 220 170
Pollock and Divers [1967] 2 Q.B. 195; [1966] 2 W.L.R. 1145; 2 All E.R. 97; 50 Cr.App.R. 149 119
Pomeroy (1935) 25 Cr.App.R. 147 136
Pople [1951] 1 K.B. 53; [1950] 2 All E.R. 679; 34 Cr.App.R. 168 147
Post Office *v.* Estuary Radio [1968] 2 Q.B. 740; [1967] 1 W.L.R. 1396; 3 All E.R. 633 10
Pountney *v.* Griffiths [1975] 3 W.L.R. 140; 2 All E.R. 881; Crim.L.R. 702 ... 16
Powles, *The Times*, March 30, 1976 .... 155, 169
Prager (1970) 121 N.L.J. 548 392
Price [1969] 1 Q.B. 541; [1968] 2 W.L.R. 1397; 2 All E.R. 282; 52 Cr.App.R. 295 197
—— *v.* Humphries [1958] 2 Q.B. 353; 3 W.L.R. 304; 2 All E.R. 725 310
Pritchard (1836) 7 C. & P. 303 170
Purdy [1975] Q.B. 288; [1974] 3 W.L.R. 357; 3 All E.R. 465; Crim.L.R. 597 64

Quartey [1975] Crim.L.R. 592 157
Quinn (1932) 23 Cr.App.R. 196 223

Radley [1974] Crim.L.R. 312; 58 Cr.App.R. 394 .... 146, 147
Rafigue [1973] Crim.L.R. 777 .... 208, 209
Rand (1866) L.R. 1 Q.B. 230 50
Randall [1960] Crim.L.R. 435 164
Raymond Lyons & Co. *v.* Metropolitan Police Commissioner [1975] Q.B. 321; 2 W.L.R. 197; 1 All E.R. 335; Crim.L.R. 92 330
Redd [1923] 1 K.B. 104; 92 L.J.K.B. 208; 27 Cox 318; 17 Cr.App.R. 36 192, 193
Reeves (1972) 56 Cr.App.R. 366 223
Reynolds [1950] 1 K.B. 606; 1 All E.R. 335; 34 Cr.App.R. 60 208
Rhodes [1899] 1 Q.B. 77; 68 L.J.Q.B. 83; 19 Cox 182 32
Rice [1963] 1 Q.B. 857; 2 W.L.R. 585; 1 All E.R. 832; 47 Cr.App.R. 79 .... 180, 187, 188, 201
—— *v.* Connolly [1966] 2 Q.B. 414; 3 W.L.R. 17; 2 All E.R. 649 21
—— *v.* Howard (1886) 16 Q.B.D. 681; 55 L.J.Q.B. 311 183
Richards [1974] Q.B. 776; [1973] 3 W.L.R. 888; 3 All E.R. 1088; Crim.L.R. 96; 58 Cr.App.R. 60 210
Richardson [1971] 2 Q.B. 484; 2 W.L.R. 889; 2 All E.R. 773; 55 Cr.App.R. 244 179
Rimmer [1972] 1 W.L.R. 268; 1 All E.R. 604; 56 Cr.App.R. 196 169
Rivers [1974] R.T.R. 31; Crim.L.R. 316 196
Roads [1967] 2 Q.B. 108; 2 W.L.R. 1014; 2 All E.R. 84; 51 Cr.App.R. 297... 33
Robert Millar (Contractors) Ltd. [1970] 2 Q.B. 54; 2 W.L.R. 541; 1 All E.R. 577; 54 Cr.App.R. 158 9
Roberts [1936] 1 All E.R. 23; 30 Cox 356; 25 Cr.App.R. 158 201
Robertson [1968] 1 W.L.R. 1767; 3 All E.R. 557; 52 Cr.App.R. 690 170
Robinson [1975] Q.B. 508; 2 W.L.R. 117; 1 All E.R. 360; 60 Cr.App.R. 108 163
Robson, Harris [1972] 1 W.L.R. 651; 2 All E.R. 699; Crim.L.R. 316 36
Roche (1944) 30 Cr.App.R. 29 218
Roe [1967] 1 W.L.R. 634; 1 All E.R. 492; 51 Cr.App.R. 10 .... 142, 294
Roff [1976] R.T.R. 7 63
Rouse [1904] 1 K.B. 184 194
Rowe [1955] 1 Q.B. 573; 2 W.L.R. 1056; 2 All E.R. 234; 39 Cr.App.R. 57... 270
—— [1975] R.T.R. 309; Crim.L.R. 245 249
Rowton (1865) Le. & Ca. 520; 34 L.J.M.C. 57; 10 Cox 25 193
Royce-Bentley [1974] 1 W.L.R. 535; 2 All E.R. 347; Crim.L.R. 308; 59 Cr.App.R. 51 197

Rudland (1865) 4 F. & F. 495 195
Rugby Justices, *ex p.* Prince [1974] 1 W.L.R. 736; 2 All E.R. 116; Crim.L.R. 252; 59 Cr.App.R. 31 332
Rumping *v.* D.P.P. [1964] A.C. 814; [1962] 3 W.L.R. 763; 3 All E.R. 256; 46 Cr.App.R. 398 33
Ryan [1976] Crim.L.R. 508, C.A. 242

S *v.* Manchester City Recorder [1971] A.C. 481; [1970] 2 W.L.R. 21; [1969] 3 All E.R. 1230 316
Sagoo [1975] 3 W.L.R. 267; 2 All E.R. 926; 61 Cr.App.R. 191 13
Salmon [1973] Crim.L.R. 707; 57 Cr.App.R. 953 .... 241, 243
Samuel (1956) 40 Cr.App.R. 8 193
Sangiovanni (1904) 68 J.P. 54 82
Sapiano (1968) 52 Cr.App.R. 674 230
Sargeant [1975] Crim.L.R. 173; 60 Cr.App.R. 74 217
Saunders [1970] Crim.L.R. 297; 54 Cr.App.R. 247 229
—— [1974] Crim.L.R. 30; 58 Cr.App.R. 248 272
Scott *v.* Baker [1969] 1 Q.B. 659; [1968] 3 W.L.R. 796; 2 All E.R. 993; 52 Cr.App.R. 566 24
—— *v.* Scott [1913] A.C. 417; 82 L.J.P. 74 154
Secretary of State for Trade *v.* Markus [1975] 2 W.L.R. 708; 1 All E.R. 958; Crim.L.R. 716; 61 Cr.App.R. 58 9
Selvey *v.* D.P.P. [1970] A.C. 304; [1968] 2 W.L.R. 1494; 2 All E.R. 497; 52 Cr.App.R. 443 194
Senat (1968) 52 Cr.App.R. 282 36
Seymour [1954] 1 W.L.R. 678; 1 All E.R. 1006; 38 Cr.App.R. 68 .... 136, 210
Shadrack [1976] Crim.L.R. 755 115
Sharkey [1976] Crim.L.R. 388 250
Sharp [1957] Crim.L.R. 821; 41 Cr.App.R. 197 170
Sheean (1908) 21 Cox 561 194
Shepherd [1975] R.T.R. 497; Crim.L.R. 336 268
Shergold *v.* Holloway (1734) Sess.Cas.K.B. 154; 2 Str. 1002 41
Sheridan [1937] 1 K.B. 223; 106 L.J.K.B. 6; [1936] 2 All E.R. 883; 30 Cox 447; 26 Cr.App.R. 1 .... 164, 318
Sheriff (1903) 20 Cox 334 181
Sibthorpe (1973) 57 Cr.App.R. 429 247
Sidhu [1976] Crim.L.R. 379 197
Simmonds [1969] 1 Q.B. 685; [1967] 3 W.L.R. 367; 2 All E.R. 399; 51 Cr.App.R. 316 249
Simms *v.* Moore [1970] 2 Q.B. 327; 2 W.L.R. 1099; 3 All E.R. 1; 54 Cr.App.R. 347 .... 290, 308, 313
Sims [1946] K.B. 531; 1 All E.R. 697; 31 Cr.App.R. 158 134
Sirros *v.* Moore [1975] Q.B. 118; [1974] 3 W.L.R. 459; 3 All E.R. 776 42
Sivalingham *v.* D.P.P. [1975] C.L.Y. 2037 346
Skipp [1975] Crim.L.R. 114 129
Skone [1967] Crim.L.R. 249; 51 Cr.App.R. 165 223
Slatter [1975] 1 W.L.R. 1084; 3 All E.R. 215 .... 86, 239
Sloggett [1972] 1 Q.B. 430; [1971] 3 W.L.R. 628; 3 All E.R. 264; 55 Cr.App. R. 532 129
Smellie (1919) 14 Cr.App.R. 128 150
Smith [1967] Crim.L.R. 59; 51 Cr.App.R. 22 267
—— [1968] 1 W.L.R. 636; 2 All E.R. 115; 52 Cr.App.R. 224 .... 180, 312
—— [1975] 2 Q.B. 531; [1974] 2 W.L.R. 495; 1 All E.R. 651 248
—— (1975) 61 Cr.App.R. 128 268
Soanes [1948] 1 All E.R. 289; 32 Cr.App.R. 136 157
Soblen. *Ex p.* [1963] 1 Q.B. 829; [1962] 3 W.L.R. 1145; 3 All E.R. 373 44
Socialist Worker Printers, *ex p.* Attorney-General [1975] Q.B. 637; 1 All E.R. 142 392
Sorrel [1971] Crim.L.R. 552 230
Southampton Justices, *ex p.* Atherton [1974] Crim.L.R. 108 290

Southampton Justices, *ex p.* Briggs [1972] 1 W.L.R. 277; 1 All E.R. 573 298
——, *ex p.* Corker, *The Times*, February 12, 1976 82
——, *ex p.* Green [1976] Q.B. 11; [1975] 3 W.L.R. 277; 2 All E.R. 1073 76, 82
Southey *v.* Nash (1837) 7 C. & P. 632 181
Southwark Juvenile Court, *ex p.* J. [1973] 1 W.L.R. 1300; 3 All E.R. 383; Crim.L.R. 511 371
Sparrow [1973] 1 W.L.R. 488; 2 All E.R. 245; 40 Cr.App.R. 83 ...... 32, 198
Spicer [1970] Crim.L.R. 695 62
—— *v.* Holt [1976] 3 W.L.R. 398; 3 All E.R. 71; Crim.L.R. 139 24
Springfield [1969] Crim.L.R. 557; 53 Cr.App.R. 608 213
Stafford *v.* D.P.P. [1974] A.C. 878; 3 W.L.R. 719; 3 All E.R. 762; 58 Cr.App.R. 256 ...... 267, 269, 270
Stanton (1851) 5 Cox 324 161
Stentiford [1976] Crim.L.R. 383 ...... 144, 145
Stephenson (1862) L. & C. 165; 31 L.J.M.C. 147; 9 Cox 156 108
Sterk [1972] Crim.L.R. 391 179
Stevenson [1971] 1 W.L.R. 1; 1 All E.R. 678 36
Stewart [1970] 1 W.L.R. 907; 1 All E.R. 689; 54 Cr.App.R. 210 23
Stirland *v.* D.P.P. [1944] A.C. 315; 113 L.J.K.B. 394; 2 All E.R. 13; 30 Cr.App.R. 40 ...... 192, 193
Stone [1970] 1 W.L.R. 1112; 2 All E.R. 594; 54 Cr.App.R. 364 222
Stratford on Avon Justices, *ex p.* Edmonds [1973] R.T.R. 356; Crim.L.R. 241 314
Sullivan [1971] 1 Q.B. 253; 54 Cr.App.R. 389 113
Sulston *v.* Hammond [1970] 1 W.L.R. 1164; 2 All E.R. 830 342
Summers [1952] 1 All E.R. 1059; 36 Cr.App.R. 14 196
Surrey Justices, *ex p.* Witherick [1932] 1 K.B. 450; 101 L.J.K.B. 203 132
Swatkins (1831) 4 C. & P. 548 178

Talgarth Justices, *ex p.* Bithell [1973] 1 W.L.R. 1327; 2 All E.R. 717; Crim.L.R. 756 327
Tancock (1876) 13 Cox 217 160
Tarry [1970] 2 Q.B. 561; 2 W.L.R. 1034; 2 All E.R. 185; 54 Cr.App.R. 323, 422 ...... 228, 241
Tasamulug (Ali) [1971] Crim.L.R. 441 155
Tavernor [1976] R.T.R. 242 254
Taylor (1974) 60 Cr.App.R. 143 231
—— *v.* Taylor [1970] 1 W.L.R. 1148 189
Telfer [1976] Crim.L.R. 562 64
Tew (1855) Dears. 429 181
Thames Magistrates' Court, *ex p.* Polemis [1974] 1 W.L.R. 1371; 2 All E.R. 1219 307
Thomas (1800) 2 East P.C. 934; 2 Leach 877 132
—— (1949) 33 Cr.App.R. 74 136
—— [1950] 1 K.B. 26; [1949] 2 All E.R. 662; 33 Cr.App.R. 200 162
—— [1975] R.T.R. 38; Crim.L.R. 296 247
——, *Ex p.* [1956] Crim.L.R. 119 78
—— *v.* Sorrell (1674) Vaughan 330 256
Thompson [1914] 2 K.B. 99; 83 L.J.K.B. 643; 24 Cox 43; 9 Cr.App.R. 252 ... 148
—— [1917] 2 K.B. 630; 86 L.J.K.B. 643; 24 Cox 43; 9 Cr.App.R. 252 178, 203
—— [1966] 1 W.L.R. 405; 1 All E.R. 505; 50 Cr.App.R. 91 193
—— [1975] 1 W.L.R. 1425; 2 All E.R. 1028; Crim.L.R. 459; 61 Cr.App.R. 108 ...... 145, 149
Thomson *v.* Knights [1947] K.B. 336; 1 All E.R. 112 129
Thomson Holidays Ltd. [1974] Q.B. 592; 2 W.L.R. 371; 1 All E.R. 823 160
Tonks [1916] 1 K.B. 443; 85 L.J.K.B. 396; 25 Cox 228; 11 Cr.App.R. 284 ... 162
Toohey *v.* Metropolitan Police Commissioner [1965] A.C. 595; 2 W.L.R. 439; 1 All E.R. 506; 49 Cr.App.R. 148 186
Tottenham Justices, *ex p.* Rubens [1970] 1 W.L.R. 800; 1 All E.R. 879; 54 Cr.App.R. 183 ...... 341, 344, 348
Tragen [1956] Crim.L.R. 332 197

Treacy [1944] 2 All E.R. 229; 30 Cr.App.R. 93 187
—— *v*. D.P.P. [1971] A.C. 537; 2 W.L.R. 112; 1 All E R. 110; 55 Cr.App.R. 113 9
Tregear [1967] 2 Q.B. 574; 2 W.L.R. 1414; 1 All E.R. 989; 51 Cr.App.R. 280 189
Tremayne (1932) 23 Cr.App.R. 191 221
Tucker [1974] 1 W.L.R. 615; 2 All E.R. 639; 59 Cr.App.R. 71 275
Tullet [1976] 1 W.L.R. 241; 2 All E.R. 1032 404
Tunde-Olarinde [1967] 1 W.L.R. 911; 2 All E.R. 491; 51 Cr.App.R. 249 ... 247
Turnbull [1976] 3 All E.R. 549 .... 35, 197, 202, 266
Turner [1970] 2 Q.B. 321; 2 W.L.R. 1093; 2 All E.R. 281; 54 Cr App.R. 352 156
—— (1975) 61 Cr.App.R. 67 19

UPTON [1973] 3 All E.R. 318 .... 265, 283
Urbanowski [1976] 1 W.L.R. 455; 1 All E.R. 679 102
U.S.A. *v*. McRae (1867) 3 Ch.App. 79 32
Uxbridge Justices, *ex p*. Burbridge, *The Times*, June 21, 1972 290

VANDERCOMB AND ABBOTT (1796) 2 Leach 708 161
Vernon *v*. Paddon [1973] 1 W.L.R. 663; 3 All E.R. 302 .... 130, 305
Verolla [1963] 1 Q.B. 285; [1962] 3 W.L.R. 132; 2 All E.R. 426; 46 Cr.App.R. 252 30
Verrier *v*. D.P.P. [1967] 2 A.C. 195; [1966] 3 W.L.R. 924; 3 All E.R. 568; 50 Cr.App.R. 315 224
Vickers [1972] Crim.L.R. 101 193
—— [1975] 1 W.L.R. 811; 2 All E.R. 945; 61 Cr.App.R. 48 .... 155, 169, 268

WAINWRIGHT (1875) 13 Cox 771 195
Wakefield Justices [1970] 1 All E.R. 1181; 114 S.J. 30 343
Walker [1950] 2 All E.R. 911; 34 Cr.App.R. 199 107
Wall [1974] 1 W.L.R. 930; 2 All E.R. 245 10
Wallwork (1958) 52 Cr.App.R. 153 .... 30, 122, 124
Walters *v*. W. H. Smith & Son [1914] 1 K.B. 595 .... 63, 67
Ward (1848) 2 C. & K. 759; 3 Cox 279 114
Ware *v*. Fox [1967] 1 W.L.R. 379; 1 All E.R. 100 130
Warren [1954] 1 W.L.R. 531; 1 All E.R. 597; 38 Cr.App.R. 44 331
Warwickshall (1783) 1 Leach 263 23
Waterfield [1975] 1 W.L.R. 711; 2 All E.R. 40; 60 Cr.App.R. 296 153
Waterfield, Lynn [1964] 1 Q.B. 164; [1963] 3 W.L.R. 946; 3 All E.R. 659; 48 Cr.App.R. 42 28
Waugh *v*. R. [1950] A.C. 203 198
Weaver [1968] 1 Q.B. 353; [1967] 2 W.L.R. 1244; 1 All E.R. 277; 51 Cr.App. R. 77 .... 180, 205
Webb [1975] Crim.L.R. 159 179
Weir [1972] 3 All E.R. 906 65
Wemyss *v*. Hopkins (1875) L.R. 10 Q.B. 378; 44 L.J.M.C. 101 .... 162, 163
Westwell [1976] 2 All E.R. 812; Crim.L.R. 441 179
Whalley [1972] Crim.L.R. 324; 56 Cr.App.R. 304 249
Wheatley *v*. Lodge [1971] 1 W.L.R. 29; 1 All E.R. 173 64
White (1960) 45 Cr.App.R. 34 209
Wilkes *v*. Lord Halifax (1769) 19 St.Tr. 1407 57
—— *v*. Wood (1763) 19 St.Tr. 1153 57
Wilkinson [1970] 1 W.L.R. 1319; 3 All E.R. 439; 54 Cr.App.R. 437 230
William (James) [1972] Crim.L.R. 436 143
Williams (1871) 12 Cox 101 108
—— *v*. Summerfield [1972] 2 Q.B. 513; 3 W.L.R. 131; 2 All E.R. 1334; Crim.L.R. 424 26
Willis [1972] 1 W.L.R. 1605; 3 All E.R. 797; 57 Cr.App.R. 1 129
—— [1976] Crim.L.R. 127 24
Wilmot (1933) 29 Cox 652; 24 Cr.App.R. 63 .... 130, 132
Wilson (1957) 41 Cr.App.R. 226 189

Wilson [1965] 1 Q.B. 402; [1964] 3 W.L.R. 593; 3 All E.R. 269; 48 Cr.App.R. 329 ... 224
— *v.* Skeock (1949) 65 T.L.R. 418 ... 328
Wiltshire *v.* Barrett [1966] 1 Q.B. 312; [1965] 2 W.L.R. 1195; 2 All E.R. 271 65
Winfield (1939) 27 Cr.App.R. 139 ... 193
Woking Justices, *ex p.* Gossage [1973] 1 Q.B. 448; 2 W.L.R. 529; 2 All E.R. 621; Crim.L.R. 306 ... 328
Wood [1972] Crim.L.R. 665 ... 247
Woods [1969] 1 Q.B. 447; [1968] 3 W.L.R. 1192; 3 All E.R. 709; 53 Cr.App. R. 30 ... 213
Woolmington *v.* D.P.P. [1935] A.C. 462; 104 L.J.K.B. 433; 30 Cox 234; 25 Cr.App.R. 72 ... 196, 266
Worley *v.* Bentley [1976] 2 All E.R. 449; Crim.L.R. 310 ... 179
Wright [1974] Crim.L.R. 324; 58 Cr.App.R. 444 ... 212
— *v.* Eldred (1971) 135 J.P. 491 ... 304
— *v.* Nicholson [1970] 1 W.L.R. 142; 1 All E.R. 12; 54 Cr.App.R. 38 ... 304
Wylie [1974] Crim.L.R. 608 ... 251

Yates (1872) 12 Cox 233 ... 148
Young [1964] 1 W.L.R. 717; 2 All E.R. 480; 48 Cr.App.R. 292 ... 202, 210
— [1973] Crim.L.R. 507 ... 150, 154
— *v.* Bristol Aeroplane Ltd. [1944] K.B. 718 ... 260
Yscuado (1854) 6 Cox 386 ... 151, 153

Zaman [1975] Crim.L.R. 710; 61 Cr.App.R. 227 ... 264

TABLE OF STATUTES

1361 Justices of the Peace Act (18 Edw. 3, St. 2, c. 2) 327, 328
1381 Forcible Entry Act (5 Ric. 2, St. 1, c. 7)........... 42
1679 Habeas Corpus Act (31 Car. 2, c. 7) 256
1689 Bill of Rights (1 Will. & M. sess. 2, c. 2) 232
1695 Treason Act (7 & 8 Will. 3, c. 3)
s. 5 14
1699 Offences by Officials Abroad Act (11 Will. 3, c. 7) 12
1750 Constables Protection Act (24 Geo. 2, c. 44)
s. 6 41
1792 Libel Act (32 Geo. 3, c. 60) 211
1814 Treason Act (54 Geo. 3, c. 46)
s. 1 .... 217, 223
1823 Judgment of Death Act (4 Geo. 4, c. 48)
s. 1 223
1824 Vagrancy Act (5 Geo. 4, c. 83)
s. 3 289
s. 4 ...... 191, 289, 306, 334
s. 5 .... 331, 334, 353
s. 10 334
1825 Juries Act (6 Geo. 4, c. 50)
s. 29 174
1826 Criminal Law Act (7 & 8 Geo. 4, c. 31) 255, 329
ss. 28, 30 252
1828 Night Poaching Act (9 Geo. 4, c. 69) 124
s. 1 130
1831 Game Act (1 & 2 Will. 4, c. 32)
s. 31 306
1837 Piracy Act (7 Will. 4 & 1 Vict. c. 88)
s. 2 223
1843 Evidence Act (6 & 7 Vict. c. 85)
s. 1 31
Libel Act (6 & 7 Vict. c. 96) 244
1848 Indictable Offences Act (11 & 12 Vict. c. 42)
ss. 12–15 59
Justices Protection Act (11 & 12 Vict. c. 44)
s. 1 ....53, 78
ss. 2, 5, 6 53
1851 Evidence Act (14 & 15 Vict. c. 19)
s. 13 ....166, 217
1857 Summary Jurisdiction Act (20 & 21 Vict. c. 43)
s. 6 .... 350, 351
Accessories and Abettors Act (24 & 25 Vict. c. 94)
s. 8 .... 121, 137
Offences against the Person Act (24 & 25 Vict. c. 100)
s. 5 218
s. 9 .... 10, 13
s. 18 ... 120, 125, 127, 142, 157
s. 20 ... 121, 126, 131, 142, 157, 297
s. 42 .... 163, 293
s. 43 163
s. 44 .... 163, 165
s. 45 .... 163, 164, 165
s. 46 163
s. 47 297
s. 57 13
s. 59 127
1862 Poaching Prevention Act (25 & 26 Vict. c. 114) 52
1865 Criminal Procedure Act (28 & 29 Vict. c. 18)
s. 2 .... 195, 199
s. 3 .... 182, 183
ss. 4–6 187
1867 Criminal Law Amendment Act (30 & 31 Vict. c. 35)
s. 6 109
s. 10 151
Justices of the Peace Act (30 & 31 Vict. c. 115)
s. 2 50
1870 Forfeiture Act (33 & 34 Vict. c. 23)
s. 2 50
Extradition Act (33 & 34 Vict. c. 52) 61, 115
s. 19 61
Foreign Enlistment Act (33 & 34 Vict. c. 90) 13
1871 Prevention of Crimes Act (34 & 35 Vict. c. 112)
s. 18 217
1873 Extradition Act (36 & 37 Vict. c. 60) 61

1875 Conspiracy and Protection of Property Act (38 & 39 Vict. c. 86)
s. 9 293
1876 Appellate Jurisdiction Act (39 & 40 Vict. c. 59)
s. 5 261
1878 Territorial Waters Jurisdiction Act (41 & 42 Vict. c. 73)
s. 2 .... 10, 15
1879 Bankers' Books Evidence Act (42 & 43 Vict. c. 11)
s. 7 26
Prosecution of Offences Act (42 & 43 Vict. c. 22) 19
s. 2 20
s. 5 105
1881 Summary Jurisdiction (Process) Act (44 & 45 Vict. c. 24)
s. 4 56
1883 Explosive Substances Act (46 & 47 Vict. c. 3)
ss. 2 and 3 .... 10, 13
Bankruptcy Act (46 & 47 Vict. c. 52)
s. 32 50
1887 Coroners Act (50 & 51 Vict. c. 71)
s. 3 (1) 37
s. 4 .... 38, 109
s. 5 .... 39, 73
s. 6 40
ss. 18, 19 38
s. 20 .... 40, 117
Sched. 2 39
1888 Oaths Act (51 & 52 Vict. c. 46)
ss. 1, 3 181
1889 Interpretation Act (52 & 53 Vict. c. 63)
s. 33 .... 159, 309
1894 Merchant Shipping Act (57 & 58 Vict. c. 60)
s. 686 .... 11, 12
s. 687 12
s. 691 110
1895 Extradition Act (58 & 59 Vict. c. 33) 61
1897 Police (Property) Act (60 & 61 Vict. c. 30) 254, 330
1898 Criminal Evidence Act (61 & 62 Vict. c. 36)
s. 1 .... 31, 201, 308
(*a*) 31, 189, 269
(*b*) 32, 190, 195
(*c*) 32, 269
1898 Criminal Evidence Act—*cont.*
s. 1 (*d*) 33
(*e*) 31, 32, 180, 190, 191, 201
(*f*) ... 32, 191, 192, 193, 194, 200, 201
(*h*) 190, 312
s. 2 180
s. 3 195
s. 4 (1) 30, 31
Sched. 30
1903 Motor Car Act (3 Edw. 7, c. 36)
s. 1 132
1908 Prosecution of Offences Act (8 Edw. 7, c. 3) ... 19
Punishment of Incest Act (8 Edw. 7, c. 45)
s. 5 153
1909 Oaths Act (9 Edw. 7, c. 39)
s. 2 181
1911 Perjury Act (1 & 2 Geo. 5, c. 6)
s. 1 .... 394, 395
s. 7 34
s. 9 .... 144, 395
ss. 12, 13 395
Protection of Animals Act (1 & 2 Geo. 5, c. 27)
s. 2 344
Official Secrets Act (1 & 2 Geo. 5, c. 28) 13, 15
s. 1 89
(2) 191
s. 9 26
1913 Forgery Act (3 & 4 Geo. 5, c. 27) 13, 91
s. 4 (1) 127
1914 Criminal Justice Administration Act (4 & 5 Geo. 5, c. 58)
s. 28 (3) 30
Bankruptcy Act (4 & 5 Geo. 5, c. 59)
s. 154 (1) 120
1915 Indictments Act (5 & 6 Geo. 5, c. 90) 133
s. 3 (1) 117
s. 4 .... 133, 139
s. 5 139
(1) 146, 159
(2) 147
(3) 133, 135, 205
(4) 147, 205
(5) 148, 205
1920 Official Secrets Act (10 & 11 Geo. 5, c. 75) ... 13, 15
s. 2 21
s. 8 (4) 94

1925 Supreme Court of Judicature (Consolidation) Act (15 & 16 Geo. 5, c. 49)
s. 9 87
s. 63 (6) 342
Criminal Justice Act (15 & 16 Geo. 5, c. 86)
s. 13 (3) 108, 109, 110
s. 20 354
s. 33 (3) 391
(6) 390, 391
1926 Coroners (Amendment) Act (16 & 17 Geo. 5, c. 59) 37
ss. 13, 14 38
s. 15 (2) 39
s. 19 40
s. 21 38
1929 Infant Life (Preservation) Act (19 & 20 Geo. 5, c. 34)
s. 2 (2) 213
1933 Children and Young Persons Act (23 & 24 Geo. 5, c. 12)
s. 1 (1) 142
s. 31 366
s. 34 .... 369, 374, 385
(1) 365
(2) 374
s. 36 154
s. 37 ...... 94, 112, 153, 369
s. 38 .... 30, 111, 181, 312
(1) 111
s. 39 ...... 112, 365, 366, 369, 371
ss. 42, 43 109
s. 46 .... 364, 365, 368
(1) 364
ss. 47, 49 .... 365, 371
s. 50 362
s. 53 (1) 366
(2) 363, 367
s. 55 (1) 368
s. 56 370
ss. 59 (1), 107 362
Sched. 1 109
Administration of Justice (Miscellaneous Provisions) Act (23 & 24 Geo. 5, c. 36) 45
s. 2 .... 107, 391
(1) 145, 146
(2) ... 104, 137, 140, 142, 144, 395
(3) ... 95, 143, 146, 148, 149
1934 Incitement to Disaffection Act (24 & 25 Geo. 5, c. 56) 25
1936 Coinage Offences Act (26 Geo. 5 & 1 Edw. 8, c. 16)
s. 5 (1) (5) 143
Public Order Act (1 Edw. 8 & 1 Geo. 6, c. 6)...15, 25
s. 5 .... 130, 306
s. 6 21
1938 Infanticide Act (1 & 2 Geo. 6, c. 36)
s. 1 (2) 214
Administration of Justice (Miscellaneous Provisions) Act (1 & 2 Geo. 6, c. 63) 45
1948 Children Act (11 & 12 Geo. 6, c. 43) 378
British Nationality Act (11 & 12 Geo. 6, c. 56) ... 244
s. 3 12
Criminal Justice Act (11 & 12 Geo. 6, c. 58)
s. 19 238
(1)–(3) (5) (7) (8)... 389
s. 20 (1) 231, 255, 335
(5) 335
s. 27 .... 373, 388
s. 31 12
s. 37 (1) 351
s. 39 217
1949 Civil Aviation Act (12, 13 & 14 Geo. 6, c. 67)
s. 62 11
Representation of the People Act (12 13 & 14 Geo. 6, c. 68)
ss. 140, 141, 163 50
Justices of the Peace Act (12, 13 & 14 Geo. 6, c. 101)
s. 1 (1) 49
s. 3 51
ss. 18, 20, 44 290
1950 International Organisations (Immunities and Privileges) Act (14 Geo. 6, c. 14) 14
1952 Diplomatic Immunities (Commonwealth Countries and the Republic of Ireland) Act (15 & 16 Geo. 6 & 1 Eliz. 2, c. 31) 14
Customs and Excise Act (15 & 16 Geo. 6 & 1 Eliz. 2, c. 44)
ss. 71, 73 320
s. 283 320
(4) 340, 344
ss. 297, 298 25

1952 Prison Act (15 & 16 Geo. 6 & 1 Eliz. 2, c. 52)
s. 28 256
s. 44 256
(1) 232
s. 45 259
(2) 231
(4) (5) 259
s. 49 (1) 63
Magistrates' Courts Act (15 & 16 Geo. 6 & 1 Eliz. 2, c. 55)
s. 1 51, 54
(1) 54
(2) ... 51, 52, 60, 291, 369
(3) 60
(4) 52
(5) 49
s. 2 (1) 291
(2) 291, 369
(3) 52, 85
s. 3 51, 291
(1)–(3) 16
s. 4 (1) 52, 85
(3) 96, 302, 390
s. 6 67
(1) 70, 95, 306
(2) 96
s. 7 (1) 100, 101
(2) 101
s. 8 73
s. 13 (1) 308, 343
(3) 316
s. 14 67
(1) 70, 307
(2) 307
(3) ... 307, 318, 331, 338, 374
(4) 70, 306, 327
s. 15 60, 309, 311
(1) 301, 315
(3) 301
ss. 16, 17 303
s. 18 ... 91, 94, 95, 111, 289, 302, 310, 311, 390
(1) ... 295, 296, 299, 302, 320, 332, 364
(3) ... 296, 299, 302, 320, 323, 330, 332, 354
(5) 296, 299
s. 19 ... 91, 95, 111, 163, 289, 291, 302, 311, 320, 323, 330, 332, 354, 390, 391
(2) 297, 299
(3) 298
(4) (7) 297
s. 20 95
s. 23 296
s. 25 ... 91, 111, 292, 294, 301, 310, 311, 334, 335, 364, 390, 391

1952 Magistrates' Courts Act—*cont.*
s. 25 (1) 292, 299
(2) 301
(3)–(5) 293
(6) 293, 295
s. 26 318
(1) 307, 318, 336
(3) 77, 220
s. 27 (3) 323
s. 28 331, 341, 353
(1) 335
s. 29 ... 296, 297, 330, 332, 333, 336, 337, 338, 341, 353
s. 31 (1) 323
s. 35 52, 291, 369
s. 38 65, 67
(1) 65, 69
(1A) 78
(2) 65, 69
(4) 64, 69
s. 40 35
s. 41 109
s. 63 (1) 323
(2) 324, 325
(3) 324
s. 64 (1) 325
s. 65 (2) 324, 325
s. 67 324
s. 68 326
s. 70 (2) 324, 325
(3) 325
s. 71 325
s. 77 98, 308
(2)–(4) 98
s. 78 107, 312
s. 83 351
(1) 344
(2) 344, 345
(3) 344
s. 86 348
s. 87 (1) 342, 349, 350
(2) 350
(4) 346, 347
(5) (6) 349
s. 88 351
s. 89 (1) 347
(1A) 350
s. 90 350
s. 91 327, 328
s. 93 58, 69
s. 96 82, 382
(4) 82
s. 98 (1) 289
(2) 324
(4) 303
(5) 289, 290
(6) 289
(7) 318
s. 99 ... 96, 301, 302, 303, 390

1952 Magistrates' Courts Act—*cont.*
s. 100 .... 55, 304, 310
(2) 96, 104
s. 101 (4) 68
s. 102 (1) 58
(2) 57, 58
(3) 58, 59
(4) 58, 59, 64
s. 104 .... 13, 306, 384
s. 105 69
(1) 70
(1A) 70, 76
(2) 67
(3) 70
(4) ... 67, 68, 70, 307, 374
(5) 68, 307
s. 106 (1) 68, 70
(2) (3) 70
s. 107 (1) 224, 319
s. 108 (1)–(4) 320
s. 109 (1) (2) 319
ss. 110, 111 319
s. 126 (5) 369
s. 131 109
Sched. 1 ... 91, 291, 297, 298
Sched. 2 .... 390, 391
Sched. 3 .... 320, 323, 326
Sched. 5 109
Visiting Forces Act (15 & 16 Geo. 6 & 1 Eliz. 2, c. 67) 15
1953 Post Office Act (1 & 2 Eliz. 2, c. 36)
s. 53 37
s. 56 15
s. 58 36
s. 87 37
1955 Food and Drugs Act (4 & 5 Eliz. 2, c. 16)
s. 106 293
Army Act (3 & 4 Eliz. 2, c. 18)
s. 70 .... 11, 13
ss. 133, 134 92
Air Force Act (3 & 4 Eliz. 2, c. 19)
ss. 133, 134 92
1956 Magistrates' Courts (Appeals from Binding-over Orders) (4 & 5 Eliz. 2, c. 44)
s. 1 346
Sexual Offences Act (4 & 5 Eliz. 2, c. 69) 153
s. 5 .... 120, 124
s. 6 .... 14, 128
ss. 10, 11 15
s. 12 (1) 119
s. 13 297
1956 Sexual Offences Act—*cont.*
ss. 30–32 293
s. 33 .... 143, 293, 295
ss. 34–36 .... 143, 295
s. 37 .... 15, 213
s. 39 .... 30, 31
ss. 42, 43 26
s. 47 178
Sched. 2 .... 14, 213
1957 Homicide Act (5 & 6 Eliz. 2, c. 11)
s. 3 157
Magistrates' Courts Act (5 & 6 Eliz. 2, c. 29)
s. 1 .... 310, 369, 391
Geneva Conventions Act (5 & 6 Eliz. 2, c. 52)
s. 1 90
Naval Discipline Act (5 & 6 Eliz. 2, c. 53)
s. 129 92
1958 Prevention of Fraud (Investments) Act (6 & 7 Eliz. 2, c. 45)
s. 13 (1) 129
1959 County Courts Act (7 & 8 Eliz. 2, c. 22)
s. 157 (1) 393
Highways Act (7 & 8 Eliz. 2, c. 25)
s. 121 292
Street Offences Act (7 & 8 Eliz. 2, c. 57)
s. 1 (3) 63
Obscene Publications Act (7 & 8 Eliz. 2, c. 66) ... 154
s. 2 (1) 125
s. 3 54
Mental Health Act (7 & 8) Eliz. 2, c. 72) 279, 282, 381, 387
s. 4 (1)–(4) 234
s. 60 ... 234, 235, 326, 336
(1) 326
(2) ... 326, 336, 337, 346
(6) 234
s. 62 .... 234, 336
ss. 65, 66 234
s. 67 .... 331, 337, 353
(3) 337
(5) 335
s. 68 (1) 337
s. 70 (1) 346
s. 71 212
s. 72 .... 171, 234, 256
(1) (6) 367
ss. 128, 141 16
1960 Betting and Gaming Act (8 & 9 Eliz. 2, c. 60
s. 5 (1) 130

1960 Administration of Justice Act (8 & 9 Eliz. 2, c. 65)
ss. 1–9 352
s. 13 394
s. 14 .... 46, 80
s. 15 .... 45, 353
s. 16 .... 46, 342
1961 Oaths Act (9 & 10 Eliz. 2, c. 21)
s. 1 181
Criminal Justice Act (9 & 10 Eliz. 2, c. 39)
s. 1 .... 181, 335
(2) 335
(3) 336
s. 3 .... 222, 225, 367
(1) 231, 232, 322
(3) 231, 232
s. 4 (1) (2) 377
s. 5 389
(1) (3) (4) (5) 377
s. 6 389
s. 10 (2) 389
s. 11 231
s. 12 .... 338, 355
(1) (2) 259
(3) (4) 338
s. 39 (3) 231
Sched. 6 231
Human Tissue Act (9 & 10 Eliz. 2, c. 54) 224
1962 Criminal Justice Administration Act (10 & 11 Eliz. 2, c. 15)
s. 13 .... 291, 298, 299
1963 Betting, Gaming and Lotteries Act (c. 2)
s. 21 130
s. 51 (1) 27, 57, 63
Children and Young Persons Act (c. 37) 106
s. 16 (1) 362
(2) 190, 191, 217
s. 17 (2) 371
s. 18 .... 365, 368
s. 25 (1) 365, 369, 374
s. 27 .... 111, 296
(1) (2) 111
s. 64 112
Sched. 5 112
1964 Continental Shelf Act (c. 29)
s. 3 11
Criminal Procedure (Right of Reply) Act (c. 34)
s. 1 (1) (2) 195
Administration of Justice Act (c. 42)
s. 2 49
1964 Administration of Justice Act—*cont.*
s. 10 50
s. 27 53
Police Act (c. 48)
s. 48 43
s. 51 293
(3) 21
Fishery Limits Act (c. 72) 10
Diplomatic Privileges Act (c. 81) 14
Criminal Procedure (Insanity) Act (c. 84)
s. 1 212
(1) 211
s. 4 .... 278, 279, 309
(2) 171, 279
(4) 171
s. 5 171
(1) 235
1965 Dangerous Drugs Act (c. 15)
s. 5 130
Backing of Warrants (Republic of Ireland) Act (c. 45)........ 59
Criminal Procedure (Attendance of Witnesses) Act (c. 69)
s. 1 (1) 106
(2) 99, 106
(3) 106
ss. 2–4 106
s. 7 38
Sched. 2 108
Murder (Abolition of Death Penalty) Act (c. 71) 62
s. 1 217
(2) 226
(5) 366
Race Relations Act (c. 73)
s. 6 15
1966 Criminal Appeal Act (c. 31)
ss. 2 (1) (3), 3 260
Armed Forces Act (c. 45)
s. 35 92
1967 Tokyo Convention Act (c. 52)
s. 1 11
s. 4 12
Criminal Law Act (c. 58)... 21
s. 2 .... 62, 66, 67
(1) (2) (3) 62
(4) (5) 63
(6) 66
(7) 63
s. 3 66
s. 4 .... 16, 122
(1) 121, 122
(2) 214

1967 Criminal Law Act—*cont.*
s. 5 .... 16, 21
s. 6 .... 213–214, 304
(1) ... 157, 158, 159, 165, 169, 170, 271
(2) ... 157, 160, 213, 214
(3) 160, 213, 214
(4) ... 120, 131, 160, 205, 214
(5) 158, 214
(7) 214
s. 10 (2) 12
s. 12 (6) 150
Sched. 2 223
Sched. 3 12
Sexual Offences Act (c. 60)
s. 4 15
s. 5 .... 15, 293
s. 7 14
s. 9 293
Fugitive Offenders Act (c. 68) 61, 115
s. 14 61
Wireless Telegraphy Act (c. 72) 10
Road Traffic Regulation Act (c. 76)
s. 80 2
Criminal Justice Act (c. 80)
s. 1 ... 93, 94, 100–101, 110, 365
s. 2 ... 93, 100, 107, 183, 296
(2) 97, 114
(3) 97
(3A)–(6) 97
(7) 110
(9) 111
(10) 106
s. 3 .... 94, 95
(3) 95
s. 4 .... 95, 365
s. 6 .... 49, 67, 86, 94
s. 7 107
s. 8 121
s. 9 .... 110, 385
(2)–(5) 110
(6) 111
(8) 110
s. 10 .... 176, 246, 308
(1)–(4) 112
s. 11 ... 93, 99, 113, 178, 180, 308
(1) 112
(2)–(7) 113
(8) 112
s. 17 .... 19, 158, 163
s. 19 .... 51, 71, 289
s. 20 .... 332, 335
s. 22 ...... 68, 79, 347, 351
(1) (2) (4) 79

1967 Criminal Justice Act—*cont.*
s. 24 .... 59, 60
(2) 60, 302, 311
(3) 56, 301
(4) 301
s. 26 ...... 302, 311, 319, 328
s. 28 291
s. 29 391
(2) 390
s. 30 .... 307, 318, 336
s. 33 35
s. 34 388
s. 35 .... 65, 94, 306
s. 43 (1) (2) 323
s. 44 (2) (3) 324
(4) 324, 326
(5) 325
(6) ... 302, 324, 325, 326
(8) 323, 325
(9) (10) 325
s. 45 326
s. 46 325
s. 56 .... 335, 339
(5) 333, 335
s. 59 257
s. 60 (1)–(3) 257
(5) (6) 258
s. 61 .... 225, 366
(1) 257
s. 62 .... 258, 338
(6) 258, 331
(7)–(10) 258
s. 67 .... 224, 257
s. 89 .... 96, 394
s. 91 (1) 291
s. 93 (1) 326
s. 103 (1) 324, 325
Sched. 2 257
Sched. 6 ...... 324, 325, 336
Companies Act (c. 81)
s. 110 25
Abortion Act (c. 87)
s. 1 127

1968 Consular Relations Act (c. 18) 14
Criminal Appeal Act (c. 19)
s. 1 265
(1) 260
(2) 262
s. 2 (1) ... 265, 266–268, 273, 277, 279
(2) 271
(3) 271, 272
s. 3 272
(2) 272, 276
s. 4 271
(3) 276
s. 5 279
s. 6 271
s. 7 272
s. 8 .... 272, 278

1968 Criminal Appeal Act—*cont.*
s. 9 .... 275, 353
s. 10 .... 353, 355
(2) 260, 353
(4) 354
s. 11 (2) 275
(3) 276
(4) 277
s. 12 .... 212, 260, 277
s. 13 (1) (2) 277
(3) 278
(4) (5) 277, 278
s. 14 (2) 278
s. 15 279
(1) 260
s. 16 (1)–(3) 279
s. 17 ...... 168, 265, 270, 273
s. 18 (2) 262, 263
s. 19 263
s. 20 .... 260, 262, 270
s. 21 .... 260, 264
s. 22 .... 263, 264, 277
s. 23 .... 269, 272
(1) 263, 269
(3) 269
(2) 269
(4) 270
s. 29 (1) 224, 273
s. 30 273
s. 31 260
(1) 263
(2) 272, 273, 274
(3) 263
s. 32 264
s. 33 280
s. 34 .... 280, 281
(1) 281, 282
s. 35 (2) 281
(3) 282
s. 36 281
s. 37 282
s. 38 281
s. 42 282
s. 44 281
s. 47 405
(2) 406
s. 50 (1) 275
(2) 276
s. 52 (1) 20
Sched. 1 .... 271, 278
Sched. 2 273
Sched. 3 279
Sched. 4 277
Sched. 5 20
Courts-Martial (Appeals) Act (c. 20) 261
Firearms Act (c. 27)
s. 46 26
s. 47 .... 21, 25
s. 48 21
s. 52 (1) 254

1968 Trade Descriptions Act (c. 29)
s. 14 (1) 160
s. 24 178
Theatres Act (c. 54)
s. 2 (2) 295
Theft Act (c. 60)
s. 1 ... 57, 119, 123, 126, 129, 141, 246
(1) 126
s. 4 291
s. 5 (1) 124
s. 7 .... 120, 218
s. 8 .... 126, 137, 298
(1) 119
(2) 218
s. 9 91
(1) 120, 123, 213
s. 11 (1) 120, 123
s. 12 246
(1) 128
(3) 63
s. 13 132
s. 14 13
s. 15 (1) 26, 125
s. 21 26
(1) 126
s. 22 55
(1) ... 126, 129, 141, 142
(2) 120
s. 25 306
s. 26 (1) (2) 25
(3) 26
s. 28 ... 252, 273, 275, 282, 318, 330
(3) 253
s. 29 (1) 297
s. 30 16
(2) 30
(3) 30, 31, 32, 33
s. 31 (1) 32
(2) 252
Civil Evidence Act (c. 64)
s. 11 250
Justices of the Peace Act (c. 69)
s. 1 (2) 49, 88
(7) 57, 115, 243
s. 5 (1) 48, 54
(3) 290
Sched. 2 49
1969 Family Law Reform Act (c. 46)
s. 1 97
Children and Young Persons Act (c. 54) 361 *et seq.*
s. 1 387
(1) 384
(2) ... 361, 374, 383, 385
(3) 382, 386, 387

1969 Children and Young Persons Act—*cont.*
s. 1 (4) 387
(5) ... 382, 384, 386, 387
(6) 384
s. 2 (1)–(4) (8) 384
(10 (11) 386
(12) 387
(13) 382, 387
s. 3 (1)–(4) 384
(5) 386
(6) 368, 387
(7) 387, 388
(8) 388
s. 4 .... 363, 369, 384
s. 5 (1) (8) (9) 363
s. 6 (1) ... 363, 364, 365, 368
(2) 292, 295
(3) 377
s. 7 (1) ... 231, 331, 367, 380
(3) 380
(5) 389
(7) ... 368, 378, 382, 387
(8) 370, 377
s. 9 375
s. 10 (3) 365
s. 11 380
s. 12 (1)–(3) 380
(4) (5) 381
s. 13 (2) 381
s. 14 380
s. 15 385
(1) (3) 381
(4) 382
(5) 381
s. 16 (1)–(3) 382
(5) 382, 385
(8) 388
s. 17 381
s. 19 380
s. 20 (1) 378
(3) 379
s. 21 (1)–(3) 379
(4) 388
s. 23 378
(1) 366, 371, 373
(2) 366, 373
(3) 366, 373
(5) 373
s. 24 (1) (2) 378
(5) (8) 379
s. 27 378
s. 28 (1) 374, 384
(2) (3) 384
(4) 384, 385
(5) (6) 384
s. 29 378
(1) 371, 372
(2) 372
(3) 373
(5) 372

1969 Children and Young Persons Act—*cont.*
s. 30 (1) (2) 366
s. 31 231
(1)–(4) 379
s. 32 .... 374, 380
ss. 32A, 32B 385
s. 34 (1) 364, 367
ss. 35–48 .... 366, 378
s. 61 370
s. 70 362
(1) 383
s. 72 (3) 364
Sched. 5 ... 97, 364, 369, 370, 373, 374, 388, 389
Sched. 6 .... 368, 389
Administration of Justice Act (c. 58)
ss. 12–16 352
1970 Taxes Management Act (c. 9)
s. 103 14
Administration of Justice Act (c. 31)
s. 1 300
s. 9 405
(1) 206
(2) ... 260, 263, 280, 281
(3) 260
s. 41 248
Sched. 1 300
Sched. 9 248
1971 Courts Act (c. 23) 352
s. 1 (1) 86
s. 2 (1) 91
s. 4 (2) (3) 86
(4) 16, 86
(5) 88
(6) 16
(7) 88, 118
(8) 393
(11) 82
s. 5 (1) 332, 341
(3) (4) 88
(6) (7) 341
(8) (9) 88, 341
s. 6 (1) 86
(4) ... 219, 222, 243, 327, 393
s. 7 (1) 101
(2) (3) 101, 118
(4) 102
(5) 101, 102
s. 9 (1) 348
(2) 346, 348
(4) 348
(6) 347
s. 10 158
(1)–(3) 351

1971 Courts Act—*cont.*
s. 10 (5) 43
s. 11 332
(1) 224, 230
(2) (3) 222
(4) 221
(5) 354
s. 12 (1) 152
s. 13 .... 332, 347
(1) 71, 151
(2) 151
(4) ... 71, 224, 351, 352
(6) 69, 152
(7) 152
(8) 56
(9) 152
s. 16 86
s. 17 (1) (2) (4) 87
s. 20 (1) (3) 86
s. 21 (1) (3)–(6) 87
s. 23 (3) 88
s. 24 (1) 87
(2) (4) 88
Sched. 8 .... 52, 110, 394
Sched. 11 .... 79, 91
Misuse of Drugs Act (c. 38) 255, 295
s. 8 130
s. 23 .... 21, 25
s. 27 254
s. 29 255
Criminal Damage Act (c. 48)
s. 1 122
s. 6 (1) (2) 26
s. 9 32
Hijacking Act (c. 70) ... 11, 223
s. 3 61
Immigration Act (c. 77)
s. 2 (1) (2) (6) 244
s. 3 (6) 328
(8) 244
s. 4 (6) 244, 367
s. 6 (2) 244
(4) 245
(5) 245, 346
ss. 12–22 245
1972 Road Traffic Act (c. 20)
s. 1 .... 91, 132
s. 2 .... 130, 295, 357
s. 3 .... 56, 293
s. 5 .... 24, 63, 295
(1) 129
s. 6 (1) 121, 123, 247
s. 7 246
s. 9 .... 24, 123
s. 93 345
(1) (2) 246, 334
(3)–(5) 246
(7) 247
s. 94 247
(2) 273
1972 Road Traffic Act—*cont.*
s. 95 247
s. 99 .... 143, 245
s. 101 (1) 247
(7) 247
s. 102 .... 237, 240
s. 103 (1)–(3) (5) 334
s. 161 21
s. 164 (2) 63
s. 168 21
s. 179 .... 14, 306
Sched. 4 ...... 245, 246, 247
Local Government Act (c. 70)
s. 216 16
s. 220 37
Sched. 27 16
Criminal Justice Act (c. 71)
s. 6 .... 220, 273, 330
(2) 252
(3) 252, 275, 318
(4) 275
(5) 330
s. 34 66
s. 35 258
s. 36 .... 5, 260, 279
s. 37 (4) (5) 280
s. 41 .... 315, 316
(1) 315
(2) 301
(3) 315, 316
(4) (5) 315
s. 42 .... 259, 354
s. 44 365
s. 45 .... 96, 302
s. 46 .... 97, 110
s. 47 297
s. 49 (2) 324
s. 58 330
s. 62 (1) 290
s. 66 (6) 280
Sched. 5 354
1973 Costs in Criminal Cases Act (c. 14)
s. 1 (1) 329
(2) 100, 329
(4) (5) (7) 329
s. 2 (1) 329
(2) 329, 367
(4) 100, 329, 345
(5) 329, 345
s. 3 274
(1) 248
(2) 345, 348
(3)–(5) (8) 248
s. 4 .... 249, 275
(2) 249
s. 5 .... 249, 351
s. 6 352
s. 7 248
(1)–(3) 274

1973 Costs in Criminal Cases Act—*cont.*
s. 8 248
(1) (2) 274
s. 9 (1) 274
s. 10 .... 248, 283
s. 11 (1) 249, 283
s. 12 275
(1) (3) 329
(5) 249, 329
s. 18 332
(4) 249
Sched. 1 274
Administration of Justice Act (c. 15) 49
s. 1 (1) 49
(2) 49, 50
(5) (6) 50
(7) 49
s. 2 (6) (7) 50
s. 3 49
s. 17 151
Sched. 1 .... 49, 50
Protection of Aircraft Act (c. 47) 11, 223
s. 5 61
Powers of Criminal Courts Act (c. 62)
s. 1 .... 222, 327, 334
(1)–(3) 242
(4) 241, 242
(7) 222, 242
s. 2 (1) ... 219, 233, 236, 253 326, 377
(3) (4) 237
(5) 237, 327
(6) 237
s. 3 238
(1) ... 219, 326, 327, 336
(5) (6) 238
s. 4 237
s. 5 (2) 240
s. 6 .... 241, 401
(1)–(3) 238
(4) 238, 339, 353
(5) 239
(6) 239, 339, 353
(8) 239
s. 7 (1) 233, 240, 253
s. 8 .... 240, 241, 401
(1) 239
(4) 240
(6) 331, 339
(7) 239, 339
(8) 339
s. 9 367
s. 11 238
s. 12 (1) 237, 240, 244
(3) 207, 239
(4) 237, 251

1973 Powers of Criminal Courts Act—*cont.*
s. 13 .... 236, 343, 345
(1) 241, 275, 345
(2) 241
(4) 241, 275, 345
s. 14 (1) 235, 367
(2) 219, 235
(3) 235
(4) 236
(5) 235
(6) 236
(8) 235, 251, 253
s. 15 (1) 236
(2) 235
(3) 236
s. 16 .... 236, 401
(3) 331, 338, 353
(5) 353
(7) 207
s. 17 401
(1) 236
(2) 236, 338, 353
(3) 236, 353
(7) 236
s. 18 (1) (2) 224
s. 19 231
(1) 225, 321, 367, 377, 393
(2) 220, 225, 231, 233, 321
(3) (4) 321
s. 20 220
(1) 225, 233, 320
s. 21 .... 153, 367
(1) 225, 321
(2) 321
s. 22 (1) 227, 334
(2) 228
(3) 228, 237
(4) 221, 228
(5) 228, 232, 277
(6) 228
s. 23 401
(1) 229, 277, 322
(2) 230
s. 24 (1) 228, 322
(2) 322, 331, 338
s. 25 229
s. 26 (1) 228
(2) 228, 319
(3) (4) 228
s. 27 .... 228, 401
s. 28 226
(3) 227
s. 29 226
s. 30 (1) 232, 255
(2) 232
s. 31 243
(1)–(4) 233
s. 32 243

1973 Powers of Criminal Courts Act —*cont.*
s. 34 ..... 249, 251
s. 35 ..... 220, 250, 275, 329
(1) ... 250, 251, 252, 318
(2) 250, 252
(3) 250
(4) 251
(5) 330
s. 36 282
(1) 251, 273
(2) 330
(3) 251, 275
s. 37 ..... 251, 401
s. 38 251
s. 39 ..... 220, 240
(1) 251, 253
(2)–(4) 253
s. 40 ..... 253, 319
(1) 275
(2) (3) 276
s. 41 ..... 253, 343
s. 42 ..... 333, 335
s. 43 ... 240, 247, 254, 319, 330, 367, 391
(1)–(4) 254
s. 44 ... 235, 240, 247, 328, 367, 376
s. 45 ..... 220, 318
s. 46 220
s. 53 56
s. 57 (1) 227, 321
(2) 230
Sched. 1 238
Sched. 2 253
1974 Legal Aid Act (c. 4) ... 401–406
s. 1 403
s. 2 (4) 403
s. 3 (2) 403
s. 4 402
s. 7 79
s. 28 71
(2) 400, 401
(3) (4) 401
(5) 399, 400
(6)–(11) 401
s. 29 71
(1) 402
(2) 402, 404
(3) 399, 404
(4) 404
(5) (5A) (6) 402
s. 30 71
(1) (2) 403
(5)–(8) 404
(11) 400
(12) 400, 401
s. 32 ..... 399, 404
(1) 405
ss. 33–35 405
s. 36 (1) (2) 400

1974 Legal Aid Act—*cont.*
s. 37 (1) 400
s. 38 (1) (2) 399
Sched. 1 400
Juries Act (c. 23)
s. 1 172
s. 2 (2) (5) 172
ss. 3 (1), 4 172
s. 5 172
(2) (3) 174
s. 6 174
s. 8 ..... 172, 173
s. 9 (2)–(4) 173
s. 10 173
s. 11 (1) 174
(3) 175
(4)–(6) 176
s. 12 (1) 174, 175
(3) 174
(4) 174, 175
(6) 174
s. 13 208
s. 16 205
s. 17 (3) 212
(4) 212, 213
s. 18 (1)–(3) 215
s. 19 173
s. 20 (5) 175
s. 21 (4) 206
Sched. 1 ..... 172, 173
Solicitors Act (c. 47)
s. 38 51
Road Traffic Act (c. 50)
ss. 1–5 21
Rehabilitation of Offenders Act (c. 53) 187
1975 Criminal Procedure (Scotland) Act (c. 21)
s. 325 59
s. 326 56
Evidence (Proceedings in Other Jurisdictions) Act (c. 34) 110
s. 1 34
s. 2 ..... 34, 394
ss. 3, 5 34
Sched. 1 394
Public Service Vehicles (Arrest of Offenders) Act (c. 53) 21
Criminal Jurisdiction Act (c. 59) 10, 59
s. 7 ..... 10, 13
Children Act 1975 (c. 72) ... 378
s. 64 385
s. 68 ..... 374, 380
Sched. 3 ..... 379, 383
1976 Prevention of Terrorism (Temporary Provisions) Act (c. 8)
ss. 1, 9, 10 65

1976 Prevention of Terrorism (Temporary Provisions) Act—*cont.*
s. 11 .... 21, 65
s. 12 .... 25, 65, 68
s. 13 26
s. 17 65
Sched. 3 .... 25, 26, 27
Police Act (c. 46)
s. 5 (1) 165
s. 11 (1) (2) 165
Bail Act (c. 63) ... 58, 68–82, 243, 263
s. 1 (1) 264, 347
s. 2 (2) 73
s. 3 264
(1) 75, 264
(2) (4) 76
(5) 76, 82
(6) 77, 364
(7) 77, 364, 382
(8) 78, 152
(9) 77
s. 4 .... 67, 370
(1) 73
(2) 72, 73, 332
(3) 73, 338
(4) 73, 375
(7) 73

1976 Bail Act—*cont.*
s. 5 373
(1) 78, 80
(2) 78
(3)–(5) 77
(6) 77, 80, 104, 332
(7)–(9) 82
s. 6 .... 75, 80
(1)–(7) 80
s. 7 80
(1) 81, 151
(2) 81
(3) 63, 81, 152
(4) 81
(5) (6) 82
s. 8 (2) 76
(3) 70, 76
(4) 76
(5) 70, 76
s. 9 76
s. 10 (1) 73
s. 11 71
(2) 400
(4) (5) (7) 402
(8) 403
Sched. 1 ... 73, 74, 75, 223, 375
Sched. 2 ... 58, 65, 69, 70, 71, 77, 78, 79, 151, 350, 351, 352, 372
Sexual Offences (Amendment) Act (c. 82) 186

TABLE OF STATUTORY INSTRUMENTS

1928 Summary Jurisdiction (Process) (Isle of Man) Order (S.I. 1928 No. 377) 56

1946 Prosecution of Offences Regulations (S.I. 1946 No. 1467) 19
reg. 9 307

1953 Coroners Rules (S.I. 1953 No. 205) 37
r. 24 39

1954 Juvenile Courts (Constitution) Rules (S.I. 1954 No. 1711) 370

1956 Coroners (Indictable Offences) Rules (S.I. 1956 No. 1692)........ 39

1963 Prison Commissioners Dissolution Order (S.I. 1963 No. 597) 259

1964 Borstal Rules (S.I. 1964 No. 387)................. 232

Prison Rules (S.I. 1964 No. 388) 257, 258

Justices of the Peace (Size and Chairmanship of the Bench) Rules (S.I. 1964 No. 1107) 85
r. 2 289

Territorial Waters Order in Council (S.I. 1965 p. 6425A) 10

1965 Coroners (Indictable Offences) Rules (S.I. 1965 No. 1668) 39

1967 Local Review Committee Rules (S.I. 1967 No. 1462) 257

1968 Legal Aid in Criminal Proceedings (Complaints Tribunal) Rules (S.I. 1968 No. 1220) 399

Legal Aid in Criminal Proceedings (General) Regulations (S.I. 1968 No. 1231) 405

Criminal Appeal Rules (S.I. 1968 No. 1262)
r. 2 262
rr. 4–6 264
r. 7 265
r. 8 .... 261, 264
rr. 9, 10 270
r. 11 269

1968 Criminal Appeal Rules—*cont.*
r. 12 263
rr. 18, 19 .... 261, 264
r. 20 264
r. 22 261
r. 23 .... 280, 281
Sched. 1 ... 262, 270, 276, 280, 281, 283

Magistrates' Courts Rules (S.I. 1968 No. 1920)
r. 1 .... 54, 303, 304
r. 3 .... 100, 113
r. 4 ... 98, 99, 101, 104, 111, 113
r. 5 .... 99, 106
r. 6 106
r. 10 105
r. 11 .... 105, 114
r. 12 54
r. 13 .... 311, 385
r. 15 315
r. 19 296
r. 22 70
r. 38 .... 323, 325
r. 46 325
rr. 65–67 .... 350, 355
r. 68 ...... 349, 350, 355, 356
r. 71 70
r. 77 104
rr. 78, 79 57
r. 80 104
r. 81 55
r. 82 .... 56, 98, 390
r. 83 .... 54, 304
r. 88 98
r. 93 57

1970 Justices' Clerks Rules (S.I. 1970 No. 231) 48, 54

Magistrates' Courts (Children and Young Persons) Rules (S.I. 1970 No. 1792)
r. 5 374
rr. 6, 7 375
r. 8 ...... 365, 374, 375, 385
r. 9 385
r. 10 .... 375, 376, 386
r. 11 376
r. 14 385
r. 15 386
rr. 16, 17 385
r. 18 386
r. 19 385
rr. 21, 22 386
r. 26 .... 365, 369, 374

1970 Legal Aid in Criminal Proceedings (General) (Amendment) Regulations (S.I. 1970 No. 1980) 405

1971 Indictments Rules (S.I. 1971 No. 1253) 123
r. 4 117
r. 5 .... 118, 121
r. 6 ...... 119, 121, 127, 178
r. 7 128
r. 8 125
r. 9 .... 133, 166
r. 10 146
Sched. 1 117

Crown Court Rules (S.I. 1971 No. 1292)
r. 4 341
r. 5 .... 88, 341
rr. 7, 8 346
r. 9 .... 139, 347
r. 10 .... 250, 348
rr. 11–16 250
rr. 17, 18 72
r. 19 102
r. 21 .... 351, 352
Sched. 2 72

Indictments (Procedure) Rules (S.I. 1971 No. 2084)
r. 4 145
r. 5 144
rr. 7–10 145

1972 Prison (Amendment) Rules (S.I. 1972 No. 1860) 224, 257

Legal Aid in Criminal Proceedings (Amendment) Regulations (S.I. 1972 No. 1975) ... 399

1973 Local Review Committee (Amendment) Rules (S.I. 1973 No. 4) 257

Magistrates' Courts (Amendment) Rules (S.I. 1973 No. 790) ... 96
Sched. 57

Criminal Appeal (Reference of Points of Law) Rules (S.I. 1973 No. 1114) 279, 280

1973 Crown Office (Commissions of the Peace) Rules (S.I. 1973 No. 2099) 49

1974 Magistrates' Courts (Forms) (Amendment) Rules (S.I. 1974 No. 444)
Form 1 54
Form 2 55
Form 3 57
Form 11 105
Form 12 99
Form 13 104
Form 17 106

Children and Young Persons Act 1969 (Transitional Modifications to Part I) (Amendment) Order (S.I. 1974 No. 1083)... 381

Borstal (Amendment) Rules (S.I. 1974 No. 1923) 232

1975 Magistrates' Courts (Amendment) (No. 2) Rules (S.I. 1975 No. 518) 349, 350, 355, 356

Police (Disposal of Property) Regulations (S.I. 1975 No. 1474)... 330

1976 Borstal (Amendment) Rules (S.I. 1976 No. 508) 232

Legal Aid in Criminal Proceedings (General) (Amendment) Regulations (S.I. 1976 No. 790) 403

1977 Costs in Criminal Cases (Central Funds) (Appeals) Rules (S.I. 1977 No. 248)......... 249, 275

Children and Young Persons Act 1969 (Transitional Modifications of Part I) (Amendment) Order (S.I. 1977 No. 420) 373

TABLE OF RULES OF THE SUPREME COURT

Ord. 52 .... 253, 392, 393
Ord. 53 .... 46, 47
Ord. 54 .... 44, 45, 151
Ord. 56 .... 342, 350
Ord. 79 .... 79, 80, 82
Forms 97, 97A 79

CHAPTER 1

INTRODUCTION

THE study of criminal procedure could almost be said to belong to constitutional law. On the one hand it provides the machinery for implementing the criminal law, which, however comprehensive and just, would be useless without it. On the other hand it has to protect the individual from unjust prosecution and unjustified punishment. Readers may therefore find much of principle that is familiar in the following pages. The very complex system of checks and alternatives in the details of criminal procedure must always be placed in this context so as to establish their proper significance. Without this they often seem meaningless and, in any event, uninteresting. I therefore intend at this stage to draw the reader's attention to some of the salient features of the English system to help him to bear the general scheme of things in mind.

Until recent times the treatment of the accused can only be described as barbarous. He was not allowed counsel to represent him in trials for felony until 1836 and was generally unable to give evidence in his defence until 1898. He had no right to appeal against conviction until 1907. Even with these iniquities removed, the natural human tendency to think " he wouldn't be there unless he's guilty " requires the utmost safeguards for the accused. First and foremost, the accused is presumed innocent until proved to be guilty. Furthermore, he must be proved guilty beyond reasonable doubt. This means, in theory at least, that if he can throw doubt on the prosecution's evidence the accused is entitled to be acquitted without having to prove a " defence " in the formal sense (insanity, mistake, etc.).

Besides the presumption of innocence, an additional safeguard is the duty of the prosecution simply to lay the facts before the court, the Crown's only interest being that the right person should be convicted. Prosecuting counsel must not press for a conviction or for punishment. The prosecution has no general right to appeal against acquittal or sentence.

The law developed also a strong bias in favour of the personal liberty of the individual. This was done by means of the writ of habeas corpus and the civil remedies for false imprisonment. For instance, an arrested person in custody must be brought before the justices within 24 hours or as soon as is reasonably practicable [1] and, if the justices order him to be kept in custody during an adjournment of the hearing, he must be brought before them again every eighth day.[2] If he is committed for trial on indictment he should be sent for trial within eight weeks of committal, unless the Crown Court orders otherwise.[3] These provisions may not be an absolute guarantee against excessive detention without trial but are in marked contrast to many continental systems where periods of detention can be much longer.

The continental system of criminal procedure is of course totally different—investigation as well as trial is carried out by judicial authorities. In England, on the other hand, an underlying factor throughout criminal procedure is the " accusatorial " nature of the trial (as opposed to " inquisitorial "). This means that by the time the case is heard the prosecutor must have got together enough evidence to substantiate his accusation and the tribunal hearing it, altogether unacquainted with the matter, decides it as if it were umpire of a contest. The judge or magistrate has no power to interrogate the accused, and does not normally ask questions except to clear up some ambiguity left unanswered by counsel's questions. If he is not guilty of the offence charged (or of one of the few available alternative offences [4]), he must be acquitted and the court cannot find him guilty of another offence on its own initiative or investigation. There is, however, some judicial control over a prosecutor in the initial stages, *e.g.* issue of warrants for arrest and search, and, indirectly, over police interrogation.[5]

The separation of " crime " from " breaches of regulations," which exists in many European countries, has a very limited application in England in the form of fixed penalty notices for minor traffic offences, *e.g.* parking tickets.[6] The result is that the procedure of trial by a court of law has to apply to every sort of offence from murder and treason to keeping an unlicensed dog. The initial division of procedure to deal with this criminal spectrum is twofold—trial by jury for serious offences and summary trial by magistrates' courts for minor offences. The formal document charging an offence which is triable

---

[1] See p. 64.
[2] See p. 67.
[3] See p. 102; in fact, the period between committal and trial is often much longer.
[4] See p. 213.
[5] See pp. 20, 25 and 57, respectively.
[6] This is a system whereby fixed penalties can be paid without trial and sentence within a certain period, and it is only their non-payment which is an offence triable by a court: Road Traffic Regulation Act 1967, s. 80.

by jury is the indictment. The most serious offences are only triable on indictment and the least serious are only triable summarily. Between these two extremes some flexibility is achieved by providing three further categories—offences which are expressly made either summary or indictable ("hybrid offences"); offences which are indictable but for which the accused may consent to summary trial; and summary offences carrying a substantial term of imprisonment for which the accused may demand trial by jury. The need for differential treatment for differing degrees of culpability can be readily understood by looking at, for example, theft and dangerous driving. Hybrid offences are effectively two offences and the prosecutor must elect which one he intends to proceed with at the outset.[7] The court also exercises a judicial control over the choice of form of trial.[8] Juvenile offenders are in a special position, except when charged with homicide.[9]

In the English system of trial, Professor Glanville Williams[10] identifies six features which are unusual from a comparative point of view: the judge's position as umpire, the defendant's freedom from being questioned, the examination of witnesses by question and answer, the exclusionary rules of evidence, trial by jury and trial by lay magistrates. The most important factor is perhaps the trial by a jury of "12 people of average ignorance" or, at any rate, with no previous training for or experience in the function which they have to perform. To some extent this explains the necessity for oral examination of witnesses, the exclusion of some classes of evidence which are relevant but considered to be too prejudicial to leave to the jury (or the lay magistrate) and the fact that the judge takes no part in the "contest" between prosecution and defence but sits aloof, impartially guiding the trial and summing up each party's case to the jury.

The two central points of the system of criminal courts are the jury and the magistrate. Both institutions are essentially amateur, though lay magistrates now receive some training and are in places replaced by professionals.

The jury has a relatively confined task—to act as judge of the facts in a trial on indictment.[11] This takes place at the Crown Court.[12] In some cases magistrates sit on trials on indictment with a legally qualified judge.[13]

---

[7] See p. 295.

[8] See p. 294 *et seq.*

[9] See Chap. 15. p. 361.

[10] *The Proof of Guilt* (3rd ed.) p. 1.

[11] See p. 206.

[12] See p. 86.

[13] See p. 88.

The criminal functions of magistrates are much more diverse. First, they exercise some judicial control over the stages in a prosecution before trial: they authorise the police to enter private property to obtain evidence or to make an arrest, they secure the presence of the accused in court and they can decide whether an accused person should be kept in custody or allowed out on bail. Secondly, they examine charges of indictable offences to ensure that the accused is not sent for trial on a flimsy allegation, and they issue orders to secure the presence of witnesses at the trial. Thirdly, they try offences in three capacities: with a jury in the Crown Court, on their own at petty sessions, or sitting as a juvenile court. They have been described, quite aptly, as "judicial beasts of burden," for in addition they have jurisdiction in some matrimonial and small civil cases and in certain administrative matters such as licensing. [14] There are various safeguards to counterbalance the magistrates' ignorance of the law: they are guided (but not bound) by the advice of a qualified clerk on the law[15]; when they sit as a court of summary trial, either party may appeal to the Divisional Court of the Queen's Bench Division on a point of law[16]; and over some of their proceedings the High Court exercises some control by the prerogative orders.[17]

One final peculiarity of criminal procedure is that, despite the accusatorial form of trial, there is no official authority for handling prosecutions, although the police usually do so. However, while any person may institute a prosecution, once he has started he cannot compromise or drop the prosecution without either the consent of the Attorney-General on an indictment or the approval of the court and the Director of Public Prosecutions in proceedings before magistrates, for all proceedings are theoretically brought by the Crown.[18] Although this sounds cumbersome, prosecutors often get round these requirements by offering no evidence at trial or on committal, which is an informal way of securing an acquittal or having the charge dismissed. Alternatively, the court of trial may order that the indictment be stayed and not proceeded with without the leave of the court.[19] The Crown, as prosecutor, only has a right of appeal in two cases (both on a point of law and not on fact or sentence): to the Divisional Court of the Queen's Bench Division from a trial in a

---

14 See p. 300.
15 See p. 290.
16 See p. 349.
17 See p. 43.
18 See p. 17.
19 See p. 166.

magistrates' court or from an appeal from a magistrates' court to the Crown Court,[20] and to the House of Lords from the Court of Appeal or from the Divisional Court.[21] The Attorney-General's power to refer a point of law to the Court of Appeal following an acquittal[22] is not an appeal because the Court of Appeal's ruling can have no legal effect on the acquittal.

---

[20] See p. 349.
[21] See pp. 280 and 352.
[22] Criminal Justice Act 1972, s. 36; see p. 279.

PART ONE

MATTERS PRELIMINARY TO TRIAL

CHAPTER 2

CRIMINAL JURISDICTION

THE first consideration when someone believes that an offence has been committed is to establish that a prosecution can be brought in an English court—where was it committed, when, by whom and what preliminary step, if any, is necessary before embarking on the prosecution? The second consideration, if the first is satisfied, is in which English court to start the proceedings.

A. GENERAL TERRITORIAL JURISDICTION

The general rule is that the criminal jurisdiction of the English courts is territorial, *i.e.* limited to offences committed within the territory of England and Wales. Several statutes make exceptions to this general rule in relation to particular places, persons or crimes, but if a crime does not fall within such an exception, it cannot be tried at all by any English court. For the purposes of the general rule Scotland and Northern Ireland are foreign countries.

To trespass for a moment in the field of the substantive law, it must be borne in mind that the place where a crime was committed is sometimes open to question. It can generally be deduced from the definition of the particular crime, coupled with the proposition that a crime is committed where the act is completed. For instance, where a person in Paris caused incorrect figures to be entered in an account in London by making false returns, the offence was committed in England.[1] Blackmail is committed where the blackmailing letter is posted [2] but the English court has jurisdiction to try a person accused of obtaining by deception through a letter posted abroad.[3] A conspiracy may be tried in England wherever it was formed provided it

---

1 *R.* v. *Oliphant* [1905] 2 K.B. 67; *R.* v. *De Marny* [1907] 1 K.B. 388; *R.* v. *Hornett* [1975] R.T.R. 256.

2 *Treacy* v. *D.P.P.* [1971] A.C. 537; this is a difficult ruling, however; two Law Lords stated it in this form; two other Law Lords disagreed and would have allowed the appeal; Lord Diplock based his agreement with the first two on a much broader principle which challenges the "general rule" of jurisdiction stated above—now that the formalities of venue have been abolished, jurisdiction is to be found in the international rules of comity, none of which prevent Parliament from prohibiting the doing of acts in England notwithstanding that their consequences take effect elsewhere.

3 *R.* v. *Ellis* [1899] 1 Q.B. 230; *R.* v. *Baxter* [1972] 1 Q.B. 1. See also *R.* v. *Robert Millar (Contractors) Ltd.* [1970] 2 Q.B. 54; *Secretary of State for Trade* v. *Markus* [1975] 2 W.L.R. 708 (Lord Diplock's dictum in *Treacy*, above, was doubted in the Court of Appeal, but the House of Lords did not discuss it in principle).

is still in existence when the conspirator is in England and provided he does acts in furtherance of the conspiracy in England, even if those acts are not in themselves unlawful.[4]

For further information, reference should be made to a work on the criminal law.[5] The creation of extra-territorial offences by the Criminal Jurisdiction Act 1975 is restricted to Northern Ireland and the Republic of Ireland, except in relation to explosives.[6]

1. Offences committed outside territorial limits

The following places outside the strict territorial limits of the United Kingdom are within the jurisdiction of the English criminal courts: territorial waters, British ships, British aircraft and installations on the continental shelf.

(a) *Territorial waters*

The Territorial Waters Jurisdiction Act 1878, s. 2, provides that an offence committed by any person on the open sea within the territorial waters of H.M. Dominions is within the jurisdiction of the English courts. This applies to offences committed by any person, British subject or foreigner, and to offences committed on board or by means of a foreign ship. "Territorial waters" means the sea adjacent to the coast within three nautical miles. It may be extended for specific purposes by statute, as, for example, by the Wireless Telegraphy Act 1967 and the Fishery Limits Act 1964; or by Order in Council, as by the Territorial Waters Order of 1964.[7]

(b) *British ships and aircraft*

The jurisdiction of the courts extends to all persons, whether or not they are British subjects, on board British ships on the high seas and in foreign rivers "below all bridges and at a point where the tide ebbs and flows and where great ships lie and hover": *R.* v. *Anderson.*[8] This

---

[4] *D.P.P.* v. *Doot* [1973] A.C. 807. See also *R.* v. *Borro* [1973] Crim. L.R. 513; *R.* v. *Wall* [1974] 1 W.L.R. 930.

[5] In the case of homicide, the most important provision is s. 9 of the Offences against the Person Act 1861; see p. 13. In *R.* v. *Coombes* (1785) 1 Leach 358 it was held that the offence is committed on the victim's side of a territorial boundary if the act was done elsewhere.

[6] s. 7 of the 1975 Act substitutes new ss. 2 and 3 of the Explosive Substances Act 1883.

[7] S.I. 1965, p. 6425A; *Post Office* v. *Estuary Radio* [1968] 2 Q.B. 740.

[8] (1868) L.R. 1 C.C.R. 161; *R.* v. *Liverpool Justices, ex p. Molyneux* [1972] 2 Q.B. 384. This may have surprising results; in *Oteri* v. *The Queen, The Times,* October 5, 1976, it was held that the English criminal law is applicable in the courts of the Australian states in respect of offences committed off shore because citizens of Australia may also be British subjects still and a boat owned by one is therefore a "British ship."

ancient extension of jurisdiction is confirmed for offences committed on the high seas by section 686 of the Merchant Shipping Act 1894. Admiralty jurisdiction is exercised by the Crown Court.[9] It was postulated by Lord Devlin in *R.* v. *Martin*[10] that some offences are of exclusively domestic application and therefore cannot be committed in any place other than England and Wales, *e.g.* on a British ship abroad. This case, which involved possession of dangerous drugs, was decided under section 62 of the Civil Aviation Act 1949 which has been repealed by section 1 of the Tokyo Convention Act 1967. The latter provides that acts and omissions which would constitute an offence in some part of the United Kingdom if committed there, do constitute that offence if committed in a British aircraft while in flight elsewhere than on or over United Kingdom territory, unless expressly or impliedly authorised to be committed outside the United Kingdom. The offence may be tried in any place where the offender is found for the time being: section 1 (3). This, like section 70 (1)[11] of the Army Act 1955 could be said to create the offence, for, as Lord Devlin stated,[12] some offences could not otherwise be committed outside United Kingdom territory. For instance, summary offences are generally deemed to be committable only in England unless it is expressly provided to the contrary.[13]

(c) *Offences against aircraft*

Unlawful acts against aircraft are justiciable in the United Kingdom wherever the offence is committed and whatever the nationality of the offender; the Hijacking Act 1971 created the offence of unlawful seizure and the Protection of Aircraft Act 1973 covers other unlawful acts intended to destroy or endanger an aircraft. Offences against aircraft in military, police or customs service are, however, outside the jurisdiction under either Act, unless the act is committed in the United Kingdom or the offender is a British subject or, in the case of hijacking, the aircraft is registered in the United Kingdom. The same exception applies to hijacking an aircraft whose place both of take-off and of landing is in the state in which the aircraft is registered.

(d) *The continental shelf*

Section 3 of the Continental Shelf Act 1964 extends the criminal

---

9 Courts Act 1971, s. 6 (2).
10 [1956] 2 Q.B. 272 at p. 286.
11 See p. 13.
12 In *R.* v. *Martin* above.
13 *R.* v. *Kent Justices, ex p. Lye* [1967] 2 Q.B. 153.

jurisdiction of the courts, regarding offences taking place on or near an installation in an area of the sea outside territorial waters designated by Order in Council for exploitation by the United Kingdom of the seabed and subsoil, of that part of the United Kingdom nearest the relevant area.

2. Offences committed outside the jurisdiction

Jurisdiction is extended to cover some persons when they commit an offence outside the jurisdiction, for instance, any British subject employed in the service of the Crown who commits an indictable offence abroad while purporting to act in the course of his employment.[14] Further, any person, British or foreign, who commits an offence against property or person either ashore or afloat in any place and who is or has been in the previous three months employed in any British ship, is amenable to the jurisdiction under section 687 of the Merchant Shipping Act 1894. Under section 686 of the same Act a British subject who commits an offence on a foreign ship to which he does not belong or in a foreign port [15] may be tried in England.

Trial in England of an offence committed abroad is limited to British subjects except, principally, in two cases (and the exceptions in the last paragraph). One is piracy which may be tried here whoever committed it in whatever place: *Re Piracy Jure Gentium*.[16] The other—treason—is more complex in that the offence can only be committed by someone who owes allegiance to the Crown. The authorities state that a "British subject" can commit treason wherever he may be,[17] but this is subject to section 3 of the British Nationality Act 1948 which provides that British subjects who are not citizens of the United Kingdom and Colonies are not guilty of an offence against English law for anything done abroad unless it would constitute an offence if committed by an alien. "Abroad" includes the Republic of Ireland and Commonwealth countries. Allegiance is correlative with the protection granted by the Crown and is distinct from nationality. An alien owes allegiance while he is in British territory and he may continue to owe it after leaving if he leaves his family and property

---

[14] Criminal Justice Act 1948, s. 31, as amended by the Criminal Law Act 1967, s. 10 (2) and Sched. 3. See also the Offences by Officials Abroad Act 1699 (colonial governors).

[15] *R.* v. *Liverpool Justices, ex p. Molyneux* [1972] 2 Q.B. 384.

[16] [1934] A.C. 586. This applies also to piracy of aircraft under s. 4 of the Tokyo Convention Act 1967; see also para. (c) above and the Geneva Convention of April 29, 1958.

[17] See *e.g. R.* v. *Casement* [1917] 1 K.B. 98.

behind or if he is in possession of a British passport.[18] There are also a few statutory exceptions, such as section 14 of the Theft Act 1968 which provides that theft of a mail bag or postal packet in the British postal area may be tried in England or Wales without proof that it was stolen there.

Other crimes triable in the English courts if committed abroad by a British subject who is also a citizen of the United Kingdom and Colonies include murder and manslaughter,[19] bigamy,[20] and offences under the Foreign Enlistment Act 1870, the Official Secrets Acts 1911–20 and the Forgery Act 1913.[21]

Section 70 of the Army Act 1955 gives British Courts-Martial jurisdiction to try members of the United Kingdom armed forces for civil (*i.e.* non-military) offences when they are serving abroad, if the offence would be punishable by English law if committed in England.[22]

If a person who has committed an offence in one state is later found in another state, extradition proceedings may be instituted by the government of the state in which it is sought to prosecute him.[23]

B. Time Limits

The general rule is that time does not run against the Crown and there is no limitation period on prosecutions unless a statute specifically provides one. This has led to some extraordinary cases; Sir James Stephen records an indictment (thrown out by the grand jury) for trivial theft committed 60 years earlier[24] and A. F. Wilcox recalls cases of burglary committed eight years before, when the accused was 14, and homicide 21 years previously in both of which the court took a lenient view.[25]

The most important statutory exception is section 104 of the Magistrates' Courts Act 1952 which provides that prosecutions for all summary offences must be brought within six months of the commission of the offence, unless it is expressly provided by statute to the

---

18 Foster's *Crown Cases* (3rd ed.), p. 185; *Joyce* v. *D.P.P.* [1946] A.C. 347.

19 Offences against the Person Act 1861, s. 9.

20 *Ibid.*, s. 57; *R.* v. *Sagoo* [1975] 3 W.L.R. 267.

21 s. 7 of the Criminal Jurisdiction Act 1975 (amending ss. 2 and 3 of the Explosives Act 1883) makes provision for explosives offences to be punished under English law and extends in particular to the Republic of Ireland.

22 *e.g. Cox* v. *Army Council* [1963] A.C. 48 (driving without due care and attention on a German road).

23 See pp. 60 and 115.

24 See Stephen's *History of the Criminal Law II*, p. 2.

25 *The Decision to Prosecute*, pp. 66–68.

contrary.[26] Time limits are attached to several other offences, for instance: treason and misprision of treason—three years [27]; homosexual offences—12 months [28]; income tax offences—six years [29]; intercourse with a girl under 16 years old—12 months.[30] A full list can be found in *Archbold.*[31]

A limitation of great practical significance relating to certain traffic offences (including dangerous and careless driving and speeding) is provided by section 179 of the Road Traffic Act 1972. If the accused has not been warned at the time of committing the offence that prosecution will be considered, he (or the registered keeper of the vehicle) must be served with either a summons or a notice of intended prosecution within 14 days of the commission of the offence. No limitation applies, however, if the driver does not stop and the prosecutor cannot, despite using due diligence, discover the necessary name and address within the 14 days.[32]

C. Immunity from Prosecution

The Queen, whether or not she is theoretically capable of committing an offence, cannot be prosecuted, for no court has jurisdiction to try her. Foreign sovereigns and their emissaries are also given immunity from prosecution but it may be expressly waived by the foreign state. It is a matter of the comity of nations and is embodied principally in the Diplomatic Privileges Act 1964 and the Consular Relations Act 1968. Members of the diplomatic staff of an embassy have full personal immunity from the criminal and civil jurisdiction, but administrative and technical staff, service staff and consuls are immune only for offences committed in the course of performing their duties. Members of Commonwealth and Irish diplomatic missions and people who work for international organisations to which the United Kingdom belongs have similar immunities (Diplomatic Immunities (Commonwealth Countries and the Republic of Ireland) Act 1952 and the International Organisations (Immunities and Privileges) Act 1950). The exercise of the privilege has great significance in relation to breaches of the motoring and highway laws and regulations.

---

[26] *N.B.*, however, that this does not include those indictable offences which may be tried summarily; see pp. 296 and 297.

[27] Except in the case of plots to assassinate the sovereign or of treasonable acts or of misprision of treason committed abroad: Treason Act 1695, s. 5.

[28] Sexual Offences Act 1967, s. 7.

[29] Taxes Management Act 1970, s. 103.

[30] Sexual Offences Act 1956, s. 6 and Sched. 2.

[31] Paras. 77–86.

[32] *Haughton* v. *Harrison* [1976] R.T.R. 208.

It was reported in July 1976 that about 6000 unpaid parking fines are incurred every month by the diplomatic staff in London.[33]

The jurisdiction over the armed forces of foreign states in the United Kingdom is subject to the Visiting Forces Act 1952 which provides for the forces of Commonwealth countries and others specified by Order in Council under defence treaty arrangements such as NATO. The jurisdiction of the English courts is only ousted in relation to offences arising in the course of service duty, offences against the person or property of a member of or the property of a visiting force and offences for which the accused has already been tried by the visiting force's service court.

D. Preliminary Administrative Action

Before prosecuting for a large number of offences, the approval of the Attorney-General, the Director of Public Prosecutions (D.P.P.) or, occasionally, the Home Secretary or other Minister, is necessary.[34] If it is withheld, although the power of arrest is often expressly preserved, then any proceedings already begun are void and, as it is an executive act, there is no appeal against a refusal.

As a broad generalisation, prosecutions requiring the sanction of the Attorney-General are for offences against the state and public order, *e.g.* under the Public Order Act 1936, the Race Relations Act 1965, s. 6, and the Official Secrets Acts, and for seditious libel and corruption of officers of public bodies. However, others do not fall into this category, *e.g.* corruption of agents. The consent of the Home Secretary is required for prosecuting an alien under the Territorial Waters Jurisdiction Act 1878 [35] and the consent of other officers of state may be specifically required.[36] Sometimes the consent of one of two officers is necessary, *e.g.* the Director of Public Prosecutions *or* the Attorney-General for prosecutions for incest.[37]

The consent of the D.P.P. is a prerequisite of prosecutions for a wide variety of offences, usually where there is a risk of abusive prosecution, such as homosexual offences,[38] assisting and concealing

---

[33] *Evening Standard*, July 22, 1976.

[34] The precise stage at which the consent must be obtained may vary, depending on construction of the statute requiring the consent; sometimes it has to be obtained before any proceedings are begun; in other cases, the defendant has first to be charged before the magistrate. The consent of the Attorney-General need not take any particular form and may be cast in quite general terms; see *R.* v. *Cain* [1975] 3 W.L.R. 131.

[35] See p. 10.

[36] *e.g.* Post Office Act 1953, s. 56.

[37] Sexual Offences Act 1956, ss. 10, 11 and 37.

[38] Sexual Offences Act 1967, ss. 4 and 5.

offenders and wasting police time,[39] theft or unlawful damage to a spouse's property,[40] and intercourse by male nurses with mental patients.[41] As to other powers of these officers, see pp. 18–20.

E. LOCAL JURISDICTION

The division of the country into metropolitan and non-metropolitan counties applies to the jurisdiction of magistrates' courts.[42] The Crown Court has jurisdiction throughout England and Wales over more serious offences; it may sit at any time and at any place and its jurisdiction is single and indivisible.[43] The day to day organisation of sittings is administered by the Lord Chancellor.[44]

A magistrates' court has jurisdiction over offences committed within its commission area, *i.e.* county. For the sake of reasonable flexibility, the county includes its boundary, land within 500 yards of its boundary, and any harbour, river, arm of the sea or other water lying between it and another county.[45] Further, an offence begun in one county and completed in another may be treated as committed wholly in either of them[46] and if the offence was committed on property or a person, or on a vehicle or vessel, journeying between two or more counties, it may be treated as committed in any one of them.[47] The detailed exceptions to the rule of local jurisdiction can be more conveniently dealt with in the context of the proceedings to which they relate.[48]

---

39 Criminal Law Act 1967, ss. 4 and 5.

40 Theft Act 1968, s. 30.

41 Mental Health Act 1959, s. 128. Leave to prosecute must be sought from the High Court under certain other provisions of this Act, *e.g.* s. 141: *Pountney* v. *Griffiths* [1975] 3 W.L.R. 140.

42 Local Government Act 1972, s. 216.

43 Courts Act 1971, s. 4 (4).

44 Courts Act 1971, s. 4 (6); see also p. 89. The places at which the Crown Court sits and the circuits have been designated by the Lord Chancellor; see (1971) 121 New L.J. 1122.

45 Magistrates' Courts Act 1952, s. 3 (1), as amended by the Local Government Act 1972, Sched. 27.

46 *Ibid.*, s. 3 (2).

47 Magistrates' Courts Act 1952, s. 3 (3), as amended by the Local Government Act 1972, Sched. 27.

48 See pp. 51, 85 and 289.

CHAPTER 3

PREPARATION FOR PROSECUTION

THE matters considered so far cannot strictly be called procedure, but are conditions precedent to criminal proceedings. Because the form of proceedings is a contest between the parties and not a judicial investigation into facts other than those produced in evidence, the intending prosecutor must prepare the case supporting his allegation before beginning proceedings against the suspect. The powers of and the controls over an intending prosecutor before he can open formal proceedings against the suspect will be considered and the consequences of bringing proceedings wrongly will be briefly described.

A. PROSECUTING AUTHORITIES

Any person may initiate criminal proceedings.[1] In practice the bulk of prosecutions is brought by the police in the name of the Crown, and all offences tried on indictment are prosecuted in the name of the Crown. The most numerous of non-police prosecutions are by companies (*e.g.* shoplifters prosecuted by shopkeepers), local authorities and government departments, such as the Commissioners of Customs and Excise and the Department of Health and Social Security; some of these departments keep their own legal staffs, while the Treasury Solicitor acts for others. The Treasury Solicitor's Office has a staff of solicitors and barristers employed to act for government departments in all legal matters.

1. Private individuals

Prosecutions by private individuals are most often found in the form of a summons for common assault in the magistrates' court because the magistrates have power to restrain the defendant from repeating the assault, whereas a civil court can award damages only and not grant an injunction.

---

[1] A report by Justice published in 1970 sets out proposals for a unified public prosecution system; see *The Prosecution Process in England and Wales*. The idea is further discussed in Sigler [1974] Crim. L.R. 642 and Bowley [1975] Crim. L.R. 442. The Australian Law Reform Commission has published a report on " Criminal Investigation " (No. 2—Interim) which comprehensively examines the law enforcement procedures prior to trial; see also Ashworth [1976] Crim. L.R. 594, *Report of the Committee on Criminal Procedure in Scotland* (Cmnd. 6218) and Adams [1976] Crim. L.R. 609.

The greatest deterrent to private prosecutions for serious offences is the cost. The prosecution must be legally represented for trial on indictment and costs for the prosecution are assessed, if awarded at all, according to what appears to be " reasonably sufficient " as compensation, which tends to fall short of the actual expenses.[2] However, the Director of Public Prosecutions has power to authorise costs and expenses to be fully reimbursed. As to costs generally, see p. 248.

2. The police

Purely in terms of court procedure the police are not in a special position as regards bringing prosecutions. But in practice they are very much at an advantage, for not only have they the funds and the necessary facilities, but they also have wider powers ancillary to prosecution [3] and arrest,[4] and greater protection from civil liability for their acts.[5] The Royal Commission on the Police which reported in 1962 [6] included in the five main functions of the police the " responsibility for the detection of crime " and " of deciding whether to prosecute suspected criminals." [7] Although the organisation of the police is still based on local forces, there are various central controls on prosecution for the purposes of co-ordination as well as to prevent abuses.

Central controls of prosecution

These controls emanate either from the Attorney-General or from the Director of Public Prosecutions. For a wide range of offences the consent of one of them is necessary, as outlined on p. 15, before proceedings can be instituted. The Attorney-General, who holds a ministerial post although his decisions in connection with prosecutions are made quasi-judicially, has power to take over private prosecutions and to stop proceedings on indictment by granting a *nolle prosequi*. Any person may request him to grant it and it may be entered on the court record after the indictment has been signed[8] and before judgment. Its effect is to stop all proceedings on that indictment, but it does not amount to an acquittal so the accused may be

---

[2] *e.g.* in *Re Central Funds Costs Order* [1975] 1 W.L.R. 1227 a private prosecutor in the Crown Court was awarded £20,000 towards his solicitors' bills, no award being made in respect of his personal expenses, where he had claimed over £29,000.

[3] See pp. 21 and 27.

[4] See p. 63.

[5] See p. 41.

[6] Cmnd. 1728.

[7] A. F. Wilcox's *The Decision to Prosecute* (1972) provides an interesting analysis of this second function.

[8] See pp. 145 and 218.

re-indicted and, if necessary, a further *nolle prosequi* granted.[9] An informal alternative is for the prosecution to offer no evidence so that the jury must acquit.[10] If the accused has not yet been committed for trial, the D.P.P. may use his power to take over the prosecution[11] before committal for trial and offer no evidence. In magistrates' court proceedings, although the prosecutor cannot drop a prosecution merely by agreement with the accused, the court may give leave for the withdrawal of the charge. The clerk of the court or to the justices must tell the D.P.P. if the charge is withdrawn or not proceeded with in a reasonable time.[12] Undertakings not to prosecute may be given to a suspect who turns Queen's evidence; the police should never give them, however, and the D.P.P. should use the practice sparingly.[13]

The courts will only interfere with a police decision not to prosecute in extreme cases.[14]

The powers and duties of the D.P.P. are laid down in the Prosecution of Offences Acts 1879 to 1908 and specified in detail in Regulations made in 1946 under the 1879 Act.[15] He is a non-political appointee of the Home Secretary. The Attorney-General superintends his activities and has power to direct him to make an inquiry, prosecute a particular offence or employ particular counsel. The D.P.P. may give advice to justices' clerks and prosecutors, whether police, private individual or government department, in cases of importance or difficulty, on their application or on his own initiative. He may take over any prosecution, summary or on indictment, if he considers it necessary. He must prosecute offences punishable by death [16] and where he considers his intervention is necessary in a case referred to him, because of its importance, difficulty or for some other reason. Chief officers of police must report to him certain offences specified in the 1946 Regulations including rape and public mischief. If he is not obliged to conduct the prosecution but advises for a prosecution against the inclination of the police, he can do it himself. In addition to advice, he may assist a private prosecutor by specially

---

[9] *Goddard* v. *Smith* (1704) 6 Mod. Rep. 261; *R.* v. *Mitchel* (1848) 3 Cox 93.

[10] A verdict of not guilty may be entered by order of the judge in those circumstances: Criminal Justice Act 1967, s. 17, see p. 158.

[11] Below.

[12] Prosecution of Offences Regulations S.R. & O. 1946 No. 1467.

[13] *R.* v. *Turner* (1975) 61 Cr. App. R. 67; *R.* v. *Arrowsmith* [1975] 2 W.L.R. 484.

[14] *R.* v. *Commissioner of Police for the Metropolis, ex p. Blackburn* [1973] 2 W.L.R. 43.

[15] Prosecution of Offences Regulations, above.

[16] See p. 223.

authorising the payment of expenses and reimbursement of costs. Further, he may defend an appeal against conviction if he prosecuted at trial, if he considers it desirable or if the Court of Appeal directs him to do so.[17]

The Attorney-General and the Solicitor-General, if he acts instead of the Attorney-General, may appear themselves in important cases or employ barristers from the nominated list of "Treasury Counsel." They are both forbidden to engage in private practice.[18] The D.P.P. keeps a staff of solicitors and barristers but he may employ any solicitor or barrister.

The Divisional Court of the Queen's Bench Division has certain powers of control over proceedings in the magistrates' courts by the issue of prerogative writs, which are described later.[19]

B. Investigation by the Police

Except in cases where an offender is caught red-handed in front of willing witnesses, the prosecution must assemble sufficient evidence for its case by inquiry and search. The obtaining of evidence and its subsequent admissibility varies according to whether or not the evidence is in the form of a confession of guilt by the accused. This applies to police and others, but the police have additional powers of questioning [20] and of searching.[21]

The Judges' Rules

Interrogation of suspected offenders is subject to the Judges' Rules.[22] They are formulated by the judges of the Queen's Bench Division and, although they do not have the force of law, evidence obtained in infringement of them is liable to be excluded at the trial judge's discretion. They supplement the general rule that a confession must be made voluntarily.

No one is obliged to go to a police station unless he is arrested. This appears to be subject to an exception, however, when the police are given a power to search and detain a person; a constable may take the person to a place where the searching may be properly done.

---

17 Prosecution of Offences Act 1879, s. 2, as amended by the Criminal Appeal Act 1968, s. 52 (1), Sched. 5.

18 Treasury Minute of 1894.

19 See p. 43 *et seq.*

20 Below.

21 See p. 27.

22 Revised in 1964 and published in Appendix A of Home Office Circular No. 31/1964.

It is desirable to do so if a male constable wishes to have a female suspect searched.[23]

Although the police are entitled to question any person about the commission of an offence (Judges' Rules, Rule I), they are entitled to demand an answer in only a few cases. Several statutes make it an offence not to answer questions. For instance, section 168 (2) of the Road Traffic Act 1972 places a duty on the owner of a vehicle to give information as to the identity of the driver at the time when an alleged driving offence was committed.[24] Section 2 of the Official Secrets Act 1920 prescribes a duty to answer the questions of a chief officer of police on official secrets matters. A person who conceals information for a consideration may commit the offence of concealing under section 5 of the Criminal Law Act 1967. Various statutes give a constable the right to demand the name and address of a person he suspects and, on failure to give them, he may arrest that person.[25] The Public Service Vehicles (Arrest of Offenders) Act 1975 gives a police constable the power to arrest a person who refuses to give his name and address if the constable suspects with reasonable cause that he is contravening regulations about the conduct of passengers. Mere refusal to answer questions, as opposed to giving false information, cannot amount to obstructing the police in the execution of their duty under section 51 (3) of the Police Act 1964.[26] Section 11 of the Prevention of Terrorism (Temporary Provisions) Act 1976 makes it an offence not to disclose information to a police constable if the person who has it knows or believes it might be of material assistance in preventing an act of terrorism or in apprehending, prosecuting or convicting a person involved in an act of terrorism. This provision, which is akin to the offence of misprision of felony abolished by the Criminal Law Act 1967, requires the person to volunteer the information.

When a police officer has reasonable grounds[27] for suspecting that a person has committed an offence he may question him after caution-

---

[23] *Farrow* v. *Tunnicliffe* [1976] Crim.L.R. 127. Such powers exist under s. 23 of the Misuse of Drugs Act 1971 and s. 47 of the Firearms Act 1968. A driver may be required to attend a police station to produce documents under s. 161 of the Road Traffic Act 1972.

[24] *Cf.* the guilt of a vehicle-owner under ss. 1–5 of the Road Traffic Act 1974 if he fails to give details of ownership in response to a notice issued for failure to pay a fixed penalty; he is also liable to pay the penalty, whether or not he was the driver when the penalty was incurred.

[25] See, *e.g.* the Public Order Act 1936, s. 6; the Firearms Act 1968, s. 48. See also Glanville Williams (1950) 66 L.Q.R. 465.

[26] *Rice* v. *Connolly* [1966] 2 Q.B. 414.

[27] This is judged objectively, *i.e.* information which could go before a court: *R.* v. *Osbourne* [1973] 2 W.L.R. 209.

ing him that he is not obliged to answer and that his words may be written down and given in evidence (Rule II). This is the first caution. The second caution must be given when the police officer charges him or informs him that he may be prosecuted.[28] The police officer may ask him if he wishes to say anything, again stating that he is not obliged to do so (Rule IIIa). However, after charging or warning of prosecution, the police officer may ask him further questions only in exceptional cases, for instance, where harm to a third party may be prevented or to clear up an ambiguity in an earlier statement (Rule IIIb). The Rules are expressly based upon the principle that the police officer must charge the suspect as soon as he has sufficient evidence. He may also show the person charged any statement made by another person charged with the same offence, but must not invite comments (Rule V). In *R.* v. *Buchan* [29] it was held permissible to question a person who is in custody for one offence about other suspected offences not already charged.

" Verbals "

Anything the suspect says to the police or is heard to say—" verbals " [30]—may be admissible as evidence. It may amount to an informal admission of guilt, and should be treated with caution by the court. The process of recording a statement quickly may lead to an innocent distortion such as the following:

" Policeman: Come along now, someone's shopped you over that job at the White House.

Innocent man in astonishment: Me? How can anyone have shopped me? "

comes out in court as:

" Policeman: I have reason to believe you were concerned in a burglary at the White House.

Accused: Who shopped me? " [31]

The feasibility of experimental tape recording was examined by a Home Office committee's report, published on October 19, 1976.

Likewise overheard conversations between accomplices or between the accused and his family should be treated with caution. In

---

[28] *Conway* v. *Hotten* [1976] 2 All E.R. 213.

[29] [1964] 1 W.L.R. 365.

[30] This is a term in popular use but has received no official sanction and should not be used in court.

[31] *Cf.* Justice Report, *Preliminary Investigations of Criminal Offences*, 1960. A new practice has arisen whereby the accused is given a written questionnaire to complete in his own handwriting in front of witnesses, such as his solicitor, so that the area of conflict can be reduced.

R. v. *Stewart* [32] a policeman sat in a neighbouring cell without his belt or bootlaces (to look like a prisoner) to listen to a conversation involving the whereabouts of stolen goods. The Court of Appeal held that the judge should consider the motive for the eavesdropping and the substance of the conversation when using his discretion to admit the evidence. In this case he was held to have admitted it rightly. The same caution and disapproval might well be meted out to evidence obtained by telephone-tapping and interception of mail.[33] It is also possible to misconstrue the silence of a suspect, although he is not bound to say anything at any stage, for silence in the face of allegations may amount to an acceptance of them.[34]

An inculpatory statement made to a person in authority, such as a police officer, must, if challenged by the defence, be proved to have been made voluntarily, *i.e.* without fear of prejudice or hope of advantage or any other oppression.[35] If not, the "confession" is inadmissible and a conviction following its improper admission will, in all probability, be quashed as unsafe and unsatisfactory.

Evidence obtained by improper means

In contrast with the restrictive rules on confessions of guilt, evidence which is obtained by improper means is admissible, although a policeman may thereby make himself liable in tort.[36] Where a confession is obtained improperly and is therefore inadmissible, a fact revealed in the course of it which can be proved without reference to it is admissible, "for a fact, if it exist at all, must exist invariably in the same manner, whether the confession . . . be in other respects true or false."[37] However, the judge has a discretion to exclude such evidence and in *R.* v. *Payne* [38] the Court of Criminal Appeal quashed the conviction of a man for drunken driving, against whom a doctor testified as to his drunkenness having examined him to establish whether his condition was due to illness. The Court felt that his consent was not freely given.

This question also arises in connection with evidence obtained by

---

[32] [1970] 1 W.L.R. 907.

[33] See p. 36.

[34] *R.* v. *Chandler* [1976] 1 W.L.R. 585. For how the court may treat silence, see p. 198.

[35] For detailed consideration of this rule, reference must be made to a work on the law of evidence, *e.g. Cross on Evidence* (4th ed.), pp. 482–495; see also p. 208.

[36] See p. 42.

[37] *R.* v. *Warwickshall* (1783) 1 Leach 263.

[38] [1963] 1 W.L.R. 637, applying dicta in *Noor Mohammed* v. *R.* [1949] A.C. 182 and *Harris* v. *D.P.P.* [1952] A.C. 694.

an unauthorised search. In *Kuruma* v. *R.*[42] the judge should have excluded evidence of ammunition found on the accused during an unlawful search. The judge's discretion to exclude evidence is based on fairness of treatment of the accused, control of unconscionable police practices and the avoidance of evidence whose probative value is slight but whose prejudicial value is considerable.

It has been contended in a number of cases that the principle should also apply to prosecution evidence where a witness has acted as *agent provocateur* or conspirator. In *R.* v. *Birtles*[39] it was held that the evidence of the *agent* must not mislead the court and that his act must not have procured an offence which would not otherwise have been committed. In *R.* v. *McEvilly*[40] this was confirmed but the evidence should not be vitiated because of a mere possibility of procurement by a prosecution witness. In *R.* v. *Willis*[41] the *Birtles* principle was doubted but not rejected; no defence of entrapment exists, however, so the exclusion of the evidence is the only means by which the court may protect an accused in these circumstances.

A situation which is analogous to the exclusion of illegally obtained evidence has arisen under the " breathalyser " procedure of the Road Traffic Act 1972, ss. 5–9. At the time of writing, *Spicer* v. *Holt*[43] was the most recent House of Lords' decision on the provisions. These require, *inter alia*, the arrest of the driver before taking him to a police station to give a specimen of blood or urine. The House of Lords ruled that the specimen is necessarily rendered inadmissible in evidence if the arrest proves to have been unlawful. The exclusion is not based, however, on the principle that it would be unjust to the accused, but the accused does not come within the terms of the sections unless the procedure is complied with.[44] The procedure must therefore be regarded, if not as unique, then at least as a juridical form from which no general principles applicable elsewhere can be drawn.[45] The reason for the complex formula to exclude the evidence if the procedure is not complied with is based, however, like the

---

[39] [1969] 1 W.L.R. 1047; *cf. R.* v. *O'Brien* (1974) 59 Cr. App. R. 222.

[40] [1974] Crim. L.R. 239.

[41] [1976] Crim. L.R. 127.

[42] [1955] A.C. 197.

[43] [1976] 3 All E.R. 71; [1976] 3 W.L.R. 398.

[44] The same would apply if, for instance, the wrong sort of breathalysing device were used: *Scott* v. *Baker* [1969] 1 Q.B. 659.

[45] Recommendations for reform have been made by the Blennerhasset Committee's Report (H.M.S.O. 1976) which the Minister of Transport announced will be implemented (*The Times*, August 5, 1976, p. 4). These leave the basic form of criminal responsibility unchanged, however. For an analysis of the case law before *Spicer* v. *Holt*, see Strachan, *The Drinking Driver and the Law* (2nd ed., 1976).

exclusion of confessions, on the reluctance of the English law to require a person to furnish evidence against himself.

C. Powers of Search

The investigator of a crime frequently needs to look for and procure real evidence for the prosecution and to keep it if necessary. Although generally search is permitted only by specific statutory authority, there is a further power at common law ancillary to arrest and lawful search, but the specific powers will be dealt with first.

1. Under statute

By no statute is a private individual given power to search person or property. Police officers are the usual recipients of the power to search, but certain public officers are given statutory authorisation in particular circumstances, *e.g.* Board of Trade officials and customs officers.[46]

The power may be given without further requirements, such as the power of the police to search persons and vehicles under the Firearms Act 1968, s. 47, and the Misuse of Drugs Act 1971, s. 23.[47] Schedule 3, paragraph 6, to the Prevention of Terrorism (Temporary Provisions) Act 1976 gives a constable power to stop and search a person whom he has power to arrest under section 12.[48] More often the statute requires the warrant (written authorisation: p. 57) of a magistrate or, exceptionally, of a High Court judge.[49]

Section 26 (1) of the Theft Act 1968 enables a magistrate, on information being laid[50] before him by any person on oath, to issue a warrant to search for and seize any stolen goods when there is reasonable cause to believe that stolen goods are in a person's possession or on his premises. It can only authorise a police constable to carry out the search, unless another enactment expressly nominates someone else. Section 26 (2) enables a police superintendent (or higher rank) to authorise a police constable in writing to search premises for stolen goods if the person in occupation has been convicted of handling, or other offence of dishonesty punishable by imprisonment, within the last five years; or, if a person who has been

---

[46] Companies Act 1967, s. 110; Customs and Excise Act 1952, ss. 297, 298.

[47] See *Farrow* v. *Tunnicliffe*, p. 21. The law is sparing in authorising search of the person, the principal power being at common law in conjunction with arrest; see p. 27.

[48] See p. 65. This provision expressly requires a woman suspect to be searched by a woman, as does search under a warrant under para. 4, p. 27.

[49] *e.g.* under the Incitement to Disaffection Act 1934 and the Public Order Act 1936.

[50] See pp. 54–55.

in occupation within the past 12 months has been convicted of handling within the last five years. " Stolen goods " are defined by section 24 to include goods obtained by deception (s. 15 (1)) and blackmail (s. 21) and goods stolen abroad. Section 26 (3) of the same Act enables a policeman who has a warrant to search premises for stolen goods to seize any goods he believes to be stolen, even though they are not identified in the warrant. This preserves the law as laid down in *Chic Fashions* (*West Wales*) *Ltd.* v. *Jones*.[51]

Many other statutes give magistrates powers to issue search warrants, including the Sexual Offences Act 1956, s. 42 (prostitution) and s. 43 (woman or girl detained for immoral purposes), the Firearms Act 1968, s. 46, the Official Secrets Act 1911, s. 9, and the Criminal Damage Act 1971, s. 6. This last section was enacted after the cases discussed below had been decided. In order to avoid the potential strictness of the common law rules, section 6 (1) enables a search warrant to be issued where there is reasonable cause to believe that a person has property which there is reasonable cause to believe has been used or is intended to be used to damage property belonging to another or in a way likely to endanger life without lawful excuse. Section 6 (2) enables the constable who carries out the search to " seize anything which he believes to have been used or to be intended to be used " for such purposes. This section is therefore broader than the common law in two respects: first, the person who has the property in his control or custody or on his premises need not be implicated in the offence; secondly, no offence need be specified in the information and, if it is, the property seized need not relate to that particular offence.

The warrant must specify the premises to be searched with tolerable accuracy, though a trivial misdescription will not vitiate it.[52] The property to be looked for should also be specified.

The court may order bank accounts and statements to be inspected under section 7 of the Bankers' Books Evidence Act 1879. The other party need not be told. In *Williams* v. *Summerfield*[53] this was held to be " a very serious interference with the liberty of the subject " only to be exercised after the most careful thought; justices should apply at least as much care to such an order as to the issue of a search warrant.

The Prevention of Terrorism (Temporary Provisions) Act 1976,

---

[51] [1968] 2 Q.B. 299.
[52] *R.* v. *Atkinson* [1976] Crim. L.R. 307.
[53] [1972] 2 Q.B. 513.

Sched. 3, para. 4, gives a magistrate power to issue a warrant to search premises for evidence of offences under the Act and it authorises search of any person found on the premises. The application for the warrant must be by a police inspector, or higher rank, and it must be made on oath. Power is also given to a police superintendent, in cases of great emergency affecting the interests of the state, to give a written order to search premises.

Section 13 of the same Act makes a novel provision for the " examination " of persons arriving in or leaving Great Britain or Northern Ireland in order to determine whether an offence under the Act has been, is being or will be committed. It includes powers of search, arrest and detention by the examining officer (constable, immigration or customs officer) and is regulated by orders of the Home Secretary. This Act requires annual renewal by order of the Home Secretary.

2. At common law

These statutory powers by no means cover the whole range of crimes. The police have further powers at common law. First, they may search a person who has been lawfully arrested and they may take and keep any property found in his possession which may form material evidence of the offence for which he is arrested or of any other serious offence which they reasonably believe he has committed. Secondly, after they have entered premises lawfully, *e.g.* with a search warrant or to make an arrest,[54] they may take property which will form evidence of the offence in respect of which they entered.[55]

A doubtful common law extension of police powers of search which went much further was laid down in *Elias* v. *Pasmore*, [56] when Horridge J. said that " the interests of the state must excuse the seizure of documents, which seizure would otherwise be unlawful, if it appears *in fact* that such documents were evidence of a crime committed *by anyone*." In *Chic Fashions* v. *Jones* [57] and in *Ghani* v. *Jones* [58] this dictum has been restricted. On the one hand, the lawfulness of the searcher's conduct must be judged at the time and not by what happens afterwards. On the other hand, the property taken must be related to the offender or offence on account of which the

---

[54] See p. 66; see also Betting, Gaming and Lotteries Act 1963, s. 51 (1), p. 63.

[55] *Crozier* v. *Cundey* (1827) 6 B. & C. 232; *Dillon* v. *O'Brien and Davis* (1887) 16 Cox 245.

[56] [1934] 2 K.B. 164.

[57] [1968] 2 Q.B. 299.

[58] [1970] 1 Q.B. 693. See also *Frank Truman Export Ltd.* v. *Metropolitan Police Commissioner*, *The Times*, December 22, 1976.

entry was lawful. " The common law does not permit police officers . . . to ransack anyone's house . . . simply to see if he may have committed some crime or other."[59] The question of entering private premises also arises in connection with arrest.[60]

A case where the power to detain property as evidence was specifically limited was *R.* v. *Waterfield, R.* v. *Lynn.*[61] The defendants smashed a car into a wall. Two policemen wished to keep it as evidence of the defendants' dangerous driving and tried to prevent the defendants from driving it away. The driver, who had not been charged, drove the car at one of the policemen and then drove away. On appeal, his conviction for assaulting a constable in the execution of his duty was quashed on the grounds that in these circumstances the police have no duty to detain property found in a public place so that it can be used in evidence.

In *Ghani* v. *Jones* [62] the police, suspecting a murder, asked for and were given letters and the plaintiffs' passports—the plaintiffs being the suspected victim's relatives—as being of potential evidential value. No arrest was made. The Court of Appeal held that keeping property for evidence without making an arrest is lawful only if the police have reasonable grounds for believing that:

(*a*) a serious offence has been committed;
(*b*) the property taken is material evidence to prove commission of the offence; and
(*c*) the possessor of the property was implicated in the offence or, at any rate, his refusal to give up the property must be quite unreasonable.

Furthermore, the police must not keep the property any longer than is reasonably necessary to complete their investigations or to produce it in evidence and the lawfulness of their conduct must be judged at the time and not by what happens afterwards.

Lord Denning M.R., in the same case, alarmingly summed up [63] the gaps in the law as follows:

> " No magistrate—no judge even—has any power to issue a search warrant for murder. . . . Not to dig for the body. Not to look

[59] Lord Denning M.R. in *Ghani* v. *Jones*, above. The New Zealand interpretation of the power of seizure is more restricted; the police are authorised to seize evidence relating only to the offence in respect of which their entry was lawful: *McFarlane* v. *Sharp* [1972] N.Z.L.R. 64, discussed by Bridge [1974] Crim. L.R. 218.

[60] See p. 66.

[61] [1964] 1 Q.B. 164.

[62] Above.

[63] [1970] 1 Q.B. 693 at p. 705.

for the axe, the gun or the poison dregs. The police have to get the consent of the householder to enter if they can; or, if not, to do it by stealth or by force. Somehow they seem to manage. No decent person refuses them permission. If he does, he is probably implicated in some way or other. So the police risk an action for trespass. It is not much risk."

It is recognised, as mentioned above, that unlawful search and seizure does not result in the inadmissibility of the evidence obtained, subject to the trial judge's discretion to exclude it.[64] It is remotely possible that the owner of property could get a civil judgment which, by a discretionary remedy, might order the return of the property so that it might not be available by the time criminal proceedings begin. As to falsely obtained search warrants, see p. 42.

By way of gruesome footnote, the police may in the course of investigation exhume a dead body with the licence of the Home Secretary.

D. Witnesses

Almost all evidence must be produced in court by a witness, either by oral testimony or by production of a thing or document.[65] While preparing a case for prosecution, therefore, the prosecutor must consider the potential value of the available witnesses. Apart from the relative credibility of a witness, there are some rules of law which may deprive a witness of any value. The means of getting witnesses to attend court is described on p. 105.

Unlike questions during investigation,[66] once the witness is summoned to court he must answer questions put to him. However, a witness may not be in a position to give evidence either at all or on a particular subject.

This occurs in three forms—incompetence, non-compellability and privilege.

1. Competence

If a witness is incompetent, that is an end of the matter; his evidence is inadmissible. Children and the mentally ill are competent if they understand the duty of speaking the truth. The mentally ill must also be aware of the nature of and the obligation imposed by an oath to

---

64 *Kuruma* v. *R.* [1955] A.C. 197.
65 See p. 106 *et seq.*
66 See p. 21.

speak the truth. It is for the judge to decide on competence, preferably before examination of the witness starts. Under section 38 of the Children and Young Persons Act 1933 a child may give unsworn evidence if he understands the duty to speak the truth, even though he does not appreciate the nature of the oath. However, his unsworn statement is insufficient evidence to support a conviction unless corroborated by other material evidence implicating the accused.[67] Thus children of any age may be competent but admission of the evidence of a child of five years has been held to be " most undesirable." [68]

In the case of evidence for the prosecution, the accused is not competent. Thus, on a joint trial one co-accused is not competent to testify against the other(s) on the prosecution's behalf. Further, the accused's spouse is generally incompetent.[69] If the spouse has been divorced, he or she is incompetent as to matters occurring before the decree [70]; the same applies to voidable, but not to void, marriages. But if a husband prosecutes his wife, or vice versa, under section 30 (2) of the Theft Act 1968, which applies to all offences, the prosecutor can give evidence. The accused's spouse is also competent on a charge of an offence relating to himself or herself or to his or her property against the accused (*ibid.* s. 30 (3)).[71] Spouses are also competent for the prosecution by statute for offences of neglect or of injuries to themselves or their children, child destruction, sexual offences and bigamy.[72] At common law a spouse is competent on charges of violence or personal injury to himself or herself, forcible abduction and marriage, and possibly high treason.[73] The husband or wife of the accused is, like the accused, incompetent to testify for the prosecution against the other co-accused(s), to the same extent as he or she is incompetent *vis à vis* his or her own spouse.

An accomplice who is not tried jointly is a competent witness for the prosecution, but the judge must warn the jury that it is dangerous to convict on his evidence alone without corroboration.[74] The crime of a witness does not make him incompetent, nor does having some

---

[67] This other evidence may not consist of another child's unsworn evidence admitted by virtue of s. 38: *D.P.P.* v. *Hester* [1972] 3 W.L.R. 910.

[68] *R.* v. *Wallwork* (1958) 52 Cr.App.R. 153.

[69] *R.* v. *Deacon* [1973] 1 W.L.R. 696.

[70] *R.* v. *Algar* [1954] 1 Q.B. 279; *Moss* v. *Moss* [1963] 2 Q.B. 799.

[71] *R.* v. *Noble* [1974] 1 W.L.R. 894.

[72] Criminal Evidence Act 1898, s. 4 (1), Sched.; Sexual Offences Act 1956, s. 39; Criminal Justice Administration Act 1914, s. 28 (3).

[73] See *e.g. R.* v. *Verolla* [1963] 1 Q.B. 285 (attempted poisoning); *R.* v. *Blanchard* [1952] 1 All E.R. 114 (buggery); and dicta in *D.P.P.* v. *Bladey* [1912] 2 K.B. 89 (treason).

[74] *Davies* v. *D.P.P.* [1954] A.C. 378; see also Archbold, paras. 1424–1435.

interest in the proceedings.[75] He may be questioned as to his convictions.[76]

In the case of evidence for the defence, the accused and his or her spouse are competent to give evidence.[77] They are also competent witnesses in relation to a co-accused and, whether their evidence goes for the co-accused or for the prosecution, it is admissible. The accused's sworn evidence is given from the witness-box but he may make an unsworn statement from the dock, which was his only chance to speak before the 1898 Act. If he decides to give evidence on oath, he is compelled to answer any questions put to him, despite their incriminating quality.[78]

2. Compellability

We come next to the compellability of witnesses. If he is competent, the prosecution or the defence must now consider whether the witness is bound to give his evidence in court if summoned by either side. The only witnesses who are competent but not generally compellable for either side are the sovereign, foreign sovereigns and people entitled to claim diplomatic privilege.[79] On behalf of the prosecution, the accused's spouse is compellable in all the cases where he or she is competent at common law, but not where competence depends on the Criminal Evidence Act 1898, s. 4 (1), or the Sexual Offences Act 1956, s. 39.[80] Under section 30 (3) of the Theft Act 1968,[81] the prosecution cannot compel a spouse to give evidence unless he or she is already compellable at common law (*e.g.* where the offence is inseparably involved in causing personal injury, or arson with intent to kill the spouse). Of course the prosecution may be able to compel an accused or his or her spouse to give evidence against other defendants by procuring a separate trial, an acquittal,[82] a plea of guilty, a *nolle prosequi* or a pardon for that accused, for he ceases to be an accused.

For the defence, one co-accused is competent but not compellable for the other(s).[83] The spouse of an accused is not generally compellable either for that accused or for his or her co-accused(s). The exceptions to this are the same as to competence—charges of violence and personal injury and treason. However, subject to these exceptions, the accused whose spouse is going to give evidence must

---

75 *e.g.* that he is owner of the property stolen: Evidence Act 1843, s. 1.
76 See p. 185.
77 Criminal Evidence Act 1898, s. 1.
78 *Ibid.*, s. 1 (*e*); see " privilege," below.
79 See p. 14. 80 See p. 30. 81 See p. 30.
82 *R.* v. *Conti* (1973) 58 Cr.App.R. 387.
83 Criminal Evidence Act 1898, s. 1 (*a*).

consent before the evidence is given:[84] A and B are charged jointly with theft; Mrs. A cannot be compelled to give evidence for A or B; Mrs. A cannot give evidence for B, even though she is willing, unless A consents.

Where the accused or his or her spouse declines to give evidence for the defence, the prosecution must not comment on the failure.[85] This does not preclude the judge from commenting on it,[86] but if he goes too far it may be a misdirection *e.g.* if he says that the accused's silence corroborates an accomplice's evidence [87] or is to be equated with guilt.[88]

3. Privilege

The third matter to be considered—privilege—may arise in the course of giving evidence, whether or not the witness has been compelled to testify. It is a sort of limited non-compellability for it excuses a witness from answering a particular question. It does not prevent the question being asked. It falls into two main categories—personal and the public interest—though only the first is privilege fully in the sense of the above definition.

(a) *Personal privilege*

The most important personal privilege is against self-incrimination, *i.e.* the refusal to answer a question when the answer would tend to expose the witness to a criminal charge or forfeiture. In criminal proceedings, this does not include a finding of adultery or other " ecclesiastical censure " or a civil claim. The privilege probably does apply to criminal process against the witness's husband or wife [89] and possibly to process under foreign law.[90] The existence of the privilege is ascertained by the judge as and when it is claimed. The failure of a witness to make use of the privilege does not vitiate his evidence.[91] The only person who cannot claim the privilege is the accused himself, so far as it relates to the offence charged.[92]

---

[84] Criminal Evidence Act 1898, s. 1 (*c*).

[85] *Ibid.* s. 1 (*b*); Theft Act 1968, s. 30 (3) (*b*); see p. 195.

[86] *R.* v. *Rhodes* [1899] 1 Q.B. 77.

[87] *R.* v. *Jackson* [1953] 1 W.L.R. 591.

[88] *R.* v. *Sparrow* [1973] 1 W.L.R. 488; see p. 198.

[89] See dicta in *R.* v. *All Saints, Worcester* (*Inhabitants*) (1817) 6 M. & S. 194.

[90] *U.S.A.* v. *McRae* (1867) 3 Ch.App. 79.

[91] *R.* v. *Kinglake* (1870) 11 Cox 499.

[92] Criminal Evidence Act 1898, s. 1 (*e*). He may also lose his privilege as to other misconduct not charged, under s. 1 (*f*), see p. 190. As to his privilege for himself and his spouse in later civil proceedings, see Theft Act 1968, s. 31 (1), and Criminal Damage Act 1971, s. 9.

Two more heads of personal privilege are relevant here—communications between husband and wife during the marriage,[93] and communications between a client and his lawyer during the time when the lawyer was acting for him on a lawful matter with proceedings in view. Again these privileges are personal, in the second case, to the client, but if a third party can prove the contents of the communication, the evidence is admissible.[94] In criminal proceedings, however, the solicitor and client privilege may be held not to be available: where a letter was prima facie privileged, the court refused an injunction to restrain its production in a Board of Trade prosecution for fraud because the duty of a department of state to prosecute outweighs the private right in equity to restrain a breach of confidence.[95] The Crown Court has ordered a solicitor to produce documents in his possession as a result of his acting as an executor when the accused wished to call them in his defence because to refuse to allow it would have been against the rules of natural justice.[96]

(b) *Privilege in the public interest*

Privilege in the public interest is effectively an exclusionary rule of evidence and not privilege in the above sense—it cannot be waived and a third party cannot give evidence of the privileged matter. It applies to a juror as to what took place in the jury room,[97] but he may give evidence of entirely extrinsic matters.[98] The judges of the superior courts are privileged but magistrates appear to be compellable.

The very broad exclusion of evidence where disclosure would be contrary to the interests of the state which applies in civil cases [99] has little or no application in criminal proceedings. Where the prosecution seeks to call such evidence, the practical expedient of excluding the public [1] is adopted, although in strict theory the evidence should not be given even in camera because it is a "privilege" which cannot be waived.

---

[93] *Ibid.* s. 1 (*d*); Theft Act 1968, s. 30 (3) (*a*).

[94] *Rumping* v. *D.P.P.* [1964] A.C. 814.

[95] *Butler* v. *Board of Trade* [1971] Ch. 680. See also *R.* v. *Barton* [1972] 2 All E.R. 1192.

[96] *R.* v. *Barton* [1974] Crim. L.R. 43; *cf.* the Law Society's statement of May 10, 1976 (*The Times*, May 11, 1976, p. 4), which advised solicitors hearing a client's confession on no account to tell the police, even if it involved the conviction of an innocent man.

[97] *R.* v. *Roads* [1967] 2 Q.B. 108.

[98] *R.* v. *Hood* [1968] 1 W.L.R. 773 (whether a juror recognised the accused's wife when she gave evidence).

[99] *Duncan* v. *Cammell Laird and Co. Ltd.* [1942] A.C. 624 as modified by *Conway* v. *Rimmer* [1968] A.C. 910.

[1] See p. 154.

Where the accused seeks to call such evidence, it would appear that the court would not allow the evidence to be excluded. A Lord Chancellor has stated [2] that "no claim of privilege is nowadays made in criminal proceedings." In *Marks* v. *Beyfus* [3] it was held that the public interest in enabling an innocent man to establish his innocence outweighs any public interest in non-disclosure of facts. The law on this subject is, however, somewhat uncertain [4]; if no form of Crown privilege can be claimed by the police, it would seem that an accused might be able to require a discovery of confidential documents made up in the preparation for prosecution.

Interference with witnesses is diversely prohibited; it is a common law offence to offer inducement by threats or persuasion to a witness not to give evidence.[5] To prevent a summoned witness from attending court amounts to contempt of court,[6] as does the wilful non-attendance of the witness himself. Anyone who bribes, procures, induces, aids or abets the commission of perjury, himself commits subornation of perjury under section 7 of the Perjury Act 1911.

Witnesses who are needed in criminal proceedings in a foreign country to give oral or written evidence or to produce a document may be ordered to do so before the High Court.[7] The proceedings must already have been instituted and it cannot be done in a trial for a political offence. The court in the foreign country makes the request and the High Court secures the attendance of the witness for examination or production of a document. As these provisions form part of a reciprocal international arrangement, it may be possible for an English prosecutor to request a particular foreign court to obtain evidence in a similar way.

E. Evidence of Identity and Miscellaneous Matters

The identity of the accused usually needs to be proved by witnesses or by real evidence (fingerprints, handwriting, etc.).

If witnesses are called to identify him the weight of their evidence will vary according to the circumstances. The court must exercise great care where visual identification is disputed by the defence; the jury must be warned about the special need for caution before convicting. The quality of the identification varies according to the cir-

---

[2] [1959] Crim. L.R. 11. [3] [1890] 25 Q.B.D. 494.
[4] For an analysis of the authorities, see Wharam [1971] Crim. L.R. 675.
[5] *R.* v. *Greenberg* (1919) L.T. 288.
[6] See p. 392.
[7] Evidence (Proceedings in Other Jurisdictions) Act 1975, ss. 1–3, 5.

cumstances in which it was made (light, closeness, recognition, etc.) but, if the quality is poor, the case should be withdrawn from the jury unless other evidence goes to support the correctness of the identification.[8]

Identification of the accused in the dock is to be discouraged unless the witness has previously identified him in rather less obvious circumstances. One of these—and probably the most satisfactory—is the identification parade, held at the police station, where about eight people of a similar appearance to the accused are lined up and the witness is asked to pick out the accused. Home Office rules provide guidelines for the conduct of identification parades and for the use of photographs.[9] This second means of identification is less satisfactory than a parade and is more often used by the police to get a lead on the identity of the offender. An album containing photographs of a number of different people should be used. It is clearly improper to show the witness photographs of the suspect before asking him to identify him.[10]

The law on identification evidence has recently been reviewed by the Devlin Committee [11] and legislation is expected to implement its recommendations. The Attorney-General has issued guidelines in the meantime to be adopted in cases where identification evidence forms all or a major part of the prosecution's case.[12] These, briefly, are (a) full oral committal proceedings should be used,[13] (b) a prosecutor should not invite a witness to make a dock identification unless there has been an identification parade, and (c) difficult cases should be referred to the D.P.P. who will attend to them personally, or through his deputy, in consultation with the Law Officers.

An expert may be called to identify fingerprints and palmprints. The prints may be taken by the police with the accused's consent or with an order of a magistrates' court under section 40 of the Magistrates' Courts Act 1952.[14] The order may be given on the application of a police inspector (or higher rank) in respect of a person at least

---

8 *R.* v. *Turnbull, The Times*, July 10, 1976; see also p. 206.

9 Home Office Circular No. 9/69 (reproduced in the Devlin Report, below); the suggestion that the photographs come from a rogue's gallery should be avoided because that implies previous convictions.

10 *R.* v. *Dwyer* [1925] 2 K.B. 799.

11 *Report to the Secretary of State for the Home Department of the Departmental Committee on Evidence of Identification in Criminal Cases* (House of Commons Paper 338); see also Glanville Williams [1976] Crim. L.R. 407.

12 Home Office Circular No. 127/1976, incorporating the Attorney General's parliamentary reply of May 25, 1976; see (1976) 126 New L.J. 863.

13 See pp. 97–100.

14 As amended by the Criminal Justice Act 1967, s. 33.

14 years old in custody, or in court answering a summons, for an offence punishable by imprisonment. The prints are then taken by a constable who may use such reasonable force as is necessary. The prints are taken in this way to match up, for instance, with prints left on stolen goods. They may also be relevant for proving previous convictions (but not, of course, before verdict [15]). Where an order is not obtained the admissibility of prints is subject to the overriding discretion of the trial judge to exclude evidence obtained oppressively or by a trick.[16] If the accused is discharged or acquitted, all records of the prints must be destroyed, unless he already has a criminal record.

Handwriting may need to be proved on an issue of identity. This may be done by someone who saw the suspect writing the actual piece of handwriting in question, by anyone who has seen him writing on any other occasion, or by anyone who has become familiar with his writing by correspondence or similar means (or by the writer himself). It may also be proved by comparison, but this should be done by an expert.[17]

Tape recordings are not inadmissible but they must be treated with caution, in the light of the possibilities of faking or tampering with them. If the question is raised, the prosecution must prove beyond reasonable doubt that the recording is the untampered original.[18] As a record of an admission by an accused, a recording could be admitted in the same way as a policeman's record of the admission.[19] In *R.* v. *Mills* [20] a noisy conversation between occupants of neighbouring cells was recorded by a policeman in the corridor. He gave evidence that he remembered the conversation anyway and used the recording to refresh his memory; the court held that the recording had served the same purpose as a notebook and pencil and was therefore admissible. In *R.* v. *Senat* [21] a tape-recording obtained by private telephone-tapping was held to be admissible.

A final word must be said on powers of telephone-tapping and interception of mail. Under section 58 of the Post Office Act 1953,

---

15 See p. 190.

16 *Callis* v. *Gunn* [1964] 1 Q.B. 495; *cf. R.* v. *Payne* [1963] 1 W.L.R. 637 and *Kuruma* v. *R.* [1955] A.C. 197.

17 *R.* v. *O'Sullivan* [1969] 1 W.L.R. 497 (where giving specimens of writing to the jury for comparison without expert guidance was disapproved).

18 *R.* v. *Stevenson* [1971] 1 W.L.R. 1. As to proof of the recording's authenticity, see *R.* v. *Robson, R.* v. *Harris* [1972] 1 W.L.R. 651.

19 See p. 22.

20 [1962] 1 W.L.R. 1152.

21 (1968) 52 Cr.App.R. 282.

the Home Secretary may issue a warrant to open and detain a " postal packet," which includes a telegram.[22] Without a warrant, the officer of the Post Office who carries out or allows the interception will be guilty of an offence under section 53. In 1957 a Committee of Privy Councillors considered that the interception of mail and wire-tapping requires the Home Secretary's authority, which will be given only where the security of the state is in jeopardy or to detect large-scale and serious criminal activities.[23]

F. Coroners' Inquests

The inquest is a fact-finding procedure conducted as an inquiry rather than as a trial. The proceedings are not criminal but sometimes play a part in the criminal process.

The coroner has survived remarkably intact from the earliest stages of the legal system when he was employed by the Crown to look after its fiscal interests. This explains his interest in treasure trove, which still exists, and his duty to hold an inquest on any dead body found within his jurisdiction. Formerly fines and forfeitures might result from a death and the object causing the death or its value—the deodand—was forfeited (this was abolished in 1846, possibly in view of the increasing number of railway casualties). His modern function is principally to identify the dead person and ascertain the cause of death. Counsel and solicitors are often called upon at the inquest to represent the deceased's relatives with a view to civil action, or the police, or a person who may be prosecuted or sued.

The Coroners Act 1887, the Coroners (Amendment) Act 1926 and the Coroners Rules 1953, made under the 1926 Act, govern the holding of inquests. There are about 350 coronerships in England and Wales with jurisdiction limited locally (there are none in Scotland). Coroners are barristers, solicitors or medical practitioners appointed by county councils.[24]

Anyone, and particularly the Registrar of Births, Deaths and Marriages, may inform the coroner of a death and the coroner, if he believes the information, must hold an inquest in the following cases: where he has reasonable cause to suspect that the death was caused by violent or unnatural means; where it was sudden and its cause unknown or suspicious (*e.g.* by poisoning); or where it occurred in prison or other place specified by enactment.[25] It is the presence of the dead body, and not the cause or place of the death, that gives him

[22] s. 87.
[23] Cmnd. 283.
[24] Local Government Act 1972, s. 220.
[25] Coroners Act 1887, s. 3 (1).

local jurisdiction. It is a common law offence to bury a body with intent to prevent a coroner's inquest being held, and, if the body is of a newly-born child, it may amount to the offence of concealment of birth.

The standard procedure is as follows:

(*a*) The coroner decides on the information whether an inquest is necessary. If the cause of death is unknown, he may order a post-mortem examination by a pathologist; if it reveals death from natural causes, he need not hold an inquest.[26]

(*b*) The coroner summons between seven and 11 jurors to attend the hearing. He may sit without a jury on an inquest into treasure trove or where he *does not* suspect the following:

(i) death by murder, manslaughter or infanticide;
(ii) death in prison or other prescribed place;
(iii) death from disease, poisoning or accident which requires notification to a government department;
(iv) death in a motor accident; or
(v) death in circumstances which, if recurrent, may be prejudicial to public health.[27]

(*c*) The coroner summons the witnesses, including a medical witness, who are liable for a fine for non-attendance or refusal to answer.[28]

(*d*) If he is sitting with a jury, *i.e.* in cases (*b*) (i)–(v) above, he must view the body. He may direct the jury to do likewise.[29]

(*e*) The jury is sworn.[30]

(*f*) The coroner calls and examines the witnesses. Being an inquiry and not a trial, no one else has a right to put questions, but the coroner may allow it. The evidence is put into writing and signed by the witness and the coroner.[31] These documents may be used later in a trial as depositions or as written evidence.[32] He may order the witnesses to attend at subsequent criminal proceedings.[33]

(*g*) The jury delivers its verdict which is also put into writing and certified by the jurors and the coroner.[34] This document is called the

---

26 Coroners (Amendment) Act 1926, s. 21.

27 *Ibid.* s. 13.

28 Coroners Act 1887, ss. 4, 19.

29 Coroners (Amendment) Act 1926, s. 14.

30 This jury differs from the jury in a trial on indictment (p. 171) in that there is no challenge and the number of jurors is smaller (seven).

31 Coroners Act 1887, s. 4.

32 See pp. 107 and 109.

33 Criminal Procedure (Attendance of Witnesses) Act 1965, s. 7.

34 Coroners Act 1887, s. 18; Coroners (Amendment) Act 1926, s. 13.

" inquisition." If there is no jury the coroner makes his own inquisition. The jury, whatever its number, may reach a valid verdict by a majority, provided the minority is not more than two. If the minority is larger, the jury must be discharged and a new one summoned, so that the whole procedure, except the coroner's view of the body, must be repeated,[35] notice being given to all persons interested.[36]

(*h*) The " inquisition " consists of three parts—caption, verdict and attestation.[37] The caption identifies the date and place of the inquest, the coroner, his entitlement to sit, and the jury. The verdict states the finding of the identity of the dead person and of the time, place and probable cause of his death. A rider may be added as to how recurrence of deaths in similar cases may be prevented. If there is insufficient evidence as to the cause of death, an open verdict may be recorded.[38] The attestation consists of the signatures of the coroner and concurring jurors.

The conflict with criminal procedure may come in the verdict, for the jury may find that the death was caused by a particular person. If this amounted to murder, manslaughter or infanticide, the inquisition is equivalent to an indictment[39] and the inquest to commital proceedings,[40] and the person accused may stand trial. This is very rarely done, but if it is, the coroner must issue a warrant for his arrest[41] or if he is present commit him for trial.[42] If charged with manslaughter, he may release him on bail.[43] The inquisition and evidence[44] are sent to the court of trial.

Where a homicidal offence is suspected, it is more usual for the coroner to adjourn the inquest when parallel committal proceedings are likely. If a chief officer of police requests the coroner to adjourn because charges are to be brought, the coroner *must* adjourn until conclusion of the criminal proceedings. On the other hand, if a lesser charge is contemplated, *e.g.* dangerous driving, the inquest should be completed first.[45] If a person is tried for an offence relating to the

---

35 Coroners (Amendment) Act 1926, s. 15 (2).
36 Coroners Rules 1953, r. 24.
37 Coroners Act 1887, Sched. 2; Coroners (Indictable Offences) Rules 1956 and 1965.
38 Home Office Circular No. 38/53.
39 See p. 117.
40 See p. 93.
41 See p. 73.
42 See p. 101.
43 Coroners Act 1887, s. 5. As to bail generally, see pp. 68–82.
44 As to depositions, see p. 107; the coroner retains custody of the body and application must be made to him for examination of it: *R.* v. *Bristol Coroner, ex p. Kerr* [1974] Q.B. 652.
45 *R.* v. *Beresford* (1952) 36 Cr.App.R. 1.

death during an adjournment of the inquest the coroner may resume the inquest after the verdict of the trial jury, but the inquisition should not charge that person with any offence for which he could have been convicted.[46] If it charges a new offence (*e.g.* manslaughter, when he has been tried for dangerous driving), the Attorney-General is likely to enter a *nolle prosequi.*[47]

An inquisition which charges a person is subject to the same rules as to contents, amendments, etc., as an indictment.[48]

The Queen's Bench Division may issue an order of certiorari [49] to quash the inquisition and order a new inquest, if it is necessary in the interests of justice by reason of fraud, rejection of evidence, irregularity or misconduct.[50] They may also do so if fresh evidence appears to upset the findings of the inquisition.[51]

Lastly, to revert to its evidential value, the inquest is not subject to the strict law of evidence, which may diminish the evidence's subsequent usefulness. The jury are asked to disregard inadmissible evidence in reaching their verdict. It is highly undesirable that the inquest should consider any issue of civil liability, although this is often why counsel is asked to appear for an interested person. The coroner has complete discretion as to whether counsel or anyone else can ask questions of witnesses, which he often allows, but he will not allow them to address the jury. Counsel should therefore ask his permission. He also has discretion to exclude the public or a particular person from the inquest.

"The office of coroner is ancient, odd, anomalous, and perhaps unnecessary." [52] A departmental committee on coroners recommended in 1936 that trial on inquisition should be abolished.[53] This was again recommended by the Broderick Committee in November 1971.[54] Both committees recommended the retention of the coroner, however.

G. Remedies for Wrongful Process

The remedies available to a person who is wrongly prosecuted, arrested, searched, etc., clearly represent a form of control over

---

[46] See pp. 157, 160 and 213.

[47] *R.* v. *Beresford*, above. As to *nolle prosequi* generally, see p. 18.

[48] Coroners Act 1887, s. 20. As to indictments generally, see p. 117 *et seq.*

[49] See p. 45.

[50] Coroners Act 1887, s. 6.

[51] Coroners (Amendment) Act 1926, s. 19.

[52] A. P. Herbert.

[53] Cmnd. 5070.

[54] Cmnd. 4801. A Home Office working party has been set up to study the Broderick ecommendations and propose changes: *The Times*, July 30, 1976, p. 3.

prosecution activities. As they properly belong to a work on the law of tort, the following is only a bare outline of this very important subject.

The law gives most protection against the deprivation of personal liberty. Any total restraint of liberty is an imprisonment and the person imposing it must prove that the restraint was justified by the law. Not only is false imprisonment a tort but it is also a common law offence, punishable by discretionary fine and imprisonment.[55] Even then the prosecutor need only prove the imprisonment and the accused has the burden of justifying it. As an offence it is relatively little known.[56] The imprisonment or restraint of liberty must be complete but it may take place anywhere, including a person's own house or a public street.[57]

The remedy in a civil action is damages. The aggrieved person may also apply for a writ of habeas corpus in the High Court which may order his release.[58]

In the context of criminal proceedings, the justification usually consists either of lawful arrest, or of lawful and reasonable detention after arrest,[59] or of detention ordered by a court. In the last case, the detention is justified if the order imposing it is valid on the face of it.[60] The criterion of lawful arrest on suspicion is the reasonableness of the cause to suspect and reasonableness is also the criterion of the lawfulness of the subsequent behaviour of the person making the arrest.[61]

If a warrant of arrest is obtained,[62] a police constable executing it is protected from action or prosecution, whether or not there were in fact grounds for obtaining the warrant [63] and even if the magistrate had no jurisdiction to issue it.[64] This is because the arrest is the result of a judicial, and not of a ministerial, process.

If a warrant of arrest was obtained on false information, a civil action for malicious prosecution may be brought. This would also avail a person whose liberty has not been restrained during a prosecution. Malicious prosecution is much more difficult to establish than

---

55 1 East P.C. 428; 1 Russell 690.

56 *R.* v. *Lesley* (1860) Bell 220; 8 Cox 269. Unlawful restraints of liberty often constitute a more precisely defined statutory offence such as abduction.

57 *Bird* v. *Jones* (1845) 7 Q.B. 742.

58 See p. 44.

59 See pp. 64–66.

60 *Henderson* v. *Preston* (1888) 21 Q.B.D. 362.

61 See p. 64.

62 See pp. 57–60.

63 *Shergold* v. *Holloway* (1734) 2 Str. 1002.

64 Constables Protection Act 1750, s. 6.

false imprisonment, for the plaintiff must prove that he has suffered damage because the defendant initiated a prosecution which resulted in an acquittal or other discharge, without reasonable or probable cause and with malice.[65] The " prosecution " need not have reached court for trial and the action covers falsely procuring a warrant of arrest; a similar action lies for falsely procuring a search warrant.[66] Lord Devlin, approving an Australian case, defined the " reasonable and probable cause " as follows: " The prosecutor must believe that the probability of the accused's guilt is such that upon general grounds of justice a charge against him is warranted." [67] The allegations giving rise to the prosecution may thus be true or false provided the prosecutor believed in them. Malice, which must also be proved, is the motive for bringing the prosecution and exists " unless the predominant wish of the accuser is to vindicate the law." [68]

Other circumstances which may subsequently give rise to an action by the aggrieved person include:

(*a*) Assault (crime or tort), when an arrest or personal search is unlawful [69];

(*b*) Trespass to land (tort) or, possibly, forcible entry (crime), when property is unlawfully searched or entered to make an unlawful arrest.[70]

(*c*) Trespass to goods (tort), when goods are taken or detained unlawfully.[71]

Judges, witnesses, counsel and jurors are exempt from civil actions for what they say and do in court, provided the proceedings are within the jurisdiction of the court. As the superior courts determine their own jurisdiction, any decision containing a wrong conclusion as to jurisdiction is still within their jurisdiction. A judge acting in his capacity as judge, albeit mistakenly, is immune from process, as are the officers whom he orders to carry out his wrong instructions.[72] The inferior courts, *e.g.* magistrates' courts and courts-martial, are largely creatures of statute and, having a limited jurisdiction, may exceed it, giving the aggrieved person a cause of action (which might include defamation for things said in wrongful proceedings). They are controlled by the prerogative writs and orders of the High

---

[65] See *Winfield and Jolowicz on Tort* (10th ed.), pp. 477–485.
[66] *Ibid.* p. 485.
[67] *Glinski* v. *McIver* [1962] A.C. 726.
[68] Winfield, *op. cit.* p. 484.
[69] See pp. 27 and 62.
[70] See pp. 25–29 and 66; and see Forcible Entry Act 1381.
[71] See p. 25 *et seq*,
[72] *Sirros* v. *Moore* [1975] Q.B. 118.

Court.[73] If a magistrate acts maliciously and without reasonable and probable cause, an action similar to malicious prosecution may lie against him.[74]

The police are given greater protection from civil action than a private prosecutor only in the execution of warrants.[75] Otherwise it is their *de facto* position which is more advantageous. Their powers of entry, search and arrest are much wider [76] and include an element of discretion in the power to act upon suspicion. If a policeman acts outside his powers he is personally liable and his Chief Constable is vicariously liable provided the policeman was acting " in the performance or purported performance of [his] functions."[77]

Although not a civil remedy, the lawfulness of arrest and detention may arise on a charge of assaulting or obstructing a police officer in the course of his duty. The fact that arrest was unlawful may amount to a defence to the charge but any detention by a police officer without an arrest must be a defence.[78]

Ex gratia compensation may be paid to a person who is wrongly convicted or charged. Application is made to the Home Secretary and the amount is assessed on the principles applied to the assessment of damages in tort, by an independent assessor to whom the applicant may make representations.[79]

H. Supervisory Jurisdiction of the High Court

The Divisional Court of the Queen's Bench Division exercises supervisory jurisdiction over the inferior courts and public officers and bodies by means of the prerogative writs and orders. For the purposes of criminal proceedings, they are usually directed at magistrates' courts, coroners, prison governors or the police. They may also be issued against the Crown Court when that court is exercising any of its jurisdiction other than trial on indictment.[80]

The procedure for issuing them is laid down in the Rules of the Supreme Court and is therefore a procedure for which legal aid [81] is available as for civil proceedings.

---

[73] See section H, below.

[74] See p. 53.

[75] See p. 41.

[76] See pp. 25, 27, 63 and 66.

[77] Police Act 1964, s. 48.

[78] *Ludlow* v. *Burgess* [1971] Crim.L.R. 238.

[79] Written parliamentary reply of the Home Secretary: *Hansard*, July 29, 1976, cols. 328–330; (1976) 120 S.J. 536.

[80] Courts Act 1971, s. 10 (5). As to the jurisdiction, see pp. 330 and 344.

[81] See p. 399.

One factor which is common to all of them is that they are issued entirely at the discretion of the court and, although an individual may start the proceedings moving, they are directed at persons performing public functions and do not represent any form of civil remedy. Although they are generally called " prerogative writs," only the first is a writ and the others are orders.

1. Habeas corpus

The writ of habeas corpus can be issued against any person who is holding another in custody or detention without legal justification.[82] The uses to which it has been put are diverse, for example, in custody of minors and slavery cases, but in criminal proceedings it is usually used to secure the release of a person imprisoned or in custody without cause, particularly under wrongful extradition proceedings,[83] and sometimes as an application for bail.[84]

The writ is not available where the grounds for the application amount to a rehearing of a wrong decision made *within* the jurisdiction of a court [85]; the proper remedy for that, if any, is an appeal. The writ is not a writ of course like a writ in a civil case, but is only issued if a prima facie case of wrongul restraint can be shown. Applications for habeas corpus are given precedence over the rest of the court's business for the day.

Procedure

The Divisional Court of the Queen's Bench is the usual tribunal for issuing the writ.[86] In cases of peculiar urgency, application can be made to a single judge in court, or, if the court is not sitting, to a judge anywhere, *e.g.* at home at night.[87]

Application is made *ex parte* the person detained, supported by an affidavit [88] made by him or by someone on his behalf describing the nature of the restraint of liberty.[89] Counsel should normally make the application but it may be made in person in exceptional cases.[90]

---

[82] *Cf.* false imprisonment, p. 41.

[83] See p. 115.

[84] See p. 68.

[85] *Ex p. Hinds* [1961] 1 W.L.R. 325 (D.C., later affirmed by the House of Lords) and *Re Corke* [1954] 1 W.L.R. 899; see also Rubenstein, "Habeas Corpus as a Means of Review" (1964) 27 M.L.R. 322.

[86] R.S.C., Ord. 54, r. 1.

[87] *e.g. ex p. Soblen, The Times,* July 27, 1962.

[88] *i.e.* a sworn written statement of evidence.

[89] R.S.C., Ord. 54, r. 1.

[90] *Re Greene* (1941) 57 T.L.R. 533 (no illustrations of the exceptional cases are suggested).

Normally no writ is in fact issued, as the court or judge to whom the application is made adjourns the hearing so that notice of it can be given to the person against whom the writ is sought, or a summons issued, normally allowing him eight clear days before resuming the hearing.[91] However, the court or the judge may order the prisoner's immediate release which will be sufficient to secure it without issuing the writ. If a single judge does not make such an order he must direct the application to be made to the Divisional Court.[92]

If a writ is issued, which will only be necessary if the person to whom it is addressed refuses to answer the notice of the application, it must be served either personally or on the person having actual charge of the prisoner.[93] If he does not appear in court on the return day[94] he is in contempt of court and the judge may issue a bench warrant.[95]

Counsel for the prisoner addresses the court or judge twice at the hearing of the application, but the other party only speaks once.[96]

Appeals

Section 14 of the Administration of Justice Act 1960 provides that, after a refusal to grant habeas corpus, no further application can be made on the same grounds and evidence to any other judge or Divisional Court or to the Lord Chancellor. Appeal lies to the House of Lords[97] under section 15 of the same Act against a decision of the Divisional Court by either party, but not against the decision of a single judge to order the prisoner's release. Leave must be obtained from the House of Lords or from the court below.

2. Certiorari

The order of certiorari is addressed to an inferior court or other body exercising a judicial function. The procedure does not involve a writ but merely the application of a person aggrieved (*i.e.* suffering a particular harm beyond the harm suffered by the general public), showing cause why an order should be made.[98] The effect of the

---

[91] R.S.C., Ord. 54, r. 2, except in cases of great urgency.

[92] R.S.C., Ord. 54, r. 4; Administration of Justice Act 1960, s. 14 (1).

[93] R.S.C., Ord. 54, r. 6.

[94] *i.e.* the date specified in the writ for entering an appearance.

[95] See p. 151.

[96] R.S.C., Ord. 54, r. 8.

[97] For appeal to the House of Lords generally, see p. 280.

[98] This and the next two procedures used also to be made by writ, which was cumbersome and was replaced by the more expeditious procedure of application and order under the Administration of Justice (Miscellaneous Provisions) Acts 1933 and 1938. The Law Commission (Law Com. No. 73) has recommended the replacement of the present procedures by a single " application for judicial review."

order is to remove the proceedings to the High Court for scrutiny and, if necessary, for rehearing. It is of particular use to inquire into proceedings before magistrates where they have acted outside their jurisdiction. As the applicant wishes to show that the decision of the inferior court was void, the effect of a finding of voidness is to quash the offending proceedings. If they are not found to be void, the order does not direct the inferior court to do anything except that, on an application involving a conviction, it can vary the applicant's sentence instead of quashing the conviction.[99] As the procedure for this and the next two orders is the same, it is dealt with jointly below.

3. Prohibition

This order is issued by the Divisional Court to prevent an inferior court from exceeding its jurisdiction or from continuing to do so. It is a preventive measure and is no longer available once the unlawful decision has become final and is therefore little used in connection with criminal proceedings. It might be used, for instance, during an adjournment to stop a magistrates' court from resuming the trial of an indictable offence when it is improper for them to try it.[1]

4. Mandamus

This order is the obverse of prohibition—it orders an inferior court or public body to do something which is either one of its duties or within its jurisdiction or competence. It may be used, for instance, to compel justices to hear an application or complaint or to compel a coroner to hold an inquest.[2]

Procedure

The procedure for applying for an order of certiorari, prohibition or mandamus is laid down in the Rules of the Supreme Court, Order 53.

Application for leave is made *ex parte* to a Queen's Bench Divisional Court [3] supported by a statement of the relief sought and the reasons for the intended application and affidavits of the facts relied on.[4]

When leave is granted the application for an order is made within 14 days by originating motion in the Divisional Court, or by origin-

---

[99] Administration of Justice Act 1960, s. 16.

[1] As to the jurisdiction of magistrates, see pp. 51 and 291.

[2] See p. 37.

[3] Except in vacation when it may be made to a judge in chambers. If the judge refuses leave, the applicant may then apply for the leave of the Divisional Court.

[4] R.S.C., Ord. 53, r. 1.

ating summons before a judge, giving eight clear days between service of the notice of motion or the summons and the date of the hearing.[5] At the hearing the judge may allow any person he considers should be heard to oppose the motion or summons.[6]

A grant of leave to apply for prohibition or certiorari operates as a stay of the proceedings in question.[7]

Time Limits

Order 53, Rule 2, imposes the following time limits on applications:

(*a*) mandamus requiring the Crown Court to hear an appeal: two months.

(*b*) certiorari for the purpose of quashing a judgment, conviction, etc.: six months.

---

[5] R.S.C., Ord. 53, r. 3.
[6] R.S.C., Ord. 53, r. 5.
[7] R.S.C., Ord. 53, r. 1 (5).

CHAPTER 4

INITIATION OF PROCEEDINGS

THE prosecutor now believes that he has sufficient evidence that the suspect has committed an offence to justify putting the allegation before a court. In this chapter the processes by which he can achieve this and bring the accused into the court to answer the charge will be considered. The question of detaining the accused in custody until trial will also be considered.

Most criminal proceedings are initiated in one of two ways. Either the suspect has been arrested summarily without a warrant, in which case he must be charged by a police officer with having committed an offence and brought before a magistrate as soon as possible, or the suspect has not been arrested and the intending prosecutor must obtain a summons or a warrant for his arrest. If he is already in custody for some other offence, he may be brought before the court in the same way as if he had been summarily arrested. The unusual procedure of the coroner's inquisition has already been dealt with[1] and the exceptional cases of contempt of court and perjury are given separate sections on pp. 392 and 394.

When the suspect is out of the jurisdiction, a further procedure—extradition—may be required to secure his presence in England, but if he is in some part of the British Isles, the summons or warrant is endorsed by a local magistrate.

Although they have already been dealt with,[2] search warrants are issued, like warrants of arrest, by laying an information before a magistrate.[3]

A. THE MAGISTRATE AND HIS JURISDICTION

The tribunal which deals with the issuing of process is the magistrate,[4] not the magistrates' court. When a person is arrested, the trial or committal proceedings begin when he is brought before the court, so the tribunal is then the magistrates' court. Although it must be in

[1] See pp. 37–40.

[2] See pp. 25–27.

[3] See p. 54.

[4] Justices' clerks may exercise certain of the magistrate's functions under s. 5 (1) of the Justices of the Peace Act 1968 and the Justices' Clerks Rules 1970; see pp. 54, 108 and 290.

open court,[5] the court may consist of a single justice and the constitution of the court will therefore be dealt with when dealing with committal and trial.[6]

Normally informations will be laid at the court building at a time when the magistrate is not sitting in open court, but they may be laid anywhere, *e.g.* at the magistrate's home. One magistrate always has power to issue process despite any statutory requirement for the information to be laid before two or more magistrates.[7] The term "magistrate" is used interchangeably with the older description "justice of the peace," or simply "justice," though it is sometimes used to distinguish a stipendiary from a lay magistrate.

The appointment of magistrates

The majority of magistrates are laymen appointed to the "commission of the peace" for a county or London commission area by the Crown through the Lord Chancellor.[8] A magistrate can normally be appointed only for a commission area where he lives or which is within 15 miles of his residence.[9] The Lord Mayor and Aldermen of the City of London are justices of the peace for the City of London, which is a separate commission area.[10]

Lay magistrates receive reimbursement of expenses and lost earnings.[11] It is nevertheless rather surprising that sufficient numbers of suitable people are prepared to perform the multifarious tasks and often monotonous routine required of magistrates. The individual magistrate does not usually sit more than once or twice a month, but if appointed since January 1, 1966, he must give up spare time in his first year for training in the form of lectures, reading, court attendance and prison visiting.[12]

Stipendiary magistrates

Qualified lawyers who are paid to do the work may be appointed as magistrates by the Crown on the recommendation of the Lord

---

[5] Criminal Justice Act 1967, s. 6.

[6] See pp. 85–86 and 289–290.

[7] Magistrates' Courts Act 1952, s. 1 (5).

[8] Administration of Justice Act 1973, s. 1 (1) and (2); the Chancellor of the Duchy of Lancaster appoints them in certain northern counties: s. 1 (7). For the London commission areas, see Administration of Justice Act 1964, s. 2. For the form of the commission, see Crown Office (Commissions of the Peace) Rules 1973 (S.I. No. 2099).

[9] Justices of the Peace Act 1949, s. 1 (1).

[10] Justices of the Peace Act 1968, s. 1 (2) and Sched. 2, as amended by the Administration of Justice Act 1973; the right to be justices for the City was conferred by charter of August 25, 1741.

[11] Administration of Justice Act 1973, Sched. 1, Pt. III.

[12] *Ibid.*, s. 3, and Cmnd. 2856.

Chancellor. They must be barristers or solicitors of not less than seven years' standing and a maximum of 60 metropolitan stipendiary magistrates (*i.e.* in Inner London)[13] and 40 stipendiary magistrates for any other commission area may be appointed.[14] A person qualified to be appointed may be made a temporary stipendiary magistrate for up to three months at a time.[15]

Stipendiary magistrates have power to try cases sitting alone.[16] Metropolitan stipendiaries also have power to deal with extradition proceedings.[17]

Removal and retirement of magistrates

Magistrates may be removed in the same way as they are appointed and justices in the City of London may be excluded from exercising their functions.[18] They may be transferred to the supplemental list for infirmity, neglect of duties or refusal to act.[19]

Magistrates are transferred to the "supplemental list" at the age of 70 (or 75 if the magistrate has held high judicial office). Thereafter they may perform minor administrative tasks and may continue, if authorised, to sit in the Crown Court.[20] Stipendiary magistrates also retire at 70, though those appointed before October 25, 1968, may continue until they are 72; the Lord Chancellor may extend the appointment until the age of 72 or 75 respectively.[21]

Disqualification of magistrates

A magistrate may become disqualified from acting generally or be unable to sit in a particular case. By statute he is disqualified if convicted of treason or corrupt practices at an election or, if adjudged bankrupt, before his discharge.[22]

He is disqualified in the particular case if he has an interest in the matter before him. If pecuniary, the interest, however small, disqualifies him.[23] If the interest is not pecuniary or proprietary, it must

13 Administration of Justice Act 1964, s. 10, as amended by the Administration of Justice Act 1973, s. 2 (6).

14 Administration of Justice Act 1973, s. 2.

15 *Ibid.* s. 2 (7).

16 See p. 289.

17 See p. 115.

18 Administration of Justice Act 1973, s. 1 (2) and (6).

19 *Ibid.* Sched. 1, Pt. II.

20 *Ibid.* s. 1 (5) and Sched. 1, Pt. II.

21 *Ibid.* Sched. 1, Pt. I.

22 Forfeiture Act 1870, s. 2; Representation of the People Act 1949, ss. 140, 141 and 163; Bankruptcy Act 1883, s. 32.

23 For instance, if he is a ratepayer in civil proceedings by the local authority (*R.* v. *Gaisford* [1892] 1 Q.B. 381; *R.* v. *Rand* (1866) L.R. 1 Q.B. 230) but not in criminal proceedings simply because the fine will be paid into local funds: Justices of the Peace Act 1867, s. 2.

afford a real likelihood of bias.[24] A solicitor who is also a magistrate, and his partners, may not act in proceedings before a magistrates' court in the petty sessional division (or, if none, in the commission area) in which he is a magistrate.[25] A magistrate is disqualified if he is a member of a local authority involved in the proceedings,[26] or if he has heard about the accused's previous convictions while deciding whether to grant him bail.[27] Expert knowledge of the background circumstances of the case (*e.g.* a magistrate who is also a doctor in a case where the effect of alcohol is in issue) raises no question of impropriety provided he uses the knowledge to interpret the evidence and does not in effect give expert evidence to himself or his colleagues.[28]

The effect of the disqualification through interest is to invalidate the proceedings, but an acquittal cannot be quashed on this ground.[29] If the disqualification is non-statutory the parties may waive the disqualification.[30]

Local jurisdiction: summons and warrant

For the purpose of issuing process the magistrate's jurisdiction is laid down in section 1 of the Magistrates' Courts Act 1952. As we have already seen, local jurisdiction is basically limited to the place where the offence was committed or is suspected of having been committed.[31]

If more than one person is involved in an offence or series of connected offences, a magistrate in the area in which one of those people is in custody or is being proceeded against, may, if he considers it expedient for the better administration of justice, issue a summons or warrant in respect of an offence committed outside that jurisdiction, so that the participants may be tried jointly or in the same place.[32] The two cases need not involve the same offence but there must be a

---

24 *R.* v. *Camborne Justices* [1955] 1 Q.B. 41; *R.* v. *Altrincham Justices, ex p. Pennington* [1975] 2 W.L.R. 450.

25 Solicitors Act 1974, s. 38.

26 Justices of the Peace Act 1949, s. 3.

27 Criminal Justice Act 1967, s. 19; see p. 71; knowledge of previous convictions from acquaintance with the person charged does not disqualify but it is desirable that the case be transferred to another magistrate: *R.* v. *McElligott, ex p. Gallagher* [1972] Crim. L. R. 332.

28 *Wetherall* v. *Harrison* [1976] 2 W.L.R. 168.

29 *R.* v. *Simpson* [1914] 1 K.B. 66.

30 *Wakefield Local Board of Health* v. *West Riding Ry.* (1865) L.R. 1 Q.B. 84.

31 Magistrates' Courts Act 1952, s. 1 (2) (*a*); see p. 16 and s. 3 regarding the extension of an area to cover boundaries, etc.

32 *Ibid.* s. 1 (2) (*b*).

sufficient nexus between them (*e.g.* theft and handling stolen goods).[33] The magistrate must consider the interests of both the prosecution and the defence; his discretion will be improperly exercised if, for instance, it is made excessively difficult for one accused to prepare his case by long distances, difficulty in getting witnesses to attend and heavy expenses.[34]

If the offence alleged in the information is indictable, a summons or warrant may be issued by a magistrate in the county in which the person lives or is, or is believed to live or to be.[35] If the offence alleged is not indictable then a summons cannot be issued solely on the ground that the accused lives or is in the area. If a warrant of arrest is issued on that ground alone, it must require him to be brought before the magistrates' court which has jurisdiction to try the offence.[36]

Section 1 (2) (*d*) preserves other enactments, such as the Poaching Prevention Act 1862, which enable an offence to be dealt with in a jurisdiction other than the one where it was committed.

For indictable offences which are triable in England and Wales although committed elsewhere[37] process can be issued where the accused is or lives[38] under section 1 (2) (*c*). Summary offences, being creatures of statute, can be committed outside England and Wales only if a statute so provides. If an offence is exclusively punishable on summary conviction[39] and was committed outside England and Wales, a magistrate for a county in which the court would have jurisdiction to try the offence if the offender were brought before it (*i.e.* Magistrates' Courts Act 1952, s. 2 (3), below) may issue a summons or warrant.[40]

Local jurisdiction: arrest without warrant

If a person has been arrested without a warrant, section 2 (3) of the Magistrates' Courts Act 1952 gives a magistrates' court jurisdiction to inquire into a charge against any person who appears or is brought before it. By section 4 (1) a single magistrate is sufficient.

---

33 See also *ibid.* s. 35 (aiding and abetting of summary offences is triable by the court having jurisdiction over either the principal or the accessory offence). As to joinder of offences and offenders in an indictment, see pp. 128–142.

34 *R.* v. *Blandford and Freestone* (1955) 39 Cr. App.R. 51.

35 *Ibid.* s. 1 (2) (*c*).

36 See p. 291.

37 See pp. 9–13.

38 Magistrates' Courts Act 1952, s. 1 (4).

39 See p. 292.

40 Magistrates' Courts Act 1952, s. 1 (2) (*e*), added by the Courts Act 1971, Sched. 8, para. 34 (2).

The rules relating to jurisdiction for trial are dealt with on pp. 85, 89 and 291.

Liability of magistrates

The magistrate's decision whether or not to issue process is made judicially. If, after consideration, he refuses to do so, his decision will not be reviewed by the High Court.[41] But if he refuses to hear the information or if he considers extraneous and non-judicial matters, the High Court may issue an order of mandamus to compel him to reconsider the information judicially.[42]

In this case the bad decision would be reviewed by the High Court in its prerogative jurisdiction.[43] A civil remedy, however, is given by the Justices' Protection Act 1848 to any person who has suffered injury as a result of the magistrate acting without or in excess of his jurisdiction.[44] There is no right of action where the magistrate is carrying out an order of mandamus,[45] nor where a conviction following the bad proceedings is confirmed on appeal. Furthermore, the plaintiff must have been acquitted or discharged and delay in securing such an outcome does not stop the right of action becoming statute-barred.[46]

Section 1 of the 1848 Act recognised an action on the case against a magistrate for things done maliciously and without reasonable and probable cause *within* his jurisdiction. The existence of such an action has been doubted.[47] In *O'Connor* v. *Isaacs*, however, Diplock J. considered that, on a review of the authorities, the action probably does exist.[48]

Indemnification of magistrates

By section 27 of the Administration of Justice Act 1964, a magistrate (or magistrates' clerk) who acted reasonably and in good faith, is, in the event of proceedings against him in his judicial capacity, entitled to be indemnified out of local funds for the damages paid and for the costs of the proceedings, or for sums paid in settlement of a

---

41 *e.g. ex p. Lewis* (1888) 21 Q.B.D. 191 (where the magistrate decided the information did not disclose an offence).

42 *R.* v. *Adamson* (1875) 1 Q.B.D. 201 (where the magistrate refused to issue process because, it was believed, he sympathised politically with the accused).

43 See p. 43.

44 s. 2; considered comprehensively in *O'Connor* v. *Isaacs* [1956] 2 Q.B. 288.

45 s. 5.

46 s. 6.

47 s. 2 proviso; *O'Connor* v. *Isaacs*, above.

48 [1956] 2 Q.B. 288 at p. 312; see also Winfield and Jolowicz on *Tort* (10th ed.), p. 598, and dicta in *Everitt* v. *Griffiths* [1921] 1 A.C. 631 at p. 666.

claim. The decision to indemnify is made by the magistrates' courts' committee for the area.

B. Laying an Information

As any person may prosecute,[49] any person may lay an information, though he must be the prosecutor in person, his counsel, solicitor or " other person authorised in that behalf." [50] In practice it is usually done by a police officer. The process involves giving the magistrate a concise statement of the suspected offence and the suspected offender (the information) and the magistrate will then issue the appropriate means to procure the presence of the suspect.[51] Justices' clerks have power to take informations and issue summonses where the information is not given on oath.[52]

An information need not be in any particular form. It may be on oath, in writing or verbal.[53] It must be in writing and on oath if a warrant of arrest is asked for,[54] or if a statute requires it for a particular purpose, *e.g.* for a search warrant under section 3 of the Obscene Publications Act 1959.

The Magistrates' Courts Rules 1968 regulate the contents of the statement of the offence, which are similar to the particulars of the offence in an indictment [55]—the information must allege only one offence or it will be bad for duplicity [56]; the offence must be described in ordinary language avoiding technical terms [57]; it must refer to the Act or other enactment which creates the offence, if any [58]; and it need not negative any exemption, proviso or excuse contained in the definition of the offence.[59]

Example [60]

Bow Street **Magistrates' Court**

Date: January 4, 1977.

Accused: Adolphus Biggs.

Address: 4 Railway Cuttings, London, N.1.

---

[49] See p. 17.
[50] Magistrates' Courts Rules 1968, r. 1 (1).
[51] Magistrates' Courts Act 1952, s. 1.
[52] Justices of the Peace Act 1968, s. 5 (1); Justices' Clerks Rules 1970 (S.I. No. 231).
[53] Magistrates' Courts Rules 1968, r. 1 (2).
[54] Magistrates' Courts Act 1952, s. 1 (1), proviso.
[55] See pp. 121–128.
[56] Magistrates' Courts Rules 1968, r. 12; but two informations may be contained in one document.
[57] *Ibid.* r. 83 (1).
[58] *Ibid.* r. 83 (2).
[59] *Ibid.* r. 1 (3).
[60] Magistrates' Courts (Forms) (Amendment) Rules 1974, Form 1. The statement, if any, taken on oath may conveniently be taken in the form of a deposition, see p. 107.

Alleged offence: Adolphus Biggs on 31st December, 1976, at the Broken Flask public-house in Skidding Road, London, N.1, dishonestly handled stolen goods by receiving a bottle of Wincarnis Tonic Wine knowing or believing the said goods to be stolen goods contrary to section 22 of the Theft Act 1968.
The information of: Percival Cubitts, Police Constable 999.
Address: St. Pancras Police Station, Euston Road, London, N.W.1.
Telephone: 034 735.

who [upon oath] states that the accused committed the offence of which particulars are given above.

Justin Porter
Justice of the Peace
[**or** Jonathan Close
Justices' Clerk]

At this stage the only really important aspect is the clear identification of the accused and the offence alleged. The information will be incorporated in the summons or warrant, but the court's power to amend a faulty information later is wide.[61]

C. Summons

The summons is addressed to the accused and requires him to attend at a magistrates' court at a specified time (the " return date ") to answer the information. When a summons is issued, the accused remains at liberty until conviction. The magistrate issuing the summons must sign it or have his name authenticated by the clerk's signature.[62] One summons may contain allegations of more than one offence, but each offence must be alleged in a separate information and each information has effect as a separate summons.[63] The circumstances which determine whether a summons or a warrant of arrest should be issued will be dealt with in the next section.[64]

Example [65]

Bow Street **Magistrates' Court**

Date: January 4, 1977.

---

[61] s. 100 of the Magistrates' Courts Act 1952 provides that an information, summons or warrant cannot be objected to for any defect in it in substance or in form or for any variance between it and the evidence adduced by the prosecutor, but the court must adjourn if it considers that the accused has been misled; for detailed consideration of this section, see p. 304.

[62] Magistrates' Courts Rules 1968, r. 81 (1); *R.* v. *Brentford Justices, ex p. Catlin* [1975] Q.B. 455.

[63] *Ibid.* r. 81 (3). As to trial for more than one offence, see pp. 304 and 309.

[64] See p. 59.

[65] Magistrates' Courts (Forms) (Amendment) Rules 1974, Form 2.

To the accused: Adolphus Biggs.
of: 4 Railway Cuttings, London, N.1.

You are hereby summoned to appear on May 27, 1977, **at** 10.30 a.m. **before the Magistrates' Court** at Bow Street to **answer to the following information** [66]

Alleged offence: You on December 31, 1976, at 7.30 p.m. in Pentonville Road, London, N.1., drove a motor vehicle without due care and attention contrary to section 3 of the Road Traffic Act 1972.

Prosecutor: Charles Inskipp, Chief Inspector of Police.
Address: St. Pancras Police Station, Euston Road, London, N.1.

Justin Porter
Justice of the Peace

A summons may be endorsed for service in Scotland and the Isle of Man.[67]

Service of summons

The summons may be served by personal delivery to the person it is addressed to, by leaving it at his last known or usual address or the address he gave for the purpose, or by sending it by registered post or recorded delivery.[68] However, if he does not appear in answer to it and the offence is indictable, such service is only to be treated as proved if it was delivered to the accused personally. Otherwise its receipt by the accused will have to be actually proved. This is because a warrant for his arrest may be issued if he fails to answer a summons for an indictable offence, and sometimes for a summary offence, if it was properly served.[69] If the accused does not appear in answer to the summons, he can make a statutory declaration that he did not know of the summons or the proceedings and serve it on the magistrates' court's clerk; without prejudice to the validity of the information, the summons and the proceedings so far are void.[70]

A summons served outside England and Wales cannot be served by

---

[66] If there is more than one information they are set out in a schedule giving the date of the information and the particulars and statute of the alleged offence.

[67] Summary Jurisdiction (Process) Act 1881, s. 4, and Summary Jurisdiction (Process) (Isle of Man) Order 1928. This also applies to process issued by the Crown Court under the Courts Act 1971, s. 13 (8), and to other process under the Powers of Criminal Courts Act 1973, s. 53; see pp. 59 and 151. An accused served with a summons in Scotland may also plead guilty by post: Criminal Procedure (Scotland) Act 1975, s. 326; see p. 310.

[68] Magistrates' Courts Rules 1968, r. 82.

[69] See p. 60; as to corporations, see p. 390.

[70] Criminal Justice Act 1967, s. 24 (3).

post, for instance, where an English magistrate issues a summons in respect of an offence committed in his jurisdiction by a person who lives in Scotland.

D. Warrant of Arrest

A warrant of arrest is addressed to the person who is to carry out the arrest, usually to the police constables of that police area.[71] It is a command to them to bring the person named in it before the court to answer the information [72] which has been laid in writing and on oath.[73] It must normally be signed by the magistrate.[74]

It is essential that the person to be arrested be named or sufficiently described to be recognised as an individual. In *Leach* v. *Money* [75] a warrant issued by a Secretary of State to apprehend the authors, printers and publishers of an allegedly seditious publication was held to be unlawful and the people arrested recovered damages for trespass and false imprisonment.[76] Section 51 (1) of the Betting, Gaming and Lotteries Act 1963, by enabling arrests to be made when carrying out a search of premises with a warrant, comes fairly close to the " general warrant " declared unlawful in this case, however. A search warrant which does not specify the property to be looked for is also unlawful.[77]

Example [78]

Bow Street **Magistrates' Court**

Date: January 4, 1977.

Accused: Adolphus Biggs.

Address: 4 Railway Cuttings, London, N.1.

Alleged offence: On December 31, 1976, at the Broken Flask public house in Skidding Road, London, N.1., the accused stole a bottle of Bell's Whisky, the property of the Waterdown Brewery Ltd., contrary to section 1 of the Theft Act 1968.

Information having been laid before me on oath by John Tapmaster of

---

[71] Magistrates' Courts Act 1952, s. 102 (2). Civilian process servers, employed by the local authority or police force, may be used instead: Magistrates' Courts (Amendment) Rules 1973, Sched.

[72] Magistrates' Courts Rules 1968, r. 79.

[73] See p. 54.

[74] Magistrates' Courts Rules 1968, rr. 78 and 93 (2).

[75] (1765) 19 St.Tr. 1001.

[76] See also *Wilkes* v. *Lord Halifax* (1769) 19 St.Tr. 1407. Secretaries of State no onger have this power: Justices of the Peace Act 1968, s. 1 (7).

[77] *Wilkes* v. *Wood* (1763) 19 St.Tr. 1153; *Entick* v. *Carrington* (1765) 19 St.Tr. 1029. As to search warrants, see pp. 25–27.

[78] Magistrates' Courts (Forms) (Amendment) Rules 1974, Form 3.

13 Skidding Road, London, N.1., on January 4, 1977, **that the accused committed the offence of which particulars are given above.**

Direction: You, the constables of St. Pancras **Police Force are hereby required to arrest the accused and to bring the accused before the Magistrates' Court at** Bow Street **immediately.**

***Bail: On arrest the accused shall be released on bail subject to a duty to appear before the** Bow Street **Magistrates' Court on** January 4, 1977, **provided that** one **surety in the sum of** £50 **is bound to secure the accused's appearance.**[79]

Justin Porter
Justice of the Peace

***Delete if bail is not granted.**

Execution of a warrant

A warrant remains in force until executed or withdrawn.[80] The warrant is executed when the arrest is made and the accused brought before the court either by the person to whom the warrant was addressed or by a police constable acting within his police area.[81] The warrant may be executed at any time, including Sunday,[82] and at any place in England and Wales. The constable making the arrest need not have the warrant with him but it must be shown to the person arrested as soon as is practicable.[83] The constable's powers and duties are considered generally in Section G.[84]

Backing for bail

According to the general principles of bail outlined in Section I,[85] it may be proper that the person to be arrested should be released after arrest on guarantee of appearing before the court on a certain date. By section 93 of the Magistrates' Courts Act 1952 [86] the magistrate endorses a direction on the back of the warrant that the officer in charge at the police station to which the arrested person is taken release him subject to the duty to appear in court as specified in the endorsement.

---

[79] The wording of this direction for bail is the invention of the author as, at the time of writing, no forms rules had been issued to implement the Bail Act 1976.

[80] Magistrates' Court Act 1952, s. 102 (1). It might be withdrawn, *e.g.* where it becomes obvious the person named in it did not commit the offence.

[81] *Ibid.* s. 102 (2).

[82] *Ibid.* s. 102 (3).

[83] *Ibid.* s. 102 (4).

[84] See p. 64.

[85] See p. 68.

[86] As amended by Sched. 2 to the Bail Act 1976.

Backing for Scotland, Northern Ireland, etc.

A warrant of arrest issued in Scotland may be executed in England, and a warrant issued in England may be executed in Scotland, without being locally endorsed.[87] If the suspect is in Northern Ireland, the Isle of Man or the Channel Islands, a warrant of arrest issued in England must be endorsed on the back by a magistrate acting in the place where the suspect is believed to be.[88]

Section 102 (4) of the Magistrates' Courts Act 1952 may not be applicable to these warrants. Under the Criminal Procedure (Scotland) Act 1975, Scottish warrants may be executed by a police constable within his area without the warrant in his possession, but the very existence of this special provision for Scotland implies that a policeman executing a Northern Irish, etc., warrant must have it in his possession.[89]

In relation to the Irish Republic, English warrants may be executed there under the Extradition Act 1963 (an Irish statute) and Irish warrants may be executed here by virtue of the Backing of Warrants (Republic of Ireland) Act 1965. This arrangement is more in the nature of extradition proceedings and does not apply to political or military offences.[90] Under the English Act the warrant must be in respect of an indictable offence or a summary offence punishable by six months' imprisonment. A magistrate may issue a provisional warrant if a constable has received an urgent request to make an arrest but is not yet in possession of the actual warrant. It must be stressed that this applies only to England and Wales; the "common law enforcement area" of Northern Ireland and the Republic is a great deal more comprehensive.[91]

When a warrant may be issued

The issue of warrants is limited by section 24 of the Criminal Justice Act 1967. They can only be issued in the following cases:

---

[87] Criminal Procedure (Scotland) Act 1975, s. 325.

[88] Indictable Offences Act 1848, ss. 12–15.

[89] The same applies to s. 102 (3)—execution on Sunday, which is expressly allowed for Scottish warrants by the 1975 Act, s. 325 (1).

[90] See pp. 61 and 115. The Irish Supreme Court gave an interesting interpretation to "political" on the application for the transfer to England of Sean Bourke who "sprang" George Blake (convicted of spying for the Soviet Union) from Wormwood Scrubs Prison, on the ground that it was an offence "connected with a political offence," see *Irish Times*, February 4, 1969, and July 10, 1969. The Divisional Court, on the other hand, held that robbing a bank to get funds for the I.R.A. did not have a political character although it would be tried by a special court: *R.* v. *Governor of Winson Green Prison, ex p. Littlejohn* [1975] 1 W.L.R. 893.

[91] Criminal Jurisdiction Act 1975.

(*a*) where the offence is indictable or punishable by imprisonment; or

(*b*) where the accused's address is not sufficiently established for a summons to be served on him; or

(*c*) where a summons has been issued in respect of a summary offence [92] and—

(i) the information for the issue of the summons was substantiated on oath, and

(ii) the accused has not appeared in answer to the summons, and

(iii) it is proved that the accused was served with the summons,[93] and *either*

(iv) the offence to which the warrant will relate is punishable with imprisonment, *or*

(v) the court, having convicted the accused, proposes to impose a disqualification on him.

The power of the court to try and convict the accused in his absence is dealt with later.[94]

A warrant of arrest may always be issued for an indictable offence, even though a summons has already been issued.[95] If the accused does not appear to answer an indictment, a " bench warrant " may be issued by the judge,[96] or a warrant of arrest issued by a magistrate for the area where the accused is or resides, or where he is believed to be, or to reside.[97]

E. Extradition

Extradition proceedings have two aspects—where the accused is wanted by a foreign state for an offence committed within that state's jurisdiction, and where the English authorities want the accused to be returned from a foreign state to stand trial here. The same principles usually apply in each case, because the procedure is based on statutes passed to give effect to reciprocal treaty arrangements.[98] The first

---

92 Magistrates' Courts Act 1952, s. 15, as amended by the Criminal Justice Act 1967, s. 24 (2).

93 See p. 56.

94 See p. 301.

95 Magistrates' Courts Act 1952, s. 1 (3).

96 See p. 151.

97 Magistrates' Courts Act 1952, s. 1 (2); see p. 52.

98 The individual treaties are brought into effect by Order in Council.

will be dealt with later,[99] but the second is a means of compelling the presence of the accused in an English court, without which the people involved in bringing him to England will be guilty of trespass and false imprisonment.[1] If he is believed to be in a Commonwealth country, the Fugitive Offenders Act 1967 applies; if he is elsewhere, the Extradition Acts 1870, 1873 and 1895 apply.

As regards proceedings in England, the prosecutor should apply to the police. Chief officers of police report particulars of the application to the Director of Public Prosecutions. He then decides whether to apply to the Home Secretary to have the relevant papers, including a warrant of arrest, forwarded to the British representative in the state where the accused is believed to be. The representative handles the matter according to the local procedure for extradition.[2] There is sometimes an arrangement for expedited extradition, whereby a provisional order is applied for similar to the provisional warrant available to the Irish authorities.[3]

Extradition will only be granted by the foreign state for an offence included in the extradition treaty, which always excludes political offences.[4] Treaties normally provide that it will be granted only for offences committed within the *territory* (which includes territorial extensions to ships, aircraft, etc.) as opposed to the *jurisdiction* of the requesting state. Unless the treaty specifies "jurisdiction" therefore, crimes committed on land abroad will not be extraditable.[5] The offender must return to England. If the application is successful, the accused cannot be made to stand trial for any offence other than the one for which his surrender was sought or for some lesser offence proved by the facts on which the surrender was granted. If the English authorities wish to try him for some other offence, he must first be given the opportunity to return to the state from which he was extradited.[6]

The prosecutor may apply for the warrant of arrest to the magistrate

---

[99] See p. 115. They are somewhat similar to committal proceedings.

[1] See p. 41.

[2] *i.e.* the counterpart of the proceedings initiated by a foreign state in England, see p. 115.

[3] See p. 59.

[4] Offences against aircraft (see p. 11) are made extraditable by the Hijacking Act 1971, s. 3, and the Protection of Aircraft Act 1973, s. 5. These offences are, by their nature, very often political in character. The Conventions implemented by these Acts (The Hague, 1970, and Montreal, 1971) imposed an obligation on states either to extradite, which is often impossible, or to prosecute the offender locally. The jurisdiction to prosecute, described in Chap. 2, is therefore extraterritorial.

[5] See pp. 9–13.

[6] Extradition Act 1870, s. 19; Fugitive Offenders Act 1967, s. 14.

having jurisdiction in the place where the offence was committed. If the offence was committed abroad (*e.g.* murder) [7] it would be necessary to move that an indictment be preferred by a judge of the High Court,[8] after which a warrant may be issued.[9]

F. Arrest without a Warrant

Most of the common law powers of arrest are superseded by section 2 of the Criminal Law Act 1967. At common law, however, any person could arrest another person committing a breach of the peace,[10] and a justice of the peace had power to apprehend or to give a verbal order to apprehend a person who committed an offence or breach of the peace in his presence.[11] These powers may survive. Otherwise arrest must be authorised by statute. The powers and duties ancillary to arrest are considered in Section G.[12]

Under the Criminal Law Act 1967, s. 2 (1), the power to arrest is confined to "arrestable offences," *i.e.* offences and attempts to commit offences for which the sentence is fixed by law [13] or for which a person not previously convicted may be sentenced to imprisonment for five years by virtue of any enactment.[14]

Arrest by private citizens

Any person may arrest another person who is in the act of committing an arrestable offence, or whom he suspects with reasonable cause is so doing.[15]

Any person may, where an arrestable offence has been committed, arrest any person who is, or whom he suspects with reasonable cause to be, guilty of committing that offence.[16]

"Any person," of course, includes a policeman. The important distinction, however, between the individual's power to arrest and the policeman's is that an offence must in fact have been committed for

---

[7] Or other offence triable in England when committed elsewhere, see pp. 12–13.

[8] See p. 144.

[9] See p. 151.

[10] *Baynes* v. *Brewster* (1841) 2 Q.B. 375; if he is not actually committing the breach of the peace, he must have done so and there must be reasonable grounds for apprehending a repetition of it. *Cf.* the power to arrest in cases of riot: *Bristol Riots Case* (1832) 3 St.Tr. (N.S.) 1; *Phillips* v. *Eyre* (1870) L.R. 6 Q.B. 1.

[11] 2 Hale 86.

[12] See p. 64.

[13] *e.g.* for murder: Murder (Abolition of Death Penalty) Act 1965.

[14] *N.B.* this part of the definition excludes common law offences, such as conspiracy, which do not have a statutory punishment: *R.* v. *Spicer* [1970] Crim.L.R. 695; see p. 224.

[15] s. 2 (2).

[16] s. 2 (3).

arrest by an individual to be lawful. This is based on the common law.[17]

Arrest by police constables

Additionally a police constable may arrest without a warrant

(*a*) where he suspects with reasonable cause that an arrestable offence has been committed, anyone whom he suspects, with reasonable cause, to be guilty of it,[18] and

(*b*) any person who is, or whom he suspects with reasonable cause to be, about to commit an arrestable offence.[19]

A policeman may therefore arrest without warrant where an arrestable offence has not in fact been committed, provided he reasonably suspects it has been or is about to be committed.

Statutory powers of arrest without warrant

Numerous statutes give power to arrest without warrant and are preserved by section 2 (7). They include: the Bail Act 1976, s. 7 (3) (a person released on bail who appears unlikely to surrender to custody —arrest by a constable)[20]; the Prison Act 1952, s. 49 (1) (a person lawfully committed to detention who is unlawfully at large—arrest by a constable); the Street Offences Act 1959, s. 1 (3) (a common prostitute loitering or soliciting in a public place for the purpose of prostitution—arrest by a constable); the Theft Act 1968, s. 12 (3) (taking a motor vehicle, etc., without authority is to be treated as an arrestable offence); the Road Traffic Act 1972, s. 164 (2) (reckless, dangerous or careless driving—arrest by a constable unless the driver gives his name and address or produces his licence).

Powers of summary arrest given by statute are strictly construed. In *R.* v. *Roff*,[21] for instance, the power to arrest a person " committing " a drunken driving offence (Road Traffic Act 1972, s. 5) means that the arrest must be contemporaneous with the offence or immediately afterwards.

Section 51 (1) of the Betting, Gaming and Lotteries Act 1963 gives a constable, executing a search warrant issued in respect of premises where it is suspected that an offence under the Act is being committed, the power to arrest persons found there.

---

[17] *Walters* v. *W. H. Smith & Son* [1914] 1 K.B. 595.
[18] s. 2 (4).
[19] s. 2 (5).
[20] See p. 81.
[21] [1976] R.T.R. 7.

G. Powers and Duties Ancillary to Arrest

A policeman making an arrest has power to search the person he arrests for any property which may form evidence in subsequent criminal proceedings against him.[22]

If a person makes an arrest with a warrant, he must show it to the accused if he has it in his possession. If he has not got it with him he must tell the accused the reason for his arrest and ensure that he sees the warrant as soon as is practicable.[23]

If the arrest is without a warrant, the accused must be told that he is being arrested[24] and of the true reason for his arrest in plain language. He need not be told if the circumstances are such that the general nature of the charge is obvious[25] or if he makes the telling impossible, for instance, by immediately running away or making a counter-attack. Otherwise, if he is not told, the arrest will be unlawful.[26]

Where, however, the person arrested suffers from a disability which prevents him from understanding what is said to him, the arrest is lawful if the constable has done everything reasonable in the circumstances, whether or not in ignorance of the disability. In *Wheatley* v. *Lodge*[27] a deaf person was arrested by a police constable but did not know that he was being arrested; the constable did not know and had no reason at that stage to realise that he was deaf. When he was taken to the police station the arrest and charge was explained in writing. The arrest was held to be lawful.

If a private person makes an arrest without a warrant, he must take the person arrested before a magistrate or to a police station as soon as he reasonably can. In *John Lewis and Co. Ltd.* v. *Tims*[28] it was found to be reasonable, and therefore lawful, for a store detective to detain the person arrested until a senior officer of the company had considered whether to call for the police.

A policeman must bring the arrested person before a magistrates' court as soon as practicable.[29] In *Dallison* v. *Caffery*[30] it was held to be

---

22 See p. 27.

23 Magistrates' Courts Act 1952, s. 102 (4). If the warrant is not for a person charged with a criminal offence (*e.g.* for non-payment of a fine), the policeman must have it in his possession: *R.* v. *Purdy* [1975] Q.B. 288; as to what is meant by "charged," see *Evans* v. *Macklen* [1976] Crim. L.R. 120.

24 *Alderson* v. *Booth* [1969] 2 Q.B. 216.

25 *e.g. R.* v. *Mayer* [1975] R.T.R. 411, where a motorist who was breathalysed must have known the general nature of the offence alleged.

26 *Christie* v. *Leachinsky* [1947] A.C. 573. For an illustration of insufficient information, see *R.* v. *Telfer* [1976] Crim. L.R. 562 (Crown Court).

27 [1971] 1 W.L.R. 29.

28 [1952] A.C. 676.

29 Magistrates' Courts Act 1952, s. 38 (4).

30 [1965] 1 Q.B. 348.

lawful for a constable who had made an arrest to carry out reasonable investigations—identification parade and attempts to verify the arrestee's alibi by visiting various places—for about 24 hours before bringing the arrested person before a magistrates' court. A practical result of excessive detention may be the inadmissibility of any statement made to the police because of a doubt of its having been made voluntarily.[31] The magistrates' court begins to make the preliminary inquiry (*i.e.* committal proceedings) as soon as the accused appears or is brought before the court.[32]

Section 12 of the Prevention of Terrorism (Temporary Provisions) Act 1976 enables a person arrested without warrant on suspicion of acts of terrorism or an offence under the Act [33] to be detained by the police for up to 48 hours of his arrest; the Home Secretary may order a further period of detention of up to five days in a particular case. Section 38 of the Magistrates' Courts Act 1952, below, is excluded in such cases. It should be noted, however, that the Act requires annual renewal by order of the Home Secretary under section 17.

If the offence is not very serious and the accused cannot or need not be brought before a magistrates' court within 24 hours, the accused must be released on bail.[34] Bail may also be granted if inquiries cannot be completed immediately.[35] If inquiries reveal that the arrested person is innocent, he must be released at once.[36] If the arrest is made with a warrant, then, unless the warrant is endorsed for bail,[37] the arrested person must be brought before the magistrates' court specified in the warrant as soon as practicable.

Further, a person arrested without a warrant should be taken to a police station as soon as possible,[38] where he is put in the charge of the station officer. If he is already there for interrogation,[39] he must be charged as soon as there is sufficient evidence against him. Before

---

[31] *R.* v. *McGregor* [1975] Crim. L.R. 514 (arrest on Thursday evening, statement made on Saturday morning, taken before the magistrate Saturday afternoon).

[32] Criminal Justice Act 1967, s. 35.

[33] Membership of a proscribed organisation, breach of an exclusion order, contribution to acts of terrorism or refusal to give information; ss. 1, 9, 10 and 11.

[34] Magistrates' Courts Act 1952, s. 38 (1), as amended by the Bail Act 1976, Sched. 2: see p. 68.

[35] *Ibid.* s. 38 (2), as amended by the Bail Act 1976, Sched. 2.

[36] *Wiltshire* v. *Barrett* [1966] 1 Q.B. 312.

[37] See p. 58.

[38] See Devlin, *The Criminal Prosecution in England*, p. 67.

[39] He cannot have been compelled to go there—he may be there voluntarily (see p. 20). An informal alternative is to arrest him for some other offence, but of course there must also be a lawful arrest in respect of that other offence. If he is already under arrest for one offence and the police wish to place him under arrest for another it is sufficient simply to tell him: *R.* v. *Weir* [1972] 3 All E.R. 906.

charging, however, he is arrested, which is done by the police officer informing him that he is being arrested;[40] the police officer must then caution him.[41]

Where a constable has a power to arrest a person for an offence involving drunkenness (drunk and disorderly, etc.), he may take him to a medical treatment centre for alcoholics instead of the police station, if there is such a centre available.[42] The offender cannot be compelled to stay there but it is deemed to be lawful custody; it does not preclude a charge and prosecution.

Entry of premises to make an arrest

Section 2 (6) of the Criminal Law Act 1967 gives a constable the power, in making an arrest under section 2, to enter and search any place where the person he wants to arrest is, or where he reasonably suspects him to be. He may, if necessary, use force to enter.

In accordance with the principles of search and taking property for use in evidence,[43] the constable may take property which will form evidence for the offence in respect of which he entered.

The use of force

Section 3 of the Criminal Law Act 1967 supersedes the common law on this subject:

> "A person may use such force as is reasonable in the circumstances in the prevention of crime, or in effecting or assisting in the lawful arrest of offenders or suspected offenders or of persons unlawfully at large."

A constable may use force to enter premises under section 2 (6).

Liability for wrongful arrest

A person who makes an arrest without the power to do so, or does so in breach of his duties,[44] commits the crimes and torts of assault and false imprisonment,[45] as to which the Criminal Law Act is silent. If an offence has been committed (or, in the policeman's case, is about to be committed) which, contrary to the arrester's belief, is not arrestable, there will be no defence to a prosecution, for the mistake is

---

[40] The duty is to ensure that the suspect understands that he is no longer a free man: *R.* v. *Inwood* [1973] 1 W.L.R. 647.

[41] See Judges' Rules, p. 22. The "charge" on an arrest made with a warrant is the statement of offence in the warrant, see p. 57.

[42] Criminal Justice Act 1972, s. 34. When it came into effect (April 1, 1976) two "detoxification centres" were planned, at Leeds and Manchester.

[43] See p. 27 *et seq.*

[44] As outlined above.

[45] See pp. 40–43.

of law and not of fact. Obversely there will be a defence if the wrong person was arrested (or, in the case of a policeman, if an arrestable offence has not been committed), provided the suspicion of the arrester was reasonable. In a civil action it is a defence for the defendant to prove that he "reasonably and honestly believed" that the circumstances justified the arrest of the plaintiff.[46] Whether this goes further than the definition in section 2 is doubtful. It may be more limited: as "reasonably" is interpreted in an objective sense, the addition of the word "honestly" makes it possible for the plaintiff to prove that the defendant did not actually believe the facts which gave the reasonable grounds for suspicion.[47]

H. Remand

When a person has been arrested he will be kept at the police station until he is brought before the magistrates' court. If the suspected offence is indictable, the court hears the charge against the accused as examining justices.[48] The court may adjourn the hearing and remand the accused before beginning to inquire into the offence.[49] If the offence is triable summarily, or if the court decides to proceed summarily,[50] the court hears the charge as court of trial, and it may adjourn and remand the accused or release him, leaving the date of resumption to be fixed later.[51]

"Remand" means commit to custody or release on bail with the requirement that the accused appear before the court on a specified date. Release on bail is considered in the next section.[52]

Duration of remand in custody

When remanded in custody, the accused is sent to the local prison. He cannot be remanded in custody for more than eight clear days.[53] When he is brought before the court again, the court may remand him in custody for a further eight days,[54] *e.g.* if the prosecution case is not

---

[46] In the case of arrest by a private person, the defence must prove that an arrestable offence has in fact been committed, albeit not by the plaintiff: *Walters* v. *W. H. Smith & Son* [1914] 1 K.B. 595.

[47] *Dallison* v. *Caffery* [1965] 1 Q.B. 348 at p. 369, *per* Diplock L.J.

[48] See pp. 93–115. The examining justices must sit in open court unless there are special reasons for not doing so: Criminal Justice Act 1967, s. 6.

[49] Magistrates' Courts Act 1952, s. 6; see p. 95.

[50] See pp. 292, 295 and 297.

[51] Magistrates' Courts Act 1952, s. 14; see pp. 95 and 307. For this purpose the court may be composed of a single justice.

[52] See p. 68.

[53] Magistrates' Courts Act 1952, s. 105 (4). "Eight clear days" means *e.g.* from Tuesday to the Thursday of the following week. (He may be remanded for a longer period for reports to be made after conviction; see p. 219.)

[54] *Ibid.* s. 105 (2).

ready for hearing. There is no statutory limitation on the number of times this may be done; if the period spent in custody without trial becomes excessive, the accused may apply to the High Court to be granted bail.[55] It is also the duty of the examining magistrate to use his discretion to commit to custody judicially and for a proper purpose.[56] It is probable, though not certain, that the accused's release would be ordered as soon as it becomes apparent to the court that the prosecution is going to be unable to substantiate its suspicion, possibly by forcing the prosecution to reveal its case by refusing an adjournment.

The court may commit a remanded person to the custody of a police constable for a period not exceeding three clear days.[57] If a person is due to come up for further remand but the court is satisfied that he cannot attend because of illness or accident, it may remand him in custody for *any* period (because section 105 (4) is expressly excluded).[58] The period of remand may also be longer if an indictable offence is charged which is also triable summarily and which the court decides to try summarily, but is not properly constituted for the trial.[59] However, section 4 of the Bail Act 1976 requires the court to remand on bail unless certain conditions are satisfied.

I. Bail

A person in custody may be released on bail before trial or committal for trial, or during any proceedings, by the police, by the magistrates' court or by the Crown Court. Historically, the term " bail " meant the security taken from a third person (surety) for the accused's attendance at court. Under the Bail Act 1976, bail is " granted " to a person in criminal proceedings who is, or is liable to be, under arrest or in custody; he is released subject to the duty to surrender to custody at the time and place specified. The security taken from the surety is called a " recognisance."

1. Bail by the police

This is available under section 38 of the Magistrates' Courts Act 1952[60] when the accused has been arrested without a warrant.

---

[55] Criminal Justice Act 1967, s. 22; see p. 78.

[56] This includes obtaining information. If the discretion is improperly exercised, an order for certiorari might be applied for; see p. 45. See also *R.* v. *Guest* [1961] 3 All E.R. 1118.

[57] Magistrates' Courts Act 1952, s. 105 (5).

[58] *Ibid.* s. 106 (1).

[59] *Ibid.* s. 101 (4) (*c*).

[60] This section is excluded when a person is arrested by a police constable under s. 12 of the Prevention of Terrorism (Temporary Provisions) Act 1976; see p. 65.

When a person is in custody at a police station after arrest without a warrant,[61] a police officer not below the rank of inspector, or the officer in charge of the station,

(*a*) *may* inquire into the offence in respect of which the arrest was made, and

(*b*) *must* inquire into that offence, if it will not be practicable to bring the arrested person before a magistrates' court within 24 hours,

and, unless the offence appears to him to be a serious one, the officer may or must[62] grant the arrested person bail subject to a duty to appear before a magistrates' court at such time and place as the officer specifies.[63]

A police officer *may* release an arrested person on bail, with or without sureties, if the inquiry into the case cannot be completed immediately; the arrested person is then under a duty to appear at the police station at a specified time unless he receives written notice from the station officer that his attendance is not required.[64] This bail is enforceable as if the person released were required to appear before the local magistrates' court.

When a warrant is issued for a person's arrest, either by a magistrate or by the Crown Court, it may be indorsed with a direction for bail. The person arrested must be taken to a police station (unless, if it issued the warrant, the Crown Court directs otherwise). The officer in charge of the station must release the arrested person if any sureties tendered in accordance with the direction for bail are approved and enter into recognisances for the amounts fixed by the endorsement.[65] Where bail is directed on a warrant of arrest, however, it is granted by the court, not by the police.

2. Bail by the magistrates' court

Section 105 of the Magistrates' Court Act 1952, which has already been considered in connection with remand in custody,[66] also

---

[61] If he was arrested with a warrant, he will only be released on bail by the police if the warrant is indorsed for bail under s. 93 of the 1952 Act.

[62] *i.e.* he must release him on bail if he cannot be brought before the court within 24 hours—(*b*) above.

[63] Magistrates' Courts Act 1952, s. 38 (1), as amended by the Bail Act 1976, Sched. 2. If he is not released on bail the accused must be brought before the court as soon as is practicable: s. 38 (4); see pp. 64–68.

[64] Magistrates' Courts Act 1952, s. 38 (2).

[65] Magistrates' Courts Act 1952, s. 93, and Courts Act 1971, s. 13 (6), as amended by the Bail Act 1976, Sched. 2.

[66] See p. 67.

provides for remand on bail during an adjournment of the hearing.[67]

The magistrates' court may remand the accused on bail, with or without sureties, directing him to appear either

(*a*) before the court at the end of the period of remand; or

(*b*) at every time and place to which the proceedings may from time to time be adjourned.[68]

Bail on the latter condition is known as "continuous bail" and each adjournment is a remand, but the court may remand him afresh. A surety's recognisance may be conditioned to secure his presence at the Crown Court as well if the magistrates' court is holding committal proceedings.

A remand on bail before trial may be for a period longer than eight days if the accused and the prosecutor consent.[69] If the accused is in custody because the chosen sureties have not yet made their recognisances, however, he must be brought before the court again in eight days.[70] The court may fix the amount of bail, commit the accused to custody and allow the surety's recognisance to be taken subsequently by a prescribed person.[71]

If the accused is absent because of illness or accident the recognisances previously taken may be enlarged and the remand may be for longer than eight days.[72] If he is absent for other reasons the recognisances may be enlarged, but notice must be given to the accused and his sureties.[73]

A person remanded in custody may wait until he next appears for remand to make or renew his application for bail, or he may apply afresh to the magistrates' court, or he may apply to a High Court judge.[74] He may also apply with fresh evidence if he was committed to custody in default of finding sureties.

A defendant who comes before the court in pursuance of a remand in custody on an occasion on which he may again be remanded or committed in custody must, if he wishes to be legally represented, be granted legal aid. A person who is remanded for inquiries and reports to be made after conviction must also be granted legal aid

---

67 Magistrates' Courts Act 1952, ss. 6 (1) (committal proceedings) and 14 (1) and (4) (summary trial), see pp. 95 and 307.

68 *Ibid.* s. 105 (1) and (3), as amended by the Bail Act 1976, Sched. 2.

69 *Ibid.* s. 105 (4) (*a*).

70 Magistrates' Courts Rules 1968, r. 22.

71 See p. 76. Magistrates' Courts Act 1952, s. 105 (1) and (1A), and Bail Act 1976, s. 8 (3)–(5) and Sched. 2.

72 Magistrates' Courts Act 1952, s. 106 (1) and (2), as amended, and see p. 68.

73 *Ibid.* s. 106 (3), as amended; Magistrates' Courts Rules 1968, r. 71.

74 See p. 78.

if he is ordered to be kept in custody. These cases of mandatory legal aid only apply to the application for bail, however, and they do not extend to representation by counsel.[75]

A magistrate is disqualified from trying the defendant summarily if he has been informed during the same proceedings of the defendant's previous convictions for the purpose of determining whether to grant bail.[76]

3. Bail by the Crown Court

Any direction to appear before the Crown Court may contain a condition that appearance be made at such time and place as may be directed by the Crown Court.[77] The Crown Court may subsequently vary the direction. This provision enables the place of trial to remain flexible as long as possible, though the accused should be tried within certain time limits.[78]

The Crown Court may itself grant a person bail in the following circumstances:

(*a*) if he has been committed in custody for appearance before the Crown Court;[79]

(*b*) if he is in custody pursuant to a sentence imposed by a magistrates' court and he has appealed to the Crown Court against conviction or sentence;[80]

(*c*) if he is in the custody of the Crown Court pending the disposal of his case by the Crown Court;[81]

(*d*) if he has applied to the Crown Court for the statement of his case for the High Court;[82] or

(*e*) if he has applied to the High Court to have the Crown Court proceedings removed to the High Court by an order of certiorari,[83] or has applied for leave to make such an application.[84]

Procedure

Bail may be asked for during the hearing of proceedings in the Crown Court, in which case an oral application is made to the judge.

---

[75] Bail Act 1976, s. 11, amending the Legal Aid Act 1974, ss. 28, 29 and 30. See pp. 399–406.

[76] Criminal Justice Act 1967, s. 19.

[77] Courts Act 1971, s. 13 (1), as amended by the Bail Act 1976, Sched. 2.

[78] See p. 102.

[79] This includes a person committed for sentence; see pp. 238 and 330.

[80] As to appeal, see pp. 344–348.

[81] *e.g.* during an adjournment of a trial or pending sentence.

[82] This only applies to a person who appears before the Crown Court on an appeal against a decision of a magistrates' court; see p. 351.

[83] See p. 45.

[84] Courts Act 1971, s. 13 (4).

Where the applicant is not before the court, application must be made at the Crown Court in the place where the proceedings in which the application arises are taking place.[85]

The applicant must give to the prosecutor a notice in writing of his intention to apply at least 24 hours before the application is made.[86] He must give a copy of the notice to the appropriate officer of the court.[87] The prosecutor then notifies the appropriate court officer and the appellant either that he wishes to be represented at the hearing of the application or that he does not wish to oppose it; alternatively he may give a written statement of his reasons for opposing the application to the court officer, sending a copy of it to the applicant.[88]

The applicant must inform the court of any earlier application for bail to the High Court [89] or to the Crown Court in the course of the same proceedings.[90]

The time for the hearing of the application is fixed by an officer of the court. The applicant is not entitled to be present at the hearing unless the court gives him leave to be present.[91] Where an applicant has been unable to instruct a solicitor to act for him, he may request that the Official Solicitor be appointed to act for him, in the meantime giving written notice to the court of his intention to apply for bail.[92]

4. Bail on appeal

Bail may also be granted by the Court of Appeal when a person in custody comes before it (pending retrial, pending the hearing of the appeal, pending appeal to the House of Lords, etc.).[93] There is no general right to bail in these circumstances, however, as the right does not avail a person who has been convicted.[94] Bail could also be

---

[85] Directions of the Lord Chief Justice of October 14, 1971, direction 15 (i).

[86] Crown Court Rules 1971, r. 17 (2). The form of the notice is prescribed in *ibid.* Sched. 2. After the heading and the name of the applicant, it gives the place of detention, particulars of the proceedings during which the applicant was committed to custody, the details of any previous applications for bail, and a full statement of the facts relied on as grounds for the application and any previous convictions. It must also give details of proposed sureties and answer any objections already raised.

[87] *Ibid.* r. 17 (4).

[88] *Ibid.* r. 17 (3).

[89] See p. 78.

[90] *Ibid.* r. 18 (1).

[91] *Ibid.* r. 17 (5).

[92] *Ibid.* r. 17 (6). An application which requests the appointment of the Official Solicitor must be heard by a Crown Court judge in London: Directions of the Lord Chief Justice, direction 15 (i). An application made through the Official Solicitor may be heard summarily without the notice under r. 17 (2) having to be served on the prosecutor.

[93] See Chap. 10, p. 260.

[94] Bail Act 1976, s. 4 (2); see below.

granted on an appeal from the magistrates' court to the Crown Court or Divisional Court, or on a committal for sentence to the Crown Court.[95]

5. Bail by coroners

Where a coroner's inquisition charges a person with homicide, he must issue a warrant of arrest if the person charged is still at large. He may also grant bail to him subject to the duty to appear at the Crown Court.[96] The general principles of bail apply to a coroner as to a court.

6. Principles of bail

Under the Bail Act 1976 all bail in criminal proceedings is subject to the general principles of bail; in some cases bail must be granted unless certain factors are present. This represents a shift in emphasis from the previous law and it was hoped that enactment of a " presumption " in favour of bail would make courts more ready to grant it than previously. It is supported by the important requirement that reasons must be given when refusing or limiting bail.

(a) *The right to bail*

In general, any person who is accused of an offence is entitled to be released on bail when he appears before the magistrates' court or the Crown Court or when he applies to a court for bail unless certain considerations, specified in Schedule 1 to the Act, are satisfied.[97] In addition, a person who is remanded for reports after conviction and a person who is before a court for breach of a requirement of a probation or community service order are entitled to bail.[98]

The people who do not have this right are:

(a) a person who is or has been convicted of the offence of which he is accused unless he is remanded for inquiries and reports [99];
(b) a fugitive offender [99];
(c) a person who is in custody following conviction under the Services Acts [1];
(d) a person who is charged with treason [2];

---

[95] See pp. 71, 330, 344 and 349, but see *R.* v. *Coe*, p. 333.
[96] Coroners Act 1887, s. 5, as amended by the Bail Act 1976, s. 10 (1).
[97] Bail Act 1976, s. 4 (1) and (2).
[98] *Ibid.* s. 4 (3) and (4); see pp. 219–220.
[99] *Ibid.* s. 4 (2). This means a person being extradited to a foreign court: s. 2 (2).
[1] *Ibid.* Sched. 1, paras. 4 of Pts. I and II.
[2] He can only be granted bail by order of a High Court judge or the Home Secretary: Magistrates' Courts Act 1952, s. 8; Bail Act 1976, s. 4 (7).

(e) a person who has already been released on bail and has been arrested for absconding or breach of bail.[3]

There is no general right to be granted bail by the police except as outlined in the first section above.[4]

(b) *Exceptions to the right to bail*

A person who is accused of an offence which is punishable with imprisonment may be refused bail if the court is satisfied that:

(a) he would fail to surrender to custody; or
(b) he would commit an offence while on bail; or
(c) he would interfere with witnesses or otherwise obstruct the course of justice in relation to himself or someone else[5]; or
(d) he should be kept in custody for his own protection (or, if he is a child or young person, for his own welfare)[6]; or
(e) it has not been practicable to obtain sufficient information to make a decision on the above grounds because of want of time since the institution of proceedings.[7]

If the defendant has been convicted and is remanded for inquiries or reports the court may refuse bail on the additional ground:

(f) that it appears to be impracticable to complete the inquiries or make the report without keeping the defendant in custody.[8]

If the court is considering refusing bail on grounds (a)–(c) above, it must consider any relevant matter, especially:

(i) the nature and seriousness of the offence (or default, if it is a breach of a probation requirement) and the probable method of dealing with the defendant;
(ii) the defendant's character, antecedents, associations and community ties;
(iii) the defendant's record of fulfilment of his obligations under previous grants of bail; and
(iv) the strength of the evidence against the defendant if the offence or default has not yet been proved in the proceedings.[9]

---

[3] Bail Act 1976, Sched. 1, Pt. I, para. 6, and Pt. II, para. 5.
[4] See p. 68.
[5] Bail Act 1976, Sched. 1, Pt. I, para. 2.
[6] *Ibid.* para. 3.
[7] *Ibid.* para. 5.
[8] *Ibid.* para. 7.
[9] *Ibid.* para. 9.

If the defendant is accused or convicted of an offence which is not punishable with imprisonment, bail may only be refused if:

(a) it appears that he has previously failed to surrender to custody when granted bail *and*, in view of that failure, the court is satisfied that it is probable he will fail to surrender to custody if granted bail on the present occasion [10]; or

(b) he should be kept in custody for his own protection (or welfare, if he is a child or young person).[11]

The guidance given by the Lord Chief Justice for granting bail to a defendant during a trial which lasts for more than a day [12] appears to remain effective within the new limits. Bail may be refused during a short adjournment (*e.g.* for lunch) if it is impossible to segregate the defendant from witnesses or jurors; it would presumably be necessary now to show a likelihood of his interfering with them. If the defendant was on bail pending trial, it would be wrong to refuse it overnight unless some new and special reason emerged, such as the increased likelihood of absconding because the case is going badly for the defence.

(c) *Incidents of bail*

The basic requirement of release on bail is the duty of the person released to surrender to the custody of the court or police at the time and place appointed.[13] Failure to perform this duty constitutes the offence of absconding under section 6 of the Act.[14]

Extra requirements must not be imposed on a grant of bail unless they appear necessary to the court to secure the defendant's surrender to custody, to prevent him committing an offence while on bail, or to prevent him interfering with witnesses or obstructing the course of justice.[15] The permitted requirements are the taking of sureties or of security from the accused, the imposition of conditions on the bail, and the requirement of a juvenile's parent or guardian to secure the juvenile's compliance with the conditions of bail.

Only a court may impose conditions but the other requirements may be made by the police or other person authorised to grant bail.

Sureties

In order to enhance the defendant's promise to appear, he may be

---

[10] *Ibid.* Sched. 1, Pt. II, para. 2.
[11] *Ibid.* para. 3.
[12] *Practice Direction* [1974] 1 W.L.R. 770.
[13] Bail Act 1976, s. 3 (1).
[14] See p. 80.
[15] *Ibid.* Sched. 1, Pt. I, para. 8

required to find one or more sureties to undertake to secure the surrender of the defendant to custody,[16] this is done by the surety entering a "recognisance"—an acknowledgment that he will owe the Crown a certain sum if the defendant fails to appear. He must not be required to deposit money because his debt does not become payable unless the defendant fails to appear.[17] It is discharged when the defendant surrenders to custody.

The factors to be taken into account when considering the suitability of a proposed surety include his financial resources, his character and previous convictions and his proximity by kinship, neighbourhood, etc., to the person for whom he is to be surety.[18] If no suitable surety can be found immediately, the court may fix the amount in which the surety is to be bound, commit the defendant to custody,[19] and direct the surety when found to enter his recognisance before a different court or officer.[20] The proposed surety who is rejected as unsuitable may himself apply to the court, or to his local magistrates' court, for approval.[21]

It is an offence for a person granted bail to agree to indemnify his surety or proposed surety in any way against any liability for his failure to surrender to custody.[22] The surety also commits the offence. "Bail-bonding" is also a common law offence (conspiracy to pervert the course of justice); it is not expressly abolished by the Act.

Security by the defendant

The defendant cannot himself be required to enter a recognisance.[23] If it appears that he is unlikely to remain in Great Britain until the time appointed for him to surrender to custody, however, he may be required to give security and it may be given by him or on his behalf.[24] It may or may not be in money and could consist, for instance, of handing over his passport.

---

16 Bail Act 1976, ss. 3 (4) and 8.

17 *R.* v. *Harrow Justices, ex p. Morris* [1973] 1 Q.B. 672; as to forfeiting the recognisance, see p. 82.

18 Bail Act 1976, s. 8 (2). In considering his resources, jointly owned property and his spouse's property should be excluded: *R.* v. *Southampton Justices, ex p. Green* [1975] 3 W.L.R. 277.

19 Magistrates' Courts Act 1952, s. 105 (1A); see p. 70.

20 Bail Act 1976, s. 8 (3). S. 8 (4) enables a magistrates' court, a justice of the peace, a justices' clerk, a police officer in charge of a police station or of the rank at least of inspector, or other person specified in rules to take the recognisance. S. 8 (5) enables it to be taken in Scotland.

21 *Ibid.* s. 8 (5).

22 *Ibid.* s. 9. The consent of the D.P.P. is necessary before proceedings may be instituted; the maximum punishment is three months and/or a fine of £400 on summary conviction, or 12 months and/or a fine on conviction on indictment.

23 *Ibid.* s. 3 (2).

24 *Ibid.* s. 3 (5).

Conditions

Additional requirements may be imposed on a person granted bail if they appear necessary to secure that:

(a) he surrenders to custody;
(b) he does not commit an offence while on bail;
(c) he does not interfere with witnesses or obstruct the course of justice in relation to himself or someone else; or
(d) he makes himself available for inquiries or reports to be made to assist the court in deciding how to deal with him.[25]

Typical conditions which might be imposed are requirements that the defendant tell the police of any change of address, stay within the jurisdiction, desist from driving or attempting to drive,[26] etc.

Parents as sureties

Normally sureties cannot be taken to secure the defendant's compliance with the conditions of his bail. In the case of a juvenile defendant, however, his parent or guardian may be required to act as surety for a sum not exceeding £50 to secure the juvenile's compliance with the conditions of bail. The parent cannot be ordered to be surety without his consent and is not bound beyond the extent of his consent.[27]

(d) *Reasons for bail decisions*

If a magistrates' court or the Crown Court withholds bail from, or imposes or varies conditions of the bail granted to, a person entitled to bail, it must give reasons for its action to the defendant with a view to his applying for bail to another court.[28] If it is a magistrates' court and the defendant is unrepresented, the court must tell him of his right to apply to the High Court, or the Crown Court if it is committing him for trial.[29]

If the defendant is legally represented, the court need only give its reasons to him on request.[30]

A record of decisions in relation to bail must be made and a copy

---

[25] *Ibid.* s. 3 (6). Conditions which secure his examination by a doctor or at an institution for the purpose of para. (d) are mandatory under the Magistrates' Courts Act 1952, s. 26 (3), as amended by the Bail Act 1976, s. 3 (9) and Sched. 2.

[26] *R.* v. *Kwame* [1975] R.T.R. 106.

[27] Bail Act 1976, s. 3 (7); this procedure must not be adopted where the defendant is not liable to surrender to custody until after his 17th birthday.

[28] *Ibid.* s. 5 (3). It must include the reasons on the record of its decision (below): s. 5 (4).

[29] *Ibid.* s. 5 (6).

[30] *Ibid.* s. 5 (5).

given to the defendant on request as soon as practicable.[31] This record must be made if bail is granted, if bail is withheld from a person who has a general right to it, or if conditions on the bail are imposed or varied.[32]

(e) *Improper refusal of bail*

If a magistrate refuses to grant or delays in granting bail when it ought to be granted, he may be guilty of a common law offence,[33] though this is virtually unknown; if the refusal or delay is malicious and without reasonable and probable cause, he may be liable in a civil action for damages.[34]

7. Variation of bail and appeal

Where a court has granted bail to a person, it may vary the conditions of the bail or impose conditions on bail granted unconditionally when an application is made by or on behalf of the person granted bail or by the prosecutor or a constable.[35] If a person has been granted bail by the police, the magistrates' court before which he is brought may only vary the bail by appointing a later time at which the defendant is to surrender to custody and extending any sureties accordingly.[36]

Jurisdiction of the High Court

" Apart from the statutory provision, there is an inherent jurisdiction in the High Court to [grant bail to] any person awaiting trial on a criminal charge . . . though judges are, as a rule, loth to interfere with the discretion of the magistrates during the preliminary hearing of indictable offences."[37] This jurisdiction grew out of the court's powers to order release by a writ of habeas corpus.[38] It is now distinct and usually more useful because the court can determine the conditions of bail, whereas habeas corpus simply orders release without imposing conditions or taking recognisances from sureties.[39]

---

[31] Bail Act 1976, s. 5 (1). Rules, which at the time of writing have not been issued, prescribe the particulars to be included.

[32] It also has to be made if a court or officer appoints a different time and place for surrender to custody from that originally appointed. The police constable who makes the arrest under a warrant endorsed for bail makes the record of it instead of the court issuing the warrant: s. 5 (2).

[33] *R.* v. *Badger* (1843) 4 Q.B. 468 at p. 472.

[34] Justices' Protection Act 1848, s. 1; *Linford* v. *Fitzroy* (1849) 13 Q.B. 240 at p. 247; see p. 53.

[35] Bail Act 1976, s. 3 (8).

[36] Magistrates' Courts Act 1952, s. 38 (1A), added by the Bail Act 1976, Sched. 2.

[37] *Supreme Court Practice 1970*. Vol. 2, para 3313.

[38] See p. 44 and *Re Kray* [1965] Ch. 736 at p. 741.

[39] *Ex p. Thomas* [1956] Crim.L.R. 119.

Section 22 (1) of the Criminal Justice Act 1967 gives the High Court power to grant a person bail, or, where he has already been granted bail, to vary the conditions subject to which he was granted bail, including the reduction of the amount in which a surety is bound or the discharge of a surety. This power avails wherever an inferior court [40] has power to grant bail in connection with any criminal proceedings and either withholds it or grants or offers to grant it on terms unacceptable to the person to be granted bail. The conditions which may be varied include the condition as to time and place of appearance.[41] Section 22 also affects bail granted pending appeal from an inferior court.[42]

Procedure

The procedure for appealing to the High Court is contained in the Rules of the Supreme Court, Ord. 79, r. 9. In brief, a person applying for bail or a variation of bail applies to the High Court by summons [43] before a judge in chambers, the application being supported by affidavit evidence, to show cause why the applicant should not be granted bail. If the applicant is in custody and has insufficient means to instruct a solicitor, he may give written notice to the judge that he wishes to apply for bail and the judge may then appoint the Official Solicitor to act for him, in which case the application can be dealt with summarily without issuing a summons or producing an affidavit. The second procedure is a substitute for legal aid,[44] the person in custody having been told of his right to appeal either by his legal

---

[40] *i.e.* a magistrates' court or a coroner: Criminal Justice Act 1967, s. 22 (4), as amended by the Courts Act 1971, Sched. 11. S. 22 has also been amended by the Bail Act 1976, Sched. 2.

[41] Criminal Justice Act 1967, s. 22 (2); see p. 70.

[42] See pp. 344 and 349.

[43] R.S.C. 1965, Appendix A, Form 97, provides the following form:
In the High Court of Justice.
Queen's Bench Division.
Let all the parties concerned attend the judge in chambers on the day of 1977 at o'clock on the hearing of an application on behalf of A.B. to be granted bail as to his commitment on the day of by a magistrates' court sitting at .
Dated the day of 1977.
This summons was taken out by of , solicitor for the said A.B.
Form 97A provides the form for an application for variation.

[44] See pp. 399–406. Legal aid as for civil cases is available for an application to the High Court (Legal Aid Act 1974, s. 7), but the second procedure, above, is probably more expeditious. Instructions on how to draw up the written notice are sometimes found on the walls of prison cells. An interesting study of appeals to the High Court and analysis of a random sample of applications was published in [1976] Crim. L.R. 541 (Bases and Smith). A major fault in the Official Solicitor procedure appears to lie in the fact that the applicant sends in his form applying for bail and the police then send in their reasons for opposing it; the applicant therefore has no opportunity to argue against the police contentions.

representative before the magistrates' court or by the court when it refused to grant him bail.[45]

The powers of the judge have already been considered. If that judge refuses bail, the applicant cannot make any further appeal, either to another judge or to the Divisional Court,[46] but an *ex parte* application for a writ of habeas corpus could be made if the withholding of bail were improper.[47]

8. Breach of bail

Failure to surrender to custody constitutes the offence of "absconding," the person granted bail may be arrested, and the surety's recognisance and the defendant's own security may be forfeited. Arrest may also be used as a preventive measure.

Absconding

If a person who has been released on bail in criminal proceedings fails without reasonable cause to surrender to custody, he is guilty of an offence.[48] If, when he first fails to surrender, he has a reasonable cause for the failure, he "absconds" if he does not surrender to custody at the appointed place as soon as is reasonably practicable after the appointed time.[49]

The offence is punishable on summary conviction in the magistrates' court by a maximum of three months' imprisonment and a fine of £400, or, when the defendant is before the Crown Court, by a maximum of 12 months' imprisonment and an unlimited fine.[50] On conviction in the magistrates' court, the court may sentence him for the summary offence or commit him to the Crown Court for sentence.[51]

If the offence is committed in relation to the Crown Court it is punishable as above as a criminal contempt of court; this avoids the necessity of preferring an indictment.[52]

---

45 Bail Act 1976, s. 5 (6); see p. 77.

46 R.S.C., Ord. 79, r. 9 (12); as to applications for habeas corpus, see Administration of Justice Act 1960, s. 14, and *Re Kray* [1965] Ch. 736.

47 See p. 44. The holding of the defendant in custody would then be a false imprisonment; see p. 41.

48 Bail Act 1976, s. 6 (1). The term "abscond" is used only in the side-heading to ss. 6 and 7 and is not sanctioned by use in the text of the statute.

49 *Ibid* s. 6 (2). The defendant must prove the reasonable cause (s. 6 (3)) and failure to give him a copy of the record of the bail decision (s. 5 (1); see p. 77) cannot be a reasonable cause: s. 6 (4).

50 *Ibid.* s. 6 (5) and (7).

51 *Ibid.* s. 6 (6); it has the power to commit where it considers a greater punishment than it has power to impose is appropriate or where it is committing him for trial in any event for another offence and it would be proper for the two offences to be dealt with together. As to committal for sentence generally, see p. 330.

52 *Ibid.* s. 6 (5), and see p. 392.

Arrest

Arrest of a person granted bail may be by warrant or summarily; it may be for failure to surrender to custody or in order to prevent him breaking his bail.

A court may issue a warrant of arrest when—

(a) the person released on bail fails to surrender to custody [53]; or

(b) the person released on bail has surrendered to custody but absents himself from court (without its leave) before the court is ready to begin or resume hearing the proceedings.[54]

Summary arrest by a police constable is generally of a preventive nature. He may arrest without warrant a person granted bail in criminal proceedings if:

(a) he has reasonable grounds for believing that that person is not likely to surrender to custody;

(b) he has reasonable grounds for believing that that person is likely to break any of the conditions of his bail, or has reasonable grounds for suspecting that that person has broken any of those conditions; or

(c) a surety to the bail notifies him in writing that that person is unlikely to surrender to custody and the surety wishes to be relieved of his obligations.[55]

When a person on bail has been summarily arrested by a constable on any of these grounds he must be brought before a magistrate in the petty sessions area in which he was arrested as soon as practicable, but in any event within 24 hours; if, however, he was due to surrender to custody within 24 hours of his arrest, he must be taken before the court at which he was to have surrendered to custody.[56] In the first case, the magistrate, if of the opinion that the arrested person is not likely to surrender to custody or has broken or is likely to break any condition of his bail, may remand him in custody, commit him to custody, or grant him bail on the same or different

---

[53] *Ibid.* s. 7 (1).

[54] *Ibid.* s. 7 (2).

[55] *Ibid.* s. 7 (3). At common law the person on bail was in the custody of his sureties and they had power to arrest him if they thought he was about to fly: 2 Hale 124. This power may survive, *e.g.* where the surety has no time to notify the constable under s. 7 (3) (c).

[56] *Ibid.* s. 7 (4).

conditions; if he is not of that opinion he must grant bail on the same conditions, if any, as were originally imposed.[57]

Forfeiture of security

If the person granted bail has been required to give security for staying in Great Britain under section 3 (5), the court may order him to forfeit the security in whole or in part, under section 5 (7)-(9), if it is satisfied that he has failed to surrender to custody.[58]

Forfeiture of recognisances

When the person granted bail fails to surrender to custody, the court may order that the sums specified in the recognisances of the sureties be forfeited (or "estreated") to the Crown. The order to forfeit is in the discretion of the court. Factors which may make it unfair and so improper to order the forfeiture of the whole sum are the surety's lack of culpability in connection with the absconding, the efforts he has made to secure the defendant's surrender to custody and the surety's means.[59]

The magistrates' court may adjudge the sureties liable to pay the whole sum, a lesser sum or nothing at all.[60] Any money payable is enforced as a fine.[61]

Where bail has been granted or approved by the High Court, it can only be forfeited by order of a Queen's Bench judge, applied for by a summons to a judge in chambers, supported by an affidavit.[62]

---

[57] Bail Act 1976, s. 7 (5); if the defendant is a child or young person, he is remanded to the care of the local authority, not "in custody": s. 7 (6).

[58] *N.B.* he does not have to have left or attempted to leave Great Britain in order for the court to order forfeiture.

[59] *R.* v. *Southampton Justices, ex p. Green* [1975] 3 W.L.R. 277; *R.* v. *Horseferry Road Stipendiary Magistrate, ex p. Pearson* [1976] 1 W.L.R. 511; *R.* v. *Southampton Justices, ex p. Corker, The Times*, February 12, 1976; *R.* v. *Sangiovanni* (1904) 68 J.P. 54.

[60] Magistrates' Courts Act 1952, s. 96.

[61] *Ibid.* s. 96 (4). In the Crown Court it is enforced by officers of the Crown Court; Courts Act 1971, s. 4 (11).

[62] R.S.C., Ord. 79, r. 8.

PART TWO

TRIAL ON INDICTMENT

CHAPTER 5

COURTS

In this chapter the jurisdiction and constitution of the courts which are involved in a trial on indictment will be considered.

The magistrate is again the corner-stone of the procedure on trial on indictment. The nature of the office and its occupant have been dealt with in Chapter 4.[1] In this chapter the magistrate appears twice —first as the examining justice in the preliminary inquiry and secondly as a member of the bench at the trial of some of the less serious offences.

A complication, which has already been indicated[2] but which, to minimise confusion, will be passed over at this stage, is the possibility of summary trial of indictable offences and trial on indictment of summary offences. The process adopted in choosing which course to follow is dealt with in Part III.[3] This part is concerned with offences which are *being tried* on indictment.

A. EXAMINING JUSTICES

Almost all trials on indictment start with a preliminary inquiry by a magistrates' court into the charge against the accused.[4]

The magistrates' court's jurisdiction to hold a preliminary inquiry into an indictable offence extends to any person who appears or is brought before it.[5] The accused "appears" in answer to a summons[6] or "is brought" after arrest with or without a warrant.[7] If the accused is before the court for summary trial of, or for a preliminary inquiry into, some other offence, the court may then hear an additional charge of an indictable offence against him when he comes before the court, and proceed with the preliminary inquiry into it. The inquiry may be by a single justice[8] and the maximum number of justices who may sit is seven.[9] If there is an even number and they disagree in even numbers, the proper course of action is to

[1] See p. 48.
[2] See p. 3.
[3] See pp. 292–299.
[4] See p. 144.
[5] Magistrates' Courts Act 1952, s. 2 (3)
[6] See p. 55.
[7] See pp. 57 and 62.
[8] Magistrates' Courts Act 1952, s. 4 (1).
[9] Justices of the Peace (Size and Chairmanship of the Bench) Rules 1964.

adjourn for a rehearing by the same or a different bench.[10] The hearing is usually in open court.[11]

The purpose of the preliminary inquiry is to eliminate charges which are not substantiated by a prima facie case. The procedure is described in detail in Chapter 6.[12]

B. The Crown Court

The Crown Court, which is part of the Supreme Court,[13] has exclusive jurisdiction over trials on indictment.[14] Unlike its predecessors —assizes and quarter sessions—it has jurisdiction over all offences committed in any place in England and Wales.[15] It is a single and indivisible court; one sitting or section cannot review or take over the decision of another section.[16]

1. Constitution

The jurisdiction and powers of the Crown Court are exercised by a High Court judge, a circuit judge, a recorder or a court consisting of one of these sitting with justices of the peace.[17] The Lord Chancellor may request a judge of the Court of Appeal to sit in the capacity of a High Court judge.[18] On all trials on indictment the court sits with a jury. Except where justices sit with the judge, all proceedings in the court are heard and disposed of by a single judge.[19]

Any judge of the High Court may sit in the Crown Court, though a judge of the Queen's Bench Division would be usual.

A circuit judge is a permanent judge of the Crown Court.[20] Appointment is by the Queen on the recommendation of the Lord Chancellor; a person is qualified for appointment if he has been a barrister for at least 10 years or a recorder for at least five years; the Lord Chancellor must be satisfied that the appointee's health is satisfactory. Circuit judges are also judges of the county court by virtue of their appointment.[21] A circuit judge vacates office at the end

---

[10] *R.* v. *Hertfordshire Justices, ex p. Larsen* [1926] 1 K.B. 191.

[11] Criminal Justice Act 1967, s. 6; see p. 94.

[12] See p. 93 *et seq.*

[13] Courts Act 1971, s. 1 (1).

[14] *Ibid.* s. 6 (1).

[15] *Ibid.* s. 4 (4) (*a*).

[16] *R.* v. *Slatter* [1975] 1 W.L.R. 1084; *R.* v. *Dudley Crown Court, ex p. Smith* (1973) 58 Cr. App. R. 184.

[17] *Ibid.* s. 4 (2).

[18] *Ibid.* s. 4 (3).

[19] *Ibid.* s. 4 (4).

[20] *Ibid.* s. 16.

[21] *Ibid.* s. 20 (1). Judges of the Court of Appeal and the High Court and recorders are also *ex officio* capable of sitting as judges of the county court: s. 20 (3).

of the year of service in which he reaches the age of 72, but the Lord Chancellor may authorise him to remain a judge until he is 75 if it is desirable in the public interest.[22] The Lord Chancellor may remove a circuit judge from office on the ground of incapacity or misbehaviour.[23]

A recorder is a part-time judge of the Crown Court. Appointment is made by the Queen on the recommendation of the Lord Chancellor; a person is qualified for appointment if he is a barrister or solicitor of at least 10 years' standing.[24] Because a recorder of at least five years' standing may be appointed as circuit judge,[25] a solicitor may become a full-time judge of the Supreme Court. A recorder is appointed for a specified term and the duration and frequency of the occasions on which he sits are specified on his appointment.[26] A recorder cannot continue in office after the end of the year of service in which he reaches the age of 72.[27] His term of office may be extended from time to time by the Lord Chancellor, but not beyond this age limit.[28] The Lord Chancellor may terminate a recorder's appointment on the grounds of incapacity, misbehaviour or failure to comply with the terms of his appointment.[29]

Both circuit judges and recorders may be requested by the Lord Chancellor to sit as High Court judges for hearing cases which should normally be heard by a High Court judge.[30] The Lord Chancellor may also appoint deputy High Court judges as a temporary measure to dispose of business in the High Court or the Crown Court.[31] Anyone qualified for appointment as a High Court judge [32] may be appointed as a deputy High Court judge, as may any person who has held office as a judge of the High Court or Court of Appeal.[33] The Lord Chancellor may also appoint a deputy circuit judge as a temporary measure to facilitate the disposal of Crown Court and county court business; the appointee must be qualified for appointment as a circuit judge or have held office as a judge of the Court of Appeal, the High Court or the county court before the Courts Act

[22] *Ibid.* s. 17 (1) and (2).
[23] *Ibid.* s. 17 (4).
[24] *Ibid.* s. 21 (1).
[25] See p. 86.
[26] *Ibid.* s. 21 (3).
[27] *Ibid.* s. 21 (5).
[28] *Ibid.* s. 21 (4).
[29] *Ibid.* s. 21 (6).
[30] *Ibid.* s. 23. See pp. 89 and 103.
[31] *i.e.* where a High Court judge must hear the case, see p. 89 *et seq.*
[32] Judicature Act 1925, s. 9.
[33] Courts Act 1971, s. 24 (1).

came into force.[34] A person asked to act as a temporary High Court judge does not acquire the status of a High Court judge but has all his powers and jurisdiction.[35]

The Crown Court consists of a High Court judge, circuit judge or recorder sitting with at least two (and not more than four) justices of the peace when dealing with certain parts of the Crown Court jurisdiction; they are required to sit when the court is exercising its appellate and sentencing jurisdiction from magistrates' courts[36] and they may be asked to sit on certain trials on indictment.[37] A justice from any commission or petty sessions area may sit in the Crown Court, as he is not disqualified on the ground that the proceedings are not related to his area.[38] He is not disqualified because he sat at the committal proceedings, though he is if the court is exercising its appellate or sentencing jurisdiction over proceedings in a magistrates' court of which he was a member.[39] There are no offences which must be tried on indictment by a court comprising justices, but any offences which are listed for trial by a circuit judge or recorder are suitable for allocation to such a court.[40]

When a judge sits with justices, the decision of the Crown Court may be a majority decision and if the members of the court are equally divided, the judge has a second and casting vote.[41] The justices participate in all matters except deciding questions of law and summing up to the jury.[42]

When the Crown Court sits in the City of London, it is known as the Central Criminal Court (popularly, the Old Bailey) and the Lord Mayor and Aldermen of the City, as *ex officio* justices, are entitled to sit at *all* proceedings arising in the City of London.[43] The composition of the court when the Crown Court sits for the purposes of appeal or sentence from the magistrates' court is described on p. 340.

---

[34] Courts Act 1971, s. 24 (2).

[35] *Ibid.* ss. 23 (3) and 24 (4).

[36] See pp. 330 and 340.

[37] See p. 90.

[38] *Ibid.* s. 5 (9).

[39] Crown Court Rules 1971, r. 5; see p. 341.

[40] See Classes 3 and 4, p. 90. Directions of the Lord Chief Justice of October 14, 1971, direction 13; the directions are made under the Courts Act 1971, ss. 4 (5) and 5 (3) and (4).

[41] Courts Act 1971, s. 5 (8). This is clearly not so important a factor in trials on indictment, where the issue to be decided is restricted to sentence, as it is on appeal from the magistrates' court. The judge may be outvoted: *R.* v. *Deary*, *The Times*, June 9, 1976.

[42] *R.* v. *Orpin* [1974] 3 W.L.R. 252.

[43] *Ibid.* s. 4 (7) and Justices of the Peace Act 1968, s. 1 (2); see p. 49.

2. Allocation of business

The country is divided for administrative purposes into six circuits[44]—Midland and Oxford, North-Eastern, Northern, South-Eastern, Wales and Chester, and Western. Each circuit has first-tier, second-tier and third-tier centres.

A first-tier centre is attended by High Court judges and deals with both civil and criminal business.[45] A second-tier centre hears only criminal business and is served by a High Court judge.[46] A third-tier centre hears only criminal business and is served by circuit judges and recorders only.[47] Circuit judges and recorders also serve at first- and second-tier centres.

A High Court judge is assigned to each circuit to have special responsibility for it. He is known as the " presiding judge."[48]

3. Jurisdiction

Offences tried on indictment are divided into four classes which are distinguished by the composition of the court trying them.[49]

Class 1

These offences can only be tried by a High Court judge:

(i) Offences for which the offender may be sentenced to death.[50]
(ii) Misprision of treason and treason felony.
(iii) Murder.
(iv) Genocide.
(v) An offence under the Official Secrets Act 1911, s. 1.
(vi) Incitement, attempt or conspiracy to commit any of the above offences.

Class 2

These offences must be tried by a High Court judge unless a particular case is released on the direction of the presiding judge to be tried by a circuit judge or recorder.[51]

---

[44] The allocation of places and circuits is subject to variation in accordance with the availability of court buildings. Facilities for sittings of the Crown Court are made, if necessary, for certain remote places, *e.g.* Penzance, Scarborough, Lampeter.

[45] *e.g.* Greater London and Norwich on the South-Eastern circuit.

[46] *e.g.* Chelmsford, Ipswich, Lewes, Maidstone, Reading and St. Albans on the South-Eastern circuit.

[47] *e.g.* Aylesbury, Bedford, Brighton, Bury St. Edmunds, Cambridge, Canterbury, Chichester and Guildford on the South-Eastern circuit.

[48] Directions of the Lord Chief Justice, direction 1.

[49] The Report of the Committee on the Distribution of Criminal Business between the Crown Court and the Magistrates' Courts (the James Committee: Cmnd. 6323) was published in 1975; it recommended the exclusion of certain offences, or offences lacking a certain gravity, from trial on indictment.

[50] See p. 223.

[51] *Ibid.* directions 1 and 12 (i); if the D.P.P. is prosecuting the presiding judge must obtain his views.

(i) Manslaughter.
(ii) Infanticide.
(iii) Child destruction.
(iv) Abortion.
(v) Rape.
(vi) Sexual intercourse with a girl under thirteen.
(vii) Incest with a girl under thirteen.
(viii) Sedition.
(ix) An offence under the Geneva Conventions Act 1957, s. 1 (the Conventions relate to the Red Cross, treatment of wounded and prisoners of war).
(x) Mutiny.
(xi) Piracy.[52]
(xii) Incitement, attempt or conspiracy to commit any of the above offences.

Class 3

All indictable offences other than those in Classes 1, 2 or 4 can be tried by a High Court judge, or by a circuit judge or recorder. Such offences must be listed by the officer responsible for listing for trial by a High Court judge, unless he considers that it should be listed for trial by a circuit judge or recorder.[53] He must consult the presiding judge or act in accordance with his directions, if choosing the latter course, and the same considerations apply to his choice as apply to justices committing the accused for trial by a High Court judge of a Class 4 offence.[54] Any offence in this class may be transferred to Class 4 on the direction of the presiding judge.[55] When allocated to a circuit judge or recorder, it may be tried by a court comprising justices of the peace.[56]

Class 4

These offences are triable by a High Court judge, circuit judge or recorder, but should normally be tried by a circuit judge or recorder.[57] They are also suitable for trial by a court comprising justices.[56] The Crown Court officer responsible for listing may list a Class 4 offence for trial by a High Court judge on the considerations to be applied by committing justices when making the same deci-

---

[52] Where not punishable by death; see Class 1, above.
[53] Directions of the Lord Chief Justice, direction 12 (ii).
[54] See p. 103.
[55] Directions of the Lord Chief Justice, direction 1 (4).
[56] *Ibid.* direction 13.
[57] *Ibid.* direction 12 (iii).

sion[58]; he must hear the views of the committing justice and consult the presiding judge or act in accordance with his directions.[57] Justices may commit an accused for trial of a Class 4 offence by a High Court judge. This is considered on p. 103

The following are Class 4 offences:

(i) All offences which may be tried on indictment or summarily.[59]

(ii) Conspiracy to commit such an offence.

(iii) Causing death by dangerous driving.[60]

(iv) Burglary.[61]

(v) Offences under the Forgery Act 1913, other than those which are triable summarily.

(vi) Conspiracy, attempt or incitement to commit offences under paragraphs (iii)–(v).

(vii) Conspiracy to commit an offence which is only triable summarily[62] or to do an act which is not a criminal offence.

C. The High Court

The powers of the High Court in criminal proceedings are purely ancillary[63]; they are exercised either by the Divisional Court of the Queen's Bench Division or by a High Court judge. As the High Court is held and exercises jurisdiction at any place in England and Wales,[64] application need not be made in London, but may be made at any place where a High Court judge or Divisional Court is.

The High Court's powers to issue prerogative orders and to grant bail have already been outlined[65]; a High Court judge's power to direct the preferment of an indictment and the Queen's Bench Divisional Court's appellate jurisdiction in connection with summary trials will be dealt with later.[66]

D. Courts-Martial

These are essentially outside the scope of this book, but as counsel is sometimes called upon to act for a defendant, it may be useful to know a few points of difference between proceedings before a court-martial and civilian proceedings.

---

58 See p. 103.
59 *i.e.* under the Magistrates' Courts Act 1952, ss. 18, 19 and 25; see pp. 292–298.
60 Road Traffic Act 1972, s. 1.
61 Theft Act 1968, s. 9, as restricted by the Magistrates' Courts Act 1952, Sched. 1, para. 11 (*c*).
62 See p. 292.
63 It has no power to try offences on indictment; Courts Act 1971, Sched. 11.
64 Courts Act 1971, s. 2 (1).
65 See pp. 43 and 78.
66 See pp. 144 and 349.

Courts-martial try military offences, over which they have exclusive jurisdiction, and non-military criminal offences committed by members of the armed forces. The members of a court-martial are judges of both law and fact and so sit without a jury. The rules of evidence are, however, the same as in civilian proceedings. The members of the court-martial are officers, one of whom is the president of the court, and a "judge-advocate." The judge-advocate does not act as a judge, but advises the court on law and procedure (like a magistrates' court clerk[67]) and sums up the evidence and the law (like a judge would do in civilian proceedings[68]). He takes no part in the deliberations of the other three members of the court.

The judgment of a court-martial does not bar proceedings in a civil court, though any sentence imposed must be taken into account, but a trial by a civil court precludes trial by court-martial for the same offence.[69] Courts-martial are inferior courts subject to the supervisory jurisdiction of the High Court.[70]

Appeal may be made to the Courts-Martial Appeal Court, which operates on similar principles to the Court of Appeal, Criminal Division,[71] but there is no appeal against sentence. The judges of the Court of Appeal and the Queen's Bench Division, their counterparts in Scotland and Northern Ireland and appointees of the Lord Chancellor sit in the Court. Leave of the Court must be obtained to appeal against conviction and the appellant must first have petitioned the appropriate minister to have his conviction quashed. Further appeal lies to the House of Lords with the leave of the Court or of the House of Lords.

---

[67] See p. 290.

[68] See p. 196.

[69] Army Act 1955, ss. 133, 134; Naval Discipline Act 1957, s. 129, as amended by the Armed Forces Act 1966, s. 35; Air Force Act 1955, ss. 133, 134. These Acts regulate the constitution, jurisdiction, and powers of, and the procedure before, courts-martial.

[70] See p. 43.

[71] See p. 260.

CHAPTER 6

COMMITTAL PROCEEDINGS

BY this stage the prosecution has prepared its case and is ready to put it before the examining justices who will inquire whether or not there is " such evidence, that if it be uncontradicted at the trial, a reasonably minded jury may convict upon it." [1] This provides a check to exclude frivolous and misconceived prosecutions for serious offences.

The proceedings may be an oral hearing or a gathering up of written evidence which may be passed on unread to the trial court under section 1 of the Criminal Justice Act 1967. The prosecution's function at committal is quite straightforward—to produce all its evidence. It may call further evidence later, but it must give notice of this to the accused.[2] The position of the defence is less clear-cut. The accused may avail himself of his right to give and call evidence, and so disclose his defence, in the hope of being discharged. As the magistrate's function is not to try the case, however, he will be inclined to leave any serious conflict of evidence for the jury to decide. Unless the accused can show that the prosecution's case is so weak that it does not disclose an issue worth trying, or that it is effectively a pack of lies, it is ill-judged to reveal his own defence, lay himself open to cross-examination and enable the prosecution to strengthen its case on the points of conflict. Even if he does succeed in demolishing the prosecution's case, he is not acquitted, *i.e.* if charged again he cannot plead *autrefois acquit.*[3]

This may seem to give the defence an unfair evidentiary advantage but this is greatly diminished by section 11 of the Criminal Justice Act 1967 which requires him to give particulars of alibi evidence to the prosecution before trial.[4]

A. COMMITTAL PROCEEDINGS—PRELIMINARY

Since the advent of written statements of evidence,[5] committal proceedings may take the following forms:

(*a*) the full oral hearing,[6] where the accused may seek to challenge

---

1 *Ex p. Bidwell* [1937] 1 K.B. 304 at p. 314.
2 See p. 114.
3 See p. 163.
4 See p. 112.
5 Criminal Justice Act 1967, s. 2.
6 See Section C, p. 97.

all or some of the items of the prosecution's evidence in the hope of having the charge dismissed;

(*b*) the oral form of committal proceedings, where the accused agrees to accept some or all of the evidence in the form of written statements. This might occur where there are several co-accused of whom one is unrepresented, or where the accused wishes to challenge one or two items of the prosecution evidence;

(*c*) the committal without consideration of the evidence provided by section 1 of the Criminal Justice Act 1967,[7] where the accused does not wish to challenge any of the evidence until trial.

However, it is only in the taking of the evidence that the traditional procedure described in paragraph (*a*) above differs from a section 1 committal. The procedure they have in common will be dealt with now and in Sections E–H on pp. 101–115.

The court

The court begins to act as examining justices as soon as the accused appears or is brought[8] before the court charged with an indictable offence.[9]

Publicity of proceedings

The examining justices must sit in open court unless an enactment provides expressly to the contrary or unless they consider that the ends of justice would not be served by their so sitting.[10] For instance, the prosecution may apply for proceedings under the Official Secrets Acts to be held in camera[11] and the court has a discretion to exclude the public when a child gives evidence.[12]

Reporting committal proceedings

The danger of committal proceedings being held in open court is that the prosecution's case may be given publicity before the accused comes to trial. Accordingly the Criminal Justice Act 1967 restricts press and broadcast reports of committal proceedings by making it

---

[7] See Section D, p. 100. [8] See p. 85.

[9] Criminal Justice Act 1967, s. 35; unless the court has already decided to try the offence summarily under the Magistrates' Courts Act 1952, s. 18, see p. 295.

[10] Criminal Justice Act 1967, s. 6.

[11] Official Secrets Act 1920, s. 8 (4).

[12] Children and Young Persons Act 1933, s. 37; see p. 153, and see also p. 98, footnote 46.

a summary offence (fine: £500) to publish reports in contravention of section 3.

A report may only contain a bare identification of the court, justices, parties, witnesses, counsel and solicitors, of the offences charged and of any decision made by the court in relation to committal for trial, remand, bail and legal aid.[13] The consent of the Attorney-General must be obtained to prosecute a newspaper company, etc. The individual reporter is not punishable.

A full report can be lawful if a defendant in the proceedings applies to the court for an order authorising publication. It is also lawful after all the persons accused have been either discharged or tried.[14]

The court also has power to order that a child who gives evidence should not be identified in any press report.[15]

Joint committal

The restrictive rules relating to joint trial [16] do not apply to committal proceedings. The question of whether or not two or more defendants can be tried together is decided when the evidence has been heard and when the indictment is drafted. If joint committal appears unsuitable from the evidence disclosed in the course of the proceedings, the magistrates' court may use its power of adjournment.[17]

One accused may be committed on several charges, but each charge is deemed to be a separate committal.[18]

Adjournment

As already mentioned,[19] the magistrates' court may adjourn before beginning to inquire into the offence and at any time during the hearing.[20] On adjournment it must remand [21] the accused and fix the

---

[13] The clerk of the court must put up a notice in a public part of the court-house stating the outcome of the proceedings, the accused and the offence charged: Criminal Justice Act 1967, s. 4.

[14] *Ibid.* s. 3 (3); if one accused is tried summarily under ss. 18–20 of the Magistrates' Courts Act 1952 (see pp. 295–298), a report of his trial may describe so much of the committal proceedings as took place before the court decided to try the accused summarily, even though other co-accused are still being committed for trial. See also *R.* v. *Blackpool Justices, ex p. Beaverbrook Newspapers Ltd.* [1972] 1 W.L.R. 95.

[15] See p. 112.

[16] See p. 137.

[17] See below.

[18] Administration of Justice (Miscellaneous Provisions) Act 1933, s. 2 (3); *R.* v. *Phillips and Quayle* [1939] 1 K.B. 63.

[19] See p. 67.

[20] Magistrates' Courts Act 1952, s. 6 (1).

[21] See p. 67.

time and place at which the hearing is to be resumed, and the time must be the same as the time fixed for the appearance of the accused in pursuance of the remand.[22]

The prosecution or the defence may request the adjournment; an exceptionally long adjournment may be overruled by the High Court on an order of mandamus [23] on the application of the aggrieved party.

The court *must* adjourn on the accused's application if the evidence discloses an offence different from the one alleged in the summons or warrant and if the variance is such as to have misled the accused.[24]

Presence of the parties

The accused must himself be present at the committal proceedings unless the justices consider that, because of his disorderly conduct before them, it is not practicable for the evidence to be given in his presence, or he cannot be present for reasons of health and is legally represented and has consented to the evidence being given in his absence.[25]

The prosecutor need not be present.[26] He may have to appear to give evidence, or he may conduct the committal proceedings himself if he wishes. The practice of policemen acting as advocates for prosecutions of anything other than minor offences has been strongly criticised.[27]

B. Written Statements of Evidence

A written statement of a witness's evidence is admissible to the same extent as that witness's oral evidence would be,[28] provided that

(*a*) the statement purports to be signed by the person who made it;

(*b*) the statement contains a declaration by the maker that it is true to the best of his knowledge and belief and that if the statement were tendered in evidence he knows he will be liable to prosecution if he knows it to be false or does not believe it to be true (*i.e.* under s. 89 of the Criminal Justice Act 1967);

---

22 Magistrates' Courts Act 1952, s. 6 (2).

23 See p. 46.

24 Magistrates' Courts Act 1952, s. 100 (2).

25 *Ibid.* s. 4 (3), as modified by the Criminal Justice Act 1972, s. 45; Magistrates' Courts (Amendment) Rules 1973 (S.I. No. 790).

26 Magistrates' Courts Act 1952, s. 99.

27 Royal Commission on the Police, Cmnd. 1728, para. 381; see also p. 18.

28 See p. 29. The process for getting the witness to attend, if he does not attend voluntarily, is the same as for witnesses who have not made written statements of their evidence, see p. 105.

(*c*) a copy of the statement has been given to the other parties to the proceedings by the party proposing to tender it in evidence before the statement is tendered in evidence; and

(*d*) none of the parties has objected to the statement before it is tendered in evidence.[29]

Thus a written statement can only be admissible if all the parties agree to it. However, the court may still require the maker of the statement to attend and give evidence, either if one of the parties applies or on its own initiative.[30] A party might wish to apply after the statement is read aloud in court, which it must be unless the committal is under section 1 or the court directs otherwise.[31]

Section 2 (3) provides further that

(*a*) a statement made by a person under 18 [32] years old must give his age [33];

(*b*) a statement made by a person who cannot read, must have been read over to him before he signs it by someone who declares that he has so read it; and

(*c*) if it refers to another document as an exhibit, a copy of that document, or information sufficient to identify it, must be given with the copy of the statement to the other parties to the proceedings.[34]

Any document or object referred to as an exhibit to a written statement is treated as though it were produced and identified by the maker of the statement in court.[35] Written statements made in Scotland or Northern Ireland are also admissible.[36] As to the subsequent use and admissibility as evidence of the statement after committal for trial, sec Section H, p. 106 below.

C. Oral Committal Proceedings

Although written statements of evidence may be accepted in all committal proceedings, this is not always the case and it is necessary

---

[29] Criminal Justice Act 1967, s. 2 (2).

[30] *Ibid.* s. 2 (4).

[31] *Ibid.* s. 2 (5).

[32] Family Law Reform Act 1969, s. 1.

[33] If the maker of the statement is under 14 years old, the declaration that the statement is true (s. 2 (2)) includes a declaration that the maker "understands the importance of telling the truth in it," not that he knows that he will be liable to prosecution: Criminal Justice Act 1967, s. 2 (3A), added by the Children and Young Persons Act 1969, Sched. 5.

[34] See s. 2 (2) (*c*), above.

[35] Criminal Justice Act 1967, s. 2 (6).

[36] Criminal Justice Act 1972, s. 46.

to consider how to secure the personal attendance of witnesses before outlining the full procedure for committal.

Witnesses

If a magistrate considers that a witness is likely to give material evidence but is unlikely to attend voluntarily, he may issue a summons addressed to the witness requiring him to attend court at the time and place appointed.[37] If he is satisfied by evidence on oath that the witness is unlikely to answer the summons, the magistrate may issue a warrant for the witness's arrest.[38] The High Court may set aside a witness summons or warrant on an application for certiorari,[39] or order its issue by mandamus if the magistrate refuses to issue a summons or warrant.[40]

The court may issue a warrant for the witness's arrest if he fails to attend in answer to a summons, provided the court is satisfied by evidence on oath that the witness is likely to give material evidence and that he has been duly served[41] with the summons and was offered a reasonable sum of money to cover his costs and expenses and provided that the court considers he had no just cause for his failure to attend.[42] The court may commit a recalcitrant witness to custody for up to seven days until he gives evidence or produces the thing required in evidence.[43]

When the accused is committed for trial, the court orders the witness to attend the court of trial.[44]

Procedure[45]

1. The prosecution calls its witnesses who give their evidence on oath. It need not call all its evidence if the evidence in fact called is sufficient to commit the accused.[46]

---

[37] Magistrates' Courts Act 1952, s. 77. The application for a summons may be made by writing to the clerk to the justices who will submit the application to the magistrate: Magistrates' Courts Rules 1968, r. 88. It need not be made on oath. *Cf.* summons to the accused p. 55.

[38] Magistrates' Courts Act 1952, s. 77 (2).

[39] See p. 45; *R.* v. *Hove Justices, ex p. Donne* [1967] 2 All E.R. 1253.

[40] See p. 46.

[41] It cannot be served by post: Magistrates' Courts Rules 1968, r. 82 (5).

[42] Magistrates' Courts Act 1952, s. 77 (3).

[43] *Ibid.* s. 77 (4). As to juvenile witnesses who cannot be imprisoned, see *R.* v. *Greenwich Justices, ex p. Carter* [1973] Crim.L.R. 444.

[44] See p. 106.

[45] Magistrates' Courts Rules 1968, r. 4.

[46] *R.* v. *Epping and Harlow Justices, ex p. Massaro* [1973] 1 Q.B. 433 (where the prosecution did not wish to subject a child to the ordeal of giving evidence twice). The prosecution must give notice of the evidence omitted to the accused; see p. 114.

2. The accused, his counsel or solicitor, may cross-examine each witness and the prosecutor may re-examine him.[47]

3. The whole of each witness's evidence is put into writing by the magistrates' clerk in the form of a " deposition," [48] which is read out to the witness in the presence of the accused and is then signed by the witness and authenticated by a certificate signed by the magistrate.[49]

4. When all the prosecution evidence has been either given orally or accepted in the form of written statements and read out to the court, the accused may submit that there is no case to answer, *i.e.* that the prosecution has not made out a prima facie case, and therefore the charge should be dismissed and the accused discharged. (If the court decides to issue a *conditional* witness order, it should now serve the order on the witness.[50])

5. If the charge is not dismissed, the court requires it to be written down, if that has not already been done, and read to the accused, and the court explains the meaning of it to him in ordinary language.

6. The court asks the accused if he wishes to say anything in answer to the charge. If he is not legally represented, it must explain to him that he need not say anything but if he does it will be written down and may be used in evidence at the trial, and it must tell him of his right to give evidence on oath and to call witnesses.

7. If the accused says anything, it is written down, read to him and signed by the magistrate and, if the accused wishes, he may also sign it himself.[51] This is sometimes known as a " magisterial confession."

8. The court warns him that he must give particulars of alibi evidence either to the court now or to the solicitor for the prosecution not later than seven days after the end of the committal proceedings.[52]

9. Whether or not the accused has made a statement, he must now be given the opportunity to give evidence himself on oath and to call witnesses. His counsel or solicitor may address the court before calling the evidence.

---

[47] As to the meaning of "cross-examine" and "re-examine," see pp. 183 and 188.

[48] See pp. 107–109.

[49] Magistrates' Courts Rules 1968, r. 4 (3). The deposition becomes an "exhibit": r. 4 (5). As to the evidence of children, see p. 111.

[50] Magistrates' Courts Rules 1968, r. 5 (1); Criminal Procedure (Attendance of Witnesses) Act 1965, s. 1 (2); see p. 106.

[51] Everything the accused says at committal should be treated in this way, so it need not be a statement in any formal sense. See also Magistrates' Courts (Forms) (Amendment) Rules 1974, Form 12.

[52] Magistrates' Courts Rules 1968, r. 4 (9), applying Criminal Justice Act 1967, s. 11; see p. 112.

10. The accused and his witnesses may be cross-examined and re-examined and their evidence, except evidence only as to his character, is written down and made into depositions.[53]

11. The accused's counsel or solicitor may, with the leave of the court, address the court for a second time. If he intends to do so, the prosecution is entitled to address the court immediately before the defence's second address.

12. If the court is of the opinion, *on consideration of the evidence* and of any statement made by the accused, that there is sufficient evidence to put the accused on trial before a jury, it *must* commit him for trial. If it is not of that opinion, it *must* discharge the accused in respect of that offence.[54] "Discharge" means that the charge is dismissed, the accused is set free and his costs may be ordered to be paid out of central funds or by the prosecutor.[55]

D. Section 1 Committal

Section 1 of the Criminal Justice Act 1967 provides for committal for trial without consideration of the evidence, which procedure is generally known as "section 1 committal." This is applicable only where all the evidence, for both prosecution and defence, is in the form of written statements tendered to the court under section 2 and, further, where the accused, or all of them, if more than one, is represented by counsel or a solicitor. The court cannot proceed under section 1 if the accused, or one of them, asks the court to consider a submission that there is no case to answer[56] (*i.e.* it must then hold full committal proceedings, though it may still accept the evidence in the form of written statements).

Procedure[57]

1. The magistrates' court causes the charge to be written down and read to the accused and then ascertains from the accused whether he wishes

(*a*) to object to any of the prosecution's written statements of evidence;

---

[53] See p. 107.

[54] Magistrates' Courts Act 1952, s. 7 (1). As to committal, see also Section F, p. 103.

[55] Costs in Criminal Cases Act 1973, ss. 1 (2) and 12 (1) and (3). S. 2 (4) enables the court to order the prosecutor to pay defence costs if it is of the opinion that the charge was not made in good faith and it dismisses the charge because of insufficient evidence. S. 12 covers cases where the proceedings are discontinued, *e.g.* by withdrawal of the charge, rather than dismissed.

[56] See p. 99, para. 4.

[57] Magistrates' Courts Rules 1968, r. 3.

(*b*) to give evidence himself or call witnesses (*i.e.* not by written statement); or

(*c*) to submit that there is no case to answer.

2. If the accused wishes to do none of these things, the court receives the written statements of evidence tendered by the prosecution. If he wishes to do one of them, the proceedings must continue as oral proceedings.[58]

3. The court tells the accused of his duty to give details of any alibi he intends to rely on.[59]

4. The court then commits the accused for trial *without considering the contents* of the written statements.[60] Section 7 (1) of the Magistrates' Courts Act 1952[61] does not apply, but the accused is committed in custody or on bail under secton 7 (2) in the usual manner.

E. Time and Place of Trial

1. Place

The place of trial by the Crown Court is selected by the magistrates' court which commits the accused. It must have regard to the following factors:

(*a*) the convenience of the defence, prosecution and witnesses.[62]

(*b*) the expediting of the trial,[62] and

(*c*) the location or locations of the Crown Court designated by the presiding judge[63] as the location or locations to which cases should normally be committed from the petty sessions area of the relevant magistrates' court.[64]

The Crown Court may itself direct that the accused be tried at a different place from the place selected by the magistrates' court (or from a place previously directed by the Crown Court.)[65]

If the accused or the prosecutor is dissatisfied with the place of trial selected by the magistrates' court or Crown Court, he may apply to the court for a direction varying the place of trial. Such an application must be made in open court to a High Court judge.[66]

---

[58] *i.e.* under r. 4; see pp. 97–100.

[59] See pp. 112–114.

[60] A s. 1 committal is not a nullity even if the statements disclose no case at all against an accused, provided the basic conditions are complied with: *R.* v. *Brooker* (1976) 120 S.J. 250.

[61] See p. 100.

[62] These two considerations are prescribed by the Courts Act 1971, s. 7 (1).

[63] See p. 89.

[64] This was specified by the Lord Chief Justice (Directions of October 14, 1971, direction 3) under the Courts Act 1971, s. 7 (1).

[65] *Ibid.* s. 7 (2). The appropriate officer of the Crown Court may make such a direction: s. 7 (5).

[66] *Ibid.* s. 7 (3).

These powers to vary the place of trial would be particularly useful if the court or the parties desired the trial to take place in London at the Old Bailey to avoid local prejudice or because witnesses need to be called from different parts of the country.

2. Time

The magistrates' court should commit the accused so that his trial does not begin either

(*a*) before the expiration of 14 days, or

(*b*) later than the expiration of eight weeks [67]

from the date of his committal.[68] The trial is deemed to begin when the accused is arraigned.[69] The accused may, however, be committed for trial in less than 14 days if both he and the prosecution consent, and he may be committed for trial later than eight weeks from committal if the Crown Court orders otherwise. Such an order must be made by a judge of the court, though not necessarily by a High Court judge.[70] The average waiting time after committal was 9·9 weeks in 1975 (10·3 in 1974); 56 per cent. waited for less than eight weeks (59 per cent. in 1974) and 90 per cent. waited less than 20 weeks (89 per cent. in 1974).[71]

3. Trial by a High Court judge

As already mentioned,[72] Class 1 offences must be tried by a High Court judge and Class 2 offences must be so tried unless the presiding judge has released a particular case for trial by circuit judge or recorder. If the offence in respect of which the accused is committed falls into Class 3, the magistrates' court should commit him to the most convenient Crown Court where a High Court judge regularly sits.[73] If the accused is committed in respect of more than one offence, and one or more of the offences falls into Classes 1, 2 or 3, he must be committed to a place where a High Court judge sits in respect of all of them.[74] The officer of the Crown Court responsible for listing may vary the order made by the committing justices in respect of a Class 3 offence.[75]

---

[67] Crown Court Rules 1971, r. 19, made under the Courts Act 1971, s. 7 (4) (i). The maximum limit is directory only, not mandatory: *R.* v. *Urbanowski* [1976] 1 W.L.R. 455.

[68] Courts Act 1971, s. 7 (4) (*a*) and (*b*).

[69] *Ibid.* s. 7 (4) (ii); as to arraignment, see p. 154.

[70] *Ibid.* s. 7 (5).

[71] Reply of the Attorney-General in the House of Commons on February 17, 1976.

[72] See p. 89.

[73] Directions of the Lord Chief Justice, direction 2 (i); trial of Class 3 offences must therefore be a first- or second-tier centre (see p. 89).

[74] *Ibid.* direction 4.

[75] See *ibid.* direction 12 (ii), p. 90.

If the offence falls into Class 4, the magistrates' court must specify the most convenient Crown Court, whether or not a High Court judge regularly sits there. The magistrates' court has power, however, to commit an accused for trial of a Class 4 offence by a High Court judge if the justices are of the view that he should be so tried.[76] The considerations which should influence the justices in committing an accused for trial of a Class 4 offence by a High Court judge are:

(i) that the case involves death or serious risk to life (excluding cases of dangerous driving having no aggravating features);
(ii) that widespread public concern is involved;
(iii) that the case involves violence of a serious nature;
(iv) that the offence involves dishonesty in respect of a substantial sum of money;
(v) that the accused holds a public position or is a professional or other person owing a duty to the public;
(vi) that the circumstances are of unusual gravity in some respect other than those indicated above;
(vii) that a novel or difficult issue of law is likely to be involved, or a prosecution for the offence is rare or novel.[77]

The officer of the Crown Court responsible for listing may list a Class 4 offence for trial by a High Court judge although it has been committed for trial by a circuit judge or recorder.[78]

In all cases where a probation order, care order, community service order or order for conditional discharge has been made or a suspended sentence has been passed by a High Court judge and the offender is committed to or brought before the Crown Court, his case should be listed for hearing by a High Court judge. The officer responsible for listing may, however, list the case for trial by a circuit judge or recorder, provided he consults the presiding judge or acts in accordance with his directions.[79]

F. Committal for Trial

Changing the charge

If the evidence called does not reveal a case against the accused for the offence originally charged but it does reveal another offence,

---

[76] Directions of the Lord Chief Justice, direction 2 (ii).
[77] *Ibid.* direction 2.
[78] See *ibid.* direction 12 (iii), p. 90.
[79] *Ibid.* direction 12 (iv) (v); this might occur where the offender is committed for trial of a subsequent offence, or where the offender is committed to the Crown Court to be dealt with or sentenced (see pp. 330–339).

the court may substitute the new charge; or it may add a new charge for an offence which is revealed in any examination or deposition before a justice, provided the new charge is one that can be lawfully joined in the same indictment.[80] The court puts the charge in writing, reads and explains it to the accused as with the original charge [81] and commits him for trial upon it. The offence to be charged is only fixed finally when enshrined in the indictment, which is drawn up on the evidence disclosed at the committal proceedings. If the evidence turns out to disclose an offence different from the one charged in the information, the court must adjourn if the accused has been misled.[82] The prosecution may adduce additional evidence at the trial provided it does not add to the charges in the indictment and provided notice is given to the accused.[83]

Committal on bail or in custody

When the court is satisfied that the accused should be committed for trial, it may grant him bail or commit him in custody.

The same presumption in favour of bail, and the same principles, apply to committal for trial as to remand.[84] If the accused is not legally represented and bail is withheld or offered on unacceptable terms, the court must tell the accused of his right to apply to the Crown Court or to the High Court.[85] If bail is granted, the accused is under a duty to appear at the Crown Court on the specified date and the sureties' recognisances, if any, extend to the same obligation.

If the court is satisfied that the accused should not be granted bail, it may commit him in custody. The magistrate issues a warrant of commitment, similar to a warrant of arrest, addressed to the constables of the area or a named person and to the governor of the prison or other place where the accused will be kept, directing the arrest of the accused, if necessary, his conveyance to the prison and his detention there until his delivery to a specified court.[86]

Witnesses

As soon as is practicable after the committal of the accused for trial, the court orders witnesses to attend the trial, see Section G, p. 105 below.

---

[80] See pp. 133–137; see also *R.* v. *Nisbet*, p. 143.

[81] Administration of Justice Act 1933, s. 2 (2), and Magistrates' Courts Rules 1968, r. 4 (12).

[82] Magistrates' Courts Act 1952, s. 100 (2), see p. 304.

[83] See p. 114.

[84] See pp. 73–78.

[85] Bail Act 1976, s. 5 (6).

[86] Magistrates' Courts Rules 1968, rr. 77 and 80. The warrant may be endorsed with a direction for bail; for the form of the warrant, see Magistrates' Courts (Forms) (Amendment) Rules 1974, Form 13.

Transmission of depositions, documents and exhibits

The clerk of the magistrates' court which commits the accused for trial sends the following documents, etc., as soon as possible to the proper officer of the court of trial (or to the Director of Public Prosecutions, if necessary):[87]

(*a*) the information, if in writing;

(*b*) the depositions and written statements with the certificate authenticating them and any formal admissions made;[88]

(*c*) all statements made by the accused before the magistrates;

(*d*) a list of the witnesses subject to witness orders;

(*e*) the recognisance of any surety, if bail is granted;

(*f*) a list of exhibits;

(*g*) the accused's particulars of alibi evidence, if any;[89]

(*h*) a statement that it was a section 1 committal, if it was;

(*i*) any order made authorising full press reporting;

(*j*) a certificate of the costs of the prosecution.[90]

The magistrate then issues a certificate of the committal to the Crown Court.[91] The officer of the trial court can have the indictment drawn up.[92]

If a conditional witness order was made, that witness's statement and exhibits, if any, are retained by the clerk and are only sent to the trial court if a notice to attend is sent to the witness.[93]

Information given to the accused

The accused may apply to the person who has custody of the various documents listed above for copies of the depositions, the list of witnesses and the information, if it is in writing.[94]

G. Witnesses

The admissibility of a witness's evidence has been considered in Chapter 3.[95] Statements of children are considered in Section H below.[96]

The provisions for compelling a witness to attend the trial if he

---

[87] Prosecution of Offences Act 1879, s. 5.
[88] See p. 112; see also Home Office Circular No. 116/1976.
[89] See p. 112.
[90] Magistrates' Courts Rules 1968, r. 10.
[91] See Magistrates' Courts (Forms) (Amendment) Rules 1974, Form 11.
[92] See p. 145.
[93] See Section G, below.
[94] Magistrates' Courts Rules 1968, r. 11.
[95] See pp. 29–34.
[96] See p. 111.

has given oral evidence at the committal proceedings apply also if he has sent in a written statement of his evidence.[97] The witness must in any event be given notice by the clerk of the court as to when and where to attend.[98]

Witness orders

The magistrates' court acting as examining justice makes an order in respect of every witness examined during the committal proceedings, except the accused and witnesses to his character only, requiring the witness to give evidence before the court at which the accused is to be tried.[99] Disobedience is punishable as a contempt of court by the court of trial.[1]

Conditional witness orders

A witness order may be conditional, *i.e.* the witness need only attend if given notice to do so, if his evidence is unlikely to be disputed or required.[2] The court may make it conditional in the first place or direct that a full order be made conditional, and it must consider any representation of the accused or the prosecutor before making a conditional witness order. It must inform the accused of his right to require the attendance of a witness by means of a conditional order and how he can enforce the attendance.[3]

Witness summons

The court of trial or the High Court may issue a witness summons to a witness to attend court either to testify or to bring something required in evidence to the court.[4] A High Court judge may issue a warrant for the arrest of a witness ordered or summoned to attend if he is satisfied by evidence on oath that the witness is unlikely to attend.[5]

H. Other Forms of Evidence

Although general consideration of the rules of evidence is outside the scope of this book, it is necessary to know how the various forms

---

[97] Criminal Justice Act 1967, s. 2 (10).

[98] Magistrates' Courts Rules 1968. r. 5; Magistrates' Courts (Forms) (Amendment) Rules 1974, Form 17.

[99] Criminal Procedure (Attendance of Witnesses) Act 1965, s. 1 (1).

[1] Criminal Procedure (Attendance of Witnesses) Act 1965, s. 3 (maximum punishment: three months or a fine); as to contempt generally, see p. 392.

[2] *Ibid.* s. 1 (2).

[3] *Ibid.* s. 1 (3). Attendance can be compelled by notifying the clerk of the magistrates' court or of the court of trial who will serve the requisite notice: Magistrates' Courts Rules 1968, r. 6.

[4] Criminal Procedure (Attendance of Witnesses) Act 1965, s. 2; the witness may apply to the court issuing the summons to annul it if he cannot give material evidence.

[5] *Ibid.* s. 4.

of evidence arising out of committal proceedings are taken and rendered admissible—depositions, written statements (whether under s. 2 of the Criminal Justice Act 1967 or made by children), formal admissions and alibi evidence. We will also consider prosecution evidence which emerges after the accused is committed for trial, and evidence which is known to the prosecution but is in the accused's favour.

Depositions

The general rule is that evidence in committal proceedings must be given on oath,[6] unless an exception is expressly made by enactment, the most important of which is, of course, section 2 of the Criminal Justice Act 1967.[7] As already mentioned, all the evidence, except evidence only as to the accused's character, is written down by the clerk to the examining justices in the form of a deposition, which is signed by the witness and certified by the examining justice.[8] Further, the accused must be present throughout and have the opportunity to cross-examine.

If there is any deviation from these requirements, not only the committal but also the subsequent indictment and trial will be null and void. For instance, where typed proofs of the witnesses' evidence were given to the magistrate and the clerk, but not to the accused, and the witness signed them, it was held that the proceedings were so irregular that no indictment could properly be preferred against the accused.[9] Again, where depositions had been taken in respect of one co-accused who was arrested later so that he could not cross-examine the witnesses, the committal was held to be a nullity.[10] On the other hand, depositions representing evidence which was elicited by leading questions [11] were held not to vitiate the committal [12]; and the same has been held to apply to evidence of an incompetent witness at committal.[13]

The signature of the justice is sufficient if he signs a certificate authenticating each batch of depositions taken, *e.g.* at one sitting.[14]

Provided the deposition was properly taken and the accused had

---

[6] Magistrates' Courts Act 1952, s. 78.
[7] Also, the written statement of the accused.
[8] See p. 99.
[9] *R.* v. *Gee* (1936) 25 Cr.App.R. 198; see Administration of Justice (Miscellaneous Provisions) Act 1933, s. 2, p. 144.
[10] *R.* v. *Phillips and Quayle* [1939] 1 K.B. 63.
[11] See p. 182.
[12] *R.* v. *Walker* [1950] 34 Cr.App.R. 199.
[13] *Ex p. Brunson* [1953] 1 Q.B. 503.
[14] Criminal Justice Act 1967, s. 7; *R.* v. *Edgar* (1958) 42 Cr.App.R. 192.

an opportunity to cross-examine the witness, the deposition is admissible as evidence at the trial in the following circumstances:

(*a*) when a witness appears in person at the trial, his deposition may be used to show a material variance between the evidence he gave at committal and the evidence he is giving now [15];

(*b*) when a witness is made subject to a conditional witness order,[16] his deposition may be used as evidence without further proof as to its contents [17];

(*c*) when a witness is proved on oath by a credible witness to be dead or insane, his deposition may be admitted as evidence without further proof [18];

(*d*) the same applies to a witness who is ill.[19] The judge must be satisfied that he is not reasonably fit to travel to attend court through illness, which includes pregnancy and the effects of childbirth [20];

(*e*) the deposition may be read without further proof if the witness is being kept out of the way by the accused or on his behalf.[21]

Further conditions are:

(*a*) that the offence charged in the indictment is substantially the same as the one with which the accused was charged before the magistrates' court, again to guarantee that the accused has been able to cross-examine on all points [22]; *e.g.* charged with robbery with violence—victim died—trial for murder [23]; or committal for obtaining by false pretences—trial for uttering a forged promissory note [24];

(*b*) that it is proved at trial by a certificate of the examining justice or his clerk, or by the oath of a credible witness, that the deposition was taken in the presence of the accused who had an opportunity to cross-examine the witness [25];

(*c*) that the deposition purports to be signed by the justice before whom it purports to have been taken.[26]

---

15 *R.* v. *Oldroyd* (1805) R. & R. 88.

16 See p. 106.

17 Criminal Justice Act 1925, s. 13 (3) (*a*), as amended by the Criminal Procedure (Attendance of Witnesses) Act 1965, Sched. 2, Part. 1.

18 Criminal Justice Act 1925, s. 13 (3) (*a*).

19 *R.* v. *Linley* [1959] Crim.L.R. 123 (where the judge used his discretion not to admit the deposition of the principal prosecution witness).

20 Criminal Justice Act 1925, s. 13 (3) (*a*), and see *R.* v. *Stephenson* (1862) 9 Cox 156.

21 *Ibid.* s. 13 (3) (*a*). The accused and his agent commit a common law offence and contempt of court, see p. 392.

22 *Ibid.* s. 13 (3).

23 *R.* v. *Abbatto and Healey* [1955] Crim. L.R. 645.

24 *R.* v. *Williams* (1871) 12 Cox 101.

25 Criminal Justice Act 1925, s. 13 (3) (*b*).

26 *Ibid.* s. 13 (3) (*c*).

The deposition cannot be read out as evidence if

(*a*) the certificate or signature required as above is proved in fact not to be the certificate or signature of the examining justice in question [27]; or

(*b*) that the witness, whose deposition it is proposed to admit as evidence, was subject to a conditional witness order and has been given notice to attend.[28]

Depositions taken before a coroner [29] are only admissible if the accused was present at the inquest and had full power to cross-examine, if the evidence contained in them was given on oath and if they are signed by the coroner and the witness.[30]

Depositions not taken in court

The dangerously ill

Section 41 of the Magistrates' Courts Act 1952 enables a deposition to be taken out of court if the examining justice is satisfied that a person who is able and willing to give material information as to an indictable offence or as to a person accused, is dangerously ill and unlikely to recover, and it is not practicable for the examining justices to take evidence orally in court. A qualified medical practitioner must give evidence as to the state of health of the sick person. The justice takes it down in writing and it must be given on oath.

The admissibility of the deposition so taken is, however, limited by the application of section 6 of the Criminal Law Amendment Act 1867 [31] which provides that it must be proved to the satisfaction of the court that the party (prosecutor or defendant) against whom the sick witness's evidence is given was given by notice a full opportunity to cross-examine the witness.

Children and young persons

Section 42 of the Children and Young Persons Act 1933 makes a very similar provision for taking the evidence of sick children. However, the section only applies to certain offences [32] and it is only admissible without further proof as evidence *against* the accused if he was given an opportunity to cross-examine.[33]

---

[27] Criminal Justice Act 1925, s. 13 (3), proviso (i).

[28] *Ibid.* s. 13 (3), proviso (ii), see p. 106.

[29] See p. 38.

[30] Coroners Act 1887, s. 4.

[31] As amended by Magistrates' Courts Act 1952, s. 131 and Sched. 5.

[32] Specified in the Children and Young Persons Act 1933, Sched. 1 (they include homicide, sexual offences and assaults).

[33] *i.e.* evidence for the defence can be taken in this way although the prosecutor did not have a chance to cross-examine: *ibid.* s. 43.

Evidence taken abroad

Depositions taken out of England and Wales are not admissible in substitution for the oral statement of the deponent except under rare statutory exceptions, the principal one being section 691 of the Merchant Shipping Act 1894. The conditions of admissibility are that the deposition was taken before a magistrate or consul and that the witness cannot be found in the place where the accused is being tried.[34]

Written statements—Criminal Justice Act 1967

The requirements for a written statement to be valid for the purposes of committal under section 2 [35] have already been considered. By section 2 (7), the provisions of section 13 (3) of the Criminal Justice Act 1925 apply to written statements as they apply to depositions, as far as admissibility at trial without further proof is concerned, but section 13 (3) (*b*) does not apply (signature of justice, swearing of oath, opportunity to cross-examine and taking in the presence of the accused).

Section 9 of the 1967 Act provides further that, in criminal proceedings other than the committal, the statement shall be admissible to the same extent as the witness's oral evidence would be.[36] Its admissibility in evidence is subject to subsections (2) and (3) which are almost identical to subsections (2) and (3)[37] of section 2, with the exception that, whereas section 2 requires a copy of the statement to be *given* to all the other parties to the proceedings before it is tendered in evidence, section 9 requires a copy to be *served* before the hearing; however, the parties may at any time before or during the hearing agree to accept the written statement.[38]

At the hearing the party tendering the statement in evidence may call the witness to give evidence in person and the court may do so on its own motion or on the application of a party to the proceedings.[39] Any statement accepted in evidence under section 9 must be

---

[34] See also Evidence (Proceedings in other Jurisdictions) Act 1975.

[35] See p. 96.

[36] Any parts of the statement which are prejudicial or inadmissible should be edited out; if anything so omitted is material, notice of it should be given to the defence: Practice Direction [1969] 3 All E.R. 1003. Written statements made in Scotland or Northern Ireland are also admissible under s. 46 of the Criminal Justice Act 1972.

[37] See p. 97.

[38] Criminal Justice Act 1967, s. 9 (2) proviso. Service is effected by personal delivery, sending by registered post or recorded delivery to or by leaving it at the last-known address of the accused or his solicitor: *ibid.* s. 9 (8).

[39] *Ibid.* s. 9 (4); the "court" is the High Court judge, circuit judge or recorder, sitting alone: *ibid.* s. 9 (5), as amended by the Courts Act 1971, Sched. 8.

read aloud in court, unless the court otherwise directs, and any part not read out must be verbally described.[40]

If a magistrates' court decides to try the accused summarily, having begun the proceedings as examining justices,[41] the written statement is not sufficient evidence and the witness must be called.[42]

Written statements—children

If a "child of tender years" is called as a witness in proceedings for any offence and the court is of the opinion that he is of sufficient intelligence to understand the duty of speaking the truth, although he does not understand the nature of an oath, his unsworn evidence may be taken at the committal proceedings in the same way as sworn evidence would be,[43] and, when it is written down, it is deemed to be a deposition.[44]

However, a child *must not* be called for the prosecution in committal proceedings for a sexual offence except in specified circumstances. Instead a statement made by him or taken from him in writing is admissible to the same extent as his oral evidence would be.[45] The excepted circumstances are that the defence objects, the prosecution requires the child's attendance to establish identity, the court is satisfied that it has been impossible to procure a written statement, or the inquiry takes place after the court has discontinued summary trial[46] and the child has given evidence at the trial.[47]

If the court proceeds to try the accused summarily having started the inquiry as examining justices,[47] the child's written statement is not enough, *i.e.* the child must be called. A child's unsworn evidence given for the prosecution must be corroborated by some other material evidence in support of it.[48]

The Children and Young Persons Acts also protect juvenile witnesses by enabling the court to direct that all persons leave the court who are not court officers, parties or their legal representatives, while the child gives evidence as to an offence against "decency or

---

[40] Criminal Justice Act 1967, s. 9 (6).
[41] *i.e.* under Magistrates' Courts Act 1952, s. 19; see p. 297.
[42] Criminal Justice Act 1967, s. 2 (9).
[43] *i.e.* under Magistrates' Courts Rules 1968, r. 4; see pp. 98–100.
[44] Children and Young Persons Act 1933, s. 38.
[45] Children and Young Persons Act 1963, s. 27 (1) (*i.e.* the magistrate must be satisfied that the child understands the duty to speak the truth).
[46] *i.e.* under Magistrates' Courts Act 1952, ss. 18 or 25; see pp. 292 *et seq.*
[47] Children and Young Persons Act 1963, s. 27 (2).
[48] Children and Young Persons Act 1933, s. 38 (1) proviso.

morality." [49] The court may also direct that no newspaper report or picture shall be published naming or identifying a child witness.[50]

Formal admissions

The need to call undisputed evidence is further removed by formal admissions whereby either prosecutor or defendant (or their legal representatives) may admit any fact of which oral evidence may be given in any criminal proceedings. Such an admission is conclusive evidence of the fact admitted,[51] not only at the proceedings at which it is made, but also in any subsequent criminal proceedings relating to the matter, including appeal and retrial,[52] but it may be withdrawn at any stage with the leave of the court.[53] The admission may be made before or at the proceedings but if it is not made in court, it must be made in writing. If made in writing by an individual it must be signed by the maker; if on behalf of a defendant, it must be signed by his counsel or solicitor; if made before trial by a defendant, it must be approved by his counsel or solicitor, before or at the proceedings, at the time of making it or subsequently. If the maker is a corporation it must be signed by a director, manager, secretary, clerk or other officer of the corporation.[54]

Alibi evidence

"Alibi evidence" is evidence tending to show that, by reason of the presence of the defendant at a particular place or in a particular area at a particular time [55] he was not, or was not likely to have been, at the place where the offence is alleged to have been committed at the time of its alleged commission.[56] This provision includes alibi evidence given only by the accused.[57]

By virtue of section 11 (1) of the Criminal Justice Act 1967, the accused will not be able to adduce evidence in support of an alibi at his trial on indictment without the leave of the court unless he gives notice of the particulars of the alibi within seven days from the end of the committal proceedings. He gives the notice to the magi-

---

[49] Children and Young Persons Act 1933, s. 37.

[50] *Ibid.* s. 39, as amended by the Children and Young Persons Act 1963, s. 64 and Sched. 5.

[51] Criminal Justice Act 1967, s. 10 (1).

[52] *Ibid.* s. 10 (3).

[53] *Ibid.* s. 10 (4).

[54] *Ibid.* s. 10 (2).

[55] Thus the section does not apply to evidence adduced by the accused to a charge of an offence of a continuing nature committed in an area such as "the city of Cardiff": *R.* v. *Hassan* [1970] 1 Q.B. 423.

[56] Criminal Justice Act 1967, s. 11 (8).

[57] *R.* v. *Jackson and Robertson* [1973] Crim. L.R. 356.

strates' court during or at the end of the committal proceedings or thereafter in writing to the solicitor for the prosecutor.[58] Notice given by the accused's solicitor is deemed to be notice authorised by the accused.[59]

The court *must* give leave to the accused to call and give alibi evidence where he has not given notice if he was not warned by the magistrates' court of his duty to give notice in accordance with rule 3 or rule 4 of the Magistrates' Courts Rules 1968.[60] Further, it was held to be "indefensible" to refuse to admit alibi evidence of an accused who was unrepresented until two days before trial and who failed to give particulars at the proper time.[61] Other conditions for admitting the evidence of a witness as to the alibi are:

(*a*) that the notice contained the witness's name and address or other means of finding him;

(*b*) that, if it did not contain the name and address, the court is satisfied the accused took and continued to take all reasonable steps to secure the name and address of the witness;

(*c*) that, if the notice did not contain the name and address, the accused gave notice of any other information which might have helped to find the witness, as soon as he received it; and

(*d*) that, after the prosecutor told him that the witness could not be traced, the accused gave notice of any information in his possession as soon as he received it.[62]

Evidence tendered to disprove an alibi may, subject to the direction of the court, be given before or after the evidence given in support of the alibi.[63]

It will be noticed from the definition that the accused need only give notice of evidence which relates to the time when the offence was alleged to have been committed. In *R.* v. *Lewis* [64] the accused was charged with receiving stolen property on a Wednesday and in the course of the trial it was alleged that he was the driver of a car used to distribute the stolen goods on the following Friday. Evidence he wished to call about his movements on the Friday was excluded under section 11 of the Criminal Justice Act 1967. His conviction

---

[58] *Ibid.* s. 11 (6).

[59] *Ibid.* s. 11 (5). Service is effected by delivering it to, leaving it at the office of or sending it by registered post or recorded delivery to the prosecutor's solicitor at his office: *ibid.* s. 11 (7).

[60] *Ibid.* s. 11 (3); see pp. 99 and 101.

[61] *R.* v. *Sullivan* [1971] 1 Q.B. 253.

[62] Criminal Justice Act 1967, s. 11 (2).

[63] *Ibid.* s. 11 (4).

[64] [1969] 2 Q.B. 1.

was quashed and it was held that the need for notice must be ascertained from the charge and evidence at the committal proceedings.

Notice of additional evidence

The accused may already have been given copies of the written statements,[65] or he may ask for copies of the depositions.[66] If the prosecutor wishes to introduce any further evidence at the trial which is not contained in the depositions or statements, he may do so provided he first gives notice to the accused. He must also send a copy of the additional evidence he intends to call to the accused and to the court. There is no statutory provision compelling this but it is such a firmly established rule of practice that, although additional evidence called without giving notice is not inadmissible,[67] the court will almost certainly adjourn the case, or, if that is inconvenient, may refuse to admit it in the exercise of its general discretion to exclude evidence which may be unfair to the accused.[68] The purpose of adjourning is to give the defence time to find evidence to rebut the new evidence.[69] In *R.* v. *Dickson* [70] the Court of Appeal quashed a conviction on the ground that it was unsafe and unsatisfactory [71] because the accused had not been given sufficient time to call an alibi witness on new counts in the indictment. In *R.* v. *Hawkins* [72] the court required proof that notice had been given before admitting the new evidence.

Prosecution to make material evidence available to accused

Where the prosecution has discovered evidence which tends to show that the accused is innocent or which is otherwise helpful to the accused,[73] and therefore does not intend to call it, the prosecutor, his counsel or solicitor, must make it available to the defence.[74] It is not certain whether the duty extends to furnishing the accused with a copy of a witness's statement,[75] but the convictions of several co-

---

[65] Criminal Justice Act 1967, s. 2 (2) (*c*), see p. 97.

[66] Magistrates' Courts Rules 1968, r. 11, see p. 105. Also, he has been present throughout the committal proceedings, see p. 96.

[67] *R.* v. *Ward* (1848) 2 C. & K. 759, and *R.* v. *Curtis*, *ibid.* 763.

[68] See p. 23.

[69] *R.* v. *Flannigan* (1884) 15 Cox 403 at p. 406.

[70] [1969] 1 W.L.R. 4095.

[71] See p. 267.

[72] (1896) Q.B.D. unreported, noted in Archbold, para. 446.

[73] *e.g.* evidence showing that a prosecution witness is of bad character, or a previous inconsistent statement which the accused might use in cross-examination, see pp. 185 and 187.

[74] *Dallison* v. *Caffery* [1965] 1 Q.B. 348 at pp. 369 and 376.

[75] See dictum of Lord Denning M.R. in *Dallison* v. *Caffery*, above, at p. 369, but Diplock L.J. at p. 376, did not consider the prosecution's duty went further than informing the accused that such evidence existed. This followed dicta in *R.* v. *Bryant and Dickson* (1946) 31 Cr.App.R. 146 at pp. 151–152.

accused were quashed in a case where a document in the police file which supported one of the accused's defence was not disclosed by the prosecution.[76]

If a witness is listed on the back of the indictment, the prosecution must take all reasonable steps to secure his presence at the trial; provided no injustice is done, the trial may, however, proceed in his absence.[77]

I. Extradition

"Inward" extradition [78] has already been dealt with and "outward" extradition, *i.e.* where a foreign state wishes to try a person who is at present in the United Kingdom, must now be considered briefly.

Again, the availability of extradition depends on treaty arrangements and the Extradition Act 1870 or the Fugitive Offenders Act 1967.[79] The principles upon which it is granted are, generally speaking, the same.

The request and the relevant documents are sent to the Home Secretary who, if he is of the opinion that the request is made lawfully, may give authority to a metropolitan stipendiary magistrate [80] to issue a warrant for the arrest of the suspected fugitive offender. If the magistrate issues a warrant he must immediately inform the Home Secretary who may confirm or cancel the warrant.[81] If the Home Secretary confirms it, the fugitive person must be brought before a metropolitan stipendiary who will hear the evidence and anything the fugitive has to say. If the magistrate is satisfied that the request is valid and that there is a prima facie case against the fugitive on the evidence, he may commit the fugitive to prison pending his return to the requesting state. If he is not so satisfied, he must discharge the fugitive.[82]

The fugitive must be informed of his right to apply to the High Court for a writ of habeas corpus.[83] The basis for issuing habeas corpus is that the Extradition Act 1870 or the Fugitive Offenders Act 1967 is not complied with; for instance, that the offence is not

---

[76] *R.* v. *Shadrack* [1976] Crim. L.R. 755.

[77] See *R.* v. *Cavanagh and Shaw* [1972] 1 W.L.R. 676 p. 178.

[78] See p. 60.

[79] Depending on whether the requesting state is foreign or Commonwealth, respectively.

[80] See p. 50.

[81] Secretaries of State, Privy Councillors or the Sovereign may not issue warrants themselves: Justices of the Peace Act 1968, s. 1 (7).

[82] Under an Irish warrant the magistrate is under no duty to inquire into the circumstances of the warrant: *Keane* v. *Governor of Brixton Prison* [1972] A.C. 204.

[83] See p. 44.

extraditable, that it is political or racial, or that it would not be an offence if committed in the United Kingdom.[84]

His return to the requesting state will be delayed pending the outcome of the habeas corpus application, but if he is not returned to the requesting state within two months of arrest he may apply for discharge.

---

[84] *R.* v. *Governor of Brixton Prison, ex p. Gardner* [1968] 2 Q.B. 399.

CHAPTER 7

THE INDICTMENT

AFTER the accused is committed for trial the indictment is drawn up.[1] It is the formal accusation against him in writing and he stands trial upon the allegations in it. It is akin to the pleadings in civil cases, for it fixes the offence charged and states the facts, but not the evidence upon which the charge is based. In the interests of the accused the power to amend is limited,[2] and there are no subsequent pleadings; the accused does not make any defence until the prosecution has presented its case at trial.[3]

The clerk of the magistrates' court sends the written evidence and the other documents to the appropriate officer of the court of trial.[4] The latter officer either drafts the indictment himself or sends it to counsel to be drafted. The prosecution may require him to have counsel draft it.[5]

The draft indictment is called thc " bill of indictment " and it must be " preferred " [6] by delivering it to the appropriate officer of the court of trial, which is, of course, a mere technicality when he has drawn it up himself. He then signs the bill and makes it into an indictment upon which the accused can stand trial.

The coroner's inquisition is an alternative, albeit very rare, to an indictment and is subject to the same rules.[7]

A. DRAFTING AN INDICTMENT

Form

The indictment is written or printed. It is in three parts: the commencement, the statement of offence and the particulars of offence.[8] One indictment may contain allegations of more than one offence but, usually, each one must be contained in a separate paragraph called a " count," consisting of the statement of offence and the particulars of offence.[9]

---

[1] This is the normal course of events; see also pp. 144, 392 and 394.

[2] See p. 146.

[3] Subject to giving notice of alibi evidence, see p. 112.

[4] See p. 105.

[5] It is theoretically possible for any person to prefer an indictment, but as it can only be preferred after committal or on the direction of a judge, it would be unusual for a layman or any other lawyer to do so; see pp. 144–146.

[6] See p. 145.

[7] Coroners Act 1887, s. 20; see also pp. 39–40.

[8] Indictments Act 1915, s. 3 (1).

[9] Indictment Rules 1971, r. 4 (1) and Sched. 1.

If allegations, facts or details are inserted in the indictment which are not essential to constitute the offence, they may be ignored by the court and treated as surplusage, provided they do not affect the charge or vitiate the indictment.[10–11]

The counts, if more than one, are numbered consecutively and set out in order in the indictment.[9] There should not be an unreasonably large number of counts because of the danger of confusing the jury and prejudicing the accused.

Commencement

This part states the name of the accused and the place of trial. This is an example:

The Crown Court at Exeter [12]
The Queen v. *A.B.*
charged as follows:

The indictment is always brought in the name of the Crown.[13] The place of trial has already been sufficiently dealt with in Chapters 2 and 6.[14] If the indictment is transferred from one place at which the Crown Court sits to another, the new place of trial is substituted by the order of the court.[15]

Statement of offence [16]

" Every indictment shall contain, and shall be sufficient if it contains, a statement of the specific offence with which the accused person is charged describing the offence shortly." [17] " Where the specific offence with which an accused person is charged in an indictment is one created by or under an enactment, then . . .

(*a*) the statement of offence shall contain reference to

(i) the section of, or the paragraph of the Schedule to, the Act creating the offence in the case of an offence created by the provision of an Act;

10–11 *R.* v. *Barraclough* [1906] 1 K.B. 201 at p. 210.

12 When the Crown Court sits in the City of London it is known as the Central Criminal Court: Courts Act 1971, s. 4 (7).

13 See p. 17.

14 See pp. 16 and 101.

15 See Courts Act 1971, s. 7 (2) and (3), p. 101.

16 All the examples of indictments given in the following pages are inventions of the author. The Lord Chief Justice is empowered by r. 5 (2) of the Indictment Rules 1971 to approve forms of indictment for specific offences.

17 Indictment Rules 1971, r. 5 (1).

(ii) the provision creating the offence in the case of an offence created by a provision of a subordinate instrument." [18]

The offence charged must be a recognisable offence precisely stated, *i.e.* the " specific offence." For instance, " attempt to commit an indictable offence " would not be valid.

If an act or omission is an offence at common law and by modern statute, the statutory offence should be charged.[19]

If an offence has a name which is commonly used, the statement of offence will use it, for instance, " murder," " manslaughter," " conspiracy to defraud." As the offence is described " shortly " it is unnecessary to state all the essentials of the offence; no mention is made, for instance, on an indictment for murder, of malice aforethought, nor, on an indictment for conspiracy, of the agreement, for the words " murder " and " conspiracy " include those factors in their ordinary meaning. These examples are common law offences and so the statement of offence will contain the name of the offence on its own.

Example

STATEMENT OF OFFENCE

Murder

If the offence is created by statute the section of the relevant Act creating the offence is added, with the words " contrary to." Again the common name for the offence is used, if there is one.

Examples

STATEMENT OF OFFENCE

Theft, contrary to section 1 of the Theft Act 1968.

STATEMENT OF OFFENCE

Robbery, contrary to section 8 (1) of the Theft Act 1968.

The name used in the statute creating the offence is usually in sufficiently ordinary language to be used, *e.g.* burglary, assault with intent to rob, rape, incest, wounding, arson, perjury. A useful guide to this is the word used in the section when prescribing the punishment, particularly when the definition is complex. For example, in

---

[18] *Ibid.* r. 6 (*a*).

[19] *R.* v. *Pollock and Divers* [1967] 2 Q.B. 195 (robbery by threats of accusations of sodomitical practices; the same would apply to buggery at common law or under the Sexual Offences Act 1956, s. 12 (1)).

the Theft Act 1968, section 7 says " a person guilty of *theft* shall on conviction . . ." and section 22 (2) says " a person guilty of *handling stolen goods* shall on conviction. . . ." [20]

Where one section creates more than one offence, the subsection and paragraph, if necessary, must be stated precisely. For instance, section 9 (1) of the Theft Act 1968 provides that a person commits burglary if

" (*a*) he enters a building . . . as a trespasser with intent to commit [an offence] . . .; or
(*b*) having entered a building . . . as a trespasser he steals . . . anything in the building. . . ."

As this section provides for two distinct offences of burglary,[21] the statement of offence must specify which one:

" Burglary, contrary to section 9 (1) (*b*) of the Theft Act 1968."

The need for this precision arises from the rule that each count of an indictment can only charge one offence. This is considered in detail below.[22]

Where the statutory offence does not have a common name, sufficient details of basic description are used.

Examples [23]

1. Sexual intercourse with a girl under thirteen, contrary to section 5 of the Sexual Offences Act 1956.
2. Wounding with intent, contrary to section 18 of the Offences against the Person Act 1861.
3. Removing an article from a place open to the public, contrary to section 11 (1) of the Theft Act 1968.

If the statutory definition is very complex but the offence belongs to a class of offences created by statute, it is permissible to say, for instance, " Bankruptcy offence, contrary to section 154 (1) paragraph (i) of the Bankruptcy Act 1914."

Attempted crimes, if specifically charged,[24] are stated with the word " attempted," *e.g.* " attempted murder," " attempted theft." An attempt is a common law offence unless the attempt is itself a

---

[20] *Griffiths* v. *Freeman* [1970] 1 All E.R. 1117; see also p. 126.
[21] See *R.* v. *Hollis*, p. 213.
[22] See Section B, p. 128.
[23] See also Examples 2 and 4, p. 123 and p. 124.
[24] The jury can convict of attempt on an indictment of the full offence, and vice versa: Criminal Law Act 1967, s. 6 (4), p. 214.

statutory creation. Thus, on an indictment for attempted theft, no statute is mentioned, whereas the statement of offence for attempting to drive with blood alcohol in excess of the prescribed limit would be: " Attempting to drive a motor vehicle with blood alcohol concentration above the prescribed limit, contrary to section 6 (1) of the Road Traffic Act 1972."

The same applies to statements of accessory offences:

Examples

1. Assisting an offender, contrary to section 4 (1) of the Criminal Law Act 1967.
2. Inciting to steal/murder/etc.

When a person is charged with aiding and abetting it is usual to indict him as a principal.[25] The offence may, however, be stated as follows:

" A.B., wounding, contrary to section 20 of the Offences against the Person Act 1861.

C.D., being aider and abettor to the same offence."

Particulars of offence

" Every indictment shall contain . . . such particulars as may be necessary for giving reasonable information as to the nature of the charge." [26] The particulars " shall disclose the essential elements of the offence " provided that an essential element need not be disclosed " if the accused person is not prejudiced or embarassed in his defence by the failure to disclose it." [27] As for the statement of offence, common names and everyday descriptions are to be used for every place, time, thing, matter, act or omission.

The " reasonable information as to the nature of the charge " required in the particulars goes back to the basic rules of criminal law and evidence. The prosecution must prove that the accused committed the actus reus of the offence charged, with the relevant mens rea. It does not have to prove the accused's state of mind in a general sense, *i.e.* that he was aware of what he was doing and foresaw the consequences of his act, unless the accused raises a doubt about it.[28] Accordingly the particulars must allege the essential facts of the offence and any intent specifically required by a statute.

---

[25] Because the aider and abettor is triable and punishable as the principal offender: Accessories and Abettors Act 1861, s. 8.

[26] Indictment Rules 1971, r. 5 (1).

[27] *Ibid.* r. 6 (*b*). *Cf.* amending an indictment, p. 146.

[28] However, any presumption in the prosecution's favour as to this general intention is excluded by the Criminal Justice Act 1967, s. 8.

It may also be necessary to give particulars which establish at the outset the court's jurisdiction and the maximum available punishment, *e.g.* impeding an offender's apprehension under section 4 of the Criminal Law Act 1967 where both factors can be determined only by knowing what the offence is that was committed by the assisted offender.[29]

For the accused to be reasonably informed the time and place of commission of the offence must also be alleged.

(a) *Essential facts*

These will vary according to the definition of the offence charged. If the offence is against the person, the victim must be identified.

Example

STATEMENT OF OFFENCE

Manslaughter

PARTICULARS OF OFFENCE

A.B., on —— in ——, unlawfully killed C.D.

If the offence is against property, the property may be identified and should be if the properly in question is a common item.

Example

(criminal damage)

PARTICULARS OF OFFENCE

A.B., on —— in ——, set fire to a haystack belonging to C.D. with intent to destroy it.[30]

The name of the town or county is usually sufficient identification of place unless the actual place of commission is relevant.[31] Where the offence charged can leave the accused in no doubt, even the county may be treated as surplusage; in one case, a charge of incest " in the county of Sussex or elsewhere " was held to be valid, despite its vagueness, as the place of commission was immaterial.[32]

Property must, in ordinary language, be identified with reasonable clearness, but it is desirable to name the owner when an offence

---

[29] *R.* v. *Morgan* [1972] 1 Q.B. 436 (the assistant's knowledge of the nature of the principal offence is immaterial under s. 4 (1), so it need not be stated).

[30] Under the Criminal Damage Act 1971, s. 1.

[31] *e.g.* where an offence is committed on board a ship in a harbour: *R.* v. *Wallwork* (1958) 42 Cr.App.R. at p. 157; see also p. 124.

[32] *R.* v. *Wallwork* (1958) 42 Cr.App.R. 153. The former practice of putting " in the county of ——" is not necessary, except for identification purposes, as the Crown Court has jurisdiction throughout the country.

depends on the particular ownership of property.[33] Thus, for instance, in theft it is necessary that the accused " appropriates property belonging to another " [34] so the particulars of theft would be: " A.B., on the —— at —— stole a watch, *the property of C.D.*" [35]

Where the definition of the offence specifies factual circumstances without which the offence cannot be committed, they must be included in the particulars of offence.

Examples

1.

STATEMENT OF OFFENCE

Removing an article from a place open to the public, contrary to section 11 (1) of the Theft Act 1968.

PARTICULARS OF OFFENCE

A.B., on ——, *without lawful authority* removed from the —— Art Gallery, *a building to which the public then had access in order to view a collection of paintings housed therein*, a painting *displayed to the public* therein entitled " The Anthropoid Jungle " by Mandrill Fitzgibbon.

2.

STATEMENT OF OFFENCE

Driving a motor-vehicle with blood alcohol concentration above the prescribed limit, contrary to section 6 (1) of the Road Traffic Act 1972.

PARTICULARS OF OFFENCE

A.B., on —— in ——, drove a motor vehicle *on a road* named ——, having consumed alcohol *in such a quantity that the proportion thereof in his blood exceeded the prescribed limit at the time when he provided a specimen under section* 9 *of the Road Traffic Act* 1972, namely that *at the said time there were* 250 *milligrammes of alcohol in* 100 *millilitres of blood.*

3.

STATEMENT OF OFFENCE

Burglary, contrary to section 9 (1) (*b*) of the Theft Act 1968.

---

[33] The former provision which required this identification is not reproduced in the 1971 Rules; it is submitted, however, that in these circumstances ownership may be an " essential element " of the offence charged. The value of the property might also become an essential element again if the James Committee's proposals are implemented (Cmnd. 6323); see Appendix.

[34] Theft Act 1968, s. 1.

[35] *R.* v. *Gregory* [1972] 1 W.L.R. 991 (a case of handling). See also example on p. 126.

PARTICULARS OF OFFENCE

A.B., on ——, having entered *as a trespasser* a building known as ——, ——, stole therein £400 in money.

4.

STATEMENT OF OFFENCE

Sexual intercourse with a girl under thirteen, contrary to section 5 of the Sexual Offences Act 1956.

PARTICULARS OF OFFENCE

A.B., on —— in ——, had sexual intercourse with C.D., *a girl of the age of twelve years.*

Other rules as to factual information are:

(i) Time: the date is sufficient [36] and if it is not known it should be described as being between stated dates. These should not be unreasonably far apart for the accused must know with some exactness the acts of his which are alleged to constitute offences.[37] Unless the date is of the essence, *e.g.* where there is a limitation period on prosecution or for offences of bankrupts before discharge, it can be amended without objection.[38]

(ii) Place: the town or county is an adequate description of place,[39] though the name of a street might be added for greater clarity. The definition of the offence may require further identification, *e.g.* " on a road " is necessary for many traffic offences which could not be committed on private ground, and the address or place of display would be alleged on charges of indecent exhibitions, keeping disorderly houses, indecent exposure, etc.

(iii) Ownership: where this is stated,[40] the name of the owner, or, if more than one, their description as " Trustees," " Club," etc., is sufficient. " Belonging to X " is sufficient for charges of theft from a person having possession or control of property, such as a bailee or servant, or a proprietary interest in it.[40a]

---

[36] Unless the time of day is of the essence, *e.g.* under the Night Poaching Act 1828.

[37] In *R.* v. *Owen* (*The Times*, April 21, 1970, p. 4) the objection of defence counsel on this ground to the following count was disallowed: " . . . between January 1 and December 31, 1967 . . . did an act preparatory to communicating to another person . . . information . . . useful to an enemy."

[38] See p. 146. This may have an inconvenient effect on alibi evidence and the requisite notice; see p. 112.

[39] *R.* v. *Wallwork* (1958) 42 Cr.App.R. 153; see also p. 122.

[40] See p. 123.

[40a] Theft Act 1968, s. 5 (1).

(iv) Identity of person: " It shall be sufficient . . . to describe a person whose name is not known as a person unknown." [41]

(v) Things: documents can be described by their usual name—" letter," " will," etc. —and money, as " money."

(vi) Special cases: in an indictment for libel, the libel should be set out verbatim,[42] and for publishing an obscene article,[43] the particulars should identify the obscenity. The particulars may be contained in a separate document attached to the indictment.

The above are guiding lines of the factual content of the particulars of offence. Because " reasonable information " is required, they may have to contain allegations of facts clarifying and identifying any general word used in the statutory definition of the offence.

Example

STATEMENT OF OFFENCE

Obtaining property by deception, contrary to section 15 (1) of the Theft Act 1968.

PARTICULARS OF OFFENCE

A.B., on ——, dishonestly obtained from C.D. the sum of £400 [44] by deception, *namely by a false oral representation that he, the said A.B., intended to use the said sum for the purchase of materials for certain work, namely the reconstruction of a cellar, which he had undertaken to carry out at the house of the said C.D. at* ——.

(b) *Intent*

The intention specified in the definition of an offence must be alleged in the particulars of offence, for it is an essential element of it. This may take the form of " maliciously," " knowing . . .," " with a view to . . .," " with intent to . . .," etc.

Examples

1. Wounding with intent, contrary to section 18 of the Offences against the Person Act 1861.

PARTICULARS OF OFFENCE

A.B., on the —— in —— Street, ——, wounded C.D., with intent to do him grievous bodily harm.

---

[41] Indictment Rules 1971, r. 8.

[42] *R.* v. *Barraclough* [1906] 1 K.B. 201.

[43] Obscene Publications Act 1959, s. 2 (1).

[44] The precise sum need not be stated; if it is incorrectly stated the count may be amended, but it is unnecessary under this section to prove the amount with precision: *Levene* v. *Pearcey* [1976] Crim.L.R. 63.

2. Wounding, contrary to section 20 of the Offences against the Person Act 1861.

PARTICULARS OF OFFENCE

A.B., on the —— in —— Street, ——, maliciously wounded C.D.

3. Blackmail, contrary to section 21 (1) of the Theft Act 1968.

PARTICULARS OF OFFENCE

A.B., on the ——, with a view to gain for himself in a letter dated —— and addressed to C.D. at ——, made an unwarranted demand of £100 from C.D. with menaces.

4. Handling stolen goods, contrary to section 22 (1) of the Theft Act 1968.

PARTICULARS OF OFFENCE

A.B., on the —— in the —— public house, ——, dishonestly received a watch, the property of C.D., knowing or believing the same to have been stolen.[45]

Where a word, such as " murder," " steal," or " rob," has been given a meaning, and one meaning only, by common use or by statute,[46] it is not necessary to allege each part of the intent required. For instance, " steal " means " dishonestly appropriate property belonging to another with the intention of permanently depriving the other of it." The state of mind and intent (*i.e.* the dishonesty and the intent permanently to deprive) need not be expressed, for the word " steal " is construed according to the above definition.[47] (The *fact* on the other hand must be alleged, *i.e.* that the property belongs to another.) The word " murder " may be used without more: " A.B., on the —— in ——, murdered C.D."; the same applies to " robbed," " assaulted," " indecently assaulted " and " conspired." By contrast, a person who " handles stolen goods " " dishonestly receives . . . or dishonestly undertakes or assists in their retention, removal, disposal or realisation by or for the benefit of another person, or . . . arranges to do so." [48] This involves 18 means of commission under two classifications (receiving and the

---

[45] As to alternatives, see Section B, p. 128. As to counts charging handling, see also pp. 129 and 141.

[46] For the meaning of " steal " and " rob," see Theft Act 1968, ss. 1 and 8.

[47] Theft Act 1968, s. 1 (1).

[48] *Ibid.* s. 22 (1). See Example 4, above, and p. 141.

rest) and, although they all constitute the offence of " handling," the sort of activity must be alleged.[49]

Other words do not have the same portmanteau quality, such as blackmail (*see* Example 3 *above*), rape (" had sexual intercourse with X, without her consent "), manslaughter (" unlawfully killed ").

An intent to defraud, deceive or injure should be alleged expressly, but it need not specify the particular object of the intent. This is again in accordance with basic principles; for instance, where A pulls the trigger of his gun aimed at Y, his lifelong enemy, but the bullet misses Y and kills an unknown passer-by, it is immaterial to A's intention to kill that the bullet missed Y. Where the intent must be stated in an indictment therefore it will be expressed as follows:

Example

Forgery of a document, contrary to section 4 (1) of the Forgery Act 1913.

PARTICULARS OF OFFENCE

A.B., on the —— in ——, *with intent to defraud*, forged a document purporting to be a cheque.

The intent is sometimes defined as being directed at " any person " (or thing) or " such person " (or thing). In the first case, it will be usual to allege the person or thing: " wounded C.D., with intent to do *him* grievous bodily harm." [50] In the second case the object of the intent must be specified: " Maliciously administered to C.D. a poison with intent to injure, aggrieve or annoy C.D." [51]

(c) *Exceptions*

When a statutory offence is charged, it is not necessary to specify or negative any exception, exemption, proviso, excuse or qualification to the operation of the statute creating the offence.[52] For instance, on a charge against a doctor of abortion under section 59 of the Offences against the Person Act 1861, it would be unnecessary to negative the exception made by section 1 of the Abortion Act 1967.[53] Nor on a charge of unlawful sexual intercourse with a girl under

---

[49] See p. 129.

[50] Offences against the Person Act 1861, s. 18. It might be " with intent to resist or prevent the lawful apprehension of the said A.B." (" any person ").

[51] As to alternatives, see Section B, p. 128.

[52] Indictment Rules 1971, r. 6 (c).

[53] *i.e.* it need not be alleged that he terminated the pregnancy *not* in good faith or *without* the agreement of a second medical practitioner, etc.

16[54] is it necessary to state that the accused is over the age of 24 (if he is).[55]

This must be distinguished from offences which specify an absence of consent, authority or other possible justification, as a constituent part of the offence. In those cases, it must be stated in the particulars of offence.

Example

Taking a conveyance without authority, contrary to section 12 (1) of the Theft Act 1968.

PARTICULARS OF OFFENCE

A.B., on the —— in ——, without the consent of the owner or other lawful authority, took a conveyance, namely a Rolls-Royce motor car registration number —— for his own use." [56]

The reader will find specimen indictments for almost all offences in Archbold and a more comprehensive example on page 141.

B. Duplicity[57]

Each count of the indictment must charge one offence and one only. Two offences cannot normally be charged either cumulatively or in the alternative in one count.[58] This apparently simple rule has the most complex effects, particularly in indictments for statutory offences.

First, it is provided that " where an offence created by or under any enactment states the offence to be the doing or the omission to do any one of any different acts in the alternative or . . . in any one of any different capacities, or . . . intentions, or states any part of the offence in the alternative, the acts, omissions, capacities or intentions or other matters . . . may be stated in the alternative in an indictment charging the offence." [59] However, this rule only applies where the offence may be committed by various alternative means, not where the statute creates two or more alternative and separate offences. The criterion of whether the prohibited alternative acts, omissions or intentions are facts constituting one offence committable in various ways, or themselves constitute two or more separate

[54] Sexual Offences Act 1956, s. 6 (1).

[55] *Ibid.* s. 6 (3), whereby it is a defence if a man is under the age of 24, if he has never been charged with a similar offence, and if he reasonably believed the girl to be 16 or older.

[56] See also Example 1 on p. 123.

[57] For a critical appraisal of the rule against duplicity, *see* Glanville Williams [1966] Crim.L.R. 255.

[58] Subject to some exceptions, see p. 131.

[59] Indictment Rules 1971, r. 7.

offences, is not entirely clear and must be decided by interpretation of the individual statute.

A very straightforward example is theft, which is a " dishonest appropriation " with the requisite intent and which may be done in all kinds of ways—by physically taking, by finding and keeping, by a trustee converting the trust fund to his own use, etc. All these are " modes " of commission and are facts proving the appropriation.[60]

Section 5 (1) of the Road Traffic Act 1972 provides a less straightforward example. The section prohibits driving while " unfit to drive through drink *or* drugs." It was held, in *Thomson* v. *Knights*,[61] that the offence was the driving while unfit, and the alternative means of becoming unfit were " merely adjectival." [62]

The case of handling is particularly difficult. Section 22 (1) of the Theft Act 1968 creates one offence, committable by eighteen different means but by two basic sorts of activity (old-style " receiving " and dishonestly undertaking or assisting in the retention, etc., of stolen goods).[63] As a matter of fairness and clarity it is desirable to state which sort of activity is alleged, although it is not strictly obligatory in law.[64] " Receiving " should, if possible, be specified.[65] A proliferation of alternative counts should, on the other hand, be avoided as it may confuse the defence.[66] The proper practice is therefore not to charge more than two counts of handling.[67]

If the count alleges handling by means of the second part of section 22 (1), it is desirable for the words " by or on behalf of " a named person (or " a person unknown ") to be added.[68]

In *R.* v. *Linnell*[69] the Court of Appeal held that a count charging the offence of " fraudulently inducing another person to enter an agreement " [70] was not bad for duplicity (*i.e.* for charging more than one offence) because it alleged that the accused had " promised " two things and " stated " two others, for both promises and statements were merely *methods* of doing the inducing, which was the offence.

---

60 Theft Act 1968, s. 1. In *R.* v. *Skipp* [1975] Crim.L.R. 114 it was held that the " assumption of the rights of an owner " may occur at one time in respect of separate items and the inclusion of all the items in one count was therefore proper.

61 [1947] K.B. 336.

62 *Per* Lord Goddard C.J., *ibid.* at p. 338.

63 See p. 126.

64 *R.* v. *Willis* [1972] 1 W.L.R. 1605; *R.* v. *Marshall* [1972] Crim.L.R. 231.

65 *R.* v. *Alt* (1972) 56 Cr.App.R. 457.

66 *R.* v. *Ikpong* [1972] Crim.L.R. 432, clarifying dicta in *Griffiths* v. *Freeman* [1970] 1 W.L.R. 659.

67 *R.* v. *Deakin* [1972] 1 W.L.R. 1618 and *R.* v. *Willis*, above.

68 *R.* v. *Sloggett* [1972] 1 Q.B. 430.

69 [1969] 1 W.L.R. 1514; see also *R.* v. *Inman* [1967] 1 Q.B. 140.

70 Contrary to the Prevention of Fraud (Investments) Act 1958, s. 13 (1) (*a*).

A count charging an offence under section 5 of the Public Order Act 1936 may allege using words *or* behaviour with intent to provoke a breach of the peace *or* whereby a breach of the peace is likely to be occasioned because the section creates a single offence consisting of " conduct conducive to breaches of the peace ".[71]

On the other hand, the following are cases where it was held that the relevant section of the statute created two offences which therefore could not be charged in one count:

(*a*) Permitting premises, of which the accused is occupier, to be used for the purpose of *smoking* cannabis or of *dealing* in cannabis, contrary to section 5 (*a*) of the Dangerous Drugs Act 1965: *Ware* v. *Fox.*[72] " [The section alleges] use for two completely different activities. . . . It is quite different from the sort of case which alleges one activity achieved in one of two different respects."[73]

(*b*) It used to be an offence unlawfully to *admit* or *allow* a person under 18 *to remain* in a betting office under section 5 (1) of the Betting and Gaming Act 1960[74]: *Mallon* v. *Allon.*[75] " There are two separate acts, first of all admitting a person, and, secondly, allowing him to remain after he has got on to the premises, and . . . it seems perfectly clear that these are two separate offences." [76]

(*c*) The accused " by night unlawfully took or destroyed game or rabbits at C *or* was in the said land by night with a gun . . . for the purpose of unlawfully taking or destroying game " [77]: *R.* v. *Disney* [78] (this charged two offences in the alternative).

(*d*) Driving a motor vehicle on a road *recklessly* or at a *speed* or in a *manner* which is dangerous to the public, contrary to section 2 of the Road Traffic Act 1927: *R.* v. *Wilmot* [79]

This last case must be contrasted with *R.* v. *Clow* [80] where it was

---

[71] *Vernon* v. *Paddon* [1973] 1 W.L.R. 663. It was said, however, that, even if two or more offences were created, they could be charged conjunctively if they arose out of a single incident.

[72] [1967] 1 All E.R. 100. A further decision reported with this case (at p. 103) applied the same principle to s. 5 (*b*) of the Act (being concerned in the management of the premises used). The Act has been replaced by the Misuse of Drugs Act 1971, s. 8.

[73] *Ibid.* at p. 102.

[74] Repealed and replaced by the Betting, Gaming and Lotteries Act 1963, s. 21.

[75] [1964] 1 Q.B. 385. This was a case concerning an information, not a count in an indictment, but the same principle would apply to a count.

[76] *Per* Lord Parker C.J. [1964] 1 Q.B. 385 at p. 392.

[77] Contrary to the Night Poaching Act 1828, s. 1, since repealed.

[78] [1933] 2 K.B. 138.

[79] (1933) 24 Cr.App.R. 63. The section probably creates two offences rather than three; see *R* *Clow*, p. 132.

[80] [1965] 1 Q.B. 598.

held that it is sometimes permissible to join charges of two or more offences in one count.[81]

Treason is not an exception to the rule against duplicity, though it may appear so, for when two or more " overt acts " are alleged in one count, they are evidence of the abstract offence of " compassing," levying war, adhering to the Queen's enemies, etc. The same applies to conspiracy where one " unlawful combination " may comprise several overt acts.

The need for this rule against duplicity, or double indictments, is primarily that the indictment does not mislead or confuse the accused so as to make him unable to defend himself against the charges, and also that the jury's verdict must be clear and unambiguous on every count, either acquitting or convicting the accused of every charge made against him. These ends are not usually served by combining several offences in one charge.

The variety of interpretation puts the drafter of an indictment at some risk of being " caught out," for if he alleges each alternative part of the definition of the offence in a separate count and the court, on appeal, holds that only one offence is created, it may hold the indictment to be bad for putting the accused to trial twice for the same offence.[82]

C. Joinder of Offences

In law two indictments can never be tried together,[83] so it is desirable, where offences are connected, to charge them in the same indictment.

1. In one count

Where this is allowed it is an exception to the rule against duplicity described in the last section.

In the first place, every allegation of a completed offence is taken to include an allegation of attempting to commit that offence.[84] This is a question not so much of duplicity in the indictment as of the jury's power to find the accused not guilty of the offence charged but guilty of an alternative (lesser) offence not expressly charged, which they may do in some circumstances.[85] For instance, there is no question of duplicity when charging unlawful wounding [86] merely because

[81] See Section C, below.

[82] See *Autrefois Convict*, p. 159, and Glanville Williams [1966] Crim.L.R. at p. 263.

[83] Two indictments may exist at the same time against the same accused alleging the same facts, but the prosecution will never be allowed to proceed on both. Practice Direction [1976] 1 W.L.R. 409.

[84] Criminal Law Act 1967, s. 6 (4); see p. 214. As to the indictment, see p. 120.

[85] See p. 213.

[86] *i.e.* Offences against the Person Act 1861, s. 20

the jury may convict of common assault, although it could be said that the allegation of the wounding includes an allegation of the lesser offence.

Secondly, if two or more offences constitute a single act, they may be charged in one count. This only applies where the charges are cumulative or " conjunctive " and the offences are so closely bound together that it is virtually impossible for them to be separated on the facts. The following cases illustrate its application:

(*a*) " Uttering " a number of forged receipts at the same time in one bundle: *R.* v. *Thomas.*[87]

(*b*) Robbery from A and B when the accused used force on both simultaneously and stole something from each of them at the time of using the force: *R.* v. *Giddings.*[88]

(*c*) Theft consisting of separate takings but which form a continuous transaction, such as misappropriating small sums of money over a period of time before having to hand over the total or account for it: *R.* v. *Balls.*[89]

(*d*) Causing the death of another person by driving a vehicle recklessly or at a speed or in a manner dangerous to the public: *R.* v. *Clow.*[90] The court considered that the statute [91] probably creates two, rather than three, offences (recklessly or dangerously driving),[92] and held that " even if these are separate offences, it is permissible to charge them conjunctively . . . if the matter relates to one single incident." [93]

In two other decisions involving reckless or dangerous driving,[93] the court held that the charge [94] was bad for duplicity if charged in the alternative, but proper if charged conjunctively " since the act of driving was one indivisible act." [95] In *R.* v. *Clow* [96] Lord Parker C.J. considered the addition of an allegation of speed " was in fairness to the

[87] (1800) 2 East P.C. 934.

[88] (1842) C. & M. 634.

[89] (1871) L.R. 1 C.C.R. 328; the same might apply to abstracting amounts of electricity over a period of time, contrary to the Theft Act 1968, s. 13. Another example is *Jemmison* v. *Priddle* [1972] 1 Q.B. 489 where a combined charge of shooting two deer with two shots was approved because the two acts were extremely close in time and place.

[90] [1965] 1 Q.B. 598.

[91] Now the Road Traffic Act 1972, s. 1.

[92] *Per* Lord Parker C.J. [1965] 1 Q.B. 598 at p. 602.

[93] *R.* v. *Jones ex p. Thomas* [1921] 1 K.B. 632 and *R.* v. *Surrey JJ.* [1932] 1 K.B. 450; see also *R.* v. *Wilmot*, p. 130.

[94] Then under the Motor Car Act 1903, s. 1.

[95] *Per* Avory J. at [1932] 1 K.B. 452.

[96] [1965] 1 Q.B. 598, see above

defence who thereby would realise that one of the allegations going to be made was that of excessive speed." [97]

Where distinct items were stolen from different parts of a large store on one shoplifting expedition, however, it was held that each taking should be charged in a separate count.[98] Two offences of burglary cannot be charged together.[99]

2. In one indictment

The charging of several offences against one accused in separate counts of one indictment is permissible [1] on a wider range than for charging them in one count. The offences must be related to each other, *i.e.* they must be " founded on the same facts or form or [be] a part of a series of offences of the same or a similar character." [2] However, where more than one count is properly joined the court has a discretion to sever the indictment and direct separate trials of one or more of the counts, if it is of the opinion that the accused may be " prejudiced or embarrassed in his defence . . . or that for any other reason it is desirable to direct that the [accused] should be tried separately for any one or more offences charged in [the] indictment." [3]

The House of Lords, in *Ludlow* v. *Metropolitan Police Commissioner*,[4] considered the effect of the Indictments Act 1915 and the general application of these rules. The following general criteria emerge from their decision:

(*a*) Two offences may constitute a " series of offences." [5]

(*b*) For the series of offences to be of a " similar character," it is necessary to look at both the law and the facts of the charges to establish similarity.

(*c*) To be of similar character there must be a " nexus " between the offences. The nexus would be established if the evidence of one offence would be admissible on the trial of the other(s), but this is not the only test for the existence of the " nexus." [6]

(*d*) The trial judge has no *duty* to order separate trials under section 5 (3) unless there is some special feature involving the prejudice

[97] [1965] 1 Q.B. 598 at p. 602.
[98] *R.* v. *Ballysingh* (1953) 37 Cr.App.R. 28.
[99] See p. 120.
[1] Indictments Act 1915, s. 4.
[2] Indictment Rules 1971, r. 9.
[3] Indictments Act 1915, s. 5 (3).
[4] [1971] A.C. 29.
[5] This confirms the decision of the Court of Appeal in *R.* v. *Kray* [1970] Q.B. 125.
[6] Approving dicta in *R.* v. *Kray*, above, at p. 131; see also *R.* v. *Clayton-Wright* (1949) 33 Cr.App.R. 22, p. 135.

and embarrassment of the accused over and above the prejudice which is inevitably associated with making more than one charge, *i.e.* the implication of bad character. Such a special feature might be

(i) the excessively large number of counts [7]; or
(ii) the difficulty of disentangling them in the summing-up and in the jury's minds [8];
(iii) the addition of a scandalous charge likely to arouse in the minds of the jury hostile feelings against the accused.[9]

The mere fact that evidence is admissible on one charge but not on the other(s) does not impose a duty on the judge to order separate trials, unless it cannot be overcome by the judge's directions to the jury.[10] He still has the *power* to direct separate trials. It was recommended in *D.P.P.* v. *Boardman* [10] that the judge should decide the question of admissibility at the outset in the absence of the jury.

(*e*) Offences should be joined in one indictment wherever there is a prima facie case that they can properly and conveniently be tried together, whether founded on the same facts or forming a series of offences of a similar character.[11] As a general rule, if offences are not joined when they should have been the judge at the second trial will direct the indictment to be stayed [12] as it may be oppressive to the accused.[13] The test for doing so is whether, had they been joined in one indictment, the judge

---

[7] *e.g. R.* v. *King* [1897] 1 Q.B. 214 at p. 216, (40 counts of obtaining by false pretences) and *R.* v. *Bailey* [1924] 2 K.B. 300 (16 indecent assaults on 16 different boys).

[8] *e.g. R.* v. *Norman* [1915] 1 K.B. 341 (seven charges of obtaining credit and property by false pretences where the evidence was admissible on some but not others of the counts and it would have been exceptionally difficult for the jury to separate the two).

[9] *e.g. R.* v. *Muir* (1938) 26 Cr.App.R. 164 (joinder of a charge of indecent assault on one woman to a charge of rape of another woman on a completely separate occasion) and *R.* v. *Fitzpatrick* [1963] 1 W.L.R. 7 (charge of indecent exposure quite separate from, though within 15 minutes of, indecent assault).

[10] Approving dicta of Lord Goddard C.J. in *R.* v. *Sims* [1946] K.B. 531 at p. 536, where four charges of gross indecency with four men, and three charges of buggery with three of them were held to have been properly tried together. See also *R.* v. *Flack* [1969] 1 W.L.R. 937 (three charges of incest where evidence on one was inadmissible on the others; separate trial desirable but not obligatory) and *Boardman* v. *D.P.P.* [1975] A.C. 421 (evidence on one count to be used as similar fact evidence on another count; separate trial desirable if the evidence is not in fact admissible as similar fact evidence).

[11] Approving *R.* v. *Kray* [1970] 1 Q.B. 125 at p. 131 and *Connelly* v. *D.P.P.* [1964] A.C 1254.

[12] *i.e.* order that it remain on the file not to be proceeded with; see p. 166. It does not amount to *autrefois acquit*, as to which, see p. 159.

[13] *Connelly* v. *D.P.P.* [1964] A.C. 1254 at p. 1360.

would have used his discretion to order separate trials under section 5 (3).

In the present case [14] the accused was tried for

(i) attempting to steal from the staff quarters of one public house on August 20, 1968, and

(ii) robbing the relief manager of a nearby public house by snatching back the money he paid for his drinks and causing the manager injuries to the face, on September 5, 1968.

The House of Lords held on these facts that—

(i) both offences had the same essential ingredient of actual or attempted theft from neighbouring public houses within 16 days of each other, and were therefore " similar " in law and in fact; and

(ii) there was no multiplicity or complexity in the indictment and so no difficulty for the judge in dealing separately with the two offences in his summing-up, *i.e.* there was no " special feature " requiring separate trials.

In *R.* v. *Kray* [15] the accused appealed against being convicted of two murders joined in one indictment, but the court, dismissing the appeal, held that the inevitable prejudice created by two charges of murder is not a conclusive consideration for granting separate trials where the two charges show unusual common features.[16] Other considerations were the public interest in the crimes charged and the degree of publicity which would have prejudiced the second of the two trials.

In *R.* v. *Clayton-Wright* [17] the accused was charged with two offences of malicious damage to a ship, one of defrauding the insurers of the ship by claiming for the damage and one of defrauding other insurers on a different occasion for the pretended theft of a furcoat from a car. The Court of Criminal Appeal held that the fourth count was properly joined because the first three counts, in substance, charged offences of insurance fraud which provided the nexus with the fourth count in law (fraudulent acts) and in fact (insurance swindles). The admissibility of similar fact evidence [18] has some bearing on this decision, since the evidence of the third charge assisted on the fourth, and vice versa, in as much as it assisted in

[14] *i.e. Ludlow* v. *Metropolitan Police Commissioner*, [1971] A.C. 29.
[15] [1970] 1 Q.B. 125.
[16] *Ibid.* at p. 131.
[17] (1949) 33 Cr.App.R. 22.
[18] See *D.P.P.* v. *Boardman*, p. 134.

establishing proof of knowledge, intent and system, although it was not conclusive as to the similarity.

Even though the offences are founded on the same facts they should not be charged together unless the offences are also of a related character. In *R.* v. *Thomas*[19] it was held that a count charging a road traffic offence should not be joined with counts charging rape, although there was a connection in that the rape took place in a car which was taken without the owner's consent. On the other hand, in *R.* v. *Andrews*[20] the Court of Appeal held that it would be proper to charge driving a stolen car while disqualified in the same indictment as a charge of handling the car, or stealing or taking it without authority, provided the accused could not be prejudiced on the latter charge by the necessary implication that he had previously been convicted of a driving offence.[21]

On an indictment for treason, several species of treason may be joined in one indictment, *e.g.* counts may charge compassing the Queen's death, levying war and adhering to the Queen's enemies. Murder and manslaughter may be joined with other offences.[22]

Counts may be joined cumulatively or in the alternative. For instance, one count may charge theft and another count, handling stolen goods. It is impossible for the jury to convict of both offences in respect of the same goods as the two offences are inconsistent. The prosecution may elect which one to proceed with and have the other count stayed.[23] If the evidence throughout points equally at either offence, *e.g.* where the prosecution evidence consists of the accused's recent possession of the goods,[24] the decision must be left to the jury with a warning that they cannot convict of both.

Finally, as to cumulative counts, the Court of Appeal has held that it is wrong and undesirable to charge an accused with all the offences which he has committed in the course of one act, for a conviction of the lesser charge merges in the graver offence. In *R.* v. *Harris*[25] the court quashed a conviction for indecent assault which was charged in the same indictment as buggery, of which the accused was also convicted, when the only indecent assault committed was that which immediately preceded and was a preliminary to the act of buggery. If

[19] (1949) 33 Cr.App.R. 74.

[20] [1967] 1 W.L.R. 439.

[21] Following dicta in *R.* v. *Pomeroy* (1935) 25 Cr.App.R. 147 (here, however, it was held that there was no prejudice because the accused's defence to both driving while disqualified and dangerous driving was that he was not driving the car at all).

[22] Practice Direction [1964] 1 W.L.R. 1244.

[23] See p. 166.

[24] *R.* v. *Seymour* [1954] 1 W.L.R. 678.

[25] [1969] 1 W.L.R. 745

convicted of both it would subsequently appear that he had committed two separate offences of that sort, causing great unfairness to the accused.[26]

An example of an indictment charging two offences can be found on page 141.

D. Joinder of Defendants

If two or more people participate in the commission of an offence or series of offences they may be indicted and tried together. If separately indicted the opportunity for joint trial is lost as two indictments cannot be tried together.[27] However, it is possible to join in the same indictment two or more defendants who have been separately committed. It is even possible to join new defendants in an indictment already signed in respect of one defendant under section 2 (2) (i) of the Administration of Justice (Miscellaneous Provisions) Act 1933.[28]

1. In one count

If the offences are carried out in concert the accused may be charged jointly in each count.

The form of commencement is:

The Crown Court at ——
The Queen v. *A.B. and C.D.*
charged as follows:

The following is an example of the statement and particulars of an offence charged against two people:

STATEMENT OF OFFENCE

Assault with intent to rob, contrary to section 8 of the Theft Act 1968.

PARTICULARS OF OFFENCE

AB and CD, on —— in —— Street, ——, assaulted EF with intent to rob him.

The fact that one is an accessory offender and another is the principal offender does not matter as aiders and abettors may be indicted, tried and punished as the principal offender.[29]

---

[26] *Quaere* where a conviction for the lesser offence cannot be returned as an alternative verdict; see p. 213.

[27] See p. 131.

[28] Practice Direction of the Court of Appeal [1976] 1 W.L.R. 409; *R.* v. *Groom* [1976] 1 W.L.R. 618; as to s. 2 (2) (i), see p. 104.

[29] Accessories and Abettors Act 1861, s. 8. As to the indictment for aiding and abetting, see p. 121.

The practical effect of the rule against duplicity is modified in the case of two or more defendants charged jointly in one count. It is open to the jury to convict each defendant of committing the offence independently. In other words, the prosecution need not prove additionally that they were acting in concert.[30] This theoretically involves charging two or more separate offences but " the rule against duplicity . . . has always been applied in a practical, rather than a strictly analytical, way." [31]

If A and B are charged with one offence in one count and the evidence proves that A committed the offence, it is open to the jury either to acquit B or to convict him. The question is simply whether the evidence against each defendant proves that he committed the offence. Lord Diplock said [32]:

> " When two men are aiding one another in doing physical acts with criminal intent, though the *mens rea* of the separate offence of each is personal to the individual charged, the physical act of either one of them is in law an *actus reus* of the separate offence of each. A 'joint offence' of two defendants means no more than that there is this connection between the separate offences of each, so that as against each defendant not only his own physical acts but also those of the other defendant may be relied on by the prosecution as an *actus reus* of the offence with which he is charged."

In *D.P.P.* v. *Merriman* [33] two accused were charged with wounding with intent to do grievous bodily harm the licensee of a night club who tried to eject them. One accused pleaded guilty. The judge, at the trial of the second accused, directed the jury not to consider the question of common purpose but to convict if they were sure that the evidence against the second accused was correct. This direction was upheld.

In *D.P.P.* v. *Shannon* [34] the House of Lords extended this principle to counts charging conspiracy. Although it would not be possible to find that A and B, charged jointly (but with no third party) with conspiracy, had each conspired independently (only one agreement having been alleged), it is perfectly possible for the jury to find one

---

[30] *D.P.P.* v. *Merriman* [1973] A.C. 584.

[31] *Per* Lord Diplock at p. 607.

[32] *Ibid.* at p. 606.

[33] Above. A New South Wales judgment, approved by the House of Lords, stated that a joint charge is to be treated as being a joint and several charge against each accused: *R.* v. *Fenwick* (1953) 54 S.R.N.S.W. 147 (where two defendants raped the same girl in the course of the same car journey).

[34] [1975] A.C. 717.

accused guilty and the other not guilty. In this case two accused alone were charged with conspiracy; one pleaded guilty and the other was later acquitted; the House of Lords upheld the conviction of the one who had pleaded guilty. The acquittal of one person is evidence only of the prosecution's failure to prove him guilty; it affects no one but that person and would not be admissible in evidence against or on behalf of any other.[35]

A count charging two or more accused jointly must still satisfy the general rule against duplicity.[36] The judge may order separate trials where accused are jointly charged.[37]

2. In one indictment

More difficulties arise in charging several offenders jointly when they are each charged with different offences which are in some way connected. In view of the opening remarks in the following case, it is of no great assistance to study the older authorities.

The question was comprehensively considered in *R.* v. *Assim.*[38] First of all, the court held that it had the power to formulate its own rules and to vary them in the light of current experience and the needs of justice, unless a statute specifically restrains it. This applies to joinder of offences in an indictment against one person within the limits imposed by the Indictments Act 1915 [39] but its application is even wider with regard to joinder of offenders as this is not expressly dealt with in the Act at all. The principles evolved are rules of practice which do not become settled or rigid.

Within this rather loose framework, Sachs J. defined the general principles as follows:

(*a*) it is no more proper to try several offenders on charges of different offences in one indictment than it would be if those offences were charged against one accused, *i.e.* there must be a connection between the offences. The Court did not consider whether the provision now incorporated in rule 9 of the Indictment Rules 1971[40] applies to joinder of offenders.

(*b*) Two or more offenders may, however, be joined where the matters constituting the individual offences are, on the available

---

[35] See *Res judicata* and issue estoppel, pp. 167–168.
[36] See p. 128. See also *R.* v. *Messingham* (1830) 1 Mood.C.C. 357.
[37] *R.* v. *Buggy* (1961) 45 Cr.App.R. 298; as to the judge's discretion, see p. 140.
[38] [1966] 2 Q.B. 881.
[39] Indictments Act 1915, ss. 4 and 5, and Indictment Rules 1971, r. 9, see pp. 133–137.
[40] See p. 133.

evidence, so related by time or by other factors that the interests of justice are best served by their being tried together.

(*c*) Among the "interests of justice" are the interests of the accused.[41]

(*d*) The joinder is most plainly proper in, but is not restricted to, cases where the accused acted in concert. The Court suggested the following examples of proper joinder:

(i) Two witnesses commit perjury as to the same or closely related facts in the same proceedings.[42]

(ii) The charges of fact are contemporaneous (*e.g.* affray) or successive (*e.g.* protection racket cases).[43]

Sachs J. contrasted example (i) with a hypothetical joinder of two burglars who independently break into the same house on the same night but at different times. It would be wrong to join the burglars.[43]

The facts of the case were that the two accused were doorman and receptionist at a night club. Two clients refused to pay the whole of an extortionate bill for champagne and beer. One of the accused viciously attacked one of the clients and the other accused assaulted the other client. They were jointly indicted the first being charged with malicious wounding and the second, with assault occasioning actual bodily harm. This joinder was held to be proper.

Defendants who are separately committed may be joined in one indictment provided no defendant is indicted on counts not appearing from the evidence forming the basis of his own committal.[44]

Separate trials

If two or more accused are jointly indicted and the judge considers that a joint trial will be prejudicial to one or more of them, he may order separate trials. The Court of Appeal will only interfere with a conviction where the judge's decision has resulted in a miscarriage of justice.[45] Separate trials might be ordered, for instance, where the evidence against one accused is inadmissible as against another accused.

---

[41] See *R.* v. *Hoggins*, below.

[42] *R.* v. *Leigh and Harrison* [1966] 1 All E.R. 687, where the facts were approximately these, was overruled by the present case (*i.e. R.* v. *Assim*, above).

[43] *Per* Sachs J. [1966] 2 Q.B. 249 at p. 261.

[44] *R.* v. *Groom* [1976] 1 W.L.R. 618; the apparently inconsistent case of *R.* v. *Brooker* (see p. 101), where no reference to an accused was made in the committal statements, was resolved by the admission of additional evidence before the indictment was signed, as described in Section E, below. The report does not reveal whether the additional evidence was taken in accordance with s. 2 (2) of the Administration of Justice (Miscellaneous Provisions) Act 1933, below.

[45] See pp. 266–268.

The question often arises in connection with the competence and compellability of the accused.[46] As one co-accused is not usually a competent witness for the prosecution, the prosecution may desire the court to order separate trials so that he can be called as a witness. Or, because of the non-compellability of the accused for the defence, one accused may wish to call another accused and ensure that he gives evidence.

However, where the accused are mutually hostile and seek to incriminate each other by their own evidence and by cross-examination, the mutual prejudice is only one factor to be considered. In *R.* v. *Hoggins*[47] three accused were indicted for murder and each sought to blame the others. It was held that the interest of the public in finding out the truth outweighed the prejudice their allegations against each other involved and therefore a joint trial was desirable.

Example of an indictment charging more than one offence

The Crown Court at Newington Causeway, London S.E.1.

The Queen v. *Adolphus Burley, Cedric Dodge, Emmanuel Findlater and Gregory Hadham*

Count 1

STATEMENT OF OFFENCE

Theft, contrary to section 1 of the Theft Act 1968.

PARTICULARS OF OFFENCE

Adolphus Burley and Cedric Dodge, on December 31, 1976, at the Broken Bottle public house, Skidding Road, London S.E.1., stole 48 bottles of Guinness, the property of the Waterdown Brewery Ltd.

Count 2

STATEMENT OF OFFENCE

Handling stolen goods, contrary to section 22 (1) of the Theft Act 1968.

PARTICULARS OF OFFENCE

Emmanuel Findlater, on January 1, 1977, dishonestly received 10 bottles of Guinness, the property of the Waterdown Brewery Ltd., knowing or believing the same to have been stolen.

---

[46] See pp. 30–32 and 189. *R.* v. *Grondkowski and Malinowski* [1946] K.B. 369.

[47] [1967] 1 W.L.R. 1223.

Count 3

STATEMENT OF OFFENCE

Handling stolen goods, contrary to section 22 (1) of the Theft Act 1968.

PARTICULARS OF OFFENCE

Gregory Hadham, on January 2, 1977, at the Broken Bottle public house, Skidding Road, London S.E.1., dishonestly undertook the disposal of stolen goods, namely 24 bottles of Guinness, the property of the Waterdown Brewery Ltd., knowing or believing the same to have been stolen, by offering the said goods for sale to the licensee of the Broken Bottle public house above for the benefit of Adolphus Burley and Cedric Dodge.

E. The Substance of the Indictment

The indictment must charge offences which are disclosed by the evidence given at the committal proceedings. Within this limitation, the charges in the indictment need not be the same as the charges made before the examining justice, nor as the committal charges, but " may include either in substitution for or in addition to counts charging the offence . . ., any counts founded on facts or evidence disclosed in any examination or deposition taken before a justice in his presence, being counts which may lawfully be joined in the same indictment." [48] This has been ruled by the Court of Appeal to extend to the addition of counts to an indictment already signed in respect of one defendant charging different defendants separately committed who are thus added to the existing indictment.[49]

A new or extra charge need not be of the same nature as the charges before the justice. For instance, an information charged the two accused with wilfully neglecting their baby daughter contrary to section 1 (1) of the Children and Young Persons Act 1933. The evidence also revealed violent assaults and the indictment contained charges of causing grievous bodily harm and wounding contrary to sections 18 and 20 of the Offences against the Person Act 1861. This was held to be correct.[50]

---

[48] Administration of Justice (Miscellaneous Provisions) Act 1933, s. 2 (2), proviso (i); see also *R.* v. *Groom*, p. 140.

[49] Practice Direction of the Lord Chief Justice [1976] 1 W.L.R. 409; the reason for this direction is the rule which precludes the trial of more than one indictment at the same time.

[50] *R.* v. *Roe* [1967] 1 W.L.R. 634 at p. 640. In an earlier case decided on assizes (*R.* v. *McDonnell* [1966] 1 Q.B. 233) Nield J. held that the new charge should not be a

New offences may be charged in addition to or in substitution for the committal offence even where the accused has elected [51] to be tried on indictment for the offence with which he was charged in the magistrates' court.[52] Offences revealed in written statements on a section 1 committal may be charged in the indictment.[53]

If there is more than one count, each count is treated as a separate indictment [54] and may be severed; if one count is good, therefore, and one bad, the good one can still be tried. However, if there is a defect in the committal charge, *e.g.* the offence charged no longer exists,[55] this cannot be rectified by charging a new offence in the indictment, even though the new one was disclosed by the evidence at the committal proceedings, for the committal itself is a nullity.[56]

If the examining justice refuses to commit the accused for trial on the charge of a certain offence, that offence may still be charged in the indictment, but should the defence object, it is a matter for the judge at trial to decide whether or not to allow its inclusion.[57] In any event the court of trial has power to amend the indictment, even by an alteration of substance, *e.g.* adding a new count.[58]

For certain rare offences it is necessary to allege a previous offence as an essential element of the offence now being charged.[59] It is included in the particulars of the offence charged: "A.B., having been previously convicted of an offence under section 5 (1) of the Coinage Offences Act 1936 on —— at the Central Criminal Court, on —— in ——, uttered, etc." The particulars of the previous offence are not alleged.

The conviction is not alleged when an indictment charges driving while disqualified,[60] though the disqualification is: "A.B., being a

---

" substantial departure " from the charge before the justices; he allowed, however, the substraction of the words " and others unknown " from a charge of conspiracy as this did not constitute such a departure.

[51] See p. 292.

[52] *R.* v. *Nisbet* [1971] Crim.L.R. 532.

[53] *R.* v. *James William* [1972] Crim.L.R. 436.

[54] *Latham* v. *R.* (1864) 9 Cox 516; *cf.* Administration of Justice (Miscellaneous Provisions) Act 1933, s. 2 (3) (*a*), see p. 146.

[55] *R.* v. *Lamb* [1968] 1 W.L.R. 1946.

[56] As to other cases in which the committal may be a nullity, see pp. 107 and 295.

[57] *R.* v. *Morry* [1946] K.B. 153; *R.* v. *Dawson* [1960] 1 W.L.R. 163 at p. 168; otherwise the prosecution would have to apply to prefer an indictment with the consent of a High Court judge, see p. 144.

[58] See p. 146.

[59] *e.g.* Coinage Offences Act 1936, s. 5 (5) (altering counterfeit coin), where the maximum punishment is greater if the accused has a previous conviction for a coinage offence. The same would presumably not apply to offences such as brothel-keeping (see Sexual Offences Act 1956, ss. 33–36, p. 295) where the offence is triable on indictment only if the accused has a previous conviction because he must necessarily have notice of the higher maximum penalty in claiming trial by jury.

[60] Road Traffic Act 1972, s. 99.

person disqualified from holding or obtaining a driving licence, on —— drove a motor vehicle on a road, namely ——."

F. Preferring the Indictment

There are two courses of action available before a bill of indictment can be preferred[61]:

(*a*) the person charged has been committed for trial of the offence; or

(*b*) the bill is preferred by the direction or with the consent of a High Court judge; it may also be preferred by the Court of Appeal[62] or by the order of a court under section 9 of the Perjury Act 1911.[63]

In the overwhelming majority of cases indictments are preferred after committal, in which case preferment must be within 28 days of committal unless the judge allows a longer period.[64]

After committal

The words " for the offence " in paragraph (*a*) of section 2 (2) are limited by the proviso described in Section E, above,[65] whereby an offence different from the offence for which the accused is committed may be added or substituted.

With the judge's consent

Although this procedure might seem to offer an opportunity to circumvent the protection against unjustifiable indictments secured by committal proceedings, it is not in practice anything of the sort. Lord Devlin, in " The Criminal Prosecution in England," examined the use to which it was put in the years 1951–56 and concluded that the reasons why it was invoked were generally of a formal nature, such as the death of the examining justice after a full hearing but before committal, or because an undisputed fact emerged after committal, such as the death of the victim after committal for inflicting grievous bodily harm. It might be necessary where the examining justice refuses, without good reason, to commit,[66] or where there

---

[61] *i.e.* delivered to the appropriate officer of the court of trial for signature; see p. 145.

[62] *i.e.* where the court orders a new trial; see p. 272.

[63] Administration of Justice (Miscellaneous Provisions) Act 1933, s. 2 (2). As to perjury, see p. 394.

[64] Inds. (Proc.) Rules 1971, r. 5; *R.* v. *Stentiford* (1975) 120 S.J. 266; but see *R.* v. *Sheerin* [1976] Crim.L.R. 689.

[65] *i.e.* Administration of Justice (Miscellaneous Provisions) Act 1933, s. 2 (2), proviso (i); see p. 142.

[66] *e.g. R.* v. *Harrison* [1954] Crim.L.R. 39.

has been a delay after committal beyond the 28 days allowed,[67] or if an indictment is quashed at trial in its entirety.[68]

As proceedings are never in open court and are usually in writing, it is not possible to ascertain the number of applications made or the reasons why applications have been granted or refused. The procedure was used in *R.* v. *Kray* [69] where two murders were charged and separate indictments were drawn up in respect of the three principal accused. As the indictments could not be tried together,[70] an application was made by the prosecution to the judge to prefer an indictment charging them jointly. It was granted. The murders were closely connected as the accused were a " gang " and it was therefore in the public interest that they should be tried together.

The applicant makes his application to a High Court judge in writing accompanied by the draft indictment and an affidavit stating his reasons for making it, proofs of evidence of his proposed witnesses and, if the application is made because committal proceedings have failed, copies of the depositions, written statements and any other evidence. The same applies, except that the reasons need not be stated in affidavit form, to applications where the accused has already been committed for trial.[71]

The judge gives his decision in writing without requiring anyone's attendance before him; he may call for the applicant or a proposed witness to attend, but the application cannot be made or heard in open court.[72]

The preferment

The preferring or " preferment " is the delivery of the bill of indictment to the " appropriate officer " of the court of trial. If he has drawn it up himself, the preferment occurs when he is satisfied with his work.[73] The officer then signs the bill of indictment[74] and the accused may be brought to the court of trial and arraigned, *i.e.* called to the bar of the court and asked how he pleads to the indictment.[75]

If it has been preferred but not signed by the proper officer, the

---

67 *R.* v. *Stentiford*, above.
68 *R.* v. *Thompson* [1975] 1 W.L.R. 1425.
69 [1970] 1 Q.B. 125 at p. 131.
70 See *R.* v. *Groom*, p. 137.
71 Indictments (Procedure) Rules 1971, rr. 7–9.
72 *Ibid.* r. 10.
73 Indictments (Procedure) Rules 1971, r. 4.
74 Administration of Justice (Miscellaneous Provisions) Act 1933, s. 2 (1).
75 See p. 154 *et seq.*

judge, provided he is satisfied it has been properly preferred,[76] may on his own or on the prosecution's motion direct that officer to sign it. If it has not been properly preferred, it is liable to be quashed.[77] If it has been properly preferred in respect of one or more of several counts, only the bad counts are to be quashed.[78]

When preferred and signed a copy of the indictment must be supplied by the clerk free to the accused on request.[79] The indictment, or the draft, if not yet preferred, should be available for inspection by both prosecution and accused at the court of trial.[80]

G. Amendment

According to section 5 (1) of the Indictments Act 1915, the court, before or at any time during trial, may order such amendments to a defective indictment as it thinks necessary to meet the circumstances of the case. This is limited, however, by the qualifying words: " unless, having regard to the merits of the case, the required amendments cannot be made without injustice." Although the subsection is in rather broad terms, the courts have given it a restrictive interpretation.

In *R.* v. *Errington* [81] an amendment adding an allegation of a new false pretence was held to be wrong. In *R.* v. *Jennings*,[82] where a count was amended to charge a completely different offence—a charge of *using* a forged ration-book was substituted for charges of obtaining by false pretences and forging an application for a ration-book—the conviction was quashed. On the other hand, where the words " with intent to defraud " were omitted, it was held to be permissible to add them by amending the indictment.[83]

The indictment must first be shown to be " defective." In *R.* v. *Radley* [84] an indictment was held to be potentially defective if it does not charge all the offences which might have been charged or charges any offence not disclosed in the depositions or committal statements.

A distinction has been drawn between amendments made before

---

[76] Administration of Justice (Miscellaneous Provisions) Act 1933, s. 2 (1).
[77] *Ibid.* s. 2 (3), and see p. 148. As to circumstances in which a committal may be void, see pp. 107 and 143.
[78] *Ibid.* s. 2 (3) (a).
[79] Indictment Rules 1971, r. 10 (1).
[80] Direction of the Lord Chief Justice [1956] 1 W.L.R. 1499.
[81] (1922) 16 Cr.App.R. 148.
[82] (1949) 33 Cr.App.R. 143.
[83] *R.* v. *Fraser* (1923) 17 Cr.App.R. 182.
[84] (1973) 58 Cr.App.R. 394.

the accused is arraigned and those made after, for the obvious reason that the accused must plead to the charge of which he is ultimately convicted or acquitted. In *R.* v. *Martin* [85] the substitution of a new count by way of amendment was considered to be permissible before arraignment, if it caused no injustice, but it was not a practice to be encouraged. In *R.* v. *Johal*,[86] however, the addition of new counts *after* arraignment but before empanelling the jury was approved as the accused had not been prejudiced. In *R.* v. *Harden*,[87] the court decided that an amendment, if it substitutes a new offence, may not be made after arraignment, but it was pointed out that the distinction between this and correcting a misdescription in a count, which is permissible, is a " matter of degree." In *R.* v. *Harris* [88] an amendment at the close of the prosecution case to correct a misdescription of a false representation but also to add an allegation of attempt was upheld because no injustice had resulted. In *R.* v. *Hall* [89] the Court of Appeal upheld the amendment *before* arraignment of a count charging receiving three paintings to one charging receiving eight paintings. In *R.* v. *Gregory* [90] an amendment deleting the name of the owner of stolen goods made at the close of the evidence was held to be improper. The proper time for amendment is in any event before arraignment,[91] for counsel for the prosecution is responsible for the indictment's correctness before opening his case. The risk of injustice naturally increases with the progress of the trial. In *R.* v. *Bonner*,[92] however, it was held to be possible to amend even as late as the summing up, but an adjournment must be granted to allow the accused to consider calling further evidence.

If amended, the indictment must be endorsed with a note of the order for amendment.[93] If substantially amended after arraignment, the accused should be arraigned again.[94] The court may order the trial to be postponed if it considers such a course of action to be expedient.[95] This power also applies where the judge orders separate trials of counts in one indictment or of various co-defendants.[96] If

[85] [1962] 1 Q.B. 221; the offence charged was not disclosed by the depositions, whereas the offence so disclosed was not charged.
[86] [1973] 1 Q.B. 475.
[87] [1963] 1 Q.B. 8.
[88] (1975) 62 Cr.App.R. 28.
[89] [1968] 2 Q.B. 788.
[90] [1972] 1 W.L.R. 991.
[91] *R.* v. *Pople* [1951] 1 K.B. 53.
[92] [1974] Crim.L.R. 479.
[93] Indictments Act 1915, s. 5 (2).
[94] *R.* v. *Radley* (1973) 58 Cr.App.R. 394.
[95] *Ibid.* s. 5 (4).
[96] See pp. 135 and 140.

the order for postponement is made after arraignment, the jury may be discharged from giving a verdict on the postponed counts, in which case the trial of those counts will proceed independently and by the normal procedure.[97]

H. Quashing the Indictment

Quashing is done by the trial judge and his order makes the indictment, or certain counts in it, void and of no effect. The grounds for making an order are various.

If the facts stated in a count do not disclose any offence, that count should be quashed. For instance, in *R.* v. *Yates*[98] a count charging libel which alleged words not prima facie libellous without alleging any innuendo to make them libellous, was quashed.

Less substantial defects may be corrected by amendment,[99] but if a count is bad for duplicity[1] it should be quashed. The fact that the evidence in the depositions could or would not support a conviction on a count is not enough in itself to quash the count[2]; the offence charged in the count must be *disclosed* by the depositions. If not, it will amount to an improper preferment for which the indictment may be quashed.[3]

As in the case of amendment, it will sometimes be against the accused's interests to propose quashing an imperfect indictment, for the Court of Appeal may quash his conviction on appeal[4]—for instance, where the count is bad for duplicity—in which case he stands in no fear of being re-indicted.[5] Defence counsel who raise the issue for the first time on appeal are rarely greeted with approval, however. The application should be made before the accused pleads, *i.e.* before arraignment, but possibly it may be made after that stage in exceptional circumstances.[6] If the prosecution still wishes to pursue the charge, prosecuting counsel should have ready a properly drafted indictment which can be preferred and signed in the court.

---

[97] Indictments Act 1915, s. 5 (5).

[98] (1872) 12 Cox 233: to be called a " rabbit and game-destroyer " is not libellous unless it is also alleged that the person is a gamekeeper.

[99] See Section G, above.

[1] See Duplicity, p. 128.

[2] *Ex p. Downes* [1954] 1 Q.B. 1; *R.* v. *McDonnell* [1966] 1 Q.B. 233.

[3] Administration of Justice (Miscellaneous Provisions) Act 1933, s. 2 (3); as to preferring, see pp. 144–146, and see *R.* v. *Brooker*, p. 101.

[4] See p. 271; but see also the power of the Court of Appeal to affirm the conviction when no miscarriage of justice has occurred, p. 267.

[5] See *Autrefois convict*, pp. 159 and 164; if acquitted, he cannot be re-tried, see p. 163.

[6] *R.* v. *Thompson* [1914] 2 K.B. 99 at p. 104; see also p. 146.

If neither party applies to quash an indictment (or counts in it) which has been improperly preferred and the accused is convicted, neither party can raise the improper preferment on appeal.[7]

If the indictment is quashed in its entirety, a new indictment must be preferred by a High Court judge; the Crown Court as such has no authority to do so.[8]

The other procedural steps which may be taken before the trial starts are dealt with in the next chapter.

---

[7] Administration of Justice (Miscellaneous Provisions) Act 1933, s. 2 (3) (*b*).
[8] *R.* v. *Thompson* [1975] 1 W.L.R. 1425.

CHAPTER 8

TRIAL ON INDICTMENT

THE preliminary matters have now been dealt with and the accused awaits the trial of his case. An experimental scheme for preliminary proceedings in which the parties may seek directions on practice from the judge was introduced in the Central Criminal Court on October 1, 1974. It was intended to avoid time wastage by, for instance, establishing which items of evidence would not be disputed.

A. PRESENCE AND REPRESENTATION OF THE ACCUSED: PRESENCE OF THE PUBLIC

Presence in court

The accused must be present when he is arraigned as he himself must plead to the accusation in the indictment.[1] After he has pleaded it is in practice the rule for him to remain in court except in certain cases when the trial may proceed in his absence, even to judgment and sentence.[2] For instance, if he is violent or disorderly [3] he may be sent from court and if he is seriously ill he need not be disturbed; neither case necessitates calling an adjournment, though the court may do so. An accused who absconds may properly be tried and sentenced in his absence.[4] If the accused is likely to intimidate a witness he may be removed from the court but kept within earshot.[5] Multiple trials do not require the presence of all the co-accused all the time.[6]

The customary but not obligatory place in court for the accused is the dock, a raised platform surrounded by a railing. He is sometimes

---

[1] See Section B, p. 154.

[2] A person accused of treason must be present, a rule preserved by the Criminal Law Act 1967, s. 12 (6).

[3] *R.* v. *Berry* (1897) 104 L.T. Journ. 110 (the accused leapt " in an almost miraculous manner over the heads of the barristers " onto the clerk's table where " he proceeded to divest himself of his clothing and to utter wild shouts and blasphemies "). It is undesirable that he should be seen in handcuffs unless absolutely necessary: *R.* v. *Young* [1973] Crim.L.R. 507.

[4] *R.* v. *Jones* (*No. 2*) [1972] 1 W.L.R. 887.

[5] *R.* v. *Smellie* (1919) 14 Cr.App.R. 128 (a father accused of assaulting his daughter was hidden from her sight on the stairs leading to the dock while she gave evidence).

[6] In the course of preparing a draft European Convention on the International Validity of Criminal Judgments, the Council of Europe Ministers' Deputies adopted a resolution (No. (75) 11) on minimum rules for proceeding in the absence of the accused; see *Forward in Europe* (No. 4, 1975), p. 70.

moved from it for obvious reasons when a witness is called upon to identify the offender for the first time in court.

A foreigner who cannot speak English must have an interpreter, however difficult it may be to find one. He cannot waive this right, though the judge has a discretion to permit the omission of certain items of evidence from translation at his request.[7] In *R.* v. *Yscuado*[8] it was thought that the accused was Spanish but, even with an interpreter, he spoke not a single word at his trial and it could not be ascertained whether or not he understood. He was presumed to understand and was convicted.

Securing the accused's presence

Depending on the circumstances, there are various ways of doing this:

(*a*) If the accused is in custody awaiting trial, the warrant of commitment issued at the committal proceedings [9] directs the prison governor to deliver the accused to the court of trial at the appropriate time.[10] The accused is then kept in the court cells until he is arraigned.

(*b*) If he is in prison under the jurisdiction of some other court, he may be brought to court by a writ of habeas corpus *ad respondendum* [11] if he is awaiting trial elsewhere or, more simply, by the written order of the Crown Court to the governor of the prison where he is in custody or serving a sentence of imprisonment.[12]

(*c*) If the accused is on bail,[13] he is under a duty to appear before the Crown Court. If the accused fails to appear at the appointed time and place in the Crown Court, the Crown Court may issue a warrant for his arrest.[14]

(*d*) Where an indictment has been signed although the person has not been committed for trial,[15] the Crown Court may issue a summons or warrant for his arrest.[16]

---

[7] *R.* v. *Lee Kun* [1916] 1 K.B. 337. The interpreter's expenses are payable out of central funds under the Administration of Justice Act 1973, s. 17. [8] (1854) 6 Cox 386.

[9] See p. 104. This may have been varied later by the Crown Court: Courts Act 1971, s. 13 (1). [10] See p. 101.

[11] The writ is issued on the application of the prosecutor on affidavit to a judge in chambers (R.S.C. Ord. 54, r. 9), otherwise the writ is the same as the writ described on p. 44.

[12] Criminal Law Amendment Act 1867, s. 10, as amended by the Bail Act 1976, Sched. 2.

[13] As to bail generally, see p. 68, and as to bail by the Crown Court, see p. 71.

[14] Bail Act 1976, s. 7 (1).

[15] *i.e.* a voluntary preferment with the consent of a judge; see p. 144.

[16] Courts Act 1971, s. 13 (2).

(*e*) If the accused is abroad, extradition proceedings may have to be instituted [17] and, if he is in another part of the United Kingdom, a warrant of arrest will have to be backed by a local magistrate.[18]

The power of a constable to arrest without warrant under section 7 (3) of the Bail Act 1976 [19] does not apply to a person who has actually failed to surrender to custody.

When the Crown Court issues a warrant and the person is arrested, he must be brought immediately before either the Crown Court or before a magistrates' court.[20] If he is brought before a magistrates' court, the court must release him on bail or commit him to custody until he can appear or be brought before the Crown Court at the time and place appointed.[21] When the Crown Court issues a warrant it may be endorsed with a direction for bail.[22] If it is endorsed for bail, but the person in custody is unable to satisfy the conditions any magistrates' court before which he is brought may vary the conditions, if satisfied that it is proper to do so.[23]

Representation of the accused

There is no need for an accused to be legally represented, though the overwhelming majority of defendants do employ counsel when tried in the Crown Court. At a trial on indictment representation is normally by counsel, for solicitors do not have the right of audience generally in the Crown Court. The Lord Chancellor has power, however, to direct that solicitors may appear in any proceedings in the Crown Court, conduct, defend a case, and address the court.[24] Solicitors may conduct proceedings in the Crown Court anywhere on appeal from magistrates' courts (see Chap. 14), but they have no right of audience in trials on indictment except in certain areas[25] where they may conduct the defence to an indictment charging a Class 4 offence. If the accused chooses to conduct his own case, the judge does all in his power to assist him on

---

[17] See p. 60. [18] See p. 59.

[19] See p. 81.

[20] Any magistrates' court has jurisdiction despite the fact that neither was the offence committed nor the arrest made in its area: Courts Act 1971, s. 13 (9).

[21] *Ibid.* s. 13 (7) (*a*). In these circumstances, the court may refuse to release him on bail under the Bail Act 1976, Sched. 1, Pt. I, para. 6.

[22] See Courts Act 1971, s. 13 (6), p. 69.

[23] *Ibid.* s. 13 (7) (*b*); Bail Act 1976, s. 3 (8).

[24] Courts Act 1971, s. 12 (1).

[25] *e.g.* Cornwall, Doncaster; in the normal course of events solicitors are, of course, employed in addition to counsel for preparation of the case and advice preliminary to the court hearing. See also Directions of the Lord Chancellor of December 7, 1971, and February 9, 1972.

legal points but the accused cannot protest on appeal that his case was not properly conducted.[26]

In view of the general availability of legal aid, which is described later,[27] the accused need never be unrepresented unless he so wishes. On any serious charge the court may request any available barrister to represent an accused, if he will accept representation.[28] If this cannot be fully arranged, the accused may choose a robed barrister in court to conduct his case on a " dock brief," an unsatisfactory arrangement giving counsel time for only a short interview with the accused and paying him only about £2.20, a fee which does not encourage the experienced and able barrister to accept the case.[29]

The right of representation is strongly reinforced by the courts. In *R.* v. *Kingston*[30] a conviction was quashed on appeal after the accused's counsel had failed to appear and the judge had refused to adjourn or appoint other counsel, treating the accused as an unrepresented person.

Public trial[31]

A trial on indictment must be held in a public court with open doors and the proceedings may be fully reported by the press.[32] To this common law rule there are the following exceptions:

(*a*) The court may exclude a person who makes a disturbance.[33]

(*b*) Under the Children and Young Persons Act 1933, section 37, the court may be cleared of all except the court officers, the parties and their representatives and bona fide press reporters when a child or young person is giving evidence of conduct contrary to decency or morality.[34]

---

[26] A case where such an appeal was rejected was discussed in the *Sunday Times*, July 26, 1970 (*R.* v. *Baisie*).

[27] See p. 399.

[28] *R.* v. *Yscuado*, 6 Cox 386 (where the accused refused to speak and so was taken to refuse representation). This discretion was at one time abused to circumvent the payment of a solicitor's fees as well as those of counsel; see Jackson, *The Machinery of Justice* (5th ed.), p. 159.

[29] The accused pays the fee himself; the practice is little used, usually only on pleas of guilty (see p. 215); the Widgery Committee on Legal Aid recommended its abolition; see Cmnd. 2934, paras. 152–153; as to the conduct of counsel when he cannot undertake the case, see Practice Direction [1964] 2 All E.R. 400.

[30] (1948) 32 Cr.App.R. 183. There is also a restriction on sentencing unrepresented defendants; see Powers of Criminal Courts Act 1973, s. 21, p. 225.

[31] As to publicity of committal proceedings, see p. 94.

[32] The " right " of the public and press to be present does not, however, entitle them to view the exhibits, *e.g.* " blue " films: *R.* v. *Waterfield* [1975] 1 W.L.R. 711.

[33] If it is very bad, the court may punish the disturber for contempt of court; see p. 392.

[34] See also p. 98 (evidence at committal proceedings). The Incest Act 1908, s. 5, required trials for incest to be held *in camera* but this provision was not reproduced in the Sexual Offences Act 1956.

(*c*) By section 36 of the same Act, children are prohibited from being present in court except when giving evidence.

(*d*) The trial may take place *in camera* where some " overriding principle which defines the field of exception and does not leave its limits to the individual discretion of the judge " applies.[35] Such cases would include evidence of classified information being given in official secrets trials and " tumult and disorder, or the just apprehension of it."[36] The outrage of public decency is not sufficient to exclude the public, although the contents of press reports may be restricted by the Obscene Publications Act 1959.

B. Arraignment and Plea

The arraignment of an accused consists of three parts:

(*a*) Calling the accused by name to the bar of the court.

(*b*) Reading the indictment, or stating the substance of it, to the accused.

(*c*) Asking him whether or not he is guilty—" How say you, are you guilty or not guilty? "—and taking down his answer.

1. Calling the accused

The " bar " of the court is the traditional barrier between the court (judge and officers) and the parties and their representatives. The accused should not be brought to it " in a contumelious manner, as with his hands tied together . . . nor even with fetters on his feet, unless there be some danger of rescous or escape."[37] If there is more than one accused, they are called at the same time.[38]

2. Reading the indictment

As might be expected from general principles,[39] each count must be put separately to the accused and he is asked to plead to each count individually. If two counts charge alternative offences, the second count need only be put to him if he pleads not guilty to the first.[40] If there is a coroner's inquisition as well as an indictment charging the accused with homicide,[41] the accused should be arraigned on both the

---

[35] *Scott* v. *Scott* [1913] A.C. 417 at p. 435 (this was a matrimonial case where different exceptions apply).

[36] *Ibid.* at p. 445.

[37] 2 Hawk. c. 28 s. 1; Kel. (J.) 10. He should not even be seen in handcuffs unless absolutely necessary: *R.* v. *Young* [1973] Crim.L.R. 507.

[38] See *e.g.* Kel. (J.) 9.

[39] *Latham* v. *R.* (1864) 9 Cox 516; see p. 143.

[40] *R.* v. *Boyle* [1954] 2 Q.B. 292 at p. 296.

[41] See p 39.

inquisition and the indictment at the same time [42] for if he is tried on one only, he must later be arraigned on the other and plead *autrefois convict* or *acquit*.[43]

3. Pleas

The plea of the accused completes the arraignment. There are at least ten courses of action open to the accused when asked how he pleads, seven of which are " pleas " in a formal sense. These will be dealt with first. One of the courses of action, however, has already been dealt with—moving to quash or applying to amend the indictment.[44] Pleas by corporations are dealt with separately.[45]

The practice of convenience whereby the accused is called to the bar of the court, agreed facts are put before the judge for a preliminary ruling of law and, because of the ruling, the accused may plead guilty, has been disapproved.[46] It usurps the function of the jury, albeit with the accused's consent, and puts him in danger of not having a right of appeal.[47] The approved practice is for the arraignment to be completed by a plea of not guilty and for the ruling to be made in the course of trial when the accused may change his plea.[48]

(a) *Guilty*

" An express confession is where a person directly confesses the crime with which he is charged, which is the highest conviction that can be . . . yet the judges, upon probable circumstances, that such confession may proceed from fear, menace or duress, or from weakness or ignorance, may refuse to record such confession and suffer the party to plead not guilty."[49]

The plea must thus be made freely,[50] in full knowledge and understanding of its implications and by the accused personally, not by his defending counsel.[51]

---

[42] 1 East P.C. 371.
[43] See p. 159 *et seq.*
[44] See p. 146.
[45] See p. 391.
[46] *R.* v. *Vickers* [1975] 1 W.L.R. 811; *R.* v. *Auker-Howlett* [1974] R.T.R. 109. See also *R.* v. *Powles*, p. 169.
[47] See *D.P.P.* v. *Shannon*, p. 268. In *Vickers*' case, however, the Court of Appeal did entertain the appeal.
[48] As in *D.P.P.* v. *Doot* [1973] A.C. 807; see also p. 169 and *cf.* demurrer, p. 159.
[49] 2 Hawk. 466.
[50] In a case where the judge put pressure on the accused to plead guilty, his conviction was quashed despite overwhelming evidence against him: *R.* v. *Barnes* (1971) 55 Cr.App.R. 100; see also p. 268.
[51] *R.* v. *Ellis* (1973) 57 Cr.App.R. 571 (a plea made improperly through defence counsel makes all subsequent proceedings a mistrial; a new trial must be ordered); *R.* v. *Heyes* [1951] K.B. 29; in *R.* v. *Ali Tasamulug* [1971] Crim.L.R. 441 it was held to be permissible for the accused to plead guilty through his counsel if he desires it and applies to do so " as a matter of grace."

In some cases, an accused may be tempted to defend on facts which are unlikely to secure an acquittal and by means which are likely to show him in a poor light if they fail, *e.g.* by attacking police witnesses. In others, he may be charged with a serious offence, the facts of which he does not contest but the gravity of which he does not wish to concede. In such cases defending counsel may advise, sometimes forcefully, a plea of guilty to the offence charged or to a milder alternative in the hope of getting a less severe sentence and, for this purpose, seek to discuss the position with the judge and prosecuting counsel. This " plea bargaining " has been considered by the Court of Appeal; at the time of writing, however, the court is reconsidering the practice [52] and may therefore modify its former ruling.

In *R.* v. *Turner* [53] a retrial was ordered after the accused changed his plea during the trial on the advice of his counsel with a view to receiving a non-custodial sentence. Defending counsel having discussed the matter with the judge advised the accused that a change of plea, *in his own personal opinion*, would be expedient. He stressed that the change of plea must be the accused's own choice but did nothing to persuade him that the arguments in favour of pleading guilty did not, in fact, emanate from the judge.

Lord Parker C.J. observed that four principles apply to plea bargaining[54]:

(*a*) Counsel must be fit to do his duty by his client's best interests, which may include strongly persuading him to plead guilty, emphasising that he must not do so if he has not committed the acts constituting the offence charged.

(*b*) The accused must have complete freedom of choice as to his plea.

(*c*) There must be freedom of access between counsel and judge, but any discussions must take place with counsel for the prosecution present.[55] On the other hand, justice should take place in open court, so circumstances justifying private discussions must necessarily be limited; it could be proper, for instance, where the accused is willing to plead guilty to a lesser offence.

---

[52] In *R.* v. *Cain* [1976] Q.B. 496, the court stated exceptions to the *Turner* principles (below); the case is being reconsidered, however, and for the time being the *Turner* principles are to prevail: Practice Direction, *The Times*, July 27, 1976.

[53] [1970] 2 Q.B. 321.

[54] [1970] 2 Q.B. 321, at p. 326.

[55] In *R.* v. *Plimmer* (1975) 61 Cr.App.R. 264 the Court of Appeal held that the practice of counsel going to see the judge is in general undesirable and should be reserved for special cases.

(*d*) The judge should never indicate the sentence which he is minded to impose if there is any suggestion whatever, explicit or implicit, that it would be different if the accused pleaded guilty or not guilty, as the case may be.[56]

When a person may by law be found guilty of an offence different from the offence expressly charged[57] to which he has pleaded not guilty, he may offer a plea of guilty to that other offence,[58] which is usually similar in its nature but less grave in its degree of culpability. For instance, A is accused of murder. The jury may find him guilty of manslaughter.[59] A will contend that he was provoked[60] and is willing to plead guilty to manslaughter. The court may allow the plea of guilty and sentence him for manslaughter, but it has a discretion to refuse it, particularly if nothing appears on the depositions to support the reduction of the offence charged.[61]

Prosecuting counsel has considerable responsibility and discretion in relation to accepting a plea of not guilty to the offence charged. On acceptance, he should apply to the judge to order that a not guilty verdict be entered or that the charge should remain on the file marked " not to be proceeded with without further order of the court."[62]

A plea of guilty which is not accepted is a nullity. In *R.* v. *Hazeltine*[63] the accused pleaded not guilty to the charge of wounding with intent but guilty to unlawful wounding.[64] The prosecution refused to accept the plea of guilty. On receiving a verdict of not guilty of wounding with intent, the judge purported to sentence him for unlawful wounding despite the fact that the jury had not even considered this nor passed verdict on it. The judge had correctly directed the jury on returning a verdict on the lesser offence at one stage in his summing up but seemed to suggest towards the end that they need not do so because the accused had already pleaded guilty to it. The

[56] In *R.* v. *Quartey* [1975] Crim.L.R. 592 the Court of Appeal ruled that a judge may only indicate whether a certain sentence will or will not be imposed *in any event* on conviction. In *R.* v. *Plimmer*, above, it refused to apply the proviso (see p. 266) to uphold a conviction where the judge indicated a fine if the accused pleaded guilty. In *R.* v. *Inns* [1975] Crim.L.R. 182 the pressure from the judge was held to be so great that the plea and trial were a nullity.

[57] See Alternative verdicts, p. 213.

[58] Criminal Law Act 1967, s. 6 (1) (*b*).

[59] *Ibid.*, s. 6 (2) (*a*); acceptance of a plea of not guilty to a charge of murder may only be done with the approval of a High Court judge (murder is, however, a Class 1 offence, so this will be no problem): *R.* v. *Jackson* [1974] Crim.L.R. 718.

[60] Homicide Act 1957, s. 3.

[61] *R.* v. *Soanes* (1948) 32 Cr.App.R. 136.

[62] *R.* v. *Moorhead* [1973] Crim.L.R. 36.

[63] [1967] 2 Q.B. 857; see also *R.* v. *Kelly* [1965] 2 Q.B. 409.

[64] Contrary to the Offences against the Person Act 1861, ss. 18 and 20 respectively.

Court of Appeal held that this was improper for only one plea and one verdict can be made to each count.[65] Had both offences been charged in the indictment in separate counts, the procedure would have been proper. The accused's plea of guilty to unlawful wounding could have stood, as it were, in reserve while the wounding with intent was tried. If acquitted of the graver offence, the judge could then have sentenced the accused for the lesser offence.[66]

Where the accused pleads guilty to an alternative offence, the court's sentence on the plea of guilty constitutes an acquittal of the offence charged, or of the other offence charged, for this rule applies equally where the two offences are charged in separate counts of the indictment.[67]

The plea of guilty must also be unambiguous and complete.[68] If it is recorded in an imperfect state the Court of Appeal will quash the conviction and either send the accused back for trial or discharge him.[69] If the accused is not represented, the judge should advise him on the law, particularly if the depositions suggest a defence.

The procedure on a plea of guilty is considered later.[70]

(b) *Not guilty*

This is sometimes called a " plea to the general issue " and the accused must himself pronounce it. When the accused pleads not guilty he joins issue with every or any part of the prosecution's case and the prosecution must prove every fact and circumstance constituting the offence charged.[71]

If the prosecution proposes to offer no evidence against the accused,[72] the accused pleads not guilty and the judge may order that a verdict of not guilty be entered on the record.[73]

(c) *To the jurisdiction*

This is a plea which is rarely used. The accused pleads it when the court hearing the indictment has no jurisdiction to do so. It might be

---

[65] This does not apply to demurrers and special pleas: Criminal Law Act 1967, s. 6 (1) (*a*); see pp. 159–169.

[66] *R.* v. *Cole* [1965] 2 Q.B. 388.

[67] Criminal Law Act 1967, s. 6 (5).

[68] *R.* v. *Ingleson* [1915] 1 K.B. 512 (on alternative charges of stealing, and receiving stolen horses, the plea of " guilty of taking horses not knowing them to be stolen " was bad); *R.* v. *Baker* (1912) 7 Cr.App.R. 217 (the accused pleaded guilty and brought out in mitigation that he had the defence of lawful authority); *R.* v. *Hussey* (1924) 18 Cr.App.R. 121 and *R.* v. *Emery* (1943) 29 Cr.App.R. 47 (" plead guilty in self-defence " was a nullity).

[69] *R.* v. *Griffiths* (1932) 23 Cr.App.R. 153.

[70] See Section F, p. 215.

[71] Subject to any formal admissions made by the accused; see p. 112.

[72] See p. 4.

[73] Criminal Justice Act 1967, s. 17. As to records, see Courts Act 1971, s. 10.

used if the alleged offence was committed outside the territorial jurisdiction or by a person who is entitled to claim immunity.[74]

(d) *Demurrer*

This is a preliminary submission to the court to decide whether, if the accused admits all the factual allegations, he can be convicted of any offence known to law.[75] It is no longer in common use[76] because the omission of some element of an offence may quite simply be cured by an amendment of the indictment under section 5 (1) of the Indictments Act 1915.[77] The accused may plead not guilty as well as make a demurrer.[78]

The following three pleas are known as " special pleas in bar," *i.e.* they are a bar to trial on the allegations of the indictment.

(e) *Autrefois acquit and autrefois convict*

The principle underlying these two pleas was expressed by Blackstone as " the universal maximum of the common law of England that no man is to be brought into jeopardy of his life, more than once, for the same offence."[79] For the words "his life," "conviction" or " punishment " would now be appropriate.

In its simplest form, an accused cannot be tried a second time for an offence of which he has previously been charged and acquitted or convicted. In more complicated circumstances, two questions must be considered. First of all, if the charge, to which the accused makes the plea, comprises factual as well as legal elements, to what extent can a charge, based on the same facts, be made after a conviction or acquittal? Secondly, what procedures, apart from a verdict of guilty or not guilty, amount to conviction or acquittal for the purposes of the plea?

Second charge on the same facts. In *Connelly* v. *D.P.P.*[80] the House of Lords considered the following facts:

---

[74] See pp. 9–15. It is likely, however, that the second of these possibilities would be dealt with informally before arraignment or at committal proceedings. See also *R.* v. *Johnson* (1805) 6 East 583.

[75] *Cf.* the modern practice, recently disapproved, where the accused admits the factual allegations before the judge for the purpose of establishing whether there is any point in defending; see p. 155.

[76] " I hope that now demurrer in criminal cases will be allowed to die naturally ": Lord Parker C.J. in *R.* v. *Deputy Chairman of Inner London Quarter Sessions* [1969] 3 All E.R. 1537, at p. 1541 (the plea in this case was improperly made as it was not in writing).

[77] See p. 146 and *R.* v. *Fraser* (1923) 17 Cr.App.R. 182.

[78] Criminal Law Act 1967, s. 6 (1) (*a*).

[79] 4 Bl.Com. 329. The Interpretation Act 1889, s. 33, restates the basic principle to cover offences which are offences by statute and at common law.

[80] [1964] A.C. 1254. The judgment of Lord Morris, at p. 1296, gives a comprehensive review of earlier law and cases.

Four robbers made an armed raid on the Mitcham Co-operative Society in the course of which a man was shot dead. Four men were charged with and convicted of murder on one indictment. Another indictment was preferred for the robbery during which the murder was committed but it was not proceeded with. The conviction of one of the accused for murder was quashed on appeal because of a misdirection to the jury. The prosecution then " revived " the second indictment against this accused and he was convicted of robbery. Before the House of Lords he contended that his plea of *autrefois acquit* to the second indictment, which had been rejected by two trial judges, should have precluded his trial and conviction.

The House of Lords held that Connelly's plea of *autrefois acquit* was rightly rejected and drew the following conclusions:

(*a*) Subsequent trial is barred for the same offence as, and for any other offence of which the accused could have been convicted,[81] at the first trial. For example, A is indicted for and acquitted of murder. The general verdict of not guilty of murder precludes any subsequent trial for manslaughter, infanticide or any other offence listed in the Criminal Law Act 1967, s. 6 (2),[82] and for attempted murder.[83]

(*b*) Even where the accused could not have been convicted of the offence charged, a subsequent trial will be barred if the offence is substantially the same.[84] This happens where the prosecution is obliged to prove that the accused committed another offence of which he has previously been convicted or acquitted.[85] One test for this proposition as expressed by Lord Morris is whether the evidence necessary to support the later charge would have sufficed to procure a conviction on the first

---

[81] See Alternative verdicts, p. 213; see also p. 271.

[82] See p. 214.

[83] Criminal Law Act 1967, s. 6 (3) and (4); *D.P.P.* v. *Nasralla* [1967] 2 A.C. 238 (a Privy Council case from Jamaica complicated by a special verdict); see also *R.* v. *Tancock* (1876) 13 Cox 217.

[84] The definition of the offence in question may need careful examination in order to establish whether an apparently identical charge is even substantially the same; under s. 14 (1) (*b*) of the Trade Descriptions Act 1968, for instance, the publication of a false statement occurs each time it is communicated to a new reader, so where two million copies of a brochure were distributed, the plea of *autrefois convict* could not be used for the second and subsequent readings of the brochure because each reading by a client was a significantly new fact: *R.* v. *Thomson Holidays* [1974] 2 W.L.R. 371. See, however, the power to stay oppressive indictments, p. 166.

[85] *Per* Lord Devlin [1964] A.C. 1254 at p. 1341.

charge, or a conviction of an offence of which he could have been convicted on that charge.[86]

In the light of decided cases, this proposition would appear to be virtually limited to what Lord Hodson described as the " ascending scale principle,"[87] except where death occurs after the first verdict, as in paragraph (*c*), below. For instance, if the accused has been charged with and acquitted of a minor offence (common assault), he cannot later be tried for the same offence in an aggravated form (assault occasioning actual bodily harm or wounding with intent) although he could not have been convicted of it at the first trial.[88] In the later trial the prosecution would again have to prove the assault, which has already been tried, in order to prove the aggravated offence.

On a " descending scale," *autrefois acquit* would normally apply because the accused could have been found guilty of the lesser offence at the first trial, as in paragraph (*a*), above. In cases where the alternative verdict is not available, it is a question of whether the later charge is of " the same offence."[89] In all the following cases where a plea of *autrefois* was put forward the two charges arose out of the same incident or course of conduct[90]:

R. v. *Vandercomb and Abbott*[91]: acquittal of burglary involving breaking and entering a house *and stealing therein*; second indictment for breaking and entering *with intent to steal*—plea failed.[92]

R. v. *Collins*[93]: acquittal of rape because of the girl's consent; second indictment for burglary involving entering with intent to commit that rape—plea failed.

R. v. *Gould*[94]: acquittal of murder alleged to be committed in the course of burglary; second indictment for the burglary—plea failed.

R. v. *Norton*[95]: acquittal of having carnal knowledge of a girl under 13; second indictment for felonious wounding—plea failed.

---

86 *Per* Lord Morris, *ibid.*, at p. 1305; see also p. 213.

87 *Ibid.* at p. 1332.

88 *R.* v. *Stanton* (1851) 5 Cox 324; *R.* v. *Miles* (1890) 24 Q.B.D. 423.

89 See quotation from Blackstone on p. 159.

90 See [1964] A.C. 1254 at pp. 1297–1330.

91 (1796) 2 Leach 708 at p. 720. In this case all the judges were called to the Exchequer Chamber to examine the plea.

92 Nor was a second indictment for stealing the same goods as were alleged to have been stolen in the first indictment barred.

93 [1976] Crim.L.R. 249.

94 (1840) 9 C. & P. 364.

95 (1910) 5 Cr.App.R. 197; the result would have been different had the wounding been an *essential part* of the sexual offence.

R. v. *Kupferberg*[96]: acquittal of conspiring to commit an offence; second indictment for aiding and abetting the same offence—plea failed.

R. v. *Coughlan*[97]: conviction of conspiracy to plant bombs in Birmingham; second charge of the same conspiracy to plant bombs in Manchester—plea failed.

R. v. *Miles*[98]: acquittal of larceny from the person; second charge of being in a public place with the intention of committing a felony—plea failed.

R. v. *Barron*[98a]: acquittal of buggery; second indictment for gross indecency—plea failed.

Wemyss v. *Hopkins*[99]: conviction of statutory assault; second charge of assault under a different statute—plea succeeded.

R. v. *King*[1]: conviction of obtaining credit by fraud; second indictment for larceny of the goods obtained—plea succeeded.

In *R.* v. *Barron*, above, the rather surprising result was reached on the ground that " acquittal of the whole offence is not an acquittal of every part of it." As gross indecency is necessarily a part of buggery, a verdict of the lesser offence would now probably be returnable under section 6 of the Criminal Law Act 1967.[2]

(*c*) If at the time of the first trial the offence to be proved is not complete, the accused may later be indicted for the complete offence. This probably only applies in homicide. In *R.* v. *Thomas*[3] a conviction of wounding with intent to murder did not bar the accused's subsequent trial for murder when the victim died of the wounds after the conviction but within a year and a day. A conviction for neglecting a child under section 1 of the Children and Young Persons Act 1933 is no bar to a later charge of manslaughter if the child dies.[4] *Quaere* whether an acquittal of dangerous driving would bar a later charge of causing death by dangerous driving if the death occurred after the first verdict.

---

[96] (1918) 13 Cr.App.R. 166.

[97] [1976] Crim.L.R. 631.

[98] (1909) 3 Cr.App.R. 13.

[98a] [1914] 2 K.B. 570.

[99] (1875) L.R. 10 Q.B. 378.

[1] [1897] 1 Q.B. 214; Hawkins J. based his argument on the offences being " practically the same, though not their legal operation." This is too wide for general application, particularly as the two offences charged were mutually inconsistent anyway.

[2] See p. 213; see also *R.* v. *Harris*, p. 136.

[3] [1950] 1 K.B. 26; see also *R.* v. *Morris* (1867) 10 Cox 480.

[4] *R.* v. *Tonks* [1916] 1 K.B. 443.

As to procedures which amount to acquittal or conviction for the purposes of an *autrefois* plea, the following must be answered [5]: Was the accused " in jeopardy " on the first indictment? Was there a final verdict? [6]

Autrefois acquit. On a plea of *autrefois acquit* six other procedures rank as an acquittal on indictment:

(*a*) A valid conviction which is quashed on appeal.[7]

(*b*) A summary conviction of the offence by a magistrates' court.[8]

(*c*) A dismissal by a magistrates' court of an information of an offence which could be tried on indictment.[9]

(*d*) A verdict of not guilty entered by order of the judge. Where the prosecution proposes to offer no evidence [10] and the accused pleads not guilty, the judge may, if he thinks fit, order a verdict of not guilty to be recorded without calling the jury.[11]

(*e*) A successful submission of no case to answer when the judge directs the jury to return a verdict of not guilty.[12]

(*f*) An acquittal by a court of competent jurisdiction outside England.[13]

The following do not amount to an acquittal:

(*a*) The dismissal of a charge at the preliminary investigation by thc examining justice.[14] This is not a final verdict; the prosecution may bring a fresh charge or apply to a judge for his consent to a voluntary preferment.[15]

---

[5] See Kenny, *Outlines of Criminal Law* (19th ed.), p. 606. He asks the third question, " Was the previous charge substantially the same as the present one? " This has been considered, above.

[6] If the verdict in question followed a trial on indictment, it must have been announced by the jury in open court: *R.* v. *Robinson* [1975] 2 W.L.R. 117.

[7] *R.* v. *Barron* [1914] 2 K.B. 570 at p. 573; and see p. 262 *et seq.*

[8] *Wemyss* v. *Hopkins* (1875) L.R. 10 Q.B. 378 at p. 381 (a case of *autrefois convict*). This is subject to the unusual feature of summary proceedings whereby the prosecution may appeal to the High Court; if an information against an accused is dismissed, the prosecutor may appeal by way of case stated and the High Court may direct that the justices convict the accused. This is not, however, an exception to the rule of double jeopardy as the proceedings at which the accused is convicted are part of the original proceedings. *See* Chap. 14, p. 349.

[9] Magistrates' Courts Act 1952, s. 19. As to offences triable summarily or on indictment, see pp. 292–299. Under the Offences against the Person Act 1861, s. 45, the dismissal of a complaint of assault under ss. 42–44 of the Act is a bar to all subsequent proceedings, civil or criminal, for " the same cause." The justices certify the dismissal (s. 44) but must not do so if it is a proper case for trial by jury (s. 46). The Criminal Law Revision Committee has provisionally recommended the repeal of these sections: *Working Paper on Offences against the Person* (H.M.S.O.).

[10] See pp. 4 and 158.

[11] Criminal Justice Act 1967, s. 17.

[12] See p. 202.

[13] *R.* v. *Aughet* (1918) 13 Cr.App.R. 101.

[14] *Flatman* v. *Light* [1946] K.B. 414 at p. 419; see also p. 100.

[15] See p. 144.

(*b*) The withdrawal with the leave of the court of a charge[16] or of a complaint of assault in a magistrates' court without having a full hearing on the merits.[17]

(*c*) The verdict of a court which lacked jurisdiction to try the offence. In this case the accused would not have been in jeopardy.[18]

(*d*) An invalid verdict,[19] such as a majority verdict on an inadequate majority.[20]

(*e*) An acquittal on a defective indictment.[21]

(*f*) The staying of proceedings on the *nolle prosequi* of the Attorney-General.[22]

(*g*) Judgment for the accused on a demurrer or a motion in arrest of judgment.[23]

(*h*) The discharge of the jury at any stage of the trial.[24]

Autrefois convict. Summary conviction by a magistrates' court counts as a conviction on indictment for the purposes of this plea[25] and the conviction by a competent foreign court would found a plea.[26]

If the accused pleaded not guilty, the jury's verdict founds the plea and it is immaterial whether or not sentence was passed.[27] If he pleaded guilty it would appear that he is convicted when the court accepts the plea.[28] However, the court has a discretion to allow him to withdraw it before sentence and there is a limited right to appeal after a plea of guilty.[29] Even so, it is probable that the conviction would be a "final verdict," for the purposes of *autrefois convict*, on

---

[16] See p. 4.

[17] Offences against the Person Act 1861, ss. 44 and 45, *Ellis* v. *Burton* [1975] 1 W.L.R. 386; see footnote 9 above.

[18] This was tentatively suggested in *R.* v. *Flower* (1956) 40 Cr.App.R. 189 at p. 193.

[19] See p. 209.

[20] *R.* v. *Randall* [1960] Crim.L.R. 435 (majority verdicts were not permissible at all then).

[21] *R.* v. *Drury* (1849) 3 C. & K. 193 (judgment on conviction was set aside on a writ of error); *R.* v. *Green* (1856) Dears. & B. 113 (stolen boots were wrongly described); *R.* v. *Marsham* [1912] 2 K.B. 362 (hearing of a charge was not brought to judgment and was then started afresh). As to defective indictments, see pp. 128–141.

[22] See p. 18.

[23] See p. 159 and 218.

[24] See p. 205.

[25] *R.* v. *Miles* (1890) 24 Q.B.D. 423.

[26] *R.* v. *Aughet* (1918) 13 Cr.App.R. 101.

[27] *R.* v. *Sheridan* [1937] 1 K.B. 223 and at p. 229 (a case where justices announced their finding of guilt only).

[28] *R.* v. *Grant* (1936) 26 Cr.App.R. 8.

[29] *R.* v. *McNally* [1954] 1 W.L.R. 933; and see pp. 265 and 273. *Archbold*, para. 426, says "a plea of guilty does not rank as a conviction until the offender is sentenced." No authority is cited and it is submitted that this relates only to the court's power to accept a plea of guilty to a lesser charge or a change of plea.

being recorded unless the plea was void [30] or was in fact upset later.

A finding of assault on a complaint counts as a conviction,[31] but the following two matters do not:

(*a*) The adjudication of a domestic tribunal, such as a professional disciplinary body. In *Lewis* v. *Morgan* [32] a ship's master held an inquiry on board and fined the accused and in *R.* v. *Hogan* [33] visiting justices made an order for loss of remission, etc., against an escaped prisoner. The trial by a court for neglect of duty and prison breach respectively was not barred. A member of a police force who is acquitted or convicted of a criminal offence cannot be charged with an offence against discipline which is in substance the same as the criminal offence.[34] As all complaints against the police which may involve the commission of a criminal offence must first be referred to the D.P.P.,[35] the police are effectively protected from double jeopardy unless the disciplinary offence consists of having been found guilty of a criminal offence.[36]

(*b*) The practice whereby a convicted person asks for an outstanding offence to be taken into consideration in sentence [37] does not bar prosecution even if he is sentenced for it.[38] This is not as likely to result in double punishment as it might seem; he would not be sentenced in this way for a serious offence and the court at the second trial could use its discretion to stay the proceedings.[38]

Procedure. The accused may make a special plea as well as a plea of not guilty.[39] Normally he would make the special plea first. It may be made informally but if the judge considers that it may be successful it should be written down with the usual commencement [40] and the words " A.B. says that the Queen ought not further to prosecute the indictment against him, because he has been lawfully acquitted [convicted] of the offence charged therein." The Crown joins

---

30 See pp. 155 and 157.
31 Offences against the Person Act 1861, s. 45; see footnote 9 p. 163.
32 [1943] K.B. 376.
33 [1960] 2 Q.B. 513.
34 Police Act 1976, s. 11 (1).
35 *Ibid.* s. 5 (1).
36 *Ibid.* s. 11 (2).
37 See p. 220.
38 *R.* v. *Nicholson* (1947) 32 Cr.App.R. 98, 127; see also p. 221.
39 Criminal Law Act 1967, s. 6 (1) (*a*).
40 The Crown Court at——

The Queen v. *A.B.*

issue in a " replication "[41] and a jury is summoned to try it. The accused bears the burden of proving the acquittal or conviction which he may do by producing a certificate of the appropriate officer of the relevant court.[42]

There are two further general considerations which can conveniently be dealt with at this stage:

Discretion to stay proceedings. " As a general rule a judge should stay an indictment (that is, order that it remain on the file not to be proceeded with [without the leave of the court]) when he is satisfied that the charges therein are founded on the same facts as the charges in a previous indictment on which the accused has been tried, or form or are a part of a series of offences of the same or a similar character as the offences charged in the previous indictment."[43]

The judge's power to intervene is founded on and limited to the restraint of an abuse of the process of the court. He cannot stop a prosecution " merely because he considers that as a matter of policy, it ought not to have been brought " [44]; the decision to prosecute is an executive decision and the constitutional division of powers is of major importance. Moreover, the accused is generally better protected by his right to the verdict of a jury, and the judge should not use this power simply because the prosecution is unlikely to succeed.[45]

In the context of this section the judge's power arises where the strict principle of *autrefois* is not applicable, for instance where the prosecution uses the same facts and evidence to found a different charge.[46] The use of the same evidence to support both indictments is as inconclusive a test on this issue as on *autrefois convict* or *acquit*. The facts of *Connelly's* case [47] illustrate this. Where the prosecution believes that an accused is lying, a later charge of perjury may be oppressive, especially if the accused is convicted of the original

---

41 " [Officer of the Court] joins issue on behalf of the Queen."

42 Evidence Act 1851, s. 13.

43 *Per* Lord Devlin in *Connelly* v. *D.P.P.* [1964] A.C. 1254 at pp. 1359–40, the words in square brackets are added from *ibid.*, p. 1354. He examines the previous case law at pp. 1340–1354. The principle is based on the Indictments Rules 1971, r. 9, as to which, see p. 133. If two indictments exist charging the same offence against the same person on the same facts, the second must necessarily be stayed: Practice Direction [1976] 1 W.L.R. 409.

44 *Per* Lord Salmon in *D.P.P.* v. *Humphrys* [1976] 2 W.L.R. 857 at p. 889. Viscount Dilhorne, at p. 871, considered that the power is even more limited.

45 *R.* v. *Chairman, London Quarter Sessions, ex p. Downes* [1954] 1 Q.B. 1.

46 In *R.* v. *Barron* [1914] 2 K.B. 570 (see p. 162) *per* Lord Reading at p. 575.

47 See p. 160.

offence. In cases such as *D.P.P.* v. *Humphrys*,[48] however, the perjury charge may be amply justified.

Res judicata and issue estoppel. In civil cases " no one should be sued twice on the same ground. The practical consequence is that, generally speaking, the order of a court of competent jurisdiction is conclusive."[49] This rule has two principal effects:

(*a*) It applies both to the retrial of the complete issue and to the repeated reliance on the grounds of that issue as a part of some other claim.

(*b*) Apart from judgments *in rem*, its applicability varies according to whether it arises between the same or different parties.

Retrial of the complete issue in a criminal case is barred by *autrefois convict* or *acquit*. " Issue estoppel "—repeated reliance on the grounds and evidence of the earlier charge—has no application in criminal proceedings. In *D.P.P.* v. *Humphrys*[50] the House of Lords considered a case in which an accused acquitted of a substantive charge (driving while disqualified) was later charged with perjury at his trial. This necessarily required the prosecution to repeat the allegations and evidence which had been given at the first trial. The accused contended that the prosecution was estopped from repeating a policeman's identification of him as the driver on that occasion because he had been acquitted, having given evidence that he had not driven at all during the year in question and which suggested that the person identified by the policeman had been someone else.

On the reasoning in *Connelly's* case explained above, *autrefois acquit* could clearly not be pleaded. He contended instead that the issue between the Crown and himself (*i.e.* whether he was driving on a particular occasion) had been finally decided by the jury's verdict: the issue was *res judicata* and the prosecution was therefore estopped from relying on the allegation.

The House of Lords rejected this contention: issue estoppel has no place in criminal proceedings. Lord Salmon summed up the reasons as follows[51]:

> "In the criminal field, however, besides being complex and technical, the doctrine of issue estoppel would, in my view, also be inappropriate, artificial, unnecessary and unfair. It would be inappropriate because there are no pleadings defining the issues and

[48] [1976] 2 W.L.R. 857; see below.
[49] Cross, *Evidence* (3rd ed.), p. 271.
[50] [1976] 2 W.L.R. 857.
[51] *Ibid.* at p. 887.

no judgments explaining how the issues (even if identifiable) were decided. . . . Since juries give general verdicts ' guilty ' or ' not guilty ' it would often be difficult, if not impossible, to do more than guess how they had decided any issue capable of identification. . . . Issue estoppel would often be artificial and unfair. Take the not infrequent case in which the jury decides an issue in the defendant's favour not because they are satisfied that their solution is correct but because they are left in doubt whether the contrary had been proved. In such a case, surely it would be artificial and unjust if the defendant, who, quite rightly in my view, enjoys many advantages, should be given the added bonus that the issue should thereafter be presumed for ever to have been irrevocably decided in his favour as between himself and the Crown. . . . Moreover, I think that it is wholly unnecessary to introduce issue estoppel into the criminal field. The doctrine of *autrefois acquit* and *convict* amply protects the accused from being brought into double jeopardy."

Distinction (*b*), above, has received less judicial attention. On the analogy of *autrefois convict*, how far could a verdict of guilty against one person bar the trial of another person for the same offence? If, for instance, in the famous cases of Evans and Christie,[52] the prosecution had charged Christie with the murder of Evans' wife (of which Evans had previously been convicted), would Christie have been able to rely on *res judicata* to bar trial of the charge? The practical answer is that the first conviction would be referred to the Court of Appeal by the Home Secretary under section 17 of the Criminal Appeal Act 1968 [53]; the second case could be proceeded with without hindrance if the first conviction was quashed.

Where a person is charged with an offence, an essential element of which is the commission by another person of an offence, and that other person is acquitted, the accused may not rely on the other's acquittal in his defence.[54] The House of Lords has ruled [55] that an acquittal is evidence only of the prosecution's failure to prove an accused's guilt.

(*f*) *Pardon*

The Royal pardon [56] is a bar to prosecution and should be pleaded

[52] See the Report of the Brabin Inquiry (1966) Cmnd. 3101.

[53] See p. 265; *quaere* whether this could be done if the first person convicted had died: the terms of the section do not preclude it.

[54] *Cf. R.* v. *Maskell* (1970) 50 Cr.App.R. 429 and *R.* v. *Close* [1977] Crim. L.R. 107.

[55] See *D.P.P.* v. *Shannon*, p. 138.

[56] See p. 256.

as soon as possible, *i.e.* if the accused obtains a pardon before arraignment, he pleads it in bar to the indictment; if he obtains it after conviction, he may move it in arrest of judgment [57] or, after sentence, in arrest of execution.[58] If he does not use it as soon as possible he may be taken to have waived it.[59]

(*g*) *Change of plea*

The court has a discretion to allow the accused to change his mind after he has pleaded guilty or not guilty. As already mentioned [60] a plea of guilty can only be withdrawn before sentence and only with the leave of the court.[61] If not withdrawn the accused may still appeal but the Court of Appeal will only hear him in limited circumstances.[62]

If the court allows the accused to change a plea of guilty, evidence of the original plea of guilty is admissible, but may be excluded in the discretion of the judge if, in his view, the prejudice necessarily flowing from its admission outweighs its probative value.[63]

The court may also give leave to an accused who has pleaded not guilty to plead guilty. The verdict of the jury must be taken before accepting the guilty plea or the trial will be a nullity.[64] The practice of changing a plea to guilty after the judge has ruled as a matter of law that a reasonable jury could not contemplate an acquittal on the evidence is to be treated with great caution.[65]

If the accused does not make a plea, two other courses of action have to be considered.

(*h*) *Standing mute*

If the accused will not answer directly or at all on arraignment, the court may order a plea of not guilty to be entered on his behalf and the trial proceeds normally.[66] This should be done, for instance, if he adheres to a plea such as " guilty in self-defence." [67] If he does not speak intelligibly or does not speak at all, the court must determine whether he is mute " of malice " or " by visitation of God," and must summon a jury of 12 to decide it.

---

[57] See p. 218.
[58] See p. 219.
[59] 2 Hawk. c. 37, s. 59.
[60] See pp. 155 and 164.
[61] *R.* v. *McNally* [1954] 1 W.L.R. 933.
[62] See p. 265.
[63] *R.* v. *Rimmer* [1972] 1 W.L.R. 268; *R.* v. *Hetherington* [1972] Crim.L.R. 703.
[64] *R.* v. *Heyes* [1951] 1 K.B. 29.
[65] *R.* v. *Powles, The Times*, March 30, 1976; *cf. R.* v. *Vickers*, p. 155, and the roles of judge and jury, p. 206.
[66] Criminal Law Act 1967, s. 6 (1) (*c*).
[67] See footnote 68, p. 158.

To be mute of malice means wilfully to refuse to speak and the prosecution must prove this beyond reasonable doubt, after which a plea of not guilty is ordered.[68] The visitation of God may take the form of deafness, dumbness or insanity; it does not bar trial, and a plea of not guilty may be entered, provided the accused will be able to understand the proceedings.

(*i*) *Fitness to plead and to be tried*

The accused will be unable to understand the proceedings if he is insane. Fitness to plead and fitness to be tried constitute one issue only. Alderson B. defined the necessary disability as " whether the prisoner is of sufficient intellect to comprehend the course of the proceedings on the trial, so as to make a proper defence . . . and to comprehend the details of the evidence." [69] This dictum has since been approved, as in *R.* v. *Robertson* [70] where a mere incapacity to act in his own best interests was held to be insufficient grounds to deprive the accused of his right to trial. An additional test is his ability to communicate with his legal advisers [71] and the existence of some certain means by which they can explain the matters to him.

Amnesia concerning the events surrounding the alleged crime cannot alone amount to insanity for the purposes of fitness to plead and standing trial.[72] A deaf-mute may be tried if he is sane. However, if he is illiterate or blind as well and cannot communicate, a finding that he is unfit to plead will have the same effect as a finding of insanity.[73] If there is a temporary interruption to communication, as by a wound in the throat, and the jury finds the accused sane, the trial may be adjourned.[74]

If the accused has stood mute, a jury would have been empanelled to try that issue. They should first be re-sworn to decide whether he is able to plead and then to decide whether he is insane.[75] If the prosecution raises the question of insanity, it must be proved beyond reasonable doubt [76]; if the accused raises it, he has to prove it on the balance of probabilities. It will normally be raised on arraignment, but the jury may postpone consideration of it until the opening of the

[68] Criminal Law Act 1967, s. 6 (1) (*c*); *R.* v. *Sharp* (1957) 41 Cr.App.R. 197.
[69] *R.* v. *Pritchard* (1836) 7 C. & P. 303 at p. 304.
[70] [1968] 1 W.L.R. 1767.
[71] *R.* v. *Sharp* (1957) 41 Cr.App.R. 197.
[72] *R.* v. *Podola* [1960] 1 Q.B. 325.
[73] *i.e.* a hospital order can be made; as to which see below and p. 234, and see *ex p. Emery* [1909] 2 K.B. 81.
[74] *R.* v. *Harris* (1897) 61 J.P. 792.
[75] *R.* v. *Pritchard* (1836) 7 C. & P. 303.
[76] *R.* v. *Robertson* [1968] 1 W.L.R. 1767.

case for the defence.[77] This enables the jury to acquit, if the prosecution does not make out its case,[78] without considering the accused's sanity.

If a plea of not guilty is entered and the accused is tried the jury which tries his fitness cannot be the jury which tries the case, unless the consideration of his fitness is postponed and the court directs that they should be the same.[79] If he is found to be insane he is removed by order of the court to a hospital specified by the Secretary of State.[80]

C. The Jury

There is no room in a book of this size to consider the general nature of the jury, its value or its drawbacks. Readers would be well advised to read further on the subject [81] as it sheds much light on the peculiarities of the English trial. At this stage only the composition of the jury and the powers of the parties to alter its composition are considered. The jury's role and verdict are considered in Sections D and E, below.[82]

The impartiality of the jury as judge of the facts is secured in as many ways as possible. For this reason the jurors are not called until after arraignment so that they do not know if the accused has pleaded guilty either to another count of the indictment or to a lesser offence.[83]

Composition of the jury

The jury consists of 12 people, male and female, aged between 18 and 65, who are qualified to serve as jurors because they are registered parliamentary or local government electors and have been resident in the United Kingdom for any period of five years since reaching the age of 13, and who are not ineligible or disqualified as

---

[77] Criminal Procedure (Insanity) Act 1964, s. 4 (2); see also p. 278.

[78] See p. 202.

[79] Criminal Procedure (Insanity) Act 1964, s. 4 (4). The trial of the issue should be postponed where there is a likelihood that the accused will be acquitted, *e.g.* on a submission of no case to answer: *R.* v. *Burles* [1970] 2 Q.B. 191.

[80] *Ibid.* s. 5; Mental Health Act 1959, s. 72; the last-mentioned section uses the words " mental illness, psychopathic disorder, subnormality or severe subnormality ": subs. (1).

[81] Particularly to be recommended are Devlin, *Trial by Jury* (1966) (Hamlyn Lectures 1956); Cornish, *The Jury* (1968); Glanville Williams, *The Proof of Guilt* (1963), pp. 253–343 (Hamlyn Lectures 1955) and the Report of the Morris Committee on Jury Service (1965) Cmnd. 2627.

[82] See pp. 206 and 208, and see pp. 266–268.

[83] See p. 157; *R.* v. *Darke* (1937) 26 Cr.App.R. 85; *R.* v. *Lashbrooke* (1958) 43 Cr App.R. 86.

defined in Schedule 1 of the Juries Act 1974.[84] The names are taken from the electoral register.[85]

The Lord Chancellor is responsible for the provision of juries to the Crown Court. The local officer responsible for the electoral register sends a copy of it to the Lord Chancellor, deleting, as far as possible, the names of those who are under 18 or over 65.[86] The Lord Chancellor then issues summonses to people on the lists [87] and prepares " panels " of the people summoned to be available at a particular court on a particular date.[88] A juror's summons may be withdrawn if his attendance appears to be unnecessary to the officer of the court responsible for managing the jury.[89]

Various classes of person must or need not serve on a jury: a person who is disqualified or ineligible must not serve and a person who is excusable need not serve. He may be excusable as of right or in the discretion of the court.[90]

(a) Disqualifications

In addition to people who do not satisfy the age or residence requirements of section 1 of the Juries Act 1974, any person who has been sentenced to imprisonment for three months or more in the last 10 years, or who has ever been sentenced to imprisonment for life or for five years or more, is disqualified.[91] If such a person serves on a jury, however, the jury's verdict is not void on that account.[92]

(b) Ineligibility

Schedule 1, Part I, of the Juries Act 1974 lists four groups of people ineligible for jury service:

Group A those who have at any time held judicial office, including justices of the peace and chairmen of tribunals.

Group B those who have carried on certain occupations in the last

[84] Juries Act 1974, s. 1. Coroners' juries are generally outside the scope of the Act; they consist of between seven and 11 people and are not subject to rules for selection. Service on a coroner's jury is not a ground for excusal from Crown Court jury service under s. 8; see p. 38. The Act also covers juries in civil cases in the High Court and county courts.

[85] *Ibid.* s. 3.

[86] *Ibid.* s. 3 (1).

[87] *Ibid.* s. 2. Regard must be had to the convenience of the person summoned and his place of residence, and to the desirability of selecting jurors within a reasonable daily travelling distance of the court: subs. (2).

[88] *Ibid.* s. 5.

[89] *Ibid.* s. 4.

[90] Representations may be made on receipt of the summons or at the court, if the juror attends: *ibid.*, s. 2 (5).

[91] *Ibid.* Sched. 1, Part II.

[92] *Ibid.* s. 18.

10 years, such as barristers and solicitors (whether or not in actual practice), their clerks and legal executives, court staff, the police, probation officers and forensic scientists.

Group C the clergy and vowed members of religious orders.

Group D the mentally ill.

Groups A, B and C are ineligible because of the undue weight that might be given to their opinions by " lay " members of the jury.

(*c*) *Excusal as of right*

Three groups of people may claim excusal as of right under Part III of Schedule 1:

(i) Members and officers of Parliament and peers and peeresses.
(ii) Full-time serving members of the armed services.
(iii) Practising members of the medical and similar professions (including veterinary surgeons and pharmacists).

(*d*) *Discretionary excusal*

Excusal as of right is, generally speaking, granted to people whose absence from their work is incompatible with the public interest. Three categories of discretionary excusal also exist:

(i) A person who has served on a jury within the last two years or longer period allowed by the court in a particular case.[93]
(ii) A person who shows good reason to be excused[94]; he should be excused if he is personally concerned in the facts of or with the parties or witnesses to a case; he may put forward personal hardship or conscientious objection; general grounds such as race, religion, political beliefs or occupation do not found a request for excusal.[95]
(iii) A person who appears to the appropriate officer of the court, in cases of doubt, to be incapable of acting effectively as a juror on account of physical disability or insufficient understanding of English.[96]

If it appears to the court that the jury is likely to be incomplete, it may require persons in, or in the vicinity of, the court to be summoned without written notice up to the number needed to make a

[93] *Ibid.* s. 8.

[94] *Ibid.* s. 9 (2); there is a right of appeal under subs. (3) and subs. (4) preserves the right of the court to which he is summoned to excuse any juror from attending. The excusal under subs. (2) is granted by an officer of the court.

[95] Practice Direction [1973] 1 W.L.R. 134. A person who serves on a jury is entitled to reimbursement at the prescribed rate for travelling and subsistence and for financial loss due to his attendance at court: Juries Act 1974, s. 19.

[96] Juries Act 1974, s. 10. The judge decides the question of capacity.

full jury after allowing for disqualifications, refusals and challenges.[97]

The parties and their representatives are entitled to inspect the panel of jurors summoned for the current sitting of the court of trial.[98] The 12 jurors who are to try the case are elected by ballot in open court from the panel, or part of the panel, of summoned jurors[99] The parties then have a power to object to them, *i.e.* to challenge.

Challenging

The challenge may be *peremptory*, *i.e.* no reason need be given for the objection, or *for cause* in which case the objection must be justified.[1] Challenges for cause are either *to the polls*, *i.e.* to an individual juror, or *to the array* where objection is taken to all the jurors in a body. Challenges for cause both to the polls and to the array may be *principal*, *i.e.* the reason for objecting is apparent, or *for favour* where a possibility of impartiality is revealed by extrinsic evidence.

A challenge to the polls must be made after the juror's name has been drawn by ballot and before he is sworn.[2] A challenge to the array, which is expressly preserved despite the transfer of responsibility to the Lord Chancellor,[3] should be made before any juror is sworn.

(*a*) *Peremptory challenges*

These challenges can only be made to individual jurors, *i.e.* to the polls, and only by the accused or his counsel.[4] There is a practice, however, whereby prosecuting counsel can ask that a juror stand by until there are no more jurors available on the panel before giving his reason for the challenge.[5] The judge has a discretion to do this himself or to allow the accused to do so.[6] The accused may make seven peremptory challenges[7] and, in a multiple trial, each accused may make seven.[8]

---

[97] Juries Act 1974 s. 6.

[98] Juries Act 1974, s. 5 (2). The right must be exercised before the close of the trial; s. 5 (3). The information contained in the panel must not include the prospective jurors' occupations: *R.* v. *Drummond* (1975) 119 S.J. 575.

[99] *Ibid.* s. 11 (1).

[1] *Ibid.* s. 12 (1).

[2] *Ibid.* s. 12 (3).

[3] *Ibid.* s. 12 (6).

[4] Juries Act 1825, s. 29; Juries Act 1974, s. 12 (1) and (4).

[5] *R.* v. *Parry* (1837) 7 C. & P. 836.

[6] *R.* v. *Chandler* [1964] 2 Q.B. 322.

[7] Juries Act 1974, s. 12 (1).

[8] If this were likely to consume a great deal of time, the prosecution might ask for separate trials.

(b) Challenges for cause

Both prosecution and defence may make these; they may be made to the polls or to the array; in either case they may be " principal " or " for favour." The juror may challenge himself, if he is disqualified or ineligible.[9]

(1) *To the polls: A principal* challenge for cause to the polls may be on the ground of the juror's disqualification to serve on a jury [10] or it may be for impartiality, *e.g.* the juror is a relative of the prosecutor or is manifestly prejudiced against the accused,[11] or because the person attending court is impersonating the juror who was impanelled.

Such a challenge *for favour* can be made where there is evidence that the juror is likely to act partially or under some prejudice, for instance, where he has been entertained in the house of one of the parties or where there is a suspicion that he has been threatened or bribed.

(2) *To the array:* This is exceedingly rare. If the challenger fails, he may challenge to the polls in respect of the same jurors.

1. A principal challenge for cause to the array may be made when the person responsible for summoning the jurors is suspected of impartial or defective selection, for instance, where he is himself the prosecutor or is acting for a party or is interested in some way in the prosecution,[12] or chose the jurors for their religious beliefs.[13]

2. A challenge to the array for favour may be made where the impartiality of the officer responsible for selecting the jury is less obvious as if, for instance, he were a close friend of the prosecutor or the accused.

(c) Effect of challenging

Challenges may be made orally by calling out " Challenge!" when the juror's name is selected by ballot but before he takes the oath.[14] A challenge for cause is tried by the judge [15] and the burden of proof is on the party making it. This may require witnesses to be called to support or rebut the challenge and the juror may himself be

---

[9] He commits an offence punishable by a maximum fine of £400 or £100 respectively if he serves on a jury knowing he is disqualified or ineligible: *ibid.*, s. 20 (5).

[10] *Ibid.* s. 12 (4).

[11] *R.* v. *O'Coigley* (1798) 26 St.Tr. 1191 at p. 1227, where a juror, looking at the accused, was heard to say " damned rascals." A person involved with the facts of the case may himself request excusal; see p. 173.

[12] *Baylis* v. *Lucas* (1779) 1 Cowp. 112.

[13] *R.* v. *O'Doherty* (1848) 6 St.Tr. (N.S.) 831.

[14] Juries Act 1974, s. 12 (3); each juror must be sworn individually: *ibid.* s. 11 (3).

[15] *Ibid.* s. 12 (1) (*b*).

examined. If the judge decides in favour of the challenge, whether it be peremptory or for cause, that juror (or the whole jury) is precluded from trying the case. If a disqualified or unfit juror is not challenged, the verdict is nevertheless generally valid.[16]

When the challenge, if any, is dismissed, the juror is sworn to " faithfully try the several issues " and to " give a true verdict according to the evidence." After that no challenge can be made. The accused is then given in charge of the jury, which means that the clerk of the court states to the jury the substance of the indictment and tells them that it is their function to return a verdict.

The jury selected by one ballot can try only one issue unless the trial of the second or last issue begins within 24 hours from the time when the jury is constituted, or unless the jury is called upon to try a special plea[17] or is directed to try the issue of the accused's fitness to plead.[18] An individual juror may be selected on more than one ballot, however, and the court may excuse an individual juror from trying a second or subsequent issue if he is likely to be challenged or excused or if the parties consent.[19]

D. The Order of Proceedings

The accused has now been arraigned and put in charge of the jury, which has been sworn in. Certain other relevant procedures may have been followed; in particular the accused may have made formal admissions[20] or either party may have moved to quash, or applied to amend, the indictment.[21]

The standard order of court proceedings where the accused is represented is as follows:

1. Prosecuting counsel opens his case.
2. He calls his first witness and examines him.
3. Defending counsel cross-examines the witness.
4. Prosecuting counsel, if he wishes, re-examines him.
   (2.–4. apply to each witness called.)
5. Defending counsel opens his case.
6. The accused, if he wishes, gives evidence.

---

16 Juries Act 1974, s. 18; see p. 172.

17 See pp. 158 and 165.

18 See p. 170.

19 Juries Act 1974, s. 11 (4)–(6).

20 Criminal Justice Act 1967, s. 10; see p. 112; see also written statements, p. 96, and alibi evidence, p. 112.

21 See p. 146 *et seq.* This should have been done before arraignment.

7. Other defence witnesses are called, examined, cross-examined by prosecuting counsel and re-examined by defence counsel.
8. Prosecuting counsel sums up the case for the prosecution.
9. Defence counsel sums up the case for the accused.
10. The judge sums up to the jury.
11. The jury retires to consider its verdict.

In this basic order variations, which will be considered after an explanation of the above steps, may arise at several stages for the following reasons:

(*a*) The accused is unrepresented.
(*b*) There is more than one accused.
(*c*) The accused submits that the prosecution has failed to prove its case.
(*d*) The prosecution wishes to rebut unexpected evidence adduced by the defence.
(*e*) Either party raises a point of law during the trial.
(*f*) The court allows the jury to visit the scene of the crime.
(*g*) The court, for some reason, orders an adjournment.
(*h*) The trial has to be stopped and re-started with a new jury.

It is also necessary to consider the division of functions between the judge and the jury.[22]

Standard Procedure

1. The case for the prosecution [23]

Prosecuting counsel's duty is to present his case objectively and moderately, not pressing for a conviction nor emphasising the iniquity of the offender.[24]

(*a*) *Opening speech*

Within these limits, counsel has a discretion in the manner and length of his opening address to the jury, but he must outline to them all the facts which the prosecution intends to prove so as to help the jury in deciding whether the evidence does in fact support the allegations in the indictment. Counsel should not, however, make any reference to evidence which defence counsel has told him will be

---

[22] See p. 206.

[23] " Case " here means opening address and evidence called. The closing speech is dealt with on p. 195.

[24] The term " as a minister of justice " has been used but in recent years this has become baffling rather than helpful.

contested as inadmissible,[25] since the jury should not be told of evidence which they may not hear. Further, they would probably be out of court while arguments as to admissibility were heard and must be if the judge thinks it would unfairly prejudice the accused and if the accused wishes them to leave the court.[26] The usual practice is for defence counsel to inform his opponent in advance if he is going to take objection to evidence.[27]

In his opening speech prosecuting counsel should outline evidence which he has prepared to rebut possible defence allegations,[28] subject to defence counsel's courtesy in telling him whether or not such matters will be put forward. He might, for instance, wish to call similar fact evidence to rebut a defence of accident or to show that he could meet an attack on the character of a prosecution witness.[29]

(b) Evidence for the prosecution

The prosecution must prove beyond reasonable doubt every fact and circumstance, including intention, necessary to constitute the offence charged. *What* must be proved is the substance of the criminal law and *how* to prove it is the law of evidence, both of which fall outside the general scope of this book.

As it does not know in advance what the defence will be except in the case of an alibi,[30] the prosecution must be ready with evidence of all that it is required to prove. This does not cover issues raised by the defence, such as insanity or statutory exceptions,[31] the burden of proof of which is on the defence, but it does cover all other " defences," as they are commonly, though inaccurately, called, by which the defence seeks to show that one or more of the prosecution's allegations is not proved. On the other hand, the prosecution can ignore any allegations in the indictment which are not necessary to prove the offence charged.[32]

The prosecution should list on the back of the indictment the

---

[25] This applies particularly to confessions: *R.* v. *Swatkins* (1831) 4 C. & P. 548; *R.* v. *Davis* (1837) 7 C. & P. 785.

[26] *R.* v. *Thompson* [1917] 2 K.B. 630 at p. 635; *R.* v. *Anderson* (1930) 21 Cr.App.R. 178.

[27] *R.* v. *Hammond* (1941) 28 Cr.App.R. 84.

[28] As to evidence in rebuttal, see p. 203.

[29] *R.* v. *Courvoisier* (1840) 9 C. & P. 362.

[30] See Criminal Justice Act 1967, s. 11, p. 112.

[31] See Indictment Rules 1971, r. 6 (*c*), p. 127; examples are the Trade Descriptions Act 1968, s. 24 (" it shall . . . be a defence for the person charged to prove . . .") and Sexual Offences Act 1956, s. 47 (" proof of the exception is to lie on the person relying on it "); see also Glanville Williams, *The Proof of Guilt* (1963), pp. 184–186.

[32] *i.e.* which are surplusage, see p. 118.

witnesses whom it intends to call and who have given evidence at the committal proceedings, and those witnesses must be present in court. Prosecuting counsel has, however, a discretion to discard a witness on the back of the indictment if he is, for instance, unlikely to be credible or to do more than repeat another witness's evidence, but such witnesses must be available for the defence to cross-examine.[33] A witness cannot be discarded in any event only because he is likely to give evidence inconsistent with the prosecution case.[34] If the prosecution knows of, but does not intend to call, a witness who might give material evidence, a copy of his statement must have been made available to the accused. Further, the prosecution should have given notice to the accused of any witness who is not on the depositions.[35]

In any case where a witness has made a record of his evidence he may wish to refer to it before giving evidence to remind himself of details. This should be allowed—it would be virtually impossible to enforce any prohibition—but the prosecution should tell the defence that a witness is doing so.[36] Failure to tell the defence alone will not found an appeal but may be relevant to the weight of the witness's evidence and of the prosecution evidence generally.[37]

A witness may refer to a document while giving evidence to refresh his memory if the record was made contemporaneously with the events recorded or soon after (but while the events were still fresh in his memory), it was made by the witness or under his supervision, it is the original and it is produced to the other party on request.[38]

After the close of its case, the prosecution can adduce further evidence only with the leave of the judge. This may be in rebuttal of the case for the defence [39] or it may be brought up in cross-examination of the accused or of defence witnesses. In the latter case the judge's discretion is very limited. He would not allow prosecuting counsel to use an accused's confession in cross-examination to contradict what the accused is saying on oath if he had not already

---

[33] The prosecution must take " all reasonable steps " to secure their presence, but the trial may, in the judge's discretion, proceed without them: *R.* v. *Cavanagh and Shaw* [1972] 1 W.L.R. 676. See also *R.* v. *Sterk* [1972] Crim.L.R. 391 where, because prosecuting counsel referred to a witness's evidence in his opening speech, the judge should have tendered the witness for cross-examination.

[34] *R.* v. *Oliva* [1965] 1 W.L.R. 1028 at p. 1035.

[35] See p. 114.

[36] *R.* v. *Richardson* [1971] 2 W.L.R. 889, approving Home Office Circular 82/1969.

[37] The Crown Court, in *R.* v. *Webb* [1975] Crim.L.R. 159, directed an acquittal when the defence was not informed.

[38] *Worley* v. *Bentley* [1976] 2 All E.R. 449; *R.* v. *Westwell, The Times*, March 13, 1976.

[39] See p. 203, in particular *R.* v. *Doran.*

proved the confession. The judge may allow it, however, where there is more than one accused and the confession elicits implications on others of the co-accused.[40]

Finally, an accused's statement [41] which the prosecution proposes to call in evidence should be " edited " of matters which are inadmissible. The statement should be in full on the depositions so that defence counsel can indicate which parts he objects to.[42] The examination of witnesses is considered separately below.[43]

2. The case for the defence

(*a*) *Opening address*

Where the accused intends to call witnesses as to facts in addition to giving evidence himself, his counsel may open his case by outlining the facts which he intends to prove. He is under no obligation to do so but it is desirable if the evidence to be called is complex. If the defence case includes no witnesses other than the accused himself and witnesses to his character only,[44] defence counsel cannot open by addressing the jury.[45]

(*b*) *Evidence for the defence*

Apart from alibi evidence [46] and the duty to put its case in cross-examination [47] the defence may keep the details of its case secret until this stage. It must be remembered that the accused has copies of the depositions and written statements, a list on the back of the indictment of the prosecution witnesses, and notice of any further evidence for the prosecution which has emerged between committal and trial.[48]

If the accused gives evidence, he should be called first whether or not he calls other evidence of fact.[49] He is a competent but not compellable witness in his own cause [50] and is to be treated as any other witness save that he cannot claim the privilege from self-incrimination *vis à vis* the offence charged [51] and he cannot generally

---

[40] *R.* v. *Rice* [1963] 1 Q.B. 857 at p. 867; see also footnote 3, p. 201.

[41] See p. 22.

[42] *R.* v. *Weaver* [1968] 1 Q.B. 353.

[43] See p. 181.

[44] See p. 193.

[45] Criminal Evidence Act 1898, s. 2; this is principally a rule of convenience to avoid having the accused's evidence repeated three times (including the defence counsel's closing speech; see p. 195).

[46] See Criminal Justice Act 1967, s. 11, p. 112.

[47] See p. 183.

[48] See pp. 107–112, 114 and 178.

[49] Criminal Evidence Act 1898, s. 2; *R.* v. *Smith* (1968) 52 Cr.App.R. 224.

[50] See pp. 30–32; see also the rules as to the accused's spouse and the accused and his spouse in multiple trials, pp. 199 and 202.

[51] Criminal Evidence Act 1898, s. 1 (*e*), and see p. 191.

be asked questions which tend to show that he is of bad character. The " rules of play " relating to character evidence are considered below.[52]

If he makes an unsworn statement to the jury from the dock, he should make it before the prosecution's closing speech and after any other witnesses whom he has called have given their evidence on oath.[53]

3. Examination of witnesses

Witnesses are normally ordered to leave the court room when the case is called on, so that they do not hear other witnesses in the case before they themselves give evidence.[54] If a witness is in court, counsel may apply to have him sent out, but, even if he is not sent out, his evidence is still admissible.[55]

Each witness is then called into the witness box and takes the oath in open court.[56] The form of the oath depends on the religion and conscience of the witness. There are no special ceremonies except that if he has a religion he should hold the bible of that religion in his uplifted hand as he pronounces the oath.[57] If his religion is unusual or he has none, he may " affirm,"[58] the words being: " I, A.B., do solemnly, sincerely and truly declare and affirm . . ." instead of: " I swear by Almighty God. . . ." Young children " promise before Almighty God," if they take the oath at all.[59]

Professor Glanville Williams has written: " In England the oath is treated with a levity that appears both remarkable and distasteful to the foreign observer."[60] Its validity is not vitiated if it later transpires that the oath-taker had no religious belief[61] and it is perhaps unrealistic to think that " an invocation of the Deity " will assist the accused in resolving the conflict between his self-interest and the truth, where they are inconsistent, more than his fear of shrewd cross-examination by prosecuting counsel.[62]

---

52 See p. 190.

53 *R.* v. *Sheriff* (1903) 20 Cox 334.

54 *Southey* v. *Nash* (1837) 7 C. & P. 632.

55 *Chandler* v. *Horne* (1842) 2 Mood. & R. 423.

56 *R.* v. *Tew* (1855) Dears. 429.

57 Oaths Act 1909, s. 2; the New Testament, Old Testament or Koran is used for Christians, Jews or Mohammedans respectively.

58 Oaths Act 1888, s. 1, as amended by the Oaths Act 1961, s. 1.

59 Children and Young Persons Act 1933, s. 38; *R.* v. *Hayes*, *The Times*, November 30, 1976; see also p. 30.

60 *The Proof of Guilt* (1963), p. 66.

61 Oaths Act 1888, s. 3.

62 A prosecution for perjury would be exceptional ; see Glanville Williams, *op. cit.*, pp. 66–71, but see *D.P.P.* v. *Humphrys*, p. 167.

(*a*) *Examination-in-chief*

This is the first examination of a witness by the party who has called him.

(1) *Relevance.* Counsel's questions must be relevant, *i.e.* they must not be such that the probable answer cannot tend to prove the matter in issue. In the case of circumstantial evidence, the matter in issue will not necessarily be one of the facts alleged in the case, but it must itself tend to prove those facts.

(2) *Leading questions.* Counsel's questions must not be leading, *i.e.* their framing must not suggest the desired answer or assume the existence of disputed facts. For instance, " when you were turning right, did you see X's car on the other side of the road?" should be split up as follows: " Where were you? What were you doing? Did you see any other traffic? Where was it? Who was the driver? " In its first form the question suggests that the answer required is " Yes, X's car was on the other side of the road " and assumes that the witness was turning right, that the vehicle was a car and that the car belonged to X.

Leading questions are allowed for convenience rather than from any rule of law on preliminary and undisputed evidence, such as the name and address of the witness; they are also often allowed on evidence of identification after the witness has described the person or thing to be identified; *e.g.* " Was this the knife you saw in A's hand? " might be allowed after ascertaining that the witness saw A, his hand and a knife in it. In any event it is counsel for the other side who must object to the question, unless the judge intervenes, and therefore leading questions may often be allowed by the tacit consent of counsel. The answer is admissible though it may be robbed of all its significance by being the answer to a leading question: *e.g.* " Is the man you saw sitting in the dock of this court? " is clearly objectionable, but the answer " Yes " will have, in theory at least, virtually no probative value.

(3) *Hostile witnesses.* A party cannot impeach his own witness by discrediting his character generally, whether by questioning, by calling other witnesses or by introducing relevant evidence.[63] If the witness does not " come up to proof," he may be a " hostile " witness or merely " unfavourable." If he is unfavourable the party calling him may call other evidence to prove what he has failed to prove or what he has disproved.[64] It is then for the jury to decide whether the

[63] Criminal Procedure Act 1865, s. 3.

[64] *Ewer* v. *Ambrose* (1825) 3 B. & C. 746.

evidence of the unfavourable witness is outbalanced by the other evidence. If he is unfavourable on one point only, the probative effect of the rest of his evidence is not of course impugned.

If, on the other hand, the witness is antipathetic to the party calling him and appears to be lying, the judge may permit him to be treated as a hostile witness, which means that counsel for the party calling him may cross-examine him.[65] Counsel is still precluded from impeaching his character in a general way, though he may need to cast doubt on his veracity on the point at issue. Whether or not the witness should be treated as hostile is entirely a matter for the judge's discretion.[66]

By a statute declaratory of the common law,[67] the term " adverse " is substituted for " hostile," which caused some confusion in early judgments.[68] The section clarifies the practice when the witness has previously made an inconsistent statement, which he now denies, by enabling the party calling him to apply to the judge for leave to prove the statement, provided he first asks the witness whether he made it. The statement is not evidence of the facts stated in it whether it was made on oath or unsworn.[69]

(b) *Cross-examination*

The purpose of cross-examination is twofold:

1. To put to the witness any facts inconsistent with what he has said in his evidence-in-chief which the party cross-examining him has sought or will seek to prove in evidence.
2. To cast doubt on the accuracy of the evidence-in-chief and elicit evidence favourable to the cross-examining party.

The first purpose is to give the witness an opportunity to explain the inconsistency; if cross-examining counsel does not do this, his opponent may contend that he has impliedly accepted the evidence-in-chief and object if he later adduces the inconsistent evidence. As a compromise cross-examining counsel may ask the judge for leave to recall

---

65 He may then ask leading questions, challenge him with previous statements and question him on collateral matters; see p. 184. See *e.g. R.* v. *Fraser and Warren* (1956) 40 Cr.App.R. 160.

66 *Rice* v. *Howard* (1886) 16 Q.B.D. 681. The witness must be shown to be hostile at the trial; a witness who shows hostility at committal proceedings cannot automatically be treated as hostile at trial: *R.* v. *Mann* (1972) 56 Cr.App.R. 750.

67 Criminal Procedure Act 1865, s. 3.

68 *See e.g. Greenough* v. *Eccles* (1859) 5 C.B.(N.S.) 786 at p. 807, line 18.

69 *e.g.* evidence given at committal proceedings as embodied in the depositions or in written statements of evidence admitted under the Criminal Justice Act 1967, s. 2 (as to which see p. 96) or a statement given to a policeman; see *R.* v. *Golder* [1960] 1 W.L.R. 1169.

the inadequately cross-examined witness.[70] Alternatively, counsel may be stopped in his closing speech [71] from relying on points which he should have brought out in cross-examination. [72] Objections as to the competence of the witness, as to whether his evidence is the best evidence available or as to the material elicited in, or the manner of, the examination-in-chief,[73] have probably already been made during the examination-in-chief, but if not, they should be dealt with first. Counsel may cross-examine a witness whether or not his opponent has examined him inchief.[74]

Although cross-examination is not in practice such an impossibly skilful and incisive matter as the popular mythology of the courtroom makes out, it does involve a considerable measure of judgment. When counsel challenges the accuracy of a witness's evidence, he may do so by questioning him on the matters in issue or by attacking the witness's credibility.

(1) *As to matters in issue.* Counsel's questions must be relevant [75] and must be directed to eliciting fact and not argument.[76] He may ask leading questions in order to bring the witness straight to the point; for instance, following the example on page 182, " You were turning right and saw X's car. Where was it?"

Counsel will usually try to get the witness to assert facts which are favourable to his case. If he cross-examines on facts not given in the evidence-in-chief, they will normally be followed up by other evidence, for this is part of the essential " putting the case " of his client to the witness. It is, however, possible to suggest alternative facts or explanations to throw doubt on the evidence-in-chief without their being part of his client's case; further, counsel may suggest fraud or misconduct on the part of the witness without substantiating it, provided it is part of his client's case, and not merely directed to credibility.[77] Random " mud-slinging " allegations of fact made without substantiation are not approved if they are not a serious part of the client's case.[78] Names of third parties should not be bandied about unless absolutely necessary.[79]

---

[70] See p. 189. [71] See p. 195.

[72] *R.* v. *Hart* (1932) 23 Cr.App.R. 202 at p. 206.

[73] *e.g.* irrelevant or leading questions or the eliciting of hearsay evidence; see p. 182.

[74] See *e.g.* p. 178.

[75] See p. 182.

[76] *e.g.* " Are you asking the jury to believe that . . . ? " is more likely to elicit arguments of self-justification: *R.* v. *Baldwin* (1925) 18 Cr.App.R. 175 at p. 178.

[77] Rules of the Bar Council of November 6, 1950, r. 2; see *Archbold*, para. 528.

[78] *R.* v. *O'Neill* (1950) 34 Cr.App.R. 108; see also p. 194, as to the effect of attacking prosecution witnesses.

[79] *R.* v. *Flynn* [1972] Crim.L.R. 428.

Counsel's judgment is often involved more in knowing when not to ask questions as to fact than in the skill with which they are framed. If a witness appears to be truthful, cross-examination will often elicit confirmation and consolidation of the evidence-in-chief with circumstantial details highly convincing to the jury. The framing of questions and their contents are very much a matter of practice and are better learned in court than in theory.

(2) *As to credit.* Counsel has considerable freedom in attacking a witness's credibility. He may ask leading questions, examine the witness on collateral matters which question his knowledge, disinterestedness, integrity or veracity, and use statements previously made by the witness to contradict what he is now saying on oath.

There are two basic limitations: first, counsel is generally bound by any answers he receives as to credit and cannot in most cases call evidence to disprove them, unless they are directly relevant to the matters in issue[80]; secondly, he cannot require an answer to a question which might tend to expose the witness to punishment.[81] The limitations on cross-examination of the accused are dealt with below.[82]

Questions may be asked relating to the sources of the witness's knowledge and to his disinterestedness without any imputation of bad character; *e.g.* questions as to how well the witness could have seen the offence or the accused, or as to whether he is in any way interested in the outcome of the trial for personal or property reasons. His answers may detract from his credit and from the weight of his evidence.

In attacking the witness's integrity and veracity, a distinction is drawn between answers which relate to matters in issue and those which are purely collateral.[83] For instance, where the defence alleges in cross-examination that the victim of an assault is and was mentally abnormal, the truthfulness of his evidence is questioned, and so also are the matters in issue, *i.e.* whether, as the defence alleges, the assault ever occurred. If, however, the defence were to suggest that that witness has tried to " fix " the other party's witnesses, the witness's denial is a collateral matter relating entirely to his credit. In the

[80] Rules of the Bar Council, above, r. 3; *R.* v. *Mendy, The Times,* June 29, 1976, below. The rule is based on convenience, as well as fairness to the witness, so that the number of issues to be tried does not proliferate unduly.

[81] See p. 32, with the exception of the accused as witness. *N.B.* the question may always be asked.

[82] See p. 191.

[83] Though collateral previous convictions may be proved; see below.

first case, cross-examining counsel may call evidence to contradict the witness. In the second case, the witness's answer will generally speaking be final. However, where a witness is examined about his bias towards one of the parties which is alleged to be so strong that he is prepared to adopt any corrupt course to assist him, cross-examining counsel may call evidence in rebuttal. In *R.* v. *Mendy* [84] a man in the public gallery was seen to be making notes during the prosecution evidence and later to talk to a defence witness in circumstances where it was clear he was describing the prosecution evidence. During cross-examination the defence witness flatly denied the exchange and the judge permitted the prosecution to call the court officer who had seen it.

A defence of consent on a charge of rape is an exceptional case. The defence may cross-examine the complainant about the sexual intercourse which she has had with the accused; this—*i.e.* consent—is a matter directly in issue. She may also be cross-examined about her sexual intercourse with other men to establish her reputation for inchastity. This generally goes only to credit and her answers must be treated as final. However, a distinction has been drawn [83] where it is alleged that she is actually a prostitute rather than simply having had sexual intercourse with another man or other men. Provided a proper foundation is laid in the course of her cross-examination, the defence may later call evidence of the fact that she is a prostitute and, moreover, may call evidence of particular acts which tend to establish that fact. As evidence of her general inchastity is evidence of character, however, it means that the accused throws away his shield against cross-examination on his own character.[86]

If evidence is called to impeach the credit of a witness for the other party, that witness must first be cross-examined as to credit; any witness called to impeach him cannot be asked to give the reasons for his belief that the evidence is incredible, but must give his reasons if asked for them in cross-examination (which will probably be by counsel for the party who called the witness whom this witness is seeking to impeach).[87]

Counsel can suggest all kinds of misconduct, unreliability, past

---

[84] *The Times*, June 29, 1976. See also *Toohey* v. *Metropolitan Police Commissioner* [1965] A.C. 595; *Harris* v. *Tippett* (1811) 2 Camp. 637; Bar Council Rules, above, r. 3.

[85] *R.* v. *Krausz* (1973) 57 Cr.App.R. 466; *R.* v. *Bashir* [1969] 1 W.L.R. 1303, a case decided on assize.

[86] See p. 191, but see the Sexual Offences (Amendment) Act 1976.

[87] As to multiple trials, see p. 200. In *Toohey's* case, above, the medical witness was allowed to give evidence-in-chief on the degree to which the witness's credibility was affected.

record, etc. He can ask about past convictions, which, if denied, he can prove in evidence.[88]

The Rehabilitation of Offenders Act 1974 has no application in criminal proceedings, whether the spent conviction is that of a witness or of the accused, but the Crown Court should respect the spirit of the Act in the following ways [89]:

(a) Counsel and the court should avoid referring to a spent conviction if it can reasonably be avoided.
(b) No one should refer in open court to a spent conviction without the authority of the judge, which should only be given if the interests of justice so require.
(c) Spent convictions in a record should be marked as such.
(d) The judge in sentencing should only refer to a spent conviction if necessary to explain the sentence being imposed.

Counsel can also suggest mental disease, drunkenness, bribery etc.; but he cannot allege past charges which have resulted in acquittals. The conduct or condition alleged, however, must be *relevant* to credibility and questions must not be asked which are intended only to insult or annoy.[90] Barristers are directed to make imputations of bad character only if told that they are well-founded by their instructing solicitor, or, if by any other person, only if he gives satisfactory reasons. The witness must answer a question, unless it tends to incriminate him, however degrading it may be.[91]

(3) *Prior inconsistent statements*. A statement made previously by a witness, whether orally, in writing or on oath, may be put to the witness by cross-examining counsel to test the veracity of his evidence on oath. The statement must in itself be admissible,[92] but it is no evidence of the facts stated in it.

The Criminal Procedure Act 1865, s. 5, enables a witness to be cross-examined on a written statement without showing it to him, provided the parts which will be used to contradict him are indicated to him. The judge always has power to make the cross-examining party produce the statement.[93] This section applies to oral statements reduced into writing and to written material used by a witness

---

[88] Criminal Procedure Act 1865, s. 6.
[89] Practice Direction [1975] 1 W.L.R. 1065. A " spent conviction " is defined by s. 5 of the Act.
[90] Rules of the Bar Council, rr. 1, 4 and 7.
[91] See pp. 29 and 32.
[92] *R.* v. *Treacy* (1944) 30 Cr.App.R. 93 and *R.* v. *Rice* [1963] 1 Q.B. 857 (see p. 201).
[93] *e.g.* in *R.* v. *Bass* [1953] 1 Q.B. 680, the judge should have ordered two policemen's records of the accused's statement to be seen by the jury as they were made in collaboration.

to refresh his memory.[94] Counsel need not make such material his evidence unless he cross-examines as to parts of the document to which the witness was not referring.[95]

Opposing counsel can demand to see the document if counsel's cross-examination on it leads for instance to inconsistency in the witness's evidence; he cannot see it if the cross-examination fails entirely. Normally, if a confession is used in this way against the accused, prosecuting counsel should have mentioned it in his opening speech or proved it in his evidence.[96] The depositions and written statements taken at the committal proceedings may be used in this way.[97]

By section 4 of the Act of 1865, evidence may be called that the witness has made an oral statement which is inconsistent with his testimony, provided he is first asked whether or not he made it (and denies it). This applies also to known but lost written statements and to statements made on oath in court.[98]

(c) *Re-examination*

Cross-examination, which has been described as " beyond any doubt the greatest legal engine ever invented for the discovery of truth," may leave a witness's testimony in a very doubtful and confused condition, particularly if cross-examining counsel has elicited damaging admissions without giving the witness a chance to qualify them. Thus, if any new fact emerges in the cross-examination of a witness, or inconsistencies which require explanation have arisen, counsel for the party calling him may re-examine him, subject to the same rules as the examination-in-chief. Leading questions, however, would probably be allowed on matters on which the witness has not been inconsistent.[99] Counsel cannot question him on any matter which has not arisen in the cross-examination[1]; nor can he refer to a previous statement of the witness which is *consistent* with the evidence-in-chief unless it has been made admissible in the cross-examination.

(d) *Examination by the judge*

The judge does not usually play an active part in the examination of witnesses, but should impartially guide it by preventing offensive

---

94 See p. 179.

95 *Gregory* v. *Tavernor* (1833) 6 C. & P 280.

96 *R.* v. *Rice* [1963] 1 Q.B. 857.

97 See pp. 96 and 107.

98 *R.* v. *Hart* (1957) 42 Cr.App.R. 47.

99 See p. 182.

1 *R.* v. *Beezley* (1830) 4 C. & P. 220.

questions being asked, allowing or disallowing counsel's objections or supplementing counsel's questions if he finds the answer ambiguous. This is the usual practice, though the judge has an almost unlimited discretion to ask questions. If he does, the questions must reflect his impartiality, though implicit bias against an accused would be more likely to provoke comment if it were contained in the summing-up, for then the Court of Appeal would quash the conviction. In *R.* v. *Clewer*,[2] however, the judge asked so many questions that it was impossible for the accused to be fairly represented and his conviction was quashed. In particular, the judge must not badger or interrupt the accused when he gives evidence. Where the judge asked 147 hostile questions out of a total of 700 in the accused's examination-in-chief, the conviction was quashed.[3] On the other hand, the judge must not appear to be asleep.[4]

The judge may himself call a witness whose evidence he deems necessary in the interests of justice. He need not have the consent of, nor allow examination by, the prosecution or the accused but he must call the witness before the jury retires.[5] He should call the witness before the close of the accused's case except in exceptional circumstances.[6] The judge may recall a witness or permit counsel for one of the parties to do so; he should recall a witness whose evidence is affected by new evidence during the trial, so that inconsistencies can be explained if possible.[7]

4. The accused as witness

(a) *The right of silence*

The accused cannot be compelled to give evidence.[8] The primary reason for keeping silent is that if he decides to give evidence he must answer all questions including those which tend to incriminate him

[2] (1953) 37 Cr.App.R. 37. See also *Taylor* v. *Taylor* [1970] 1 W.L.R. 1148.

[3] *R.* v. *Perks* [1973] Crim.L.R. 388; *R.* v. *Hulusi* (1973) 58 Cr.App.R. 378.

[4] *R.* v. *Langham* [1972] Crim.L.R. 457.

[5] *R.* v. *Wilson* (1957) 41 Cr.App.R. 226; *R.* v. *Corless* (1972) 56 Cr.App.R. 341.

[6] See *R.* v. *Cleghorn* [1967] 2 Q.B. 584, where it was held to be wrong, and *R.* v. *Tregear* [1967] 2 Q.B. 574, where it was approved. In *Phelan* v. *Back* [1972] 1 W.L.R. 273, the judge was held to have a discretion to recall a prosecution witness after the close of the defence case.

[7] *R.* v. *Grant* [1958] Crim.L.R. 42, where evidence came to light that two prosecution witnesses were lying. In *R.* v. *Doran* (1972) 116 S.J. 238, the Court of Appeal approved the calling of two witnesses for the prosecution during the presentation of the defence case, but held that the court must be vigilant to avoid prejudice to the accused. In *R.* v. *Joseph* (1971) 56 Cr.App.R. 60, the Court of Appeal approved the recall of a prosecution witness whose identification evidence was attacked as mistaken in the defence's opening but had not been questioned in cross-examination.

[8] See p. 31; Criminal Evidence Act 1898, s. 1 (*a*).

of the offence charged.[9] The obvious implication to the jury of his not giving evidence is that he has something to hide. Furthermore, if he is convicted, it is rare for him to be allowed to give evidence on appeal which he could have given at trial.[10] The implication from an unsworn statement from the dock is as bad as that formed from a refusal to give evidence, for he cannot be cross-examined on it. Nor does it have any evidential value, *i.e.* it cannot establish facts not otherwise proved.[11] In some cases, however, where the accused is likely to do much damage to his case by the way he gives evidence, it may be advisable to keep silent if there is any other evidence in his favour.

To what extent can the inference of guilt be emphasised by others? The prosecution is not allowed to comment upon the accused's silence at all.[12] The judge, however, is. His comment is permissible provided it does not amount to a misdirection; this is dealt with under "summing-up" on page 197. A co-defendant whose defence conflicts with that of another co-defendant, who does not give evidence, may comment on the fact.[13]

(b) *The accused's character*

The general rule is that evidence cannot be given as to the bad character of the accused. The reason for this is that, where bad character is relevant to the principal issue, its probative value is greatly outweighed by the prejudice likely to be caused to the accused in the minds of a lay jury.[14]

The accused's character may be brought up at two stages—in the course of the prosecution's case and in the cross-examination of the accused as to credit.

(1) *Prosecution case*. Because of the general exclusionary rule, the prosecution is only allowed to call evidence of bad character (i) when past conduct or a previous conviction[15] is a matter in issue or (ii) when proof of previous offences or a bad disposition is admissible.

---

[9] See p. 32; Criminal Evidence Act 1898, s. 1 (*e*).

[10] *R.* v. *Malvisi* (1909) 2 Cr.App.R. 251; as to fresh evidence on appeal, see p. 269.

[11] Criminal Evidence Act 1898, s. 1 (*h*). The practice is due to historical factors no longer relevant and it is not often used. See also *R.* v. *Coughlan* [1976] Crim.L.R. 628.

[12] *Ibid.* s. 1 (*b*). The same applies to the failure of the accused's spouse to give evidence.

[13] *R.* v. *Ferrara* (1971) 55 Cr.App.R. 199.

[14] Bad character, or evidence "showing a disposition towards wrong-doing in general," may not even be relevant; *e.g.* evidence of convictions for being drunk and disorderly are unlikely to be relevant on a charge of obtaining by deception.

[15] Children and Young Persons Act 1963, s. 16 (2), applies to convictions of adult accused; see p. 217.

Exception (i) applies where a statutory offence can only be committed by a person who has already been convicted of an offence or has misconducted himself in a particular way.[16] Exception (ii) arises, in the first place, when the accused himself raises the matter in his examination-in-chief by denying that he has a particular disposition or that he has committed specified acts. His raising the matter is treated as being voluntary and the prosecution may ask for leave to call evidence in rebuttal.[17] More important is the second case where the exception may apply, namely the admissibility of " similar fact evidence " whereby the prosecution can call evidence of past conduct of a sort specifically similar to the offence charged to rebut any suggestion of accident, mistake, ignorance or involuntary conduct. The prosecution may lead such evidence in chief[18] or call it in rebuttal, if allowed to do so, after the defence has asserted one of these matters.

(2) *Cross-examination*. The accused is protected against cross-examination as to his character by section 1 (*f*) of the Criminal Evidence Act 1898. He must not be asked, and, if asked, need not answer, any question tending to show that he has committed or been convicted of or charged with any offence other than the one charged, or that he is of bad character. (He may still be cross-examined in the ordinary way,[19] *e.g.* on prior inconsistent statements, provided his character is not invoked.)

Section 1 (*e*) of the 1898 Act requires the accused to answer questions tending to incriminate him as to the offence charged.[20] On a broad view this would include past offences if they indirectly prove the offence charged. In *R.* v. *Cokar*,[21] however, the paragraph was restrictively interpreted as " tending *directly* to incriminate," for, as mentioned above,[22] the prosecution can sometimes call evidence of the accused's character, and he can be cross-examined on such evidence anyway under section 1 (*f*) (i), below. In *Jones* v. *D.P.P.*[23] it was held that a question " tending to show " meant a question " tending to reveal to the jury " some fact about the accused's character; so if he brings it up in his own evidence-in-chief a question in cross-examination will not " make it known " to the jury.

16 *e.g.* a " rogue and vagabond " under the Vagrancy Act 1824, s. 4; or a person whose purposes in obtaining classified information appear to be prejudicial to the state " from his conduct or known character as proved ": Official Secrets Act 1911, s. 1 (2).

17 See p. 203.

18 *Harris* v. *D.P.P.* [1952] A.C. 694.

19 See p. 183.

20 See also p. 32.

21 [1960] 2 Q.B. 207.

22 See p. 190.

23 [1962] A.C. 635.

The application of the rule to previous convictions is relatively simple; it includes, for instance, questions which would reveal that the accused had been in prison.[24] Under section 16 (2) of the Children and Young Persons Act 1963, a finding of guilt against the accused when he was under the age of 14 is to be disregarded as a previous conviction.[25]

Questions about offences previously *charged* do not include allegations made outside court proceedings, *e.g.* by an employer as justification for dismissing an employee,[26] nor, generally, charges which have resulted in an acquittal.[27]

Questions as to bad character and the *commission* of offences are difficult to distinguish as character is usually classified as " bad " if it is criminal. A suggestion that the accused deserted from the army was held to be inadmissible.[28] In *R.* v. *Bishop*[29] an allegation of homosexuality without any implication of a criminal offence was held nevertheless to be an imputation of bad character. Drunkenness might amount to bad character and might be relevant, *e.g.* on a charge of drunken driving.

Section 1 (*f*) provides that the accused loses this protection in three circumstances:

(i) When proof that he has committed or been convicted of another offence is admissible to show that he is guilty of the offence charged.

(ii) When he or his counsel has sought
  (*a*) to establish his own good character, or
  (*b*) to cast imputations on the character of the prosecutor or prosecution witnesses.

(iii) When he has given evidence against another person charged with the same offence.

(i) GUILTY OF THE OFFENCE CHARGED. This is a part of the exception already described[30] and enables the accused to be cross-examined on evidence of character which would have been admissible as similar fact evidence, etc. This subparagraph has been construed literally.[31]

---

24 *R.* v. *Haslam* (1916) 12 Cr.App.R. 10.
25 See p. 217.
26 *Stirland* v. *D.P.P.* [1944] A.C. 315.
27 *Maxwell* v. *D.P.P.* [1935] A.C. 309 at p. 322; *R.* v. *Flynn* [1972] Crim.L.R. 428.
28 *R.* v. *Redd* [1923] 1 K.B. 104.
29 [1975] Q.B. 274.
30 See " 1. Prosecution case," p. 190.
31 *Jones* v. *D.P.P.* [1962] A.C. 635

(ii) PUTTING CHARACTER IN ISSUE. The term " character " means disposition and reputation.[32]

(*a*) The Accused's Good Character. The accused may assert his good record and disposition in his own evidence-in-chief or try to elicit such assertions from the prosecution witnesses in cross-examination, or call other witnesses to testify to his good reputation and, possibly, their good opinion of him.[33] If he follows the third course of action, he would already have been cross-examined [34] so section 1 (*f*) (ii) does not apply. He does, however, " put his character in " and the witnesses may be cross-examined on it; if the judge allows, evidence of bad character and past convictions may be called in rebuttal.[35] Neither this nor section 1 (*f*) (ii) applies if a witness voluntarily and independently testifies to the accused's good character, or if the accused suggests that a third party with previous convictions who is not called as a witness could have committed the offence.[36]

If the accused asserts, or examines prosecution witnesses on, his good character, he cannot expect to be immune from questions tending to show the opposite, for his character is indivisible.[37] There are two aspects of good character evidence—that it tends to show that the accused did not commit the offence charged, and that the accused's evidence ought on that account to be believed; both aspects appear to be treated in the same way, even though from the first aspect the relevance of past offences of a totally different kind from the one charged must be minimal. For instance, in *R.* v. *Winfield*,[38] the accused, in meeting a charge of indecent assault, called a witness to testify to his respectful behaviour with women generally. The prosecution then proved a previous conviction for larceny, which was allowed; the approval of the Court of Criminal Appeal, however, was *obiter* and it was not decided on section 1 (*f*) (ii). A clear case of an accused putting in his character was *R.* v. *Samuel* [39] where, on a charge of larceny by finding, he asserted that on two previous occasions he had found property and returned it to its owner. In *R.* v. *Thompson* [40] the rule was not applied to an accused who gave evidence

[32] *Stirland* v. *D.P.P.* [1944] A.C. 315 at pp. 324–326.

[33] *Jones* v. *D.P.P.* [1962] A.C. 635; Lord Devlin, at p. 699, considered that it was confined to reputation, as in *R.* v. *Rowton* (1865) Le. & Ca. 520.

[34] See p. 176.

[35] *R.* v. *Redd* [1923] 1 K.B. 104; this is rather doubtful authority; see also p. 203.

[36] *R.* v. *Lee* [1976] 1 W.L.R. 71.

[37] *Stirland* v. *D.P.P.* [1944] A.C. 315 at p. 324. The prosecution must take care not to suggest that character evidence admitted under this section has probative value as admissible evidence of disposition: *R.* v. *Vickers* [1972] Crim.L.R. 101.

[38] (1939) 27 Cr.App.R. 139.

[39] (1956) 40 Cr.App.R. 8.

[40] [1966] 1 W.L.R. 405.

of a previous conviction (and unpaid fine) as the reason for part of the offence charged (running away from a policeman); he had not put his character in evidence, but in such a case the judge should anyway have used his discretion to prevent the revelation of his past record.[41]

(*b*) Prosecution Character. The relevant words of section 1 (*f*) (ii) are: " The nature or conduct of the defence is such as to involve imputations on the character of the prosecutor or the witnesses for the prosecution." Although given a restrictive interpretation [42] in the past, the broadness of the words " nature or conduct of the defence " led to many conflicting decisions. The case of *Selvey* v. *D.P.P.*[43] clarified the position:

1. The words should be given their natural meaning.[44]
2. They apply equally where the accused casts imputations to show the unreliability of a witness and where such an allegation is part of his defence.[45]
3. In cases of rape a defence of consent on the part of the prosecutrix does not remove the accused's protection from cross-examination.[46]
4. If what is said amounts to no more than a denial of the charge, it is not an imputation.[47]
5. The judge has a discretion to exclude the accused's character in spite of his casting imputations on the prosecution; it is desirable that he should warn the defence as soon as it becomes apparent that imputations are being made. (Defence counsel should always take the utmost care not to put character in inadvertently.)

At first sight this part of the rule appears to contain sporting rather than rational elements. The reason for its inclusion, however, is based on credibility—if the accused invites the jury to disbelieve the prosecution because of a witness's unreliability, it is only proper that

---

[41] See p. 23.

[42] *e.g.* a suggestion on a charge of murder that the victim had made improper overtures was not within the section, as the deceased was not a witness: *R.* v. *Biggin* [1920] 1 K.B. 213. See also *R.* v. *Lee*, above.

[43] [1970] A.C. 304.

[44] *Cf. R.* v. *Bishop*, p. 192, which arose from the accused's allegation that a prosecution witness was a homosexual.

[45] *e.g.* where he contends that one of the prosecution witnesses committed the offence: *R.* v. *Hudson* [1912] 2 K.B. 464.

[46] See *R.* v. *Sheean* (1908) 21 Cox C.C. 561 and see p. 186.

[47] Where an accused simply protests his innocence he may well imply that the prosecutor is lying; he may even say so: *R.* v. *Rouse* [1904] 1 K.B. 184.

they should be able to judge whether he is a fit person to make such an invitation.

(*c*) Co-accused's Character. This exception is dealt with on page 200.

5. Closing speeches

When prosecution and defence have finished calling their evidence,[48] each side has a right to address the jury (provided the accused is represented by counsel).[49] Counsel aims in his closing speech to sum up the evidence in favour of his client's case thoroughly, succinctly and persuasively.[50]

(a) *Prosecution*

Prosecuting counsel's closing speech is made after all the defence evidence has been given.[51] He cannot make one if an unrepresented accused does not call any witnesses as to fact,[52] and even if the accused is represented, there may be no need to sum up the case, for prosecuting counsel must maintain his impartial role to the end.[53] There are certain matters he must not mention—the failure of the accused or his wife (or her husband) to give evidence,[54] the failure to call any other evidence, or any indication that the prosecutor or a witness would be adversely affected by an acquittal.[55]

(b) *Defence*

Defence counsel always has the right to the last word; *i.e.* if prosecuting counsel makes a closing speech, defence counsel has a right to reply to it.[56] He acts purely as an advocate and may urge an acquittal and comment not only on the evidence but on any matter in the case which seems proper, though obviously he must not assert as fact anything which has not been adduced in evidence.[57] He must not

---

[48] This may include, subject to the judge having allowed it, the prosecution calling evidence in rebuttal; see p. 203.

[49] See p. 199.

[50] He should not raise new matters or suggest explanations which cannot be tested in evidence: *R.* v. *Bircham* [1972] Crim.L.R. 430.

[51] The right was given by the Criminal Procedure Act 1865, s. 2, as amended by the Criminal Evidence Act 1898, s. 3, and the Criminal Procedure (Right of Reply) Act 1964, s. 1 (2).

[52] See p. 199.

[53] See pp. 177 and 216.

[54] See Criminal Evidence Act 1898, s. 1 (*b*), p. 190.

[55] *R.* v. *Rudland* (1865) 4 F. & F. 495. *Cf. R.* v. *Culbertson* (1970) 54 Cr.App.R. 310 where the judge wrongly suggested that an acquittal would ruin a police witness.

[56] Criminal Procedure (Right of Reply) Act 1964, s. 1 (1); the right was originally given by the Criminal Procedure Act 1865, s. 2.

[57] *R.* v. *Wainwright* (1875) 13 Cox 171; *R.* v. *Bircham*, above.

refer to the consequences of conviction, for the jury is concerned only with fact, and punishment and personal losses are not relevant.[58]

6. The judge's summing-up

When the evidence and arguments are over, the judge addresses the jury. Until the nineteenth century he tended only to explain the relevant law. It has long been recognised now that the judge's duties —and his powers of controlling the verdict—extend much further. The reasons for this are twofold: First, the judge must direct the jury on the law relating to proof; not only must the verdict be supported by the evidence but also it must not be contrary to the weight of the evidence; further, he must direct them on the burden of proof. Necessarily this involves some evaluation of the evidence.[59] Secondly, it is his duty to summarise the relevant evidence for each party, directing the jury to disregard worthless evidence and reminding them of evidence which they may otherwise forget or overlook.

He *must* direct the jury on the following:

(*a*) The law applicable to the offence charged; *i.e.* the act or omission and intent required to be proved by the prosecution. If there are several counts, he must direct the separate consideration of each.[60]

(*b*) The burden of proof; the proper direction is that the jury must be satisfied by the evidence so that they *are sure* that the prosecution has established the accused's guilt.[61] In cases where accident or lack of intention on the part of the accused is raised, the judge must direct the jury to acquit if they feel that such an explanation *may* be true.[62] The judge must point out the different standards of proof[63] if the accused raises a

---

[58] *R.* v. *Black* [1963] 1 W.L.R. 1311 (counsel reminded the jury of its power to add a recommendation of mercy to their verdict).

[59] For discussion of this function, see Devlin, *Trial by Jury* (1966), Chaps. 4 and 5.

[60] *R.* v. *Fisher* [1965] 1 W.L.R. 464.

[61] *R.* v. *Summers* (1952) 36 Cr.App.R. 14 (where the use of the words " reasonable doubt " was disapproved) and *R.* v. *Hepworth and Fearnley* [1955] 2 Q.B. 600 (where being " satisfied " of guilt was held to be an inadequate direction). It is important to avoid any phrase or formula which sounds like an approved incantation: *R.* v. *Lock*, *The Times*, October 9, 1974. See also *R.* v. *Johnson* [1972] Crim.L.R. 180 and *R.* v. *Gray* (1973) 58 Cr.App.R. 177 (where " the sort of doubt that might affect you in the conduct of your everyday affairs " was held to suggest too low a standard of proof).

[62] *R.* v. *Murtagh and Kennedy* (1955) 39 Cr.App.R. 72; *Woolmington* v. *D.P.P.* [1935] A.C. 462, at p. 481.

[63] *i.e.* that the prosecution must prove its case beyond reasonable doubt and the defence, on the balance of probabilities; see above for the forms of words to be avoided, however. See *R.* v. *Brown* (1971) 55 Cr.App.R. 478, where a direction that the burden passed " to some extent " was held to be incomplete, and *R.* v. *Rivers* [1974] R.T.R. 31.

special defence, *e.g.* under a statute. If no burden rests on the accused, the judge must direct accordingly.[64]

(*c*) Corroboration; the judge must explain what is meant by, and whether there is evidence capable of being, corroboration; he must not say that such evidence is corroboration in law for it is the jury's function to decide whether to accept the evidence.[65] The direction must clearly point out the danger of convicting on the uncorroborated evidence of an accomplice.[66] However, if the accomplice's evidence is favourable to the accused, the judge should not give a direction on it.[67]

(*d*) Inadmissible evidence; the judge should direct the jury to disregard any evidence which does not constitute proof, *e.g.* the contents of prior inconsistent statements used in cross-examination.[68]

(*e*) Identification evidence; the judge must warn the jury of the special need for caution where the prosecution case rests wholly or substantially on the correctness of visual identification; he must direct them to examine closely the circumstances in which the identification was made; he must avoid suggesting that failure of an alibi supports the identification evidence.[69]

(*f*) In all cases except those where the issue of guilt can be stated in the simplest terms,[70] the judge must sum up the evidence for the prosecution and the defence. He must not say that the evidence has proved (or failed to prove) any part of the case.

The judge may comment on the accused's failure to give evidence or to call witnesses, as long as the comment does not amount to a misdirection as it would plainly be if he suggested that the accused's silence amounted to corroboration.[71] It would also be a misdirection to equate silence with guilt. There is a fine distinction, examined in

---

[64] *R.* v. *Cameron* [1973] Crim.L.R. 520; on the burden of proof, see also *R.* v. *Brown* [1972] 2 Q.B. 229 (direction on provocation) and *D.P.P.* v. *Shannon* [1975] A.C. 717 at pp. 1041 and 1049.

[65] *R.* v. *Tragen* [1956] Crim.L.R. 332 and *R.* v. *Goddard* [1962] 1 W.L.R. 1282. He must indicate which parts of the evidence require corroboration (*R.* v. *Charles* [1976] 1 W.L.R. 248); and it is helpful to explain the meaning of "corroboration," "accomplice," etc., rather than to use the words strictly: *R.* v. *Sidhu* [1976] Crim. L.R. 379.

[66] *R.* v. *Price* [1969] 1 Q.B. 54.

[67] *R.* v. *Royce-Bentley* [1974] 1 W.L.R. 535; but see *R.* v. *Peach* [1974] Crim.L.R. 245.

[68] *R.* v. *Golder* [1960] 1 W.L.R. 1169; and see p. 187.

[69] *R.* v. *Turnbull* [1976] 3 All E.R. 549; see p. 35.

[70] *R.* v. *Artfield* (1961) 45 Cr.App.R. 309.

[71] *R.* v. *Jackson* [1953] 1 W.L.R. 591; *R.* v. *Blank* [1972] Crim.L.R. 176.

R. v. *Sparrow*,[72] between this and commenting on the accused's absence from the witness box; this is often necessary because some explanation of what they may infer from it is due to the jury, for reasons of common sense. " In our experience of trials, juries seldom acquit persons who do not give evidence when there is a clear case for them to answer and they do not answer it."[73] Similar care must be exercised when commenting on the accused's failure to call witnesses.[74]

It is permissible for the judge to point to lack of innocent explanation, for instance, where the prosecution case calls effectively for a " confession and avoidance." Where the defence relies on a straight denial, however, it is likely to be a misdirection.[75]

The judge may not infer that the accused's silence outside court is evidence of guilt; on arrest and during committal proceedings the accused has a right to say nothing.[76] However, it is possible for silence in the face of allegations to amount to acceptance of those allegations particularly if accompanied by evasive action.[77] A direction on the accused's silence before caution as amounting either to an exercise of his common law right or " to avoid incriminating himself " was disapproved.[78] The distinction is again a fine one.

A direction that, even if the jury accepts the accused's explanation, there cannot be an acquittal may, on the facts, be proper.[79] An explicit direction to convict must not be made in cases involving a dishonest intention.[80]

The judge has no duty to refer to the accused's good character in evidence,[81] a direction to consider it in relation to his credibility as a witness may be included.[82]

A mistake in the summing-up must be corrected by redirecting the

---

[72] [1973] 1 W.L.R. 488.

[73] *Per* Lawton L.J., *ibid.* at p. 493.

[74] *R.* v. *Gallagher* [1974] 1 W.L.R. 1204; in *R.* v. *Brigden* [1973] Crim.L.R. 579 the judge admitted evidence that an alibi notice was served but no witnesses came forward under it.

[75] *R.* v. *Mutch* [1973] 1 All E.R. 178; *Waugh* v. *R.* [1950] A.C. 203.

[76] *R.* v. *Davis* (1959) 43 Cr.App.R. 215 (" Can you imagine an innocent man . . . not saying something to the police . . . ? " was a misdirection); *R.* v. *Hoare* [1966] 1 W.L.R. 762 (where the accused did not reveal an alibi until trial; for the law on alibis now, see p. 112; see also *R.* v. *Lewis* (1973) 57 Cr.App.R. 860 and *R.* v. *Foster* [1975] R.T.R. 553.

[77] *Parkes* v. *The Queen* [1976] 3 All E.R. 380.

[78] *R.* v. *Chandler* [1976] 1 W.L.R. 585.

[79] *R.* v. *Larkin* [1943] K.B. 174 (the accused contended, on a charge of murder that the death resulted from his unlawful act); *cf.* alternative verdicts, p. 213.

[80] *R.* v. *Clemo* [1973] R.T.R. 176.

[81] *R.* v. *Pico* [1971] Crim.L.R. 531.

[82] *R.* v. *Falconer-Atlee* (1973) 58 Cr.App.R. 348

jury and allowing them to retire again; questioning the jury on their reasons will not do.[83]

Special Procedures

1. An unrepresented accused

The judge has a duty to assist an accused who is not defended by counsel. He should tell him in ordinary language of his power to cross-examine prosecution witnesses, of his choice between giving evidence on oath, making an unsworn statement and remaining silent, and of his right to call witnesses[84] and to address the jury.[85]

The order of proceedings is the same as for a represented accused (save that it is the accused himself who opens and sums up the defence case), except where he does not call any witnesses as to fact. In that event, the prosecution has no right of reply to the case for the defence.[86] In a case, however, where prosecuting counsel was allowed by the court to make a closing speech in breach of this rule, the conviction was not quashed.[87] If the judge refuses the accused's request to make a closing speech after he has given evidence, it is a denial of justice for which the conviction will be quashed.[88] The judge has power, however, to curb an irrelevant discourse.

If the accused puts his character in issue, the judge must explain the effect of it to him; if a previous conviction is disclosed, the accused may ask for the jury to be discharged and a new trial started.[89]

2. Joint trials [90]

(a) *The order of proceedings*

Where two or more accused are tried on the same indictment, the order of proceedings is generally the same as for one accused, save that the co-accused are called upon to cross-examine prosecution witnesses, give evidence and address the jury in the order in which their names appear on the indictment.[91] Where all accused are represented by the same counsel and co-operate in their defence, the proceedings follow the regular course. Where they are separately

---

[83] *R.* v. *Plimmer* (1975) 61 Cr.App.R. 264.

[84] *R.* v. *Carter* (1960) 44 Cr.App.R. 225 (a conviction was quashed because the accused had not been told of his right to call witnesses).

[85] Under the Criminal Procedure Act 1865, s. 2.

[86] *Ibid.* s. 2, *i.e.* prosecuting counsel cannot make a second speech either before or after the case for the defence, see p. 195.

[87] *R.* v. *Pink* [1971] 1 Q.B. 508.

[88] *R.* v. *Middlesex Crown Court, ex p. Riddle* [1975] Crim.L.R. 731.

[89] *R.* v. *Featherstone* (1942) 28 Cr.App.R. 176.

[90] As to joint trial generally, see pp. 137–141.

[91] *R.* v. *Barber* (1844) 1 C. & K. 434 at p. 438.

defended, however, the case of each accused is taken as a whole before turning to the next accused, whether or not every accused calls other witnesses. For instance:

(i) The prosecution finishes calling its evidence.
(ii) A's counsel opens A's case (if he wishes), calls A to give evidence (if A wishes) and then calls A's other witnesses as to fact and character.
(iii) B's counsel calls B to give evidence.
(iv) Prosecuting counsel sums up the prosecution case.
(v) A's counsel addresses the jury.
(vi) B's counsel addresses the jury.

If one co-accused is unrepresented and calls other witnesses as to fact, the order of proceedings is the same. If he only gives evidence himself, however, the order is as follows:

(i) and (ii) As (i) and (ii), above.
(iii) B gives evidence (and calls witnesses as to character only).
(iv) The prosecution sums up the *case against A*.
(v) A's counsel addresses the jury.
(vi) B addresses the jury.[92]

(b) *Examination of co-accused*

The reasons for the separate treatment of each accused's case are that the jury must consider the charges against each accused separately and that the accused may be mutually hostile. Counsel for one co-accused may cross-examine the other co-accused(s) whether or not the other co-accused's evidence-in-chief was unfavourable to his client [93]; in practice this precedes any cross-examination by the prosecution. He may also cross-examine any witness called by a co-accused.

An accused loses the protection of section 1 (*f*) of the Criminal Evidence Act 1898 against having his previous record and bad character put to him in cross-examination if he gives " evidence against any other person charged with the same offence." [94] In *Murdoch* v. *Taylor* [95] the House of Lords considered the meaning of " evidence against." Although not in unanimous agreement, the House considered that it is evidence which supports the prosecution's case in a material respect, which undermines the other accused's

[92] The order of the (v) and (vi) may, in the discretion of the judge, be reversed.
[93] *R.* v. *Hilton* [1971] Crim.L.R. 530.
[94] See also p. 141; if a co-accused is acquitted (*e.g.* on a submission of no case to answer, p. 202), he is no longer " a person charged ": *R.* v. *Conti* (1973) 58 Cr.App.R. 387.
[95] [1965] A.C. 574.

defence or which, if accepted by the jury, would warrant the conviction of the other accused. This test is objective and the evidence need not be given with hostile intent; if the circumstances are such that a denial by one accused implies that the other accused must have committed the offence, the denial is treated as evidence against the other.[96] The throwing away of the protection of section 1 (*f*) is for the benefit of the co-accused, not for the prosecution; the co-accused can cross-examine him on his bad character as of right, but the prosecution must ask for the leave of the judge.[97]

This rule may involve a hard choice for defence counsel; it may be a justification for asking for separate trials.[98] In an earlier case,[99] section 1 (*f*) (iii) was interpreted strictly, so that an accused charged with fraudulent conversion did not lose his protection by giving evidence against a co-accused charged with obtaining by false pretences, for they were not " charged with the same offence."

A co-accused is affected by the protection and the exception in section 1 (*f*) whether he is giving evidence on his own behalf or for a co-accused; this is due to the wording of the Act—" a person charged and called as a witness in pursuance of this Act. . . ." Further, if one accused calls another to give evidence on his behalf,[1] the prosecution may then cross-examine the accused giving evidence to show his own guilt of the offence charged.[2]

(c) *Evidence*

A statement of one accused not made on oath which implicates a co-accused is not evidence against the co-accused.[3] If the accused gives evidence on oath it should be treated with caution by the jury if it is only directed to show the guilt of a co-accused, but it is not accomplice evidence if an accused incidentally incriminates a co-accused in giving evidence on his own behalf.[4]

---

96 *R.* v. *Davis* [1975] 1 W.L.R. 345.

97 [1965] A.C. 574, *per* Lord Donovan at p. 593.

98 *R.* v. *Miller* (1952) 36 Cr.App.R. 169; defence counsel ought to approach his colleague in advance to enable him to consider what course of action is best. As to separate trials, see p. 140.

99 *R.* v. *Roberts* (1936) 25 Cr.App.R. 158.

1 " This Act " enables him to give evidence " for the defence," which includes " for a co-defendant "; *see* Criminal Evidence Act 1898, s. 1, p. 31.

2 *i.e.* he is not protected from incriminating questions directed to the offence charged in his capacity as witness for a co-accused; see Act of 1898, s. 1 (*e*), p. 191.

3 *R.* v. *Gunewardene* [1951] 2 K.B. 600. *Cf. R.* v. *Rice* [1963] 1 Q.B. 857 (see p. 188), where cross-examining counsel used such a statement to elicit evidence against a co-accused from the accused on oath.

4 *R.* v. *Barnes and Richards* (1940) 27 Cr.App.R. 154. Evidence of accomplices must generally be treated with caution; see pp. 30 and 197.

(d) *Summing-up*

Finally, the verdict against each accused is a separate entity. The judge must direct the jury accordingly.

3. Submission of no case to answer

At the close of the prosecution case, the defence may submit to the judge that the evidence adduced by the prosecution is insufficient to found a conviction and should therefore not be left to the jury. A judge must withdraw the case from the jury if the prosecution case rests substantially on unsupported evidence of identification which is of poor quality.[5] If the prosecution has not proved its allegations and the judge overrules the submission, the Court of Appeal will quash a conviction even where a co-accused then gives evidence supporting the prosecution,[6] subject to the court's power to affirm a conviction where no miscarriage of justice has occurred.

The submission may be made on one or more counts or in respect of the whole indictment. It should be made in the absence of the jury.[7] The proper procedure is for the judge, if he allows the submission, to direct the jury to return a verdict of not guilty immediately or to hold it over until summing-up on the other counts when he will direct the jury to return a verdict of not guilty on the submitted count.[8]

A count withdrawn on a submission and held over until the summing-up cannot be revived by further evidence.[9] The jury has a power, rarely exercised, to stop a case if they feel that the prosecution has not proved its allegations.[10]

This procedure is an interesting illustration of the judge's control of the jury. Lord Devlin expressed it in terms of the " reasonable lawyer," as opposed to the " reasonable man." " When twelve men unanimously return a certain verdict, they must believe that there is evidence to support it. When the judge rejects their verdict, he is not really telling them that not a single one among them is a reasonable man. What he is telling them is that there is a certain minimum of evidence which the law requires and that as a trained lawyer he is a

---

[5] *R.* v. *Turnbull* [1976] 3 All E.R. 549.

[6] *R.* v. *Abbott* [1955] 2 Q.B. 497.

[7] *R.* v. *Falconer-Atlee* (1973) 58 Cr.App.R. 348.

[8] The judge, clearly, must not use this power to usurp the jury's function: *R.* v. *Barker* [1976] Crim.L.R. 324. As to the judge's powers to refuse an unsupportable verdict, see p. 210.

[9] *R.* v. *Plain* [1967] 1 W.L.R. 565 (where it was also held that one only of alternative counts cannot be withdrawn).

[10] See *R.* v. *Young* [1964] 1 W.L.R. 717 (where Lord Parker C.J. doubted whether the power should ever be used).

better judge than they are of what that minimum should be. What the minimum should be is not a question of law but a question for lawyers."[11]

4. Evidence in rebuttal

Where the defence has introduced new matters which the prosecution could not have foreseen, the judge may give leave to the prosecution to call evidence in contradiction. If the accused has put his character in issue, the judge may allow evidence of bad character to be called.[12] The judge will probably refuse to allow the prosecution to call any evidence which is not clearly and directly relevant, but even clearly relevant evidence would not be allowed if the need for it had been obvious throughout the case.[13] In any event, the admission of evidence in rebuttal is entirely within a sparingly-used discretion of the judge and prosecuting counsel cannot demand it.

The judge may allow a prosecution witness to be recalled in the light of matters which have arisen unexpectedly in the defence case and the Court of Appeal will only interfere where injustice to the accused has resulted.[14] In *R.* v. *Doran*[15] the Court of Appeal allowed fresh evidence which was not of a rebutting character after the close of the prosecution case and even after the defence had called two of its six witnesses. Such evidence, however, must not prejudice the accused and must not deprive him of the " last word ".

5. Legal arguments

It is usually proper to send the jury to the jury room while legal arguments are heard, for the jury might learn of evidence or allegations which are not later adduced or substantiated. The accused should be asked for his consent if he has not himself requested their exclusion. It is almost invariably the practice when argument relating to the admissibility of evidence is heard,[16] though it continues to be heard in open court so that it may appear on the transcript. The judge may also order the jury to leave when a party asks for leave to treat his witness as a hostile witness,[17] and must do so when an accused submits that there is no case to answer.[18]

[11] Devlin, *Trial by Jury* (1966), p. 63.

[12] See p. 192.

[13] *R.* v. *Levy and Tait* (1966) 50 Cr.App.R. 198; *R.* v. *Day* [1940] 1 All E.R. 402 and *R.* v. *Pilcher* (1974) 60 Cr.App.R. 1 (where it was held that it should only be allowed in favour of the prosecution in respect of matters arising " ex improviso ").

[14] See p. 189; *R.* v. *Grant* [1958] Crim.L.R. 42.

[15] (1972) 116 S.J. 238.

[16] *R.* v. *Thompson* [1917] 2 K.B. 630.

[17] See p. 182.

[18] See p. 202.

6. View

The judge may allow the jury to visit the place at which the offence is alleged to have been committed. The jury must of course be kept isolated from the parties and their witness. Any suggestion of improper contact will vitiate the trial.[19] The accused's presence is not essential provided he has an opportunity to cross-examine prosecution witnesses who did attend.[20] The jury must make the view as a body; a direction by the judge that one juror who knew the area should make the view and report back to her fellow jurors was wholly irregular and the conviction could not stand.[21]

Although " viewing the *locus in quo* " involves a special expedition out of court, it is as much a part of the general law relating to real evidence as the inspection of exhibits sufficiently portable to be brought to court. The view must be made before the jury retire to consider their verdict,[22] for there is a strict rule of evidence that no fresh evidence can be adduced after retirement.[23] In *R.* v. *Nixon*[24] a conviction was not quashed on this ground, however, because the view was at the express wish of the defence. The inference is always likely to be that the jury have relied on the fresh evidence obtained by a view because they have asked for it, and it is impossible to look behind their verdict.

7. Adjournment

The powers of a court to adjourn before arraignment have already been described on page 150 and the power to adjourn after verdict but before sentence is described on page 219. After arraignment the powers of adjournment are more limited because of the dangers of an interruption to the attention and impartiality of the jury. Short adjournments are obviously necessary over the lunch-hour, until the next day or over a weekend if the trial is not finished in one sitting; it is usual for the judge to warn the jury not to talk to anyone about the case. Circumstances in which a trial might be adjourned include the sudden but temporary illness of a juror or the accused, a request for the prosecution to produce an item of real evidence or an attempt by the prosecution to adduce evidence not called at committal.[25] If the adjournment is likely to be long, the judge may discharge the jury.

---

[19] The Court of Appeal may order a new trial; see p. 272.
[20] *Karamat* v. *R.* [1956] A.C. 256 (where witnesses but not the judge were present).
[21] *R.* v. *Gurney* [1976] Crim.L.R. 567.
[22] *R.* v. *Lawrence* [1968] 1 W.L.R. 341.
[23] *R.* v. *Corless* (1972) 56 Cr.App.R. 341.
[24] [1968] 1 W.L.R. 577.
[25] See pp. 114 and 150; as to bail for the accused, see p. 75.

8. Discharge of the jury

In some cases an event occurring during trial is so irregular that it is not safe for a jury who have witnessed it to return a verdict. One of the most frequent events of this sort is the accidental disclosure of the accused's past convictions,[26] but the decision to discharge the jury is for the judge and the need for it depends on the facts of each case.[27]

If a juror personally knows of the accused's bad character[28] and it is discovered before verdict, it is likely that the judge will discharge that juror or even the whole jury. If a jury separates without authority, *e.g.* by a juror leaving the jury room after retirement, the judge must discharge the whole jury and order a new trial; discharge of the juror alone is not sufficient.[29] Other misbehaviour on the part of, or improper contact with, a juror would have the same effect. A juror leaving the room to get an exhibit did not warrant quashing a conviction, however.[30]

If a juror dies or is discharged because he is ill or for some other reason, the trial may continue with a diminished jury, provided the number of jurors is not reduced below 9.[31] On a trial for murder or treason[32] the written assent of the prosecution and of every accused must be obtained to the trial continuing with a diminished jury and the judge always has a discretion to discharge the whole jury, which he probably would do if a juror were discharged for, for instance, misconduct or because he had no right to be on the jury.[33]

If separate trials are ordered or a trial is postponed under section 5 (3) or 5 (4) of the Indictments Act 1915,[34] the court may order that the jury be discharged in respect of the postponed parts of the indictment or of all parts of it.[35]

The discharge of a jury means that those jurors are released from the case and from giving a verdict. The trial of the accused may be restarted with a fresh jury, for he cannot plead *autrefois acquit*.[36] To

---

26 *R.* v. *Peckham* (1935) 25 Cr.App.R. 125.

27 *R.* v. *Weaver* [1968] 1 Q.B. 353.

28 *R.* v. *Box and Box* [1964] 1 Q.B. 430 (where, however, the juror's knowledge discovered after the verdict was held, on the facts, to be insufficient to quash the conviction).

29 *R.* v. *Goodson* [1975] 1 W.L.R. 549. The judge has to give leave for the jury to separate under the Juries Act 1974, s. 13.

30 *R.* v. *Alexander* [1974] 1 W.L.R. 422.

31 Juries Act 1974, s. 16.

32 The Act refers to " offences punishable by death "; treason (and possibly piracy) is the only significant offence in this class; see p. 223.

33 *R.* v. *Kelly* [1950] 2 K.B. 164; see also p. 172.

34 See p. 147.

35 Indictments Act 1915, s. 5 (5).

36 See p. 159 *et seq.* The judge may also discharge the jury under the Criminal Law Act 1967, s. 6 (4); see p. 214.

institute a new trial with a fresh jury, the court issues an order of "*venire de novo*."[37]

Judge and Jury

A study of the division of function between judge and jury is essential to an understanding of the English criminal process. It is unfortunately beyond the range of a book of this size to do more than pinpoint basic principles and identify some interesting exceptions. (In summary proceedings, of course, as in most civil cases, this division does not exist.)

The function of the jury is basically limited to determining the questions of fact in a proceeding in which the accused has joined issue with the Crown on questions of fact. The function of the judge covers the conduct of the trial, all decisions of law, guidance of the jury and passing sentence.

The division is most clearly illustrated by the judge's summing-up [38]: the jury decides whether the facts in issue have been proved by the evidence while the judge instructs them on the law to be applied to those facts, *i.e.* whether on the finding of certain facts the legal result will be guilt or innocence. The division is also clear between the judge's function on a plea of demurrer (or an informal preliminary ruling on agreed facts) [39] and the decision whether the accused is mute of malice or fit to plead.[40] However, in many other areas the division is not so readily identified:

(*a*) Submission of no case to answer [41]—the judge must decide whether, according to the law of evidence, the prosecution has adduced sufficient evidence to disclose a case against the accused. Yet a jury, having heard the evidence and having been properly directed on the law, would logically be capable of deciding this question within the terms of their basic duty.

(*b*) Stopping a trial—in certain circumstances the judge may, and sometimes should, stop the trial and direct the entry of a not guilty verdict. This may be done where the defence could have, but has not, submitted that there is no case to answer. In other cases, such as poor identification evidence,[42] he necessarily takes on the jury's

---

[37] Juries Act 1974, s. 21 (4); the order or writ may take such form as the court considers appropriate.

[38] See p. 196.

[39] See p. 155; *N.B.* the latter practice is generally disapproved as a usurpation of the jury's function. The judge's older powers to reject a verdict or require a special verdict on the facts are now obsolete; see pp. 210 and 211.

[40] See p. 169 *et seq.*

[41] See p. 202, especially the remarks of Lord Devlin.

[42] See pp. 35 and 197.

function as judge of fact and evidence. He may also decide that the accused has not adduced sufficient evidence of insanity and withdraw that issue from the jury.

(*c*) Exclusion of evidence—the judge has an analogous discretion to exclude certain items of evidence, *e.g.* where it has been illegally obtained, is unduly prejudicial or is being called in rebuttal.[43] This is in addition to his duty to exclude inadmissible evidence.

(*d*) Pleas—although the jury decides the factual issue in a plea of *autrefois*, the judge has the discretion to withdraw the charge from the jury without letting them hear or decide it.[44]

(*e*) Discharge of the jury [45]—the judge may discharge the jury if damaging inadmissible evidence is revealed or in circumstances where he considers that the accused will not receive a fair trial.

(*f*) Mitigation—the judge is judge of the facts in issue raised on mitigation.[46] He is also judge of the facts, when a probationer comes before him allegedly in breach of a probation order; he should hold a trial, asking the defendant whether he admits the breach and, if not, whether he wishes to give and call evidence.[47]

(*g*) Trial within a trial—this may occur when a decision has to be made during a trial on a point of law.[48] In most cases, however, such a decision involves a judgment of fact also; although the application of the law of evidence is a matter of law, it includes determining preliminary matters of fact which bear on the admission of evidence; *e.g.* facts relating to the taking of the oath and the competence and privileges of witnesses, the facts which may have to be ascertained before admission of hearsay (the death of the person making the declaration, etc.), and deciding whether a witness is giving contrary evidence-in-chief so as to be treated as a hostile witness.[49]

When the judge takes evidence for these purposes it is said to be " on the *voir dire* " as the appropriate oath was formerly different from the witness's usual oath. The burden of proof is on the party seeking to call the disputed evidence and the judge decides the issue beyond reasonable doubt if the prosecution tenders the evidence; if

---

[43] See pp. 23 and 203.

[44] See p. 166.

[45] See p. 205.

[46] See p. 217.

[47] *R.* v. *Devine* [1956] 1 W.L.R. 236; the judge is expressly made sole judge of the issue by the Powers of Criminal Courts Act 1973, s. 12 (3); similar provision is made for community service orders (s. 16 (7)), etc.

[48] See p. 203.

[49] See p. 182.

the accused does so, it would seem reasonable to decide on the balance of probabilities.

When hearing such evidence it is usual for the judge to dismiss the jury while hearing it if it is impossible to take the evidence without disclosing matters which would otherwise be inadmissible. In some cases, however, they should remain as the evidence may have some bearing on credibility, as when the judge ascertains whether a child is old enough to give evidence.[50]

The admission of a confession also depends on the judge ascertaining that it was made voluntarily. The existence of a confession should not be known to the jury as the judge may refuse its admission. Once admitted, the evidence heard by the judge can only be treated by the jury as lessening the weight of the confession as evidence; they cannot be left to decide whether it was voluntary.

Sometimes a specific provision requires the judge to consider a matter which necessarily involves a judgment of fact or the evaluation of evidence, such as whether a statement in proceedings was material for the purposes of a prosecution for perjury.[51]

One other issue which in exceptional cases may have to be determined by the judge is the question of reasonableness; for instance he may decide whether the defendant to a charge of false imprisonment had reasonable cause to suspect the commission of an offence, etc.[52]

E. Verdict

When the judge has concluded his summing-up, the jury consider their verdict. If not immediately in agreement, they retire to the jury room where they must stay, in the custody of a court officer, without interruption until they agree on a verdict or come back to the court to say they cannot agree. There can be no adjournment or further calling of evidence after the retirement of the jury.[53]

If they find difficulties in reaching their verdict the jury may come back into court and ask the judge in open court for further directions [54] on the law or on the evidence. If irregularities occur and the

---

[50] See p. 30; see also *R.* v. *Reynolds* [1950] 1 K.B. 606.

[51] Perjury Act 1911, s. 11 (6).

[52] See p. 63.

[53] The judge cannot give the jury leave to separate after retirement: Juries Act 1974, s. 13. If they are unlikely to reach agreement on the same day, they should be segregated in hotel accommodation: *R.* v. *Kalia* (1975) 60 Cr.App.R. 200.

[54] In *R.* v. *Green* (1949) 34 Cr.App.R. 33 the conviction was quashed because the jury communicated with the judge in his private room and he sent back a note to them without telling counsel or the accused. The judge's direction must be adequate to clear any confusion expressed by the jury: *R.* v. *Rafique* [1973] Crim.L.R. 777.

accused is convicted, the Court of Appeal will not necessarily quash the conviction if the accused has not been unfairly prejudiced.[55]

The doctrine of *functus officio* [56] is applicable to the jury's verdict. It means that when the jury finally deliver their verdict it cannot be changed; if it were an invalid verdict, it and the proceedings upon which it was based would be void. The jury are not *functus officio*, however, the very instant after the foreman has pronounced the verdict. Slips can certainly be corrected after formal pronouncement [57] but it is probably too late after the discharge of the jury or the passing of sentence.

The verdict may be general, partial or special; it may be reached unanimously or by a majority; it may be a verdict of guilty of an offence not expressly charged. If the jury are unable to reach any agreement, they are discharged and the accused may be tried again.

1. General verdict

A general verdict is a verdict on the whole charge in the indictment. If the indictment contains several counts or charges several people, the verdict should be taken for each count and for each accused separately.

The verdict must not be ambiguous. Verdicts of " guilty, but of unconscious mind " [58] and " guilty of obtaining . . . under false pretences, but whether there was any intent to defraud the jury consider there is not sufficient evidence," [59] are clearly ambiguous. If accepted by the judge, such a verdict is treated as an acquittal for the jury have not found proved one of the constituent parts of the offence. The proper course is for the judge to refuse to accept it, redirect the jury on what they have to find proved and ask them to reconsider their verdict.[60] Alternatively, he may question them on what they mean by an ambiguous word or phrase and obtain an unambiguous verdict in that way.[61]

If there are several counts or several accused, the verdict on each

---

[55] As *e.g.* in *R.* v. *Furlong, French and Pickard* (1950) 34 Cr.App.R. 79 where the accused knew the contents of a private communication between the judge and jury, *R.* v. *Nixon* [1968] 1 W.L.R. 577 where the accused expressed a wish that the jury should inspect an object after retirement (see p. 204), and *R.* v. *Lamb* (1974) 59 Cr.App.R. 196 where the jury communicated with the judge in writing and he sent a verbal message through the clerk. See also *R.* v. *Goodson* and *R.* v. *Alexander*, above.

[56] More often considered in relation to magistrates' courts, see p. 316.

[57] *R.* v. *Bateson* [1969] 3 All E.R. 1372; *R.* v. *Barry* [1975] 1 W.L.R. 1190.

[58] *R.* v. *Crisp* (1912) 7 Cr.App.R. 173 (a case of attempted suicide).

[59] *R.* v. *Gray* (1891) 17 Cox 299.

[60] *R.* v. *Hawkes* (1931) 22 Cr.App.R. 172.

[61] *R.* v. *White* (1960) 45 Cr.App.R. 34; *R.* v. *Rafique* [1973] Crim.L.R. 777.

must be consistent with the others. Conviction as a single conspirator is no longer, as a matter of law, an inconsistent verdict, and two accused may be found guilty of committing an offence, charged jointly, independently of one another.[62] Where conspirators are tried separately, no inconsistency arises from different verdicts; indeed, one person alone may be charged if the person he is alleged to have conspired with did not commit the offence because he did not have the intention to carry it out.[63] Where two conspirators are charged jointly, however, the House of Lords by a majority considered that a direction to acquit both if the jury is going to acquit one of them would be the proper course.[64]

If the indictment charges alternative counts, *e.g.* theft and handling, the accused cannot be convicted on both.[65] Factual, as opposed to legal, inconsistency of verdicts will not automatically result in a conviction being quashed, for the jury's verdict as to fact is inscrutable; however, where two counts alleged handling a stolen cheque and obtaining money on a forged instrument (the same cheque) and the accused contended that he had been too drunk to form the necessary intent, the Court of Appeal held that conviction of the first and acquittal of the second was so inconsistent that the conviction could not stand.[66]

If a verdict of guilty is agreed prematurely by the jury before hearing the judge's summing-up of the defence case, the conviction must be quashed.[67]

The former power of the judge to refuse to accept a verdict which is clear in its terms has long been in disuse. The verdict may be unsupportable on the evidence and contrary to the judge's clear direction but the judge must accept it. If it is a verdict of guilty, for instance where he has directed them to return a verdict of not guilty because there is no case to answer,[68] the proper course is for the judge

---

[62] *D.P.P.* v. *Shannon* [1975] A.C. 717; *D.P.P.* v. *Merriman* [1973] A.C. 584; see p. 138.

[63] *R.* v. *O'Brien* (1974) 59 Cr.App.R. 222.

[64] *D.P.P.* v. *Shannon*, above. The difficult case of accessory offenders was considered in *R.* v. *Richards* [1973] 3 W.L.R. 888 where it was held that an accomplice who was not present at the scene of the crime could not be convicted of an offence more serious than the one of which the principal offender was convicted.

[65] *R.* v. *Seymour* [1954] 1 W.L.R. 678 (if a verdict of guilty is returned on one, the jury should be discharged from giving a verdict on the other count, as a verdict of not guilty would preclude the Court of Appeal from altering the verdict on appeal); *R.* v. *Haddock* [1976] Crim.L.R. 374; as to alternative counts, see p. 136.

[66] *R.* v. *Durante* [1972] 1 W.L.R. 1612; see also *R.* v. *Hunt* [1968] 2 Q.B. 433. The appellant has to establish inconsistency: *R.* v. *Kirby* (1972) 56 Cr.App.R. 758.

[67] *R.* v. *Young* [1964] 1 W.L.R. 717 (where the foreman of the jury said that the jury had already made up their minds).

[68] See p. 202.

to postpone sentence, grant the accused bail and certify that his case is fit for appeal.[69]

Questioning the jury on an unambiguous verdict is disapproved. In *R.* v. *Larkin* [70] the judge sought to establish, on a verdict of manslaughter, whether it was a negligent killing or a killing under provocation; the questions revealed a certain amount of confusion in the jury's minds as to whether it was an accidental killing. The conviction, however, was not quashed.

Finally, the judge must put no pressure of any sort on the jury; where a judge said he was leaving the court in 10 minutes and the jury would be locked up in their room all night if they did not return a verdict before the 10 minutes were up, the conviction had to be quashed.[71]

2. Partial verdict

The jury may find the accused guilty or not guilty of a limited part of the indictment. Clearly they may acquit on one count of an indictment and convict on the others, but they may also acquit him of the offence charged and find him guilty of an offence not charged, or say that they have disagreed as to whether he is guilty of an alternative offence. In the latter case he may be indicted afresh for the alternative offence.[72] Alternative verdicts are considered on page 213.

3. Special verdict

A special verdict may take the form of a verdict on certain facts only, but not on the legal conclusion to be drawn from them, or of a verdict of insanity. The first form is only to be used in the most exceptional cases,[73] for it was once used as a weapon of oppression in political trials.[74] The judge asks whether or not the jury find certain factual issues to be proved and on their answers finds the accused guilty or not guilty in law. The jury may refuse to answer and return a general verdict.[75]

The verdict of insanity is " not guilty by reason of insanity." [76]

---

[69] See Devlin, *Trial by Jury* (1966), p. 79 *et seq.* and Glanville Williams, *The Proof of Guilt* (1963), p. 263.

[70] [1943] K.B. 174.

[71] *R.* v. *McKenna* [1960] 1 Q.B. 411.

[72] See *Autrefois acquit*, p. 160.

[73] *R.* v. *Bourne* (1952) 36 Cr.App.R. 125.

[74] The right given to the jury by Fox's Libel Act 1792 to return a general verdict in all libel cases, was created on this account.

[75] In *R.* v. *Jameson* (1896) 12 T.L.R. 551 at p. 593, the jury returned a general verdict as well; see also Glanville Williams, *The Proof of Guilt* (1963), pp. 264–266.

[76] Criminal Procedure (Insanity) Act 1964, s. 1 (1).

The two reasons why the verdict takes this form are, firstly, that the accused is not discharged but is kept in confinement for treatment [77] and, secondly, that he may appeal against the verdict, which he could not do if he were generally acquitted.[78]

4. Majority verdict

Section 17 of the Juries Act 1974 provides that a verdict may be reached, in a jury of 11 or 12, by the agreement of 10 jurors or, in a jury of 10, by the agreement of 9 jurors.[79] The judge in his summing-up must still direct the jury to return a unanimous verdict, but he should mention the possibility of accepting a majority verdict at a later stage, stressing that they must first try to be unanimous.

The jury may not return a majority verdict unless they have deliberated for at least two hours or such longer period as the court thinks reasonable.[80]

The Lord Chief Justice issued a practice direction in July 1967 explaining the procedure.[81] If the jury returns before the expiry of two hours the judge asks if they are agreed; if they are not, they are sent out for further deliberation. If the jury returns after two hours have elapsed, they should be sent out again for a reasonable time to try again to reach a unanimous verdict, but, if they cannot, to return a majority verdict. When the jury finally return to court, the form is:

(i) " Have at least ten (or nine) of you agreed upon your verdict? "
If yes,
(ii) " What is your verdict? "
(iii) If Not Guilty, the verdict is accepted without more ado.
(iv) If Guilty—" Is the verdict of you all or by a majority? "
(v) If Guilty by a majority—" How many of you agreed to the verdict and how many dissented? "

This rather complicated formula is made necessary because section 17 (3) requires the number of jurors in agreement to be stated in open court on a majority verdict of guilty but it is undesirable that a verdict

---

77 Criminal Procedure (Insanity) Act 1964, s. 1 (under the Mental Health Act 1959, s. 71).

78 Criminal Appeal Act 1968, s. 12.

79 A jury of nine (see Juries Act 1974, s. 16) must be unanimous.

80 Juries Act 1974, s. 17 (4). Any time spent asking the judge for further directions (see p. 208) is included: *R.* v. *Adams* [1968] 1 W.L.R. 106. Under a Practice Direction (*The Times*, May 12, 1970) the jury must spend at least two hours and ten minutes in deliberation before returning a majority verdict, but a further retirement (below) may be dispensed with in very straightforward cases (*R.* v. *Wright* (1974) 58 Cr.App.R. 444) as it is only recommended, not required. *Cf. R.* v. *Elia* [1968] 2 All E.R. 587.

81 [1967] 1 W.L.R. 1198.

of not guilty should be shown to be a majority verdict. If the section is not complied with, a majority verdict of guilty is invalid and must be quashed.[82]

5. Alternative verdict

Under section 6 of the Criminal Law Act 1967 the jury has certain powers to return a verdict of guilty of an offence not charged in the indictment. The availability of an alternative in any given case is a problem of the substantive law and is outside the scope of this book.

Section 6 lays down the general rule but some statutes provide specific alternatives.[83] Alternatives on a charge of murder are listed in section 6 (2); there is no alternative verdict available on a charge of treason. For all other offences section 6 (3) provides that the jury may find the accused not guilty of the offence specifically charged in the indictment but guilty of another offence, where the allegations in the indictment amount to or include, expressly or by implication, an allegation of that other offence; or they may find him guilty of any offence of which he could have been convicted on a specific charge of that other offence. Although potentially susceptible to a broad interpretation, the words of the subsection have in fact been interpreted restrictively, particularly the words " allegations in the indictment." The " red pencil " approach, approved in *R.* v. *Lillis*,[84] is to delete averments in the indictment which are not proved and see whether what remains alleges an offence which has been proved. In *R.* v *Woods* [85] a verdict of receiving could not be returned on a charge of larceny (now handling and theft respectively); indecent assault may be found on a charge of unlawful intercourse [86]; common assault is not an alternative verdict on a charge of robbery [87]; indecent assault is an alternative on a charge of rape but unlawful intercourse is not [88]; burglary under section 9 (1) (*b*) is not an alternative on a charge of burglary under section 9 (1) (*a*) of the Theft Act 1968.[89]

---

[82] *R.* v. *Barry* [1975] 1 W.L.R. 1190; this applies to both subss. (3) and (4).

[83] *e.g.* Sexual Offences Act 1956, s. 37 and Sched. 2; Infant Life (Preservation) Act 1929, s. 2 (2).

[84] [1972] 2 W.L.R. 1409.

[85] [1969] 1 Q.B. 447.

[86] *R.* v. *McCormack* [1969] 2 Q.B. 442.

[87] *R.* v. *Springfield* [1969] Crim.L.R. 557. Assault occasioning actual bodily harm is not an alternative on a charge of causing grievous bodily harm if the particulars of that harm are not included or do not include an assault: *R.* v. *Austin* (1973) 58 Cr. App.R. 163.

[88] *R.* v. *Hodgson* [1973] 2 W.L.R. 570; *R.* v. *Fisher* [1969] 2 Q.B. 114 (an assize case).

[89] *R.* v. *Hollis* [1971] Crim. L.R. 525; *see* p. 120.

Attempt

A verdict may always be returned finding the accused guilty of an attempt to commit the offence charged in the indictment, for the allegation of a completed offence always includes an allegation of an attempt to commit it; where attempt is charged, or where an assault or preliminary offence is charged, the jury may convict of the attempt or preliminary offence notwithstanding that the evidence proves that the accused committed the completed offence.[90] This is subject to the judge's discretion to discharge the jury with a view to indicting the accused for the completed offence.

Murder

On a charge of murder the accused can be found guilty of the following offences only[91]: Murder, manslaughter, causing grievous bodily harm with intent, any offence specifically made an alternative by statute, such as infanticide,[92] an attempt to commit any of these offences or assisting the murderer.[93]

Effect of an alternative verdict

Section 6 applies to each count of an indictment as if it were a separate indictment.[94] The form of verdict required by section 6 (3) includes an acquittal of the offence charged. If the accused pleads guilty to the alternative, the acceptance of his plea constitutes an acquittal of the offence charged.[95] A conviction or acquittal of one of a series of available alternative offences can be pleaded in bar to an indictment for another of those offences.[96]

6. Disagreement of the jury

If a jury is in hopeless disagreement and is unable to reach even a majority verdict, they must tell the judge so and he will discharge them from giving a verdict.[97] The accused may be tried again on the same indictment. The procedure for majority verdicts[98] has not altered the practice where the jurors are more or less evenly divided, *i.e.* they need not spend two hours trying to resolve irreconcilable differences before coming back to court to say so.[99]

---

[90] Criminal Law Act 1967, s. 6 (4).
[91] *Ibid.* s. 6 (2).
[92] Infanticide Act 1938, s. 1 (2).
[93] *i.e.* under the Criminal Law Act 1967, s. 4 (2).
[94] *Ibid.* s. 6 (7).
[95] *Ibid.* s. 6 (5).
[96] See *Autrefois acquit* and *convict*, p. 159 *et seq.*
[97] See p. 205.
[98] See p. 212.
[99] *R.* v. *Elia* [1968] 2 All E.R. 587.

7. Validity of the verdict

A judgment cannot be upset because the provisions for impanelling or selecting the jury were not complied with or because an individual juror was not qualified or was misnamed or mis-described or unfit to serve.[1] Objection to the verdict may be made, however, if a member of the jury was an impostor.[2] If the jury has been improperly summoned, impanelled or selected, however, and objection was taken at the time the irregularity occurred, the judgment may be objected to if the irregularity was not corrected.[3]

F. Procedure on a Plea of Guilty [4]

Once the accused's plea of guilty is accepted by the court, none of the matters described in Sections C–E above are involved and the court proceeds straight to sentence. Evidence of the offence confessed to need not be given, but the prosecution normally states the facts in open court to enable the judge to pass an appropriate sentence. Evidence may be called by either party, in which case the judge decides the issues himself if they relate to mitigation, *e.g.* whether the accused was a ringleader as contended by the prosecution. If prosecution evidence reveals further offences to which the accused does not wish to confess it is quite wrong to sentence him on those offences.[5] Moreover, the evidence may be such that the court should accept a change of plea and proceed to trial with a jury.[6] Where a sentence is mandatory, as is the life sentence for murder, and the committal proceedings have received no publicity,[7] the prosecution must state the facts in open court before the sentence is pronounced.[8] This is done to protect the public interest in knowing that justice has been done.

The procedure on sentence is the same as the procedure when the jury have returned a verdict of guilty. This is considered in the next chapter.

---

1 Juries Act 1974, s. 18 (1).
2 *Ibid.* s. 18 (3).
3 *Ibid.* s. 18 (2).
4 See also p. 155.
5 *R.* v. *Hutchison* [1972] 1 W.L.R. 398.
6 See p. 169.
7 See p. 94.
8 Practice Direction [1968] 1 W.L.R. 529.

CHAPTER 9

SENTENCE

IF the accused has been found not guilty by the jury, he is immediately a free man.[1] The court has no further business with him unless an application in connection with the costs of the trial is made.[2] Where the jury returns a verdict of guilty or where the accused has pleaded guilty, counsel for both sides still have to perform certain duties in court and the judge has to impose an appropriate punishment or order suitable treatment of the offender.

Although the choice of treatment of the offender and its efficacy is equal in importance to the court's function of adjudication, it cannot be dealt with as fully as it deserves in a book of this size.[3-4] The following is confined to the appropriate classes of punishments and orders and the procedural requirements for, and effects of, their imposition.

Defence counsel sometimes discusses the quantum of punishment, *e.g.* the length of imprisonment, with the judge, but it must be done tactfully as it may be considered discourteous and presuming in a field which is entirely the court's.[5] Prosecuting counsel has no interest in sentence, but remains in court to deal with the matters described in Section A below.

A. JUDGMENT

1. Matters to be put before the judge

The information which the prosecution must lay before the judge to assist him in passing sentence includes the accused's past convictions and character. The prosecution should prepare a proof of evidence containing particulars of the accused's age, education,

---

[1] Unless he has been found not guilty by reason of insanity, as to which, see pp. 211 and 277.

[2] See p. 248.

[3-4] Readers are recommended to refer to specialist books, especially Thomas, *Principles of Sentencing*, and Fallon, *Crown Court Practice: Sentence*; for a stimulating comparative examination of the court's powers in sentencing, see Stockdale, *The Court and the Offender*. H.M.S.O. publishes two booklets on sentence: *The Treatment of Offenders in Britain* and *The Sentence of the Court*.

[5] The practice of plea bargaining (*i.e.* offering the judge a plea of guilty with a view to a lighter sentence) is disapproved; see p. 156.

employment and previous convictions,[6] the date of arrest and a statement of whether the accused was granted bail. The proof should be given to the judge and a copy of it to the accused before giving it in evidence.[7]

The prosecution does not need to prove the accused's previous convictions unless the accused denies them, which naturally is rare, but simply asks a police officer to read them out in court.[8] The police should always give defence counsel details of previous convictions before trial so that he will know whether it is safe to put the accused's character in issue.[9]

2. Plea in mitigation

During trial many matters which are important in assessing the culpability of the accused are irrelevant and inadmissible on the issue of guilt. For instance, the fact that, shortly before committing the offence, the accused's wife and two children were killed in a fire, is not relevant to show that he did or did not commit the offence (unless he were trying to prove insanity to which the tragedy was conducive). If such matters were put to the jury, they might acquit the accused on compassionate grounds and not on the facts proved before them.[10] Personal circumstances, however, are by no means ignored by the criminal courts. Except in cases, such as treason and murder,[11] where the judge has no choice but to impose a certain punishment, the plea of defence counsel to mitigate the severity of the judge's sentence, and any evidence he calls at this stage, is important. The judge may be called upon to judge issues of fact at this stage; the defence may contest facts presented by the prosecution

---

[6] Including those findings of guilt excluded from the details of previous convictions by the Children and Young Persons Act 1963, s. 16 (2), as to which, see p. 192. This proposition is clearly stated in the practice direction cited in the next footnote. S. 16 (2), however, states that " in any proceedings for an offence *committed* . . . by a person . . ., any offence of which he was found guilty while under the age of fourteen shall be disregarded for the purposes of *any evidence* of his previous convictions." There would appear to be some inconsistency, therefore, in allowing evidence of such findings of guilt to be given to the judge.

[7] Practice Direction [1966] 1 W.L.R. 1184; *R.* v. *Sargeant* (1974) 60 Cr.App.R. 74.

[8] Proof of conviction is by production of the certificate of the previous court and a copy of the court record (Evidence Act 1851, s. 13), production of a certified extract of the record and proof of identity (Prevention of Crime Act 1871, s. 18), or a certificate that the fingerprints of the accused are identical with those of the person previously convicted (Criminal Justice Act 1948, s. 39).

[9] See p. 193 *et seq.*

[10] A skilful defence counsel may try indirectly to bring out such matters with this in mind, but it is an unofficial question of tactics and discretion and could hardly be formulated in a textbook.

[11] Treason—the death penalty (Treason Act 1814, s. 1); murder—life imprisonment (Murder (Abolition of Death Penalty) Act 1965, s. 1).

which reveal aggravating circumstances, or prosecuting counsel may wish to question defence evidence in mitigation. A particular issue which the judge is required to decide is the existence of special reasons not to disqualify from driving where the disqualification is mandatory.[12]

Defence counsel, in his plea, puts forward almost any matter which shows mitigating circumstances surrounding the offence such as the accused's desire to " go straight " and the likelihood of his doing so, for instance, by now having a regular job and a stable home life. Most indictable offences carry a relatively high maximum penalty which is imposed only in the worst cases[13] and the judge may choose from the variety of less severe punishments and remedial treatments, right down to discharging him without punishment. In this way " the crudity of the criminal law, with its clutter of legal debris and statutory additions, can be tolerated simply because . . . legal liability is only one part of the legal process."[14] Defence counsel may be very free in his plea in mitigation; he may call witnesses, who may give hearsay evidence,[15] and documentary evidence of character[16] and evidence of motive, or he may simply address the judge himself about the accused's circumstances, character and motives. If the accused is unrepresented he should be asked by the judge if he wishes to say anything.

There are still several matters which may arise before the judge actually pronounces the sentence and these may occur before the defence makes the plea in mitigation; in the case of a probation officer's report, it must be read before then as defence counsel may wish to examine the officer on it.[17]

3. Motion in arrest of judgment

This is a rare and archaic procedure whereby the accused objects to the formal parts of the court record—the indictment and the recording of the verdict of guilty—and is applied if, for instance, a pardon is granted to the accused. Uncertainty or inaccuracy in the indictment should have been removed by amending or quashing it[18]

---

[12] *e.g.* driving with a prohibited level of alcohol in the blood disqualification on a " totting-up " endorsement; see pp. 245–246.

[13] *e.g.* manslaughter—life imprisonment (Offences against the Person Act 1861, s. 5); theft—10 years' imprisonment (Theft Act 1968, s. 7); or robbery—life imprisonment (*ibid.* s. 8 (2)).

[14] Jackson, *Enforcing the Law* (1967), p. 100.

[15] *R.* v. *Marquis* (1951) 35 Cr.App.R. 33.

[16] *e.g.* an army record: *R.* v. *Roche* (1944) 30 Cr.App.R. 29.

[17] *R.* v. *Kirkham* [1968] Crim.L.R. 210.

[18] See pp. 146 and 148.

before arraignment, or at least during the trial. The accused cannot put forward an irregularity during the trial in arrest of judgment, but should appeal against his conviction.[19] A successful motion in arrest of judgment causes the proceedings to be set aside[20]; it does not bar the accused from being re-indicted.[21]

4. Reports

In some cases the judge will receive reports from non-legal specialists on the mental, physical, social and personal condition of the accused to help him to select the appropriate sentence.[22] If these are not ready when verdict is returned, the judge may adjourn[23] the case to enable inquiries to be made by a probation officer or a doctor or psychiatrist. The prison where the accused has been kept in custody may also make a report.

To avoid wasting doctors' and probation officers' time on an acquitted accused, the reports are most conveniently made after conviction; on the other hand, when the current sitting of the court of trial is not likely to last for the two or three weeks necessary for compiling the reports, difficulty and delay may be experienced in finding the judge who is due to pass sentence. A different judge may pronounce sentence,[24] but this is naturally undesirable if it can be avoided.

The system for obtaining reports is generally governed by administrative directions, based largely on the Report of the Streatfield Committee of 1961.[25] Reports are obtained in a wide variety of cases but they are more desirable in certain classes of case than in others. They are most obviously desirable if the court is considering making a probation order,[26] and are obligatory before it makes a community service order.[27] Medical reports must be taken before imposing a treatment condition on a probation order.[28] Where the offender is under 21 years old, the court should obtain information

---

[19] See p. 262 *et seq.*
[20] 4 Bl.Com. 385.
[21] See p. 164; if it is made because of a pardon, the pardon is pleaded in bar; see p. 169.
[22] As to juvenile offenders where reports are usually obligatory, see p. 375.
[23] See p. 204.
[24] Courts Act 1971, s. 6 (4) (*a*).
[25] Cmnd. 1289. The system came into operation on October 1, 1963, and guidance to courts is given by Home Office Circular 30/1971 and in the Home Office publication, *The Sentence of the Court.* For a concise description of the system, see Jackson, *Enforcing the Law* (1967), p. 126 *et seq.*
[26] Powers of Criminal Courts Act 1973, s. 2 (1); see p. 236.
[27] *Ibid.* s. 14 (2); see p. 235.
[28] *Ibid.* s. 3 (1); see p. 237. See also Hospital orders, p. 234.

about the circumstances of the case and must consider any information available about his character and physical and mental condition before imposing a sentence of imprisonment.[29] A report will almost certainly be obtained before an adult who has not previously been sentenced to imprisonment is so sentenced.[30] In neither of these cases, however, is it mandatory to obtain a report.[31] Other cases where a report would be desirable are where the offender has recently been in touch with the probation service or where, as in a case such as arson, there is a suspicion of mental unbalance. A copy of the report of a probation officer must be made available to the offender or his legal representative (or parent or guardian, if he is under 17 years old).[32]

Special considerations apply to granting bail on an adjournment to obtain reports.[33] A pre-trial medical report may be made by the prison doctor, if the accused is in custody; if the accused is remanded on bail, the court must impose conditions enabling the report to be made.[34]

Section 45 of the Powers of Criminal Courts Act 1973 enables the Home Secretary by rules to make " social enquiry reports " obligatory in specified cases where the court considers imposing a custodial sentence.[35] A social inquiry report or a probation officer's report looks into, among other things, the accused's personal and family circumstances, the availability of employment and the likelihood of a non-custodial sentence benefiting the accused.

5. Taking offences into consideration

Where the accused wishes to confess to other untried offences without being convicted, he may ask the judge to take them into consideration in passing sentence. This practice is not enacted, but has received statutory recognition in relation to compensation, restitution and criminal bankruptcy orders.[36] The accused may ask for offences of a nature similar to the offence of which he is convicted to be taken into consideration and he must himself admit his guilt

---

[29] Powers of Criminal Courts Act 1973, s. 19 (2); see p. 225.

[30] *Ibid.* s. 20. See also Criminal Justice Act 1961, s. 1 (3), p. 336.

[31] *R.* v. *Ampleford* (1975) 61 Cr.App.R. 325 (where the accused refused to co-operate before trial and the judge proceeded immediately to sentence him to imprisonment on the verdict of guilty).

[32] Powers of Criminal Courts Act 1973, s. 46; see also *R.* v. *Kirkham*, p. 218.

[33] See pp. 74 and 223

[34] Magistrates' Courts Act 1952, s. 26 (3); see p. 77.

[35] Certain cases are specified in Home Office Circulars Nos. 188 and 189/1968.

[36] Powers of Criminal Courts Act 1973, ss. 35 and 39; Criminal Justice Act 1972, s. 6; see pp. 250 and 253.

before the judge,[37] but the prosecution may prepare a list containing particulars of the offences and the judge may ask whether the accused admits each offence.

The effect of this practice is not equivalent to a conviction and does not bar a subsequent charge or indictment.[38] The judge cannot in general impose a penalty greater than he could have imposed for the offence or offences of which the accused has been convicted,[39] nor can the judge invoke this practice if a prosecution is pending. He can, however, make a compensation or restitution order in respect of the offence " t.i.c." and he may take a " t.i.c." into account in making the offender bankrupt.[36] A court of limited jurisdiction, *e.g.* a magistrates' court, cannot take into consideration offences outside its jurisdiction.[40]

6. Sentence

The sentence is pronounced in open court by the presiding judge. It is most unusual for the accused not to be present.[41] In accordance with the general principle,[42] sentence is pronounced separately for each count of the indictment of which an accused has been convicted.[43]

The content of the sentence must be considered under the appropriate class of punishment or order. General principles of sentencing fall outside the scope of this book, *e.g.* the balancing of restraint, deterrence and reformation as the aim of the sentence; other aspects are dealt with in the following pages, *e.g.* concurrent and consecutive sentences on page 229.

Postponement, Alteration and Deferment

Alteration or rescission of a sentence by the court of trial [44] is permissible by statute within 28 days from the day on which the sentence

---

[37] *R.* v. *Nelson* [1967] 1 W.L.R. 449; *R.* v. *Davis* [1943] K.B. 274.

[38] *R.* v. *Nicholson* (1947) 32 Cr.App.R. 98; see p. 165.

[39] *R.* v. *Tremayne* (1932) 23 Cr.App.R. 191.

[40] *R.* v. *Anderson* (1958) 42 Cr.App.R. 91 (where civilian offences also triable by a court-martial were considered).

[41] As to trial in his absence, see p. 150. The terms of some sentencing provisions presuppose the offender's presence; *e.g.* s. 22 (4) of the Powers of Criminal Courts Act 1973 requires the court to explain to the offender his liability under a suspended sentence (see p. 227).

[42] See p. 209.

[43] This also enables the sentence on other counts to stand if the Court of Appeal quashes a conviction on one count.

[44] The court must be constituted (*i.e.* High Court judge or circuit judge) as it was when sentence was passed (Courts Act 1971, s. 11 (4)), but there is no need for the same judge to be sitting: *R.* v. *Dudley Crown Court, ex p. Smith* (1973) 58 Cr.App.R. 184.

was passed.[45] Where two or more defendants are tried jointly, the sentence may be varied either within 28 days of the conclusion of the joint trial or within 56 days from the day on which the sentence was imposed, whichever period is the shorter.[46] The Crown Court has a common law power to postpone sentence in addition to this and to the power to defer sentence.[47] It avails the court when the exigencies of the particular case require a postponement for longer than 28 days and it cannot be used with the same flexibility as the statutory power. In *R.* v. *Annesley*[48] it was held to be proper to deal with a " totting-up " disqualification more than 28 days after the original sentence because, as the driving licence was missing, it took some considerable time to check the computerised record. Such an exercise of the power is distinct from an improper use of the deferment procedure in order to split up the sentence for a single offence to deal with different elements separately. There is also power at common law, expressly preserved by section 6 (4) (*b*) of the Courts Act 1971, for the judge to release a convicted person on respite of judgment on a recognisance to come up for judgment if called upon, but meanwhile to be of good behaviour.[49]

An important power to postpone sentence for up to six months is the power to defer under section 1 of the Powers of Criminal Courts Act 1973. A sentence can only be deferred, however, for the purpose of enabling the court to consider the offender's post-conviction behaviour and circumstances, and, as this is in the nature of granting a probationary period, its description is postponed to page 242.

The exercise of the power to vary or rescind is a matter for the court's discretion and so must be proper. In *R.* v. *Stone*,[50] it was held that the judge should not have recalled a co-accused to increase his sentence merely because that co-accused, who had pleaded guilty and been sentenced before the trial of the other co-accused, failed to give the anticipated evidence; in *R.* v. *Gillespie*[51] it was held that an increase in the sentence is not invalid for that reason alone, but the judge's second thoughts must result in a sentence which is appropriate in all the circumstances.

[45] Courts Act 1971, s. 11 (2). This is a statutory exception to the rule of *functus officio* (see p. 316) whereby a person (or court) is unable to reopen his decision after his duty is performed.

[46] *Ibid.* s. 11 (3).

[47] See p. 242.

[48] [1976] 1 W.L.R. 106.

[49] See also pp. 243 and 327. It is also preserved by s. 1 (7) of the Powers of Criminal Courts Act 1973.

[50] [1970] 1 W.L.R. 1112.

[51] [1973] 1 W.L.R. 1483 (where a sentence was increased after the judge became aware of the effect of s. 3 of the Criminal Justice Act 1961, as to which, see p. 231).

An abuse of sentencing discretion which formerly caused some concern was the use of a remand in custody for reports when the likelihood of a custodial sentence being appropriate was remote.[52] The Bail Act 1976 has probably removed this possibility because bail must be granted on such an adjournment unless it would be impracticable to make the reports if the accused were not in custody[53]; if the accused consents to the making of the reports, this exception would not often apply.

Subject to the fairly wide range of matters already described which the judge may legitimately take into account, certain other matters must not influence him. In some reported cases the following matters were improperly considered; allegations against the police (*R.* v. *Skone*)[54] pleading not guilty, or, conversely, not showing leniency when the accused pleaded guilty and showed remorse (*R.* v. *Harper*; *R.* v. *de Haan*)[55]; election of trial by jury (*R.* v. *Jamieson*)[56]; inability of the accused to pay a substantial fine where the sentence was of imprisonment (*R.* v. *Reeves*)[57]; passing a severe sentence so that in future a court might impose an extended sentence (*R.* v. *Lycett*)[58]; and passing a severe sentence because the judge considered that the accused had committed perjury (*R.* v. *Quinn*).[59]

B. Punishments

This chapter does not deal with punishments and orders relating to children and young persons under the age of 17; they are dealt with separately in Chapter 15.[60]

1. Sentence of death

Death remains the sentence for treason and piracy with violence.[61] It is carried out by hanging but, in the case of piracy, it may be recorded without actual execution taking place.[62]

---

52 See, *e.g.*, *R.* v. *Neville* [1971] Crim.L.R. 589; as to reports, see p. 219.
53 Bail Act 1976, Sched. 1, Pt. I, para. 7 see p. 74.
54 (1965) 51 Cr.App.R. 165.
55 [1968] 2 Q.B. 108.
56 [1975] Crim.L.R. 248.
57 (1972) 56 Cr. App.R. 366.
58 [1968] 1 W.L.R. 1245; as to extended sentences, see p. 226.
59 (1932) 23 Cr.App.R. 196 at p. 198.
60 See p. 361.
61 Treason Act 1814, s. 1, and Piracy Act 1837, s. 2.
62 Judgment of Death Act 1823, s. 1, as amended by the Criminal Law Act 1967, Sched. 2. Piratical acts against aircraft are punishable by imprisonment for life; see Hijacking Act 1971 and Protection of Aircraft Act 1973, p. 11.

2. Imprisonment

Imprisonment is not normally available as a punishment for offenders under 21 years old; these are dealt with in Section 3 below [63] and in Chapter 15.[64] All indictable offences are punishable by imprisonment and usually the maximum term is laid down by statute. For common law offences, such as conspiracy, where no maximum is prescribed, the court may impose any term reasonable in the circumstances.[65] If a statutory offence carries no maximum term, the sentence of imprisonment must not exceed two years [66] and the conviction for an attempt cannot be punished by a longer term than the maximum prescribed for the completed offence.[67] Although magistrates' courts generally have a statutory minimum term of five days' imprisonment,[68] courts trying offences on indictment may impose a nominal sentence of one day. The length of time actually spent in prison is determined by the Home Secretary's power to release prisoners [69]; for these purposes the length of a sentence is computed to include any time spent in custody before trial or sentence[70] but from the court's point of view, the sentence starts on the day on which the sentence is passed.[71] If the judge imposes a longer term than is appropriate in order to counteract the offender's, in his view, possible premature release, the sentence should be reduced on appeal.[72] With the exception of life imprisonment,[73] all

---

[63] See p. 231.

[64] See p. 361.

[65] *e.g.* 30 years for armed robbery from a mail train: *R.* v. *Wilson* [1965] 1 Q.B. 402 (£2,500,000 was stolen from the train); seven years for conspiracy to defraud: *Verrier* v. *D.P.P.* [1976] 2 A.C. 195 (in this case the House of Lords decided that in exceptional cases a conspiracy to commit a statutory offence could receive a greater punishment than was available for the offence; *cf.* Law Com. 76 in which the Law Commission propose a maximum for conspiracy which is the same as the maximum available for the offence conspired about, and see Criminal Law Bill, Appendix).

[66] Powers of Criminal Courts Act 1973, s. 18 (1). Offences within this subsection are rare as the omission of a specific penalty must be due to legislative oversight. The Human Tissue Act 1961 prohibits unauthorised removal of parts of a body; no offence is specified. In *R.* v. *Lennox-Wright* [1973] Crim.L.R. 529 a contravention of this prohibition was held to be a common law offence, not a statutory offence without a specific penalty.

[67] *Ibid.* s. 18 (2).

[68] Magistrates' Courts Act 1952, s. 107 (1); see p. 319.

[69] See p. 257.

[70] Criminal Justice Act 1967, s. 67; see also Criminal Appeal Act 1968, s. 29 (1), p. 273, and Prison (Amendment) Rules 1972 (S.I. No. 1972/1860) which allow time spent in custody to count for the purposes of remission. Any period spent on bail granted by the Crown Court is not counted as part of any sentence of detention: Courts Act 1971, s. 13 (4).

[71] Courts Act 1971, s. 11 (1).

[72] *R.* v. *Maguire and Enos* (1956) 40 Cr.App.R. 92.

[73] And detention during H.M. pleasure; see p. 366

sentences of imprisonment must be determinate, *i.e.* for a specified period.[74]

There are five restrictions on the Crown Court in sentencing to imprisonment:

(i) A person under 17 years old cannot be sentenced to imprisonment.[75]

(ii) A person under the age of 21 may not be sentenced to imprisonment unless the court is of the opinion that no other method of dealing with him is appropriate.[76] The court must obtain and consider information about the circumstances, and take into account any information before the court which is relevant to the offender's character and his physical and mental condition.[77]

(iii) A person of borstal age (under 21) may only be sentenced to imprisonment for six months or less, or three years or more; if the offender has previously been sentenced to imprisonment or borstal training, the second limit is reduced to 18 months or more.[78]

(iv) A person who is 21 or over and who has not previously been sentenced to imprisonment in the United Kingdom may not be so sentenced unless the court is of the opinion that no other method of dealing with him is appropriate.[79]

(v) A person who is not legally represented may not be sentenced to imprisonment (or borstal or detention) if he has not previously been so sentenced in the United Kingdom, unless he applied for legal aid and it was refused on the grounds of his means, or he was informed of his right to apply for legal aid and given the opportunity but he refused or failed to apply.[80]

(a) *Life imprisonment*

In theory this sentence involves incarceration for the rest of the offender's life. In practice the executive power to release prisoners on licence[81] gives the life prisoner a prospect of release on licence

---

[74] *R.* v. *McCauliffe* (1970) 54 Cr.App.R. 516.

[75] Powers of Criminal Courts Act 1973, s. 19 (1). As to permissible sentences, see p. 376.

[76] *Ibid.* s. 19 (2).

[77] This does not necessarily mean obtaining medical or social inquiry reports; see *R.* v. *Ampleford*, p. 220.

[78] Criminal Justice Act 1961, s. 3; as to borstal, see p. 231.

[79] Powers of Criminal Courts Act 1973, s. 20 (1). The court must consider the circumstances, etc., as under s. 19 (2) above and footnote 77 applies to this provision.

[80] *Ibid.* s. 21 (1); *R.* v. *McGinlay* (1975) 62 Cr.App.R. 156.

[81] See Criminal Justice Act 1967, s. 61, p. 257.

after about 10 years unless, on a conviction for murder, the judge has recommended that he should serve a minimum number of years.[82] Once the sentence is passed, however, the court is not concerned with release and there is no appeal against the judge's recommendation.[83]

Where a life sentence is not mandatory, *e.g.* for manslaughter, the judge should pass a sentence of a specified number of years and should not leave the length of sentence to others except where the offence and the offender are of such a nature that the public requires protection for a considerable time unless the offender's condition changes.[84]

(b) *Extended sentence*

If a person convicted of an offence punishable by at least two years' imprisonment is a " persistent offender," the court may impose a term of imprisonment longer than the maximum laid down for the offence of which he is convicted.[85] If that maximum is between five and 10 years, he may be imprisoned for up to 10 years, and if it is less than five years, for up to five years.[86] A " persistent offender " is a person from whom the court considers the public should be protected for a substantial time because of his previous conduct and the likelihood of his committing further offences. Three conditions must be satisfied:

(i) that the offence was committed before the expiration of three years from his prior conviction of an offence punishable by at least two years' imprisonment or before the expiration of three years from his final release[87] from prison on a sentence passed for such an offence;

(ii) that he has been convicted of such offences on at least three occasions since he reached the age of twenty-one; and

(iii) that the total length of the sentences passed on him on those three occasions was not less than five years, and—

---

[82] Murder (Abolition of Death Penalty) Act 1965, s. 1 (2); this recommendation cannot be made on a life sentence for any offence other than murder: *R.* v. *Flemming* [1973] 2 All E.R. 401.

[83] *R.* v. *Aitken* [1966] 1 W.L.R. 1076.

[84] *R.* v. *Picker* [1970] 2 Q.B. 161; *R.* v. *Beever* 115 S.J. 465. A recidivist arsonist whose mental state might be susceptible to treatment and cure was a proper subject for a sentence of life imprisonment: *R.* v. *Lishman* [1971] Crim.L.R. 548.

[85] Powers of Criminal Courts Act 1973, s. 28.

[86] This must be a single term; two consecutive sentences cannot be certified (s. 29) as an extended term: *R.* v. *McKenna* [1974] 1 W.L.R. 267.

[87] It need not be *after* the final release, *e.g.* if the offender escapes from prison before release, because that is still " before the expiration of three years " from final release: *R.* v. *Johnson* [1976] 1 W.L.R. 426.

(*a*) on at least one of those occasions he was sentenced to preventive detention,[88] or

(*b*) on at least two of those occasions he was sentenced to imprisonment (not being a suspended sentence which was not brought into effect) or to corrective training,[88] and *one* of them was a sentence of not less than three years' imprisonment, or on *two* of them he was sentenced to at least two years' imprisonment for each offence.[89]

Combining an extended term with other sentences was considered in *R.* v. *Jackson*[90] where the Court of Appeal laid down the following principles of sentencing practice:

(a) It is wrong in principle to impose an extended term and, on the same occasion, a non-extended term consecutive to it or concurrent with it but of a longer duration.

(b) When a court imposes a sentence of imprisonment to run consecutively to an existing extended term, it should be expressed "to run from the date upon which, but for the imposition of this sentence, you would be released from prison either on licence or finally."

(c) A non-extended sentence of imprisonment can properly be ordered to run consecutively to the unexpired portion of an extended sentence imposed on another occasion.

Apart from the possibility of exceeding the maximum term specified for an offence, the distinguishing feature of an extended sentence is that, if released on licence, the offender remains subject to the licence until the expiry of the extended term.[91]

(c) *Suspended sentence*

On passing a sentence of imprisonment of not more than two years,[92] the court may order that the sentence shall not take effect, *i.e.* that the offender shall not be actually imprisoned, unless he commits a further offence within a specified period.[93] This period, known as the "operational period," may be between one and two years from the date of the order suspending the sentence.

---

[88] Preventive detention and corrective training were the predecessors of the extended sentence.

[89] Powers of Criminal Courts Act 1973, s. 28 (3).

[90] [1974] Q.B. 802.

[91] As to release on licence, see p. 257.

[92] If consecutive terms are imposed, the total sentence must not exceed two years: Powers of Criminal Courts Act 1973, s. 57 (1); *R.* v. *Arkle* [1972] Crim.L.R. 582.

[93] *Ibid.* s. 22 (1).

Where a sentence of more than six months is considered, the court may make a " suspended sentence supervision order " which places the offender under the supervision of a probation officer for a period not exceeding the operational period of the suspended sentence.[94] The offender is under a duty to keep in touch with the probation officer as instructed by him and to notify him of any change of address.[95] The order ceases to have effect if the suspended sentence is activated or if the order is discharged or varied under section 26 (8)–(10). Breach of the requirements of the order (contact with the probation officer) makes the offender liable to a maximum fine of £50.[96]

The effect of a suspended sentence is that the offender goes free and is not liable to have his sentence executed if he behaves well.[97] Where a suspended sentence is imposed, it ranks as a sentence of imprisonment, whether or not it has taken effect.[98] It can only be imposed where the court considers that a sentence of imprisonment would have been appropriate had there been no power to suspend it.[99]

A suspended sentence for one offence cannot be combined with a probation order for another offence,[1] and a borstal sentence passed on a person subject to a suspended sentence removes his liability under the suspended sentence.[2] Concurrent and consecutive suspended sentences are considered on page 230.

If he is convicted [3] of a further offence punishable by imprisonment during the operational period of the original order, the court [4] trying that further offence may make one of four orders:

(i) that the sentence of imprisonment which was suspended shall be brought into effect unaltered; the court must do this unless

---

[94] Powers of Criminal Courts Act 1973, s. 26 (1) and (3). The minimum length precludes the imposition of such an order by a magistrates' court, but the Home Secretary may in future reduce the length by order under s. 26 (2).

[95] *Ibid.* s. 26 (4).

[96] *Ibid.* s. 27; his presence before the court is secured by summons or warrant under this section.

[97] This must be explained to him in ordinary language: Powers of Criminal Courts Act 1973, s. 22 (4).

[98] *Ibid.* s. 22 (6) (*a*).

[99] *Ibid.* s. 22 (2).

[1] *Ibid.* s. 22 (3).

[2] *Ibid.* s. 22 (5).

[3] If he is given a probation order or discharge on the later conviction, it does not rank as a conviction and the court may not make any order on the suspended sentence: *R.* v. *Tarry* (1970) 54 Cr.App.R. 323; see also p. 240.

[4] The Crown Court may deal with any suspended sentence: s. 24 (1); as to magistrates' courts, see p. 322.

it would be unjust in the light of all the circumstances, including the facts of the subsequent offence, to do so[5];

(ii) that the suspended sentence order shall take effect for a shorter term than was originally ordered;

(iii) that the suspended sentence order shall be varied by substituting an operational period of not more than two years starting from the date of variation; or

(iv) that the original order shall be unaffected.[6]

If the court does not know of the existing suspended sentence when it deals with the later offence but subsequently information is laid that such an order was in force, a judge or justice of the peace may issue a summons or warrant of arrest to secure the offender's presence before the court which made the suspended sentence order or before a magistrates' court for committal to that court.[7]

At the later trial, the court must not activate the suspended sentence unless it has information about the original offence and the circumstances of it.[8]

(d) *Consecutive and concurrent sentences*

When the accused is convicted of several offences on different counts of an indictment, the court may order that the sentences of imprisonment passed on each count should be served at the same time or one after the other, *i.e.* concurrently or consecutively. The court must specify in which way they are to run. Cases where two different punishments or orders are imposed, *e.g.* imprisonment and a fine, are dealt with in the following pages and on page 255.

As a general rule terms of imprisonment are ordered to run consecutively when the appropriate or the maximum sentence for each offence would not protect the public from the offender for a sufficiently long time.[9]

A sentence cannot run consecutively to an indeterminate

---

[5] In *R.* v. *Saunders* (1970) 134 J.P. 371, the fact that the offences were of a different character was not a sufficient ground for not activating the suspended sentence, but the triviality of the later offence combined with its different nature may be grounds for not activating the suspended sentence; *R.* v. *Moylan* [1970] 1 Q.B. 143. The court must give its reasons for not activating the sentence.

[6] Powers of Criminal Courts Act 1973, s. 23 (1).

[7] *Ibid.* s. 25.

[8] *R.* v. *Munday* (1971) 115 S.J. 965.

[9] *e.g. R.* v. *Blake* [1962] 2 Q.B. 377 (42 years on five counts, the maximum for any of which was 14 years; as to the sequel to this case, see p. 59).

sentence,[10] such as detention at Her Majesty's pleasure [11] or life imprisonment,[12] and a term of imprisonment, effective or suspended, should not be imposed on a person currently undergoing borstal training.[13] If, at the time of passing sentence, the offender is already serving a sentence of imprisonment, the judge may order that the sentence now being imposed should run " consecutive[ly] to the total period of imprisonment to which [he is] already subject." [14] In passing a sentence on a later conviction to run concurrent with an existing sentence, the judge cannot order the later sentence to start at a date earlier than the date it is pronounced.[15]

The power to pass consecutive sentences applies also to suspended sentences and extended terms of imprisonment.[16] In *R.* v. *Sapiano*,[17] it was held to be wrong to impose an effective sentence at the same time as a suspended sentence and, in *R.* v. *Flanders*,[18] it was held to be improper to order that a suspended sentence run consecutively to a term of imprisonment already being served; if a person is subject to a suspended sentence and is convicted of an offence committed before it was imposed, an effective sentence can be passed on the second conviction.[19] Two suspended sentences ordered at the same time may, however, be ordered consecutively.[20] On a later conviction during the operational period the court may order that the suspended sentence shall take effect immediately or after the sentence for the later offence has expired [21]; on sentencing during the operational

---

[10] An " indeterminate sentence " is one the length of which is not decided until it has been served (*cf.* a hospital order, which comes to an end when the relevant authorities consider the patient is cured); it is not correct therefore to describe a sentence with a defined maximum, *e.g.* borstal training (see below), as an indeterminate sentence, although the offender may be released before the term expires.

[11] See p. 366.

[12] *R.* v. *Foy* [1962] 1 W.L.R. 609.

[13] *R.* v. *Dick* [1972] Crim.L.R. 58. Successive sentences of borstal cannot be ordered: *R.* v. *Beamon* (1948) 32 Cr.App.R. 181.

[14] Practice Direction [1959] 1 W.L.R. 491; the reason for this is to avoid the new sentence running consecutively to the first sentence if the offender is already serving consecutive sentences. For the purposes of the Powers of Criminal Courts Act 1973, two or more sentences passed concurrently or consecutively are treated as a single term: s. 57 (2).

[15] *R.* v. *Gilbert* [1975] 1 W.L.R. 1012, applying the Courts Act 1971, s. 11 (1).

[16] See p. 226.

[17] (1968) 52 Cr.App.R. 674; *R.* v. *Butters* (1971) 55 Cr.App.R. 515.

[18] (1968) 52 Cr.App.R. 676.

[19] *R.* v. *Sorrel* [1971] Crim.L.R. 552.

[20] *R.* v. *March* [1970] 2 W.L.R. 998; the court must specify which way they are to run if it is the same court in both instances: *R.* v. *Wilkinson* [1970] 1 W.L.R. 1319. The aggregate must not exceed 2 years; see p. 227.

[21] Powers of Criminal Courts Act 1973, s. 23 (2). The court should consider the appropriate sentence for the later offence first then deal with the suspended sentence: *R.* v. *Ithell* [1969] 1 W.L.R. 1319.

period, it is undesirable, although lawful, for suspended and immediate sentences to be mixed.[22]

3. Borstal training

A person who is under 21 and is not less than 15[23] years old and who is convicted on indictment of an offence punishable by imprisonment may instead be sentenced to borstal training.[24] If he is to receive a custodial sentence, he must be sentenced to borstal unless the appropriate prison sentence is for a term of six months or less, or of three years or more[25]; to impose such a prison sentence the court must consider that no other method of dealing with the offender would be appropriate.[26] If the young person has previously served a term of imprisonment or a borstal sentence, the court may impose a sentence of eighteen months or longer.[27] To impose two or more sentences of imprisonment to take effect consecutively so that the aggregate is over the prescribed limit is nevertheless an unlawful sentence if one of the sentences does not comply with these provisions.[28]

Borstal training is a sentence varying in length between six months and two years[29] and is imposed where the court considers that a custodial but reformative sentence of not less than six months is appropriate.[30] Being of uncertain length the sentence should not be ordered to run consecutively with any other sentence[31] and a

---

[22] *R.* v. *Goodlad* [1973] 1 W.L.R. 1102.

[23] The Children and Young Persons Act 1969, s. 7 (1), will eventually raise this age limit to 17. In some cases a 15-year-old person may be transferred to a borstal institution; *ibid.* s. 31, see p. 379. The age of the offender is judged by the available evidence and, if a mistake is made reasonably, a sentence of imprisonment passed on a person who is in fact under 21 will not be invalid: *R.* v. *Farndale* (1973) 58 Cr.App.R. 336, explaining the Criminal Justice Act 1961, s. 39 (3). Similar provision is made in the Powers of Criminal Courts Act 1973, s. 19; see p. 225.

[24] Criminal Justice Act 1948, s. 20 (1), as substituted by the Criminal Justice Act 1961, Sched. 6.

[25] Criminal Justice Act 1961, s. 3 (1); *R.* v. *Parc* [1974] Crim.L.R. 720.

[26] Powers of Criminal Courts Act 1973, s. 19 (2); see p. 225.

[27] Criminal Justice Act 1961, s. 3 (3).

[28] *e.g.* a sentence of 12 months added to a sentence of six months is unlawful (see s. 3 (3) above) but a sentence of 18 months passed concurrently with a sentence of six months is lawful: *R.* v. *Halse* [1971] 3 All E.R. 1149. A sentence for breach of probation added to the sentence for the offence constituting the breach need not both satisfy the section, however, provided the aggregate does so: *R.* v. *Taylor* (1974) 60 Cr. App. R. 143.

[29] Prison Act 1952, s. 45 (2), and Criminal Justice Act 1961, s. 11.

[30] The Home Secretary may release him before the expiration of six months: Prison Act 1952, s. 45 (2).

[31] See p. 229 and *R.* v. *Hart* [1960] Crim.L.R. 277 (where borstal was wrongly ordered to run after a sentence of imprisonment; the unexpired prison term merges in the borstal sentence).

suspended sentence order ceases to be enforceable if the offender is subsequently sentenced to borstal.[32]

Borstal training is a form of imprisonment (it took its name from the prison in Kent where the first segregation of " juvenile adults " took place), but the regime aims at training offenders for some activity after they are released and is rather more relaxed than an adult prison regime.[33] In view of the minimum period, borstal training is inappropriate for an offence for which the maximum term of imprisonment is less than six months. For offences committed after the offender has served a borstal sentence, or while he is on release during the sentence, the court should consider whether a further borstal sentence would benefit the offender.[34] The Home Secretary may transfer an offender from prison if satisfied that he might with advantage be detained in a borstal institution; consultations with the judge who passed the sentence should be held if practicable.[35]

The post-release supervision for two years of borstal trainees is an integral part of the sentence, as to which see page 259. The Crown Court's powers to pass a borstal sentence on an offender committed for sentence by a magistrates' court are considered in Chapter 13.[36]

4. Fine

A monetary fine may be imposed in lieu of or in addition to any other punishment, on all persons convicted on indictment of an offence for which the sentence is not fixed by law.[37] The amount of the fine must be reasonable in the circumstances.[38] Many statutes prescribe a maximum sum for a particular offence; a person convicted of an attempt cannot be sentenced to a fine larger than the maximum for the completed offence.[39]

A fine cannot be imposed at the same time as ordering probation

---

[32] Powers of Criminal Courts Act 1973, s. 22 (5).

[33] The regime is regulated by rules of the Home Secretary (Borstal Rules 1964 (S.I. 1964 No. 387) as amended by S.I. 1974 No. 1923 and 1976 No. 508).

[34] *R.* v. *Noseda* [1958] 1 W.L.R. 793 (where the principles to be applied in such a case were considered at length). He may then be sent to prison for any term longer than 18 months (Criminal Justice Act 1961, s. 3 (3)) *i.e.* instead of a minimum of three years; see *ibid.* s. 3 (1) p. 225.

[35] Prison Act 1952, s. 44 (1).

[36] See p. 335.

[37] Powers of Criminal Cases Act 1973, s. 30 (1); the life sentence for murder is " fixed by law."

[38] Bill of Rights 1688. In *R.* v. *Platt Bros.* [1970] Crim.L.R. 656, a fine of £50,000 was upheld on a conviction for sanction-breaking exports to Rhodesia.

[39] Powers of Criminal Courts Act 1973, s. 30 (2).

or discharge of the offender, for they are by statute imposable only " instead of sentencing " or where " it is inexpedient to inflict punishment."[40]

A fine can be imposed when making a suspended sentence order.[41] In the case of a young offender or an offender who has not previously been sentenced to imprisonment, the court must be wary of fining as well as imprisoning, for it must consider that " no other method of dealing with [him] is appropriate " before sentencing him to imprisonment.[42] However if the prison sentence is regarded as the primary punishment, whether suspended or immediate, circumstances may justify a fine in addition.[43]

A fine is enforceable by sending the offender to prison if he does not pay. Magistrates' courts are restricted[44] in ordering imprisonment but the Crown Court may order up to 12 months' imprisonment.[45] The court, when it sentences the offender to a fine, may make[46] an order giving him time to pay and directing payment by instalment[47] and it must specify the term of imprisonment to be served if he defaults in payment.[48] He cannot simply be kept in custody until he pays the fine.[49] If he is in prison anyway, the judge may order that the imprisonment for non-payment should start after he has served his current sentence.[50]

C. Non-Punitive Orders

This Section and Section D, below, contain miscellaneous orders, designed for particular types of offender or dealing with matters ancillary to sentence, which the judge can make instead of, or in addition to, sentencing an offender to a punishment.[51] The

---

[40] *Ibid.* s. 2 (1) and 7 (1) respectively, and see pp. 236 and 240.

[41] *R.* v. *King* [1970] 1 W.L.R. 1016.

[42] Powers of Criminal Courts Act 1973, ss. 19 (2) and 20 (1); *R.* v. *Ankers* (1975) 61 Cr.App.R. 170.

[43] *R.* v. *Genese* [1976] 2 All E.R. 600.

[44] See p. 323.

[45] Powers of Criminal Courts Act 1973, s. 31 (3).

[46] *Ibid.* s. 31 (1). Under s. 31 (3) such an order must be made unless the offender appears to have sufficient means to pay immediately or to be unlikely to remain in the U.K. long enough for means other than immediate payment to be effective, or unless he is already serving a sentence of imprisonment or detention.

[47] It is wrong to impose a large fine payable by instalments over a long period (*R.* v. *Hewitt* (1971) 55 Cr.App.R. 433) and a fine should not be so large in relation to the offender's capacity to pay that he may be tempted to commit further offences to pay it.

[48] Powers of Criminal Courts Act 1973, s. 31 (2).

[49] *R.* v. *Brook* [1949] 2 K.B. 138.

[50] Powers of Criminal Courts Act 1973, s. 31 (4).

[51] *i.e.* death, imprisonment or fine. This is not perhaps a general distinction but is convenient when considering the classification of penalties and orders and their effects.

complexities required for the treatment of juveniles are postponed to Chapter 15.[52]

1. Hospital order

The court may find that an offender, though not insane under the M'Naghten Rules,[53] suffers from a mental disorder which requires or would benefit from special treatment or training. " Mental disorder " is defined by section 4 (1) of the Mental Health Act 1959 as including mental illness, arrested or incomplete development of mind, psychopathic disorder or any other disorder or disability of the mind.[54]

Under section 60 of the same Act the court may order that a person, convicted of an offence punishable by imprisonment but for which the sentence is not fixed by law,[55] be admitted to and detained in a specified hospital or be placed in the guardianship of a local health authority. The court must consider that this is the most suitable order in all the circumstances of the offender's case and must be satisfied by the evidence of two doctors[56] that he is suffering from a mental disorder or subnormality which warrants his detention or guardianship.

The court must further be satisfied that arrangements have been made for the order to be carried out.

In less serious cases the court may order probation with psychiatric treatment.[57] A hospital order cannot be made at the same time as a sentence of imprisonment, detention or fine, or as a probation order.[58] The order is of indeterminate length but the court may, where the safety of the public is endangered by the prospect of the offender's release, order that his discharge be restricted indefinitely or for a specified period.[59]

---

52 See pp. 369 and 376.

53 *i.e.* where a verdict of " not guilty by reason of insanity " can be returned; see pp. 211 and 235.

54 " Severe subnormality," " subnormality " and " psychopathic disorder " are further defined in subss. (2)–(4). The definitions of mental disorder are reviewed in *A Review of the Mental Health Act* 1959 (H.M.S.O., 1976), a consultative document of an inter-departmental committee.

55 A convicted murderer must be sent to prison for life but the Home Secretary may direct his removal to a hospital under the Mental Health Act 1959, s. 72.

56 See *ibid.* s. 62; copies of any report made must be given to defence counsel and solicitor and the two doctors who give evidence should be those who will in fact have care of the offender: *R.* v. *Blackwood* (1974) 59 Cr.App.R. 170.

57 See p. 237.

58 Mental Health Act 1959, s. 60 (6).

59 *Ibid.* s. 65; the Home Secretary may direct that the restriction shall cease to have effect: s. 66. The Butler Committee's *Report* (Cmnd. 6244) considered the treatment of mentally abnormal offenders.

Once ordered to hospital, the matter is no longer a concern of the court. Mental Health Review Tribunals [60] can hear applications for the patient's discharge and the Home Secretary has overall control. Although a hospital order may involve a longer period of detention than a term of imprisonment imposed by the judge, the Court of Appeal may substitute a hospital order on appeal against the prison sentence, for its purpose is remedial, not punitive.[61]

Where a verdict of " not guilty by reason of insanity " is returned [62] the court must make an order that the accused be admitted to hospital,[63] as it must do when he is found unfit to plead.[64] A hospital order is made in the usual way under section 60 of the 1959 Act.

2. Community service order

A person who is at least 17 years old may be required to perform unpaid work for between 40 and 240 hours, within 12 months, under a community service order.[65] It is expressed to be " instead of dealing with him in any other way," which is broader than the terms used in relation to probation orders and discharges,[66] and would clearly preclude the court from combining it with any other principal sentence or order; the power to make an order for costs, disqualification, compensation, bankruptcy, forfeiture of property used in crime, disqualification under section 44 of the 1973 Act or restitution of property at the same time, is expressly stated.[67] If the court makes an order in respect of two or more offences, the aggregate of hours to be spent in community service must not exceed 240, but individual orders may be made consecutive or concurrent.[68]

The court must consider a probation officer's report on the offender's suitability for such an order and it must be satisfied that facilities for its performance exist.[69] The offender must consent and the effect of the order must be explained to him in ordinary language.[70] The performance of the order is supervised, usually by a probation officer, and the offender reports to him, notifies him of any

---

[60] These were considered in the *Review* of the 1959 Act mentioned in footnote 54 above. See also *Report on the Review of Procedures for the Discharge and Supervision of Psychiatric Patients subject to Special Restrictions* (Cmnd. 5191).

[61] *R.* v. *Bennett* [1968] 1 W.L.R. 988; see also p. 277.

[62] See p. 211.

[63] Criminal Procedure (Insanity) Act 1964, s. 5 (1).

[64] See p. 170.

[65] Powers of Criminal Courts Act 1973, ss. 14 (1) and 15 (2).

[66] See pp. 236 and 240.

[67] *Ibid.* s. 14 (8).

[68] *Ibid.* s. 14 (3).

[69] *Ibid.* s. 14 (2).

[70] *Ibid.* s. 14 (2) and (5).

change of address and performs his hours of duty in accordance with his instructions.[71]

A community service order may be amended to extend the period in which the work may be done to more than 12 months.[72] Alternatively, the order may be simply revoked or revoked at the same time as dealing with the offender in any other way in which he could have been dealt with had the order not been made.[73] The court must in both cases consider the interests of justice. These powers of review arise on application independently of any misbehaviour on the part of the offender.

If the offender fails to comply with the requirements of the order, he may be summoned, or arrested, to appear before the magistrates' court specified in the order which has power to fine him up to £50, revoke the order and deal with him in any way in which it could have dealt with him instead of imposing the order or, if the order was made by the Crown Court, commit him to the Crown Court (which, in turn, may fine him up to £50 or revoke the order and substitute any other sentence which it could have imposed on conviction).[74]

3. Probation order

A probation order is procedurally similar to a discharge and the effect, that the conviction does not operate as such for later sentencing, is the same.[75] Both orders are made when the offender is unsuitable for punishment because, for instance, he is a first offender, or he shows an inclination not to repeat his criminal activities, or the offence was not serious or dangerous. A probation order releases the offender from custody but requires him to be under the supervision of a probation officer for a period of between one and three years.[76] It is imposed " instead of sentencing him," though it

---

[71] Powers of Criminal Courts Act 1973, ss. 14 (4) and 15 (1); the hours to be performed must, as far as possible, avoid any conflict with the offender's religious beliefs, working hours or school or college attendance: s. 15 (3).

[72] *Ibid.* s. 17 (1). Application to the magistrates' court may be made by the offender or the " relevant officer " and it is based on circumstances which have arisen since the order was made.

[73] *Ibid.* s. 17 (2). Application is made as under s. 17 (1). If the order was made by the Crown Court, the magistrates' court specified in the order (s. 14 (6)) may commit the offender to the Crown Court to be dealt with under s. 17 (3). The offender's presence may be compelled by summons or, failing appearance in answer to the summons, by warrant of arrest: s. 17 (7).

[74] *Ibid.* s. 16. Similar general provisions apply as apply to breach of probation or discharge (below): the judge determines the issue of breach, the committing justice's certificate of the breach is admissible but not conclusive evidence of the breach and the offender may appeal against any sentence substituted by the magistrates' court.

[75] Powers of Criminal Courts Act 1973, s. 13.

[76] *Ibid.* s. 2 (1).

may be combined with a disqualification from driving.[77] If the offender is convicted on more than one count of an indictment, no sentence of imprisonment should be made on the others if a probation order is made in respect of one offence; otherwise the conviction counts towards the imposition of an extended term on a later conviction.[78] Probation officers are organised in the petty sessional divisions[79] and the probationer is allocated to a local officer and supervised by the local magistrates' court.

The probation order contains conditions for the supervision and conduct of the offender while on probation. These must not include any provision for the payment of damages or compensation,[80] but may include any requirements for residence, reporting to the officer, home visiting or being of good behaviour and keeping the peace[81]; any reasonable condition which may help the probationer to behave well and not to commit further offences may be included, but it must be definite and capable of enforcement.[82] The prospective probationer must be told in ordinary language the effect of the order and he must express his willingness to comply with the requirements.[83]

If appropriate, the court may investigate the offender's home surroundings and order him to live in a probation hostel or approved home or institution for not more than twelve months from making the order.[84] The order may include a requirement that the probationer attend at a specified day training centre during the probation period. The court must have been informed that appropriate facilities exist. The probationer may be required to attend on up to sixty days and, while at the centre, must comply with the instructions of the person in charge of it. Such a requirement cannot be made at the same time as a condition for medical treatment.[85]

If a doctor gives evidence that the offender's mental condition, though not warranting a hospital order,[86] requires and may be

---

77 Road Traffic Act 1972, s. 102; see also p. 245. Sureties for good behaviour may be taken at the same time: Powers of Criminal Courts Act 1973, s. 12 (1).

78 *R.* v. *Isherwood* (1974) 59 Cr.App.R. 162. A suspended sentence cannot be imposed: Powers of Criminal Courts Act 1973, s. 22 (3).

79 See p. 290.

80 This may be ordered at the same time as the probation order but not as a part of it: Powers of Criminal Courts Act 1973, ss. 2 (4) and 12 (4); see also p. 250.

81 Practice Note (1952) 35 Cr.App.R. 207 (a condition to " lead an honest and industrious life " was disapproved).

82 Powers of Criminal Courts Act 1973, s. 2 (3).

83 *Ibid.* s. 2 (6); *R.* v. *Marquis* [1974] 1 W.L.R. 1087.

84 *Ibid.* s. 2 (5). The probationer uses a hostel as his residence from which he goes out to work, whereas a home or institution provides work on the premises.

85 *Ibid.* s. 4.

86 See p. 234.

susceptible to medical treatment, the court may order treatment for up to twelve months in a non-security hospital, as an out-patient in a specified institution, or by a qualified doctor.[87] The court must be satisfied that such facilities for treatment are available but the order does not specify the type of treatment to be given.

While under a psychiatric probation order, the probationer remains in contact with the probation officer but the supervision is shared with his doctor. The doctor may, for instance, with the consent of the probationer and after giving notice to the probation officer, arrange for him to be admitted as a resident in a home not ordered by the court.[88]

There are several ways in which a probationer may appear before the court before the expiry of the probation period. First, the probationer or the probation officer may apply to the supervising court or the court which made the order for a conditional discharge [89] to be substituted for the probation order, the period of the conditional discharge ending at the same time as the probation period would have expired.[90] Secondly, the terms of the order may be varied, and the order itself may be discharged, on an application under Schedule 1 of the Powers of Criminal Courts Act 1973.[91]

Thirdly, if the probationer does not comply with the terms of the order, a justice of the peace on information laid may issue a summons or warrant of arrest to bring him before a magistrates' court in the same division as the supervising court or the court which made the order.[92] On proof of the probationer's failure to comply, that court may either fine him up to £50, make a community service order in respect of him,[93] require him to attend at an attendance centre,[94] or commit him in custody or on bail [95] to appear before the Crown Court, if the order was made by the Crown Court. If it was made by a magistrates' court, the court may deal with him as if he had just been convicted of the offence.[96] The Crown Court dealing with him may also deal with him as if he had just been convicted,

---

[87] Powers of Criminal Courts Act 1973 s. 3.

[88] *Ibid.* s. 3 (5) and (6).

[89] See p. 240.

[90] *Ibid.* s. 11.

[91] Generally the power to discharge or amend lies with the supervising court and the probationer must consent if the requirements are changed or made more onerous.

[92] *Ibid.* s. 6 (1) and (2).

[93] See p. 235.

[94] A non-residential local authority run institution for periodical visits by released offenders: Criminal Justice Act 1948, s. 19.

[95] Powers of Criminal Courts Act 1973, s. 6 (4).

[96] *Ibid.* s. 6 (3) (this includes a new probation order).

fine him up to £50 or make a community service order in respect of him.[97] Unless the court deals with him as if he had just been convicted, the probation order continues unaffected.[98]

Fourthly, if a probationer commits a further offence, the court which made the order may deal with him in respect of the offence for which the probation order was made as though he had just been convicted of that offence.[99] If information is laid before that court that he has been dealt with in respect of an offence committed during the probation period, it may issue a summons or a warrant for his arrest.[1] If the court which is trying him for the later offence is the Crown Court, it may deal with him as if he had just been convicted. Once the Crown Court has dealt with the offender in respect of the offence for which he was put on probation, even if it decides to make no order, it cannot later reconsider the same breach of probation because the Crown Court has a single and indivisible jurisdiction and one sitting has no power to review the decisions of another sitting.[2] If it is a magistrates' court, not being the court which made the order, it may commit him to appear before that court; or if the court making the order was a magistrates' court, but the present court is neither that court nor the supervising court, it may deal with the probationer with the consent of the court which made the order or of the supervising court.

The procedure for dealing with a breach of probation, whether by commission of a further offence or not, is for the judge without a jury to decide whether the probationer is in breach.[3] If he denies the breach, the probationer may give and call evidence.[4] The magistrates' court, committing an offender for breach of the requirements of a probation order where the order was made by the Crown Court, sends a certificate to this effect to the Crown Court; it is admissible as evidence of the breach but is not conclusive.[5] If a severe sentence is imposed for a further offence, the punishment for breach of probation may be nominal[6] or concurrent. If sentenced for the offence for which the offender was put on probation, the

---

[97] *Ibid.* s. 6 (6). See also p. 235.
[98] *Ibid.* s. 6 (8).
[99] *Ibid.* s. 8 (7).
[1] *Ibid.* s. 8 (1).
[2] *R.* v. *Slatter* [1975] 1 W.L.R. 1084.
[3] *Ibid.* s. 12 (3).
[4] *R.* v. *Devine* [1956] 1 W.L.R. 236.
[5] *Ibid.* s. 6 (5); *R.* v. *Chapman* [1960] 1 W.L.R. 147.
[6] A nominal fine of £1 would usually be preferable, unless one day's imprisonment can be imposed concurrently: it is necessarily a fine for offenders under 17 (see p. 225: *R.* v. *James* [1970] 1 W.L.R. 1304).

probation order is discharged.[7] The same procedure applies to breach of a conditional discharge, below.

The probation officer's supervision ceases at the expiry of the probation period and the only special treatment of the ex-probationer is that reports should be made about him before sentence if he is again convicted.[8]

4. Discharge

There are two forms of discharge—absolute and conditional. The word " discharge " means release from custody and exemption from punishment. It is ordered when it is inexpedient to inflict punishment and probation is inappropriate,[9] though a recommendation for deportation,[10] an order for costs, compensation, restitution or disqualification from driving may be made at the same time.[11] It would seem possible that a criminal bankruptcy order, an order to forfeit property used for the purposes of crime or a disqualification from driving under section 44 of the 1973 Act could be combined with a discharge (or a probation order). In none of the relevant provisions[12] is the word " punishment " (or, in the case of probation, " sentence ") used in relation to those orders.

When given an absolute discharge, the offender is immediately free and absolved from sentence. A conditional discharge is an order that he shall be released immediately but subject to the condition that he does not commit another offence within a specified period of not more than three years from making the order.[13] If he does commit an offence during that period, he is liable to be dealt with for the original offence in any manner in which the court making the conditional discharge order could have dealt with him.[14] If a conditional discharge was ordered in a magistrates' court and is being considered by the Crown Court, the latter is limited to the sentences and orders which the magistrates could have imposed.

If a discharge is ordered the conviction of that offence does not

---

[7] Powers of Criminal Courts Act 1973, s. 5 (2).

[8] See p. 219.

[9] Powers of Criminal Courts Act 1973, s. 7 (1).

[10] *R.* v. *Akan* [1973] 1 Q.B. 491.

[11] Road Traffic Act 1972, s. 102; see also Section D, p. 245. Sureties for good behaviour may be taken: Powers of Criminal Courts Act 1973, s. 12 (1).

[12] Powers of Criminal Courts Act 1973, ss. 39, 43 and 44; see pp. 247, 253 and 254.

[13] *Ibid.* s. 7 (1).

[14] *Ibid.* s. 8; see above (the same applies as applies to probation orders). If a person is dealt with for the offence for which he was conditionally discharged, the discharge order ceases to have effect: s. 8 (4).

rank as a conviction except for the proceedings relating to that offence.[15] This does not mean that the accused cannot appeal or plead *autrefois convict* if re-indicted,[16] nor even that the prosecution cannot prove the conviction at a later trial,[17] but it does not rank as a conviction for the purposes of later sentencing, *e.g.* extended terms of imprisonment,[18] or where, being subject to a suspended sentence,[19] the court orders the offender's discharge[20] or defers sentence[21] on the later conviction.

The procedure on the later conviction for dealing with the original offence is the same as for a breach of a probation order and is dealt with on page 238.

The conditional discharge bears some superficial resemblance to a suspended sentence of imprisonment, a deferment of sentence and binding over to keep the peace. It differs from the first in its effects and in the greater degree of flexibility: the suspended sentence ranks as a conviction for all purposes; it is also a fixed term of imprisonment only ineffective in its execution, whereas a conditional discharge is an absolution from sentence, as well as from execution of sentence, and when the offender makes himself liable for the sentence to be passed, the later court has complete freedom in sentencing him for the original offence. It differs from deferment in being a conditional absolution; a deferment is a means of postponing consideration of sentence and the offender remains fully liable to be sentenced during the deferment; moreover, his total conduct after conviction may be taken into account, whereas a conditionally discharged offender is obliged only to avoid committing a further offence. It differs from binding over to keep the peace (described in paragraph 6 below) because recognisances only make the offender liable to forfeit fixed sums of money for breach of condition, not to be sentenced for the offence. Binding over is a supplementary order, whereas a discharge with or without conditions is a principal order which cannot be combined with a punishment.

---

[15] *Ibid.* s. 13 (1). If he was of or over 17 years of age at the time and the offence is later dealt with as if he had just been convicted (s. 8 or s. 6, in the case of probation), the conviction ranks fully as such thereafter: s. 13 (2).

[16] *Ibid.* s. 13 (4) (*a*); as to *autrefois*, see p. 159. It does not affect any right of appeal against conviction (see p. 262) nor does it prevent the restoration of property by the offender: s. 13 (4) (*b*).

[17] Either in cross-examination (see p. 191) or as one of the accused's antecedents (see p. 217).

[20] *R.* v. *Tarry* [1970] 2 Q.B. 561 (*i.e.* the suspended sentence is not brought into effect).

[21] *R.* v. *Salmon* (1973) 57 Cr.App.R. 953; see Powers of Criminal Courts Act 1973, s. 1 (4), p. 242.

5. Deferment of sentence

The court may defer passing sentence on an offender for not more than six months after the date of conviction in order to be able to consider, in determining his sentence, his conduct after conviction and any change in his circumstances; " conduct " expressly includes making reparation for his offence, where appropriate.[22] The court may only defer sentence if the accused consents and if it is satisfied that it would be in the interests of justice to do so, having regard to the nature of the offence and the character and circumstances of the offender.[23]

The court may pass sentence on the date to which the passing of sentence has been deferred[24]; on that date, however, it may not use its power to defer again.[25] The court's powers to postpone sentence otherwise than under this provision are expressly preserved.[26] There seems to be no reason why these powers should not be exercised on a deferment to obtain a further postponement, for instance, to await the outcome of further charges against the offender.[27] There is no restriction on the sentence which may be passed after a deferment. In the nature of the power, however, it is desirable to avoid making the offender feel an injustice has been done, as where an offenders' conduct has been satisfactory and he is to some extent entitled to think that he will avoid a substantial custodial sentence.[28] A deferment should not be used to separate different elements of a single offence so that the court may deal with them on separate occasions.[29]

The judge who defers sentence should, if possible, reserve the case to himself or leave a note with the sentencing court stating the sentence he had in mind; the same counsel should appear so that the court may be fully informed.[30]

If the court has deferred sentence, it may pass sentence before the expiration of the period of deferment if, during that period, he is convicted of an offence in Great Britain.[31] The court should pass

---

22 Powers of Criminal Courts Act 1973, s. 1 (1) and (2).

23 *Ibid.* s. 1 (3); *R.* v. *McQuaide* [1975] Crim.L.R. 246.

24 The importance of the precise date was questioned in *R.* v. *Ingle* [1974] 3 All E.R. 811.

25 Powers of Criminal Courts Act 1973, s. 1 (2).

26 *Ibid.* s. 1 (7). Other powers include the power to adjourn for reports, to bind over to come up for judgment and the inherent power to postpone sentence in order to deal with the particular matters arising in a case; see p. 221.

27 See *R.* v. *Ingle* above.

28 *R.* v. *Jacobs* (1975) 62 Cr.App.R. 116.

29 *R.* v. *Fairhead* [1975] 2 All E.R. 737 (*i.e.* the whole sentence must be deferred).

30 *R.* v. *Jacobs*, above, and *R.* v. *Ryan*, *The Times*, March 11, 1976.

31 Powers of Criminal Courts Act 1973, s. 1 (4).

sentence on the original offence in these circumstances.[32] It cannot do so, however, if a probation order or discharge is made in respect of the later offence, as that does not count as a conviction. If the court decides to defer a sentence on an offence committed during the operational period of a suspended sentence, the activation of the suspended sentence should also be deferred.[33]

6. Binding over

This is a procedure akin to bail before the passing of the Bail Act 1976—recognisances are entered into by the convicted person and, if necessary, by sureties. It may be used for two purposes.

First, the court may bind the offender over to answer to judgment when called upon to do so.[34] This is a means of postponing sentence and might be used, for instance, where the accused wishes to appeal against conviction and the court does not consider that he should be kept in custody. If he fails to appear for judgment after being given notice of the date, the sums fixed in the recognisances are forfeited; it is not a punishment but a means of conditioning his release. A condition of keeping the peace may be added; if he fails to do so, he may be brought before the court before the date fixed for judgment to have his recognisances estreated.[35]

The second purpose for which this procedure is used is as an order supplementary to or instead of any other sentence or judgment passed.[36] The recognisances are conditioned to the offender's keeping the peace and being of good behaviour for a specified and reasonable period. The Crown Court has this power after trial on indictment but it is used for a variety of purposes by magistrates, even where no offence has been committed.[37]

The conditions may specify prohibited acts but the general purpose of keeping the peace or being of good behaviour must be served; for instance, recognisances should not be used to secure repayment of a civil debt.[38] Imprisonment is only a sanction if money

---

[32] Practice Direction [1974] 1 W.L.R. 441.

[33] *R.* v. *Salmon* (1973) 57 Cr.App.R. 953; *R.* v. *Dwyer* (1975) 60 Cr.App.R. 39 (even an " order to make no order " on the suspended sentence should not be made because the whole sentence should be deferred).

[34] Courts Act 1971, s. 6 (4) (*b*). *Cf.* remand on bail for reports, p. 220.

[35] *i.e.* the sums forfeited. They are then enforced as an unpaid fine: Powers of Criminal Courts Act 1973, ss. 31 and 32; see p. 233.

[36] Justices of the Peace Act 1968, s. 1 (7).

[37] *e.g.* against a husband or wife after hearing a matrimonial complaint: see p. 327.

[38] *R.* v. *Peel* (1943) 29 Cr.App.R. 73.

to pay off the recognisance is not forthcoming.[39] In *R.* v. *Finch*[40] the offender was bound over on a recognisance of £25 to be of good behaviour; the attempt of the judge in dealing with a breach of the recognisance to sentence him to 9 months' imprisonment was held to be a nullity, the forfeiture of £25 being the only penalty that could be imposed for the breach.

Sureties for good behaviour may be taken in respect of a person made subject to a probation order or a conditional discharge.[41]

7. Deportation

Any person who has no right of abode in the United Kingdom may, on conviction of an offence which is punishable with imprisonment, be recommended by the court to be deported; he must be aged 17 or over.[42] A person with a right of abode in the United Kingdom is known as a "patrial."[43] A patrial is a person who is either a citizen by birth, adoption, naturalisation or registration or the child of such a person or whose parent had been born or legally adopted by a person who was a citizen. A patrial is also any citizen of the United Kingdom and Colonies who has been settled in the United Kingdom and Islands[44] and has at that time been ordinarily resident there for the past five years or more, or a Commonwealth citizen born to or adopted by a citizen of the United Kingdom and Colonies.[45] A woman has a right of abode in the United Kingdom if she is a Commonwealth citizen and is married to a patrial, as defined above, or has at any time been the wife of a citizen or a British subject (prior to the British Nationality Act 1948).[46]

Before the recommendation for deportation is made, the court must give the offender not less than seven days' notice in writing stating that he is not liable to deportation if he is a patrial and describing the persons who are patrial.[47]

A person who seeks to claim that he should not be deported because he is a patrial bears the burden of proving that he is.[48] A

---

39 Some statutory provisions specifically provide for binding over (*e.g.* Libel Act 1843), by which imprisonment is for not more than one year.

40 (1962) 47 Cr.App.R. 58.

41 Powers of Criminal Courts Act 1973, s. 12 (1).

42 Immigration Act 1971, s. 4 (6).

43 *Ibid.* s. 2 (6).

44 This means the United Kingdom, the Isle of Man and the Channel Islands.

45 Immigration Act 1971, s. 2 (1).

46 *Ibid.* s. 2 (2). The term " citizen " is restricted in this subsection in the case of citizens by registration.

47 *Ibid.* s. 6 (2).

48 *Ibid.* s. 3 (8).

person is not liable to deportation if he is a Commonwealth citizen or a citizen of the Irish Republic and, at the time of the coming into force of the Act, had been ordinarily resident in the United Kingdom and Islands for the past five years.[49]

A recommendation for deportation may be made at the same time as imprisonment or a fine is imposed.[50] The person subject to the recommendation may appeal against it to the Court of Appeal, or other appropriate court. Appeal can only be made against the recommendation itself (it is treated as a sentence) or against the conviction; appeal against the recommendation is treated in the same manner as an appeal against sentence.[51]

Once the Home Secretary has made the deportation order, the Commonwealth immigrant or alien has a right of appeal under the Immigration Act 1971, ss. 12–22. Adjudicators[52] appointed by the Home Secretary hear the appeal against the order in the first instance[53]; if dissatisfied with this adjudication the appellant or the Home Secretary may appeal to the Immigration Appeals Tribunal, a body appointed by the Lord Chancellor.[54] The Queen's Bench Divisional Court exercises supervisory jurisdiction over the proceedings.[55]

D. Miscellaneous Orders

1. Disqualification from driving—Road Traffic Act 1972

When an accused is convicted of certain offences involving a motor vehicle, the court may or must make an order disqualifying him from holding or obtaining a driving licence for a period; if he then drives or applies for a licence he is guilty of an offence.[56]

On the conviction of a person of one of seven road traffic offences listed in Schedule 4 to the Road Traffic Act 1972, the court must order disqualification from driving for at least 12 months; the

---

49 *Ibid.* s. 7 (1) (*c*). Such a person might, however, have no immunity from deportation if he is subject to an exclusion order under the Prevention of Terrorism (Temporary Provisions) Act 1976. Such an order is entirely executive.

50 Including life imprisonment: Immigration Act 1971, s. 6 (4).

51 *Ibid.* s. 6 (5); as to appeal, see p. 274. The grounds must relate to the propriety of the recommendation; possible ill-treatment of the offender in his country of origin is a matter for the Home Secretary: *R.* v. *Antypas* (1972) 56 Cr.App.R. 207.

52 *Ibid.* s. 12.

53 *Ibid.* s. 19.

54 *Ibid.* ss. 20 and 21.

55 See pp. 43–47.

56 Under the Road Traffic Act 1972, s. 99; the maximum penalty is imprisonment for six months and/or a fine of £50 on summary conviction or imprisonment for 12 months and/or a fine of £100 on indictment. Disqualification for 12 months may be ordered.

offences are manslaughter by a driver, causing death by dangerous driving, dangerous driving within three years of a previous conviction for dangerous driving, driving under the influence of drink or drugs, driving or attempting to drive with a prohibited level of alcohol in the blood, racing on the highway and refusing to give a specimen under section 7 of the Road Traffic Act 1972. The court has a discretion, however, if there are " special reasons," not to order disqualification or to order it for a shorter period.[57] A special reason is tested objectively; it must be a mitigating circumstance, not a defence to the charge, and it must relate to the offence, not to the particular circumstances of the offender.[58] The previous good character of the offender is not a special reason though it may mitigate any punishment imposed at the same time.[59] Special reasons should be supported by evidence on oath, unless the prosecution formally admits them.[60]

Disqualification for at least six months is usually obligatory where the offender has been *convicted* on at least two occasions within the three years preceding *commission* of the offence.[61] This is often called a " totting-up " disqualification. If already disqualified, the six months must be in addition to the existing period.[62] The court need not impose it, however, where it " is satisfied, having regard to all the circumstances, that there are grounds for *mitigating* the normal consequences of the conviction." When an offender has a prior conviction for a drinking and driving offence, within 10 years of committing the same offence, he must be disqualified for three years.[63]

Schedule 4 of the 1972 Act also contains a list of offences for which disqualification may be ordered for any period.[64] These include careless driving, speeding and other summary driving offences, dangerous driving, being in charge of a vehicle when under the influence of drink or with a prohibited level of alcohol in the blood, and stealing or taking a motor vehicle without authority.[65]

---

[57] Road Traffic Act 1972, s. 93 (1).

[58] *e.g.* the involuntary taking of alcohol or a drug may be a special reason not to disqualify (*Brewer* v. *Metropolitan Police Commissioner* (1968) 112 S.J. 1022) but driving to assist a friend is not (*R.* v. *Baines* [1970] Crim.L.R. 590). A great many cases have been reported since the advent of the " breathalyser " procedure; recourse to the *Criminal Law Review* or *Current Law* is recommended.

[59] *R.* v. *Steel* (1968) 52 Cr.App.R. 510.

[60] *i.e.* under the Criminal Justice Act 1967, s. 10; see p. 112.

[61] Road Traffic Act 1972, s. 93 (3).

[62] *Ibid.* s. 93 (5).

[63] Road Traffic Act 1972, s. 93 (4).

[64] *Ibid.* s. 93 (2).

[65] *i.e.* under the Theft Act 1968, ss. 1 and 12, respectively.

The court may order disqualification for life[66] or for any period certain; it may also order or impose a condition on the disqualification that the offender be disqualified until he has passed, or re-passed, the driving test[67]; two or more separate periods of disqualification can only be ordered to take effect consecutively under the "totting-up" procedure.[68] The disqualified person may appeal against the order,[69] or apply to the court during the period to have the disqualification removed.[70] He may not apply until the expiry of two years, if the disqualification is for less than four years, or of half the period, if it is between four and ten years, or of five years in all other cases.[71]

Particulars of the disqualification must be entered or endorsed on the offender's licence; particulars of any conviction for which he may or must be disqualified[72] must be endorsed on his licence unless the court finds special reasons for not doing so.[73] Endorsements are prima facie evidence of the conviction or disqualification and are transferred to any new licence issued. However, the driver may, when three years have elapsed since conviction, apply to have them removed.[74]

Disqualification is a purely statutory penalty and cannot be imposed for a common law offence such as an attempt (unless the attempt is also a statutory offence).[75]

2. Disqualification from driving—Powers of Criminal Courts Act 1973

If a person is convicted of an offence punishable on indictment with imprisonment for two years or more, the court may order him to be disqualified from holding or obtaining a driving licence, for such period as it thinks fit, provided the court is satisfied that a motor vehicle was used for the purpose of committing the offence in question.[76] The offender who is ordered to be disqualified need not

---

[66] *R.* v. *Tunde-Olarinde* [1967] 1 W.L.R. 911. There must, however, be "unusual circumstances" for otherwise disqualification for life is "wrong in principle": *R.* v. *Wood* [1972] Crim.L.R. 665. See also *R.* v. *North* [1971] Crim. L.R. 429.

[67] Road Traffic Act 1972, s. 93 (7).

[68] *R.* v. *Meese* [1973] 1 W.L.R. 675; *R.* v. *Sibthorpe* (1973) 57 Cr.App.R. 447.

[69] Road Traffic Act 1972, s. 94.

[70] *Ibid.* s. 95. This applies equally to discretionary and mandatory disqualifications: *Damer* v. *Davison* [1975] Crim.L.R. 522.

[71] Road Traffic Act 1972, s. 95 (2).

[72] *i.e.* under Sched. 4, above.

[73] *Ibid.* s. 101 (1).

[74] *Ibid.* subs. (7).

[75] *R.* v. *Cockermouth Justices, ex p. Patterson* [1971] R.T.R. 216; an example of a statutory attempt is s. 6 (1) of the Road Traffic Act 1972, see p. 121.

[76] Powers of Criminal Courts Act 1973, s. 44; see also *R.* v. *Thomas* [1975] R.T.R. 38 and *R.* v. *Brown* [1975] R.T.R. 36. This section is closely related to s. 43, as to which see p. 254.

have used the vehicle himself in the course of committing the offence, and the vehicle may have been used to facilitate the commission of the offence, including the disposal of any property to which the offence relates and the avoidance of apprehension or detection.

3. Costs

Two types of orders for costs may be made—out of central funds or by one of the parties—and either may be ordered for the prosecution or for the defence.[77] The Crown Court may order costs to be paid personally by a solicitor if he causes unnecessary expense, but, as there is no appeal, he must be given an opportunity to be heard.[78]

(a) *Out of central funds*

The Crown Court may always order that the prosecution's costs be paid out of central funds, but can only make such an order in favour of the defence if the accused is acquitted.[79] Costs are assessed on the basis of reasonable compensation for the expenses of carrying on the proceedings and for the expense, trouble and loss of time of witnesses.[80] Witnesses as to character only may be awarded costs if the court certifies that the interests of justice required their attendance[81]; defence witnesses may be compensated whether or not the accused's costs are awarded.[82] A witness may be awarded costs if he attends court, even though he did not give evidence.[83] The accused's costs may be ordered where he is legally aided and, on a successful appeal, the Court of Appeal may order his costs to be paid for the trial as well as for the appeal.[84] If intended to cover committal proceedings, the order must so specify.[85]

The award of costs for an acquitted accused is entirely discretionary; it would clearly be suitable to award them in his favour where the prosecution was unfounded or where a mistake was made, but there is no general presumption for or against awarding them.[86] The

[77] Enforcement, which is outside the scope of this book, is governed by the Administration of Justice Act 1970, s. 41 and Sched. 9. Because of the provisions for attachment of earnings in place of imprisonment, an accused ordered to pay costs (see below) may ultimately be imprisoned for non-payment, whereas a prosecutor cannot be.

[78] *R.* v. *Smith* [1975] Q.B. 531.

[79] Costs in Criminal Cases Act 1973, s. 3 (1).

[80] *Ibid.* s. 3 (3).

[81] *Ibid.* s. 3 (5).

[82] *Ibid.* s. 3 (4).

[83] *Ibid.* s. 3 (8).

[84] *Ibid.* ss. 7 and 8; the power extends to witnesses' and the prosecution's costs. Costs on appeal to the House of Lords may be ordered out of central funds under s. 10.

[85] *R.* v. *Michael* [1975] 3 W.L.R. 731.

[86] Practice Directions (1952) 36 Cr.App.R. 13 and [1959] 1 W.L.R. 1090.

judge makes an entire award and it is for the taxing officer to assess the *quantum*; the judge cannot award part only of that sum.[87] A person awarded costs out of central funds may apply for a review of their assessment and appeal against the reviewed assessment.[88]

Costs may be ordered to be paid out of central funds to a party to proceedings in the Queen's Bench Divisional Court in a criminal case.[89]

(b) *Against the prosecutor or the accused*

Under section 4 of the Costs in Criminal Cases Act 1973, the Crown Court may order a convicted accused to pay all or any part of the prosecution costs and may order the prosecutor to pay the whole or any part of an acquitted accused's costs. In both cases the costs include the committal proceedings. Unless a specific amount is ordered, the costs are assessed by an officer of the Crown Court.[90] If the court specifies the amount, it must take into account the means of the accused.[91] If there are several accused convicted, the order to pay prosecution costs may be joint and several, but the individual order should bear a relation to the proportion of the costs incurred for prosecuting each accused.[92]

Where a person committed for trial is not ultimately tried, the Crown Court has the same power to order costs out of central funds or against the prosecutor as if the accused had been tried and acquitted.[93]

Costs may be awarded against a person convicted during the operative period of a suspended sentence order or while he is on probation or subject to a conditional discharge[94] for the proceedings at which the order was made as well as for the present proceedings.[95] An unsuccessful applicant for leave to appeal to the House of Lords may be ordered to pay the prosecution's costs.[96]

The procedure for taxing costs and for review of the taxation and for appeal against the review is laid down in the Crown Court Rules

---

[87] Practice Direction (1968) 52 Cr.App.R. 196.

[88] Costs in Criminal Cases (Central Funds) (Appeals) Regulations 1977.

[89] Costs in Criminal Cases Act 1973, s. 5.

[90] *Ibid.* s. 4 (2).

[91] *R.* v. *Whalley* (1972) 136 J.P. 162; *R.* v. *Rowe* [1975] R.T.R. 309. The court may allow time to pay or payment by instalments under the Powers of Criminal Courts Act 1973, s. 34.

[92] *R.* v. *Simmonds* [1969] 1 Q.B. 685. The length of unduly long cross-examinations may be reflected in the taxation of the costs: *R.* v. *Kalia* (1975) 60 Cr.App.R. 200.

[93] Costs in Criminal Cases Act 1973, s. 12 (5).

[94] See pp. 228, 239 and 241.

[95] *Ibid.* s. 18 (4).

[96] *Ibid.* s. 11 (1).

1971, rr. 10–16. An officer of the Crown Court is assigned to the assessment of costs which have not been quantified by the court; he may be asked to review his assessment and the taxing master may be asked to make a further review, if a party is still dissatisfied. If the taxing master certifies that the question to be decided involves a point of principle of general importance appeal may be made by originating summons to a judge of the Queen's Bench Division.

4. Compensation

If a person is injured or his property is damaged or lost through a proven crime, he will almost certainly be able to ground a civil action against the offender.[97] The prospect of getting satisfaction for the judgment is of course proportionally low. If his injuries are personal and arise from a violent crime, he may apply to the Criminal Injuries Compensation Board for compensation. This is a scheme, not embodied in statute, for awarding *ex gratia* payments from public funds on the same basis as civil damages would be awarded.[98]

The court may order the offender to pay compensation to the victim of his offence under section 35 of the Powers of Criminal Courts Act 1973. The compensation may be ordered to cover " any personal injury, loss or damage." [99] Loss suffered by dependants on a person's death, and injury, loss or damage due to an " accident arising out of the presence of a motor vehicle on a road " are expressly excluded, except where damage to property has resulted from an offence under the Theft Act 1968.[1] Where property is damaged while it is out of the owner's possession due to an offence under the Theft Act 1968, all the damage is treated as having resulted from the offence in question, " however and by whomsoever the damage was caused." [2] A compensation order against the handler of stolen goods has been held to be improper, however, unless it is shown that the owner suffered damage as a result of the handling.[3] It has also been held that the victim cannot recover the costs of a civil action as " loss " under a compensation order.[4]

The injury, loss or damage must result from a specific offence with

---

97 *Cf.* Civil Evidence Act 1968, s. 11.

98 See Williams, *Criminal Injuries Compensation* (1972), which includes the text of the scheme and other useful information as well as an account of the scheme. Readers may also refer to *Current Law* for the " case law " of the Board.

99 Powers of Criminal Courts Act 1973, s. 35 (1).

1 *Ibid.* s. 35 (3).

2 *Ibid.* s. 35 (2).

3 *R.* v. *Sharkey*, *The Times*, January 16, 1976.

4 *Hammertons Cars* v. *Redbridge L.B.C.* [1974] 1 W.L.R. 484.

which the offender is charged, or from any other offence which is taken into consideration in determining the sentence for the offence charged.[5] The victim must also be clearly identifiable and the sum to be paid must be specified.[6] This is particularly important where there are several offences charged or taken into consideration; for analogous reasons, it is desirable that several rather than joint compensation orders should be made against joint defendants.[7]

The court must take into account the offender's means both in deciding whether to make a compensation order at all and in determining the amount.[8] An order should not be made if it might result in the offender committing further crimes to discharge his obligations under it.[9] The amount and the number of instalments by which it is to be paid must also be conducive to the offender's rehabilitation.[10] Within these limits it is not wrong in principle to make a compensation order which will become effective on the offender's release from prison if his prospects of employment are good.[11]

Although a compensation order cannot be imposed at the same time as a criminal bankruptcy order,[12] it is expressly provided that it may be imposed with a community service or probation order or a discharge.[13]

Where civil proceedings are also brought in respect of the injury, loss or damage covered by the compensation order, the damages are limited to the amount by which the civil award exceeds the amount already paid; the leave of the court is needed to enforce the civil judgment for the excess amount.[14] The magistrates' court which has the function of enforcing the order may discharge or reduce the order if a smaller sum is later awarded in civil proceedings than the amount specified in the compensation order or if the property lost is recovered.[15]

[5] Powers of Criminal Courts Act 1973, s. 35 (1). The order in respect of a " t.i.c." ceases to have effect if the conviction is quashed on appeal; further, he may appeal against that order alone as if it were an appeal against sentence: s. 36 (3).

[6] *R.* v. *Oddy* [1974] 1 W.L.R. 1212.

[7] *R.* v. *Grundy* [1974] 1 W.L.R. 139.

[8] Powers of Criminal Courts Act 1973, s. 35 (4).

[9] *R.* v. *Oddy*, above.

[10] *R.* v. *Daly* [1974] 1 W.L.R. 133; s. 34 of the 1973 Act enables the court to allow time to pay or payment by instalments of costs and compensation orders.

[11] *R.* v. *Bradburn* (1973) 57 Cr.App.R. 948; *R.* v. *Wylie* [1974] Crim.L.R. 608.

[12] Powers of Criminal Courts Act 1973, s. 39 (1).

[13] *Ibid.* ss. 12 (4) and 14 (8).

[14] *Ibid.* s. 38.

[15] *Ibid.* s. 37; the order is suspended for 28 days after conviction, in case of an appeal; the same principles apply as apply to restitution orders: *ibid.* s. 36 (1); see p. 273.

The person who has suffered the injury, loss or damage may make an application to the court for a compensation order to be made, but the court may equally make the order on its own motion.[16] If the accused has strenuously denied having caused the loss of particular items, the court should not make an order unless an application is made and proof given; even so, the criminal courts should not take on complicated issues of law or fact in dealing with compensation.[17]

Other forms of compensation which still exist are compensation or a reward out of local funds for being active in apprehending an offender and similar compensation to the family of a person killed while apprehending an offender.[18] The third type of restitution order, below, also savours of compensation.

5. Restitution

The title to stolen goods is governed by the civil law.[19] If it is still vested in the owner and a person is convicted of an offence with reference to the theft of the goods,[20] or has such an offence taken into consideration on sentence,[21] the court may make an order under section 28 of the Theft Act 1968 for one of the following:

(*a*) That the person having possession or control of the goods restore them to any person entitled to recover them;

(*b*) That other goods which directly or indirectly represent the stolen goods be transferred to any person entitled to recover the stolen goods;

(*c*) That the convicted person pay, out of the money in his possession[22] at the time of his apprehension, a sum not exceeding the value of the stolen goods to any person entitled to recover them.

No application need be made to the court.[23] A compensation order and a restitution order may probably be made in respect of the same goods if the owner recovers them in a damaged condition.[24]

---

[16] Powers of Criminal Courts Act 1973, s. 35 (1). In *R.* v. *Ali* (1972) 56 Cr.App.R. 301 it was recommended that the police take particulars of property stolen from the complainant so that the prosecution could make the application on his behalf.

[17] *R.* v. *Kneeshaw* [1975] Q.B. 57.

[18] Criminal Law Act 1826, ss. 28 and 30, as amended by the Criminal Law Act 1967; see *R.* v. *Beard*, p. 255.

[19] Theft Act 1968, s. 31 (2).

[20] This includes *e.g.* obtaining by deception, handling, blackmail or conspiracy to steal.

[21] Criminal Justice Act 1972, s. 6 (3).

[22] Unless the money is in his hands or in his pockets the court must be satisfied beyond reasonable doubt that it belongs to him, *e.g.* if it is in his house or in a safe-deposit: *R.* v. *Ferguson* [1970] 1 W.L.R. 1246.

[23] Criminal Justice Act 1972, s. 6 (2).

[24] Powers of Criminal Courts Act 1973, s. 35 (2).

A bona fide purchaser (or pledgee) of the goods is protected by section 28 (3), which enables the court, on the application of such a person, to order payment to him out of the money in the possession of the convicted person, of the amount he has paid for the goods or lent on their security. An order for restitution is enforceable by committal to prison for contempt of court.[25]

6. Criminal bankruptcy order

Where loss or damage to property has been caused to a person whose identity is known to the court and the amount involved exceeds £15,000, the court may make a criminal bankruptcy order against the person convicted of an offence which caused or was conducive to the loss or damage.[26] The loss must be due to the offence or offences of which the offender is convicted or to an offence or offences taken into consideration on sentence or to all or some of those offences together.[27] The loss or damage cannot include damage attributable to personal injuries. The order must specify the amount of the loss, the identity of the person suffering that loss, and the amount of loss suffered by each of the victims, if more than one.[28] The order may be made against two or more offenders in respect of the same loss or damage.[29]

The order is administered by the " Official Petitioner " who is the Director of Public Prosecutions.[30] The offender is deemed to have committed an act of bankruptcy on the date on which the order is made.[31] No appeal lies against the order as such but, on a successful appeal against conviction, the Court of Appeal must rescind the order unless a part of the appellant's conviction remains upon which a bankruptcy order could still be made.[32]

The order may not be made at the same time as a compensation order,[33] and the terms used (" where a person is *convicted* . . . the court may, in addition to *dealing with* the offender in any other way ") make it unlikely that it could be made at the same time as a probation order or discharge.[34] It can, however, be made at the same time as a community service order.[35]

---

[25] See R.S.C., Ord. 52.
[26] Powers of Criminal Courts Act 1973, s. 39 (1).
[27] *Ibid.* s. 39 (2).
[28] *Ibid.* s. 39 (3).
[29] *Ibid.* s. 39 (4).
[30] *Ibid.* s. 41.
[31] *Ibid.* Sched. 2, para. 1; this Schedule regulates the bankruptcy proceedings.
[32] *Ibid.* s. 40.
[33] *Ibid.* s. 39 (1).
[34] See *ibid.* ss. 2 (1) and 7 (1), pp. 236 and 240.
[35] *Ibid.* s. 14 (8).

7. Forfeiture

Various statutory powers of forfeiture exist,[36] the most important of which are section 43 of the Powers of Criminal Courts Act 1973 and section 27 of the Misuse of Drugs Act 1971.

(a) *Property used for the purposes of crime*

The court may order an offender to be deprived of property when he is convicted of an offence which is punishable with imprisonment for two years or more if the court is satisfied that it has been used for the purpose of committing or facilitating the commission of any offence, or was intended by him to be used for that purpose; the property must have been in his possession or under his control at the time of his apprehension.[37]

The order operates to deprive the offender of his rights, if any, in the property and to transfer possession to the police.[38] The police hold the property for six months and, if no one makes a claim in that time, they dispose of it.[39] If they have possession under this provision, however, a claimant cannot succeed in his claim unless he can show that he did not consent to the offender's possession of the property or that he did not know, and had no reason to suspect, that the property was likely to be used for criminal purposes.[40]

The section is broadly defined; " for the purpose of . . . facilitating the commission of an offence " is further defined [41] to include steps taken after an offence has been committed to dispose of property or to avoid apprehension or detection. The courts have tended to give the section a restrictive interpretation, however, in four cases concerning the forfeiture of a car:

(i) The order was not proper where the offence was committed on the spur of the moment by a man of good character.[41a]

(ii) It was not proper where the offence was not intended when the journey began and the car was not used to commit the offence.[41b]

(iii) It was not proper where the car was bought out of damages for an accident and the offender still needed it because of those injuries.[42]

---

[36] *e.g.* Firearms Act 1968, s. 52 (1).
[37] Powers of Criminal Courts Act 1973, s. 43 (1).
[38] *Ibid.* s. 43 (3).
[39] Police (Property) Act 1897; see also p. 330.
[40] Powers of Criminal Courts Act 1973, s. 43 (4).
[41] *Ibid.* s. 43 (2).
[41a] *R.* v. *Miele* [1976] R.T.R. 238.
[41b] *R.* v. *Lucas* [1976] R.T.R. 235.
[42] *R.* v. *Tavernor* [1976] R.T.R. 242.

(iv) It was proper, on the other hand, when the accused was selected by thieves on account of the suitability of his car for transporting the stolen goods.[43]

(b) *Drugs offences*

Anything shown to the satisfaction of the court to relate to an offence committed against the Misuse of Drugs Act 1971 may be ordered by the court to be forfeited and either destroyed or dealt with as the court directs. Anyone who claims to own or be interested in the thing forfeited must be given an opportunity to be heard before the order is made.[44] In *R.* v. *Beard*[45] the court ordered forfeiture of cash admitted to be the proceeds of sale of drugs.

E. Combinations of Punishments and Orders

In describing the various possible punishments and orders the inconsistency of combining them has repeatedly been mentioned. Two general points emerge:

(*a*) Most of the ancillary orders (described in Section D, above) may be made at the same time as a punishment is imposed or a non-punitive order is made.

(*b*) A punishment, *i.e.* fine or imprisonment, cannot be imposed at the same time as a non-punitive order (hospital, community service or probation order or discharge), though it may be combined with binding over.

A combination of two or more prison sentences has been dealt with separately[46]; a court may impose a fine in addition to imprisonment, whether or not the sentence is suspended.[47] Borstal training cannot be ordered at the same time as any other punishment[48] and, being a form of imprisonment, it could not be imposed at the same time as a non-punitive order.

Community service, probation, discharge, hospital orders and borstal are, by definition, inconsistent with other orders; an extended sentence of imprisonment is also inconsistent with other

[43] *R.* v. *Lidster* [1976] R.T.R. 240.

[44] Misuse of Drugs Act 1971, s. 29.

[45] [1974] 1 W.L.R. 1549. Most of the money was paid to the Commissioners of Customs and Excise but £500 was ordered to be paid through the City of London to the investigating officer under the Criminal Law Act 1826.

[46] See p. 229.

[47] Powers of Criminal Courts Act 1973, s. 30 (1).

[48] Criminal Justice Act 1948, s. 20 (1), the words " in lieu of any other sentence " being used.

punishments except, possibly, a fine; a suspended sentence is inconsistent with any custodial sentence.[49] A recommendation for deportation may be made at the same time as a conditional discharge, although it might seem illogical to make it at the same time as a rehabilitative order such as probation.[50]

F. Pardon, Release, etc.

1. Pardon, reprieve and commutation

A pardon is part of the Crown's prerogative powers. Its effect is not altogether clear; the accused cannot be tried[51] or, if already convicted, punished; if already punished, it has no procedural significance.[52]

A reprieve is the temporary withdrawal of a sentence and the suspension of its execution; the Crown or the court may grant it if for instance the prisoner becomes insane after sentence is passed so that appropriate action may be taken by the court or the Home Secretary.[53] Reprieves were more common when the death penalty was more widely available; alternatively the Crown had power to commute the death sentence to a term of imprisonment. The term " commute " is also used to describe the Home Secretary's power to transfer an " incorrigible " borstal trainee to prison for the unexpired part of his training. He may also transfer a prisoner under the age of twenty-one to a borstal institution[54] and he may transfer a prisoner to a mental hospital,[55] but neither of these powers is called a commutation.

2. Release of prisoners

(a) *Temporary discharge*

Under section 28 of the Prison Act 1952, the Home Secretary may authorise the temporary discharge on conditions of a prisoner whose state of health makes his discharge desirable. This may be ordered before or after sentence is passed, the discharge being conditioned to his attendance in court or his return to prison, respectively.

---

[49] See p. 230.
[50] *R.* v. *Akan* [1973] 1 Q.B. 491.
[51] See p. 168.
[52] *Quaere* whether it could found an action in defamation against an allegation of having committed the offence. It cannot be granted if a person will thereby be deprived of his rights (*Thomas* v. *Sorrell* (1674) Vaughan 330) nor for the offence under the Habeas Corpus Act 1679 of sending a prisoner out of the jurisdiction.
[53] Hale 412 and see also pp. 171 and 234.
[54] Prison Act 1952, s. 44; see p. 232.
[55] Mental Health Act 1959, s. 72; see pp. 171 and 234.

(b) *Remission*

A prisoner has for a long time been able to earn remission, *i.e.* a cancellation of part of his term of imprisonment, for his good behaviour in prison. In the normal case, the prisoner is made free without supervision; in the case of an extended sentence he can only be released on licence.[56] At present he may earn remission of up to one third of his sentence under the Prison Rules.[57] There can be no remission of life sentences. For a person serving an extended sentence[58] or for a person serving more than 18 months' imprisonment who was under 21 at sentence, remission is replaced by release on licence.[59]

(c) *Release on licence*

Remission is an unconditional release; parole is not. The Criminal Justice Act 1967, s. 59, set up a Parole Board, whose members include a present or past member of the judiciary, a psychiatrist, a person with experience in the after-care of discharged prisoners and a person trained in the causes of delinquency or the treatment of offenders,[60] to supervise the release of prisoners before the expiry of their terms of imprisonment. The Parole Board gives advice on their release and the conditions for it when the Home Secretary refers a case to the Board; it considers reports and other documents and any other evidence, oral or in writing, relating to the prisoner, and a member of the Board may interview the prisoner if necessary. The prisoner may apply to the Board for release. Preliminary investigations are carried out by local review committees who refer their findings to the Home Secretary.[61]

A person is eligible for release, if he is serving a determinate sentence, after he has served 12 months or one third of his sentence, whichever expires the later.[62] The length of time served includes time spent in custody permitted by statute.[63] A person sentenced to imprisonment for life may be released by the Home Secretary but only on the advice of the Parole Board and after consultation with the Lord Chief Justice and the trial judge, if available.[64]

---

[56] *R.* v. *Shirley* [1972] Crim.L.R. 259.

[57] S.I. 1964 No. 388, para. 5; time spent in custody before conviction may be taken into account for the purposes of remission: S.I. 1972 No. 1860.

[58] See p. 226.

[59] Criminal Justice Act 1967, s. 60 (3).

[60] *Ibid.* Sched. 2.

[61] See Local Review Committee Rules (S.I. 1967 No. 1462) as amended by S.I. 1973 No. 4.

[62] Criminal Justice Act 1967, s. 60 (1).

[63] *Ibid.* ss. 67 and 60 (2).

[64] Criminal Justice Act 1967, s. 61 (1).

The conditions of the licence on which the prisoner is released must be approved individually or as a class by the Parole Board.[65] Power is given to the Home Secretary in appropriate cases not to refer the applicant to the Parole Board but simply to release him by his own order.[66] The licence remains in force until the time when the released prisoner would have been released had he been granted remission for good behaviour under the Prison Rules. If he is serving an extended sentence or if he was under 21 years old when sentenced to a term of 18 months or more, the licence does not expire until the date when the sentence expires.[67]

While a prisoner is released on licence, he is subject to the administrative power to recall him, which may be exercised by the Home Secretary either

(i) on the recommendation of the Parole Board; or
(ii) without consultation where it appears to him to be expedient to recall a prisoner before consultation is practicable.[68]

The recalled prisoner may make written representations which are referred to the Parole Board. If at this stage the Board recommends his immediate release on licence, the Home Secretary must carry out the recommendation.

If a prisoner released on licence commits an offence punishable on indictment by imprisonment, the court[69] dealing with him has power to revoke the licence. He then returns to prison and any further sentence imposed on him may be ordered to run consecutively.[70] Moreover, the Home Secretary must not release him on licence again until one year has elapsed from the date of revocation or the expiry of one third of the period during which he would have been released on licence but for the revocation, whichever is the later.[71]

The court which deals with an offender for a later offence first considers whether it should sentence him to prison for as long as the remaining effective part of his original sentence (*i.e.* subtracting remission). If it decides that it should, it should revoke the licence, then consider whether a further sentence should be imposed concurrently or consecutively. If a sentence of imprisonment is imposed, but the

[65] Criminal Justice Act 1967, s. 60 (5).
[66] Criminal Justice Act 1972, s. 35.
[67] *Ibid.* s. 60 (6).
[68] *Ibid.* s. 62.
[69] The Crown Court either as court of trial or on committal for sentence from a magistrates' court, as to which see p. 330.
[70] See p. 229.
[71] Criminal Justice Act 1967, s. 62 (6)–(10).

licence is not revoked, a court dealing with him on a later occasion cannot make its sentence run consecutively to the original sentence.[72]

3. Release of borstal trainees

A " juvenile adult " sentenced to borstal training is always released at the discretion of the Home Secretary.[73] Under section 45 of the Prison Act 1952 he is subject to supervision for two years after his release which is subject to conditions and requirements. If he fails to keep to the conditions he may be at once recalled to borstal for six months or until the expiration of two years from the date of sentencing, whichever is the later. After recall, he may again be released.[74]

If a released borstal trainee commits an offence punishable by imprisonment while under supervision or while unlawfully at large,[75] the court which deals with that offence may order his return to the borstal under the original order.[76] He may appeal against the order of return to borstal.[77] If a sentence of borstal training is passed for the later offence, the original sentence of borstal automatically ceases to have effect.[78] The court may sentence the offender to imprisonment, either for a long term (over 18 months)[79] for a serious offence, or for a short term with a view to recalling him to borstal after he has served it.[80]

In this chapter only the punishments and orders on a conviction on indictment have been considered; for the powers of magistrates' courts, see pages 317–339, and for the treatment of juveniles (under 17 years old), see Chapter 15, page 361.

---

72 *Practice Direction* (1975) 119 S.J. 28.

73 See p. 230. The maximum is two years; the Home Secretary may direct release before the minimum of six months.

74 Prison Act 1952, s. 45 (4), as amended by the Criminal Justice Act 1961, Sched. 4, and the Prison Commissioners Dissolution Order 1963 (S.I. 1963 No. 597).

75 This includes being at large after the Home Secretary has ordered his recall: Prison Act 1952, s. 45 (4).

76 Criminal Justice Act 1961, s. 12 (1); he is then treated as if he had been recalled under the Prison Act 1952, s. 45; *ibid.* s. 12 (2).

77 Criminal Justice Act 1972, s. 42.

78 Prison Act 1952, s. 45 (5).

79 See p. 231.

80 *R.* v. *Noseda* [1958] 1 W.L.R. 793.

CHAPTER 10

APPEALS

A. COURTS

1. Court of Appeal

The Court of Appeal consists of the Civil Division and the Criminal Division; the Criminal Division entertains appeals from trial on indictment or sentence passed by the Crown Court. The prosecution cannot appeal to the Court of Appeal, although the Attorney-General may refer a point of law to it following an acquittal[1]; the accused can appeal against conviction, against a finding of insanity or disability or against sentence.[2]

The judiciary of the division consists of the judges of the Court of Appeal (Lords Justices) and any of the judges of the High Court.[3] Any number of courts may sit at the same time[4]; a full court is constituted by an uneven number of judges, being not less than three[5]; for matters which do not require the decision of a full court, the court consists of one or two judges,[6] depending on the nature of the proceedings. One judgment only is delivered unless the presiding judge states that on a question of law it would be convenient to have separate judgments given. No judge may sit in the court who sat as a judge in the proceedings at which the conviction was returned or the sentence passed.[7]

The Criminal Division, unlike the Civil Division, is not strictly bound by its previous decisions, but may depart from them when it considers that the law was misapplied or misunderstood in the previous decision.[8]

The Registrar of Criminal Appeals, his assistants and other staff deal with the administration of the division; he sorts out applications, prepares the case (documents, exhibits, etc.) for hearing, arranges hearings and gives notice to the parties of proceedings in the division.[9]

---

[1] Criminal Justice Act 1972, s. 36; see p. 279.

[2] Criminal Appeal Act 1968, ss. 1 (1), 10 (2), 12 and 15 (1).

[3] Administration of Justice Act 1970, s. 9 (3).

[4] Criminal Appeal Act 1966, s. 2 (1).

[5] Administration of Justice Act 1970, s. 9 (1).

[6] *Ibid.* s. 9 (2), and Criminal Appeal Act 1968, s. 31. See also footnote 27, p. 263.

[7] Criminal Appeal Act 1966, s. 2 (3).

[8] *R.* v. *Gould* [1968] 2 Q.B. 65 and see *Young* v. *Bristol Aeroplane Ltd.* [1944] K.B. 718.

[9] See Criminal Appeal Act 1966, s. 3, Criminal Appeal Act 1968, ss. 20 and 21, and

If the appellant himself has applied and has no solicitor, the Registrar appoints counsel to represent him without appointing a solicitor.

2. The House of Lords

The House of Lords hears appeals in criminal cases from the Court of Appeal and, in some cases, from the High Court.[10] When hearing appeals at least three Law Lords must be sitting; these are life peers who are specifically appointed (Lords of Appeal in Ordinary),[11] the Lord Chancellor and any peer who has held high judicial office (this category includes ex-Lord Chancellors). There is no rule that lay peers may not sit, but tradition excludes them. When hearing an appeal the House forms an Appellate Committee which sits separately.

The usual number of Law Lords to sit at the hearing of an appeal is five. Each may deliver an opinion (the appeal is always on a point of law) and the appeal is won or lost by a majority vote. The House of Lords used to bind itself by its own decisions but since 1966 it may depart from a previous decision where " it appears right to do so " bearing in mind " the especial need for certainty as to the criminal law." [12] There is no statutory prohibition on a Law Lord who has been involved in earlier stages of the proceedings from sitting on an appeal.

3. Courts-Martial Appeal Court

This court hears appeals from the courts-martial of the armed services. The judges of the Court of Appeal and nominated Queen's Bench judges sit in it as well as judges specifically appointed. By and large the right of appeal and the powers of the Appeal Court are similar to those of the Court of Appeal, save that appeal does not lie against sentence alone; further appeal may be made to the House of Lords. The court is regulated by the Courts-Martial (Appeals) Act 1968 and is a superior court of record. Its existence is noted here but details are beyond the scope of this book.

Criminal Appeal Rules 1968, rr. 8, 18, 19 and 22. A pamphlet called "Preparation for Proceedings in the Court of Appeal Criminal Division " was issued by the Registrar in June 1974; it deals comprehensively with the procedural steps of an appeal. Some practical guidance drawn from the pamphlet is given on p. 283.

[10] Where the Queen's Bench Divisional Court has heard an appeal on a case stated (see pp. 349–353) and where it has exercised the High Court's supervisory jurisdiction (see pp. 43–47).

[11] Appellate Jurisdiction Act 1876, s. 5.

[12] Practice Statement [1966] 1 W.L.R. 1234.

B. Appeal Against Conviction

1. Making the appeal

The procedural requirements for making an appeal vary according to whether the appeal is based on law only or involves a question of fact.

(a) *Appeal on law only*

If no issues of fact are involved, the appeal lies as of right [13] and is heard without any intervening procedure except the service of a notice of appeal by the appellant, or his legal advisers, on the Registrar at the Criminal Appeal Office.[14] The notice of appeal must be served within 28 days of conviction [15] or an application for an extension of time must be made giving reasons for the delay.[16] The grounds of the appeal are submitted with the notice of appeal [17]; if they turn out to involve questions of fact, the court may treat the notice of appeal as an application for leave to appeal [18]; if the Registrar finds that the grounds do not show any substantial ground of appeal, he may refer the appeal to the court for summary determination.[19]

(b) *Appeal involving fact*

An appeal on a question of fact alone or of mixed fact and law cannot be made as of right; it requires either the leave of the Court of Appeal or the certificate of the trial judge that the case is fit for appeal.[20] In the latter case the certificate is served on the Registrar with the appellant's notice of appeal.[21] An application to the Court of Appeal for leave to appeal [22] is accompanied by a statement of the grounds of appeal.[23] If the appellant is appealing against more than one conviction returned on the same indictment, the grounds for the

---

[13] Criminal Appeal Act 1968, s. 1 (2) (*a*).

[14] Criminal Appeal Rules 1968, Sched. 1, Form 2. The forms issued by the Criminal Appeal Office (or available at the Crown Court) have been given letters to identify them. The notice of appeal is Form N.

[15] Criminal Appeal Act 1968, s. 18 (2).

[16] Criminal Appeal Rules 1968, r. 2 (3).

[17] An example of a statement of grounds may be found on p. 284. The forms for appeals do not indicate the need to state grounds involving questions of law only. In view of s. 20 of the 1968 Act and r. 2 (7) of the Rules (below), however, such a statement is clearly necessary.

[18] Criminal Appeal Rules 1968, r. 2 (7).

[19] Criminal Appeal Act 1968, s. 20.

[20] Criminal Appeal Act 1968, s. 1 (2) (*b*). The court has a residuary discretion to grant leave to appeal against conviction " on any other ground which appears to the court . . . to be a sufficient ground of appeal."

[21] See above.

[22] Criminal Appeal Rules 1968, Sched. 1, Form 2, Appeal Form N.

[23] *Ibid.* Form 3, Appeal Form G.

appeal and the notice of appeal against each must be separately stated. The notice of appeal or the application for leave must be served within 28 days of conviction or an application for an extension of time must be made.[24] The court may give leave to vary or extend the grounds of appeal after the period has expired, however.[25]

A single judge of the court may determine an application for leave or for an extension of time.[26] If he refuses the application, the appellant is entitled to have the application heard by at least two judges of the Court of Appeal.[27] If the application has been heard in the first instance by the full court of three judges (*e.g.* if an appeal on law only reveals issues of fact), its decision is final.

The Court of Appeal has jurisdiction to alter its decision or order at any time before the proper officer of the court of trial has entered the decision on the record, the decision having been transmitted to the court by the Registrar; thereafter the Court of Appeal is *functus officio*.[28]

(c) *Ancillary applications*

Apart from the notice of appeal or the application for leave, the appellant may apply before the hearing for bail,[29] to be present at the hearing of the appeal [30] or to have witnesses ordered to attend or evidence to be produced.[31] The single judge also hears these applications and the same provision as to re-hearing applies as applies to applications for leave or for an extension of time. As to legal aid for the appellant, see Chapter 17, below.[32]

Bail may be granted pending the determination of the appeal on the same general principles as apply at other stages of the proceedings,[33] though it is possibly granted more rarely and the Bail Act 1976 does not operate to give the appellant a general right to

---

[24] Criminal Appeal Act 1968, s. 18 (2).

[25] *R.* v. *Haycraft* (1973) 58 Cr.App.R. 121; it is a discourtesy to the court to add new grounds at the last minute even before the period has expired: *R.* v. *Kalia* (1975) 60 Cr.App.R. 200.

[26] Criminal Appeal Act 1968, s. 31 (1).

[27] *Ibid.* s. 31 (3), Administration of Justice Act 1970, s. 9 (2), and Criminal Appeal Rules 1968, r. 12. The only functions which the two-judge court cannot perform are the determination of the appeal, the determination of an application for leave to appeal to the House of Lords and the refusal of an application for leave to appeal otherwise than after a single judge has refused it.

[28] *R.* v. *Cross* [1973] Q.B. 937.

[29] Criminal Appeal Act 1968, s. 19. The Crown Court has no jurisdiction to grant bail pending appeal.

[30] *Ibid.* s. 22.

[31] *Ibid.* s. 23 (1).

[32] See p. 399.

[33] See Chap. 4, Section I, p. 68.

bail.[34] Such bail is "bail in criminal proceedings," however, and the restrictions on taking a recognisance from the appellant, etc., under section 3 apply.[35] Sureties may be ordered by the court and recognisances are entered before the Registrar, a justice of the peace, a police inspector or the person having custody of the appellant.[35a] The appellant is entitled to be present in court except in four cases; where he is in custody he needs the leave of the court to attend if the appeal is on law only, if the hearing is of an application for leave or other preliminary matter or if he is in custody following a finding of insanity or disability.[36]

The court has power to order the production of documents, exhibits or other things which appear necessary in the case, or to order the presence of a witness who would have been compellable at the trial [37] for attendance at the appeal, whether or not he was called at the trial. This provision enables the court to hear fresh evidence. It may also receive oral evidence from a competent but non-compellable witness.

It is the Registrar's duty to obtain the documents, etc., and lay them before the court.[38] He must supply a copy of all the written material to the appellant and respondent on request or allow them to inspect it.[39] A transcript of the shorthand note or recording of the proceedings at trial must be made available when asked for by the Registrar.[40] The trial judge may direct the exclusion of parts of the proceedings or the inclusion of the opening and closing speeches of counsel, which are normally omitted. The Registrar or appellant may ask for a transcript of some parts only, such as the formal parts

---

[34] One criterion for granting bail is the likelihood of a custodial sentence being quashed on appeal or having been effectively served by the time the appeal is heard (*i.e.* by the appellant being in custody). After the court has dealt with an appeal, it has no jurisdiction to grant bail and application must be made to the court of trial; an appellant might wish to apply for bail at this stage if, for instance, he is awaiting the making of a deportation order in custody: *R.* v. *Zaman* (1975) 61 Cr.App.R. 227.

[35] Bail Act 1916, s. 1 (1) and 3 (1); see p. 75

[35a] Criminal Appeal Rules 1968, r. 4. The grant may be varied or revoked and the recognisances forfeited under rr. 5 and 6.

[36] Criminal Appeal Act 1968, s. 22. He should be brought within the precincts of the court if he is in custody, if the appeal is likely to be heard immediately after the application for leave or if it is the most convenient means of enabling him to have a conference with his legal advisers.

[37] Literally "the proceedings from which the appeal lies," for appeal also lies against sentence in the Crown Court where the accused was convicted by magistrates; see pp. 353 and 355.

[38] As to the assistance given by the appellant's legal advisers, see *Preparation for Proceedings in the Court of Appeal, Criminal Division*, footnote 9 on p. 261 and p. 285.

[39] Criminal Appeal Act 1968, s. 21, and Criminal Appeal Rules 1968, r. 8.

[40] Criminal Appeal Act 1968, s. 32, and Criminal Appeal Rules 1968, rr. 18, 19 and 20. R. 20 applies to verification of the transcript.

and the summing-up, where the appeal does not warrant the expense and delay involved in obtaining the complete transcript. The officer of the court of trial retains exhibits in his custody for 35 days after the conviction unless the judge orders otherwise or the Registrar asks for them to be sent to him earlier.[41]

(d) *Defence of appeals*

The Crown is entitled to defend the actual appeal.[42] Where an unusual or complex point of law is raised, the Director of Public Prosecutions may be the proper officer to undertake the defence,[43] otherwise the body or person who handled the prosecution may defend it.

(e) *Reference by the Home Secretary*

Under section 17 of the Criminal Appeal Act 1968 the Home Secretary may refer a case to the Court of Appeal when an accused has been convicted, or found not guilty by reason of insanity or found to be under disability. He may refer the whole issue, in which case it is treated as the appeal of the accused, or he may request that the court's opinion on a point arising in the case be furnished for his use. He may refer it on his own initiative or on the application of the accused. This provision may help the Home Secretary in determining the proper treatment of an offender where it is left to him.

(f) *Appeal after a plea of guilty*

If the accused pleaded guilty, it is quite likely that he has no right of appeal under section 2 (1) below. Although he has undoubtedly been convicted for the purpose of section 1, there is no verdict of a jury and, if the plea was made without preliminary argument and was properly accepted, the other two grounds do not apply. " In any other case [the Court of Appeal] shall dismiss the appeal." [44]

In any event, the Court of Appeal is wary of quashing the conviction unless it finds that the appellant did not appreciate the nature of the charge or did not intend to plead guilty to that offence, or that he could not in law have been convicted of the offence on the facts.[45]

---

[41] Criminal Appeal Rules 1968, r. 7.

[42] *R.* v. *Upton* [1973] 3 All E.R. 318.

[43] See p. 19.

[44] Criminal Appeal Act 1968, s. 2 (1); *D.P.P.* v. *Shannon* [1975] A.C. 717; see p. 273 and below.

[45] *R.* v. *Forde* [1923] 2 K.B. 400 at p. 403; *cf.* the power of the accused to change his plea at trial, p. 169, and on committal for sentence to the Crown Court, p. 344.

In such a case the plea and subsequent trial are a nullity and the Court of Appeal may order a new trial on a *venire de novo.*[46]

2. Grounds of appeal

Under section 2 (1) of the Criminal Appeal Act 1968, the only grounds of appeal against conviction are:

" (*a*) that the verdict of the jury should be set aside on the ground that under all the circumstances of the case it is unsafe and unsatisfactory; or

(*b*) that the judgment of the court of trial should be set aside on the ground of a wrong decision of any question of law; or

(*c*) that there was a material irregularity in the course of trial."

This is subject to the proviso that the court may dismiss an appeal, even though it might be decided on the above grounds in favour of the appellant, if it considers that " no miscarriage of justice has actually occurred."

Allegations in support of these grounds are many and varied, but perhaps the most common are of a misdirection by the judge or of a wrongful admission of evidence.

A misdirection of law might be a misdirection on the burden of proof,[47] or a non-direction on the danger of convicting on unsupported identification evidence [48] or on accomplice evidence without corroboration.[49] An almost infinite range of misdirections can be envisaged in which the judge's words do not reflect correctly the rules of the substantive law or of the law of evidence or procedure. Where the wrong or misleading direction is of minor importance and, balanced with the rest of the case, would not alone have swayed the jury into convicting, the Court of Appeal may apply the proviso to section 2 (1).

The total omission of the defence of an accused from the summing-up would be a misdirection for which the Court of Appeal would quash the conviction, but the understatement of the defence case need not have this result.[50]

---

[46] *R.* v. *Inns* (1974) 60 Cr.App.R. 231; *R.* v. *Peace, The Times,* November 28, 1975; as to *venire de novo,* see p. 273.

[47] *e.g. Woolmington* v. *D.P.P.* [1935] A.C. 462 and *R.* v. *Murtagh and Kennedy* (1955) 39 Cr.App.R. 72. As to summing-up, see p. 196.

[48] See *R.* v. *Turnbull*, p. 35.

[49] *e.g. Davies* v. *D.P.P.* [1954] A.C. 378.

[50] *R.* v. *Badjan* (1966) 50 Cr.App.R. 141 and the case of Craig and Bentley, noted in Glanville Williams' *The Proof of Guilt*, p. 304, for the affirmation of a conviction where the summing-up dealt with the prosecution case in four or five pages of transcript while dealing with the defence case in one sentence.

Wrongful admission of evidence may render the verdict unsafe and unsatisfactory, or amount to a wrong decision of law, if the judge says that it is admissible evidence, or constitute a material irregularity in the trial. The wrongful exclusion of evidence in the accused's favour might be a ground under section 2 (1) (*a*) or 2 (1) (*c*).

It is clearly important to be able to show that the verdict is unsafe and unsatisfactory for then it would be impossible for the court to apply the proviso that no miscarriage of justice has occurred; logically the two propositions are mutually exclusive. The Court of Appeal considers the case as a whole and in cases which are not clear, if it finds that it has a lurking doubt that injustice has been done, it will quash the conviction.[51] This is decided by the court on the basis of what it thinks of the safeness of the verdict: no test is applied of whether a jury would inevitably have convicted even if the defective aspect of the trial had been absent, or whether they would probably have acquitted.[52] A verdict may be unsafe and unsatisfactory where several accused tried jointly should have been tried separately[53] or where the verdict is inconsistent as between co-accused.[54] It may be contended that a verdict is unreasonable; a verdict of guilty after the judge has directed that the prosecution has not made out a case or after the judge has wrongly overruled a submission of no case to answer may be unreasonable.[55] The verdict itself must be unsafe and unsatisfactory; circumstances outside the conduct of the trial must bear immediately and directly upon it if they are to be taken into consideration.[56]

Matters which may amount to a " material irregularity " in the trial include defects in the indictment,[57] undue interference by the judge in the conduct of the defence,[58] wrongful revelation of the accused's previous convictions,[59] a suspicion of bribery or other impartiality of the jurors[60] or the absence of a juror from the

---

[51] *R.* v. *Cooper* [1969] 1 Q.B. 267.

[52] *Stafford* v. *D.P.P.* [1974] A.C. 878.

[53] See p. 140.

[54] *R.* v. *Smith* (1966) 51 Cr.App.R. 22.

[55] *R.* v. *Abbott* [1955] 2 Q.B. 497 and see p. 202.

[56] *R.* v. *Graham* [1975] Crim.L.R. 699 (where an irregular first trial was held to have no bearing on the new trial).

[57] See *e.g.* pp. 107 and 146.

[58] See p. 189.

[59] Where an accused was wrongly cross-examined on his record, but in the circumstances it would otherwise quite properly have been revealed, the Court of Appeal applied the proviso: *R.* v. *Lovett* [1973] 1 W.L.R. 241. In *R.* v. *Box and Box* [1964] 1 Q.B. 430 the conviction was also upheld when a juror, who knew of the accused's past form, gave evidence that it did not affect his judgment.

[60] *R.* v. *Gash* (No. 2) [1967] 1 W.L.R. 454.

juryroom during retirement.[61] Again a large range of irregularities can be envisaged which are "material" in the process of conviction, but on this ground the court may apply the proviso. For instance, where prosecuting counsel was wrongly allowed to make a closing speech at the trial of an unrepresented accused, the Court of Appeal applied the proviso.[62]

The jurisdiction of the Court of Appeal in a case where the accused has pleaded guilty, as mentioned above, may arise if the judge's acceptance of the plea can be said to amount to a decision of law; this may occur where he gives a preliminary ruling on admitted facts as a result of which the accused pleads.[63] A mere acceptance of the plea, however, where the allegations in the indictment, if admitted, justify the conviction and where the plea is freely given without argument, cannot amount to a decision of law.[64] In *D.P.P.* v. *Shannon* [65] the House of Lords recommended immediate legislative amendment to change the words "verdict of the jury" to "conviction," [66] but, at the time of writing, no such amendment has been made.

In *R.* v. *Barnes*,[67] the conviction of a man against whom the prosecution evidence was overwhelming was quashed because of an outburst by the judge, albeit in the absence of the jury, against defendants contesting "quite hopeless cases." It was putting improper pressure on the accused to plead guilty, it made him think that it would be impossible to obtain a fair trial and it induced his counsel to reveal that he had advised the accused to plead guilty (advice of this sort should never be revealed). Lord Parker C.J. concluded that the proviso should not be applied because "there are cases . . . in which the principles involved are more important than the case itself." [68]

3. Powers of the Court of Appeal

When applications for leave to appeal or for other matters are made, the single judge holds an informal hearing which need not be

[61] *R.* v. *Goodson* [1975] 1 W.L.R. 549.
[62] *R.* v. *Pink* [1971] 1 Q.B. 508; see p. 195.
[63] *R.* v. *Vickers* [1975] 1 W.L.R. 811; see p. 155.
[64] *R.* v. *Shepherd* [1975] R.T.R. 497.
[65] [1975] A.C. 717 (in which the Court of Appeal had entertained and allowed the appeal without considering this point).
[66] *Ibid.* at pp. 773–774. The pre-1966 law enabled the Court of Appeal to allow an appeal in any case where it thought there was a miscarriage of justice.
[67] (1971) Cr.App.R. 100.
[68] See also *R.* v. *Smith* (1975) 61 Cr.App.R. 128, where a pupil had a full conference with the defendant, then sat behind the prosecuting counsel at trial; justice was not seen to be done.

in open court.[69] If the appellant is represented, his counsel or solicitor may address the judge and expand on the grounds of the application.

The hearing of the appeal itself takes place in open court. The appellant opens the case and, if the appeal is defended, the respondent replies. The order of proceedings is flexible; the judges, having already studied the papers in the case, look to counsel to assist them on the law by their arguments, rather than to inform them of the issues of fact.

(a) *Fresh evidence*

The appellant must apply for leave to call evidence not called at the trial. If leave is granted, the Court of Appeal, unless satisfied that it would not afford any ground for allowing the appeal, must hear it if it seems likely to be credible and would have been admissible at the trial, and if it is satisfied that there is a reasonable explanation for it not having been adduced at the trial.[70] If the evidence would have been compellable at trial, the witness or the person having possession of a document, exhibit or other thing, may be ordered to attend by the single judge.[71] If the witness was non-compellable, such as the accused or his spouse, the requirements for his evidence to be given are the same as at trial.[72] The reception of fresh evidence has the important procedural effect of enabling the court to order retrial of the appellant.[73] A new trial should be ordered if evidence in rebuttal of the fresh evidence is also to be called so that a jury can evaluate it.[74]

In *Stafford* v. *D.P.P.*[75] the House of Lords considered that the Court of Appeal should have the maximum flexibility in dealing with an appeal in accordance with its view of the case in the light of all the circumstances. It has a discretion which goes beyond its duty to admit fresh evidence under section 23, above.[76] It is not bound, on the other hand, to admit evidence of matters which were not in issue at trial.[77]

---

[69] Criminal Appeal Rules 1968, r. 11.

[70] Criminal Appeal Act 1968, s. 23 (2); in general it must be satisfied that the evidence could not with reasonable diligence have been obtained for use at the trial: *R.* v. *Beresford* (1971) 56 Cr.App.R. 143.

[71] See p. 31.

[72] Criminal Appeal Act 1968, s. 23 (1) (*c*) and (3); *i.e.* it must be on the appellant's application; see Criminal Evidence Act 1898, s. 1 (*a*) and (*c*), pp. 31 and 32.

[73] See p. 272.

[74] *R.* v. *Merry* [1971] Crim.L.R. 91.

[75] [1974] A.C. 878.

[76] *R.* v. *Lattimore* (1975) 62 Cr.App.R. 53.

[77] *R.* v. *Melville* [1976] 1 W.L.R. 181, where diminished responsibility was raised on appeal from a trial where provocation was the only issue raised by the defence.

The court may call evidence on its own motion without the appellant's application. If the witness would have been compellable, the court may order his examination by an examiner and use the deposition taken from him as evidence.[78] The deposition is taken in the same manner as before an examining justice, which means that the examination should be conducted in public unless the ends of justice would not be served by a sitting in open court.[79]

(b) *Dismissal of an appeal*

The Court of Appeal has power under section 20 of the 1968 Act to dispose of and dismiss an appeal summarily, *i.e.* without attendance of the appellant or of the Crown, where the Registrar has referred an apparently insubstantial appeal on grounds of law only to the court and the court considers the appeal to be frivolous or vexatious.

If the appellant wishes to abandon his appeal or application for leave, he serves a notice of his intention on the Registrar.[80] The appeal or application is then treated as having been dismissed or refused.[81] The court has power to give leave for the notice of abandonment to be withdrawn if it can be regarded as a nullity in the sense that it was not the result of a deliberate and informed decision [82]; it will be a nullity if the appellant has been led into a fundamental error by bad legal advice, but mistaken legal advice alone will not necessarily have this effect.[83] He may abandon it orally at the hearing, but once the appeal itself has opened, the discontinuation of the appeal or any part of it, such as an application to call fresh evidence, is in the discretion of the court.[84] If the appellant dies before the appeal or application is heard, the right of appeal dies with him,[85] though if the conviction involved a fine, it has been suggested that the accused's personal representatives could appeal to save the estate from paying the fine.[86] The proper procedure for, *e.g.* a widow would be to petition the Home Secretary to make a reference under section 17 of the Criminal Appeal Act 1968.[87] The court may not alter its decision after it has been entered

---

[78] Criminal Appeal Act 1968, s. 23 (4).

[79] Criminal Appeal Rules 1968, r. 9, *R.* v. *Stafford* [1972] 1 W.L.R. 1649 (the " ends of justice " will usually require a private sitting), and see p. 107.

[80] *Ibid.* Sched. 1, Form 14, Appeal Form A.

[81] *Ibid.*, r. 10.

[82] *R.* v. *Medway* [1976] 2 W.L.R. 528.

[83] *R.* v. *Munisamy* [1975] 1 All E.R. 910; *R.* v. *Peters* (1973) 58 Cr.App.R. 328.

[84] *R.* v. *de Courcy* [1964] 1 W.L.R. 1245.

[85] *R.* v. *Jeffries* [1969] 1 Q.B. 120.

[86] *R.* v. *Rowe* [1955] 1 Q.B. at p. 573.

[87] See p. 265.

in the court record [88] and, once an application for leave to appeal has been finally rejected,[89] the court has no jurisdiction to entertain a renewed application.[90]

If the appeal fails entirely, it is dismissed by the court and the appellant serves his sentence in the ordinary way. The court may allow the appeal wholly or in part or vary the effect of the conviction, as described in the following paragraphs; the effect of making an appeal against sentence, the costs and other matters are considered in Section 4.[91]

(c) *Quashing the conviction*

If an appeal against conviction is allowed the court must quash the conviction; the order operates as a direction to the court of trial to enter a judgment and verdict of acquittal on the record.[92] If the appellant was convicted on one indictment of more than one offence, the court may allow an appeal against one or more of the convictions, the appellant remaining convicted on the rest. The court may pass a new sentence on the remaining convictions but it must not be of greater severity than the sentence taken as a whole which was passed on the convictions at trial.[93]

(d) *Finding of insanity*

Where the Court of Appeal considers that the proper verdict should not have been " guilty " but should have been " not guilty by reason of insanity," or where it considers that there should have been a finding of disability and that there should not have been an acquittal, it must make an order that the appellant be admitted to a specified hospital.[94]

(e) *Alternative conviction*

The Court of Appeal may, where the appellant has been convicted of an offence but where the jury could have returned a verdict of guilty of some other offence,[95] substitute a conviction of that other offence in place of the conviction returned by the jury. This is only possible where it appears to the court that, on the finding of the jury, the jury must have been satisfied of facts which proved him

[88] See p. 263.
[89] See p. 262.
[90] *R.* v. *Ashdown* [1974] 1 W.L.R. 270; the only means of re-opening the case is for the Home Secretary to refer it.
[91] See p. 273.
[92] Criminal Appeal Act 1968, s. 2 (2) and (3). This enables the accused to plead it in bar if re-indicted; see p. 159.
[93] *Ibid.* s. 4, and see p. 276.
[94] *Ibid.* s. 6 and Sched. 1, and see pp. 277 and 278.
[95] See Criminal Law Act 1967, s. 6, pp. 213–214.

guilty of the substituted offence.[96] This necessarily precludes the court from substituting the more serious offence which was charged in the indictment when the jury has convicted of an alternative and lesser offence; for instance, if on a charge of unlawful intercourse the jury returned a verdict of guilty of indecent assault, it would not be possible for the Court of Appeal to substitute a verdict of guilty of unlawful intercourse because the finding of the jury clearly reveals that they were not satisfied that intercourse took place.[97] The court passes sentence for the substituted offence but it must not be of greater severity than the sentence passed on the conviction at trial.[98] This applies in cases where the appellant was charged on counts for alternative offences in the indictment [99]; if convicted on both counts, the court would quash the conviction which is less clearly supported by the evidence.

(f) *Retrial*

Where the Court of Appeal has allowed an appeal because of fresh evidence received or available under section 23 of the Criminal Appeal Act 1968 [1] and it considers that the interests of justice require it,[2] the court may order that the appellant be retried for the offence of which he was convicted and against which his appeal is made, or for any offence of which he could have been convicted whether as an alternative by law [3] or on an alternative count in the indictment.[4]

An indictment for this purpose is preferred [5] by direction of the Court of Appeal.[6] The original conviction is not quashed but suspended, for clearly the subsequent indictment would otherwise be barred.[7] The court, or a single judge [8] of the court, makes the necessary orders for detention of the appellant or for his release on bail, and for the retention of the documents and exhibits. If the appellant was subject to a hospital order, it continues until he is retried.

---

[96] Criminal Appeal Act 1968, s. 3; *R.* v. *Deacon* [1973] 1 W.L.R. 696.

[97] *Cf. R.* v. *McCormack* [1969] 2 Q.B. 442 (see p. 213).

[98] Criminal Appeal Act 1968, s. 3 (2), and see p. 276.

[99] See p. 136.

[1] See p. 269.

[2] Lapse of time may make it wrong to order a retrial after receiving fresh evidence: *R.* v. *Saunders* (1973) 58 Cr.App.R. 248.

[3] See p. 213.

[4] Criminal Appeal Act 1968, s. 7.

[5] See p. 145.

[6] *Ibid.* s. 8.

[7] *Ibid.* s. 2 (3).

[8] *Ibid.* s. 31 (2).

At the fresh trial the depositions and written statements [9] of witnesses at the original trial are no longer admissible, but the transcript of the evidence they gave on oath may be read as evidence with the leave of the judge and the agreement of the prosecution and defence, or on the judge's finding that the witness is unobtainable through death, illness or disappearance.[10]

The sentence of the court on retrial and conviction must not be of greater severity than that passed on the original conviction.[11]

The power of the Court of Appeal to order a new trial by the writ of *venire de novo* was not abolished by the Criminal Appeal Act 1968. It used to be used where the trial was so irregular that it was a nullity. It might therefore be used where a plea of guilty was accepted, although not freely made, and the appellant has no right of appeal under section 2 (1).[12]

4. Effects of the appeal

Pending the determination of an appeal against sentence, an order for compensation or restitution of property under section 28 of the Theft Act 1968 is suspended.[13] A fine would not be enforced until the appeal had been determined. A disqualification from driving may be suspended pending an appeal against the order.[14]

If the appellant is in custody, a special provision applies to the period spent pending determination of the appeal. Under section 29 (1) of the Criminal Appeal Act 1968, the period shall be reckoned as part of any sentence to which the appellant is for the time being subject, unless the Court of Appeal gives a direction to the contrary. (This applies equally to time spent in custody pending determination of an application for leave to appeal.) [15] The court must state its reasons for giving a contrary direction and it cannot give it at all if leave to appeal or a certificate of the trial judge has already been granted in the case,[16] or if the Home Secretary referred the case for appeal.[17]

The Lord Chief Justice in March 1970 made a statement of policy of the court that the judge dealing with an application for leave "has

---

[9] See pp. 107 and 110.
[10] Criminal Appeal Act 1968, Sched. 2, para. 1.
[11] *Ibid.* Sched. 2, para. 2, and see p. 276.
[12] See p. 268.
[13] Powers of Criminal Courts Act 1973, s. 36 (1), Criminal Appeal Act 1968, s. 30, and Criminal Justice Act 1972, s. 6; see also p. 252.
[14] Road Traffic Act 1972, s. 94 (2).
[15] Criminal Appeal Act 1968, s. 31 (2).
[16] See p. 262.
[17] See Criminal Appeal Act 1968, s. 17, p. 265.

no reason to refrain from directing that time shall be lost " where " an application which is unarguable is made notwithstanding that advice on appeal is available . . . if he thinks it right so to exercise his discretion in all the circumstances of the case." This is a policy to be considered in the light of the general availability of legal aid for appeals.[18]

Costs

The Court of Appeal may, and normally will,[19] order costs in favour of an appellant whose appeal against conviction [20] is allowed, for the appeal and for his defence at committal and at trial.[21] Costs may also be granted where his appeal is not successful on all the convictions appealed against. If he is not in custody, he may have the expenses of his attendance at court ordered out of central funds.[22] If his appeal is dismissed, the court may order him to pay costs to a person named in the order.[23] Witnesses' expenses may be ordered out of central funds.[24] Where retrial is ordered and on retrial the appellant is acquitted, costs for the original trial and for the appeal, in addition to the costs of the retrial, may be ordered out of central funds by the Crown Court when dealing with the retrial.[25] The Court of Appeal may order costs in favour of the prosecution to be paid out of central funds or, if it dismisses the appeal or application, to be paid by the appellant.[26]

C. Appeal Against Sentence and Other Matters

1. Sentence

Sentence is defined in the Criminal Appeal Act 1968 to include " any order made by a court when dealing with an offender (including a hospital order . . .) and . . . a recommendation for deport-

[18] See p. 401. If the grounds of appeal have been settled by counsel, the single judge is unlikely to direct loss of time, but such a direction might be proper where further application is made to a two-judge or full court. Even then, it would be improper if the appellant had been misled into thinking he was not at risk: *R.* v. *Howitt* [1975] Crim.L.R. 588.

[19] Practice Direction [1973] 1 W.L.R. 718; *R.* v. *Arron* [1973] 1 W.L.R. 1238.

[20] There is no power to order costs if the appeal is against sentence only: Costs in Criminal Cases Act 1973, s. 7 (1).

[21] *Ibid.* s. 7 (1)–(3).

[22] *Ibid.* s. 8 (2).

[23] *Ibid.* s. 9. The single judge may make orders under this section and s. 7: Criminal Appeal Act 1968, s. 31 (2), as amended by the 1973 Act, Sched. 1.

[24] Costs in Criminal Cases Act 1973, s. 8 (1).

[25] *i.e.*, under the Costs in Criminal Cases Act 1973, s. 3; see p. 248.

[26] *Ibid.* ss. 7 (2) and 9 (1), respectively.

ation." [27] If two or more sentences are passed in the same proceedings, they are treated as one for the purposes of appeal.[28]

Unless given a sentence fixed by law, a person who is convicted on indictment may appeal to the Court of Appeal against the sentence passed on him at conviction or in subsequent proceedings [29] (*e.g.* where a suspended sentence is later made effective).[30] The sentence must be imposed on the appellant for an offence of which he has been convicted: there is no right of appeal against an order made in respect of another person which adversely affects the appellant.[31] If other offences have been taken into consideration on conviction, the sentence is generally treated as a whole for the offence of which the appellant has been convicted.[32] If a compensation or restitution order has been made in respect of an offence taken into consideration,[33] the order ceases to have effect if a successful appeal against conviction is made, and the appellant may appeal against the order " as if it were part of the sentence imposed in respect of the offence " of which he was convicted.[34]

There is no right of appeal against a probation order or conditional discharge as a " sentence "; the accused can only appeal against the conviction.[35] An appeal may be heard, however, when a probation order or discharge was not validly made.[36] There is no appeal against the making of a criminal bankruptcy order.[37] If an appeal against conviction is successful, the Court of Appeal must

[27] Criminal Appeal Act 1968, s. 50 (1). This includes all the punishments and orders described in Chap. 9, including disqualification from driving, an order to pay compensation (*R.* v. *Parker* [1970] 2 All E.R. 458) and costs awarded against the accused (*R.* v. *Hayden* [1975] 1 W.L.R. 852). A prosecutor ordered to pay costs under s. 4 or s. 12 of the Costs in Criminal Cases Act 1973 appears to have no right of appeal, because the order is not made on his conviction of an offence. If costs are awarded in his favour out of central funds, he may appeal under S.I. 1977 No. 248 (see p. 249).

[28] Criminal Appeal Act 1968, s. 11 (2). As to variation of sentence, see Courts Act 1971, s. 11, p. 221.

[29] Criminal Appeal Act 1968, s. 9.

[30] See p. 228.

[31] *R.* v. *Ioannou* [1975] 1 W.L.R. 1297 (the owner of premises had no right of appeal against an order, made on conviction of the licensee, prohibiting the use of the premises for the sale of liquor).

[32] See p. 220.

[33] Theft Act 1968, s. 28, as supplemented by the Criminal Justice Act 1972, s. 6 (3), and the Powers of Criminal Courts Act 1973, s. 35; see pp. 251 and 252.

[34] Criminal Justice Act 1972, s. 6 (4), and Powers of Criminal Courts 1973, s. 36 (3). The words from these sections would enable an appellant to appeal against such an order without appealing against any other part of the sentence.

[35] Powers of Criminal Courts Act 1973, s. 13 (1) and (4) (as to which, see p. 241); *R.* v. *Tucker* [1974] 1 W.L.R. 615.

[36] *R.* v. *Marquis* [1974] 1 W.L.R. 1087.

[37] Powers of Criminal Courts Act 1973, s. 40 (1).

rescind the order; if it is successful in part, or an alternative verdict is substituted, the court must rescind the order, if it could no longer be made on the basis of the surviving convictions, or amend the terms of the order to fit the new conviction if it could still be made in respect of the new and surviving convictions.[38]

The leave of the Court of Appeal is always necessary to make an appeal against sentence.[39] The application for leave is made in the same way as an application for leave to appeal against conviction and the procedural provisions relating to the appeal are in all ways the same [40] except, of course, the effects of the appeal. If the court substitutes an alternative conviction or dismisses part of the appeal, but allows it on another part, the court may vary the sentence of the court of trial. In the case of an alternative conviction, the sentence on the conviction of the offence being replaced is considered alone, whereas if the appeal is allowed in part, the sentence passed on all the convictions is considered as a whole. In neither case must the sentence passed by the Court of Appeal be more severe than the former sentence, or total of sentences.[41]

If it considers that the appellant should be sentenced differently, the court may quash the original sentence and substitute such order as it thinks appropriate, provided the issuing of that order would have been within the powers of the court below. This is subject to the important proviso that on changing the sentence, the appellant must not be more severely dealt with by the Court of Appeal, taking the case as a whole, than he was dealt with by the court below.[42]

This proviso is subject to limitations but, except for the third exception below, they are not true limitations for they are based on the distinction between punishments and other orders mentioned in Chapter 9, " severity " relating to punishments. First, the Court of Appeal has power to add a recommendation for deportation provided " the court from which the appeal lies had power to make such a recommendation." [43] Secondly, a remedial sentence may be passed

[38] Powers of Criminal Cases Act 1973, s. 40 (2) and (3). [39] *Ibid.* s. 11 (1).

[40] See pp. 262–265, and see Criminal Appeal Rules 1968, Sched. 1, Forms 2 and 3, Appeal Forms N and G.

[41] Criminal Appeal Act 1968, ss. 3 (2) and 4 (3); see pp. 271 and 273. In *R.* v. *Craig* [1967] 1 W.L.R. 645, for instance, an appellant was sentenced on two counts of an indictment to a total of five years' imprisonment; on appeal the Court of Appeal quashed one of the convictions, leaving a sentence of three years' imprisonment on the other. It altered the sentence of three years' to a sentence of five years' imprisonment.

[42] *Ibid.* s. 11 (3). This includes, for instance, making a term of imprisonment into an extended sentence, for more " severe " conditions apply to an extended sentence: *R.* v. *Dolan* [1971] Crim.L.R. 297.

[43] *Ibid.* s. 50 (2); *R.* v. *Kruger* [1973] Crim.L.R. 133.

by the Court of Appeal to replace a punitive sentence; in *R.* v. *Bennett* [44] a sentence of three years' imprisonment was replaced by an indefinite hospital order. This was based on the remedial nature of the order; the same principle would apply, for instance, to the substitution of a probation order for a fine. Thirdly, the Court of Appeal may bring a suspended sentence into effect [45] when the court below, in dealing with a subsequent offence, has made no order on the suspended sentence, either because it passed on the offender a sentence of borstal which the Court of Appeal has quashed,[46] or because it declined to make an order.[47]

Sentence of death

Special provisions are made by Schedule 4 of the Criminal Appeal Act 1968 for appeals in capital cases. Execution cannot take place until the period for appealing has elapsed or the appeal has been determined, but the accused cannot apply for extra time. If, in the unlikely event of an accused being found not guilty of treason by reason of insanity and the verdict is replaced on appeal by a conviction,[48] the Court of Appeal must sentence him to life imprisonment, not to death.[49]

2. Insanity

Although on a finding of insanity the accused is acquitted,[50] he may appeal against the verdict for it is adverse. As on an appeal against conviction, he may appeal on a question of law alone without leave, but he needs leave or the certificate of the trial judge that it is a case fit for appeal if it involves a question of fact or of mixed fact and law.[51] The grounds of appeal are effectively the same as under section 2 (1) of the 1968 Act.[52]

From a point of view of procedure, it will be remembered than an appellant who is in custody and appealing against a verdict of not guilty by reason of insanity must apply for leave to be present at the hearing of the appeal [53] and that a hospital order passed by the court

44 [1968] 1 W.L.R. 988; see also *R.* v. *Marsden* [1968] 1 W.L.R. 785.
45 Criminal Appeal Act 1968, s. 11 (4).
46 Powers of Criminal Courts Act 1973, s. 22 (5); see p. 232.
47 *Ibid.* s. 23 (1); see p. 229.
48 See Criminal Appeal Act 1968, s. 13 (4), p. 278.
49 *Ibid.* s. 13 (5).
50 See p. 211.
51 Criminal Appeal Act 1968, s. 12.
52 Criminal Appeal Act 1968, s. 13 (1) and (2), the latter subsection containing what is the proviso to s. 2 (1) enabling the Court to uphold the verdict where there has been no miscarriage of justice. As to s. 2 (1), see pp. 266–268.
53 See *ibid.* s. 22, p. 264.

below endures until retrial, if retrial is ordered by the Court of Appeal.[54] Otherwise the procedure is the same as on an appeal against conviction.[55]

The Court of Appeal has power to uphold the verdict of not guilty by reason of insanity if it finds that the proper verdict should have been that the appellant was guilty of some other offence, but that the grounds which found the appeal do not concern the question of insanity.[56]

If the court allows the appeal, it either substitutes a verdict of acquittal or, if it finds that the jury's finding of insanity ought not to stand but ought to be replaced by a verdict of guilty of the offence charged or of an alternative offence available to the jury, it substitutes a verdict of guilty of that offence.[57] It may then pass any sentence and make any order which the court below could have passed or made.[58] Save that it cannot impose the death penalty,[59] no limitation on severity of sentence applies.

If the court dismisses the appeal generally or under section 13 (3),[60] the hospital order made by the court below continues in effect. If the court allows the appeal but substitutes a verdict of guilty, it may itself make a hospital order under the provisions as to sentence described above. It may still order the appellant's detention, however, where it substitutes a verdict of acquittal, provided it is of the opinion that the appellant is suffering from a mental disorder which warrants his detention in hospital under observation "for at least a limited period" and that the interests of his own health and safety and the protection of others require his detention.[61] The order for detention in hospital is treated in the same way as a hospital order made at trial.[62]

3. Disability

Where, under section 4 of the Criminal Procedure (Insanity) Act 1964, the jury has found the accused to be suffering from such a disability that he is not fit to be tried, the accused may appeal against the jury's finding. Again, he may appeal without leave on law alone, but

---

[54] See Criminal Appeal Act 1968, s. 8, p. 272.
[55] See pp. 262–274.
[56] Criminal Appeal Act 1968, s. 13 (3).
[57] *Ibid.* s. 13 (4) (*a*).
[58] Criminal Appeal Act 1968, s. 13 (4) (*a*) (ii).
[59] See *ibid.* s. 13 (5), p. 277.
[60] See above.
[61] *Ibid.* s. 14 (2).
[62] *Ibid.* Sched. 1. As to hospital orders, see p. 234.

he requires leave of the Court of Appeal or a certificate of the trial judge if the appeal involves a question of fact [63] and, again, the grounds of the appeal are an unsafe and unsatisfactory verdict, a wrong decision of law or a material irregularity, subject to the appeal being dismissed if no miscarriage of justice has actually occurred.[64] Where consideration of the accused's fitness was postponed until after arraignment,[65] the Court of Appeal may allow the appeal, even though the finding of disability was a proper one, if it considers that the appellant should have been acquitted, as, for instance, where the prosecution failed to make out its case.[66] A verdict of acquittal is then recorded. (A verdict of not guilty by reason of insanity may not be made.)

If the appeal is allowed otherwise than by entry of acquittal, the appellant is returned to the court below to stand trial on the existing indictment. The Court of Appeal may grant him bail, keep him in ordinary custody or continue the hospital order which was made when he was found to be unfit to be tried.[67]

4. Special verdict

If in an exceptional case the jury returns a special verdict, *i.e.* where it has made specific findings of fact on the judge's questions,[68] and the Court of Appeal finds that the conclusions drawn by the judge were wrong, the court may order the conclusion that appears to it to be correct to be recorded and pass sentence accordingly.[69]

D. Attorney-General's Reference on a Point of Law

After a person is acquitted of an offence, the Attorney-General may, under section 36 of the Criminal Justice Act 1972, refer a point of law arising out of that acquittal to the Court of Appeal to obtain its opinion. The reference has no effect whatever upon the trial or acquittal. The person acquitted may appear or be represented in the Court of Appeal, if he so wishes, to argue the point. No mention must be

---

63 *Ibid.* s. 15. As to the Criminal Procedure (Insanity) Act 1964, s. 4, see p. 171.

64 Criminal Appeal Act 1968, s. 16 (1). *Cf. ibid.* s. 2 (1), p. 266.

65 See Criminal Procedure (Insanity) Act 1964, s. 4 (2), p. 171.

66 Criminal Appeal Act 1968, s. 16 (2). As to failure to make out a case, see p. 202.

67 *Ibid.* s. 16 (3) and Sched. 3, which applies the provisions of the Mental Health Act 1959, Part V, to these cases.

68 See p. 211.

69 Criminal Appeal Act 1968, s. 5; the sentence is only limited to " such sentence . . . as may be authorised by law."

made, either in the written reference or at the proceedings, of the proper name or identity of the respondent unless he consents.[70]

The written reference specifies the point of law, summarises the arguments intended to be put to the court and specifies the authorities to be cited. Notice is served on the respondent inviting him to state whether he wishes to present any argument; 28 days must be given unless he previously replies in the negative.[71]

After the Court of Appeal has given its opinion, it may on its own motion, or on application by the Attorney-General or the respondent, refer the point to the House of Lords.[72] The respondent is entitled to have his costs in the Court of Appeal and the House of Lords, if the point is referred to it, paid out of central funds.[73]

E. Appeal to the House of Lords

Appeal lies to the House of Lords from the decision made on an appeal to the Criminal Division of the Court of Appeal. It lies at the instance of the defendant or of the prosecution, and leave of the Court of Appeal or of the House of Lords is always necessary. Before leave can be applied for, however, the Court of Appeal must certify that a point of law of general public importance is involved.[74] Furthermore, the Court of Appeal or the House of Lords, when considering whether to grant leave, must decide whether the point of law is one which ought to be considered by the House of Lords.[75]

1. Procedure

A person wishing to appeal to the House of Lords may ask for the certificate of the Court of Appeal at the hearing of the appeal or with his application to the court for leave. The application to the Court of Appeal for leave must be made to a full court.[76] It must be made orally at the hearing or within 14 days of the decision of the Court of Appeal against which the applicant wishes to appeal, but the court may, on application by the defendant, extend that time.[77]

---

[70] Criminal Justice Act 1972, s. 66 (6) (*b*), and Criminal Appeal (Reference of Points of Law) Rules 1973 (S.I. 1973 No. 1114), rr. 3 (1) and 6.

[71] *Ibid.* rr. 3 and 4.

[72] Criminal Justice Act 1972, s. 37 (4).

[73] *Ibid.* s. 37 (5).

[74] It is not the practice of the Court of Appeal to give reasons for a refusal to certify: *R.* v. *Cooper* (1975) 61 Cr.App.R. 215.

[75] Criminal Appeal Act 1968, s. 33.

[76] Administration of Justice Act 1970, s. 9 (2). See also *R.* v. *Mealey and Sheridan* [1975] Crim.L.R. 154.

[77] Criminal Appeal Act 1968, s. 34; and see Criminal Appeal Rules 1968, r. 23 and Sched. 1, Form 17.

Under section 44 of the Criminal Appeal Act 1968 a single judge may hear the application for extra time, and, on his refusing it, the applicant is entitled to have it heard by a two-judge or full court.[78] The same provision applies to applications for bail [79] or for leave to an applicant to be present at any proceedings preliminary or incidental to the appeal.[80]

An application for leave can only be made to the House of Lords after refusal of leave by the Court of Appeal. Such an application must be made within 14 days of the Court of Appeal's refusal though the House of Lords may extend the time on the application of the defendant.[81]

The application is heard by the Appeals Committee of the House of Lords, consisting of three Law Lords.[82] Counsel may appear before the Committee to argue about the application. The appeal is initiated by a petition for leave [83]; five copies of every document must be sent to the Judicial Office which administers appeals to the House of Lords. It is possible to petition for extra time if the parties' cases are not ready for hearing in time (usually six weeks) after leave has been granted.[84] When prepared, the cases are lodged at the Judicial Office, this time in eight copies.[85] An appeal may be withdrawn either if it has not been set down for hearing or if the House grants leave to withdraw on a petition to that effect.[86]

An application for leave to appeal by the prosecutor cannot be made later than 14 days from the decision of the Court of Appeal.[87] If he applies for and is granted leave immediately or if he gives notice that he intends to apply for leave, the defendant may and, in some cases, should [88] be ordered by the Court of Appeal to be

---

[78] Criminal Appeal Act 1968, s. 44, and Administration of Justice Act 1970, s. 9 (2).

[79] This may be granted under the Criminal Appeal Act 1968, s. 36, and recognisances may be ordered: Criminal Appeal Rules 1968, r. 23 and Sched. 1, Forms 18 and 19.

[80] A person who is detained pending appeal must ask the Court of Appeal or the House of Lords for leave to be present at preliminary proceedings and at the appeal unless the House of Lords by order authorises him to be present: Criminal Appeal Act 1968, s. 38. The section is silent on the presence of an appellant who is released on bail or otherwise.

[81] Criminal Appeal Act 1968, s. 34.

[82] Criminal Appeal Act 1968, s. 35 (2). The procedure is laid down in detail in House of Lords Directions as to Procedure 1975 and in the *Supreme Court Practice* 1976.

[83] House of Lords Appeals Directions as to Procedure, App. B, as amended by Practice Directions of May 18 and 20, 1976.

[84] *Ibid.* Direction No. 18.

[85] *Ibid.* Direction No. 19. Direction No. 11 was revised and set out in [1969] 2 All E.R. 875; it deals with the preparation of the case.

[86] *Ibid.* Direction No. 29.

[87] Criminal Appeal Act 1968, s. 34 (1).

[88] See dicta of Lord Diplock in *D.P.P.* v. *Merriman* [1973] A.C. 584 at p. 606.

detained pending appeal to the House of Lords provided he would have been detained but for the decision in his favour of the Court of Appeal. Alternatively it may grant him bail.[89]

2. The hearing

At least three Law Lords must sit on an appeal,[90] but five is a common number. Although counsel for each side appear before them for oral argument, they must, before the hearing, submit their "cases,"[91] *i.e.* the statement in writing of their contentions, which are sent to the House of Lords with the other relevant documents in the case (transcript of the trial, transcript of the Court of Appeal hearing, etc.).[92]

The decision of the House of Lords is not delivered immediately but the judgment is reserved, written down and given to counsel for the parties in draft before the House of Lords holds the final hearing in which the result of the appeal is announced.[93] Each Law Lord may deliver a judgment whether he concurs in or dissents to the majority judgment.

The House of Lords may exercise any of the powers of the Court of Appeal in disposing of the appeal, or they may remit the case to the Court of Appeal.[94] They may consider any matter which appears to be worthy of consideration even though that matter was not certified by the Court of Appeal as a point of law of general public importance.[95]

3. Ancillary matters

A restitution or compensation order[96] is suspended until the time for applying for leave has elapsed, until refusal of an application for leave or until determination of the appeal.[97] Costs may be ordered in the prosecutor's or the defendant's favour when an application for leave to appeal is made or where an appeal to the House of Lords is heard. They are ordered out of central funds and can be

---

[89] Criminal Appeal Act 1968, s. 37. If the order of detention involved hospital internment, its continuation pending the appeal is ordered and the Mental Health Act 1959 applies, as to which see pp. 234 and 277. Any other detention order expires when it would have expired had it run its course or when the appeal is decided in the defendant's favour.

[90] Criminal Appeal Act 1968, s. 35 (1).

[91] Directions as to Procedure No. 14.

[92] *Ibid.* Direction No. 15.

[93] *Ibid.* Directions Nos. 36 and 37.

[94] Criminal Appeal Act 1968, s. 35 (3); see also Section C, p. 274.

[95] *Att.-Gen. for Northern Ireland* v. *Gallagher* [1964] A.C. 349 at pp. 364–368.

[96] See Theft Act 1968, s. 28, p. 252, and Powers of Criminal Courts Act 1973, s. 36, p. 251.

[97] Criminal Appeal Act 1968, s. 42.

ordered to cover all the proceedings at committal, trial, before the Court of Appeal and before the House of Lords.[98] The defendant may be ordered to pay the prosecution's costs in the discretion of the Court of Appeal or the House of Lords if his application for leave to appeal is unsuccessful.[99] As to legal aid in the House of Lords, see page 401.

F. Drafting Grounds of Appeal

Unlike indictments, there are no special rules for drafting grounds of appeal. It is quite usual for the defendant himself to do it. The statement of the grounds should be simple and clear, quoting, where necessary and where available, the words used at trial to which the defendant takes objection. They should identify the particular matters to be considered; if a general formula is used such as " the verdict was unsafe or unsatisfactory " or " the sentence was too severe," the Registrar may return the forms and require amplification of the grounds.[1] The point of the appeal should be stated if it is on law but it is unnecessary to spell it out at length; it should be clear enough for the Registrar to be able to see whether it is on law only, for in that event it will proceed directly to the appeal and the prosecution must be notified as the Crown is entitled to be represented at the appeal.[2]

Grounds of appeal settled by counsel are set out on a separate form [3] and are sent to the Registrar of Criminal Appeals with the notice of appeal. Where counsel is unable to settle adequate grounds of appeal, a notice of application for leave to appeal should be sent to the Registrar accompanied by a note indicating what the provisional grounds of appeal are and the further information required (*e.g.* the transcript or parts of it) to settle detailed grounds. When the grounds are perfected, they are sent to the Registrar. They must be received before the hearing of the application, or appeal if no application for leave is necessary. Where a transcript or documents have been obtained, they should be referred to accurately, naming the page number or exhibit number as appropriate in the grounds of appeal.

The short form of grounds of appeal which was illustrated in the

---

[98] Costs in Criminal Cases Act 1973, s. 10.
[99] *Ibid.* s. 11 (1).
[1] See " Preparation for Proceedings " (footnote 9, p. 261), para. 5.
[2] *R.* v. *Upton* (*Practice Note*) [1973] 3 All E.R. 318.
[3] Criminal Appeal Rules 1968, Sched. 1, Form 3 (Appeal Form G).

previous edition of this book is no longer acceptable except as provisional grounds. The perfected grounds should explain the point of the appeal, giving as much information of the circumstances as is necessary for the judge to decide whether there is an arguable case. Accordingly, no more than a simple illustration can be included in a book of this size.

Example

The applicant and a co-accused, Bert Beamish, were tried jointly on this indictment, charged with burglary. After arrest and under caution, the co-accused made a statement to the police to the effect that he had not committed the offence but that he had heard that the applicant had been involved in it (see transcript of the trial, p. 14).

The applicant applied before arraignment to be tried separately from the co-accused. The learned judge rejected the applicant's contention that the admission of the co-accused's statement would prejudice the applicant in a way which could not be cured by directing the jury to disregard that evidence in relation to the applicant, and declined to order separate trials (see transcript, p. 5).

The co-accused did not give evidence at the trial but made a statement from the dock in which he repeated the substance of the statement he had made to the police (see transcript, p. 37).

The learned judge directed the jury to disregard as much of the co-accused's statements as implicated the applicant (see transcript, p. 39).

The applicant will contend that:

(a) the learned judge, in order to secure the fair trial of the applicant, should have ordered separate trials of the applicant and the co-accused;

(b) in view of the prejudicial nature of the co-accused's statements and the want of opportunity to examine the co-accused, the fair trial of the applicant was prejudiced;

(c) the learned judge failed to direct the jury that the co-accused's statement from the dock was not evidence against the applicant; and

(d) in all the circumstances of the case, the verdict of guilty against the applicant is unsafe and unsatisfactory.

The following are some practical details affecting the making of an appeal, drawn from " Preparation for Proceedings in the Court of Appeal, Criminal Division," [4] which help to illustrate the duties of an appellant's legal representatives at this stage.

1. Counsel should be briefed to advise on appeal at the conclusion of the trial in the event of conviction and a conference with the defendant should, if possible, be arranged then.
2. Counsel must not assume responsibility for grounds of appeal unless they are reasonable (*i.e.* afford some real chance of success) [5] nor unless he is prepared to support them by oral argument.
3. Where advice against appeal is given after provisional grounds have been sent with the notice of application for leave to the Registrar, counsel should draw up his advice in a further written opinion for transmission to the appellant, warning him that, if he proceeds with the appeal, he will be doing so without the benefit of grounds settled by counsel.
4. Where fresh evidence may be called on appeal, counsel should give a written opinion on it to the solicitor; the solicitor may then obtain statements or affidavits for further advice by counsel or, if the case warrants it, for the settling of final grounds of appeal.
5. Where the prospective appellant is not legally represented, the Registrar may, on application, assign a solicitor for advice and assistance, but he must already have received the notice of application.
6. The taxation of costs in the Court of Appeal takes into account work actually and reasonably done.[6]

---

[4] See footnote 9, p. 261.
[5] See *e.g.* *R.* v. *Morsom* (1976) 62 Cr.App.R. 236.
[6] See Practice Note [1974] C.L.Y. 2982; Practice Direction [1976] 8 C.L. 36.

PART THREE

SUMMARY TRIAL

CHAPTER 11

MAGISTRATES' COURTS

SUMMARY trial means trial by a court without a jury. Apart from trial for contempt of court,[1] the only court which tries criminal offences summarily is the magistrates' court. As a court of trial it may be sitting in one of three capacities: (i) as a court of petty sessions for the trial of adults for criminal offences; (ii) as a juvenile court for deciding issues in relation to children and young persons below the age of seventeen; or (iii) as a domestic, civil or administrative court for trial of matrimonial cases, affiliation claims, small civil claims or administrative matters such as licensing. In this Part the first capacity only is considered; the second is considered in Chapter 15 [2]; the third is outside the scope of this book, but readers will find a short section on magistrates' non-criminal jurisdiction on page 300.

A. CONSTITUTION

The magistrates' court consists of magistrates, an office which has already been described in Chapter 3.[3] A single stipendiary magistrate or at least two lay justices must sit.[4] They must sit throughout the hearing, though if one justice leaves during it and takes no more part in it the others may continue provided that they are sufficient in number to constitute a proper court.[5] Not more than seven justices may sit.[6]

A justice who, in the course of hearing an application by the accused for bail, has been informed of his previous convictions, may not sit at the trial. This disqualification applies whether the trial commenced as a trial or arose from committal proceedings.[7]

The court is only fully empowered when sitting in the usual place, the petty sessional court-house; if they sit in an " occasional

---

[1] See p. 392.

[2] See p. 361.

[3] See p. 48.

[4] Magistrates' Courts Act 1952, s. 98 (1), subject to some statutory exceptions such as the Vagrancy Act 1824, ss. 3 and 4 (being idle and disorderly or a rogue and a vagabond), when a single justice may sit but his powers are limited to imprisonment for 14 days and ordering payment of £1: *ibid.* s. 98 (5).

[5] *Ibid.* s. 98 (6).

[6] Justices of the Peace (Size and Chairmanship of the Bench) Rules 1964, r. 2 (2).

[7] Criminal Justice Act 1967, s. 19. It may start as committal proceedings under the Magistrates' Courts Act 1952, ss. 18 or 19; see pp. 295–298.

court-house," *i.e.* a place temporarily designated as such, their powers of sentencing are limited to imposing 14 days' imprisonment and ordering payment of £1.[8]

A petty sessions area is the county (if not sub-divided)[9] or the petty sessional division of a county.[10] A petty sessional division is an area designated by the Home Secretary on the application of the local magistrates' court committee to be administered as a separate part of the county.[11] Magistrates are appointed for the whole county, however, for that is the commission area, and where petty sessional divisions apply they are not confined to one division.

The magistrates' court clerk, or " clerk to the justices," plays an important part in the proceedings for, apart from dealing with the administration of the court in serving summonses, arranging hearings, collecting fines, etc., he also advises lay justices on the law, practice and procedure to be applied, either on their request or on his own initiative when he thinks it necessary.[12] His participation in the proceedings was considered at length in *Simms* v. *Moore*.[13] The clerk must not, however, take any part in the adjudication of the case. It would be wrong, for instance, for him to retire with the justices when they consider the facts of the case,[14] or to give them any argument on the facts, though they may ask him to give them advice on particular matters at that stage.[15]

B. General Jurisdiction

The magistrates' court is an entirely statutory creation; the justices have no powers except those specifically given to them by Act of Parliament.

The general and local jurisdiction of the magistrates' court has been considered in Chapters 2 and 4.[16] The initiation of all criminal proceedings is the same, *i.e.* they are started by information being laid

---

8 Magistrates' Courts Act 1952, s. 98 (5).

9 *i.e.* the commission area, as to which see pp. 16 and 51.

10 Justices of the Peace Act 1949, s. 44.

11 *Ibid.* s. 18.

12 Justices of the Peace Act 1968, s. 5 (3). He must be qualified under s. 20 of the 1949 Act and he may have been subject to courses of instruction under s. 62 (1) of the Criminal Justice Act 1972.

13 See p. 313.

14 *R.* v. *Southampton Justices, ex p. Atherton* [1974] Crim.L.R. 108.

15 *R.* v. *East Kerrier JJ., ex p. Mundy* [1952] 2 Q.B. 719. Suspicion of prejudice on the part of the clerk is not necessarily fatal to a conviction, however: *R.* v. *Uxbridge Justices, ex p. Burbridge, The Times*, June 21, 1972.

16 See pp. 16 and 51.

and a summons or warrant being issued [17] or by bringing a summarily arrested person before the court.[18] In the case of summary offences, however, the magistrates have no jurisdiction to issue process against a person only on the ground that he lives or is believed to live in the area. They cannot issue a summons at all in such a case, and if they issue a warrant of arrest it must direct that the arrestee be taken before the court having jurisdiction.[19] If a person has been arrested without a warrant and is brought before a magistrate, it will in most cases be for an indictable offence.[20] If it can be tried summarily, the magistrates may proceed to try it instead of hearing the charge as examining justices.[21] If the arrest was for a summary offence (*e.g.* being drunk and disorderly under section 91 (1) of the Criminal Justice Act 1967) and the arrestee is taken to a magistrates' court without jurisdiction to try the offence, he may be transferred to the competent court by remand.[22]

The jurisdiction for trial of offences is more limited than for examining charges prior to committal. The magistrates' court has jurisdiction to try offences committed within its commission area [23] and to try charges against a person brought before the court on a summons or warrant for trial jointly with, or in the same place as, another person who is charged.[24] Furthermore, it may try the charge of any summary offence against a person already being tried by the court.[25] An aider and abettor of a summary offence may be tried either by the court which is competent to try the principal offender or by a court which would have jurisdiction otherwise to try the aider and abettor.[26]

The magistrates have no jurisdiction to try disputes involving title to real property. Although at first sight this appears rather obscure, an issue of this sort could easily arise under the Theft Act 1968, s. 4, which defines " property " in relation to theft, or on a prosecution for poaching or criminal damage. However, where the offence is tried exclusively by magistrates' courts, such as the obstruc-

[17] See pp. 54–60.
[18] See p. 62.
[19] Magistrates' Courts Act 1952, s. 1 (2) proviso.
[20] See p. 62.
[21] See Magistrates' Courts Act 1952, s. 19, as amended by the Criminal Justice Administration Act 1962, s. 13, p. 297.
[22] See p. 67.
[23] Magistrates' Courts Act 1952, s. 2 (1), as extended by s. 3, as to which see p. 16.
[24] *Ibid.* s. 2 (2); see also s. 1 (2) (*b*), p. 51.
[25] Criminal Justice Act 1967, s. 28.
[26] Magistrates' Courts Act 1952, s. 35. Aiding and abetting an indictable offence which is being tried summarily is also triable summarily under s. 19 and Sched. 1, as to which see p. 297.

tion of highways,[27] the statute is treated as a mandatory direction to the magistrates to try the case, despite their lack of jurisdiction arising from the real property dispute involved.[28]

C. Criminal Jurisdiction and the Classification of Offences

Some flexibility is achieved in the trial and treatment of offenders by enabling indictable offences to be tried summarily and vice versa.[29] The magistrates' court has jurisdiction in four of the five classes of offence:

(1) offences which can only be tried summarily;
(2) summary offences which may be tried on indictment;
(3) offences which are by definition triable on indictment or summarily;
(4) indictable offences which may be tried summarily; and
(5) indictable offences which can only be tried on indictment.

1. Summary offences

Because summary trial in the magistrates' court is a creature of statute, summary offences consist only of those created expressly [30] as summary offences. Their number is vast but, in view of the second class of offence, below, only the most minor offences are tried exclusively by magistrates' courts.

2. Summary offences triable on indictment

All summary offences for which an adult accused may be sentenced to imprisonment for more than three months may be tried by jury at the instance of the accused. It is the *right* of the accused to claim trial by jury, provided he has reached the age of 17.[31] This class

[27] Highways Act 1959, s. 121, and see Magistrates' Courts Act 1952, s. 25, below.
[28] *R.* v. *Ogden* [1963] 1 W.L.R. 274.
[29] The James Committee's Report (Cmnd. 6323) recommended replacing the existing classification by a three-way division of offences into summary offences, indictable offences, and indictable offences triable summarily with the consent of the accused. It would require lowering the maximum penalty for certain offences and, in effect, re-introducing the concept of " petty " crimes (such as theft of less than £20 or criminal damage worth less than £100). Certain other offences (*e.g.* drinking and driving) would expressly be made triable only summarily. The Committee also recommended that the prosecution case should be revealed in advance, as in a trial on indictment.
[30] The statutory definition usually takes the indirect form: " A person who [commits specified acts] shall be guilty of an offence . . . and shall be liable on summary conviction to a fine not exceeding £x."
[31] Magistrates' Courts Act 1952, s. 25 (1), as amended by the Children and Young Persons Act 1969, s. 6 (2).

expressly excludes assault [32] and certain summary offences connected with prostitution.[33] The effect of this exclusion is to deprive the accused of his right to be tried by a jury but it does not preclude such trial at the instance of the prosecution, for all the relevant offences are " hybrid," *i.e.* are expressly triable on indictment or summarily.[34] The class is extended to cover certain summary offences which would not otherwise fall into the category.[35] It must be emphasised that the right avails only where the possible prison sentence *exceeds* three months, for many summary offences have a maximum of three months' imprisonment, such as careless driving [36] and food and drugs offences.[37]

To claim the right the accused must appear in person and claim trial by jury before he pleads to the charge, though his legal representative may actually pronounce his decision provided he is in court.[38] In all cases where it is open to the accused to do so, the court *must* explain to him the consequences of exercising the right before asking whether he wishes to be tried by jury; he must be told of his right before he is asked whether he pleads guilty.[39] If he chooses to " go for trial," the magistrates' court proceeds as if the offence were indictable, *i.e.* it hears the information as examining justices and commits the accused for trial.[40]

The concluding words of this section—" and the offence . . . shall . . . be deemed to be an indictable offence "—have led to some difficulty

---

[32] As common assault is punishable by a maximum of only two months' imprisonment (Offences against the Person Act 1861, s. 42), this exception applies to other assaults such as aggravated assault under s. 43 of the 1861 Act and assault on a policeman under the Police Act 1964, s. 51. The James Committee (above) recommended that these assaults with an additional element should be triable summarily only with the consent of the accused. The Criminal Law Revision Committee in its Working Paper on Offences against the Person (see p. 163) recommended that common assault should remain a purely summary offence but with an increased maximum penalty of six months' imprisonment.

[33] *Viz.* living on immoral earnings, bawdry and soliciting by men otherwise than for a homosexual act, under the Sexual Offences Act 1956, ss. 30, 31 and 32, and the Sexual Offences Act 1967, ss. 5 and 9.

[34] See para. 3, below.

[35] *e.g.* the Conspiracy and Protection of Property Act 1875, s. 9, which prohibits intimidation usually in relation to trade disputes and is punishable by three months' imprisonment or a fine of £20. In some other cases the prosecution may also claim trial by jury.

[36] Road Traffic Act 1972, s. 3.

[37] Food and Drugs Act 1955, s. 106.

[38] *R.* v. *Kettering Justices, ex p. Patmore* [1968] 1 W.L.R. 1436.

[39] Magistrates' Courts Act 1952, s. 25 (3) and (5). Explanation is specifically required under s. 25 (4) where the existence of past convictions may make the accused liable for a heavier penalty as, *e.g.*, under the Sexual Offences Act 1956, s. 33 (brothel-keeping).

[40] *Ibid.* s. 25 (6), and see Chap. 6, p. 93.

of interpretation. Although there are undoubted advantages in being tried by a jury, the accused may find that he has fallen into a trap in exercising his right by becoming liable to greater penalties and additional charges. Where the offence charged is by definition punishable only on summary conviction and is being tried on indictment only by virtue of section 25, it has been held that counts in the indictment may charge further offences which are indictable and even the charge upon which the accused made his election may be altered to a more serious offence.[41] In *R.* v. *Furlong*,[42] however, it was held that in these circumstances the court of trial cannot impose a heavier penalty than the justices could have imposed.

In trials of offences which by express definition may be tried summarily or on indictment the principles to be applied are different.[43] Where a particular sentence may be imposed " on conviction on indictment," it matters not by what procedure the accused has come to be convicted there even though it is by his own choice and contrary to the original intention of the prosecution.[44] In *R.* v. *Roe* [45] this proposition was extended to cover the addition of new charges to the indictment when the accused has elected to go for trial on a hybrid offence; in that case, charges of causing grievous bodily harm were added to charges of neglecting a child.

Once the accused has elected trial by jury, the court usually has no opportunity to change to summary trial thereafter. However, if the offence is only triable on indictment by virtue of section 25, the justices may have power to substitute a charge of a lesser offence which is only triable summarily.[46] In *Conn* v. *Turnbull* [47] the justices reduced the charge from an offence triable only on indictment to an offence triable only summarily; this is the proper course where the prosecution evidence does not disclose the graver offence. Under section 25, however, it might be wrong to change the charge if the accused objects, as it is his right to be tried by jury on that information [48] and the justices have no inherent right to find an alternative

---

41 *R.* v. *Nisbet* [1972] Q.B. 37, disagreeing with dicta in *R.* v. *Phillips* [1953] 2 Q.B. 14.

42 [1962] 2 Q.B. 161. Sentences were ordered to run consecutively for a period longer than the justices could have imposed.

43 See para. 3, below.

44 *R.* v. *Gibbs* [1965] 2 Q.B. 281. It was held to be impossible to read into the simple words " on conviction on indictment " the additional words: " other than a conviction following the accused's election to be tried by jury."

45 [1967] 1 W.L.R. 634 (see also p. 142).

46 The summary offences to which this might apply are rare, for most modern offences punishable summarily by more than 3 months are hybrid (*e.g.* dangerous driving, driving with a prohibited blood alcohol).

47 (1925) 89 J.P. 300.

48 See also p. 166 (abandonment of charges).

charge proved. If the offence is by definition triable either on indictment or summarily and, being charged with the summary offence, the accused elects trial by jury, the court has no discretion to revert to summary trial while hearing the charge of the indictable offence.[49]

Finally, where a summary offence is punishable by three months' imprisonment or less on first conviction but more on subsequent convictions,[50] the accused necessarily reveals his past convictions in claiming jury trial. This does not, however, disqualify the magistrates from committing him for trial, although it must be obvious to the judge at trial that he has past convictions,[51] nor even from trying him if he renounces his claim to jury trial after being warned of the consequences.[52]

3. Offences triable either summarily or on indictment

Offences of this sort, which are known as hybrid offences, only occur where a statute expressly provides for the alternative form of trial. An example is the staging of an obscene performance in the theatre,[53] for which an offender may on summary conviction be sent to prison for six months but on conviction on indictment he may be sent to prison for three years. Other more common examples are dangerous driving, drunken driving, and being in possession of dangerous drugs[54] and there are a great many more.

When dealing with an information charging such an offence it is the prosecution which initially chooses the form of proceedings; the court proceeds as if the indictable offence were charged unless the prosecutor applies to the court for summary trial before calling any evidence.[55] The provision applies where the accused is at least 17 years old.[56] Unlike the accused's election of trial by jury, the choice of the mode of trial in this case is always in the discretion of the court and it is not bound to grant the prosecution's application. As in all matters, it must exercise its discretion judicially and is not

---

[49] Magistrates' Courts Act 1952, s. 25 (6).

[50] *e.g.* Sexual Offences Act 1956, ss. 33–36 (brothel-keeping). Where an alleged brothel-keeper's first conviction turned out not to have been a conviction because she had been put on probation (see p. 236), the committal for trial on the second charge was a nullity: *R.* v. *Maizone* [1974] Crim.L.R. 112.

[51] The jury should obviously not be told.

[52] See p. 298.

[53] Theatres Act 1968, s. 2 (2). This example is also illustrative of the type of offence affected by *R.* v. *Gibbs* [1965] 2 Q.B. 281; see above.

[54] Road Traffic Act 1972, ss. 2 and 5, and Misuse of Drugs Act 1971.

[55] Magistrates' Courts Act 1952, s. 18 (1).

[56] Children and Young Persons Act 1969, s. 6 (2).

obliged to follow the course agreed by the parties.[57] If it grants the application but the prosecution subsequently changes its mind, the court may grant its application to revert to the preliminary inquiry into the indictable offence at any time before the prosecution evidence is completed.[58]

If the prosecution decides to proceed on indictment, the accused has no power to demand summary trial but the court has a discretion during the inquiry to change the proceedings into a summary trial. Under section 18 (3) it may do so where it considers it to be the proper course after hearing any representations by the parties (in the presence of the accused) and having regard to the nature of the case. Thus either the prosecution or the defence may ask for summary trial, though it is in the court's discretion whether or not to order it. If the Director of Public Prosecutions is prosecuting, his consent to the change is necessary.[59]

If the court changes to summary trial while it is hearing the information as for an indictable offence, the accused may be committed to the Crown Court for sentence if the court finds that its own powers of sentencing are inadequate.[60] In this event the accused may be sentenced as if he had been tried on indictment. The court *must* inform the accused of this power; if it fails to do so, the trial, conviction and committal for sentence will be a nullity.[61] The power is not available when the prosecution initially applied for and was granted summary trial.[62]

When the form of proceedings is changed after the hearing has begun, either for summary trial or for committal proceedings, the evidence already taken may generally be treated as evidence for the new proceedings,[63] provided it was given orally and on oath and provided the witnesses are recalled if the prosecution or defence wishes to cross-examine them.[64] This clearly excludes written statements given at committal proceedings under section 2 of the Criminal Justice Act 1967 [65] or by a child under section 27 of the Children and

---

57 *Ex p. Munday* [1970] Crim.L.R. 601 (where the prosecution agreed to drop the more serious charge and the defence to plead guilty to the lesser offence; the magistrates were right in refusing to accept the " deal ") and *R.* v. *Greater Manchester Justices, ex p. Martyn* [1976] Crim.L.R. 574.

58 Magistrates' Courts Act 1952, s. 18 (5).

59 *i.e.* under the Magistrates' Courts Act 1952, s. 18 (3) or (5), above.

60 *Ibid.* s. 29; see pp. 330 and 332.

61 *R.* v. *Kent Justices, ex p. Machin* [1952] 2 K.B. 355.

62 *i.e.* under the Magistrates' Courts Act 1952, s. 18 (1).

63 *Ibid.* ss. 23 (change to summary trial) and 18 (5) (change to committal proceedings).

64 Magistrates' Courts Rules 1968, r. 19.

65 See pp. 96 and 110.

Young Persons Act 1963.[66] It may also necessitate the recall of a witness who has given evidence to have it taken in the form of a deposition.[67]

4. Indictable offences triable summarily

A large number of indictable offences may be tried summarily with the consent of the accused. Schedule 1 of the Magistrates' Courts Act 1952 contains a list of such offences [68] and more recent Acts have added further offences.[69]

In this case the court uses its discretion in choosing which way to proceed but it must have the consent of the accused (if he is 17 years old or more) before it can proceed as for summary trial. It must consider any representations made by the accused or by the prosecution in the presence of the accused so that, although either party may take the initiative, it is principally the decision of the accused. The prosecution merely proposes it or persuasively argues against it or accepts it, though where the prosecution affects public property, the prosecution must consent, and where the prosecution is brought by the Director of Public Prosecutions, he must consent.[70]

The court must consider judicially [71] whether the case is a proper one for summary trial in view of the seriousness of the offence and the circumstances in which it was committed, and whether the magistrates' powers of sentencing will provide adequate punishment.[72] This last consideration is, of course, made without knowledge of the accused's previous convictions. If they turn out to justify a sentence more severe than the magistrates can impose, the accused may be committed to the Crown Court for a heavier sentence to be passed.[73]

---

[66] See p. 111.

[67] See p. 107.

[68] *e.g.* unlawful wounding and assault occasioning actual bodily harm (Offences against the Person Act 1861, ss. 20 and 47) various criminal damage offences, indecent assault, indecency between men (Sexual Offences Act 1956, s. 13, as modified by the 1967 Act), etc.

[69] *e.g.* Theft Act 1968, s. 29 (1), which enables all offences under that Act to be tried summarily except robbery, aggravated burglary, blackmail, assault with intent to rob, burglary when combined with certain factors and handling goods stolen abroad; and the Criminal Justice Act 1972, s. 47, which adds arson committed without an intention to endanger life to the list.

[70] Magistrates' Courts Act 1952, s. 19 (7).

[71] *e.g. R.* v. *Bodmin Justices* [1947] K.B. 321, where justices interviewed a witness privately in their own room.

[72] Magistrates' Courts Act 1952, s. 19 (2). Facts revealed by the court's enquiry into whether to proceed summarily, which it takes into account in making its decision to do so, cannot later be used to justify a committal for sentence: *R.* v. *Lymm Justices, ex p. Brown* [1973] 1 W.L.R. 1039.

[73] Under Magistrates' Courts Act 1952, s. 29 (as to which, see p. 330): *ibid.* s. 19 (4).

Failure to warn the accused of this power renders his trial, conviction and committal invalid.[74]

In *R.* v. *Coe* [75] two accused consented to summary trial, pleading guilty to shopbreaking involving £3,500 of goods and taking cars on eleven occasions in connection with the shopbreakings and for joy-rides. The Lord Chief Justice said: " This court is quite unable to understand how it came about that the prosecution invited the justices, as they did, to deal summarily with the[se] indictable offences. . . . There is something more involved than convenience and expedition." Furthermore, " while . . . the prosecution were at fault, and while no doubt the invitation to the justices was a temptation to them to deal with it summarily, that is no excuse for the justices."

The change-over from committal proceedings to summary trial may be made at any stage during the inquiry. The charge must be written down and read to the accused, the court [76] explaining his choice between consenting to summary trial and being tried by jury, the result of giving his consent to summary trial and the power in that event of committing him for sentence to the Crown Court.[77]

After the court has decided to proceed as for summary trial, it still has power to revert to hearing the information as examining justices.[78] This might be done, for instance, where the prosecution evidence turned out to be more serious than the court had believed at the time of allowing summary trial. The court may also allow the accused to withdraw his consent at any stage of the proceedings, but is under no duty to do so at his request.[79]

5. Indictable offences

Indictable offences are either common law offences, such as conspiracy, or statutory offences for which no provision for summary trial is made in their definition, such as robbery.[80] If such offences are not made triable summarily with the consent of the accused,[81] they are triable only on indictment. The principal subdivisions of

---

[74] *R.* v. *Kent Justices, ex p. Machin* [1952] 2 K.B. 355.

[75] [1968] 1 W.L.R. 1950; see also p. 333.

[76] Usually in the person of the clerk to the justices.

[77] Magistrates' Courts Act 1952, s. 19 (3).

[78] Criminal Justice Administration Act 1962, s. 13.

[79] *R.* v. *Southampton Justices, ex p. Briggs* [1972] 1 W.L.R. 277; *R.* v. *Bradfield and Sonning Justices, ex p. Jones* [1976] R.T.R. 144.

[80] Theft Act 1968, s. 8.

[81] *i.e.* those which are neither contained in the Magistrates' Courts Act 1952, Sched. 1, nor are directed to be treated as though they were by subsequent statutes.

these offences are between those which are triable by a High Court judge, a circuit judge, a recorder or a court sitting with justices; these have already been described on page 89.

Summary

Although the first and fifth classes above cause little difficulty, the procedure relating to the others tends to be confusing. The first essential is to ascertain which class a particular offence belongs to by reference to the definition, punishment and ancillary provisions. Thereafter the following steps may arise during the magistrates' court proceedings:

1. The proceedings start as committal proceedings. Before the prosecution calls evidence
   (*a*) the prosecution may apply for summary trial (type 3 offence) [82] or
   (*b*) either party may ask the court for summary trial if the accused gives his consent (type 4 offence).[83]
2. The committal proceedings continue.
   (*a*) The prosecution or defence may ask the court to try the case summarily (type 3 offence),[84] or
   (*b*) the court may proceed to try the offence with the accused's consent (type 4 offence).[85]
3. The proceedings start as a summary trial. Before he pleads, the accused may claim trial by jury (type 2 offence).[86] Committal proceedings continue. Later, the court may be able to substitute a lesser summary offence and proceed to summary trial.[87]
4. The proceedings start as a summary trial because the prosecution has applied for it (type 3 offence—1 (*a*) above). The prosecution may apply to have the offence tried on indictment before the close of its evidence.[88]
5. The proceedings continue as a summary trial. The court may change the hearing to committal proceedings (type 4 offence).[89]

---

[82] Magistrates' Courts Act 1952, s. 18 (1).
[83] *Ibid.* s. 19 (2).
[84] *Ibid.* s. 18 (3).
[85] *Ibid.* s. 19 (2).
[86] *Ibid.* s. 25 (1).
[87] *Conn* v. *Turnbull* (1925) 89 J.P. 300; see p. 294.
[88] *Ibid.* s. 18 (5).
[89] Criminal Justice Administration Act 1962, s. 13.

D. Non-Criminal Jurisdiction

Apart from issuing process, committal proceedings, summary trial of criminal offences and dealing with juveniles,[90] the magistrates' courts have several other tasks not all of which are strictly "jurisdiction."

Proportionally the greatest of these is probably their matrimonial, affiliation and guardianship jurisdiction. The procedure is started by a "complaint," which is a bare assertion of the aggrieved spouse's, mother's or applicant's cause and is analogous to the information; the process is by summons. No pleadings are exchanged and the matter is heard in a way similar to summary trial of an information. Appeal on a case stated [91] against these orders lies to the Family Division of the High Court [92] and appeal by way of rehearing of the facts lies to the Crown Court.[93] When sitting as a domestic court, the court sits in private and is composed, if lay justices are sitting, to include at least one woman justice.

The magistrates' courts also hear very small claims for civil debts, such as arrears of rates, though such claims are often taken to the county courts. The magistrates' court retains the important function of enforcing maintenance orders and other payments by court order which under the Administration of Justice Act 1970 may be registered for enforcement in the magistrates' court although made elsewhere.

The main administrative function of the magistrates is licensing, *i.e.* granting licences to people in their area to sell or serve alcohol, provide gaming and betting facilities, etc. They also have some functions connected with highways, which include hearing certain disputes between the highway authority and the aggrieved person by way of appeal. For their other functions readers are recommended to refer to Stone's *Justices' Manual.*

---

[90] See Chap. 15, p. 361, especially as to the cases in which juveniles are tried by the adult magistrates' court, p. 368.

[91] See p. 349.

[92] See Administration of Justice Act 1970, s. 1 and Sched. 1.

[93] See also p. 344.

CHAPTER 12

SUMMARY TRIAL

MANY of the principles and procedures applicable in summary trial are the same as those applicable in trial on indictment and criminal procedure generally. To avoid unnecessary repetition, readers will find that they are referred back to previous chapters where possible.

A. PRESENCE AND REPRESENTATION OF PARTIES: PRESENCE OF PUBLIC

1. Presence and representation of the parties

(a) *The accused*

As a general rule (with important exceptions) the accused need not be present at any stage of the proceedings; the court may proceed to try an information of a *summary* offence in his absence provided it is satisfied by evidence on oath that the summons was served so as to give the accused reasonable notice of the proceedings.[1] He may object, however, during or after the trial in his absence by making a statutory declaration, under section 24 (3) of the Criminal Justice Act 1967, to the effect that he did not know of the summons or the proceedings until a specified date (after the proceedings had begun) and serving[2] it on the clerk to the justices within 14 days. Alternatively the magistrates' court may, within 14 days of convicting the accused in his absence, order a new trial by a different bench of magistrates if it appears to be in the interests of justice to do so.[3]

The principal exceptions to the general rule stated above are as follows:

(i) Where the accused wishes to claim trial by jury,[4] he may only do it if present in court. Otherwise the court may proceed to try him summarily.[5]

(ii) Where the accused has been granted bail with a duty to appear at trial, he must appear in person.[6]

[1] Magistrates' Courts Act 1952, s. 15 (1) and (3). As to service, see p. 56.

[2] This service may be by delivery to the clerk or his office or by registered post or recorded delivery: Criminal Justice Act 1967, s. 24 (4).

[3] Criminal Justice Act 1972, p. 41 (2); see also p. 315.

[4] *i.e.* the second class of offence above under the Magistrates' Courts Act 1952, s. 25; see p. 292.

[5] *Ibid.* s. 25 (2).

[6] Magistrates' Courts Act 1952, s. 99. As to bail, see p. 69.

(iii) Where the offence is indictable and the proceedings have started as committal proceedings, the accused must generally be present when evidence is given at the committal proceedings unless his own disorderly conduct or ill-health require him to be absent.[7] It is also essential that the accused be present

(*a*) if representations are made during the inquiry to try a hybrid offence[8] summarily,[9] and

(*b*) if representations are made to try an indictable offence summarily.[10]

If the application for summary trial is granted and the accused released, the trial may be held in his absence.

(iv) Where the court intends to impose a sentence of imprisonment, a suspended sentence or a disqualification on the accused[11] or where it wishes to commit him to prison for non-payment of a fine or other order,[12] he must be present.

If the prosecution in the first instance applies for summary trial of a hybrid offence, the accused need not be present, though in fact he will be unless the prosecution has informed him of its intention because the proceedings start as committal proceedings and only become trial proceedings on the prosecution's successful application to that effect.[13]

If the accused is absent but represented, which in magistrates' courts may be by a barrister or solicitor, he is deemed to be present,[14] though not for the purposes of the above exceptions. If he is absent and unrepresented, the courts are wary of trying all except the most straightforward minor offences in his absence, unless he has previously explained it by letter or otherwise. This is limited, however, by the difficulty in securing his presence against his will. Where a summons has been issued charging a summary offence a warrant of arrest can only be issued where the offence is punishable by imprisonment or where the court, having convicted the accused, proposes to disqualify him.[15]

---

[7] Magistrates' Courts Act 1952, s. 4 (3), as amended by s. 45 of the Criminal Justice Act 1972; see p. 96.

[8] *i.e.* is an offence in the third class of offences above under *ibid.* s. 18; see p. 295.

[9] *Ibid.* s. 18 (3); see p. 296.

[10] *i.e.* if it is an offence in the fourth class of offences above under *ibid.* s. 19; see p. 297.

[11] Criminal Justice Act 1967, s. 26. As to these sentences, see pp. 224, 227 and 245.

[12] *Ibid.* s. 44 (6).

[13] *i.e.* under the Magistrates' Courts Act 1952, s. 18 (1); see p. 295.

[14] *Ibid.* s. 99.

[15] Criminal Justice Act 1967, s. 24 (2), and see p. 60.

His presence may also be dispensed with if he pleads guilty by post, a procedure which is described on page 310. As to legal aid for representation in magistrates' courts, see page 400.

(b) *Prosecution*

As already mentioned,[16] the prosecutor may be a private individual, the police, a private corporation, a government department, a local authority, the Director of Public Prosecutions, etc., and the informant who actually initiated the proceedings may have been anyone authorised to do so by the prosecutor.[17] If the prosecutor is an individual or is represented by an individual (*e.g.* factory inspector) he may conduct the case himself or be represented by a barrister or solicitor. If legally represented he is deemed not to be absent.[18] There is no case where his physical presence is obligatory except, of course, in his capacity as a witness.

If no one appears for the prosecution, the court may dismiss the information, which operates for subsequent proceedings as an acquittal,[19] or, if evidence has been taken at a previous hearing which was adjourned,[20] proceed with the trial in the absence of the prosecution.[21] The same applies if no one appears for either party.[22]

2. Public trial

Summary trials must be held in open court with as much access given to the public as is conveniently possible.[23] Apart from juvenile courts to which special provisions apply,[24] the same provisions for *in camera* sittings apply here as apply to trials on indictment.[25]

B. The Information

By way of résumé, for most aspects of this subject have already been dealt with, the information is the material upon which the accused is tried. It contains a statement of the offender, the offence and the facts in brief and it is laid by the prosecution before a magistrate when a summons or warrant is applied for.[26] Subject to the greater

---

[16] See p. 17.
[17] See Magistrates' Courts Rules 1968, r. 1 (1), p. 54.
[18] Magistrates' Courts Act 1952, s. 99.
[19] *Cf. Autrefois acquit*, p. 159.
[20] As to adjournment, see p. 307.
[21] Magistrates' Courts Act 1952, s. 16.
[22] *Ibid.* s. 17.
[23] *Ibid.* s. 98 (4). The fact that no member of the public attends is immaterial: *R.* v. *Denbigh Justices, ex p. Williams* [1974] Q.B. 759.
[24] See p. 370.
[25] See p. 153.
[26] See p. 54.

flexibility and informality of an information, the same general principles apply to the information as apply to the statement and particulars of offence in an indictment[27]; in particular the provisions as to joinder of offences in one count and duplicity and as to the joinder of defendants apply.[28] The accused cannot, however, be tried on more than one information at the same time unless he gives his consent.[29]

The most important provision relating to informations as regards the actual process of summary trial is section 100 of the Magistrates' Courts Act 1952, whereby objections cannot be made to an information or complaint, or to a summons or warrant to procure the presence of the defendant, for any defect of substance or in form or for any variance between it and the evidence adduced by the prosecution at the hearing. On this last point, however, the court may grant the accused an adjournment if the variance may have misled him.

Despite the wide terms of the section, however, it is limited by several factors. First, an information which is void *ab initio* cannot be cured and must be dismissed.[30] It may be void *ab initio* for failing to charge any offence.[31] Secondly, the defect may be so fundamental to the charge that the information should be dismissed, and not merely adjourned or amended. For instance, where an accused charged with an indecent assault on August 17 was convicted of indecent assault "on a day in August," although he had concentrated his defence on an alibi for the 17th, the conviction was quashed on the ground that it was a " fundamental " defect, though the basis of the decision was justified by the fact that the hearing should have been adjourned.[32] Thirdly, because magistrates have no common law, non-statutory powers or discretions and because there is no counterpart in summary trial to section 6 of the Criminal Law Act 1967 (returning an alternative verdict),[33] the information must charge the same *offence* as the evidence of the prosecution discloses. In

[27] See Magistrates' Courts Rules 1968, rr. 1 (3) and 83, p. 54, and see Chapter 7, p. 117.

[28] See pp. 128, 131 and 137 respectively. See also *Criminal Procedure: Statement and Trial of Multiple Offences*, by I. R. Scott.

[29] *Brangwynne* v. *Evans* [1962] 1 W.L.R. 267 (trial of two or more informations against one defendant); *Aldus* v. *Watson* [1973] Q.B. 902 (trial of informations against two or more defendants).

[30] This does not bar a subsequent information based on the same facts as the accused has not been " in jeopardy." *Cf. Autrefois acquit*, p. 159 and see p. 55.

[31] *e.g. Garman* v. *Plaice* [1969] 1 W.L.R. 19.

[32] *Wright* v. *Nicholson* [1970] 1 W.L.R. 142; it is generally assumed that a power to amend the information exists. This was confirmed in *Wright* v. *Eldred* (1971) 135 J.P. 491. Technically it requires the withdrawal and re-issue of the charge.

[33] *e.g.* a finding of assault on a summons for malicious wounding was quashed although the ingredients of assault were included in the wounding charge: *Lawrence* v. *Same* [1968] 2 Q.B. 93.

other words the facts need not be the same but the magistrates have no power to find proved an offence less serious than, or otherwise different from, the offence charged.

These limitations need cause no practical difficulty, however, because if the court feels that the more serious charge cannot be substantiated it may dismiss that information before hearing the evidence or during it and issue a summons for the lesser offence.[34] If the court heard the whole case before dismissing it, it could not follow this course as the dismissal would amount to an acquittal, whereas dismissing it at an earlier stage has an effect similar to staying proceedings on an indictment.[35] Further, an accused can acquiesce in the defect in which case he loses his power to object,[36] though this cannot cure the above faults in an information.

An amendment, made as described in footnote 32 above, may be made at any time before sentence, provided it is not fundamental.[37] A new charge cannot be substituted, however, after the conviction is recorded. In *Garfield* v. *Maddocks*[38] the accused was charged with using threatening behaviour with intent to cause a breach of the peace. The prosecution sought to amend this to allege threatening behaviour whereby a breach of the peace was likely to be occasioned. The magistrates' court refused to allow the amendment and found the accused guilty; the accused appealed. The Crown Court purported to amend the information as requested by the prosecution and affirmed the conviction. The Divisional Court held that this was not permissible because, whether or not the two offences were technically the same in law,[39] the appeal had not been conducted in respect of the same offence in the sense of the same misdoing. An amendment may be made after the six-month limitation period, below, has expired.[40]

The limitation of prosecutions by time, described in Chapter 2,[41] is important in relation to the laying of informations, in particular

---

[34] In *Lawrence* v. *Same* [1968] 2 Q.B. 93 at p. 99, Lord Parker C.J. said: " as soon as they are minded to acquit the defendant of the substantial charge . . . [the prosecution] can immediately ask for a summons to be preferred for the lesser offence." *Cf. Conn* v. *Turnbull* (1925) 89 J.P. 300, p. 294.

[35] See p. 166.

[36] *Eggington* v. *Pearl* (1875) 40 J.P. 56. In *R.* v. *Brentford Justices, ex p. Catlin* [1975] Q.B. 455 the accused's appearance to answer a summons which had been issued without an information having been laid was held to be acquiescence sufficient to cure the defective process because she did not protest at the time.

[37] *Allan* v. *Wiseman* [1975] R.T.R. 217.

[38] [1974] Q.B. 7.

[39] See *Vernon* v. *Paddon*, p. 130.

[40] *R.* v. *Newcastle-upon-Tyne Justices, ex p. John Bryce* [1976] 1 W.L.R. 517.

[41] See p. 13.

the general period of six months on all summary offences[42] and the need to serve a summons or give notice of intended prosecution within fourteen days before prosecuting certain road traffic offences.[43] A delay between the laying of the information and the issue of the summons may make the summons defective and void if the delay is such as to prejudice the accused.[44]

C. Preliminary Procedure, Adjournment and Evidence

1. Initiation of proceedings

The process for initiating summary proceedings is the same as for proceedings on indictment, *i.e.* summons or arrest with or without a warrant.[45] In view of the restrictions on issuing a warrant of arrest,[46] summary offences are generally proceeded against by summons, though arrest without a warrant is available for a few summary offences such as loitering as a suspected person and other vagrancy offences,[47] failure to give the correct name and address when asked to do so after disorderly behaviour at a public meeting[48] and poaching.[49]

If the proceedings are commenced by a summons, the accused is at liberty throughout or until being sent to prison on conviction. The summons specifies the date of trial. If he is arrested and brought before the court for an indictable offence or for a hybrid offence, the magistrate opens the preliminary inquiry[50] so that the accused must be remanded, in custody or on bail, whether or not summary trial is later applied for.[51] The same applies where the accused is arrested for a summary offence, though the court proceeds at once to the hearing of the charge, which it may adjourn, and it need not remand the accused; instead it may release him without granting bail and fix a date for the trial to be held.[52] As the purpose of remand is to secure the accused's presence where it will be necessary, the court should remand him when it is likely to impose a prison sentence.

If the period of remand is to be short, the court may commit the

---

[42] *i.e.* under the Magistrates' Courts Act 1952, s. 104.

[43] *i.e.* under the Road Traffic Act 1972, s. 179.

[44] *R.* v. *Fairford Justices, ex p. Brewster* [1975] 3 W.L.R. 59.

[45] See pp. 55–60.

[46] See Criminal Justice Act 1967, s. 24, p. 59.

[47] Vagrancy Act 1824, s. 4 (not to be confused with " going equipped " under the Theft Act 1968, s. 25, which is indictable).

[48] Public Order Act 1936, s. 5.

[49] Game Act 1831, s. 31 (this applies to poaching by day).

[50] See Criminal Justice Act 1967, s. 35, p. 94.

[51] Magistrates' Courts Act 1952, ss. 6 (1) and 14 (4); see also p. 70.

[52] See p. 67.

accused to the custody of a police constable for a period of up to three days.[53]

2. Adjournment

The court may, at any time before or during the trial of an information, adjourn the trial. It has this power even when only one justice is sitting.[54] It must adjourn if the accused needs time to prepare his defence.[55] Neither party need be present.

(a) *Before the hearing*

This may occur when an arrested person is brought before the court or when, on the date fixed for trial, the parties are not ready for the hearing. If the accused is remanded, the date of trial must be fixed in his bail or it must be the date on which he is brought to the court again from custody.[56] If the accused is at liberty, the court need not fix a date immediately but may leave the time and place to be determined later,[57] giving adequate notice of it to the parties.

There is no absolute time limit on an adjournment, but if the information is not proceeded with or dismissed by the court within a reasonable time, the clerk to the justices must report the case to the Director of Public Prosecutions.[58]

(b) *During the hearing*

The court may adjourn before it reaches its decision in the same way as it may before the hearing. If it has convicted the accused, however, but has not yet sentenced him, it may adjourn for not more than four weeks, or three weeks if he is in custody, to consider how to treat him and to enable inquiries to be made for that purpose[59] or to enable the accused to be examined medically.[60] At this stage the court must remand the accused.

3. Evidence

The presence of witnesses to give evidence or to produce documents or things in the magistrates' courts, whether at committal proceedings or at a summary trial, is secured by summons or warrant under

[53] Magistrates' Courts Act 1952, s. 105 (5).
[54] Magistrates' Courts Act 1952, s. 14 (1).
[55] *R.* v. *Thames Magistrates' Court, ex p. Polemis* [1974] 1 W.L.R. 1371.
[56] *i.e.* within eight days; see Magistrates' Courts Act 1952, s. 105 (4), p. 67.
[57] *Ibid.* s. 14 (2). When a date is not fixed it is known as adjourning *sine die*.
[58] Prosecution of Offences Regulations 1946 (S.R. & O. 1946 No. 1467/L.17), reg. 9; see p. 19.
[59] Magistrates' Courts Act 1952, s. 14 (3), as amended by the Criminal Justice Act 1967, s. 30.
[60] *Ibid.* s. 26 (1), as amended by the Criminal Justice Act 1967, s. 30.

section 77 of the Magistrates' Courts Act 1952.[61] If committal proceedings change into summary trial, the evidence may have to be taken afresh.[62] As at a trial on indictment, the accused gives his evidence first and witnesses should be ordered out of the court before being called to give their evidence.[63]

If a party examines a witness from a written proof of evidence, it is courteous to allow the other side to see it or a copy of it for its potential value in cross-examination; this must be done if for any reason a copy is handed to the clerk of the court.[64]

The general rules of evidence at a summary trial are the same as in any other criminal proceedings, though in practice they are sometimes relaxed, particularly when the parties are not legally represented. Of the statutory rules already considered in relation to committal and trial by jury, all except the rule requiring notice of alibi evidence to be given to the prosecution [65] apply (with the exception, of course, of the rules relating to the preservation of evidence between committal and trial),[66] in particular formal admissions under section 10 of the Criminal Justice Act 1967,[67] and the non-compellability of the accused and his spouse under section 1 of the Criminal Evidence Act 1898.[68]

An important difference between summary trial and trial by jury is the lack of any advance disclosure of the prosecution case in summary proceedings. The James Committee [69] considered that some measure of disclosure should be introduced to avoid a proliferation of jury trials where the accused simply wants to be prepared to meet the case against him.

D. Order of Proceedings

If the accused is present, the substance of the information is read to him and he is asked whether he pleads guilty or not guilty.[70] If he is absent, pleads guilty in an ambiguous fashion or refuses to plead, the

---

[61] *Cf.* the process for securing witnesses' presence at a trial on indictment, p. 105.

[62] See p. 111. As to a child's evidence given in writing, see p. 111.

[63] See p. 181.

[64] *Simms* v. *Moore* [1970] 2 Q.B. 327 at p. 330; see p. 313.

[65] See Criminal Justice Act 1967, s. 11, p. 112.

[66] *i.e.* the taking of depositions, etc., described on pp. 107–115, with the exception of " Formal Admissions " on p. 112.

[67] See p. 112.

[68] See p. 30.

[69] See Appendix.

[70] Magistrates' Courts Act 1952, s. 13 (1).

court proceeds to try him as though he had pleaded not guilty.[71] Section 4 of the Criminal Procedure (Insanity) Act 1964[72] only applies to jury trial and the question of fitness to be tried has apparently not been resolved in relation to summary trial. Although the accused need not be present, it is doubtful whether a trial would be in accordance with the rules of natural justice if his absence were involuntary and based on his inability to understand. Though not a solution of this question, it would be possible for the court to treat him as having pleaded not guilty, try him and, if it finds that he committed the act or omission which constitutes the offence charged, commit him to the Crown Court with a view to medical treatment.[73]

1. Plea

The accused may plead guilty or not guilty or submit that the magistrates have no power to try him. An oral plea of guilty or not guilty is governed by the same principles as the plea at a trial on indictment.[74] The rule that the plea must be made personally does not apply with the same rigour, however, and an accused's solicitor or counsel may properly answer a charge which is properly put, even if contrary to his instructions, provided that the accused does not indicate dissatisfaction.[75]

Although the pleas of *autrefois acquit* and *convict*[76] in the formal sense apply only to trial on indictment, the principle of double jeopardy applies to summary trial, *i.e.* if, on a factual allegation, the accused has been in jeopardy and if there has been a final decision of his case, he cannot be tried again on the same facts. The Interpretation Act 1889, section 33, states the common law rule that, where an act constitutes an offence under two different statutes (or under a statute and at common law), the offender can only be tried and punished once in respect of that act.

A situation which frequently arises in road traffic cases is where two informations are laid on the same facts, one for a substantive offence such as dangerous driving, and the other for an absolute offence such as speeding. The proper course is for the court to hear the evidence, even where the accused has pleaded guilty, find him guilty of whichever offence is justified by the evidence and dismiss the other information or adjourn it *sine die*.[77]

---

71 Magistrates' Courts Act 1952, s. 15.
72 See p. 170.
73 See p. 336.
74 See pp. 155–158.
75 *R.* v. *Gowerton Justices, ex p. Davies* [1974] Crim.L.R 253.
76 See pp. 159–165.
77 *R.* v. *Burnham Justices* [1959] 1 W.L.R. 1041.

Other objections which the accused may put forward are based on want of jurisdiction, either territorial or by time or otherwise,[78] or on a defect in the information.[79] There is no formal procedure for making an objection—the accused or his legal representative asks the court to dismiss the information either before pleading to the charge or, if that opportunity was missed, at a later stage. A formal objection should be made before the close of the prosecution evidence, but objections on the merits may be made at any time.[80]

A magistrates' court may accept a change of plea during the trial on the same principles as may a court trying an indictment [81]; it is considered further on page 316. The change must be made before sentence is passed,[82] but it may be made at the Crown Court in exceptional circumstances after the accused has been committed for sentence.[83]

Plea of guilty by post

For offences which are only triable summarily [84] and which are not charged in a juvenile court, a procedure was introduced by the Magistrates' Courts Act 1957 whereby the accused may plead guilty without being present in court. Whenever a summons is issued requiring the accused to appear to answer an information charging such an offence, the prosecution must serve on the accused:

(i) a concise statement of the facts [85] which will be placed before the court if the accused pleads guilty without appearing,
(ii) a notice stating the effect of doing so, and
(iii) a form for the accused to send to the clerk of the court expressing his intention of doing so and containing, if he wishes, a submission with a view to mitigation of sentence.[86]

When the accused uses this procedure, the clerk informs the prosecution and the court proceeds to hear and dispose of the case in the

---

[78] See pp. 9–16 and 290–299.
[79] See Magistrates' Courts Act 1952, s. 100, p. 304.
[80] *Price* v. *Humphries* [1958] 2 Q.B. 353 at p. 358.
[81] See p. 169.
[82] *R.* v. *Jones* [1971] 2 Q.B. 456.
[83] *R.* v. *Fareham Justices, ex p. Long* [1976] Crim.L.R. 269 (the Crown Court remits the case for trial in the magistrates' court).
[84] *i.e.* which are not punishable by imprisonment for more than three months and which are not by definition triable also on indictment, under the Magistrates' Courts Act 1952, ss. 25 and 18; see pp. 292–297.
[85] It must be a statement of *all* the facts upon which the prosecution will seek to rely, whether relating to the offence or to a penalty: *R.* v. *Liskerrett Justices, ex p. Child* (1971) 135 J.P. 693. Further facts may not be placed before the court at the hearing.
[86] Magistrates' Courts Act 1957, s. 1.

usual way.[87] The prosecution need not attend as the accused has admitted the facts which are stated to the court and on which his conviction will be based.

However, the court is not bound to accept the accused's plea. It may decide not to on the accused's informing the clerk that he wishes to withdraw it or on its own initiative. If it decides not to, the court adjourns the hearing and informs the accused of the date of the adjourned hearing and proceeds in every way as if the accused had not pleaded guilty by post; the hearing at which it decides not to accept the plea does not count as a hearing for the purposes of issuing a warrant for the accused's arrest.[88]

If the court intends to disqualify or sentence the accused to imprisonment, it must adjourn and secure his presence.[89] This may not be done in the first instance by warrant of arrest, but only if satisfied at the resumed hearing that he was properly served with the summons for the resumed hearing [88] and that he had notice of the reasons for the adjournment.

2. Order of evidence and speeches [90]

This section applies only where the accused has pleaded not guilty; procedure on a plea of guilty is described on page 316. Further, the provisions of sections 18, 19 and 25 of the Magistrates' Courts Act 1952 for changing the mode of trial, described on pages 292–299, must be remembered in this context.

As magistrates' court proceedings are considerably less formal than proceedings on indictment, the " speeches " are usually shorter and less important. In particular, the prosecution has no duty to state its case in its opening address.[91] The following is the full procedure where both parties appear; where the accused does not appear, stages (3)–(7) and (9) do not apply.

(1) The prosecution, if it wishes to do so, addresses the court.
(2) The prosecution calls its evidence. The witnesses are examined, cross-examined and re-examined in the usual way.[92]
(3) The accused or his representative, if he wishes, addresses the court.
(4) The accused, if he wishes, makes an unsworn statement.

---

[87] See p. 316.
[88] Criminal Justice Act 1967, s. 24 (2), and Magistrates' Courts Act 1952, s. 15; see p. 60.
[89] Criminal Justice Act 1967, s. 26; see p. 302.
[90] Magistrates' Courts Rules 1968, r. 13.
[91] *Cf.* this speech in a trial on indictment, p. 117.
[92] See pp. 181–189.

(5) The evidence for the defence, if any, is called. If the accused gives sworn evidence, he must do so before other witnesses are called.[93]
(6) The prosecution calls evidence in rebuttal, if any.
(7) If it has not already been done ((3) above), the defence may address the court.

The power to make a second address where evidence is called for the defence depends in any event on the leave of the court. Refusal to allow an accused to address the court may vitiate the conviction because it may amount to a denial of justice.[94] Either party may apply but if one is granted leave, the other cannot be refused; the defence always has the last word, so if the prosecution has not made an opening address and wishes to make a closing address, the defence must be allowed to make a second speech. If both parties have made an opening address, the order is:

(8) The prosecution addresses the court.
(9) The defence addresses the court.

Evidence must be given on oath[95] except where the witness is allowed to give unsworn evidence under the general law.[96]

A submission of no case to answer[97] may be made at the close of the prosecution evidence, but the defence must take care to make it clear that it is a submission, *not* the defence's address in the absence of evidence.[98]

The prosecution's power to call evidence in rebuttal does not depend on the leave of the court,[99] for very little advance preparation for a summary trial is possible and the defence evidence may reveal unexpected facts. The evidence in rebuttal must, however, relate to unexpected evidence, and not merely reinforce the prosecution's case.[1] Otherwise, the prosecution *may* be allowed to call evidence after the close of its own case if it was omitted and whether it is a

---

[93] *R.* v. *Smith* [1968] 1 W.L.R. 636 (an appeal against conviction on indictment, but the principle was stated to apply to all criminal proceedings).
[94] *R.* v. *Great Marlborough Street Magistrate, ex p. Fraser* [1974] Crim.L.R. 47; *cf. R.* v. *Middlesex Crown Court*, p. 199.
[95] Magistrates' Courts Act 1952, s. 78.
[96] *e.g.* children under the Children and Young Persons Act 1933, s. 38 (see p. 30), and the accused under the Criminal Evidence Act 1898, s. 1 (*h*) (see p. 190).
[97] See p. 202.
[98] *R.* v. *Essex Justices, ex p. Final* [1963] 2 Q.B. 816 and Practice Note [1962] 1 All E.R. 448.
[99] See p. 203.
[1] *R.* v. *Day* [1940] 1 All E.R. 402.

formal or substantial element of it.[2] Further evidence may not be admitted after the magistrates have retired to consider their verdict.[3]

Finally, it should be said that the magistrates are in control of the hearing; they may ask people to leave the court, refuse to accept inadmissible evidence, ask questions of witnesses and call witnesses themselves.[4] They may do this personally, through the chairman of the court[5] or through the clerk. They must act judicially and impartially, not " descending into the arena " or interfering improperly with the conduct of the parties' cases. Irregular or unjudicial behaviour can be remedied later for they are subject to the supervision of the High Court.[6] In *Simms* v. *Moore*[7] the Queen's Bench Divisional Court held that the clerk to the justices had rightly taken over the examination of prosecution witnesses from the policeman who was the informant and conducting the case, and who was also a possible witness. Lord Parker C.J. laid down the following general principles for examination of witnesses by the court itself or through the clerk:

(1) The court should not intervene except to clear up an ambiguity.
(2) It should never examine witnesses if the party concerned is legally represented or is competent himself to conduct the examination.
(3) Where the party is incompetent by reason of his ignorance or otherwise, the court may authorise the clerk to examine witnesses for him.
(4) If there is a proof of the witness's evidence,[8] the clerk may use this in examination if the other party has seen it or a copy of it.
(5) It should be arranged that someone else takes notes of the evidence.
(6) Examination by the clerk should only be allowed where it is in the interests of justice, care being taken to avoid infringements of the rules of natural justice or of the rule that justice must be seen to be done.

---

[2] *Piggott* v. *Sims* [1973] R.T.R. 15.

[3] See p. 314.

[4] After the defence evidence is given, however, they may only call evidence in rebuttal: *R.* v. *Godstone Justices, ex p. Dickson* (1971) 115 S.J. 246.

[5] *i.e.* a lay magistrate chosen by his fellow lay magistrates to preside at trials; this is an informal local arrangement and he may be elected to preside in the court for a period or at the actual hearing by the other magistrates sitting.

[6] See p. 43 and the appeal by case stated, p. 349.

[7] [1970] 2 Q.B. 327.

[8] See p. 308.

Lord Parker C.J. preceded this analysis by the words: " The court was informed by counsel on both sides that the examination of witnesses by the justices' clerk was happening constantly at magistrates' courts up and down the country."

3. Decision

After hearing the evidence and the parties' speeches, the magistrates reach their decision of whether or not the accused was guilty of the offence charged. If they are not in immediate agreement, they may retire to their private room to discuss the case. It is only in the most exceptional circumstances that further evidence may be admitted after they have retired.[9] In no circumstances must a witness, such as the prosecutor or a social worker, enter the magistrates' room after retirement, however innocent the actual purpose may be.[10] If they are in difficulties over the law or over the law to be applied to a question of fact, they may ask the clerk of the court to assist.[11]

Only two courses are open to them—to convict the accused or to dismiss the information, and to convict on, or dismiss, each information if there is more than one.[12] The usual form of words for conviction is " we find the case proved." Reaching the decision is a collective process; in a case involving 34 allegedly obscene books,[13] it was held to be unnecessary for each magistrate individually to read every book provided a collective opinion could be formed on each book. However, the decision may be reached by a majority vote, the chairman having no casting vote greater than the vote of any of the others. If they are equally divided and unable to compromise, they must adjourn for a rehearing before a court composed of different justices.[14] As the decision may be by majority, this rule is presumably unaffected by the principle stated in *R.* v. *Bridgend Justices, ex p. Randall*[15]—that it is the duty of a bench of magistrates to convict if it is satisfied that the prosecution has proved the accused's guilt, but to acquit in any other event. This case involved a bench of three magistrates (capable in itself of deciding the case

[9] *French's Dairies (Sevenoaks) Ltd.* v. *Davis* [1973] Crim.L.R. 630. *Cf.* the effect of jury retirement, p. 208.

[10] *R.* v. *Stratford on Avon Justices, ex p. Edmonds* [1973] R.T.R. 356; *R.* v. *Aberdare Justices, ex p. Jones* [1973] Crim.L.R. 45—" justice must be seen to be done."

[11] See p. 290.

[12] *R.* v. *Bridgend Justices, ex p. Randall* [1975] Crim.L.R. 287.

[13] *Olympia Press* v. *Hollis* [1973] 1 W.L.R. 1520.

[14] *Bagg* v. *Colquhoun* [1904] 1 K.B. 554.

[15] [1975] Crim.L.R. 287.

finally) which failed to agree and purported to remit the case for rehearing by a different bench. If it had such a doubt about the prosecution case that it was unable to make a decision, the accused was entitled to the benefit of it. It is clearly undesirable for a bench to consist of an even number of magistrates. A stipendiary magistrate of course reaches his decision on his own. As already mentioned,[16] the magistrates can only make a decision on the offence charged, not on any other offence which the evidence has revealed.

If an appeal is being considered by either party,[17] the court must draw up a conviction form in writing.[18] Otherwise it need not.

A magistrates' court's decision, once made, is final, subject to its power under section 41 of the Criminal Justice Act 1972 to rescind or vary it. There is also a " slip rule " whereby the magistrates may correct a slip of the tongue immediately, but it must be a genuine correction, not a change of mind.[19]

The power under section 41 must be exercised within 14 days, beginning with the day on which the decision was made.[20] It must be exercised by a court consisting of the same magistrates or a majority of the original magistrates.[21] The decisions which may be varied under section 41 are:

(a) a sentence or other order made when dealing with an offender[22];
(b) a conviction after the accused has pleaded not guilty;
(c) a conviction of the accused in his absence under section 15 (1) of the Magistrates' Courts Act 1952.[23]

In the case of a sentence or order, it may be either rescinded or varied; if varied it takes effect from the day on which it was originally imposed unless otherwise directed.[24] It may be rescinded or varied because it was invalid in its original form or because the court has had second thoughts.

In the case of a conviction ((b) and (c) above) the court only has power to direct that the case be reheard by different magistrates; it

[16] See *Lawrence* v. *Same*, p. 304.
[17] See Chap. 14, p. 340.
[18] Magistrates' Courts Rules 1968, r. 15.
[19] *R.* v. *Newcastle Justices, ex p. Swales* [1972] Crim.L.R. 111.
[20] This time limit is absolute: s. 41 (3); the magistrates cannot extend it by notifying the defendant within the period but making the actual variation later: *Bradburn* v. *Richards* [1976] R.T.R. 275.
[21] Criminal Justice Act 1972, s. 41 (4).
[22] *Ibid.* s. 41 (1).
[23] *Ibid.* s. 41 (2); as to s. 15 (1), see p. 301.
[24] *Ibid.* s. 41 (5).

may not simply quash the conviction on its own motion. The effect of such a direction is to make the conviction of no effect and the accused is released or remanded as if the trial had been adjourned.[25]

The use of this simple summary procedure has been urged on aggrieved defendants instead of applying for certiorari, for instance where the magistrates' decision is allegedly in breach of the rules of natural justice.[26] It was enacted to avoid the worst effects of the doctrine of *functus officio*, *i.e.* the rule that, once a person has discharged a duty, he cannot reopen the matter to alter what he did in performance of the duty. In a magistrates' court, the doctrine applies to any decision—to issue process, commit for trial, convict, etc.[27]—and still applies fully to any decision not included in section 41. If the accused wishes to change his plea of guilty to a not guilty plea, the magistrates may allow it before the final decision of the case. This effectively occurs on the passing of sentence.[28] Where conviction was pronounced on a defence submission of no case to answer, it was held that the court retained jurisdiction over all matters before it until it had passed sentence and that the magistrates could remedy the error by immediately adjourning the case for rehearing by a different bench.[29] Once the sentence is passed and the statutory power to amend it has expired, however, the magistrates cannot make any further alteration in the light of fresh evidence.[30]

E. Plea of Guilty

Where the accused pleads guilty, the magistrates need hear no evidence before convicting him.[31] It is quite usual, however, for them to hear a brief outline of the facts given unsworn by the prosecutor or his representative. If the accused is present,[32] the magistrates ask him whether he has anything to say and he or his representative addresses the court with a view to mitigation of sentence.[33] This and subsequent procedures are described in the next chapter.

---

[25] Criminal Justice Act 1972, s. 41 (3); see p. 307.
[26] *Ex p. Haygarth*, *The Times*, October 29, 1975; as to certiorari, see p. 45.
[27] As to changing the form of trial (summary proceedings to committal, or vice versa), see pp. 292–299.
[28] *S.* v. *Manchester City Recorder* [1971] A.C. 481 (" magistrates only have one *officium*—to carry the case before them to a conclusion ": *per* Lord Reid at *ibid.* p. 490). The sentence may be varied under s. 41 (1), so the period in which a change of plea might be accepted is extended by 14 days.
[29] *R.* v. *Midhurst Justices* [1974] Q.B. 137.
[30] *R.* v. *Northamptonshire Justices, ex p. Nicholson* [1974] R.T.R. 97.
[31] Magistrates' Courts Act 1952, s. 13 (3).
[32] As to the plea of guilty by post, see p. 310.
[33] See p. 217.

CHAPTER 13

SENTENCE

MANY of the principles and procedures involved in sentencing are again the same as in trial by jury and to avoid unnecessary repetition, readers will be referred back to the relevant parts of Chapter 9[1] wherever possible. The sentences which may be imposed by a magistrates' court are essentially the same, save that the maximum degree of punishment is considerably less. In some cases the court has power to send the offender to be sentenced by the Crown Court so that a more severe punishment may be imposed. This is dealt with in Section C, below.

A. PROCEDURE BEFORE SENTENCE

In this section steps occurring between the pronouncement of the court's decision and the imposition of sentence or committal for sentence are considered.

1. Matters to be put before the court

It is usual for the prosecution to prepare a statement of the accused's character and previous convictions. The practice recommended by the Lord Chief Justice in 1966[2] may be adopted in the magistrates' courts, though if the accused has a clean record, there would be no need to put anything in writing. If there are convictions, they should be written down and a copy given to the accused, if he is present, so that he can object to any which he does not admit.

Further, the magistrates must not pass sentence until any reports they have requisitioned are available.[3]

2. Plea in mitigation

Before deciding how to deal with the accused, the court must ask him whether he has anything to say. The same matters may be

---

[1] See p. 216.

[2] See footnote 6, p. 217: preparation by the prosecution of a proof of evidence containing details of the accused's record, etc. The practice direction does not make any reference to the type of proceedings except in one reference to the retirement of the jury. Because of the greater informality in summary proceedings, the direction is presumably not mandatory.

[3] See pp. 307 and 318.

brought up as on a conviction on indictment, dealt with on page 217.

3. Taking offences into consideration

The practice described on page 220, whereby the accused may admit offences of which he has not been convicted with a view to having them taken into consideration in passing sentence on the offence charged, also operates in magistrates' courts. Unless a compensation or restitution order is made in respect of an offence taken into consideration,[4] the court cannot sentence the accused to a greater penalty than it could for the offence of which he has been convicted and it cannot take into consideration any offence outside its jurisdiction.

4. Adjournment

As already mentioned,[5] the court may adjourn after conviction to consider the best way to treat the offender. It may adjourn because the magistrates on the bench cannot agree on the sentence to be imposed. For this purpose they adjourn for any period if the offender is at liberty. The conviction still ranks as a conviction for the purposes of a later charge of the same offence even though sentence is never passed.[6]

When the hearing is resumed, the court may be composed of different magistrates. As the new bench must consider the evidence and circumstances of the case before passing sentence,[7] the division between the functions of adjudication and sentencing should cause no injustice. It is perhaps more than usually desirable for the accused or his legal representative to be present at the resumed hearing.

Other reasons for adjourning are to obtain medical or psychiatric reports.[8] In this case the offender must be remanded but not for a period of more than four weeks on bail or three weeks in custody.[9]

The hearing may also need to be adjourned to secure the presence of the accused before passing a sentence of imprisonment or a disqualification.[10]

---

[4] Powers of Criminal Courts Act 1973, s. 35 (1); Theft Act 1968, s. 28; Criminal Justice Act 1972, s. 6 (3); see pp. 251 and 252.

[5] See p. 307.

[6] See *R.* v. *Sheridan*, p. 164.

[7] Magistrates' Courts Act 1952, s. 98 (7).

[8] *Ibid.* s. 26; see p. 219. See also Powers of Criminal Courts Act 1973, s. 45, p. 220.

[9] Magistrates' Courts Act 1952, s. 14 (3) and s. 26 (1) as amended by the Criminal Justice Act 1967, s. 30.

[10] See p. 302.

B. Punishments and Orders

Of the sentences available on conviction on indictment described in Chapter 9, the only sentences which are totally outside the power of magistrates to impose are life imprisonment, extended sentences of imprisonment, disqualification under the Powers of Criminal Courts Act 1973,[11] criminal bankruptcy orders[12] and of course, the death penalty. In the case of borstal training and hospital orders, the court may only impose them itself to a limited extent but may commit the offender to the Crown Court with a view to the necessary full order being made by that court.[13]

1. Imprisonment

Magistrates' courts' powers of sentencing an offender to imprisonment, where that is a punishment available for the offence being tried, are restricted in five general ways. In addition, their powers are limited in relation to an existing suspended sentence where the offender before them has committed the offence of which he is convicted during its operational period.

The accused must be present in court when the court imposes a sentence of imprisonment.[14]

(a) *General limitations on the term*

On summary conviction a court may not sentence the offender to less than five days in prison,[15] but it may order his detention for a shorter period in some other place where a very short sentence is appropriate. Police cells may be certified by the Home Secretary as a suitable place of detention for not more than four days,[16] detention in the cells of the court may be ordered for one day[17] and detention overnight at the police station may be ordered for failure to pay a sum of money adjudged to be paid by conviction.[18]

As far as the maximum sentence is concerned, the length depends on the nature of the offence being charged. In the case of summary

[11] See p. 247.
[12] See p. 253; suspended sentence supervision orders are also effectively outside the magistrates' courts' jurisdiction, but the Secretary of State has power to reduce the minimum term upon which a supervision order may be made under s. 26 (2) of the Powers of Criminal Courts Act 1973. The magistrates' court has power to deal with an offender during the operational period.
[13] See pp. 335 and 336.
[14] Criminal Justice Act 1967, s. 26.
[15] Magistrates' Courts Act 1952, s. 107 (1).
[16] *Ibid.* s. 109 (1) and (2).
[17] *Ibid.* s. 110 (1).
[18] *Ibid.* s. 111.

offences, whether purely summary or being proceeded against summarily under section 18 (1) of the Magistrates' Courts Act 1952,[19] the court may imprison for any period up to the maximum prescribed. This is in some cases longer than six months,[20] though these are unusual. Where the court wishes to impose consecutive sentences,[21] the aggregate must not exceed six months.[22] This maximum is subject to the exception of a sentence of imprisonment imposed for failure to pay a fine in addition to a sentence of imprisonment, where the fine and imprisonment were ordered for the same offence.[23]

In the case of offences which were initially proceeded against as indictable offences but which were subsequently tried summarily, *i.e.* where section 18 (3) or 19 of the Magistrates' Courts Act 1952[24] was invoked, the court may not impose more than six months' imprisonment for one offence. It may sentence for up to 12 months, however, where there is a conviction of at least two indictable offences.[25] Alternatively, the magistrates may commit him for sentence to the Crown Court.[26]

Where the offender is already serving a sentence of imprisonment, the magistrates' court may order a sentence of imprisonment to start at the end of the existing sentence.[27]

(b) *People who have not previously served a prison sentence*

Unless of the opinion that no other method of dealing with him is appropriate, the magistrates' court, like the Crown Court, may not impose a sentence of imprisonment on a person of or over the age of 21 who has not been sentenced to imprisonment by a United Kingdom court before.[28] If it does so sentence him, a magistrates' court must state the reasons for its opinion and enter them on the warrant of commitment and court register. Although a suspended sentence

---

19 See pp. 292 and 295.

20 *e.g.* certain smuggling offences under the Customs and Excise Act 1952, ss. 71, 73 and 283. The aggregate sentences for such offences passed consecutively must not exceed the maximum for one such offence: Magistrates' Courts Act 1952, s. 108 (3).

21 See p. 229.

22 Magistrates' Courts Act 1952, s. 108 (1).

23 *Ibid.* s. 108 (4). The aggregate may then be six or twelve months plus the period for non-payment of the fine prescribed by the Magistrates' Courts Act 1952, Sched. 3; see p. 326.

24 See pp. 296 and 297. *N.B.* this does not apply where the prosecution applied in the first instance for summary trial under s. 18 (1).

25 Magistrates' Courts Act 1952, s. 108 (2). This can only occur where the accused has consented to trial of more than one information at the same hearing; see *Brangwynne* v. *Evans*, p. 304.

26 See p. 332.

27 *Ibid.* s. 108 (1).

28 Powers of Criminal Courts Act 1973, s. 20 (1). The court must consider any available information as described on p. 317.

counts as a sentence of imprisonment on the later occasion, a suspended sentence which has not been activated does not count as a previous sentence of imprisonment; *i.e.* this section applies to people who have not actually been to prison before.

(c) *Unrepresented defendants*

If a person who has not previously been sentenced to imprisonment in the United Kingdom is unrepresented, he cannot be sentenced to imprisonment (or borstal training or detention) unless either he applied for but was refused legal aid on account of his means, or he was informed of his right to apply for legal aid but refused or failed to do so.[29] Suspended sentences are treated in the same way as under (b) above. Legal representation, for the purpose of this provision, is representation by counsel or solicitor after the finding of guilt and before sentence.[30]

(d) *Young persons*

The magistrates' court may not sentence a person under the age of seventeen to imprisonment.[31]

(e) *Juvenile adults*

Unless it is of the opinion that no other method of dealing with him is appropriate, the magistrates' court may not order a person under the age of 21 to be imprisoned; it must obtain and consider information about the circumstances and take into account any available information about his character and health.[32] In the context of this provision and paragraph (d) above, though not for the other restrictions on imprisonment,[33] the term " imprisonment " includes a committal to prison in default of payment or for failure to obey an order (*e.g.* binding over).[34]

If a magistrates' court is of the opinion that no other method of dealing with the offender is appropriate, it must state its reason for holding that opinion and enter it on the warrant of commitment and court register.[35]

A magistrates' court does not normally have power to sentence to imprisonment for longer than six months, but in the case of juvenile

---

[29] *Ibid.* s. 21 (1).

[30] *Ibid.* s. 21 (2); if committed for trial or sentence, it makes no difference whether the accused was informed of his right to legal aid by the magistrates' court or the Crown Court.

[31] *Ibid.* s. 19 (1); as to the sentences it may impose, see p. 369.

[32] *Ibid.* s. 19 (2); as to the effect of the second part of this provision, see p. 220.

[33] *Ibid.* s. 57 (1).

[34] *Ibid.* s. 19 (4).

[35] *Ibid.* s. 19 (3).

adults it cannot do so at all by virtue of section 3 (1) of the Criminal Justice Act 1961.[36]

(e) *Suspended sentences*

At proceedings for an offence which was committed during the operational period of a suspended sentence, the magistrates' court has power to deal with the suspended sentence only if it was passed by a magistrates' court, though it need not be the same one.[37]

Where the suspended sentence was passed by the Crown Court, a magistrates' court dealing with the offender for an offence punishable by imprisonment during the operational period may either

(*a*) commit him in custody or on bail to be dealt with by the Crown Court, or
(*b*) give notice of the offender's subsequent conviction to the appropriate officer of the Crown Court.[38]

The person subject to the suspended sentence is committed to the Crown Court sitting in the same place as the court which passed the sentence, unless it is inconvenient or impracticable to do so.[39]

The option contained in paragraph (*b*) means that the magistrates' court ignores the suspended sentence, except in as far as it gives notice. It does *not* mean that the court " makes no order with respect to the suspended sentence "[40] for to make no order amounts to " dealing with " the sentence, which the magistrates' court is unable to do.[41]

Where it has power to deal with the suspended sentence, the magistrates' court sentences the offender in the normal way for the subsequent offence and may bring the suspended sentence into effect; limitations on the aggregate of the terms of imprisonment [42] that magistrates' courts can impose do not apply in this respect.

2. Fine

The overwhelming majority of summary offences are punishable by a fine with a fixed maximum, with or without a provision for imprisonment. Where a sentence involving detention is the only punishment and no fine is prescribed by the statute creating the sum-

---

[36] See p. 231.
[37] Powers of Criminal Courts Act 1973, s. 24 (1).
[38] *Ibid.* s. 24 (2).
[39] See Directions of the Lord Chief Justice of October 14, 1971, directions 6 and 7, p. 339.
[40] Powers of Criminal Courts Act 1973, s. 23 (1) (*d*); see p. 229.
[41] *i.e.* under *ibid.* s. 24 (1), above.
[42] See p. 319.

mary offence, the magistrates' court may impose a fine of not more than £100, provided the period of imprisonment to which the offender may be sentenced if he defaults in payment [43] does not exceed the period to which he could have been sentenced on conviction.[44]

Where an indictable offence is tried summarily under section 18 (3) or 19 of the Magistrates' Courts Act 1952[45] the court may impose a fine of not more than £400.[46]

Where a magistrates' court proposes to sentence an offender to a fine, it must take his means into consideration.[47] It may ask him to supply a statement of his means.[48] Unless he is willing to pay immediately on sentence being passed, the court may allow him time to pay or order payment by instalments.[49] If the offender is not present, the clerk must give him written notice of the fine and how it is to be paid.[50]

Enforcement

The enforcement of fines is subject to rather complex provisions. Although the subject is not generally of interest to practising lawyers, a brief summary of the provisions may be useful.

(1) *In the first instance*. At the hearing at which the court passes sentence, three courses of action may be followed:

- (i) the offender immediately pays the fine himself or through someone on his behalf;
- (ii) the court allows the offender time to pay or orders payment by instalments [51];
- (iii) the court issues a warrant for the offender's committal to prison for non-payment; it can only do this in three cases:
    - (*a*) the offence is punishable by imprisonment and he appears to have means to pay immediately;
    - (*b*) it appears that he is unlikely to stay in the United Kingdom long enough to enforce payment by any means other than imprisonment; or

[43] Magistrates' Courts Act 1952, s. 27 (3), and Criminal Justice Act 1967, s. 43 (2). Such offences are exceptional. Many statutes impose a maximum which is greatly in excess of the general limit.

[44] See Magistrates' Courts Act 1952, Sched. 3, p. 326.

[45] See pp. 296 and 297.

[46] Criminal Justice Act 1967, s. 43 (1).

[47] Magistrates' Courts Act 1952, s. 31 (1).

[48] *Cf*. Criminal Justice Act 1967, s. 44 (8), below.

[49] Magistrates' Courts Act 1952, s. 63 (1).

[50] Magistrates' Courts Rules 1968, r. 38.

[51] Magistrates' Courts Act 1952, s. 63 (1).

(*c*) he is at the same time sentenced to an immediate term of imprisonment or other detention.[52]

If course (i) is followed, no further proceedings are necessary.

If the offender is given time to pay, under (ii) above, but fails to do so, he may apply to the court for further time or for payment by instalments.[53] Alternatively, the court may require his attendance at court for an inquiry into his means before deciding how to deal with him.[54]

If course (iii) is followed, the court may postpone the issue of the warrant of commitment and fix a term of imprisonment for the offender to serve if he defaults in payment.[55]

If the offender is committed to prison immediately, his liability to pay the fine is absolved after serving the term of imprisonment; if he pays during his imprisonment, his term is reduced according to the proportion of the whole which he has paid.[56] If the committal to prison is suspended,[57] then he may be arrested on default on the warrant of commitment without any further court proceedings.[58]

The magistrates' court may make a community service order instead of committing the defaulter to prison.[59] Payment of the amount due makes the order cease to have any effect and the payment of part reduces the number of hours to be worked proportionately.[60]

(2) *At a later hearing*. If committal to prison has not been ordered, and if no term of imprisonment to be served in default of paying the fine has been fixed and the offender defaults, the court must hold an inquiry into his means unless he is already serving a sentence of imprisonment.[61] Default on one instalment is treated as default on all outstanding instalments.[62]

To hold the means inquiry the court must consist of at least two justices sitting in open court[63]; they may secure the offender's

---

[52] Criminal Justice Act 1967, s. 44 (2).

[53] Magistrates' Courts Act 1952, s. 63 (2).

[54] *Ibid.* s. 70 (2), as amended by the Criminal Justice Act 1967, s. 103 (1) and Sched. 6, para. 13.

[55] *Ibid.* s. 65 (2); this power is only available in those cases where the offender may be committed to prison immediately: Criminal Justice Act 1967, s. 44 (3).

[56] Magistrates' Courts Act 1952, s. 67.

[57] See *ibid.* s. 65 (2), above.

[58] Criminal Justice Act 1967, s. 44 (6).

[59] Criminal Justice Act 1972, s. 49; as to community service orders, see p. 235.

[60] The community service order operates normally, save that the fine of £50 for failure to comply cannot be imposed: *ibid.* s. 49 (2).

[61] Criminal Justice Act 1967, s. 44 (4). If he is in prison, the warrant of commitment need not be served on him at once but may be postponed until he is released: *R.* v. *Leeds Prison Governor, ex p. Huntley* [1972] 1 W.L.R. 1016.

[62] Magistrates' Courts Act 1952, s. 63 (3).

[63] *Ibid.* s. 98 (2).

presence by summons or warrant,[64] or by warrant if he fails to answer the summons,[65] and may require him to supply a statement of his means.[66] He must be present if committal to prison in default is ordered unless he is already serving a term of imprisonment or other detention.[67]

The court may only commit the offender to prison after inquiring into his means in two cases:

(i) where the offence is punishable by imprisonment and the offender appears to have sufficient means; or

(ii) where the court has already unsuccessfully considered and tried other methods of enforcing payment.[68]

It may postpone the operation of the warrant of commitment and fix a term to be served in default.[69]

If the court cannot commit him to prison after the means inquiry, it may order one of the following:

(i) distress, *i.e.* seizure of the offender's goods in satisfaction of the fine[70];

(ii) further time to pay or payment by instalments[71];

(iii) attachment of earnings, *i.e.* deduction at source from the offender's earned income to be paid by the employer to the court[72];

(iv) payment subject to the supervision of a person appointed by the court[73];

(v) remission of the whole or any part of the fine, having regard to any change in the circumstances of the offender since conviction[74];

---

[64] *Ibid.* s. 70 (2), as amended by the Criminal Justice Act 1967, s. 103 (1) and Sched. 6, para. 13.

[65] *Ibid.* s. 70 (3).

[66] Criminal Justice Act 1967, s. 44 (8), which is punishable by a £50 fine if he fails to supply it: *ibid.* s. 44 (9).

[67] *Ibid.* s. 44 (6).

[68] *Ibid.* s. 44 (5).

[69] Magistrates' Courts Act 1952, s. 65 (2).

[70] *Ibid.* s. 64 (1). A distress warrant may be issued without a means inquiry being held, the only pre-requisite being the notice given to the offender of the fine under the Magistrates' Courts Rules 1968, r. 38. If the distress levied is insufficient, the court must proceed by other means.

[71] *Ibid.* s. 63 (2).

[72] Criminal Justice Act 1967, s. 46.

[73] Magistrates' Courts Act 1952, s. 71. It is the duty of the supervisor to " advise and befriend the offender with a view to inducing him to pay the sum ": Magistrates' Courts Rules 1968, r. 46 (2).

[74] Criminal Justice Act 1967, s. 44 (10).

(vi) recovery of the fine by the clerk of the court in the High Court or in a county court.[75]

If the offender defaults yet again, the court need not hold a further means inquiry but may commit him to prison if no other means of enforcement appear likely to succeed.[76] If he is not already in prison, however, the court can only do so in his presence.[77]

Finally, the court may at any time when the offender is present or under arrest order his search and the application of any money found on him (which belongs to him) towards payment of the fine.[78]

(3) *Length of imprisonment in default*. The maximum terms of imprisonment which can be ordered for default in paying a fine are seven days (£2 fine), 14 days (£5 fine), 30 days (£20 fine), 60 days (£50 fine) and 90 days (fine exceeding £50).[79]

3. Other orders

(a) *Hospital order*

Where an offence tried summarily is punishable by imprisonment, the magistrates' court has the same power to make a hospital or guardianship order as a court trying the accused on indictment, on finding that he is suffering from mental illness, subnormality, etc.[80] The magistrates' court may make the order on conviction[81] or as soon as it finds that the accused committed the act or omission constituting the offence without convicting him.[82] Appeal lies despite the lack of conviction.

Alternatively the magistrates' court may commit the offender to the Crown Court with a view to its making a restriction order (*i.e.* a hospital order with a restriction on his discharge).[83] In cases where more normal psychiatric treatment is desirable, the court may make a probation order with a condition for medical treatment in a hospital or by a doctor. In that case the accused must be convicted.[84]

---

75 Criminal Justice Act 1967, s. 45.

76 *Ibid.* s. 44 (4).

77 *Ibid.* s. 44 (6). He need not be present if the court fixed a term of imprisonment at the means inquiry to be served in default.

78 Magistrates' Courts Act 1952, s. 68.

79 *Ibid.* Sched. 3, para. 1, as amended by the Criminal Justice Act 1967, s. 93 (1).

80 See Mental Health Act 1959, s. 60, p. 234. The law is summarised by Lord Parker C.J. in *R.* v. *Gardiner* [1967] 1 W.L.R. 464 at p. 468.

81 *Ibid.* s. 60 (1).

82 *Ibid.* s. 60 (2). This gives the court a chance of finding the accused to be not guilty by reason of insanity.

83 See p. 336.

84 See Powers of Criminal Courts Act 1973, ss. 2 (1) and 3 (1).

(b) *Community service, probation and discharge*

Community service, probation and discharge (absolute or conditional) may be ordered on summary conviction in the same way as on conviction on indictment.[85] In a probation order for a single offence a condition of residence in a probation hostel or home for up to twelve months may be imposed [86] for it is not treated as "detention" in a punitive sense. Hospital residence may be ordered for the whole period of the probation order.[87]

(c) *Deferment of sentence*

The magistrates' court has the same power as the Crown Court to defer passing sentence for up to six months.[88] The court is not obliged to remand the accused, as it might have to do on an adjournment,[89] but simply releases him. The magistrates' court has no inherent power to postpone sentence, although it has power to adjourn after conviction for certain purposes.[90] In view of the terms of this statutory power to defer, it has been held that the court which defers sentence must also pass sentence, *i.e.* a magistrates' court cannot commit for sentence after a deferment.[91]

(d) *Binding-over*

Taking sureties to keep the peace, which in the Crown Court is a common law power,[92] is governed in the magistrates' courts principally by the Justices of the Peace Act 1361 and by section 91 of the Magistrates' Courts Act 1952. Under the 1361 Act " all them that be not of good fame " may have taken from them " sufficient surety and mainprise of their good behaviour towards the King and his people."

Under section 91 of the 1952 Act, a magistrates' court may on complaint adjudge a person to enter into a recognisance, with or without sureties, to keep the peace or to be of good behaviour towards the complainant. If the person against whom the order is made does not comply with the order he may be committed to prison for up to six months. Although primarily designed for complaints by an individual not necessarily based on the commission of a criminal

---

[85] See pp. 235, 236 and 240.
[86] *Ibid.* s. 2 (5).
[87] *Ibid.* s. 3 (1).
[88] See *ibid.* s. 1, p. 242.
[89] See Magistrates' Courts Act 1952, s. 14, p. 67.
[90] *R.* v. *Talgarth Justices, ex p. Bithell* [1973] 1 W.L.R. 1327; as to adjournment, see p. 307.
[91] *R.* v. *Gilby* [1975] 1 W.L.R. 924.
[92] Statutorily recognised in the Courts Act 1971, s. 6 (4) (*b*).

offence, this procedure or the procedure under the 1361 Act may be used against any person who has been brought before the court, provided there is material justifying a fear of a breach of the peace.

The limits of these powers of binding over are by no means certain. It would appear that the 1361 Act may be invoked against anyone appearing before a magistrate, including the defendant, the complainant, the prosecutor or a witness.[93] If a person is already before the court, an oral complaint can be made and, if proved, the power under the 1952 Act arises. It is clearly established that an acquitted accused may be bound over.[94]

The courts have concentrated, however, on the natural justice aspect of the power, in particular the exercise of the power without giving the person bound over an opportunity to be heard. A successful complainant or witness must be warned of the magistrate's intention to bind him over[95]; it is wise, but not obligatory, to warn a defendant (whether convicted or acquitted)[96]; it is unnecessary to warn the person if he consents to the binding over[96] or if the reason for doing it is a disturbance in the face of the court.[97]

Finally, it should be mentioned that there is no maximum sum in which a person can be bound over and there is no maximum term for the binding over to last.[98]

(e) *Deportation and disqualification from driving*

A magistrates' court may make a recommendation for deportation in the same way as a court convicting on indictment.[99] It may order disqualification from driving,[1] though special provisions apply to this where the offender is at the same time committed to the Crown Court for sentence.[2] The accused must be present in court when the court imposes a disqualification.[3] The magistrates' court has no power to disqualify a person under section 44 of the Powers of Criminal Courts Act 1973.[4]

---

[93] *Wilson* v. *Skeock* (1949) 65 T.L.R. 418; *R.* v. *Aubrey-Fletcher, ex p. Thompson* [1969] 1 W.L.R. 872; *R.* v. *South West London Magistrates' Court, ex p. Brown* [1974] Crim.L.R. 313.

[94] *R.* v. *Woking Justices, ex p. Gossage* [1973] 1 Q.B. 448.

[95] *R.* v. *Hendon Justices, ex p. Gorchein* [1973] 1 W.L.R. 1502.

[96] *R.* v. *South West London Magistrates' Court, ex p. Brown* [1974] Crim.L.R. 313.

[97] *R.* v. *North London Metropolitan Magistrate, ex p. Haywood* [1973] 1 W.L.R. 965.

[98] A short analysis of the power to bind over was published in 1976: Bowden, *Binding over in the Magistrates' Court*, which also examines various specific statutory powers to bind over. As to probation combined with binding over, see p. 237.

[99] Immigration Act 1971, s. 3 (6).

[1] See p. 245.

[2] See p. 334.

[3] Criminal Justice Act 1967, s. 26.

[4] *i.e.* where a vehicle was used in the commission of the offence; see p. 247.

(f) *Costs*

The type of costs order varies in the magistrates' court according to the type of offence before the court.

An award out of central funds may only be made in respect of an indictable offence; such an order may be made in favour of the prosecution in any event, but the court may only order defence costs if the information is dismissed (if the proceedings are for summary trial) or if the examining magistrate decides not to commit the accused for trial.[5] Witnesses' costs may be ordered whether or not they give evidence but a defence witness to character only must receive a certificate that the interests of justice required his attendance.[6]

On the dismissal of an information following summary trial, the court may order the prosecutor to pay costs to the accused as it thinks just and reasonable.[7] On conviction, the accused may be ordered to pay costs to the prosecutor as the court thinks just and reasonable.[8]

If the court decides not to commit the accused for trial on the ground that the evidence is not sufficient and the court is of the opinion that the charge was not made in good faith, it may order the prosecutor to pay all or part of the defence costs.[9] If the prosecutor is ordered to pay more than £25 under this provision; he may appeal to the Crown Court.[10]

If an information charging an indictable offence is not proceeded with, either by summary trial or by committal proceedings, the court (or another court in the area) may order the prosecutor to pay the defence costs as it thinks just and reasonable.[11] Alternatively, the court may order payment out of central funds of the costs properly incurred in preparing the defence and the reasonable expenses of defence witnesses.[12] The Crown Court may order defence costs if the accused is committed but not ultimately tried as if he had been tried and acquitted.[13]

(g) *Compensation, restitution, forfeiture*

A magistrates' court has power to impose a compensation order in the same way as the Crown Court,[14] but subject to a maximum of

---

[5] Costs in Criminal Cases Act 1973, s. 1 (1) and (2).
[6] *Ibid.* s. 1 (4), (5) and (7).
[7] *Ibid.* s. 2 (1).
[8] *Ibid.* s. 2 (2).
[9] *Ibid.* s. 2 (4).
[10] *Ibid.* s. 2 (5).
[11] *Ibid.* s. 12 (3).
[12] *Ibid.* s. 12 (1).
[13] *Ibid.* s. 12 (5); costs on appeal are dealt with on pp. 348 and 351.
[14] See Powers of Criminal Courts Act 1973, s. 35, p. 250, orders under the Criminal Law Act 1826 (see p. 252) are not available in the magistrates' court.

£400 in respect of each conviction. If an order is made in respect of an offence taken into consideration, it and any other order made on the same conviction must not exceed £400 in all.[15] The order is suspended pending the determination of any appeal or the expiry of the period allowed for giving notice.[16]

Restitution orders may also be made.[17] An order made by a magistrates' court is suspended pending appeal, or the expiry of the period for giving notice, but the court may order that the transfer of the property in question or other property representing the stolen property take effect immediately if it is of the opinion that the title is not in dispute.[18]

A magistrates' court may order the delivery to the owner of property which has come into the possession of the police in connection with their investigation of any offence; the application is made by a claimant (the owner)[19] or by the police to protect themselves from civil action.[20] Property which remains unclaimed in police possession for a year may be sold or otherwise disposed of by them.[21] The procedure is not suitable where any dispute of legal or factual difficulty may arise.

Finally, the magistrates' court has power, where appropriate, to order forfeiture of property used for criminal purposes.[22]

C. Committal for Sentence

Where a magistrates' court considers that the appropriate sentence for the offender is outside its power to impose, the court may, in some cases, send him to the Crown Court to be sentenced. The cases in which it may do so are:

(i) where the offender has been tried summarily[23] for an indictable offence[24];

---

[15] Powers of Criminal Courts Act 1973, s. 35 (5).

[16] *Ibid.* s. 36 (2).

[17] Theft Act 1968, s. 28, and Criminal Justice Act 1972, s. 6; see p. 252.

[18] Criminal Justice Act 1972, s. 6 (5).

[19] *i.e.* the person entitled to the goods: *Raymond Lyons and Co.* v. *Metropolitan Police Commissioner* [1975] Q.B. 321.

[20] Police (Property) Act 1897, as amended by the Criminal Justice Act 1972, s. 58.

[21] Police (Disposal of Property) Regulations 1975 (S.I. 1975 No. 1474); property in police possession under the Powers of Criminal Courts Act 1973, s. 43 (below), may be disposed of in six months.

[22] See Powers of Criminal Courts Act 1973, s. 43, p. 254.

[23] *i.e.* under the Magistrates' Courts Act 1952, ss. 18 (3) or 19; see pp. 296 and 297.

[24] *Ibid.* s. 29.

(ii) under section 5 of the Vagrancy Act 1824 for being an incorrigible rogue [25];

(iii) where the magistrates' court has convicted a person of an offence punishable on summary conviction by imprisonment and the offender is not younger than 17 and not older than 20 and a borstal sentence is appropriate for him [26];

(iv) where a magistrates' court has convicted a person over the age of 14 of an offence punishable by imprisonment it may commit him to the Crown Court with a view to a hospital order with a restriction on discharge being made [27];

(v) where a magistrates' court convicts a person during the operational period of a suspended sentence,[28] while subject to a community service order,[29] or on probation or conditional discharge [30] or while released on licence, [31] he may be committed to the Crown Court to be dealt with.[32]

Committal for sentence is not an order subject to appeal to the Crown Court,[33] nor should appeal be made against the sentence imposed by the Crown Court after an invalid committal to the Court of Appeal.[34] The proper course is to apply to the Queen's Bench Divisional Court for an order of certiorari [35] if the committal appears to be improper.

Where an offender is committed in custody, the warrant of commitment directs his custodian to bring him before a specified sitting of the Crown Court. The limit of three weeks which applies where the offender will be brought back to the magistrates' court on adjournment [36] does not apply. The appropriate officer of the Crown Court or the judge may direct the transfer of proceedings from one sitting of the Crown Court to another; if a party is dissatisfied, he may apply to the judge, who hears the application in chambers.[37]

---

[25] A Home Office Working Party published a report on vagrancy and street offences on September 8, 1976, in which the abolition of this power and the repeal of the Vagrancy Acts were recommended.

[26] Magistrates' Courts Act 1952, s. 28, as amended by the Children and Young Persons Act 1969, s. 7 (1).

[27] Mental Health Act 1959, s. 67.

[28] Powers of Criminal Courts Act 1973, s. 24 (2); see p. 322.

[29] *Ibid.* s. 16 (3).

[30] *Ibid.* s. 8 (6).

[31] Criminal Justice Act 1967, s. 62 (6).

[32] See Directions of the Lord Chief Justice of October 14, 1971 (as amended by a Practice Direction of January 1, 1973), directions 5–9.

[33] *R.* v. *London Sessions, ex p. Rogers* [1951] 2 K.B. 74; see also p. 345.

[34] *R.* v. *Birtles* [1975] 1 W.L.R. 1623, applying *R.* v. *Warren* [1954] 1 W.L.R. 531.

[35] See p. 45.

[36] Magistrates' Courts Act 1952, s. 14 (3); see p. 318.

[37] Directions of the Lord Chief Justice of October 14, 1971, direction 14.

For the purposes of sentencing, the Crown Court is constituted as for an appeal[38]; it sits without a jury but with two, three or four justices of the peace presided over by a circuit judge or recorder.[39] A solicitor may represent the accused if he has acted for him before.[40] The provisions for variation of sentence applicable to sentence after trial on indictment apply to a sentence passed on a person committed from a magistrates' court.[41]

The Costs in Criminal Cases Act 1973 applies to committals for sentence. It applies to committals under 1, 3 and 4 below as it applies to a person convicted before the Crown Court; it applies to committals under 2 below as if the incorrigible rogue were committed for trial by examining justices; and it applies to committals under 5 below (except prisoners released on licence) and other dealings with such offenders as if they had been tried in the proceedings at which the order was made or sentence passed.[42]

1. Indictable offences triable summarily

When an offender has been tried summarily for an indictable offence,[43] the magistrates' court may discover after conviction that his character and antecedents are such that a severe punishment is appropriate.[44] "Antecedents" includes not only previous convictions but also any matters disclosed in the course of trial which reflect on the accused's character.[45]

The court commits him for sentence in custody or on bail.[46] The general right to bail does not apply because the offender has been convicted,[47] though an unrepresented accused must be told of his right to apply for bail to the Crown Court or High Court.[48] The Crown Court may grant him bail.[49]

---

[38] Courts Act 1971, s. 5 (1), and Directions of the Lord Chief Justice, direction 12 (v); see p. 340.

[39] See p. 86.

[40] Direction of the Lord Chancellor of February 9, 1972; see p. 152.

[41] See Courts Act 1971, s. 11, p. 221.

[42] Costs in Criminal Cases Act 1973, s. 18.

[43] Under the Magistrates' Courts Act 1952, ss. 18 (3) or 19, but not under s. 18 (1) for that is treated as a summary offence throughout; see pp. 292–298.

[44] *Ibid.* s. 29. See also *R.* v. *Rugby Justices, ex p. Prince* [1974] 1 W.L.R. 736. As to the magistrates' powers, see p. 319 (imprisonment) and p. 322 (fine).

[45] *R.* v. *King's Lynn Justices* [1969] 1 Q.B. 488. Facts revealed in the magistrates' inquiry into whether or not to proceed summarily cannot be used to justify a committal, but, if the facts came to light after the inquiry (or if no inquiry was made), they may be considered: *R.* v. *Lymm Justices, ex p. Brown* [1973] 1 W.L.R. 1039.

[46] The power to commit on bail was introduced by the Criminal Justice Act 1967, s. 20.

[47] Bail Act 1976, s. 4 (2). As to bail generally, see p. 73.

[48] *Ibid.* s. 5 (6).

[49] Courts Act 1971, s. 13; see p. 71.

In *R.* v. *Coe* [50] one offender was committed on bail after summary trial of six shopbreakings and 11 takings of motor vehicles and, while on bail, committed three further offences of shopbreaking and larceny. In addition he was in breach of an earlier probation order. The Lord Chief Justice said: " The cases must be rare when justices can properly commit for that purpose [*i.e.* under the Magistrates' Courts Act 1952, s. 29] on bail because the whole purpose of the committal is to have the accused sent to prison. . . . This applicant had no business to be committed on bail."

The offender must normally be committed to the sitting of the Crown Court which is most convenient; this is considered in the light of the places designated by the presiding judge as suitable for the committal of cases from the petty sessions area in which the magistrates' court sits.[51] As there is no time limit on committal for sentence, choosing the most convenient sitting presumably entails consideration of time and the avoidance of delay.

The Crown Court inquires into the circumstances of the case and has power to deal with the offender as if he had just been convicted of the offence on indictment.[52]

Where an offender is tried summarily for more than one offence and the magistrates' court intends to commit him for sentence on one of those offences, it must also leave the sentencing on the other offence or offences to be done by the Crown Court,[53] provided they are punishable by imprisonment, carry disqualification from driving or were committed during the operational period of a suspended sentence. The Crown Court does not have any greater power of sentencing in respect of those other offences than the magistrates' court would have had; the purpose of this provision is to secure that the sentence is taken as a whole and is consistent within itself. Ancillary matters such as compensation orders must also be left to the Crown Court.[54] An additional reason for this is that the offender has no right of appeal against the order made by the magistrates' court.[55] The sentence on other offences of which the offender has been convicted, but which could not be sent to the Crown Court for

---

[50] See also p. 298.

[51] Directions of the Lord Chief Justice of October 14, 1971, directions 8 and 9.

[52] Powers of Criminal Courts Act 1973, s. 42; this may mean that the offender is eligible for a different sentence for which he was not eligible at the date of committal, *e.g.* because of his age: *R.* v. *Keelan* (1975) 61 Cr.App.R. 212.

[53] Criminal Justice Act 1967, s. 56 (5).

[54] *R.* v. *Brogan* [1975] 1 W.L.R. 393; *R.* v. *Blackpool Justices, ex p. Charlson* [1972] 1 W.L.R. 1456.

[55] See p. 353.

sentencing,[56] may be adjourned *sine die* until the Crown Court's sentence has been passed.

If the magistrates' court has deferred passing sentence under section 1 of the Powers of Criminal Courts Act 1973, it may not deal with the offender after the deferment by committing him for sentence.[57]

If disqualification from driving is an obligatory or optional part of the sentence [58] for the offence for which the offender is committed or for another offence of which he is convicted, the magistrates' court may order disqualification until he is sentenced by the Crown Court.[59] If the Crown Court orders disqualification, the period during which he was disqualified by the magistrates' court is deducted from the total period.[60]

These provisions are also applicable to the other forms of committal for sentence described below.

2. Incorrigible rogues

The exceptional nature of this offence or, rather, status, gives it greater theoretical than practical significance. It applies to " rogues and vagabonds," as listed in section 4 of the Vagrancy Act 1824, of whom suspected persons loitering with intent are probably the most important item. On a first conviction a rogue and vagabond can be sentenced to three months' imprisonment or to a fine of £25. On a second conviction, or if he violently resisted his apprehension or escaped from legal confinement as a rogue and vagabond, he becomes an incorrigible rogue [61] and is liable to be committed to the Crown Court where he may be imprisoned for up to 12 months.[62] He has no right to claim trial by jury on his second trial, although the punishment exceeds three months' imprisonment,[63] for he is sent to the Crown Court for a sentence related to his status, not to the offences which have caused him to acquire that status. For the same reason, there is no power to suspend the imprisonment.[64] Indeed, unless

[56] *i.e.* trivial offences for which neither imprisonment nor disqualification is appropriate.

[57] *R.* v. *Gilby* [1975] 1 W.L.R. 924; as to deferment, see pp. 242 and 327.

[58] See Road Traffic Act 1972, s. 93 (1) and (2), pp. 245 and 246.

[59] *Ibid.* s. 103 (1). The endorsement provisions of s. 101 do not apply to this temporary disqualification (s. 103 (3)) but his driving licence is taken and sent to the Crown Court (s. 103 (2)).

[60] *Ibid.* s. 103 (5).

[61] Vagrancy Act 1824, s. 5.

[62] Vagrancy Act 1824, s. 10.

[63] See Magistrates' Courts Act 1952, s. 25, p. 292.

[64] The Powers of Criminal Courts Act 1973, s. 22 (1), refers to a " sentence of imprisonment . . . for an offence " *R.* v. *Graves*, *The Times*, April 7, 1976.

section 56 of the Criminal Justice Act 1967 applies so that the Crown Court may sentence him for other offences, there is no power to deal with the incorrigible rogue except by an effective sentence of imprisonment.[65] The Crown Court has specific statutory power, however, to make a hospital order with or without a restriction on his release.[66] The incorrigible rogue may be committed on bail [67] and he must be committed to the most convenient sitting of the Crown Court.[68]

3. Committal for a borstal sentence

Borstal training [69] is not a sentence which a magistrates' court can itself impose.[70] Where an offender over 16 but under 21 years old is convicted of an offence punishable by imprisonment on summary conviction and a substantial period of detention is an appropriate sentence, he may be committed to the Crown Court to have a sentence of borstal passed on him.[71] He may be committed on bail [72] and the particular sitting of the Crown Court is determined in the same way as for committal for sentence.

The Crown Court inquires into the circumstances of the case and may either sentence him to borstal or deal with him in any way in which the magistrates' court could have dealt with him[73]; it may order disqualification from driving under section 56 of the Criminal Justice Act 1967. It should be noticed that this power is available where the offence tried summarily is not indictable by definition.[74] The fact that the offence carries only a short term of imprisonment does not preclude a borstal sentence [75] where it is otherwise appropriate on consideration of the accused's character and previous conduct,[76] but where the offence is not unduly serious and the maximum sentence is three months' imprisonment, borstal may be improper.[77]

---

[65] *R.* v. *Jackson* [1974] Q.B. 517 (where the Court purported to make a probation order).

[66] Mental Health Act 1959, s. 67 (5).

[67] Criminal Justice Act 1967, s. 20.

[68] Directions of the Lord Chief Justice of October 14, 1971, directions 8 and 9; see p. 333.

[69] Criminal Justice Act 1961, s. 1; see p. 231.

[70] Unless he is at the time subject to a borstal sentence; see p. 338.

[71] Magistrates' Courts Act 1952, s. 28 (1).

[72] Criminal Justice Act 1967, s. 20.

[73] Criminal Justice Act 1948, s. 20 (5). *R.* v. *O'Connor* [1976] 1 W.L.R. 368.

[74] *i.e.* is a purely summary offence punishable by not more than three months' imprisonment, or is a summary offence for which the accused has not claimed trial by jury under the Magistrates' Courts Act 1952, s. 25, as to which, see p. 292.

[75] *R.* v. *Amos* [1961] 1 W.L.R. 308.

[76] Criminal Justice Act 1961, s. 1 (2).

[77] *R.* v. *James* [1960] 1 W.L.R. 812 (where a rogue and vagabond was put on probation and was in breach of the probation order, borstal was inappropriate).

If the offence of which the offender is convicted is indictable, it is a better course for the magistrates' court to commit him under the Magistrates' Courts Act 1952, s. 29,[78] however, because the Crown Court can then treat him as though he had just been convicted on indictment[79] and is not restricted to the sentence which the magistrates' court could have passed, if it decides against borstal. The usefulness of the power to commit with a view to a borstal sentence was seriously questioned in *R.* v. *Hannigan.*[80]

If the magistrates' court commits an offender with a view to borstal on one offence, it must leave any other offences punishable by imprisonment or disqualification to be sentenced by the Crown Court[81]; it would be inappropriate to sentence him for any other offences of which he is convicted, as borstal training is to be " in lieu of any other sentence."[82]

Before passing a sentence of borstal training, the Crown Court must consider any report made on behalf of the Home Secretary concerning the offender.[83]

4. Committal for a restriction order

Where the accused's mental condition is in doubt but the court is satisfied that he committed the act charged, it may adjourn for a medical report for three weeks if the accused is in custody, or for four weeks if he is on bail.[84] This should be done before conviction so that the magistrates' court may itself pass a hospital order without convicting him.[85]

The magistrates' court may, however, commit a person to the Crown Court on conviction if—

(*a*) the offence charged is punishable by imprisonment,

(*b*) the medical reports[86] reveal that a hospital order would be appropriate,[87] and

(*c*) it appears, in view of the nature of the offence, the antecedents

---

[78] See Section 1., p. 332.

[79] Powers of Criminal Courts Act 1973, s. 42.

[80] [1971] Crim.L.R. 302.

[81] Criminal Justice Act 1967, s. 56 (5).

[82] Criminal Justice Act 1948, s. 20 (1).

[83] Criminal Justice Act 1961, s. 1 (3).

[84] Magistrates' Courts Act 1952, s. 26 (1), as amended by the Criminal Justice Act 1967, s. 30 and Sched. 6, para. 10.

[85] See Mental Health Act 1959, s. 60 (2), p. 326. If a psychiatric probation order is suitable, the court must convict him first: Powers of Criminal Courts Act 1973, s. 3 (1); see p. 237.

[86] Under the Mental Health Act 1959, s. 62; see p. 234.

[87] See *ibid.* s. 60, pp. 234 and 326.

of the offender and the risk of his committing further offences if set at large, that an order restricting his discharge from hospital should also be made.[88]

From a theoretical point of view, there is a certain anomaly in this section for this power to commit is only exercisable *after* conviction; a person may in law be not guilty of an offence by reason of insanity and be sufficiently dangerous to merit a restriction order. Procedurally, the following steps could therefore follow: the court need only be satisfied that the accused " did the act or made the omission charged " before making a hospital order [89]; they need be satisfied of no more than this before committal to the Crown Court, but before conviction, they must be satisfied of the accused's *guilt*; they must therefore hear any submissions he has to make about his insanity and, if he establishes it, they must dismiss the information, for he is not guilty in law; alternatively they must make an unrestricted hospital order without convicting him. From a practical point of view this is unlikely to arise as insanity is rarely raised to any offence other than homicide and in any event a hospital order may be available even though the mental condition does not give rise to a defence of insanity. Furthermore, on an unrestricted hospital order the Home Secretary need not order the accused's discharge until he is cured.

The requirement for conviction is included so that the Crown Court can sentence him otherwise than by hospital order.

The Crown Court, when it has considered the circumstances of the case, may make a hospital order, with or without restrictions, but if it does not make a hospital order it can only deal with the offender as the magistrates' court could have dealt with him.[90] However, the magistrates' court may commit him under this provision at the same time as committing him under section 29 of the Magistrates' Courts Act 1952.[91]

He must be committed in custody which, if available, may be in a hospital [92]; he is committed to the most convenient sitting of the Crown Court.[93]

5. Other forms of committal for sentence

A number of sentencing powers involve some (in a general sense) probationary period during which the offender must not commit a further offence or, if he does, he must face a further order in respect

[88] *Ibid.* s. 67. [89] *Ibid.* s. 60 (2). [90] Mental Health Act 1959, s. 67 (3).
[91] See p. 332. [92] Mental Health Act 1959, s. 68 (1).
[93] See Directions of the Lord Chief Justice, p. 333.

of the original offence. Such powers arise in the case of a prisoner released on licence, a released borstal trainee, and an offender who is subject to a suspended sentence, a community service order, a probation order or a conditional discharge. If a magistrates' court is dealing with the offender on the later occasion and the original order was made by the Crown Court, a power to commit him for sentence arises. No uniform rules apply to all these cases.

In the case of a prisoner released on licence who is convicted by a magistrates' court of an offence which is punishable on indictment with imprisonment, the magistrates' court may commit him to the Crown Court for sentence under section 29 of the Magistrates' Courts Act 1952.[94] The Crown Court may revoke the licence.

If a person who has been sentenced to borstal commits a further offence punishable by imprisonment while under supervision after release or while unlawfully at large, the court convicting him of the later offence may return him to borstal.[95] Where it is a magistrates' court that has convicted him and where reports on his response to borstal so far are not available[96] the magistrates' court must adjourn and commit him to custody.[97] Thereafter it may send him back to borstal without committing him to the Crown Court, or it may deal with him in any other way within its powers.

If the offender is convicted by a magistrates' court during the operational period of a suspended sentence which was imposed by the Crown Court, the magistrates' court may commit him to the Crown Court or send notice of his new conviction to the appropriate Crown Court officer.[98] The offender may be committed on bail.

If the offender is subject to a community service order made by the Crown Court, the power to commit arises either if he has failed to comply with the requirements of the order or if, on application, the court wishes to revoke the order or sentence him afresh.[99] If he has failed to comply with the order, he is generally entitled to bail[1]; otherwise he may be committed in custody or on bail.

A probation order or conditional discharge made by the Crown Court enables the magistrates' court to commit the offender to the Crown Court if he is convicted of a further offence during the

---

[94] Criminal Justice Act 1967, s. 62; see p. 257.
[95] Criminal Justice Act 1961, s. 12; see p. 259.
[96] Under the Criminal Justice Act 1961, s. 12 (3).
[97] *Ibid.* s. 12 (4). Adjournment is for not more than three weeks under the Magistrates' Courts Act 1952, s. 14 (3), as to which see p. 307.
[98] Powers of Criminal Courts Act 1973, s. 24 (2); see also p. 322.
[99] *Ibid.* ss. 16 (3) and 17 (2); as to the requirements, see p. 236.
[1] Bail Act 1976, s. 4 (3).

relevant period or if he is in breach of the requirements of the probation order.[2] In the second case the offender is generally entitled to bail.[1]

The magistrates' court must commit the offender to the most convenient sitting of the Crown Court, with a High Court judge if such a judge made the original order.[3] Section 56 of the Criminal Justice Act 1967 applies to these forms of committal.[4]

---

[2] Powers of Criminal Courts Act 1973, ss. 8 (6) and 6 (4) respectively; if the offender has committed a further offence, the court which deals with him has power to deal with him in any way in which it could have dealt with him had he just been convicted: s. 8 (7); if the order was made by a magistrates' court, the sentencing court is restricted to the magistrates' court's powers of sentencing: s. 8 (8); if the offender is in breach of the requirements of the order, he may be fined £50, have a community service order imposed or be dealt with in any way in which the Crown Court could have dealt with him if it had just convicted him: s. 6 (6).

[3] Directions of the Lord Chief Justice of October 14, 1971, directions 6 and 7.

[4] See pp. 333 and 335.

CHAPTER 14

APPEALS

APPEAL from the decision of a magistrates' court in summary criminal proceedings lies in two directions—the Crown Court and the High Court. Appeal to the High Court has several unusual features, not the least being the power of the prosecution to initiate it, but these stem from the supervisory nature of the proceedings. The procedure is directed at misapplications of law or procedure by magistrates. As in the case of the prerogative orders [1] (which also play an important part at this stage) the appeal arises from the need for a central judicial control of trials at which there may be no legally qualified person except the clerk whose advice on the law is not binding on the bench.

The appeal to the Crown Court is more in the nature of the appeals against conviction on indictment—it lies at the instance of the accused only,[2] reviews the whole case, if necessary, and may be on fact, fact and law or sentence. This appeal, in turn, is subject to review by the High Court. However, where the Crown Court has handled the case because the accused has been committed to them for sentence, appeal against the sentence imposed lies to the Court of Appeal, Criminal Division.

This chapter is therefore divided into six sections, the first dealing with the courts which may be involved in an appeal from a magistrates' court, the second with appeal to the Crown Court, the third with appeal to the High Court, the fourth with appeal from the High Court and the fifth with appeal when the accused has been committed for sentence. An example of a case stated is given in the sixth part.

A. COURTS

1. The Crown Court

When the accused has been convicted and sentenced by a magistrates' court, he may appeal against conviction or sentence to the Crown Court. His appeal may be transferred to a different sitting of the Crown Court in the same way as proceedings on committal for sentence.[3] When hearing appeals, the Crown Court sits without a

[1] See pp. 43–47.

[2] In some rare cases, however, the prosecution can appeal, *e.g.* under the Customs and Excise Act 1952, s. 283 (4).

[3] See Directions of the Lord Chief Justice of October 14, 1971, direction 14, p. 331.

jury; justices sit on the bench, presided over by a circuit judge or recorder.[4] They give their judgment by majority, and the recorder or circuit judge has a casting vote if they are equally divided.[5] A solicitor who has represented the appellant in the magistrates' court may conduct the appeal.[6]

A justice is not disqualified from sitting at the Crown Court on the grounds that the proceedings are not related to the area in which he is appointed as a justice of the peace.[7] Appeals must normally be listed for hearing by a court presided over by a circuit judge or recorder and they must be heard by a court comprising not less than two and not more than four justices of the peace. Improper constitution of the court is not a ground for objecting to proceedings unless the irregularity was objected to at the time [8] and in certain circumstances the court may be constituted without all the requisite members.[9]

If an accused is committed for sentence, he cannot appeal to the Crown Court against the committal,[10] but he can still appeal against the conviction.[11] Although there is no statutory provision regarding which should come first, the appeal or the sentence, the usual practice is for both issues to be referred to the same court for the same day and, naturally enough, the appeal against conviction will be dealt with first. If appeal has not been made in time, however, and the court sentences the offender first, there is nothing to prevent the Crown Court from giving leave to appeal out of time and dealing with the appeal after sentencing him.[12] The justices sitting in the Crown Court must be changed as a justice is disqualified from sitting at the appeal if he has sat at the proceedings on committal for sentence.[13]

---

4 Courts Act 1971, s. 5 (1), and Directions of the Lord Chief Justice of October 14, 1971, direction 12 (v).

5 Courts Act 1971, s. 5 (8). His vote has no greater weight than that of each justice, however; see p. 88.

6 Direction of the Lord Chancellor of February 9, 1972. This right extends to the solicitor's partners or others employed in the same firm.

7 Courts Act 1971, s. 5 (9).

8 *Ibid.* s. 5 (7).

9 The Crown Court may consist of a judge and a single justice if it could not be properly constituted without unreasonable delay. Further, it may continue proceedings which were commenced with a properly constituted court if one or more of the justices initially comprising the court has withdrawn or is absent for any reason: Crown Court Rules 1971, r. 4, made under the Courts Act 1971, s. 5 (6).

10 See *R.* v. *London Sessions*, p. 345.

11 The appeal from the Crown Court to the Court of Appeal is on sentence only. If he wishes to challenge the committal he must go to the High Court: *R.* v. *Birtles* [1975] 1 W.L.R. 1623.

12 *R.* v. *Tottenham Justices, ex p. Rubens* [1970] 1 W.L.R. 800.

13 Crown Court Rules 1971, r. 5. This only applies to committals under the Magistrates' Courts Act 1952, s. 28 or s. 29; see pp. 335 and 332.

The decision on appeal has no general effect as a precedent. If the accused desires an authoritative ruling on the law, he should appeal to the High Court on that point of law.

2. The High Court

The jurisdiction of the High Court in hearing appeals from magistrates' courts in criminal cases is dealt with by the Divisional Court of the Queen's Bench Division.[14] At least two Queen's Bench judges[15] sit in the Divisional Court, but it is usual for there to be three judges of whom one is the Lord Chief Justice. If the court is evenly divided, the judgment of the judge who agrees with the decision of the court below prevails.[16]

It is necessary, but not easy, to distinguish between the appeal jurisdiction described in Section C below[17] and the supervisory jurisdiction by prerogative order already described in Chapter 3.[18] An appeal is made at the instance of a party and is principally aimed at correcting a misapplication of the substantive law to the evidence in the case. A prerogative order is aimed at preventing the inferior court from acting outside its jurisdiction or correcting it, if it has already occurred. In very simple terms, the appeal is concerned with a wrong decision whereas the prerogative order is concerned with a void decision.

In practice, however, the distinctions between the circumstances in which one procedure or the other is preferable are by no means clear, particularly in the case of certiorari. (Prohibition and mandamus are more likely to be appropriate before the final determination of the case, whereas certiorari can be used after decision and sentence to review the whole case.[19]) Where the magistrates' court has applied the wrong procedure, either course may be open as an appeal expressly lies where the decision of the magistrates is in excess of jurisdiction.[20] For instance, appeals were heard in *D.P.P.* v. *Burgess*[21] against a prosecution wrongly instituted without the consent of the Director of Public Prosecutions and in *Sulston* v. *Hammond*[22] against a prosecution instituted without the apparently necessary notice of intended

---

[14] R.S.C. 1965, Ord. 56, r. 5.
[15] Supreme Court of Judicature Consolidation Act 1925, s. 63 (6).
[16] *Flannagan* v. *Shaw* [1920] 3 K.B. 96 at pp. 107 and 108.
[17] See p. 349.
[18] See pp. 43–47.
[19] See p. 46, in particular the power to reduce sentence under the Administration of Justice Act 1960, s. 16.
[20] See Magistrates' Courts Act 1952, s. 87 (1), p. 349.
[21] [1971] Q.B. 432.
[22] [1970] 1 W.L.R. 1164.

prosecution. On the other hand, certiorari was applied for in *R.* v. *Wakefield Justices*[23] where the accused having consented to summary trial was never himself actually asked whether or not he pleaded guilty, a procedure required by the Magistrates' Courts Act 1952, s. 13 (1). It is difficult to draw any clear line of distinction between the issues in these cases—all of them potentially rendered the proceedings void.

The distinction is clearer where the magistrates' court reaches an erroneous conclusion by misinterpreting a statutory offence. For instance, in *Hill* v. *Baxter*[24] the magistrates' court interpreted an offence as requiring the intention of the accused, whereas on appeal the Queen's Bench decided the offence was one of strict liability. This was clearly a case for appeal. On the other hand, if the magistrates were to misinterpret section 7 of the Powers of Criminal Courts Act 1973[25] and impose a fine on the same conviction as a conditional discharge, this would be a misapplication of the law and an act in excess of jurisdiction. A clear case for applying for a prerogative order is where a denial of natural justice is alleged. However, the parties should, if possible, use the summary procedure for review by the magistrates' court itself.[26]

There is also the procedural difference between the two processes that appeals are brought by parties whereas prerogative orders are made exclusively within the discretion of the High Court, although initiated by a person aggrieved.

The decisions of the Divisional Court are binding on magistrates' courts, in as far as they are capable of being so, and generally speaking later Divisional Courts follow their previous decisions. However, like the House of Lords and the Court of Appeal, Criminal Division, they do not regard themselves as bound in all cases where in changed circumstances rigid adherence to precedent could lead to injustice.

3. Other appeal courts

Appeal lies to the House of Lords from the decision of the Queen's Bench Divisional Court and to the Court of Appeal against a sentence passed by the Crown Court after committal for sentence. These courts have already been described in connection with appeals against conviction and sentence on indictment[27]; their constitution for the purposes of this chapter is the same.

---

[23] (1969) 114 S.J. 30.
[24] [1958] 1 Q.B. 277.
[25] See p. 240.
[26] See Powers of Criminal Courts Act 1973, s. 41, p. 315.
[27] See pp. 260 and 261.

B. Appeal to the Crown Court

1. The right of appeal

Apart from some unusual cases [28] where the prosecution can appeal under a statute, the right of appeal only avails a person convicted by a magistrates' court and he may appeal to the Crown Court

(*a*) if he pleaded guilty, against his sentence, or

(*b*) if he did not, against the conviction or sentence.[29]

This provision is extended to include any sentence passed for breach of a probation or conditional discharge order; whether or not a further conviction is involved, the sentence may be appealed to the Crown Court.[30]

Although he cannot contest the conviction after pleading guilty, an appellant may ask to change his plea on the ground that the plea of guilty was equivocal and should have been refused by the magistrates. In *R.* v. *Tottenham Justices, ex p. Rubens*,[31] for example, the accused had pleaded guilty to obtaining by false pretences but, in a statement made to the police and read to the court, there was evidence that he did not have the requisite intent. Quarter sessions (now the Crown Court) rightly remitted the case to the magistrates' court for trial after recording a plea of not guilty. This is also the proper course where he has been committed for sentence on a plea of guilty.[32] There must be some objection on the evidence to the plea of guilty, however, and he cannot arbitrarily change his mind. The same principles apply as apply at trial.[33]

The term " sentence " is further defined as " any order made on conviction by a magistrates' court," except—

" (*a*) a probation order or order for conditional discharge;

(*b*) an order for the payment of costs;

(*c*) an order . . . [for the] destruction of an animal [34]; or

(*d*) an order made in pursuance of any enactment under which the court has no discretion as to the making of the order or its terms."[35]

The offender may only appeal against *conviction* if a probation or conditional discharge order is made; this is in accordance with

---

28 *e.g.* under the Customs and Excise Act 1952, s. 283 (4).
29 Magistrates' Courts Act 1952, s. 83 (1).
30 *Ibid.* s. 83 (2). As to breach of probation, see p. 238.
31 [1970] 1 W.L.R. 800.
32 *R.* v. *Mutford and Lothingland Justices, ex p. Harber* [1971] 2 Q.B. 291.
33 See pp. 169 and 316.
34 *e.g.* Protection of Animals Act 1911, s. 2.
35 Magistrates' Courts Act 1952, s. 83 (3).

section 13 of the Powers of Criminal Courts Act 1973, which provides that where such an order is made the conviction does not rank as a conviction, but that this does not affect the accused's right to appeal against conviction.[36] The order is merged into the conviction, so that a person who pleads guilty and is conditionally discharged or put on probation has no right of appeal, unless he is later sentenced in a different way for breach of the order.[37]

The second exception precludes any appeal against a costs order alone. However, as an appeal to the Crown Court operates as a rehearing of the whole issue and the court may set aside the whole or any part of the magistrates' court's decision, the costs order may be varied or revoked provided another aspect of the decision is also appealed against.[38] The Crown Court also has power to order the costs of the defence (*i.e.* including the costs of the trial) to be paid out of central funds if an appeal against conviction of an indictable offence is successful.[39] The prosecution has a right of appeal to the Crown Court against an order to pay costs of more than £25 if magistrates decide not to commit the accused for want of sufficient evidence and if they are of the opinion that the charge was not made in good faith.[40]

The other two exceptions do not require explanation save that the fourth exception does not necessarily apply to disqualification from driving for, even in the cases where it is generally mandatory, the offender may contend that he has " special reasons " not to be disqualified.[41] Non-discretionary orders are sometimes found in regulatory fields such as public health legislation.

A committal for sentence has been held not to be " an order made on conviction " and therefore the offender cannot appeal against it.[42] If the committal is improper the proper course is to apply to the Divisional Court for certiorari or prohibition.[43] If the committal is lawful and the offender is not appealing against conviction, he must wait until sentence is passed and then appeal to the Court of Appeal.[44]

---

[36] See Powers of Criminal Courts Act 1973, s. 13 (1) and (4), p. 241.

[37] See Magistrates' Courts Act 1952, s. 83 (2), above. This must also be distinguished from a case where the probation order or discharge was void; see p. 275.

[38] As to the Crown Court's powers on appeal, see p. 348.

[39] Costs in Criminal Cases Act 1973, s. 3 (2).

[40] *Ibid.* s. 2 (4) and (5).

[41] See Road Traffic Act 1972, s. 93, p. 246. As the definition of " special reasons " is a matter of law, however, the appellant should appeal to the Divisional Court unless he wishes to contest the evidence of facts which are acknowledged special reasons.

[42] *R.* v. *London Sessions, ex p. Rogers* [1951] 2 K.B. 74.

[43] See pp. 45 and 46.

[44] See p. 353.

Where a person is bound over to keep the peace he may appeal to the Crown Court whether or not the binding-over order was made on conviction.[45] A recommendation for deportation is also subject to appeal,[46] and if a deportation order is made, the offender may appeal to the Immigration Appeals Tribunal.[47]

Lastly, when a magistrates' court makes a hospital order without convicting the accused,[48] the accused may appeal against the order as if it had been made on conviction. The Crown Court deals with him as though he were appealing against conviction and sentence.[49] This enables the court to hear the whole case and acquit or convict; it may pass any sentence which the magistrates' court could have passed had they fully heard the case and convicted him.[50]

The right to appeal to the Crown Court is lost if the accused begins proceedings for appeal to the Divisional Court.[51]

2. Making the appeal and ancillary applications

The appellant gives notice of appeal to the clerk of the magistrates' court and to the prosecution within 21 days of the decision of the magistrates' court.[52] If the trial has been adjourned after conviction, the relevant date is the day when sentence was passed.[53] The notice of appeal must state whether the appeal is against conviction or sentence or both.[54] The Crown Court may grant extra time for giving the notice of appeal on the appellant's written application; the application must specify the grounds of the application and must be sent to the appropriate officer of the Crown Court.[55]

When the appropriate officer of the Crown Court receives the notice of appeal he enters it on the list and gives notice of the time and place of the hearing to the appellant, the prosecution and the clerk of the magistrates' court.[56]

---

[45] Magistrates' Courts (Appeals from Binding-Over Orders) Act 1956, s. 1. As to binding-over, see p. 243.

[46] Immigration Act 1971, s. 6 (5).

[47] See p. 245.

[48] See Mental Health Act 1959, s. 60 (2), p. 326.

[49] *Ibid.* s. 70 (1).

[50] Courts Act 1971, s. 9 (2).

[51] Magistrates' Courts Act 1952, s. 87 (4), and see Section C, p. 349. This is probably limited to the issues contested on appeal to the Divisional Court, however; in *Sivalingham* v. *D.P.P.* [1975] C.L.Y. 2037 it was held to be permissible to appeal to the Crown Court against sentence after dismissal of a substantive appeal to the Divisional Court.

[52] Crown Court Rules 1971, r. 7 (2) and (3).

[53] *Ibid.* r. 7 (4).

[54] *Ibid.* r. 7 (3).

[55] *Ibid.* r. 7 (5) and (6). There is no set form of words. The officer of the Crown Court then gives notice of the extension of time to the appellant and to the clerk of the magistrates' court; the appellant gives notice to the prosecution: *ibid.* r. 7 (7).

[56] *Ibid.* r. 8.

The appellant may abandon the appeal any time up to the third day before the date fixed by giving written notice to the clerk of the magistrates' court and to the prosecution; he must also send a copy of the notice to the appropriate officer of the Crown Court.[57]

As the right to appeal to the Crown Court is lost if an appeal to the Divisional Court is begun,[58] where the appellant wishes to contest the conviction on the evidence and on the law, he should appeal first to the Crown Court then to the Divisional Court.

If the appellant is in custody and has given notice of appeal, the magistrates' court may grant him bail with a duty to appear at the hearing of the appeal.[59] If the magistrates' court refuses it or offers it only on unacceptable terms, the appellant may apply to the High Court to grant it or vary the conditions.[60] Alternatively he may apply to the Crown Court to be admitted to bail.[61] Bail granted pending appeal is " bail in criminal proceedings "[62] and the general principles of bail apply, although the appellant has no general right to bail. As it would be wrong to seek to enforce a non-custodial order after a notice of appeal has been served,[63] so would it be wrong to keep the appellant in custody unless a substantial term of imprisonment had been imposed.

3. The hearing and the powers of the Crown Court

The appeal to the Crown Court takes the form of a rehearing.[64] Except where evidence is admitted, witnesses may be recalled and new evidence may be adduced. Where appeal is solely against sentence only that evidence which is relevant to the sentence will be heard.[65] Though with less adherence to formality,[66] the proceedings follow the same order as they followed at trial, *i.e.* the respondent opens the proceedings. The hearing may be adjourned if necessary.

---

[57] Crown Court Rules 1971, r. 9.

[58] Magistrates' Courts Act 1952, s. 87 (4), but see footnote 51 above.

[59] *Ibid.* s. 89 (1), as amended by the Bail Act 1976, Sched. 2.

[60] Criminal Justice Act 1967, s. 22; see p. 79.

[61] See Courts Act 1971, s. 13, p. 71.

[62] " Bail grantable . . . in connection with proceedings for an offence to a person who is . . . convicted of the offence ": Bail Act 1976, s. 1 (1) (*a*); see generally pp. 68–82.

[63] *Kendall* v. *Wilkinson* (1855) 19 J.P. 467.

[64] This was a traditional practice not embodied in any statute which is now recognised by the Courts Act 1971, s. 9 (6). With a few exceptions the same subsection preserves the customary practice and procedure.

[65] *Paprika Ltd.* v. *Board of Trade* [1944] 1 K.B. 327.

[66] The court must adhere to the principles of natural justice and any lack of formality must not constitute a denial of justice to the appellant: *R.* v. *Knightsbridge Crown Court, ex p. Martin* [1976] Crim.L.R. 463.

The powers of the Crown Court are broad; effectively it may do anything which the magistrates' court could have done. It may correct any error or mistake in the order or judgment incorporating the magistrates' court's decision.[67] It may confirm, reverse or vary the decision of the magistrates' court. Two factors are unusual [68]:

(*a*) The Crown Court may remit the case to the magistrates' court with its opinion as to how to proceed; *e.g.* with a direction to enter a plea of not guilty and try the appellant.[69]

(*b*) As it can impose any sentence or make any order within the magistrates' court's jurisdiction,[70] it may impose a heavier sentence on dismissing the appeal than the magistrates' court imposed on conviction.[71]

It may make any ancillary order within the magistrates' court's jurisdiction as it thinks just, including an order for costs.[72]

The Crown Court cannot commit the appellant to itself for sentence,[73] however, or for a restricted hospital order or borstal training. It has " no power . . . to go behind, as it were, the election of the magistrate and to treat the matter as if he had not given a sentence at all." [74]

The decision of the Crown Court, unless it amounts to acquittal, is enforced as if it has been made by the magistrates' court against whose decision the appeal was brought; *i.e.* a warrant of commitment will be issued or a fine collected by the magistrates' court, etc.[75] The Crown Court may, however, enforce it itself if necessary.

If the appeal is against conviction by a magistrates' court of an indictable offence, the court may order the payment of costs out of central funds in favour of the prosecution, in any event, and in favour of the defence, if the defendant's appeal is successful.[76] If the appellant abandons an appeal by giving the proper notice, he cannot be ordered to pay the prosecution's costs.[77]

---

[67] Courts Act 1971, s. 9 (1).
[68] *Ibid.* s. 9 (2) (*a*).
[69] *Ibid.* s. 9 (2) (*b*); *R.* v. *Tottenham Justices, ex p. Rubens* [1970] 1 W.L.R. 800.
[70] Courts Act 1971, s. 9 (2) (*c*).
[71] *Ibid.* s. 9 (4).
[72] *Ibid.* s. 9 (2) (*c*), and Crown Court Rules 1971, r. 10.
[73] *R.* v. *Bullock* [1964] 1 Q.B. 481.
[74] *Ibid.* at p. 488.
[75] Magistrates' Courts Act 1952, s. 86.
[76] Costs in Criminal Cases Act 1974, s. 3 (2).
[77] Crown Court Rules 1971, r. 10 (4); an order may be made against the appellant if he improperly abandons the appeal or if it is dismissed: *ibid.*, r. 10 (5).

C. Appeal to the High Court

This appeal lies to the Queen's Bench Divisional Court from the magistrates' court and from the Crown Court when it has heard an appeal from a magistrates' court. The appeal cannot be founded on factual disputes but only on questions of law. The procedure is known as " stating a case " or " appeal on a case stated," for the court whose decision is challenged draws up for the opinion of the Divisional Court a statement of the facts found to be proved, the decision made, and the reasons for it. The evidence is not stated unless the appeal is based on a misapplication of the law to the evidence or to particular items of evidence.[78] A draft case stated may be found on page 356.

1. From a magistrates' court

A person who is aggrieved by any proceedings, other than committal proceedings,[79] in a magistrates' court may question the proceedings by applying to the magistrates to state a case for the opinion of the High Court; the only grounds for questioning the conviction, order, determination or other proceeding are that it is wrong in law or in excess of the magistrates' court's jurisdiction.[80]

The magistrates' court can only refuse to state a case where it considers that the application is frivolous [81]; if it does so refuse, it must give the applicant a certificate to that effect; in any event he can apply to the Divisional Court to make an order of mandamus [82] to compel the magistrates to state a case.[83]

Either of the parties to the proceedings, *i.e.* the accused or the prosecution, may make this appeal. Even a third party may make an appeal if he is a " person aggrieved," but he must have legal rights which are directly affected by the decision, such as, for instance, the ownership of stolen goods for which he desires a restitution order. Occasionally a collective appeal is made where the same point has been at issue in a number of cases heard by the magistrates' court on the same day.[84] Appeal by case stated does not lie in committal proceedings,[85] though a prerogative order might be appropriate.[86]

---

[78] Magistrates' Courts Rules 1968, r. 68, as amended by S.I. 1975 No. 518 (see footnote 92 below); Practice Direction of the Lord Chief Justice of December 16, 1971.

[79] *Dewing* v. *Cummings* [1971] R.T.R. 295; *Atkinson* v. *U.S. Government* [1971] A.C. 197.

[80] Magistrates' Courts Act 1952, s. 87 (1).

[81] *Ibid.* s. 87 (5).

[82] See p. 46.

[83] Magistrates' Courts Act 1952, s. 87 (6).

[84] *D.P.P.* v. *Lamb* [1941] 2 K.B. 89.

[85] *Dewing* v. *Cummings* [1971] Crim.L.R. 295.

[86] See pp. 43–47.

An appeal by the prosecution is effectively an exception to the principle of double jeopardy or *autrefois* [87] for the appeal is made after the magistrates' court has reached a final decision in the case.[88] As will be seen later, the Divisional Court can remit the case to the magistrates' court for retrial and, if necessary, for conviction, or it can alter the decision of the magistrates' court itself with the effect of a conviction, even though the accused has been in jeopardy and his case has been finally dealt with already.

Procedure

On the application by a convicted accused to have a case stated, the magistrates' court may grant him bail to reappear before the magistrates' court within 10 days of the decision of the Divisional Court, unless the conviction is reversed.[89] Further, the magistrates' court may refuse to state a case until the applicant (prosecutor, accused or otherwise) has entered into a recognisance to prosecute the appeal without delay.[90]

The appellant must apply for the case to be stated by the magistrates' court within 14 days of the decision [91] and it must be stated within a maximum of 11 weeks of the application.[92] The clerk prepares a draft case which he submits to the parties so that they can make representations on it. The magistrates may then adjust the case and it is signed and sent to the appellant in its final form. Within 10 days of receiving it back, the appellant must lodge the case stated in the Crown Office of the High Court and serve notice on the respondent.[93]

The procedure at the hearing of the appeal is informal, consisting as it does of legal argument only. The judges call on counsel for either side to argue for or against the appeal. The justices may only argue their point of view through counsel as *amicus curiae*, *i.e.* to assist the court.

Powers of the Divisional Court

The Divisional Court may affirm, reverse, vary or remit the decision of the magistrates' court.[94] If it is affirmed, reversed or varied,

---

[87] See pp. 159–167.

[88] It cannot be made if a statute expressly provides that the decision shall be final: Magistrates' Courts Act 1952, s. 87 (1), proviso.

[89] Magistrates' Courts Act 1952, s. 89 (1A), as substituted by the Bail Act 1976, Sched. 2.

[90] *Ibid.* s. 90.

[91] *Ibid.* s. 87 (2).

[92] This is a total of the maximum periods allowed under the Magistrates' Courts (Amendment) (No. 2) Rules 1975 (S.I. No. 518), substituting new rr. 65–68 of the 1968 Rules.

[93] R.S.C. 1965, Ord. 56, r. 6.

[94] Summary Jurisdiction Act 1857, s. 6.

the order or decision is enforced after the appeal by the magistrates' court from which the appeal was made as though it were its own decision.[95] The Divisional Court may make ancillary orders as necessary, for instance, a costs [96] or restitution order,[97] but this does not extend apparently to a reduction of the punishment imposed if the conviction is affirmed.[98] This is because, if sentence has to be reconsidered, the magistrates' court is the proper tribunal to do it, hearing the statements of the accused and police and any other evidence available.

Remission to the magistrates' court is necessary where an error has been made which requires the magistrates' court to hear or to rehear evidence. If the Divisional Court makes a decision on the law or procedure to be applied, the magistrates' court must, of course, follow it for otherwise mandamus or prohibition would automatically be available. The new hearing begins with the calling of the evidence; preliminaries such as pleas and consents need not be repeated.[99]

2. From the Crown Court

Where the accused has appealed to the Crown Court against conviction or sentence [1] either the prosecution or the accused may appeal to the High Court on a point of law arising in the appeal to the Crown Court.[2]

The procedure is similar to the appeal from a magistrates' court—it lies by way of case stated (by the Crown Court [3]) on the ground that a decision in proceedings before the Crown Court is wrong in law or in excess of jurisdiction.[4] An appealing defendant may be granted bail by the Crown Court [5] and, if refused, he may apply to the High Court.[6] The appeal cannot be made by anyone other than the prosecutor or the accused, however, and the application must be made within 14 days of the Crown Court's decision.[7]

---

[95] Magistrates' Courts Act 1952, s. 88.

[96] Costs in Criminal Cases Act 1973, s. 5; this also applies to appeals from the Crown Court, below; the payment of costs is out of central funds and covers costs in the Divisional Court and below.

[97] Summary Jurisdiction Act 1857, s. 6.

[98] *Evans* v. *Hemingway* (1887) 52 J.P. 134.

[99] *R.* v. *Bradfield and Sonning Justices, ex p. Jones* [1976] R.T.R. 144.

[1] See Magistrates' Courts Act 1952, s. 83, p. 344.

[2] Courts Act 1971, s. 10 (1). The right to have a case stated applies to all Crown Court proceedings except those on indictment and on certain licensing matters.

[3] *Ibid.* s. 10 (3). [4] *Ibid.* s. 10 (2). [5] *Ibid.* s. 13 (4) (*d*).

[6] Criminal Justice Act 1948, s. 37 (1) (*b*), and Criminal Justice Act 1967, s. 22, as amended by the Bail Act 1976, Sched. 2.

[7] Crown Court Rules 1971, r. 21 (1). The applicant may apply to the Crown Court to extend the time for the application: r. 21 (2).

The application is made in writing to the appropriate officer of the Crown Court. The appellant may be required by the court to enter a recognisance, before the case stated is delivered to him, to prosecute the appeal without delay. Sureties may be ordered.[8] The accused as appellant may not be ordered to enter a recognisance, if he is granted bail on applying for a case to be stated, as an incident of that bail.[9]

The Crown Court may refuse to state a case if it considers that the application is frivolous; if it does refuse to do so it must, on application, give a certificate to that effect for the decision is subject to the High Court's supervisory jurisdiction.[10]

The powers of the Divisional Court are not specified in the Courts Act 1971. However, assuming that the law previously applicable to this procedure is retained, its powers here are similar to its powers on appeal from a magistrates' court, but subject to no restrictions in varying the orders passed on conviction.[11] It may remit the case for rehearing by the Crown Court,[12] as it may not review the case generally or interfere with findings of fact or the conclusions drawn from the evidence unless these are clearly wrong in law.[13]

D. Appeal to the House of Lords

An appeal from the decision of the High Court lies to the House of Lords. Either party may apply to appeal and it lies only where a point of law of general public importance is involved.[14]

Application must first be made to the Divisional Court for certification of the point of law [15] and then application must be made for leave to appeal. The procedure is the same as in the case of an application to the Court of Appeal, Criminal Division.[16]

---

[8] Crown Court Rules 1971, r. 21 (4).

[9] Courts Act 1971, s. 13 (4) (*d*), as amended by the Bail Act 1976, Sched. 2. The power to order the accused to enter a recognisance is presumably available if it is not an incident of bail, because it is directed to the expeditious disposal of the appeal, not to his conditional release from custody.

[10] Crown Court Rules 1971, r. 21 (3).

[11] *Cf.* p. 351.

[12] *Norwich Rating Authority* v. *Norwich Assessment Committee* [1941] 2 K.B. 326.

[13] *Canabe* v. *Walton-on-Thames U.D.C.* [1914] A.C. 102 at p. 114.

[14] Administration of Justice Act 1960, s. 1. In civil cases which are being heard by a Divisional Court on a case stated from magistrates or the Crown Court (on appeal), further appeal sometimes lies to the Court of Appeal, Civil Division, or, if ss. 12–16 of the Administration of Justice Act 1969 apply, it lies to the House of Lords by the " leapfrog " procedure.

[15] There is no appeal against refusal to do this.

[16] See p. 280, Administration of Justice Act 1960, ss. 1–9, and *Supreme Court Practice 1976*, para. 57/1/4. The House of Lords may order the accused's or the prosecutor's costs out of central funds if it hears and determines the appeal: Costs in Criminal Cases Act 1973, s. 6.

If the Divisional Court refuses to grant leave, the appellant may apply for leave to the House of Lords. The procedure at that stage is the same as after appeal to the Court of Appeal[17] as is also the procedure at the appeal if leave is granted.

The appeal to the House of Lords also lies from decisions of the Divisional Court on applications for habeas corpus in any criminal cause or matter.[18]

E. Appeal to the Court of Appeal

Section 10 of the Criminal Appeal Act 1968 gives an offender convicted in a magistrates' court and sentenced by the Crown Court a right to appeal to the Court of Appeal against his sentence. This appeal may be made when the offender, convicted of an offence by a magistrates' court,

(*a*) is committed by the court to be dealt with for his offence at the Crown Court[19]; or

(*b*) having been made the subject of a probation order, conditional discharge or suspended sentence, appears or is brought before the Crown Court to be further dealt with for his offence.[20]

The right of appeal under this section does not always apply to a sentence passed on committal to be further dealt with after a probation order has been made, for, if it was made on conviction on indictment, the offender may appeal under section 9.[21] Where a community service order is revoked and replaced by a substantial sentence, the offender would have to come within the terms of section 10 (2) (*a*) in order to be able to appeal because no amendment of section 10 (2) (*b*) has been made to take account of such orders imposed by the Crown Court on committal from the magistrates' court.[22] Appeal under section 10 does not apply where an offender is

[17] See Directions as to Procedure, pp. 280–282.

[18] Administration of Justice Act 1960, s. 15; see also pp. 44–45.

[19] See pp. 330–339 (*i.e.* Magistrates' Courts Act 1952, ss. 28 and 29, Mental Health Act 1959, s. 67, and Vagrancy Act 1824, s. 5).

[20] Criminal Appeal Act 1968, s. 10 (2).

[21] This allows appeal " against any sentence . . . passed on him for the offence, whether passed on his conviction *or in subsequent proceedings* "; see p. 275.

[22] See Powers of Criminal Courts Act 1973, ss. 6 (4) and (6) and 16 (3) and (5), pp. 236 and 238. The same applies to a variation of a community service order under s. 17 (2) and (3); see p. 236. There seems to be no significant difference in the wording of the power to commit for breach of the requirements of a probation order and failure to comply with a community service order. If an offender subject to the second may be committed under s. 10 (2) (*a*), the words " further dealt with " would have to be implicitly included in the provision.

sentenced by the Crown Court on appeal from a magistrates' court, the only appeal in that case being on a point of law to the High Court and thence, possibly, to the House of Lords.[23]

The right of appeal is restricted by the type and severity of the sentence imposed by the Crown Court. The appeal only lies where

(*a*) the sentence of imprisonment is for six months or more, or

(*b*) the sentence passed is outside the power of the court which *convicted* him,[24] or

(*c*) the court makes

 (i) a recommendation for deportation,[25]

 (ii) a disqualification from driving order,[26] or

 (iii) an order dealing with a previously imposed suspended sentence,[27] or

(*d*) the court orders the return of the offender to borstal.[28]

Under paragraph (*a*) two sentences are treated as a single sentence if they are passed on the same day or are expressed by the court to be a single sentence; consecutive sentences are treated as a single term.[29] Detention does not count as imprisonment for the purpose of appeal.[30] A sentence takes effect from the beginning of the day on which it is imposed; if it is varied, it still takes effect from that day but for the purposes of time limits on appealing against it, it is treated as having been imposed on the day on which it was varied.[31]

Paragraph (*b*) has especial significance where the offender has been tried summarily for a hybrid offence.[32] Special provision had to be made for a suspended sentence because the sentence is not passed but only made effective on conviction of the later offence; for a breach of a probation order or an order for conditional discharge, on the other

---

[23] See Criminal Justice Act 1925, s. 20, above and Section D, above.

[24] *N.B.* If the committal itself was invalid, no right of appeal lies because both committal and sentence are void. The proper procedure would be to apply for certiorari: *R.* v. *Jones* [1969] 2 Q.B. 53; *R.* v. *Birtles* [1975] 1 W.L.R. 1623.

[25] See pp. 244 and 328.

[26] See p. 328.

[27] See p. 322.

[28] Under the Criminal Justice Act 1961, s. 12 (see p. 259): Criminal Justice Act 1972, s. 42 and Sched. 5.

[29] Criminal Appeal Act 1968, s. 10 (4).

[30] *R.* v. *Keelan* [1976] Crim.L.R. 455; *R.* v. *Moore* (1966) 52 Cr.App.R. 180.

[31] Courts Act 1971, s. 11 (5).

[32] *i.e.* under the Magistrates' Courts Act 1952, s. 18 (3); see p. 296. Where the accused has consented to summary trial under s. 19, the magistrates' court may impose up to six months' imprisonment for one offence, so the offender could probably appeal under para. (*a*) anyway.

hand, the court " passes sentence " at the later hearing.[33] The same need for an express provision for *return* to borstal arose because it is not a new sentence imposed by the Crown Court.

It is most important that the magistrates' court which convicts an offender and commits him to the Crown Court for sentence refrains from making any order at all. If it does (*e.g.* a subsidiary order such as compensation) the Crown Court has no power to review it and the offender therefore has no right of appeal in respect of it.[34]

The procedure for appealing under section 10 of the Criminal Appeal Act 1968 and the Court of Appeal's powers are in every respect the same as for an appeal against sentence passed on conviction on indictment,[35] including the need for leave to be granted.

F. Drafting a Case Stated

It is the function of the clerk of the magistrates' court to draft the case stated on the information given in the application to him of the prospective appellant; this must identify the questions of law or jurisdiction to be referred to the High Court and, if appropriate, specify any finding of fact which it is claimed cannot be supported by the evidence before the magistrates' court.[36] The magistrates amend the clerk's draft case in the light of any representations made by the parties and sign it, or give authority for the clerk to sign it. The final case stated contains the following information:

(*a*) The names of the parties and the court.
(*b*) Particulars of the charge or charges (if more than one, it must state that the informations were tried together by consent).[37]
(*c*) The findings of fact made by the magistrates' court.
(*d*) Any relevant submissions of the parties.
(*e*) Any authorities referred to.
(*f*) The decision of the court.
(*g*) The request for the opinion of the High Court on the case, identifying the question or questions of law or jurisdiction on which the opinion is sought.

The case stated does not contain a statement of the evidence unless

---

[33] See p. 239.
[34] *R.* v. *Brogan* [1975] 1 W.L.R. 393.
[35] See pp. 274–277.
[36] Magistrates' Courts (Amendment) (No. 2) Rules 1975, substituting rr. 65–68 of the 1968 Rules.
[37] See p. 304.

one of the questions is whether there was evidence on which the magistrates' court could come to its decision.[38]

Example
In the High Court of Justice
Queen's Bench Division (Divisional Court)

Between A.B. (Appellant) and C.D. (Respondent)

CASE STATED by the Justices for the Inner London Commission Area in respect of their adjudication as a magistrates' court sitting at Euston Road on 12 December 1976.

1. The respondent preferred an information against the appellant alleging that the appellant on October 1, 1976 at 11.30 a.m., drove a motor vehicle, registration no. ZIZ 000, in Baker Street, London W.1., in a manner which was dangerous to the public, contrary to section 2 of the Road Traffic Act 1972. The respondent applied for the case to be tried summarily and the appellant pleaded not guilty.
2. We found the following facts:

(*a*) The appellant was the driver of a motor vehicle, registration no. ZIZ 000, on October 1, 1976, at 11.30 a.m. He had turned into Baker Street from George Street and proceeded in a northerly direction.

(*b*) Baker Street is a one-way street in which the traffic flow is restricted to a southerly direction.

(*c*) At the junction of George Street and Baker Street there was on the said date no sign or indication to the traffic entering Baker Street from George Street that the northerly traffic flow in Baker Street was prohibited.

(*d*) At the time alleged, the appellant had no prior knowledge of the restrictions in existence in George Street and Baker Street.

3. The respondent contended that the appellant's driving was objectively dangerous and that his fault was not relevant to the charge. The appellant contended that he was not at fault in driving in the wrong direction along Baker Street.
4. We were referred to the following authorities:

Hill v. *Baxter* [1958] 1 Q.B. 277
R. v. *Evans* [1963] 1 Q.B. 412

---

[38] Magistrates' Courts Rules 1968, r. 68, as substituted by S.I. 1975 No. 518, above.

R. v. *Ball, R.* v. *Loughlin* (1966) 50 Cr.App.R. 266

5. We agreed with the respondent's contention and accordingly we convicted the appellant of the offence charged in the information.

QUESTION

The question for the opinion of the High Court is whether, upon the above-mentioned statements of fact we came to a correct determination and decision in point of law, namely, whether a person may be convicted of dangerous driving contrary to section 2 of the Road Traffic Act 1972 in the absence of proof of fault; if not, the Court is respectfully requested to reverse or amend the said decision or to remit the matter to us with the opinion of the Court thereon.

PART FOUR

SPECIAL CASES

CHAPTER 15

JUVENILES

THE procedure for dealing with adult offenders is in many ways inappropriate for dealing with people under the age of 17. The ordinary rules of procedure and evidence have therefore been supplemented by special provisions, but a considerable measure of overlapping tends to make them complicated and, on occasion, confusing. It is especially complicated by the implementation in part only of the Children and Young Persons Act 1969 which substantially amended the former law.[1]

In a general sense, the treatment of juveniles who have become involved in criminal activities is dealt with in the field of public and social welfare: " It has become increasingly clear that social control of harmful behaviour by the young, and social measures to help and protect the young, are not distinct and separate processes. The aims of protecting society from juvenile delinquency and of helping children in trouble to grow up into mature and law-abiding persons, are complementary and not contradictory." [2] As a result of the enactment of this principle, the procedure for the treatment of a person in this age group on the grounds that " his proper development is being avoidably prevented " or that " he is exposed to moral danger " has been extended to cover proceedings for treatment on the grounds that he is guilty of an offence.[3] These are " care proceedings," of which a description will be found in Section F [4]; to cover the field of child welfare in any depth, however, is clearly outside the scope of this book.

Juveniles continue to be answerable to the ordinary criminal procedures in certain circumstances and this chapter will cover these circumstances, the court which normally deals with them and the methods of treatment available if they are found to be in need of it.

---

[1] The extent to which the Act was brought into force on January 1, 1971, and the meaning of the Act are explained in a Home Office guide entitled " Part I of the Children and Young Persons Act 1969." Mumford's *Guide to Juvenile Court Law* also describes the new provisions.

[2] " Children in Trouble," Cmnd. 3601. This Home Office report outlined the basis upon which the Children and Young Persons Act 1969 was drawn up.

[3] Children and Young Persons Act 1969, s. 1 (2). *N.B.* these are not the only grounds for bringing proceedings, but are merely illustrative; see p. 383.

[4] See p. 382.

The juvenile witness also receives special treatment, but this, in as far as it is relevant to this book, has already been dealt with.[5]

A. The Responsibility of Juveniles

The term " juvenile " is used here for convenience to mean anyone under the age of 17. The term is not used in the Children and Young Persons Act 1969; in relation to care proceedings, a person under the age of 17 is called " the relevant infant." A " young person " is anyone between the ages of 14 and 16 (inclusive) and a " child " is anyone under 14.[6] A " juvenile adult " is a person who is 17 or more but under 21. He is treated as an adult for the purposes of trial, but the special provisions as to treatment may conveniently be summarised in this Chapter.[7]

Although the terms " person convicted," " conviction " and " sentence " are used when a juvenile is tried on indictment, they must not be used where a juvenile is tried summarily by a magistrates' court or juvenile court. In that case the proper terms are " a person found guilty of an offence," " a finding of guilt " and " an order made upon a finding of guilt."[8]

1. Children

Children are divided into two groups: those who are under 10 and those who are 10 or over, but are still less than 14. A child under the age of 10 is conclusively presumed not to be guilty of any offence[9] and so cannot be prosecuted at all.[10]

A child between the ages of 10 and 13 (inclusive) may be prosecuted. The prosecution must, however, prove that he was of a " mischievous discretion," *i.e.* that he knew that what he was doing was wrong, for there is a rebuttable presumption that a child of this age group is incapable of forming the necessary *mens rea*. The prosecution must therefore *prove* both that the child was aware of the moral turpitude of his act and that he appreciated the natural and probable results of that act. If the prosecution does not succeed in doing this, the child must be acquitted.

---

[5] See pp. 30 and 153.

[6] Children and Young Persons Act 1933, s. 107, and Children and Young Persons Act 1969, s. 70.

[7] See p. 388. As to borstal, which is the principal provision relating to this age group, see pp. 231 and 259.

[8] Children and Young Persons Act 1933, s. 59 (1).

[9] *Ibid.* s. 50, as amended by the Children and Young Persons Act 1963, s. 16 (1).

[10] Or be made the subject of care proceedings instituted on the offence condition see p. 383.

The proposal enacted by the 1969 Act that a child cannot *be charged* with any offence unless it is homicide [11] is not yet in force. The Home Secretary is empowered, however, to raise the age of prosecutability for offences other than homicide in stages; *i.e.* it need not be raised immediately to 14, but might first be raised to, say, 12 and later to 13 or 14.[12] Care proceedings would still be available on the ground that the child had committed an offence for the new provision would only affect the charging and prosecution of a child, not his responsibility for criminal acts.

If a child of 10 or over is charged with murder or manslaughter,[13] he is tried on indictment as if he were an adult, though the preliminary procedure is different.[14] A child of prosecutable age may also be tried on indictment if he is charged jointly with a person of 17 or over and the court considers that it is in the interests of justice to commit them both for trial by jury.[15]

2. Young persons

A young person is fully responsible to the criminal law. One of the major proposals enacted by the 1969 Act—that a young person could only be prosecuted on the information of a " qualified informant "[16]—has not yet been brought into effect. The informant would have to give notice of his decision to lay an information to the local authority in whose area the offence was committed or in whose area the young person appeared to live.[17]

A young person may be tried on indictment only if:

(i) he is charged with homicide [18]; or

(ii) he is charged with an offence which, in the case of an adult, is punishable by imprisonment for 14 years or more (not being a sentence which is fixed by law) and he ought to be sentenced to a long term of detention if found guilty [19]; or

---

[11] Children and Young Persons Act 1969, s. 4.

[12] *Ibid.* s. 34 (1) (*a*). To add to the terminological complexity of this branch of the law, some of the provisions of the Act which relate to the treatment of young persons who are charged apply also to children who are prosecuted: *ibid.* s. 34 (1) (*b*) and (*c*).

[13] Other killings are described as " homicide," but, though possible, are unlikely to be committed by a child, *e.g.* infanticide.

[14] See Section B, below.

[15] Children and Young Persons Act 1969, s. 6 (1) (*b*); *R.* v. *Newham Justices, ex p. Knight* [1976] Crim.L.R. 323.

[16] *Ibid.* s. 5 (1) and (9); the term includes designated servants of the Crown, police forces, county councils and public bodies, the local authority and the Attorney-General and D.P.P.

[17] Children and Young Persons Act 1969, s. 5 (8) and (9).

[18] On a charge of homicide he *must* be tried on indictment. The other two cases where he may stand trial on indictment are discretionary, depending on the proper sentence if found guilty and on the interests of justice.

[19] *i.e.* under the Children and Young Persons Act 1933, s. 53 (2); see below.

(iii) he is charged jointly with a person who has reached the age of 17 and it is necessary in the interests of justice [20] to try them together.[21]

The prosecution has no election to proceed on indictment on a hybrid offence [22] and the accused has no right to elect trial by jury on a charge of a summary offence punishable by more than three months' imprisonment.[23] In all cases except those listed above, therefore, he must be tried summarily by a magistrates' court or a juvenile court as described below.[24]

B. Trial on Indictment

As most of the procedure for trial of juveniles on indictment is the same as for adults, only the points at which the procedure differs will be dealt with in this section.

1. Process

A juvenile can be arrested without a warrant or he can be brought to court by a summons or on a warrant of arrest. If he is granted bail, his parent or guardian may secure the juvenile's compliance with any special requirements of the bail but only if he (the parent or guardian) consents, only within the terms of his consent and only to a maximum of £50.[25] The special provisions described on pages 371–382 apply to his detention or release thereafter.

2. Committal for trial

A charge made jointly against a juvenile and an adult must be examined by an adult magistrates' court and not by a juvenile court.[26] An adult magistrates' court may examine the charge against a juvenile if a person of 17 or over is charged at the same time with:

(*a*) aiding, abetting, causing, procuring or permitting the offence [27]; or

---

[20] As to the criteria for allowing joint trials, see pp. 137–141.

[21] Children and Young Persons Act 1969, s. 6 (1).

[22] *i.e.* under the Magistrates' Courts Act 1952, s. 18 (1); see p. 295.

[23] *i.e.* under *ibid.* s. 25; see p. 292.

[24] See p. 371.

[25] Bail Act 1976, s. 3 (7); as to bail generally, see pp. 68–82, and as to the " requirements," see s. 3 (6), p. 77.

[26] Children and Young Persons Act 1933, s. 46 (1), as amended by the Children and Young Persons Act 1969, s. 72 (3) and Sched. 5, para. 4.

[27] *Ibid.* s. 46.

(*b*) committing the offence of which the juvenile is charged as aider, abettor, procurer, etc.; or

(*c*) an offence arising out of circumstances which are the same as or connected with those giving rise to the charge against the juvenile.[28]

Otherwise the charge must be examined by a juvenile court.[29] Although not expressly stated, this presumably includes a charge of homicide.

The juvenile's parent or guardian must be required to attend and must be allowed to assist the juvenile in his case.[30] If he is unrepresented and wishes to cross-examine prosecution witnesses, the court must do it for him, if, as is most likely, he is incompetent to do it himself.[31]

At the hearing of the committal proceedings, the court must be cleared of all except the parties, their representatives, court officers, newspaper reporters and anyone specially authorised by the court to be present.[32] No reports identifying the juvenile may be published unless the court or the Home Secretary directs otherwise.[33] The publicity of the proceedings is even less than is usual in committal proceedings[34] for the notice to be posted outside the magistrates' court giving particulars of the result of the committal proceedings[35] must not include the name or address of the juvenile unless the magistrates order it to avoid injustice to him, *e.g.* if the charge is dismissed.[36] The procedure for committal without consideration of the evidence under section 1 of the Criminal Justice Act 1967[37] applies to young persons and to children charged jointly with an adult as it applies to a person over the age of 17.[38]

It must be stressed that a juvenile can only be committed for trial on a charge of homicide or, if he is a young person, if he is charged with a grave offence or, if he is a child or young person, if he is charged jointly with a person who has reached the age of 17.[39]

---

[28] Children and Young Persons Act 1963, s. 18. *Cf.* joint indictments of adult offenders, pp. 137–141.

[29] Children and Young Persons Act 1933, s. 46.

[30] See *ibid.* s. 34 (1), as substituted by the Children and Young Persons Act 1963, s. 25 (1), and Magistrates' Courts (Children and Young Persons) Rules 1970, r. 26, p. 374

[31] Magistrates' Courts (Children and Young Persons) Rules 1970, r. 8 (2).

[32] Children and Young Persons Act 1933, s. 47.

[33] *Ibid.* s. 39.

[34] *Ibid.* ss. 47 and 49; see p. 94.

[35] Criminal Justice Act 1967, s. 4; see p. 95.

[36] Children and Young Persons Act 1969, s. 10 (3).

[37] See p. 100.

[38] Criminal Justice Act 1972, s. 44.

[39] See Children and Young Persons Act 1969, s. 6 (1), pp. 363 and 364.

When committed for trial, the juvenile is committed to the care of a local authority.[40] It may decide to keep him in a community home. If the juvenile is a young person and is so unruly that he cannot safely be committed to care, the court may commit him to a remand centre, if there is one available, or otherwise to prison.[41] The local authority may itself apply for an order to this effect if the young person turns out to be unruly.[42]

3. Trial

No special provisions apply to the actual trial of juveniles on indictment save that the court may direct that no newspaper or broadcast report reveal any particulars by which the juvenile might be identified[43] and that the juvenile must be segregated from adults, other than his relatives, who are charged with any offence when he is being taken to or from court and while waiting in court.[44]

4. Sentence

A child or young person who is found guilty of murder must be sentenced to be detained during Her Majesty's pleasure[45]; this is an indeterminate sentence, *i.e.* with no temporal limit at the outset, but, as the juvenile is subject to the directions and instructions of the Home Secretary,[46] he may be released on licence at any time when his progress is such that he is fit for release, but only after the Home Secretary has consulted with the Lord Chief Justice and the trial judge, if available.[47]

The place of detention at first may be a local authority community home[48] but this cannot be continued after the offender has reached the age of 19. At that age or before the Home Secretary may direct his transfer to prison.[49] If, on the evidence of two doctors, he is shown to be in need of medical treatment, the Home Secretary may

---

[40] Children and Young Persons Act 1969, s. 23 (1).

[41] *Ibid.* s. 23 (2).

[42] *Ibid.* s. 23 (3). The committal of juveniles to adult prisons was severely criticised in a White Paper (Cmnd. 6494) which also recommended that the court should give the local authority directions on the sort of institution to which the juvenile should be committed.

[43] Children and Young Persons Act 1933, s. 39.

[44] *Ibid.* s. 31.

[45] Children and Young Persons Act 1933, s. 53 (1), as amended by the Murder (Abolition of Death Penalty) Act 1965, s. 1 (5).

[46] *Ibid.* and Children and Young Persons Act 1969, s. 30 (2).

[47] Criminal Justice Act 1967, s. 61. See " Release on Licence," p. 257.

[48] Under the Children and Young Persons Act 1969, ss. 35–48; see p. 378.

[49] *Ibid.* s. 30 (1).

order his transfer to a hospital.[50] A verdict of not guilty by reason of insanity would also involve detention in a special hospital.[51]

If convicted of some other serious offence on indictment, the court may order detention under the direction of the Home Secretary, but only if the offence would be punishable in the case of an adult by fourteen years' imprisonment or more but not by a fixed sentence.[52] The sentence should be determinate, *i.e.* for a fixed term not exceeding the maximum penalty, but it may be ordered for life.[53] The prohibition on sentencing to any form of detention if the accused is not legally represented and has not previously been sentenced to detention (Powers of Criminal Courts Act 1973, section 21) [54] applies to juveniles, but the restrictions on the term under section 3 of the Criminal Justice Act 1961 do not.[55]

Where appropriate the court may order payment of a fine or make a hospital order, an order for conditional or absolute discharge,[56] a disqualification from driving order,[57] a forfeiture order,[58] or an order to pay costs or compensation or to make restitution.[59] The court may not order imprisonment,[60] community service,[61] probation (which is replaced by supervision orders for juveniles) or deportation.[62] If the juvenile is fifteen or sixteen, the court may still order borstal but the minimum age is to be raised first to 16 and then to 17.[63]

In the case of fines, costs or compensation the court may order the juvenile's parent or guardian [64] to pay it instead of the juvenile unless the parent or guardian cannot be found or has not conduced to the commission of the offence by neglecting to take due care of the

---

[50] Mental Health Act 1959, s. 72 (1) and (6).

[51] See p. 235.

[52] Children and Young Persons Act 1933, s. 53 (2).

[53] *R.* v. *Abbott* [1964] 1 Q.B. 489; *R.* v. *Bryson* (1973) 58 Cr.App.R. 464. In *R.* v. *McCauliffe* [1970] Crim.L.R. 660, the court disapproved a sentence for detention " not exceeding 14 years ", and substituted detention for six years.

[54] See p. 225.

[55] *R.* v. *Bosomworth* (1973) 57 Cr.App.R. 708; as to s. 3, see p. 225.

[56] Special provision is made for subsequent sentence on a person conditionally discharged while a juvenile and sentenced when over the age of 17: Powers of Criminal Courts Act 1973, s. 9.

[57] Including an order under *ibid.* s. 44; see p. 247.

[58] *Ibid.* s. 43; see p. 254.

[59] See Chap. 9, pp. 248–253. The amount of costs must not exceed any fine imposed on the young person himself: Costs in Criminal Cases Act 1973, s. 2 (2) (*b*).

[60] Powers of Criminal Courts Act 1973, s. 19 (1) (this includes suspended sentences).

[61] *Ibid.* s. 14 (1).

[62] Immigration Act 1971, s. 4 (6); see p. 244.

[63] Children and Young Persons Act 1969, ss. 7 (1) and 34 (1) (*d*).

[64] If the juvenile is in care and living in a local authority home, the local authority is the " guardian ": *R.* v. *Croydon Juvenile Court Justices, ex p. Croydon L.B.C.* [1973] 1 Q.B. 406.

juvenile. The order cannot be made if the parent or guardian is not given an opportunity to be heard; the fine is treated as though ordered on conviction of the parent or guardian and he may appeal to the Court of Appeal.[65]

The court may also order the juvenile to be detained in a detention centre or attend an attendance centre, or it may make a care or supervision order or, with the consent of his parent or guardian, order the juvenile's parent or guardian to enter a recognisance to take proper care of and exercise proper control over him.[66] These orders are dealt with later.[67] Alternatively the court of trial may remit the case for sentence to the juvenile court. This is dealt with below.[68]

C. Summary Trial by Magistrates

In all cases other than those for which he may be tried on indictment, a juvenile must be tried summarily[69] which normally means trial by a juvenile court. However, he may be tried by an adult magistrates' court in six cases[70]:

(i) if he is charged jointly with a person who has reached the age of 17;

(ii) if a person of 17 or over is charged at the same time with aiding and abetting, causing, procuring, allowing or permitting the offence with which the juvenile is charged;

(iii) if he (the juvenile) is charged with aiding and abetting, etc., an offence with which a person of 17 or over is charged at the same time[71];

(iv) if he is charged with an offence arising out of the same or connected circumstances which gave rise to an offence with which a person of 17 or over is charged[71];

(v) if, an accused's age being unknown or mistaken, it transpires during trial that he is a child or young person[72];

---

[65] Children and Young Persons Act 1933, s. 55 (1). In the case of children who are found to be guilty of an offence in care proceedings (see p. 382), the parent of guardian must be ordered to pay any compensation awarded: Children and Young Persons Act 1969, s. 3 (6) (*b*). The Act makes provision for abolishing this power in the case of children (Sched. 6) but this will only be implemented when the age for prosecution is raised.

[66] Children and Young Persons Act 1969, s. 7 (7).

[67] See pp. 376–382.

[68] See p. 369.

[69] *Ibid.* s. 6 (1).

[70] Children and Young Persons Act 1933, s. 46.

[71] Children and Young Persons Act 1963, s. 18.

[72] The magistrates' court may continue if it thinks fit to do so, or it may adjourn the case to a juvenile court.

(vi) if the accused notifies the clerk that he wishes to plead guilty by post[73] and the court has no reason to believe that he is a juvenile.[74]

The usual principles for joinder of defendants [75] apply in (i) above but the interests of justice, including as they do the interests of the accused, may of course require a juvenile's separate trial before a juvenile court. (If the 1969 Act were fully in force, the charge against a young person could only be made by a qualified informant [76] so that the cases would not be common where a young person and an adult were jointly charged.[77]) Although, if they are jointly charged, the court *must* try the juvenile, the power to try him if he has an adult accomplice or instigator is discretionary. It is based on convenience as in the cases of trial of offenders and of aiders and abettors over whom a magistrates' court would not otherwise have jurisdiction.[78] For the purposes of the last two exceptions, a person's age is established by any evidence available to the magistrates' court,[79] but the question would not arise unless the court was put on inquiry or the accused raised it himself.

If tried summarily as an adult, the procedure for trial follows the normal course,[80] subject to the restrictions on reporting and publicity which may be implemented [81] and the power to compel the attendance of the young person's parent or guardian.[82]

Treatment of young persons

On finding a juvenile guilty, the magistrates' court must remit the case to a juvenile court for sentence, unless it deals with him as follows:

(*a*) by awarding a conditional or absolute discharge;
(*b*) by the imposition of a fine; or
(*c*) by issuing an order requiring his parent or guardian to enter a recognisance to take proper care of him and exercise control

[73] See Magistrates' Courts Act 1957, s. 1, p. 310.
[74] Children and Young Persons Act 1969, Sched. 5, para. 4.
[75] See pp. 137–141 and 304.
[76] See p. 363.
[77] Except in the case of a joint charge of homicide, a child could never be tried jointly with an adult: see *ibid.* s. 4, p. 363.
[78] See Magistrates' Courts Act 1952, ss. 1 (2) (*b*), 2 (2) and 35, pp. 51 and 52.
[79] Magistrates' Courts Act 1952, s. 126 (5).
[80] See Chapter 11, pp. 308–316.
[81] See Children and Young Persons Act 1933, ss. 37 and 39, p. 371.
[82] See *ibid.* s. 34, as substituted by the Children and Young Persons Act 1963, s. 25 (1), and Magistrates' Courts (Children and Young Persons) Rules 1970, r. 26, p. 365.

over him, with or without any other order that the court has power to make when absolutely or conditionally discharging an offender.[83]

The case is sent to the juvenile court for the area in which the offender was tried summarily (or committed for trial, if he is tried on indictment) or where he habitually resides. He may be committed in detention or on bail [84] and the court which has found him guilty must send particulars of the offence and offender to the juvenile court. The juvenile court may deal with him in any way in which it could have dealt with him had he been tried and found guilty there.[85]

D. The Juvenile Court

1. Constitution

The juvenile court is not an independent court but is the magistrates' court sitting in a special capacity. A panel of justices who are suitably qualified to deal with juveniles is drawn up for each commission area; they are appointed by their fellow justices at their annual meeting and serve on the panel for three years. Stipendiary magistrates are *ex officio* on the panel.[86]

The court consists of not more than three justices, at least one of whom must be a woman and one a man.[87] This rule may be waived, however, where it would be necessary to adjourn to obtain the proper constitution of the bench and where such an adjournment would not be in the interests of justice. A stipendiary magistrate, despite his power to sit alone in other proceedings, must sit with one or two other justices in the juvenile court, although he may sit alone if an adjournment would not be in the interests of justice.[88]

2. Publicity of proceedings

The proceedings in a juvenile court are regulated so that the minimum publicity is given to them. If the hearing is held at the petty sessional court-house, an hour must elapse between the close of any

---

[83] Children and Young Persons Act 1969, s. 7 (8). As to the " other orders " which are permissible, see p. 376.

[84] He does not have a right to bail (Bail Act 1976, s. 4; see p. 73), but is subject to the same general principles as, for instance, a person committed for sentence.

[85] Children and Young Persons Act 1933, s. 56, as amended by the Children and Young Persons Act 1969, Sched. 5, para. 6: see p. 376.

[86] Juvenile Courts (Constitution) Rules 1954 (S.I. 1954 No. 1711), rr. 1–5; for further details of the juvenile court, see Mumford, *Guide to Juvenile Court Law*. New rules may be made under s. 61 of the 1969 Act.

[87] *Ibid.* r. 9.

[88] *Ibid.* r. 12.

other proceedings and the commencement of the juvenile court proceedings.[89] At the hearing the court must be cleared of all except the court officers, the parties and their representatives, witnesses, bona fide press and broadcasting reporters and anyone authorised by the court to be present,[90] though the court or Home Secretary may dispense with this provision if it is in the interests of justice to do so.[91] Press and broadcast reports must not give details identifying the juvenile, in particular, his name, address or school.[92]

3. Jurisdiction

The juvenile court has jurisdiction over all charges against young persons except in those cases listed on pages 364 and 368 where the juvenile may or must be tried on indictment or by an adult magistrates' court. The court's jurisdiction, however, extends to all juveniles when they are brought before the court for care proceedings. This is not really within the scope of this book, but its inclusion is necessary to give a proper description of the functions of the juvenile court.[93]

E. Procedure before Juvenile Courts

The procedure at trial is basically the same as the procedure at the summary trial of adults,[94] but several special provisions apply during the proceedings.

1. Process and remand

The following provisions apply not only to juveniles who are to be tried by a juvenile court, but also to a juvenile who is:

(*a*) charged with homicide[95];
(*b*) charged with an offence for which he may be tried on indictment[96];
(*c*) charged with an offence in such circumstances that he may be tried by an adult magistrates' court[97]; and
(*d*) remitted to the juvenile court[98] for sentence.[99]

---

89 Children and Young Persons Act 1933, s. 47, as amended by the Children and Young Persons Act 1963, s. 17 (2).

90 *Ibid.* s. 47. A social worker who has had responsibility for the supervision of the juvenile under the direction of a local authority is entitled to be present: *R.* v. *Southwark Juvenile Court, ex p. J.* [1973] 1 W.L.R. 1300.

91 *Ibid.* s. 49.

92 *Ibid.* s. 39.

93 See p. 382.

94 See pp. 308–316.

95 See p. 363.

96 See p. 363.

97 See p. 368.

98 See p. 370.

99 Children and Young Persons Act 1969, ss. 23 (1) and 29 (1).

The term " juvenile " is used here because children are still subject to these provisions. When the 1969 Act is fully implemented, these provisions will only apply to a child who is arrested for homicide.

A juvenile may be arrested without a warrant in the same circumstances as an adult.[1] When brought to a police station, the officer in charge or a police officer not below the rank of inspector may detain him if it is in his own interest,[2] if he is reasonably suspected of having committed homicide or a grave offence, if his release would defeat the ends of justice or if he would fail to appear to answer the charge.[3] If released, it need not be on bail, but a juvenile has a right to bail pending trial in the same way as an adult.[4]

Otherwise proceedings must be started by the issue of a summons or warrant of arrest based on an information laid.[5] If arrested with a warrant the station officer or police inspector may release him on the same conditions as if he were arrested without a warrant save that a recognisance may be taken from his parent or guardian to secure his attendance at the hearing of the charge. Sureties may be taken and, where the police officer thinks fit, the recognisance may be conditioned for the parent's attendance also.[6] A warrant of arrest may be backed for bail.[7]

When arrested, the juvenile must be brought before a justice within 72 hours from arrest unless he is too ill, in which case a police officer of the rank of inspector or above must certify his illness.[8] When the juvenile or the police officer with the certificate appears before the court, the court or justice either proceeds to inquire into the case (as an examining justice or as a court of trial, depending on the offence charged) or it releases him without remand or it remands him. A juvenile can only be remanded if the court or justice considers that it is in his own interests to be detained or has reason to believe that he has committed a grave offence, or that his release would defeat the ends of justice, or, if he was arrested without a warrant, that he would fail to appear to answer the charge. If remanded, he may be remanded in detention or on bail. If unrepresented, and ordered to be detained, the court must inform him of

[1] See pp. 62–63.

[2] This is envisaged as meaning circumstances such as being arrested a long way from home: Home Office Guide (see footnote 1, p. 361), para. 208.

[3] Children and Young Persons Act 1969, s. 29 (1).

[4] See pp. 68–82.

[5] See pp. 54–60 and, as to informants, p. 363.

[6] *Ibid*. s. 29 (2), as substituted by the Bail Act 1976, Sched. 2, para. 47; see also p. 374.

[7] See p. 58.

[8] *Ibid*. s. 29 (5).

his right to apply to the High Court for bail; it must also give him a written note of the reason for remanding him.[8a]

In the context of arrest without warrant " release " means release without bail. The power to do this with juveniles, both of the police and of the court, does not exist in the case of adults.

If a juvenile is detained, either by the police[9] or on the order of the court,[10] he must be committed to the care of the local authority. The court may, however, commit him to the custody of a police constable for not more than 24 hours.[11] Further, if the juvenile is a young person and is of so unruly a character that he cannot safely be committed to the care of the local authority, he may be committed to a remand centre, if there is one available,[12] or otherwise to prison.[13] A police officer who is dealing with an arrested juvenile and who decides to detain him must make arrangements for him to be taken into the care of the local authority unless he certifies that it would be impracticable or that the juvenile is of so unruly a character that committal to care would be inappropriate.[14]

After committal by the court to the care of the local authority, the local authority may itself apply to a local magistrates' court to have the young person committed to a remand centre or prison if his unruly character and behaviour makes his committal to care unsafe.[15]

A remand centre is a secure institution where juvenile adults are sent when remanded in custody before trial or before sentence so that they need not be sent to an adult prison except in those cases where it is the only appropriate course. As they are not available in all areas, young people have to be committed to prison unless the court is notified by the Home Secretary that a remand centre is available.[16–17]

The normal period of eight days for remand in detention before trial and for other short periods during adjournments applies to juveniles who are brought before a justice or juvenile court on a

---

8a Bail Act 1976, s. 5; see p. 78.

9 Children and Young Persons Act 1969, s. 29 (3).

10 *Ibid.* s. 23 (1).

11 *Ibid.* s. 23 (5).

12 See below.

13 *Ibid.* s. 23 (2); this provision does not apply to prosecutable children.

14 *Ibid.* s. 29 (3). Girls under the age of 15 may not be certified unruly and may not be remanded to an adult prison; such girls are the responsibility of the local authority: S.I. 1977 No. 420.

15 *Ibid.* s. 23 (3).

16–17 Criminal Justice Act 1948, s. 27, as replaced by the Children and Young Persons Act 1969, Sched. 5, para. 24.

criminal charge after arrest with or without a warrant.[18] Where the juvenile's character, circumstances and home surroundings are such that he ought to be taken into care,[19] however, the period of detention may be ordered for up to 28 days by a justice on the application of a person authorised to detain him.[20] This provision is designed for care proceedings in which the commission of an offence is not relevant, but it could occur when a juvenile from a bad home is detained prior to the decision of whether or not to make a charge.

If a juvenile has been ordered to be detained in the care of a local authority and he is absent without leave, he may be arrested without a warrant by a constable anywhere in the United Kingdom.[21]

2. Representation

A juvenile has the same right to be legally represented as an adult but if he is unrepresented, his parent or guardian must be allowed to assist him in his defence [22] and the court itself must conduct the cross-examination of prosecution witnesses if the juvenile is not competent to do so.[23]

3. Presence of parent or guardian

The parent or guardian of the juvenile must be required to attend at all stages of the proceedings unless the court is satisfied that such a requirement would be unreasonable.[24] It might be unreasonable if, for instance, he or she were ill, but in that case some other relative may be allowed to take his or her place.[25] To secure the presence of the parent or guardian, the court may issue a summons or warrant as if an information had been laid requiring his presence as a defendant; a summons to a juvenile may include a summons to his parent or guardian.[26]

If a juvenile is arrested, the person who arrests him must inform at least one person whose attendance at the proceedings could be compelled, of the arrest.[27]

---

[18] See Magistrates' Courts Act 1952, ss. 14 (3) and 105 (4), p. 67.

[19] See Children and Young Persons Act 1969, s. 1 (2) (*a*)–(*d*), p. 383.

[20] *Ibid.* s. 28 (1).

[21] Children and Young Persons Act 1969, s. 32, as amended by the Children Act 1975, s. 68; see also p. 380.

[22] Magistrates' Courts (Children and Young Persons) Rules 1970, r. 5.

[23] *Ibid.* r. 8 (2).

[24] Children and Young Persons Act 1933, s. 34, substituted by the Children and Young Persons Act 1963, s. 25 (1).

[25] Magistrates' Courts (Children and Young Persons) Rules 1970, r. 5 (2).

[26] *Ibid.* r. 26; as to summonses and warrants, see pp. 55–60.

[27] Children and Young Persons Act 1933, s. 34 (2), as amended by the Children and Young Persons Act 1969, Sched. 5, para. 3.

4. Plea

The court must explain to the juvenile the substance of the charge in simple language suitable to his age and understanding.[28] If he admits it then this amounts to a finding of guilt and the court proceeds immediately to deal with him as described in section 6, below.

5. Procedure at trial

If the juvenile does not admit the charge, the procedure is basically the same as the procedure for trial of adults in magistrates' courts.[29] The juvenile, his representative or the court[30] may cross-examine each witness giving evidence in support of the charge at the close of his evidence-in-chief.[31] If a prima facie case is made out the court must tell the juvenile of his right to give and call evidence or make a statement.[32] The court then considers the case and makes its decision in the normal way, except that a conviction is known as a "finding of guilt."[33]

6. Procedure after a finding of guilt

Special provisions are made for the proceedings at this stage[34]:

(*a*) The juvenile and his parent or guardian must be given an opportunity to make a statement. This serves roughly the same purpose as a plea of mitigation in adult proceedings.[35]

(*b*) The court must consider such information about the juvenile's general conduct, home surroundings, school record and medical history as will enable it to deal with the case *in his best interests*. This includes a doctor's medical report. It is the duty of the local authority or local education authority to provide this information if it has brought the charge.[36]

(*c*) If such information is not fully available, the court considers whether the juvenile ought to be remanded for further inquiry.[37]

(*d*) Any probation officer's, local authority's or medical report

---

[28] Magistrates' Courts (Children and Young Persons) Rules 1970, r. 6.
[29] *Ibid.* r. 7.
[30] See p. 368.
[31] See Magistrates' Courts (Children and Young Persons) Rules 1970, r. 8 (2), p. 365.
[32] *Ibid.* r. 8 (1).
[33] See p. 362.
[34] Magistrates' Courts (Children and Young Persons) Rules 1970, r. 10.
[35] See p. 217.
[36] Children and Young Persons Act 1969, s. 9.
[37] The remand would be on bail under the Bail Act 1976, s. 4 (4), unless the conditions of Sched. 1 of that Act were fulfilled; see pp. 73 and 74.

which is produced may be accepted without being read aloud. The court may order the withdrawal of the juvenile or his parent or guardian at this stage. In either of these cases the court must

(i) tell the juvenile of such material parts of the reports which bear on his character or conduct as the court considers practicable in view of his age and understanding, and

(ii) tell the parent or guardian of the material parts of the reports which bear on the juvenile's character, conduct, home surroundings or health.

If the person who made the report is not present and if either the juvenile or the parent or guardian wishes to produce further evidence, the court must adjourn to enable the person who made the report to attend and the evidence to be called.[38]

(*e*) Before finally disposing of the case and dealing with the juvenile, the court, unless it considers it to be undesirable, must explain to the juvenile and his parent or guardian the manner in which it intends to deal with him and the general nature and effect of any order it intends to make and must allow them to make representations.[39]

7. Treatment of juveniles [40]

When a young person is found to be guilty of an offence by a juvenile court, the following orders which have already been considered,[41] may be made where appropriate: fine, hospital order, absolute or conditional discharge, disqualification [42] and endorsement, an order to pay costs or compensation or to make restitution, or to forfeit property used in crime or an order that the parent or guardian pay the fine, compensation or costs. Where appropriate the court may remit the juvenile to a different juvenile court,[43] *e.g.* if he was tried by a court in the area where the offence was committed, he may be remitted to a court in the area where he lives.

---

[38] Magistrates' Courts (Children and Young Persons) Rules 1970, r. 10 (2).

[39] *Ibid.* r. 11.

[40] Former sentences, which are being phased out by the Children and Young Persons Act 1969, are approved schools, remand homes (as opposed to remand centres), fit person orders and detention in a detention centre for default of payment.

[41] See pp. 232 *et seq.* and 322 *et seq.*

[42] Not being a disqualification under s. 44 of the Powers of Criminal Courts Act 1973, because that can only be imposed by the Crown Court; see p. 247.

[43] See p. 370.

In addition, the court may order detention in a detention centre or attendance at an attendance centre, or it may make a care or supervision order; this last order is the juvenile equivalent of probation, which is not available for juveniles. Attendance at an attendance centre is described in Section H.[44]

If the offence is indictable and the juvenile is sentenced by a juvenile court,[45] the court may sentence him in any way in which it could have sentenced him for a purely summary offence,[46] or it may impose a fine of £50.[47] In no circumstances may a sentence of imprisonment be imposed.[48]

(a) *Detention centres*

Detention centres provide for a short custodial sentence whose object is primarily deterrent. The regime is rigorous and provides training and education, though the maximum term of detention restricts the possibility of serious training.

The order can be made on a finding of guilt of an offence for which the court would, in the case of an adult, have been able to sentence the offender to imprisonment.[49] The term of detention is normally three months but, where the offence is punishable by more than three months' imprisonment, the term must be between three and six months.[50] Consecutive terms of detention may be ordered but the aggregate must not exceed six months if the two terms are ordered at the same time.[51] If the offender is already subject to detention in a detention centre at the time he is found guilty of an offence, the court may order the later term to start at the expiration of the earlier term provided the aggregate does not exceed nine months.[52] If necessary to make up the aggregate the court can order a term of detention shorter than three months but otherwise the minimum term is three months.[53] Juvenile adults may also be sent to a detention centre.[54]

---

[44] See p. 389.

[45] *i.e.* after being remitted under s. 7 (8) of the 1969 Act, p. 370.

[46] *i.e.* the orders which a magistrates' court may make under s. 7 (8), above, a hospital order, detention centre, care or supervision order; the orders which are outside the court's sentencings powers are imprisonment (see below), probation orders (Powers of Criminal Courts Act 1973, s. 2 (1); see above), committal for sentence (this is not available for purely summary offences (see p. 330) and recommendations for deportation (see p. 367).

[47] Children and Young Persons Act 1969, s. 6 (3).

[48] Powers of Criminal Courts Act 1973, s. 19 (1).

[49] Criminal Justice Act 1961, s. 4 (1).

[50] *Ibid.* s. 4 (2).

[51] *Ibid.* s. 5 (1) and (4).

[52] *Ibid.* s. 5 (1) and (5).

[53] *Ibid.* ss. 4 (2) and 5 (3).

[54] See p. 388.

It is intended to replace detention and attendance [55] centres by intermediate treatments within the system of community homes.[56]

(b) *Care orders*

A care order, or " order committing the offender to the care of a local authority," [57] may always be made in respect of a juvenile who has been tried summarily or who has been remitted to the juvenile court for sentence.[58] Care orders may be " interim care orders " which are limited to 28 days in length, but such orders cannot be made on a finding of guilt.[59]

When a care order has been made (and this includes a juvenile who has been committed to their care at any stage of the proceedings) [60] the local authority has the same powers and duties with respect to the juvenile as his parent or guardian would have but for the order. This includes restriction of liberty to the extent which the authority considers appropriate.[61] The parent or guardian cannot claim any right of control over or access to the juvenile while he is in care.[62]

The local authority must decide what course is in the best interests of the juvenile and the choice of treatment is flexible.[63] He may be allowed to live at home with provisions for visiting or supervision by a local authority officer. Alternatively he may be required to live in a community home or a voluntary home or to live with a foster parent.

Community homes are regulated and approved by the Home Secretary and are planned and provided on a regional basis.[64] They are administered by the local authority and vary in the form of treatment and accommodation which they provide and the degree of restriction which they impose on the inmates. Voluntary homes, *i.e.* homes provided by voluntary organisations, are brought within

---

[55] See p. 389.

[56] See below. See *Children in Trouble*, Cmnd. 3601.

[57] Children and Young Persons Act 1969, s. 20 (1).

[58] *Ibid.* s. 7 (7); as to orders on conviction on indictment, see p. 366 (children and young persons); care and supervision orders may be made.

[59] Nor at the conclusion of care proceedings: see p. 386. They are made before the hearing when a juvenile is in need of care; see p. 383.

[60] See Children and Young Persons Act 1969, ss. 23 and 29, p. 372.

[61] *Ibid.* s. 24 (2).

[62] *Ibid.* s. 24 (1).

[63] It is generally regulated by the Children Act 1948, as amended by the Children Act 1975. See also the Children and Young Persons Act 1969, s. 27, which enables local authorities on the direction of the Home Secretary or in their own discretion to deal with a child in a manner not in accordance with their general duties to further his best interests and proper development if it is required to do so for the purpose of protecting members of the public.

[64] Children and Young Persons Act 1969, ss. 35–48.

the regional plan for community homes by regulations of the Home Secretary and are designated as " controlled " or " assisted " community homes.

A complete account of the regime within community homes is beyond the range of this book. The period to be spent inside one is a matter for the local authority's discretion, depending on the progress of the juvenile and the quality of his surroundings and circumstances if he is sent home. Parents must keep the authority informed of their changes of address. If the parents do not visit a juvenile in a community home, the authority must appoint a visitor to advise and befriend the juvenile while he is in the home.[65]

Care orders may cease to be in force in the following ways:

(i) when the juvenile reaches the age of 18 or, if he was 16 when the order was made, when he reaches the age of 19[66];

(ii) when the local authority or the juvenile applies to the juvenile court and it appears to the court that it is appropriate to do so, the court may discharge the care order. If the juvenile is under 18 years old the court may substitute a supervision order[67];

(iii) if the juvenile has reached the age of 15 and is accommodated in a community home and if his behaviour is such that it will be detrimental to other people accommodated in the home, the local authority may apply to the juvenile court to have him transferred to a borstal institution. The local authority must have the consent of the Home Secretary.[68] The juvenile is then treated as if he had been sentenced to borstal for two years from the date of the care order.[69]

A care order may be extended after the person in a community home has reached the age of 18 until he is 19 if it is in his interest by reason of his mental condition or behaviour or if it is in the public interest to do so. The local authority applies to the juvenile court for such an extension but the juvenile must be present.[70]

---

[65] Children and Young Persons Act 1969, s. 24 (5) and (8).

[66] *Ibid.* s. 20 (3).

[67] *Ibid.* s. 21 (2). If the application is dismissed, it cannot be renewed for at least three months after dismissal: *ibid.* s. 21 (3). The court must be satisfied that the supervision order will be combined with the juvenile being under proper care and control: Children Act 1975, Sched. 3, para. 69.

[68] Children and Young Persons Act 1969, s. 31 (1) and (2).

[69] *Ibid.* s. 31 (3). The court may make an order for his destination in a remand centre for up to 21 days before deciding whether he should be transferred to borstal: *ibid.* s. 31 (4).

[70] *Ibid.* s. 21 (1).

If a juvenile detained under a care order goes absent without leave he may be arrested without a warrant by a police constable anywhere in the United Kingdom.[71]

(c) *Supervision orders*

A supervision order may be made by the court after trying a juvenile or after care proceedings.[72] The juvenile is placed under the supervision of a local authority or of a probation officer.[73] The order is similar to a probation order,[74] though the conditions differ to some extent and the supervisor need not be a probation officer.

The supervisor's general duty is to " advise, assist and befriend " the supervised person.[75] The conditions which may be imposed are:

(i) Residence: the order may require the supervised person to live with a named individual or it may empower the supervisor to give binding directions to the supervised person to live for a period in a specified place.[76] The places to be made available for residence are planned by the children's regional planning committee and approved by the Home Secretary.[77] The maximum period or aggregate of periods spent in a residential home are calculated on rather a complex basis, but in any event cannot exceed 90 days.[78]

(ii) Activities: the order may empower the supervisor to require the supervised person to report to a named person and/or to participate in specified activities on a day or days specified.[79] The extent and the exact form of these requirements are left to the supervisor's discretion.

(iii) Psychiatric supervision: where the court is satisfied on the evidence of a medical practitioner that the supervised person's mental condition requires and may be susceptible to treatment but is not such as to warrant a hospital order, it may include a requirement in the supervision order that he should submit to treatment. The treatment may be

---

[71] Children and Young Persons Act 1969, s. 32, as amended by the Children Act 1975, s. 68. If someone is keeping the juvenile, he may be compelled to produce the juvenile and may be guilty of an offence.

[72] Children and Young Persons Act 1969, ss. 7 (7) and 1 (3).

[73] *Ibid.* s. 11.

[74] See pp. 236–240.

[75] Children and Young Persons Act 1969, s. 14.

[76] *Ibid.* s. 12 (1) and (2) (*a*).

[77] *Ibid.* s. 19.

[78] *Ibid.* s. 12 (3).

[79] *Ibid.* s. 12 (2) (*b*).

(*a*) by or under the direction of a registered medical practitioner,
(*b*) as a non-resident patient at a specified place, or
(*c*) as a resident patient in a hospital or mental nursing home provided under the Mental Health Act 1959, not being a " special " hospital under that Act.[80]

If the proposed supervised person has reached the age of 14, his consent to such a condition must be obtained; the condition automatically ceases when the supervised person reaches the age of 18.[81] The condition may be cancelled or varied or its duration extended on the evidence of a medical practitioner that the treatment is complete, ineffective or inappropriate or that different or further treatment is necessary.[82]

A probation officer can only be appointed, in the case of a child under 13, if a probation officer has been or is already exercising duties as a probation officer in relation to some other member of the child's household.[83]

The supervision order may be made for any period up to three years; if it is made after trial of a juvenile it continues after he has reached the age of 18 until the period expires but if it was made in care proceedings it automatically expires when he reaches the age of 18.[84]

During the period of the order, however, the supervisor or the supervised person may apply to the court to vary the conditions of the order or to discharge it. If discharged, it may be replaced by a care order.[85] When the supervised person reaches the age of 18 an adult magistrates' court may discharge or vary the order on the application of the supervisor or supervised person. The court may insert a new provision for the duration of the order, appoint a new supervisor or vary or cancel the conditions.[86] If the supervisor of a person who has reached the age of 18 applies to the court and it is proved that he is in breach of the order, the court may impose a fine of not more than £20 or order him to attend an attendance centre.[87] If it also discharges the supervision order, it may impose

80 *Ibid.* s. 12 (4). 81 *Ibid.* s. 12 (5). 82 *Ibid.* s. 15 (5).
83 *Ibid.* s. 13 (2) as amended by S.I. 1974 No. 1083.
84 *Ibid.* s. 17.
85 *Ibid.* s. 15 (1).
86 *Ibid.* s. 15 (3).
87 See p. 389.

any punishment on him which it could have imposed had it convicted him of the offence for which the supervision order was made.[88]

The presence of the supervised person at the hearing of an application to vary or discharge a supervision order is normally necessary [89] and may be secured by a justice's summons or warrant.[90] If he is arrested and cannot be brought to the court immediately he may be detained for up to 72 hours in a place of safety during which time he must be brought before a justice who may make an interim care order [91] or, if he is 18 or over, remand him.[92] In his absence, the court can discharge the order, cancel a condition, reduce the order's duration or change the supervisor or the area in which the order is administered.[93]

(d) *Recognisances*

Recognisances to be entered by a juvenile's parent or guardian may be ordered on conviction on indictment,[94] after a finding of guilt by a magistrates' or juvenile court [95] or after care proceedings.[96] The condition is that the parent or guardian will take proper care of and exercise proper control over the juvenile.[97] The parent or guardian must consent to enter the recognisance.[98] The recognisance cannot be made for more than £50 or for a period exceeding three years. If the juvenile will reach the age of 18 within three years, it must not be made so as to extend beyond that event.[99] The recognisance may be forfeited in the same way as a recognisance to keep the peace.[1]

F. Care Proceedings

The object of care proceedings is to provide a judicial process for dealing with children and young persons who are deprived of the stability and favourable conditions necessary for a proper upbringing.

---

[88] Children and Young Persons Act 1969, s. 15 (4). If the offence would have been beyond the court's jurisdiction it may order imprisonment for not more than six months or a fine of £400.

[89] *Ibid.* s. 16 (1).

[90] *Ibid.* s. 16 (2).

[91] See p. 378.

[92] *Ibid.* s. 16 (3).

[93] *Ibid.* s. 16 (5).

[94] See p. 368.

[95] See pp. 369 and 375.

[96] See p. 386. Children and Young Persons Act 1969, s. 1 (3) (*a*).

[97] *Ibid.* s. 7 (7).

[98] *Ibid.* ss. 1 (5) and 7 (7). *Cf.* the recognisance of the parent pending proceedings under the Bail Act 1976, s. 3 (7), p. 77.

[99] *Ibid.* s. 2 (13).

[1] See Magistrates' Courts Act 1952, s. 96, p. 243.

The aim of the proceedings is to protect the juvenile himself and to make up for the failings of a bad home through the welfare services. Penal proceedings against juveniles should only be used when the most serious of offences have been committed or if the shock of penal proceedings is more appropriate in the particular case, *e.g.* where the young person shows tendencies to recidivism.

The basic condition for bringing care proceedings is that the " infant " is in need of care or control [2] which he is unlikely to receive unless the court makes an order.[3] Six of the grounds upon which care proceedings may be brought relate principally to the conditions in which the infant lives:

(*a*) he is being ill-treated or his proper development is being avoidably prevented or neglected or his health is being avoidably impaired or neglected;

(*b*) it is probable that he will be treated as in (*a*) above because a person who has been convicted of an offence involving ill-treatment of a child has or is to become a member of the same household[4];

(*c*) it is probable that he will be neglected as above because he or another infant in his household has been found by a court to be so neglected;

(*d*) he is exposed to moral danger;

(*e*) he is beyond the control of his parent or guardian;

(*f*) if he is of school age, he is not receiving the full-time education suitable to his age, ability and aptitude;

(*g*) he is guilty of an offence other than homicide.

Ground (*g*) is the only one which brings these proceedings within the scope of this book and, for the sake of brevity, only proceedings brought on this ground—known as the " offence condition "—will be considered.

1. The offence condition

Care proceedings brought on the ground that an offence has been committed are subject to provisions to protect the infant from double jeopardy [5]:

---

[2] " Care " includes protection and guidance and " control " includes discipline: Children and Young Persons Act 1969, s. 70 (1).

[3] *Ibid.* s. 1 (2).

[4] Added to the 1969 Act by the Children Act 1975, Sched. 3, para. 67.

[5] See " *Autrefois,*" pp. 159–167.

(*a*) if the offence condition was satisfied in previous care proceedings in respect of the offence now being alleged [6];

(*b*) if, but for the restrictions on prosecuting children,[7] the infant would be entitled to plead *autrefois acquit* or *convict* [8]; and

(*c*) if the offence condition was satisfied in previous care proceedings in respect of an offence for which someone is now seeking to bring a charge.[9]

Further, care proceedings cannot be brought if the period of limitation [10] on a summary offence alleged has expired [11] and an offence cannot be alleged as grounds for the proceedings unless they are brought by a local authority or police constable.[12]

The burden of proof is the same as in criminal proceedings; the juvenile court has to be satisfied beyond reasonable doubt that the infant is guilty as if he had been charged with the offence in an information.[13]

2. Initiation of proceedings

The local authority or police constable may bring the infant before a juvenile court if they reasonably believe that there are grounds for making an order.[14] The local authority for the area in which the infant lives, if it is not bringing the proceedings, must be informed.[15] Anyone may give information to the local authority that grounds for bringing care proceedings exist and the local authority must make inquiries; if it finds that there are grounds it must bring care proceedings unless satisfied that it would not be in the infant's or the public interest or that someone else is going to bring proceedings.[16]

The infant's presence may be secured by summons or warrant; if arrested he may be detained for up to 72 hours in a place of safety.[17] Notice of an infant's detention and of impending proceedings must

---

[6] Children and Young Persons Act 1969, s. 3 (1) (*a*).

[7] See *ibid.* s. 4, p. 362.

[8] *Ibid.* s. 3 (1) (*c*) and see footnote 5, above.

[9] *Ibid.* s. 3 (4).

[10] See Magistrates' Courts Act 1952, s. 104, p. 13.

[11] Children and Young Persons Act 1969, s. 3 (1) (*b*).

[12] *Ibid.* s. 3 (2). This does not prevent evidence of an offence being adduced in proceedings where the grounds are of neglect, etc., and the offence condition is not sought to be satisfied.

[13] *Ibid.* s. 3 (4).

[14] *Ibid.* s. 1 (1) and (6).

[15] *Ibid.* s. 2 (3) and (8).

[16] *Ibid.* s. 2 (1) and (2).

[17] *Ibid.* s. 2 (4) and (5). Where the proceedings are not brought on the offence condition, anyone may apply to a justice to have the infant taken to a place of safety for up to 28 days: *ibid.* s. 28 (1). In some cases a police constable may detain a juvenile: *ibid.* s. 28 (2)–(6).

be given to the infant (if he is old enough to understand), his parent or guardian, the local authority and any supervisor or probation officer already involved with the infant.[18]

3. The proceedings

The infant or his parent or guardian may be legally represented,[19] the parent or guardian may conduct the case or the court may allow some other relative or responsible person to do so.[20] If it appears to the court that there is likely to be a conflict of interest between the infant and his parent or guardian, the court may order that the parent or guardian be treated as not representing the infant.[21] The court may appoint a guardian ad litem.[22] The procedure is the same as for the original hearing of the care proceedings or for any subsequent application, such as an application to vary a supervision order,[23] though if the infant is the applicant he, instead of the local authority or constable, is the complainant.

The order of evidence and speeches at the hearing is the same as that used by magistrates' courts for criminal proceedings.[24] The court must explain to the infant in simple language the substance of the alleged offence and ask him whether he admits that he is guilty of it.[25] If he does not admit it, evidence is called and the proceedings are explained to the infant as if he were being tried by the juvenile court.[26] Written statements of evidence are admissible.[27]

Generally speaking the infant must be present at the hearing,[28] but at some proceedings other than the care proceedings themselves, the infant need not attend.[29] His parent or guardian may also be compelled to attend.[30] Where evidence to be given should not in the court's opinion be given in his presence, the court may hear such evidence in the absence of the infant or of his parent or guardian, save that the infant must be present while evidence of his conduct

---

[18] *Ibid.* s. 28 (4), and Magistrates' Courts (Children and Young Persons) Rules 1970, r. 14.
[19] As to legal aid, see p. 401.
[20] Magistrates' Courts (Children and Young Persons) Rules 1970, r. 17.
[21] Children Act 1975, s. 64 (adding a new s. 32A to the 1969 Act).
[22] *Ibid.* s. 64 (adding a new s. 32B to the 1969 Act).
[23] See Children and Young Persons Act 1969, s. 15, p. 381.
[24] Magistrates' Courts (Children and Young Persons) Rules 1970, r. 16 (2) (*c*); see Magistrates' Courts Rules 1968, r. 13, pp. 311–314.
[25] *Ibid.* r. 16 (2).
[26] See *ibid.* rr. 8, 9, 16 (2) (*d*) and 19, p. 375.
[27] See Criminal Justice Act 1967, s. 9, p. 110.
[28] Children and Young Persons Act 1969, s. 1 (2).
[29] *e.g.* discharge of a supervision order: *ibid.* s. 16 (5).
[30] See Children and Young Persons Act 1933, s. 34, p. 374.

or character or that the offence condition is satisfied is being given.[31] In particular, the parent or guardian may be asked to withdraw while the infant makes any allegations against him, though the court must inform him of their substance.[32]

The court may adjourn at any time before or during the proceedings fixing, if it makes an interim care order [33] for the infant, the date and place for resuming the proceedings.[34] It may adjourn after it is satisfied that the applicant's case has been proved if information relating to the infant's general conduct, home surroundings, school record and medical history is not immediately available.[35] The court must consider such information before deciding how to deal with the infant.[36] When it has decided it must explain in simple language the nature and effect of the order it intends to make.[37]

4. Powers of the court

At the conclusion of care proceedings, the following are the various ways in which the court may deal with the case:

(*a*) It may dismiss the application if the allegation of the offence is not proved.

(*b*) It may adjourn for reports and, if appropriate, make an interim care order.[38]

(*c*) If it has found that the offence condition has been satisfied, it may remit the case to another juvenile court.[39] This must be done where the court is not the court for the area in which the infant lives.[40]

(*d*) It may order the infant's parent or guardian to enter a recognisance to take proper care of and exercise proper control over the infant. This can only be done if the parent or guardian consents.[41]

(*e*) It may make a supervision order.[42]

---

[31] Magistrates' Courts (Children and Young Persons) Rules 1970, r. 18 (1).
[32] *Ibid.* r. 18 (2).
[33] See p. 378.
[34] Magistrates' Courts (Children and Young Persons) Rules 1970, r. 15 (1).
[35] *Ibid.* r. 20 (1).
[36] *Ibid.* r. 20; see also *ibid.* r. 10, p. 375, which makes similar provision for the procedure for receiving reports.
[37] *Ibid.* r. 21.
[38] Children and Young Persons Act 1969, s. 2 (10), and Magistrates' Courts (Children and Young Persons) Rules 1970, r. 20 (see above).
[39] Children and Young Persons Act 1969, s. 3 (5).
[40] *Ibid.* s. 2 (11).
[41] *Ibid.* s. 1 (3) (*a*) and (5) (*a*); as to recognisances, see p. 382.
[42] *Ibid.* s. 1 (3) (*b*); as to supervision, see p. 380.

(*f*) It may make a care order other than an interim order.[43]

(*g*) It may make a hospital order under Part V of the Mental Health Act 1959.[44]

(*h*) It may make a guardianship order under the Mental Health Act 1959.[45]

(*i*) If the offence condition is satisfied in consequence of an indictable offence, it may order
 (i) that the infant pay compensation of up to £400[46]; and
 (ii) that his parent or guardian pay compensation unless his conduct did not conduce to the commission of the offence (if the infant is a child this provision is mandatory).[47]

(*j*) If the offence condition is satisfied, it may order the infant to enter a recognisance for not more than £25 or for a period of not more than one year to keep the peace and be of good behaviour. The infant must consent.[48]

If the infant has reached the age of 16 and is or has been married, orders under paragraphs (*d*)–(*h*) cannot be made.[49]

More than one of the orders listed in paragraphs (*d*)–(*h*) cannot be made concurrently except that a care order and a hospital order can be made at the same time. If there is a pre-existing order at the time of the later proceedings, the court may discharge the earlier order unless it is a hospital or guardianship order.[50] An order to pay compensation may be made at the same time as any other order.[51]

G. Appeals

Where a juvenile is tried and sentenced by a court, he has the same rights of appeal as an adult would have.[52] Where care proceedings are brought the infant may appeal to the Crown Court[53] against any order made under section 1 of the 1969 Act except an order that his parent or guardian enter a recognisance.[54] He has no right to appeal

---

43 *Ibid.* s. 1 (3) (*c*); as to care orders, see p. 378.

44 *Ibid.* s. 1 (3) (*d*); as to hospital orders, see p. 234.

45 *Ibid.* s. 1 (3) (*e*).

46 Children and Young Persons Act 1969, s. 3 (6), and Powers of Criminal Courts Act, s. 35; see p. 250.

47 Children and Young Persons Act 1969, s. 3 (6).

48 *Ibid.* s. 3 (7).

49 *Ibid.* s. 1 (5) (*c*).

50 *Ibid.* s. 1 (4).

51 *Ibid.* s. 3 (6).

52 See pp. 260–285 and 340–357. A juvenile court is in the same position as a magistrates' court for this purpose.

53 As to the appeal, see pp. 344–348.

54 Children and Young Persons Act 1969, s. 2 (12); *i.e.* he can appeal against a care, supervision, hospital or guardianship order. There is no appeal against recognisances as they can only be ordered with the consent of the subject: *ibid.* ss. 1 (5) (*a*), 2 (13), 3 (7) and 7 (7) (*c*).

against an order that he should himself enter a recognisance if the offence condition has been satisfied.[55]

Where the court has found that the offence condition is satisfied and the infant did not admit the offence, he may appeal to the Crown Court against the finding that he is guilty if the court decides to make no order in respect of him.[56] Otherwise he appeals against the order and the Crown Court deals with the appeal as a rehearing of the relevant parts of the proceedings.

He may also appeal against an adverse decision on an application to discharge, vary or extend a care order[57] or on an application to discharge or vary a supervision order.[58]

H. Juvenile Adults

Although juvenile adults are generally subject to the same proceedings and provisions as adults, there are various special provisions applying to people who are 17 or over but under 21.

1. Remand

When a court remands a juvenile adult in custody, he is committed to a remand centre,[59] rather than a prison, if there is one available.[60] The same applies to committal prior to extradition.[61]

2. Treatment

The restriction on imposing imprisonment as a punishment on a juvenile adult has already been described.[62] The special treatments or sentences which will be peculiar to this age group when the 1969 Act is fully implemented are borstal training[63] and attendance at an attendance centre. Juvenile adults may be sent to a detention centre for up to six months[64] and probation hostels and homes[65] are principally designed for juvenile adult offenders.[66]

---

[55] Children and Young Persons Act 1969, s. 3 (7).

[56] *Ibid.* s. 3 (8). If the court which made the finding remitted the case to another court, he may appeal against the finding if the court to which he was remitted decides to make no order.

[57] *Ibid.* s. 21 (4); see p. 379.

[58] *Ibid.* s. 16 (8); see p. 381. The right of appeal does not apply if the variation was such that it could be made in the supervised person's absence; see p. 382.

[59] See p. 373.

[60] Criminal Justice Act 1948, s. 27, as replaced by the Children and Young Persons Act 1969, Sched. 5, para. 24. This may occur after arrest or when committed for trial or sentence or during an adjournment or after sentence.

[61] Criminal Justice Act 1967, s. 34.

[62] See p. 225.

[63] See p. 231.

[64] See p. 377.

[65] See p. 237.

[66] See *The Sentence of the Court*, H.M.S.O.

If a juvenile adult defaults in paying a fine or other monetary order and he is at the time detained in a detention centre under a previous sentence or order, the court may order that he be detained in the detention centre for the default.[67] Extended sentences cannot be passed on juvenile adults: one of the conditions for passing such a sentence is that the offender has been convicted three times since he reached the age of 21.[68]

3. Attendance centres

Where offenders in this age group do not require punishment by a custodial sentence but do require something more restrictive than a fine or other treatment which effectively releases the offender, attendance at an attendance centre may be suitable. It cannot be ordered against a person who has previously been sentenced to imprisonment, borstal training or detention in a detention centre or approved school.[69] It may be ordered as a sentence where imprisonment could be ordered in the case of an adult, for a breach of a probation order or for default in paying a sum of money.[70] The court must have been notified by the Home Secretary that an attendance centre is available.

The offender is ordered to attend outside his working or school hours for up to three hours on each occasion to be arranged by the officer in charge of the centre.[71] The total number of hours spent at the centre must be not less than 12 but not more than 24 hours.[72]

The order may be discharged or varied (in the time of attendance) by a justice for the area in which the centre is situated on the application of the offender or the officer in charge of the centre.[73] If the offender fails to attend or acts in breach of the centre rules, a court or a justice in the same area as the court which made the order may on information summon the offender to appear or issue a warrant for his arrest.[74] The court, if satisfied that he is in breach of the order, may deal with him in any other way in which it could have dealt with him originally.[75]

---

67 Criminal Justice Act 1961, ss. 5 and 6, as amended by the Children and Young Persons Act 1969, Sched. 5, para. 44, and Sched. 6.

68 See p. 226.

69 This is a form of sentence made obsolete by the Children and Young Persons Act 1969, s. 7 (5).

70 Criminal Justice Act 1948, s. 19 (1) and (5), as amended by the Children and Young Persons Act 1969, Sched. 5, para. 23.

71 *Ibid.* s. 19 (2).

72 Criminal Justice Act 1961, s. 10 (2).

73 Criminal Justice Act 1948, s. 19 (3).

74 *Ibid.* s. 19 (7).

75 *Ibid.* s. 19 (8).

Chapter 16

CORPORATIONS, CONTEMPT AND PERJURY

The procedures applicable to corporations, contempt of court and perjury are dealt with together here as miscellaneous short topics and not because of any connection between them.

A. Corporations

It must be remembered that corporations are not always capable of being prosecuted [1]; this section deals with special procedures applicable when a corporation is answerable to the criminal law.

In proceedings before magistrates' courts, the procedure applicable to corporations is, with some exceptions, the same as the procedure applicable to individuals.[2]

1. Preliminary proceedings

Prosecutions against corporations must, of course, be initiated by summons. Service is made on the corporation's registered office.[3]

The corporation may be legally represented [4] and it may be present in court through a duly appointed lay representative.[5] If such a representative does not appear, however, any requirement for a natural person to attend, *e.g.* at committal proceedings,[6] does not apply to the corporation.[7]

At committal proceedings a representative may make a statement in answer to the charge. He may also consent or object to summary trial on behalf of the corporation, or claim trial by jury for it.[8] If no representative appears, the court may proceed to summary trial without the corporation's consent,[9] unless the corporation is charged jointly with an individual.[10]

---

[1] See *e.g.* Kenny's *Outlines of Criminal Law* (19th ed.), p. 75 *et seq.*

[2] Magistrates' Courts Act 1952, Sched. 2, para. 8.

[3] Magistrates' Courts Rules 1968, r. 82 (3).

[4] Magistrates' Courts Act 1952, s. 99; see pp. 301–303.

[5] *Ibid.* Sched. 2, para. 4. As to the appointment of representatives, see Criminal Justice Act 1925, s. 33 (6), and Criminal Justice Act 1967, s. 29 (2), p. 391.

[6] See Magistrates' Courts Act 1952, s. 4 (3), p. 96.

[7] *Ibid.* Sched. 2, para. 5.

[8] *Ibid.* para. 3; as to consent to summary trial and claiming trial by jury, see *ibid.* ss. 18, 19 and 25, pp. 292–299.

[9] *Ibid.* Sched. 2, para. 5.

[10] See below.

At the conclusion of committal proceedings, the court makes a written order empowering the prosecution to prefer a bill of indictment against the corporation.[11] The corporation is then committed for trial as if it were an individual being committed on bail.[12]

2. Trial

(a) *Magistrates' courts*

If the information against the corporation is tried summarily the procedure follows the normal course.[13] If a representative is present he may plead guilty or not guilty on behalf of the corporation; the corporation may plead guilty by post[14] without appearing.[15]

If a corporation is charged jointly with an individual, neither may be tried summarily for an indictable offence[16] unless both consent to it, and neither may be tried summarily if one or the other claims trial by jury[17] of a summary offence.[18]

In passing sentence the magistrates' court is naturally limited to orders which involve a monetary penalty, *i.e.* fines, costs, compensation and restitution.[19] A corporation cannot be committed for sentence to the Crown Court for a heavier penalty to be imposed.[20]

(b) *On indictment*

If a corporation is tried on indictment, its corporate name is used in the indictment: "The Queen v. A.B. Co. Ltd."[21]

The corporation need not appear at trial. It may appear through a representative authorised by someone in the corporation who has or takes part in the management of the corporation.[22] On arraignment such a representative may enter a plea in writing on behalf of the corporation. Otherwise a plea of not guilty is entered on the order of the court.[23]

---

[11] Magistrates' Courts Act 1952, Sched. 2, para. 1. The order specifies the offence but a different offence may be substituted or added in the indictment: *ibid.* para. 2; see Administration of Justice (Miscellaneous Provisions) Act 1933, s. 2, p. 142.

[12] Magistrates' Courts Act 1952, Sched. 2, para. 6; see p. 104.

[13] See pp. 308–316.

[14] See Magistrates' Courts Act 1957, s. 1, p. 310.

[15] Criminal Justice Act 1967, s. 29.

[16] See Magistrates' Courts Act 1952, s. 19, p. 297.

[17] See Magistrates' Courts Act 1952, s. 25, p. 292.

[18] *Ibid.* Sched. 2, para. 9.

[19] See pp. 322–326 and 329–330. A forfeiture order under s. 43 of the Powers of Criminal Courts Act 1973 would not be inapplicable *per se*, but the order is expressed to be exercisable over property in the offender's possession or control " at the time of his apprehension," which is not appropriate to a corporation.

[20] *Ibid.* Sched. 2, para. 7.

[21] See p. 118.

[22] Criminal Justice Act 1925, s. 33 (6).

[23] *Ibid.* s. 33 (3).

B. Contempt of Court

The term " contempt of court " covers a wide range of activities which interfere with or obstruct the administration of justice. This section considers only the forms of contempt which are committed either by physical disruption of or offensive behaviour during court proceedings or by activities outside the court which prejudice fair trial or interfere with the proper course of justice. In this range certain forms of contempt may also amount to individual offences, *e.g.* interference with witnesses, conspiracy to pervert the course of justice or libel of a judge.[24] The term is also used to mean disobedience to a court order, such as an injunction or an order to pay a civil debt, for which the delinquent may be committed to prison, but this form of contempt need not be considered here.[25]

Contempt of court may be prosecuted on indictment or by proceedings in the Queen's Bench Divisional Court brought by a person aggrieved.[26] The Divisional Court then has power to commit the person in contempt to prison. There is also power to fine the person and to bind him over to be of good behaviour.[27] Either course might be suitable where the acts constituting the contempt take place outside the court, for instance, where a newspaper includes a report of matters which are *sub judice* when court proceedings are pending or being heard.[28] There are many cases, however, where " the undoubted possible recourse to indictment . . . is too dilatory and too inconvenient to afford any satisfactory remedy."[29] This occurs principally where the contempt is committed " in the face of the court," *i.e.* where the offence is committed in the court itself.

The powers of the judge depend on the court in which the contempt is committed. In the High Court or Court of Appeal the judge or judges may deal with the offender summarily without trial or other

---

[24] The Law Commission is reviewing all offences against the administration of justice and has published Working Paper No. 62 on the subject.

[25] See Langan and Lawrence, *Civil Procedure*, 2nd edition.

[26] R.S.C. 1965, Ord. 52, prescribes the procedure for the application.

[27] See p. 243.

[28] The Phillimore Committee's *Report on Contempt of Court* (Cmnd. 5794) dealt principally with this sort of contempt. Reported examples include menacing a witness outside court after she had given evidence (*Moore* v. *Clerk of Assize, Bristol* [1971] 1 W.L.R. 1669), newspaper speculations as to what had gone on while the court was sitting in camera (*R.* v. *Prager* 121 N.L.J. 548) and publication of the true names of witnesses after a court has directed that they should be substituted by " Mr. X " or " Mrs. Y " (*R.* v. *Socialist Worker Printers, ex p. Attorney-General* [1975] Q.B. 637).

[29] *Per* Wills J. in *R.* v. *Davies* [1906] 1 K.B. 32, at p. 41. As to when it is proper to deal with the matter summarily, see *Balogh* v. *St. Albans Crown Court* [1975] Q.B. 73; *R.* v. *Owen* [1976] 1 W.L.R. 840.

inquiry. In *Morris* v. *The Crown Office* [30] 22 Welsh students invaded a Queen's Bench court in the Royal Courts of Justice, shouting slogans, singing songs and scattering pamphlets about a Welsh language movement to which they were devoted. The trial which was in progress had to be adjourned and the judge committed those who refused to apologise to prison for three months. Eleven of them appealed to the Court of Appeal which reviewed the power of High Court judges to commit people to prison summarily for contempt. The sentences were held to have been correct though the Court of Appeal substituted binding-over orders for 12 months.

In the Supreme Court, a judge has power to order any term of imprisonment, a fine or binding over to keep the peace and be of good behaviour and to come up for judgment if called upon to do so. The Crown Court has the same powers in relation to contempt of court as the High Court.[31] A county court judge has power to order imprisonment for not more than one month or a fine of not more than £20.[32] Magistrates' courts have no power to commit a person to prison for contempt of the court, though they may exclude him from the court room and bind him over to keep the peace.[33] If a person does disrupt proceedings or insult the court, an application must be made to the Divisional Court which can punish him for contempt.[34]

The case of *Morris* v. *The Crown Office* [35] was primarily concerned with the legality of the sentences of imprisonment. It was argued that the judge was limited by statute not to impose imprisonment on a person under 21 years old unless satisfied by evidence of his character and condition that it is appropriate.[36] The Court of Appeal held that because the judge was acting immediately and on matters of which he had personal knowledge and gave the offenders credit for being of excellent character, he was not required to have evidence called. Unless an indictment is preferred, the power to commit for contempt is outside the normal sentencing procedure—probation or other conditional forms of sentence, for instance, could not be ordered for they are usually available only on conviction—and the power to bind over [37] is effectively the judge's power to impose a suspended or conditional sentence.

30 [1970] 2 Q.B. 114.
31 Courts Act 1971, s. 4 (8).
32 County Courts Act 1959, s. 157 (1).
33 See p. 243.
34 R.S.C. 1965, Ord. 52.
35 [1970] 2 Q.B. 114.
36 See Powers of Criminal Courts Act 1973, s. 19 (2), p. 225.
37 As to the Crown Court, see Courts Act 1971, s. 6 (4) (*b*), p. 222.

Appeals [38]

Oppressive committals for contempt are averted by the provision of an appeal from the order. Because the power is essentially a power to imprison without trial, the appeal is given top priority; in *Morris's* case the appeal was heard within a week of the committal. The appeal, generally speaking, follows the same course as an appeal in the proceedings where it is committed:

(*a*) If the contempt occurs in the High Court or in a court having the powers of the High Court, or before a High Court judge in a civil case or in a county court, appeal lies to the Court of Appeal, Civil Division.[39] If the contempt occurs in the Crown Court appeal is expressed to lie simply to the Court of Appeal.[40]

(*b*) If the contempt occurs in the Court of Appeal or in a Divisional Court, appeal lies to the House of Lords and leave must be sought, though no other restrictions apply.

(*c*) If proceedings are brought in the Divisional Court for an order relating either to contempt in an inferior court or to contempt outside court proceedings, appeal lies to the House of Lords; leave must be sought and the usual restrictions on the appeal apply.[41]

If an appeal is made under (*a*), a further appeal lies to the House of Lords with the restrictions on making it which apply to criminal appeals.[42]

C. Perjury

A prosecution for perjury may proceed in the usual way by information, committal and trial, but if it was committed in a court [43] it may be initiated there by order.

---

[38] Administration of Justice Act 1960, s. 13.

[39] As in *Morris's* case, above.

[40] Administration of Justice Act 1960, s. 13 (2) (*bb*), added by the Courts Act 1971, Sched. 8, para. 40.

[41] See p. 352.

[42] See pp. 280–283.

[43] Perjury may also be committed at the hearings of tribunals or before anyone who examines witnesses on oath (Perjury Act 1911, s. 1), and other provisions, *e.g.* false written statements under the Criminal Justice Act 1967 (see p. 96), bring certain other false statements into the same procedure. Its scope is extended to evidence obtained in other parts of the United Kingdom by the Evidence (Proceedings in Other Jurisdictions) Act 1975, s. 2 and Sched. 1. The Criminal Law Revision Committee examined the law of perjury in 1964 (see Cmnd. 2465).

A judge or person presiding in a court of record, a justice of the peace or a petty sessional court which is of the opinion that a person has been guilty of perjury in proceedings before him or it, may order a prosecution against that person. As perjury is an indictable offence which is tried by the Crown Court, the judge may immediately perform the functions preliminary to preferring the indictment. Provided reasonable cause for the prosecution appears,[44] he may commit the accused to custody or grant him bail and order the proposed prosecutor to enter a recognisance to prosecute the accused.[45] He gives the prosecutor a certificate that an order to prosecute has been made. The prosecutor then applies to a judge of the High Court to prefer the bill of indictment and the procedure on a voluntary bill follows.[46] If the perjury is committed in proceedings before a High Court judge, the indictment, if prepared, could be preferred in the course of those proceedings.

In the indictment the substance of the offence and the proceedings at which it was committed are stated simply without setting out the details at length.[47]

Example

STATEMENT OF OFFENCE

Perjury, contrary to section 1 (1) of the Perjury Act 1911.

PARTICULARS OF OFFENCE

A.B., on the —— being a witness upon the trial of an action in the Barchester County Court in which C.D. was plaintiff and E.F. was defendant, knowingly swore falsely that he had paid £100 to the said C.D. on the 31st December 1976.

---

44 At a trial for perjury corroboration of the evidence against the accused is necessary: Perjury Act 1911, s. 13.

45 Perjury Act 1911, s. 9.

46 See Administration of Justice (Miscellaneous Provisions) Act 1933, s. 2 (2) (*b*), p. 144.

47 Perjury Act 1911, s. 12.

PART FIVE

LEGAL AID

CHAPTER 17

LEGAL AID ORDERS

THE provision of financial assistance for people to be legally represented before the courts plays a far-reaching role in the administration of justice and in the activities of practising lawyers. It has perhaps had a more noticeable effect on civil litigation where the provision of legal aid may make the difference between suing or defending and settling an action or dropping it altogether. In criminal cases the accused has no choice in whether or not to proceed, but legal aid makes a significant contribution to his chance of having a fair trial and hearing.

Although his costs may be ordered to be paid out of central funds,[1] a prosecutor can only be granted legal aid to resist an appeal to the Crown Court against the conviction or sentence of a magistrates' court.[2] The accused, however, is entitled to apply for it at every stage of the proceedings against him and on appeal. He may be required to pay back some or all of the money paid to his representatives on his behalf.[3]

A legally assisted person may effectively employ any lawyer who is prepared to act for him. Any solicitor or barrister may be assigned by the court to represent the accused under a legal aid order unless he is excluded from acting because he has been declared to be unfit by the Complaints Tribunal.[4] This is a tribunal set up by the Lord Chancellor which hears complaints against barristers and solicitors based on their conduct when acting for a legally assisted person or on their professional conduct generally[5]; it has power to exclude a barrister or solicitor from acting for legally assisted persons permanently or temporarily or to reduce or cancel his fee in the case in which he acted for the legally assisted person.[6]

The public cost of legal aid in magistrates' courts is borne by the legal aid fund—a central fund administered by the Law Society. For

---

[1] See Costs in Criminal Cases Act 1973, pp. 248 and 329.

[2] Legal Aid Act 1974, s. 28 (5).

[3] *Ibid.* s. 32. A contribution to the cost may be required as a condition precedent to the grant of legal aid: s. 29 (3).

[4] *Ibid.* s. 38 (1).

[5] *Ibid.* s. 38 (2).

[6] Legal Aid in Criminal Proceedings (Complaints Tribunal) Rules 1968, as amended by S.I. 1972 No. 1975.

other criminal proceedings—trial by the Crown Court, appeals to the Crown Court or the Court of Appeal, etc.—it is paid by the Home Secretary from central funds.[7] Legal aid for appeals to the High Court by way of case stated and for applications for prerogative orders is paid out of the legal aid fund.[8]

Orders for costs out of central funds operate quite separately from the legal aid scheme. An order for costs in the accused's favour may be made whether or not he was legally aided, but only subject to limitations[9]; in any event they are not ordered until the conclusion of the proceedings. If he is legally assisted and is awarded costs, the fund which is paying his legal fees recovers them.[10]

If an accused is not granted legal aid, he may be able to secure the services of a barrister at trial, for a small payment, on a dock brief.[11] He may, of course, decline to be represented at all.[12]

A. Availability

Legal aid may be ordered in the following proceedings:

(*a*) When a person is charged with an offence, or appears or is brought before a magistrates' court to be dealt with, legal aid may be ordered by the magistrates' court for the relevant proceedings and for the purposes of proceedings relating to the grant of bail, if the accused is in custody.[13]

(*b*) When a person convicted or sentenced by a magistrates' court wishes to appeal to the Crown Court, legal aid for the appeal may be ordered by the magistrates' court or by the Crown Court.[14]

(*c*) If notice of an appeal is given after legal aid has been granted under (*b*), legal aid for the person who is to resist the appeal

---

[7] Legal Aid Act 1974, s. 37 (1).

[8] *Ibid.* Sched. 1. This form of legal aid falls into the provisions for civil cases and is not dealt with in any detail here. Application is made to the Local Committee, run by the Law Society, and the applicant has to satisfy them that the appeal should be made on the merits of his case. This does not apply to legal aid in criminal proceedings.

[9] *e.g.* not if he were convicted; see p. 248.

[10] Legal Aid Act 1974, s. 36 (1). If the proceedings cost less than the contributions of the legally assisted person, the excess must be returned to him: *ibid.* s. 36 (2).

[11] See p. 153.

[12] See p. 152.

[13] Legal Aid Act 1974, s. 28 (2), as amended by the Bail Act 1976, s. 11 (2); this includes a person summoned or arrested or under a duty to appear or a liability to be brought to the magistrates' court in respect of an offence and a person brought to the court under a binding-over order or for extradition proceedings: *ibid.* s. 30 (11) and (12).

[14] *Ibid.* s. 28 (5).

(*i.e.* the prosecutor) may be ordered by the magistrates' court or by the Crown Court.[14]

(*d*) Where a juvenile is, or is to be brought, before a juvenile court for care proceedings or related applications, the juvenile court can make a legal aid order in his favour.[15]

(*e*) Where a juvenile wishes to appeal to the Crown Court from a juvenile court, the Crown Court or the juvenile court may make a legal aid order in his favour.[16]

(*f*) When a person is committed to, or appears or is brought before, the Crown Court for trial or sentence, legal aid may be ordered by the court which commits him or by the Crown Court.[17]

(*g*) When a person is convicted or sentenced by the Crown Court and wishes to appeal to the Court of Appeal, legal aid may be ordered by the Court of Appeal for the appeal and any incidental and preliminary proceedings.[18]

(*h*) If either party to an appeal in the Court of Appeal wishes to appeal to the House of Lords, the Court of Appeal may make a legal aid order for the appeal and incidental proceedings in favour of the person to whose conviction or sentence the appeal relates.[19]

(*i*) Where the Court of Appeal or House of Lords orders that a person be retried by the Crown Court, the Court of Appeal, House of Lords or the court by which he is to be retried may make a legal aid order in his favour for the retrial.[20]

The only occasions upon which the grant of legal aid is mandatory are—

(i) when the accused is committed for trial on a charge of murder [21];

(ii) when the prosecutor seeks to appeal to the House of Lords;

---

15 *Ibid.* s. 28 (2) and (3).

16 *Ibid.* s. 28 (6).

17 *Ibid.* s. 28 (7); this includes proceedings arising out of a probation or community service order or a conditional discharge or a suspended sentence or a suspended sentence supervision order (Powers of Criminal Courts Act 1973, ss. 6, 8, 16, 17, 23 or 27): Legal Aid Act 1974, s. 30 (12). Legal aid is also available for a review of a compensation order (see s. 37 of the 1973 Act) under s. 28 (4) of the Legal Aid Act 1974.

18 *Ibid.* s. 28 (8); *Practice Note* [1974] 1 W.L.R. 774; it is also available on appeal to the Courts-Martial Appeal Court: s. 28 (9).

19 *Ibid.* s. 28 (10).

20 *Ibid.* s. 28 (11).

21 As to the extent of such an order, see p. 403.

(iii) when a person, charged with an offence before a magistrates' court, is brought before the court on a remand in custody and is liable to be again remanded or committed in custody and wishes to be legally represented; and

(iv) when a person is committed in custody after conviction for reports.[22]

Otherwise the court may make an order when it appears to be desirable to do so in the interests of justice[23]; it may not do so unless it appears that the applicant's means are such that he is in need of assistance in meeting the costs of the proceedings.[24] No strict limits are prescribed for the financial resources available to the accused applying for legal aid, but for legal advice, below, limits of income and capital resources are imposed for determining whether the applicant is eligible for any legal assistance or what his contribution should be.[25] If any doubt arises as to the granting of legal aid, it must be resolved in favour of the applicant.[26]

In the few cases where the courts have considered legal aid orders they have been liberal to the accused in laying down guidelines for when an order should be made. In *R.* v. *Howes*[27] the Court of Criminal Appeal held that it must be rare for justice not to demand that an accused charged with a serious offence be granted legal aid for solicitor and counsel.[28] In *R.* v. *Green*[29] the Court of Appeal held that an accused should be offered legal aid in any case where it is likely that he may be sentenced to a substantial term of imprisonment (*in casu* 30 months), even if he pleads guilty.

B. Extent

1. Legal advice

Legal aid can only be claimed in connection with court proceedings. Before he is able to ask for legal aid, therefore, a person may find himself in need of the assistance and advice of a lawyer, for instance,

---

[22] Legal Aid Act 1974, s. 29 (1), as amended by the Bail Act 1976, s. 11 (4) and (5).

[23] *Ibid.* s. 29 (1). Special provision is made for juveniles by s. 29 (5) and the Bail Act 1976, s. 11 (7) (which adds a s. 29 (5A)).

[24] *Ibid.* s. 29 (2)).

[25] *Ibid.* s. 4; the actual figures are frequently revised by regulations.

[26] *Ibid.* s. 29 (6).

[27] [1964] 2 Q.B. 459.

[28] Howes was convicted of breaking and entering and maliciously placing explosives in a government building and was sentenced to three and seven years' imprisonment concurrent.

[29] [1968] 1 W.L.R. 673; see also *R.* v. *Derby Justices*, footnote 37 below, and *R.* v. *Guildhall Justices*, footnote 36 below.

immediately after being arrested and taken to a police station.[30] He may be able to make use of the legal advice and assistance provisions of Part I of the Legal Aid Act 1974—the " green form " scheme. Under this scheme he may obtain advice on the law to be applied to his circumstances and on any steps which he might appropriately take; he may also obtain assistance in making an application, *e.g.* for bail or for a legal aid order.[31] When he appears in a magistrates' court, the court may assign to him a solicitor who is present in court and who agrees to represent or otherwise assist him.[32] Although representation under this provision is more akin to legal aid, it is still within the limits of the advice and assistance scheme. The principal limitation is the maximum amount of cost which the solicitor (or counsel, if need be) is entitled to give: at present the maximum is £25.[33] Another important facility at this stage is the availability of information concerning the legal aid and advice which may be claimed. Police stations and prisons in particular should inform people in their charge and have informative literature available.[34]

2. Legal aid

Legal aid is available when the accused is to appear or appears before a court. It consists of representation by a solicitor and counsel and advice preparatory to the proceedings in court.[35]

In a magistrates' court the order must not include representation by counsel as well as a solicitor unless the offence is an indictable offence and the court is of the opinion that it would be desirable because the case is unusually grave or difficult.[36] It must not cover two counsel unless the accused is charged with murder; in this case, however, it must cover counsel as well as a solicitor.[37] Where orders are made in favour of co-defendants, it may be proper to make them only for joint representation.[38] In the Crown Court or in the

---

[30] See p. 65.
[31] Legal Aid Act 1974, ss. 1 and 2.
[32] *Ibid.* s. 2 (4). This provision is intended to enable " duty solicitors " to attend in magistrates' courts.
[33] *Ibid.* s. 3 (2). This may be raised by regulations.
[34] See the recommendations of the Widgery Committee on Legal Aid in Criminal Proceedings (1966), Cmnd. 2934, some of which are incorporated in the Legal Aid Act 1974.
[35] Legal Aid Act 1974, s. 30 (1).
[36] *Ibid.* s. 30 (2); a hybrid offence (see p. 295) which is being tried summarily counts as an indictable offence for this purpose: *R.* v. *Guildhall Justices, ex p. Marshall* [1976] 1 W.L.R. 335. Legal aid for bail does not include counsel: Bail Act, 1976, s. 11 (8).
[37] Legal Aid in Criminal Proceedings (General) (Amendment) Regulations 1976 (S.I. No. 790); *R.* v. *Derby Justices, ex p. Kooner* [1971] 1 Q.B. 147.
[38] Home Office Circular 93/1976 which explains the effect of the Divisional Court's rejection of an application for certiorari where joint representation was ordered contrary to the defendants' wishes.

Court of Appeal, however, the legal aid order may cover representation by counsel alone; at trial this is only to be ordered if the case is urgent and there is no time to instruct a solicitor.[39]

The Crown Court may order legal aid at any stage before the final conclusion of the trial; it may be ordered, therefore, to take effect retrospectively.[40]

Apart from representation in court and advice immediately connected with it, the legal advice and assistance which may be covered by a legal aid order includes the following:

(*a*) In proceedings before a magistrates' court—advice on whether there are reasonable grounds for appealing and assistance in giving notice of appeal or applying for the case to be stated.[41]

(*b*) Where legal aid is ordered for an appeal to the Crown Court—advice on whether there are reasonable grounds for having a case stated from the Crown Court and assistance in applying for it.[42]

(*c*) Where legal aid is ordered for trial or sentence by the Crown Court—advice on whether there are grounds for appealing to the Court of Appeal and assistance in making the necessary notices and applications.[43]

(*d*) Where a person wishes to appeal to the Court of Appeal—advice on whether there are grounds and assistance in making applications.[44]

C. Contributions

When applying for a legal aid order, the applicant must satisfy the court that he is in need of assistance in meeting the cost of the proceedings.[45] If he has some means he may be required to make a contribution towards the cost.[46] The court can require the applicant to furnish a written statement of his means [47] and, if it appears that he is likely to be required to make a contribution, it can refuse to make the order until he makes payment on account of the contribution.[48]

[39] Legal Aid Act 1974, s. 30 (3) and (4).
[40] *R.* v. *Tullet* [1976] 1 W.L.R. 241.
[41] *Ibid.* s. 30 (5).
[42] *Ibid.* s. 30 (6).
[43] *Ibid.* s. 30 (7).
[44] *Ibid.* s. 30 (8). The legal aid order may in this event be back-dated to cover advice already given by a solicitor or counsel not assigned by the court: s. 30 (9).
[45] *Ibid.* s. 29 (2).
[46] *Ibid.* s. 32.
[47] *Ibid.* s. 29 (4).
[48] *Ibid.* s. 29 (3).

When assessing the amount of the contribution, the court must consider his resources and commitments and may order him to pay the full amount of the legal aid.[49] The assessment of resources is computed in accordance with regulations which *inter alia* enable a spouse's and, if the applicant is an infant, parents' resources to be taken into account, prescribe the maximum income and capital resources to qualify for a wholly non-contributory order and regulate the assessment of his commitments.[50]

A contribution order may be made after the proceedings have been disposed of so that the total actual costs and the proportion to be contributed by the legally assisted person can be assessed.[51] The court may order a means inquiry by the Supplementary Benefits Commission.[52]

Payment of the contribution is made to the clerk of the magistrates' court in which the proceedings started, or other nominated magistrates' court, and it is recovered as a sum adjudged by a magistrates' court to be paid as a civil debt.[53]

D. The Application

An application for legal aid in the magistrates' court may be made in writing to the clerk or orally to the court, which may refer it to the clerk for determination. The clerk may make the order, refuse to make it unless he receives a payment towards the contribution or refer it to the court or to a justice for decision. The order cannot be made until the clerk or the court or justice has considered a statement of the applicant's means.[54]

In proceedings before the Crown Court application is made to the appropriate officer and may be made orally or in writing. Alternatively the application may be made after the conclusion of the proceedings to the magistrates' court. In the Court of Appeal applications may be made at any time to the Registrar or to a judge of the Court.[55] If the judge refuses the application, the applicant may have it re-heard by a two-judge court.[56]

---

49 *Ibid.* s. 32 (1).

50 *Ibid.* s. 34.

51 *Ibid.* ss. 32 (1) and 34.

52 *Ibid.* s. 33; it must be ordered if the legally aided person applies for it.

53 *Ibid.* s. 35. It cannot be enforced by imprisonment.

54 The detailed procedure for making an application is provided by the Legal Aid in Criminal Proceedings (General) Regulations 1968 as amended by the Legal Aid in Criminal Proceedings (General) (Amendment) Regulations 1970 (S.I. 1970 No. 1980)

55 Criminal Appeal Act 1968, s. 47.

56 See Administration of Justice Act 1970, s. 9, p. 263.

The court officer and the Registrar cannot completely refuse an application but must refer it to a justice or a judge. The Registrar has power to report to the Court of Appeal, or to a Court of Appeal or High Court judge, any case where he considers that legal aid ought to be granted although no application has been made.[57]

The Regulations prescribe forms to be used when an application is made in writing.

---

[57] Criminal Appeal Act 1968, s. 47 (2).

APPENDIX

THE following summary of the relevant proposals in the Criminal Law Bill is based on the Bill as amended only by the House of Lords, in committee (April 20, 1977). Clause numbers are only included as a general indication; page numbers are references to this book.

Conspiracy

As Part I consists of a restatement of the substantive law, only a few of its proposals fall within the scope of this book. Clause 1 (4) provides that, with the exception of murder, an agreed course of conduct to take place outside the territorial jurisdiction will not amount to conspiracy (as redefined) unless it would amount to an offence triable in England and Wales " if committed in accordance with thc intentions of the parties to the agreement " (pp. 9–10).

The maximum punishment for conspiracy will be no graver than the punishment for the offence involved in the agreement of the conspirators, with a lower limit of one year's imprisonment; if such offence is indictable and has no fixed maximum, the punishment will be imprisonment for life; the maximum for offences concerning an industrial dispute will be three months (pp. 224–226; ss. 3 and 9 of the Conspiracy and Protection of Property Act 1875 will be repealed: p. 293). The consent of the D.P.P. will be necessary for the prosecution of conspiracies involving summary offences (p. 15).

The law as stated in *D.P.P.* v. *Shannon* (pp. 138 and 210: acquittal of one conspirator, valid conviction of the other) is spelt out in clause 5 (7) and (8).

Entry on property

Part II again relates predominantly to the substantive law. *Inter alia*, it will repeal and replace the Forcible Entry Acts (p. 42) and it will include various provisions for summary arrest (p. 62 *et seq.*). The magistrates' courts will expressly be given jurisdiction regardless of any dispute as to title to property (p. 291).

Classification of offences

Part III contains the provisions of most importance to criminal procedure; it is based, by and large, on the recommendations of the

James' Committee's *Report on the Distribution of Criminal Business between the Crown Court and Magistrates' Courts* (Cmnd. 6323).

The present five-fold classification of offences will be replaced by a three-fold division: offences triable only on indictment, offences triable only summarily, and "offences triable either way"—intermediate offences.

The only offence, previously triable summarily with consent, which will become triable only on indictment is libel by newspaper proprietors and editors. A number of offences will become triable only summarily; these are listed in Schedule 1 and include conduct conducive to a breach of the peace, criminal diversion of mail (*cf.* p. 36), solicitation by men, assault on the police (at present triable on indictment only at the election of the prosecution, a position described by the James' Committee as "indefensible": Cmnd. 6323, para. 156), and drinking driving offences. Many of these carry a sentence in excess of three months' imprisonment, so the Bill will effectively take away the accused's right to elect trial by jury (p. 292). Schedule 3 will make certain offences (criminal damage and accessory offences), which would otherwise be triable either way, triable only summarily if the value involved is less than £200. The court will consider the value before proceeding to trial or committal.

The class of offences triable either way will be enlarged to include a number of (at present) purely indictable offences such as burglary, unlawful sexual intercourse, causing death by dangerous driving and bigamy (Schedule 2). Such offences will in a general way be treated as indictable rather than summary.

The procedure for determining which way a charge should be tried will, in brief, be as follows:

(a) The court will consider whether the case is more suitable for summary or jury trial, taking into account any representations of the prosecutor or accused, the nature of the case, its particulars circumstances, the adequacy of the magistrates' sentencing powers, etc.

(b) If the court finds that summary trial is more suitable it will have to ask the accused if he consents to summary trial, explaining the power to commit him for sentence. If he does not consent, it will continue as committal proceedings.

(c) If the court considers that the charge should be tried on indictment, it will inform the accused and invite him to make representations for summary trial, if he has not already done so.

(d) After the court has considered the matter and has begun the proceedings (whether for trial or committal), it will have power to change the form of proceedings:

(i) to committal proceedings, at any time before the conclusion of the prosecution evidence, or

(ii) to summary trial, at any time provided the accused consents.

Provision will also be made for proceeding in the accused's absence, for adjournment and for a single justice to proceed unless the case becomes a summary trial (pp. 93–96 and 306–308). The court will have power to proceed to summary trial of an intermediate offence in the absence of a *represented* accused who signifies his consent. If the case appears more suitable for summary trial but the accused has not consented, the court will have power, in his absence, to proceed as examining justices but to adjourn without remanding him.

Sentencing powers

The magistrates' courts' sentencing powers will be strictly limited to six months' imprisonment (unless the relevant provision is expressly excluded by statute) and a fine of £1,000, but their power under section 108 of the Magistrates' Courts Act 1952 (p. 320) and the power to order imprisonment for non-payment of fines will not be affected. Clauses 28–30 prescribe their powers in detail, and a general increase will take effect in fines for offences under pre-1949 enactments.

On a conviction on indictment, there will be no limit on the fine in any case.

Juveniles

A magistrates' court before which a juvenile is brought jointly with " an older accused " will have power to remit the juvenile for trial by a juvenile court if his co-accused pleads guilty (and he does not) or if the juvenile is to be tried summarily on his own (pp. 364–370). The remission itself will not be subject to appeal. Clause 35 makes proposals for the enforcement of fines against juveniles, including the imposition of an attendance centre order. Further, the maximum sum which may be imposed as a fine on a juvenile or taken from a parent or guardian as surety will be increased to £200.

Appeal

The gap in the law pinpointed in *D.P.P.* v. *Shannon* (p. 265)—that the Court of Appeal usually has no jurisdiction to hear an appeal after a plea of guilty—will be filled by changing the words " verdict of the jury " in section 2 (1) of the **Criminal Appeal Act 1968** to " conviction."

Coroners

Coroners will be deprived of their power to charge a person on an inquisition (pp. 37–43). An inquest will have to be adjourned if the coroner is informed that a charge is pending against a person in connection with the death in question.

Miscellaneous

A magistrates' court will be able to impose a compensation order of up to £1,000 (p. 330). The Home Secretary will be given power by order to vary the minimum and maximum periods of probation and conditional discharge orders (pp. 236–241) and to vary certain sums (including the £1,000 limit mentioned above and the maximum fine which a magistrates' court may impose on conviction of an intermediate offence) without the need for an Act of Parliament.

The Crown Court, on a committal for sentence, will have power to deal with all offences of which the accused has been convicted, including summary offences not punishable by imprisonment (see p. 332 *et seq.*).

The James' Committee

By and large, this Bill follows the general scheme recommended by the James' Committee, with a number of variations in detail. An important recommendation which was wholly omitted (in the original Bill, at least) was the introduction of a form of advance disclosure of the prosecution case on a charge of an offence for which the accused may refuse his consent to summary trial. The Committee recommended that the accused should have the right on request to receive copies of the statements of prosecution witnesses, if available, subject to a prosecution application to a magistrate to refuse disclosure. Failing copy statements, the accused should be entitled to receive a summary of the facts on which the prosecution would seek to rely. Apart from the obvious benefit to the accused in knowing what case he has to meet, this provision might have helped to reduce the number of cases going for trial by jury.

The Committee also noticed with concern the large number of cases committed for trial without consideration of the evidence neither by the court nor even by the parties, and the high rate of directed acquittals in the Crown Court.

INDEX

Absolute discharge, *see* Discharge
Accessory offences, 52, 121, 122, 137, 214
 juveniles, 364–365
Accomplice evidence, 30–31, 197, 201
Accused,
 character, *see* Character.
 consent, *see* Indictable offences (summary trial).
 duty to inform, 105, 114–115, 146, 179, 376
 election of trial on indictment, 223, 292–295, 301
 incapacity, *see* Fitness to plead.
 silence, *see* Silence.
 statements, 20–25, 99, 180, 188, 208
 unrepresented, 113, 153, 158, 195, 199, 268, 302, 308, 367, 372–373
  sentence, 225, 321
 witness, as, 30, 32, 99, 180, 189–195, 201, 308, 312
Additional evidence,
 notice of, 104, 114, 180
Adjournment,
 committal proceedings, 95–96
 coroner's inquests, 39
 magistrates' courts, 86, 307
 remand on, *see* Remand
 sentence, before, 219–220, 223, 242, 307, 318, 402
Administrative control, *see* Attorney-General, D.P.P.
Admiralty jurisdiction, 10–11
Admissibility of evidence,
 arguments as to, 134, 203
Admissions,
 formal, 112, 308
Affirmation, 181
Agent provocateur, 24
Aircraft,
 offences against, 11, 12, 61, 223
 offences committed on, 11
Alibi evidence, 93, 99, 105, 112–114, 124, 178, 180
Aliens, *see* Deportation, Diplomatic immunity, Extradition, Jurisdiction.
Alternative verdicts, 132, 156–160, 162, 210, 213–214,
 appeal, 271–272, 276, 278
 summary trial, 304–305
Amendment, *see* Indictments, Information.
Antecedents; *see* Character, Previous convictions.
Appeals, 1, 4, 260–288, 340–357, 387–388
 abandonment, 270–271
 ancillary applications, 263–265
 bail; *see* Bail.
 committal for sentence, 331, 353–355
 contempt, 394
 conviction, against, 262–274, 344
 costs; *see* Costs.
 Crown Court; *see* Crown Court.
 defence of, 265, 269
 deportation, 274–275, 276, 346, 354
 discharge, 241, 275, 344, 354–355
 disqualification from driving, 345, 354
 evidence for, 264
 fact, 262–263
 fresh evidence, 269–270
 grounds of appeal, 148, 149, 263, 266–268, 283–285
 habeas corpus proceedings, 45
 Home Secretary, 168, 265, 270, 273
 insanity; *see* Insanity.
 law, 262, 280–282, 283, 349–351
 leave to; *see* Leave to appeal.
 legal aid, 401, 405
 miscarriage of justice, proviso, 140, 266, 279
 plea of guilty, after, 155, 265, 268, 344
 prosecution, 4, 281–282, 349–353
 remission of case, 282, 344, 348
 retrial, 269, 272–273, 274
 sentence, 274–277, 283, 344–346, 353–355
  severity, 271, 276, 348
 time spent in custody; *see* Custody.
 unsafe and unsatisfactory verdict; *see* Verdict.
Arraignment, 147, 148, 154, 169, 170, 171, 279
 corporation, 391
 see also Pleas.
Arrest, 57–60, 64–67
 arrestable offence, 62
 bail on, 58, 68–69
 common law powers, 62
 disabled person, 64
 private individual, by, 62–63, 64
 summary, 52, 62–63, 306
  bailed person, 81, 152
  juveniles, 364, 372, 380
 wrongful,
  liability for, 41, 64–66; *see also* False imprisonment.
 see also Warrants.

Arrest of judgment, 164, 169, 218
Arrest without warrant; *see* Arrest (summary).
Armed forces, 15; *see also* Courts-Martial.
Attempts, 120, 121, 131, 214, 224, 232, 247
Attendance centres, 238, 368, 378, 388–389
Attorney-General, 4, 5, 15, 18, 95
  reference to the Court of Appeal, 5, 279–280
  see also Nolle prosequi.
Autrefois, 93, 159–168, 205, 207, 214, 219, 221, 241, 309, 318, 350, 384
autrefois acquit, 163–164
autrefois convict, 164–165
  form of plea, 165–166

Bail, 68–82, 217, 224, 301
  appeal, pending, 71, 72–73, 263–264, 347
  application to the High Court, 44, 68, 70, 72, 77, 78–80, 373
  arrest, 81–82, 151
  bail-bonding, 76
  breach, 74, 75, 80–82, 151
  committal for sentence, 238, 332–333, 335, 338
  committal on, 104, 333
  conditions, 77, 78–80
  continuous, 70
  coroner's, 39, 73
  defendant's security, 76, 82
  duration, 70
  incidents, 75–77
  juveniles, 77, 372
  notice of application, 72
  police, 68–69
  reasons for refusal, 73, 74–75, 77–78
  remand for reports, 73, 74, 77, 220, 223
  sureties, 70, 75–76, 81, 82, 104, 264
  warrant backed for, 58, 65
Bank accounts, inspection, 26
Bar Council,
  Rules of November 6, 1950,
    r. 1, 187
    r. 2, 184
    r. 3, 185, 186
    rr. 4 and 7, 187
Barristers; *see* Defence Counsel, Legal representatives. Prosecuting counsel.
Bill of indictment; *see* Indictment, Preferring an Indictment.
Binding-over,
  appeal, 346
  to come up for judgment, 222, 242, 243, 393
Binding-over—*cont.*
  to keep the peace, 241, 243–244, 327–328, 393
Borstal training, 225, 231–232, 338, 388
  appeal, 354, 355
  combined sentence, 228, 230, 255
  committal for, 331, 335–336
  release of trainees, 259
  transfers, 256, 379
Burden of proof, 1, 170, 178, 207, 384
  judge's direction, 196–197. 266
Burglary, 120, 123, 133, 161, 213, 297

Care,
  committal to, 366, 373
Care orders, 378–380, 386, 387
Care proceedings, 363, 368, 382–387
  legal aid, 401
  offence condition, 361, 383–384
  see also Juveniles.
Case stated, 349–352
  application for, 350
  drafting, 355–357
  parties, 349, 351
  remission, 351, 352
  see also Divisional Court.
Caution, 20–23
Central funds, *see* Costs
Certiorari, 40, 45–46, 316, 342–343, 345
Challenge of jurors, 174–176
Change of plea; *see* Pleas.
Channel Islands, 59
Character,
  accused's, 190–192, 193–194, 198, 203, 317
  co-accused's, 200–201
  prosecution, 194–195
  witnesses', 185–187
  see also Cross-examination.
Character evidence, 100, 107, 193–194
Charge, 101, 103–104, 108, 142
  arrest, on, 66
  new charges at trial, 147, 294
  see also Committal, Indictment, Information.
Children,
  criminal responsibility, 362–363
  presumption of innocence, 362
  witnesses, as, 29–30, 95, 97, 109, 111, 153, 154, 181, 296
  see also Juveniles.
Circuit judges, 86
  deputy, 87
Circuits of the Crown Court, 89
  see also Juveniles.
Circuit judges, 86
  deputy, 87
Circuits of the Crown Court, 89
Civil jurisdiction of magistrates, 300

Classifications of offences, 2–3 ,89–91, 102–103, 152, 292–299
see also Hybrid offences, Indictable offences, Summary offences.
Co-accused,
comment on accused's silence, 190
examination of, 200–201
see also Accused, Character, Joint trials. Separate trials.
Committal for sentence, 296, 297, 330–339
appeal, 331, 341, 345, 348, 353–355
borstal, 331, 334–335
community service order, 236, 352
corporations, 391
hospital order, 309, 326
legal aid 401
see also Conditional discharge, Probation orders, Suspended sentence
Committal for trial,
charge on; *see* Charge.
new evidence; *see* Additional evidence.
void, 101, 107, 143
Committal proceedings, 85–86, 93–115, 291, 364–365
change to summary trial, 111, 296, 298, 299, 302, 308
corporations, 390–391
dismissal, 93, 99, 163; *see also* Submission of no case
evidence at, 35, 98–100
hybrid offences, 294
juveniles, 364–365
oral, 93, 97–100
public hearing, 94, 365
reporting of, 94–95, 105
section 1, 94, 100–101
speeches, 99–100
summary offences, 293–295; *see also* Accused (election).
time and place of trial, 101–103
written statements; *see* Written statements of evidence.
see also Presence of the accused.
Community homes, 366, 378–379
Community service orders, 235–236, 239, 251, 253, 255, 367
Compensation,
criminal injuries, 250
rewards, 252, 255
wrongful process, 43
Compensation orders, 250–252, 273, 282, 329–330, 333, 367, 376, 387, 391
civil proceedings and, 251
combined sentence, 235, 240, 251, 253
offences taken into consideration, 220, 251, 275
Complaint procedure, 300
Concurrent sentences, 229–231; *see also* Consecutive sentences, Sentence (combined).
Conditional discharge, 238, 240–241, 249, 255, 256, 327, 367, 369, 376
appeal, 275, 344, 354–355
committal for sentence, 331, 338
see also Discharge.
Conduct,
evidence of, *see* Character, Similar fact evidence.
Confessions, 20–23
cross-examination on, 188
editing of, 180
voluntariness of, 208
Consecutive sentences, 226, 229–231, 320, 354, 377; *see also* Sentence (combined).
Conspiracy, 131, 138–139, 162, 210, 224, 298
Contempt of court, 45, 80, 106, 108 392
procedure, 392–394
Continental shelf, 11–12
Coroner, 37–40
bail by, 39, 73
inquest, 37–40
inquisition, 39, 117, 154
Corporations, 390–391
formal admissions by, 112
Corroboration, 30, 111, 201
judge's direction, 197
Costs, 235, 240, 248–250, 329, 344, 345, 348, 367, 376, 391
appeal on, 249, 274, 282, 285, 345, 352
central funds, out of, 248–249, 282, 329, 348, 400
committal proceedings, 100, 249, 329, 332
defence, 248, 249, 274, 280, 329
prosecution, 18, 105, 248, 249, 274, 283
review of, 249, 250
witnesses', 248, 274
Court of Appeal,
Civil Division, 260
Criminal Division, 260–261, 263
Attorney-General's reference, 5, 279–280
bail by, 72–73
committal for sentence, 345, 353–355
contempt, 392
House of Lords; *see* House of Lords.
legal aid, 401, 404, 405
powers, 267, 268–274, 278, 353–355
preferring an indictment, 272
sentence; *see* Appeals (se,ntence).
single judge 263, 268–269, 272, 274

Court of Appeal—*cont.*
two-judge court, 263
see also Appeals.
Courts-martial, 13, 91–92
Courts-Martial Appeal Court, 92, 261
Criminal bankruptcy orders, 235, 240, 251, 253–254
appeal, 275–276
offence taken into consideration, 220, 221
Criminal Injuries Compensation Board, 250
Cross-examination, 114, 183–188
accused, 191–195
co-accused, 200–201
confession in, 188
credit, as to, 185–187
hostile witness, 182–183, 203, 207
opportunity to cross-examine, 107–109, 204
prior inconsistent statements, 183, 187–188, 197
see also Character, Leading questions.
Crown Court, 86–91, 332–339
allocation of offences, 89–91, 333, 340
appeal to, 300, 340–343, 344–348, 387–388, 400
bail by, 71–72, 347
case stated, 351–352
legal aid application, 404, 405–406
majority decision, 88
sentencing powers; *see* Committal for sentence, Sentence.
warrant of arrest, 69, 81, 151
see also Trial on indictment.
Custody, 67–68
appeal, pending, 273–274, 281, 347
committal in, 104, 152, 159
duration, 2, 67; *see also* Bail, Habeas corpus.
juveniles, 372–374, 382, 384
remand in; *see* Remand.
taking time into account, 257, 273–274
unlawful *see* False imprisonment.

Day training centres, 237
Death penalty, 89, 223, 277, 278
Defence counsel, 180–181, 195–196, 216, 217–218, 285
Demurrer, 159, 164
Deportation,
recommendation for, 244–245, 328, 367
appeal, 274–275, 276, 346, 354
combined sentence, 245, 256
Depositions, 99, 105, 107–110, 180, 183, 273, 297
authentication of, 107, 108, 109
Depositions—*cont.*
child's, 109
evidence taken on examination, 270
sick people, 108, 109
taken abroad, 110
Detention; *see* Arrest, Custody.
Detention centres, 368, 377–378, 389
Detention during H.M. pleasure, 230, 366
Detoxification centres, 66
Diplomatic immunity, 14, 31
Director of Public Prosecutions, 4, 18–20, 35, 61, 105, 165, 265, 307
consent of, 15–16
Official Petitioner, 253
Disability; *see* Arrest (disabled person), Fitness to plead, Insanity.
Discharge, 240–241, 327
absolute, 240
combined sentence, 240, 243, 253, 255
juvenile, 367, 369, 376
see also Conditional discharge.
Disqualification from driving, 235, 237, 240, 245–248, 328, 333–334
appeal, 345, 354
criminal use of vehicle, 247–248, 328
juvenile, 367, 376
life, for, 247
presence of accused, 60, 302, 311
road traffic offences, 245–247
special reasons, 246, 345
totting-up, 222, 246
Divisional Court,
Family Division, 300
Queen's Bench Division, 43–47, 342–343
appeals, 349–352
appeal to the House of Lords, 352–353
contempt, 392–394
costs, 249
prerogative orders, 43–47, 342–343
see also Case stated.
Dock, 150; *see also* Unsworn statement.
Dock brief, 153
Documentary evidence, 97, 105, 106–112
see also Depositions. Written statements.
Domestic tribunals, 165
Double jeopardy; *see Autrefois*.
Driving offences, 130–131, 132, 295, 309, 356
compensation orders and, 250
drinking offences, 24–25, 63, 123, 129
driving while disqualified, 136, 143–144

Driving offences—*cont.*
  notice of intended prosecution, 14, 306, 342
  see also Disqualification, Endorsement.
Drugs offences, *see* Forfeiture.
Drunken offences, 66, 291
Duplicity, 54, 128–131, 138–139, 148; *see also* Joinder of offences.

Endorsement of driving licences, 247, 376
Endorsement of warrants, 58–59, 69, 78
Enforcement; *see* Fines (enforcement).
Entry of premises, 27–29, 66
Estoppel; *see* Issue estoppel, *Res judicata.*
Evidence,
  admissibility; *see* Admissibility.
  foreign proceedings, 34
  fresh; *see* Appeal (fresh evidence).
  identity, 34–35, 111, 197
  improperly obtained, 23–25
  judicial discretion to exclude, 20, 23–25. 36, 114, 169, 194
Examination of witnesses, 98–100
  cross-examination; *see* Cross-examination.
  examination-in-chief, 182–183, 191
  joint trials, 200–201
  re-examination, 188
  see also Rebuttal.
Examining justices; *see* Committal proceedings.
Exhibits, 97, 105, 204, 264, 265, 283
Exhumation, 29
Ex parte proceedings, 43–47, 343
Extended sentence, 223, 226–227, 230, 237, 241, 257, 258
  combined sentence, 227, 255
Extradition proceedings, 60–62, 115–116
  bail, 73

False imprisonment, 1, 41, 44, 61, 66, 208
Fines, 232–233, 277, 322–326, 367, 369, 370, 376, 391
  combined sentence, 233, 255
  enforcement of, 323–326
  imprisonment for non-payment, 302, 321, 324, 326, 389
Fingerprints, 35–36, 217
First offenders, 225, 320, 367
Fitness to plead, 170–171, 278, 309; *see also* Hospital orders, Insanity.
Force,
  use of, 66
Forfeitures, 235, 254–255, 330, 367, 376
  drugs offences, 255
  see also Recognisances (forfeiture).
Formal admissions; *see* Admissions.
Fresh evidence; *see* Appeal (fresh evidence).
Fugitive offenders; *see* Extradition.
Functus officio, 209, 222, 263, 271, 315–316

Grounds of appeal; *see* Appeal.
Guardianship order, 234, 387

Habeas corpus, 1, 41, 44–45, 78, 115, 116, 353
  ad respondendum, 151
Handling, 126, 129, 136, 141, 142, 147, 213, 250
  see also Restitution.
Handwriting,36
High Court, 91, 342–343
  evidence taken by, 34
  Judge,
    bail application; *see* Bail.
    consent to preferring indictment; *see* Preferring an indictment.
    deputy, 87
    trial by, 89–91, 102–103
    warrant of arrest, 98, 106
  supervisory jurisdiction, 43–47; *see also* Certiorari, Habeas corpus, Mandamus, Prohibition.
Hijacking; *see* Aircraft.
Home Secretary,
  appeal referred by; *see* Appeal.
Hospital orders, 171, 230, 234–235, 309, 326, 336–337
  appeal, 271, 272, 274, 277–278, 326, 345
  combined sentence, 255
  juveniles, 367, 376, 387
  restricted release, 331, 336–337
  vagrant, 335
  see also Insanity.
Hostile witnesses, 182–183, 203
House of Lords, 261, 280–283, 343, 352
  Attorney-General's reference, 280
  legal aid, 401
  petition to 281
Hybrid offences, 293, 295–297, 302, 354

Identification parade, 35
Identity,
  evidence of, 34–35, 111, 197, 206–207
Immigration appeals 245; *see also* Deportation.
Immunities, 14–15, 31, 159; *see also* Diplomatic immunity.
Imprisonment, 224–231
  combined sentence, 255–256
  consecutive terms; *see* Consecutive sentences.

Imprisonment—*cont.*
contempt, 393
fines, 233, 389
juvenile adults, 224, 231; *see also* Borstal, Juvenile adults.
juveniles, 224, 367, 373
magistrates' court's powers, 319–322
presence of accused, 60, 221, 302, 311, 318, 325; *see also* Accused (unrepresented).
transfer to hospital, 256
see also First offenders, Life imprisonment, Release on licence, Sentence.
In camera proceedings, 94, 154; *see also* Public hearing.
Indictable offences, 297–299
hybrid offences; *see* Hybrid offences.
summary trial, 296, 297–298, 320, 323, 330, 332–334, 391
see also Accused (consent), Classifications of offences.
Indictment, 3, 117–149, 395
amending, 143, 146–148, 218
commencement, 118
contempt of court, 393
corporations, 391
counts, 117, 154, 158, 196, 202, 210, 211, 214, 221
duplicity; *see* Duplicity.
essential facts alleged in, 122–125
exceptions, 127–128
intent, 125–127
joinder of offences; *see* Duplicity, Joinder of offences.
joining defendants, 140; *see also* Joint trials.
ownership, 123, 124, 147
particulars of offence, 121–128
place, 122, 124
preferring; *see* Preferring an indictment.
quashing, 148–149, 218
severing, 133, 143; *see also* Separate trials.
statement of offence, 118–121
staying; *see* Staying proceedings.
surplusage in, 118, 178
trial on; *see* Trial on indictment.
witnesses on back of, 114–115, 178–179
see also Charge, Duplicity, Joint trials, Trial on indictment.
Information, 54–57, 303–306
amendment, 55, 305
defective, 304–305
duplicity, 304
election of trial by jury on; *see* Accused (election).
laying, 54–55, 57, 290
trial of; *see* Summary trial.
Inquest, Inquisition; *see* Coroner.
Insanity, 207, 211–212, 234–235, 337
appeal, 271, 272, 277–278
juvenile, 367
see also Fitness to plead, Hospital orders.
Interception of mail, 23, 36–37
Interpreters, 151
Interrogation, 20–23; *see* Confessions, Judges' Rules, Police, Silence.
Ireland, Republic of, 10, 12, 13, 59
backing of warrants, 59
depotation, 245
Extradition Act 1963, 59
warrant, 59, 61, 115
Isle of Man,
backing of warrants, 59
summons, 56
Issue estoppel, 167–168

Joinder of offences, 131–137
summary trial, 304
see also Duplicity.
Joint trials, 51–52, 137–141, 154, 199–202, 267, 284, 304
accomplice evidence, 30, 201
committal proceedings, 95
corporation, 391
juvenile, 364, 368–369
legal aid, 403–404
presence of accused, 150
sentence, 222
see also Separate trials.
Judge,
counsel's access to, 156–157
discretion to exclude evidence; *see* Evidence.
discretion to stay proceedings; *see* Staying proceedings.
duty to unrepresented accused, 199
examination of witnesses by, 2, 30, 188–189, 267
immunity and privilege, 33, 42
improper behaviour of, 189, 268
judgment; *see* Summing-up, Sentence.
rulings on law by, 155, 203, 207
sentence; *see* Sentence.
consultation on, 232, 257, 366
summing-up; *see* Summing-up.
Judge and jury, 134, 198–199, 202, 203, 205, 206–208, 217
Judge-advocate, 92
Judges' Rules, 20–22; *see also* Confessions, Police.
Jurisdiction, 9–16, 51–53, 86–91, 152, 290–299, 300, 310, 371
excess of; *see* Case stated, Magistrates (liability).

Jurisdiction—*cont.*
plea to the, 158–159
territorial, 9–13, 52, 61–62, 159
Jury, 3, 171–176, 202, 267
absence from court, 134, 203–204, 207–208
addressing; *see* Speeches.
coroner's, 38
direction to; *see* Summing-up.
disagreement, 211, 214–215
discharge of, 204, 205–206, 207, 209
fitness to plead, 169–171
immunity and privilege, 33, 42
oath, 176
retirement, 204, 208
selection, 172–174, 215
view of the *locus in quo*, 204
see also Judge and Jury.
Justices; *see* Magistrates.
Justices' clerks' powers and duties, 4, 48, 53, 54, 105, 106, 117, 290, 307, 310, 313, 350, 355, 405
Juvenile adults, 225, 258, 321–322, 335, 362, 377, 388–389; *see also* Borstal.
Juvenile courts, 370–371
procedure before, 371–382
remission to, 371, 376
see also Care proceedings.
Juvenile offenders, 292, 361–389
appeal, 387–388
bail, 77, 372
committal, 364–365
legal aid, 401
parent or guardian, 220, 367, 368, 374, 375, 376, 377, 378, 382, 385–387
remand and process, 372–374
responsibility, 362–364
treatment, 225, 321, 366–368, 369–370, 376–382, 386–387
trial by magistrates' court, 368–370
see also Children.

Land,
magistrates' jurisdiction, 291–292
Leading questions, 107, 182, 184, 188
Leave to appeal, 262–263, 268, 276, 278–279, 355
House of Lords, 280–282, 352
Legal advice and assistance, 402–403
Legal aid, 43, 153, 225, 321, 399–406
bail applications, 70–71, 79, 400
contributions, 404–405
Legal representatives, 1, 152–153, 156–157, 199–200, 293, 302, 399–406
Complaints Tribunal, 399
coroner's inquests, 37
corporations, 390
deferred sentence, 242
Legal representatives—*cont.*
duties, 112, 174, 187, 194, 216, 285, 350
immunity, 42
jury service, 172–173
juveniles, 367, 374, 385
pleas made by, 155, 309
see also Defence counsel, Dock brief, Prosecuting counsel, Solicitors.
Licensing, 300
Life imprisonment, 225–226, 257
Limitation periods; *see* Time limits.
Local authorities,
juveniles in care; *see* Care.
Locus in quo; *see* View.
London, City of, 49, 88

Magistrates, 4, 48–54, 85–86, 289
Crown Court, 88
disqualification of, 50, 71, 289, 341
examining, 85–86; *see also* Committal proceedings.
excess of jurisdiction, 43, 46, 53, 342–343
liability of, 42, 43, 53, 78
privilege of, 33
stipendiary, 49–50, 289, 315, 370
metropolitan, 50, 115
Magistrates' courts, 289–290
adjournment, 86, 307; *see also* Adjournments.
bail, 69–71, 152
binding-over; *see* Binding over.
bringing accused before, 2, 64–65, 69, 94, 291, 372
case stated; *see* Case stated.
civil jurisdiction, 300
contempt procedure, 393
decision, 314–316
examination of witnesses, 313
form of trial, 264, 265; *see also* Accused (election), Hybrid offences, Indictable offences (summary trial).
jurisdiction, 16, 290–299
juvenile courts, 370–371
legal aid, 400, 404
majority decision, 85–86
probationers, 220, 221
retirement, 290
sentence, 221, 224, 319–330; *see also* Sentence.
see also Justices' clerks.
Majority verdict, 212–213, 214
Malicious prosecution, 41, 78
Mandamus, 46. 53, 342, 349, 351
Matrimonial proceedings, 300
Means,
compensation order, 251
fines, 323
inquiry, 324

Mental illness, 234–235
  jury service, 173
  witnesses, 29–30
  see also Fitness to plead, Hospital orders, Insanity.
Misdirection; *see* Summing-up.
Mitigation, 207, 215, 217–218, 310, 317–318
Murder, 119, 126, 135, 157, 159, 162, 205, 217
  alternative verdicts, 213, 214
  juveniles, 363, 371
  legal aid, 401
  term of imprisonment, 226
Mute,
  standing, 169–170, 308

Name and address,
  duty to provide, 21
Nolle prosequi, 18–19, 40, 164
Northern Ireland,
  backing of warrants, 59
  evidence, 110
Notice of additional evidence; *see* Additional evidence.
Notice of alibi evidence; *see* Alibi.
Notice of intended prosecution, 14, 306, 342

Oath, 107–110, 181
  child's evidence on, 29–30
  interpreter's evidence, 151
  juror's, 176
  laying informations, 54, 57
Obscenity, 125, 154
Offence condition; *see* Care proceedings.
Offering no evidence, 4, 19, 158
Official secrets, 89, 191
Official Solicitor, 72, 79
Open court, 49, 86, 145; *see also* Public hearing.

Pardon, 168–169, 218, 256
Parole Board, 257–258; *see also* Release of licence.
Particulars of offence; *see* Indictment.
Perjury, 34, 96, 166, 208, 394–395
Persistent offenders; *see* Extended sentence.
Petty sessions; *see* Magistrates' courts, Summary trial.
Photographic evidence,
  identification from, 35
Piracy, 12, 223; *see also* Aircraft.
Plea bargaining, 156–157
Plea in mitigation; *see* Mitigation.
Plea of guilty, 155–158, 214
  acceptance, 157, 164
  ambiguous, 158

Plea of guilty—*cont.*
  appeal after, 155, 169, 265–266, 268, 344
  postal, 310–311, 391
  procedure, 215, 316
Pleas, 155–169, 207, 308–311, 375
  ambiguous, 158, 308
  autrefois; *see* Autrefois.
  change of, 156, 157, 164, 169, 215, 310, 316, 344
  corporation, 391
  demurrer, 159
  jurisdiction, to the, 158–159
  not guilty, 158
  sentence not affected by, 223
  standing mute; *see* Mute.
Police, 4, 17, 96
  arrest, 62–63, 64–67, 78, 81; *see also* Arrest, Warrant.
  bail, 65, 68–69
  complaints, 165
  confessions to; *see* Confessions, Judges' Rules.
  duty to answer, 21
  forfeited property, 254, 330
  interrogation, 20–23; *see also* Confessions, Judges' Rules.
  juveniles and, 372–374
  liability of, 41, 43
  prosecution by, 18
  undertakings not to prosecute, 19
Police station, 20–21, 64–66, 67, 372, 403
  bail at, 65
Political offences; *see* Extradition, Official secrets, Terrorist offences, Treason.
Postal plea; *see* Plea of guilty.
Preferring an indictment, 144–146, 148, 395
  consent of High Court judge, 62, 144–145, 149, 163
  Court of Appeal, 272
Prerogative orders, 43–47, 53, 92, 342–343; *see also* Certiorari, Habeas corpus, Mandamus, Prohibition.
Presence of the accused, 96. 107, 109, 150–152, 301–303, 311, 318, 325
  appeal, 264, 270, 277
  Attorney-General's reference, 279–280
  bail application, 72, 79
  committal proceedings, 96
  corporation, 391
  election of jury trial, 293
  juvenile, 385
  juvenile's parent or guardian, 385–386
  sentence, 60, 221, 302, 311, 318, 325

Press reports, 94–95, 105, 153, 154
  contempt of court, 392
  juveniles, 365, 366, 369, 371
Preventive detention, 227
Previous convictions, 143, 187, 192, 216–217, 267, 295, 297, 332, 336
  findings of guilt, 217
  proof of, 36, 217
  spent convictions, 187
Prison; *see* Imprisonment.
Privilege, 32–34
  communications between spouses, 33
  lawyer and client, 33
  public interest, 33
  self-incrimination, 32, 180, 191, 201
Probation hostels, 237, 327, 388
Probation officers, 228, 235, 381; *see also* Reports.
Probation orders, 236–240, 249, 327
  appeal, 275, 277, 344, 354–355
  breach of, 73, 74, 207, 338
  combined sentence, 228, 233, 243, 251, 253, 256
  conditions, 237, 238
  juveniles; *see* Supervision.
  medical treatment, 219, 237–238
  psychiatric, 234, 238, 326
  reports; *see* Reports.
  variation, 238
Process to compel appearance; *see* Summons, Warrant of arrest.
Prohibition, 46, 342, 345, 351
Prosecuting authorities; *see* Attorney-General, D.P.P., Police.
Prosecuting counsel, 1, 157, 177, 195, 216
Prosecution case, 177–180, 188, 190–191
  abandonment, 4, 19, 158
Prosecutor, 17–20, 303
  appeal by, 5, 163, 281–282
  choice of form of trial, 295–296, 298, 299; *see also* Hybrid offences, Indictable offences (summary trial).
  legal aid, 400, 401
  presence of, 96, 303
  recognisance to prosecute, 352
Public hearing, 153–154, 215
  appeals, 269
  committal proceedings, 86, 94, 111–112
  coroners' inquests, 40
  juveniles, 365, 369, 370–371
  laying informations, 49
  preferring an indictment, 145
  summary trials, 303, 324
Punishments and orders; *see* Sentence.

Quashing indictments; *see* Indictment.

Rape,
  consent, 186, 194
Real property,
  magistrates' jurisdiction, 291–292
Rebuttal,
  answers as to credit, 186
  evidence in, 178, 179, 191, 203, 269, 312
Recognisances, 243–244, 264, 327–328, 352
  appeals, 346, 387
  discharge, 76
  forfeiture, 82, 241
  juvenile, 382
  juvenile's parent or guardian, 77, 369–370, 382, 386
  sureties, 243, 244; *see also* Bail (sureties).
Recorders, 87
Re-examination; *see* Examination of witnesses.
Refreshing memory; *see* Witnesses (refreshing memory).
Registrar of Criminal Appeals, 260–261, 262, 283, 285
Release on licence, 224, 225, 227, 257–258, 331, 338, 366
  temporary, 256
Remand, 67–68, 69, 70, 388
  juvenile, 365, 372–374
  legal aid, 400, 402
  reports, for, 219–220, 307, 318, 375
  summary trial, 306
Remand centres, 366, 373, 379, 388
Remission, 257
Remission to juvenile court, 371, 376
Reports,
  adjournment for, 219–220, 242, 307, 318, 402
  bail, 73, 74, 77, 220, 223
  juvenile, on, 375–376, 386
  medical, 219, 234, 375
  probation, 218, 219, 220, 235, 375
  psychiatric, 336
  social inquiry, 219
Representation; *see* Legal representatives.
Reprieve, 256
Res judicata, 167–168
Respite, 222; *see also* Sentence (postponement).
Restitution orders, 235, 240, 252–253, 273, 282, 330, 349, 351, 367, 376
  offence taken into consideration, 220, 275
Restriction order; *see* Hospital order.
Retrial; *see* Appeal.
Road traffic; *see* Driving offences.

Scotland,
  evidence, 110

Scotland—*cont.*
 process, 56, 59
Search, 24, 25–29
 personal, 27, 64
 premises, 27–29
 warrants, 25–27, 48, 57
  gaming premises, 57, 63
 women, 21, 25
Sentence, 216–259, 317–330, 366–368, 369–370, 375–382, 386–387, 388–389
 alteration of, 221–222, 315–316, 354
 appeal; *see* Appeal (sentence).
 combined, 228, 229–231, 233, 235, 236–237, 240, 241, 255–256
 committal for; *see* Committal for sentence.
 consecutive and concurrent; *see* Consecutive sentences.
 custody; *see* Custody (taking into account).
 deferment, 241, 242–243, 327, 334
 determinate, 225, 367
 evidence for, 216–217, 317; *see also* Mitigation, Reports.
 juveniles, 366–368, 369–370, 386–387; *see also* Care orders.
 postponing, 221–223, 242; *see also* deferment, *above*.
 see also Fines, Imprisonment, Taking into consideration.
Separate trials, 133–134, 135, 139, 140–141, 143, 147, 201, 205, 267, 284, 369
Service,
 alibi notice, 112; *see also* Alibi.
 summons, 56
  statutory declaration, 56, 301
 written statements, 110
Ships,
 offences committed on, 10–12
Silence,
 constituting an offence, 21
 judge's comment on, 197–198
 prosecution comment on, 32, 190
 right of, 20–23, 99, 189–190, 197–198
Similar fact evidence, 134, 135, 191, 192
Solicitors, 51, 87, 285
 rights of audience, 152
 see also Legal representatives.
Solicitor-General, 20
Speeches, 264
 defence, 180, 195–196
 prosecution, 177–178, 195
 summary trial, 311–314
Spent convictions, 187
Spouse,
 accused's, 30, 31, 308
 communications to, 33
 deportation, 244
Spouse—*cont.*
 incrimination of, 32
 offences against, 16, 30, 31
Staying proceedings, 134, 157, 166–167; *see also* Prosecution (abandonment).
Stolen goods; *see* Handling, Restitution, Search.
Submission of no case to answer, 99, 100, 163, 171, 202–203, 206, 210, 267, 312
Summary offences, 292–295, 310
 hybrid offences; *see* Hybrid offences.
 limitation period, 13, 305–306, 384
 territorial jurisdiction, 11, 52
 trial by jury; *see* Accused (election).
 warrant of arrest for, 60, 291
Summary trial, 289, 301–316
 absence of accused, 301–303, 310–311
 change to committal proceedings, 111, 296, 298, 299
 contempt, 392, 394
 corporations, 390–391
 hybrid offence; *see* Hybrid offences.
 indictable offences, *see* Indictable offences.
 juveniles, 368–370, 371–382, 375
 prosecutor's election, 293–299
 see also Adjournments, Bail, Indictable offences (summary trial), Magistrates' courts.
Summing-up, 196–199, 202, 206, 266, 284
Summons, 51–52, 55–57, 291, 300, 302, 306
 Crown Court, 151
 jury, 172
 juvenile, 364, 372, 374, 382, 384
 service, 55–56, 301
 suspended sentence, 229
Supervision,
 Borstal trainees, 232, 259
 care orders, 378
 payment of fines, 325
 probationers, 236–237, 239
 release from prison, 257–259; *see also* Release on licence.
 suspended sentence, 228
Supervision orders, 367, 377, 379, 380–382, 386
 psychiatric, 380–381
Sureties, 243, 244; *see also* Bail (sureties), Recognisances.
Suspended sentences, 221, 227–229, 230, 232, 249, 275, 277, 302, 322, 338, 354
 activation, 228, 241, 322
 combined sentence, 228, 241, 322
 committal, 322, 331, 333
 vagrant, 334–335

Suspended sentence supervision orders, 228, 319

Taking offences into consideration, 165, 220–221, 251, 275, 318, 330
Tape recordings, 22, 36
Telephone-tapping, 23, 36–37
Territorial jurisdiction; *see* Jurisdiction
Territorial waters, 10
Terrorist offences, 26–27, 61, 65; *see also* Aircraft
Theft, 13, 119, 120, 126, 129, 132, 133, 136, 141, 213
Time limits, 13, 47, 305–306, 333
Transcript, 203, 264, 273, 283–285
Treason, 12, 73, 131, 136, 205, 213, 217, 223, 277
Treasury Counsel, 20
Treasury Solicitor's Office, 17
Treatment of offenders; *see* Sentence.
Trial on indictment, 152–215
  accused's election; *see* Accused (election).
  corporations, 391
  hybrid offence; *see* Hybrid offences.
  juveniles, 364–368
  place of, 89, 101–103
  postponement, 147, 205
  preliminary proceedings for directions, 150
  preliminary rulings on law, 155, 159, 169
  procedure at, 176–196, 199–202
  time, 102; *see also* Time limits.
  trial by High Court judge; *see* High Court (judge).

Unfairly obtained evidence; *see* Evidence (judicial discretion).
Unfit to plead; *see* Fitness to plead.
Unrepresented accused; *see* Accused (unrepresented), Legal representatives.
Unsafe and unsatisfactory verdict, *see* Verdict.
Unsworn statement of the accused, 181, 190, 284, 311

Vagrancy, 191, 289, 331, 334–335
Venire de novo, 206, 266; *see also* Appeal (retrial), Jury (discharge).
Verdict, 208–215
  alternative; *see* Alternative verdict.
  ambiguous, 209, 211
  coroner's jury's, 38
  entry by order of the judge, 19, 158, 163, 202, 206
  inconsistent, 209–210; *see also* Joint trials, Separate trials.

Verdict—*cont.*
  insanity, 211–212, 234–235
  majority; *see* Majority verdict.
  rejection of, 202–203, 210
  special, 211, 279
  unsafe and unsatisfactory, 267, 283
  validity, 172, 215
View of the *locus in quo*, 204
Visiting forces, 15
Voir dire,
  examination on, 207

Warrant,
  arrest, of, 41, 51–52, 54, 57–60, 291
    backing, 58–59, 69, 78
    bailed person, 81, 151
    bench, 45, 60
    coroner's, 39
    execution, 43, 58
    extradition proceedings, 61–62, 115
    general, 57
    juvenile, 364, 372, 382, 384
    summary trial, 302, 306, 311
    suspended sentence, 229
    witness, for, 98, 106, 307
  commitment, of, 104, 151, 320, 323, 325, 331
  provisional, 59, 61
  search; *see* Search warrants.
Witnesses, 29–32, 98, 104–106, 307–308
  accused; *see* Accused.
  attendance of, 98, 263, 264, 269
  compellability, 31–32, 141, 308
  competence, 29–31, 104, 141
  coroner's inquest, 38
  costs, 98
  credit; *see* Cross-examination (credit).
  foreign proceedings, 34
  hostile, 182–183, 203, 207
  indictment, listed on, 114–115, 178–179
  interference with, 34, 392
  privilege, 32–34, 42, 180, 185, 187
  refreshing the memory, 36, 179
Witness orders, 105–106
  conditional, 99, 106
Witness summons, 98, 106, 307
Written statements of evidence, 94, 96–97, 100–101, 105, 110–111, 180, 183, 273
  editing of, 110
  exchange of, 96–97, 110
  summary trial, 111, 296

Young persons,
  criminal responsibility, 363–364
  witness, as, 97
  see also Juveniles.